Applications of Partial Differential Equations

Applications of Partial Differential Equations

Editor

Patricia J. Y. Wong

Basel • Beijing • Wuhan • Barcelona • Belgrade • Novi Sad • Cluj • Manchester

Editor
Patricia J. Y. Wong
School of Electrical and
Electronic Engineering
Nanyang Technological
University
Singapore, Singapore

Editorial Office
MDPI
St. Alban-Anlage 66
4052 Basel, Switzerland

This is a reprint of articles from the Special Issue published online in the open access journal *Mathematics* (ISSN 2227-7390) (available at: https://www.mdpi.com/si/mathematics/applications_partial_differential_equations).

For citation purposes, cite each article independently as indicated on the article page online and as indicated below:

Lastname, A.A.; Lastname, B.B. Article Title. *Journal Name* **Year**, *Volume Number*, Page Range.

ISBN 978-3-0365-9564-1 (Hbk)
ISBN 978-3-0365-9565-8 (PDF)
doi.org/10.3390/books978-3-0365-9565-8

© 2023 by the authors. Articles in this book are Open Access and distributed under the Creative Commons Attribution (CC BY) license. The book as a whole is distributed by MDPI under the terms and conditions of the Creative Commons Attribution-NonCommercial-NoDerivs (CC BY-NC-ND) license.

Contents

About the Editor vii

Edgardo Alvarez, Hernan Cabrales and Tovias Castro
Optimal Control Theory for a System of Partial Differential Equations Associated with Stratified Fluids
Reprinted from: *Mathematics* **2021**, *9*, 2672, doi:10.3390/math9212672 1

José L. Díaz, Saeed Ur Rahman, Juan Carlos Sánchez Rodríguez, María Antonia Simón Rodríguez, Guillermo Filippone Capllonch and Antonio Herrero Hernández
Analysis of Solutions, Asymptotic and Exact Profiles to an Eyring–Powell Fluid Modell
Reprinted from: *Mathematics* **2022**, *10*, 660, doi:10.3390/math10040660 25

Bienvenido Barraza Martínez, Jonathan González Ospino, Rogelio Grau Acuña and Jairo Hernández Monzón
Parameter–Elliptic Fourier Multipliers Systems and Generation of Analytic and C^∞ Semigroups
Reprinted from: *Mathematics* **2022**, *10*, 751, doi:10.3390/math10050751 41

Farah M. Al-Askar, Wael W. Mohammed, Mohammad Alshammari and Mahmoud El-Morshedy
Effects of the Wiener Process on the Solutions of the StochasticFractional Zakharov System
Reprinted from: *Mathematics* **2022**, *10*, 1194, doi:10.3390/math10071194 61

Xuhao Li and Patricia J. Y. Wong
$gL1$ Scheme for Solving a Class of Generalized Time-Fractional DiffusionEquations
Reprinted from: *Mathematics* **2022**, *10*, 1219, doi:10.3390/math10081219 73

Chein-Shan Liu, Chih-Wen Chang, Yung-Wei Chen and Jian-Hung Shen
To Solve Forward and Backward Nonlocal Wave Problems with Pascal Bases Automatically Satisfying the Specified Conditions
Reprinted from: *Mathematics* **2022**, *10*, 3112, doi:10.3390/math10173112 87

V. Subburayan and S. Natesan
Parameter Uniform Numerical Method for Singularly Perturbed 2D Parabolic PDE with Shift in Space
Reprinted from: *Mathematics* **2022**, *10*, 3310, doi:10.3390/math10183310 103

Ben Mansour Dia, Mouhamadou Samsidy Goudiaby and Oliver Dorn
Boundary Feedback Stabilization of Two-Dimensional Shallow Water Equations with Viscosity Term
Reprinted from: *Mathematics* **2022**, *10*, 4036, doi:10.3390/math10214036 123

Ali Algarni, Afnan D. Al Agha, Aisha Fayomi and Hakim Al Garalleh
Kinetics of a Reaction-Diffusion Mtb/SARS-CoV-2 Coinfection Model with Immunity
Reprinted from: *Mathematics* **2023**, *11*, 1715, doi:10.3390/math11071715 145

R. Soundararajan, V. Subburayan and Patricia J. Y. Wong
Streamline Diffusion Finite Element Method for Singularly Perturbed 1D-Parabolic Convection Diffusion Differential Equations with Line Discontinuous Source
Reprinted from: *Mathematics* **2023**, *11*, 2034, doi:10.3390/math11092034 171

Alejandro León-Ramírez, Oswaldo González-Gaxiola and Guillermo Chacón-Acosta
Analytical Solutions to the Chavy-Waddy–Kolokolnikov Model of Bacterial Aggregates in Phototaxis by Three Integration Schemes
Reprinted from: *Mathematics* **2023**, *11*, 2352, doi:10.3390/math11102352 189

Jinyang Liu, Boping Tian, Deqi Wang, Jiaxing Tang and Yujin Wu
Global Boundedness in a Logarithmic Keller–Segel System
Reprinted from: *Mathematics* **2023**, *11*, 2743, doi:10.3390/math11122743 . . . . **213**

Aly R. Seadawy, Syed T. R. Rizvi and Hanadi Zahed
Lump-Type Solutions, Lump Solutions, and Mixed Rogue Waves for Coupled Nonlinear Generalized Zakharov Equations
Reprinted from: *Mathematics* **2023**, *11*, 2856, doi:10.3390/math11132856 . . . . **225**

Mi Jin Lee and Jum-Ran Kang
General Stability for the Viscoelastic Wave Equation with Nonlinear Time-Varying Delay, Nonlinear Damping and Acoustic Boundary Conditions
Reprinted from: *Mathematics* **2023**, *11*, 4593, doi:10.3390/math11224593 . . . . **243**

About the Editor

Patricia J. Y. Wong

Dr. Patricia J. Y. Wong joined the School of Electrical and Electronic Engineering in 2000. She received all her degrees, BSc (first class honours), MSc, MSc (Financial Engineering) and PhD, from the National University of Singapore. Her research interests include differential equations, difference equations, integral equations, and numerical mathematics. She has conducted significant research and published 4 monographs and more than 200 research papers in international refereed journals. Presently, Dr Wong serves on the editorial boards of *Mathematics* (Switzerland), *Axioms* (Switzerland), *Abstract and Applied Analysis* (USA), *Advances in Dynamical Systems and Applications* (USA), and the *International Journal of Differential Equations* (USA).

Article

Optimal Control Theory for a System of Partial Differential Equations Associated with Stratified Fluids

Edgardo Alvarez [1,*], Hernan Cabrales [2,†] and Tovias Castro [3,†]

1   Departamento de Matemáticas y Estadística, Universidad del Norte, Barranquilla 081007, Colombia
2   Departamento de Ciencias Naturales y Exactas, Universidad de la Costa, Barranquila 081007, Colombia; hcabrale@cuc.edu.co
3   Departamento de Matemáticas, Universidad del Atlántico, Barranquila 081007, Colombia; toviascastro@mail.uniatlantico.edu.co
*   Correspondence: ealvareze@uninorte.edu.co
†   These authors contributed equally to this work.

Abstract: In this paper, we investigate the existence of an optimal solution of a functional restricted to non-linear partial differential equations, which ruled the dynamics of viscous and incompressible stratified fluids in $\mathbb{R}^3$. Additionally, we use the first derivative of the considered functional to establish the necessary condition of the optimality for the optimal solution.

Keywords: non-linear optimal control; stratified fluids; energy functional; optimal condition; state variable

1. Introduction

Following the results of the modern calculus of variations, in this article, we study the optimal solution of an energy functional constraint to a partial differential equations system, which models the dynamic of an exponential stratified fluid in a three-dimensional space. To do this, we investigate the existence of solutions of a non-homogenous and non-linear partial differential system, extending the result obtained in [1], where only a potential external force was considered. Being more specific, for a $\Omega \subset \mathbb{R}^3$, non-empty, open, connected, and bounded set, with boundary $\Sigma = \partial\Omega \times (0, T)$ that is smooth enough (at least Lipschitz continuous) and letting ν be the normal vector outside the boundary, we define $Q := \Omega \times (0, T)$ as the domain of our model where the motion of the fluid takes place. Here, $T > 0$, $(0, T)$ is the time interval and $t \in (0; T)$ is the temporal variable.

We are interested in establishing the existence of the solution for the following non-linear problem in a weaker sense:

$$\begin{cases} \dfrac{\partial y_1}{\partial t} - \mu \Delta y_1 + y \cdot \nabla y_1 + \dfrac{\partial p}{\partial x_1} = u_1, \\ \dfrac{\partial y_2}{\partial t} - \mu \Delta y_2 + y \cdot \nabla y_2 + \dfrac{\partial p}{\partial x_2} = u_2, \\ \dfrac{\partial y_3}{\partial t} - \mu \Delta y_3 + g\rho + y \cdot \nabla y_3 + \dfrac{\partial p}{\partial x_3} = u_3, \\ \dfrac{\partial \rho}{\partial t} - \dfrac{N^2}{g} y_3 = u_4, \\ \dfrac{\partial y_1}{\partial x_1} + \dfrac{\partial y_2}{\partial x_2} + \dfrac{\partial y_3}{\partial x_3} = 0, \end{cases} \quad (1)$$

where $x = (x_1, x_2, x_3)$ denotes the spatial variable, $y = y(x,t) = (y_1(x,t), y_2(x,t), y_3(x,t))$ denotes the velocity field of the fluid and $u(x,t) = (u_1, u_2, u_3, u_4)$ corresponds to a known function from $L^2(\Omega)$. We also have the parameter $\mu > 0$ as the kinematic viscosity, and N

Citation: Alvarez, E.; Cabrales, H.; Castro, T. Optimal Control Theory for a System of Partial Differential Equations Associated with Stratified Fluids. *Mathematics* **2021**, *9*, 2672. https://doi.org/10.3390/math9212672

Academic Editor: Patricia J. Y. Wong

Received: 10 September 2021
Accepted: 11 October 2021
Published: 21 October 2021

Publisher's Note: MDPI stays neutral with regard to jurisdictional claims in published maps and institutional affiliations.

Copyright: © 2021 by the authors. Licensee MDPI, Basel, Switzerland. This article is an open access article distributed under the terms and conditions of the Creative Commons Attribution (CC BY) license (https://creativecommons.org/licenses/by/4.0/).

and g are positive constants. The last equation for the non-linear system is because our fluid is incompressible, p denotes the scalar field of the dynamic pressure and ρ represents the dynamic density. For an ideal case, the Equation (1) can be founded in [2,3]. For a viscous compressible fluid, the system (1) is deduced, for example, in [4].

When we study optimal control problems, we start from a dynamical system that evolves temporarily in a period time $[t_0, t_f]$, described by a state equation of a specific variable $y(t)$, called a state variable with an initial condition y_0. This evolution of the system depends on a particular function $u(t)$, called a control variable, and what is sought with it is to influence the evolution of $y(t)$ such that we can optimize (maximize or minimize) a given functional, which depends on both the state and control variables, called the *energy functional*. To be more related to these terms of the theory of optimal control, we can see [5,6].

The primary motivation of this paper is to minimize an energy functional of the form $J(y, u)$, which depends on a control variable u and the velocity field y subject to a state equation that corresponds in our case, to a non-linear system of partial differential equations given in (1).

The functional that we are going to minimize is defined by:

$$J = \frac{1}{2} \int_0^T \|(y, \rho)^T - y_d\|_{L^2(\Omega)}^2 \, dt + \frac{\lambda}{2} \int_0^T \|u - u_d\|_{L^2(\Omega)}^2 \, dt,$$

where $y_d \in L^2(\Omega)^4$ is the desired state, $u_d \in L^2(\Omega)^4$ is the desired control (or also called control change) and $\lambda > 0$ is a constant. From a mathematical perspective, most of the control systems involve a set of ordinary differential equations or linear partial differential equations in their restrictions, see for example [7].

In this case, we consider a non-linear model, which makes this proposal novel and attractive. On the other hand, there is some progress associated with the Navier–Stokes systems [5,8]. However, not much seems to be known about works that deal with non-linear exponential stratified fluids, making our results an open door to consider new parameters such as salinity, rotation, and temperature in future works.

This paper is distributed in five sections. In Section 1, we introduce and describe the problem; later, in Section 2, we show the essential background information to understand the problem. In Section 3, we introduce the weak formulation of the problem. In Section 4, we study the existence of solutions for the optimal problem, and finally, in Section 5, we establish the optimal condition.

2. Previous Definitions and Notations

Before starting the study and analysis of our optimal control problem, we introduce some previous elements and necessary notation to understand the non-linear motion in the dynamics of viscous and incompressible stratified fluids in $\mathbb{R}^3$ that will be considered this paper.

Let Ω be a domain of the space $\mathbb{R}^3$, and let p in $\mathbb{R}$, such that $1 \leq p \leq \infty$. A function $y : \Omega \longrightarrow \mathbb{R}$ (or $\mathbb{C}$), is said to belong to $L^p(\Omega)$, if y is measurable and the norm

$$\|y\|_{L^p(\Omega)} = \begin{cases} \left(\int_\Omega |y(x)|^p \, dx \right)^{1/p} & \text{if } 1 \leq \infty \\ \operatorname*{ess\,sup}_{x \in \Omega} |y(x)| & \text{if } p = \infty, \end{cases}$$

is finite. The spaces $L^p(\Omega)$ are Banach spaces (see [9]). Furthermore, in the spaces $L^p(\Omega)$ the Hölder Inequality is fulfilled, which ensures that, for $y \in L^p(\Omega)$ and $v \in L^q(\Omega)$ with $\frac{1}{p} + \frac{1}{q} = 1$ for $1 \leq p, q \leq \infty$, it holds:

$$\int_\Omega |y(x)v(x)|\,dx \leq \|y(x)\|_{L^p(\Omega)} \cdot \|v(x)\|_{L^q(\Omega)}.$$

In particular, when we have that $p = 2$, then $L^2(\Omega)$ is a Hilbert space with the scalar product

$$(y,v)_2 = \int_\Omega y(x) \cdot v(x)\,dx.$$

It is known that $L^2(\Omega)$ is one of the essential Hilbert spaces in the mathematical analysis since they appear very frequently in the study of partial differential equations, and it is the space where the kinetic energy is automatically well defined. As the variational form of a mathematical physics problem appears, we cross the Sobolev's spaces denoted by $W^{k,p}(\Omega)$, and defined as the set of all functions $y(x) \in L^p(\Omega)$ that have all the generalized derivatives up to the order p, which also belongs to $L^p(\Omega)$. The associated norm defined in this space is given by

$$\|y\|_{W^{k,p}(\Omega)} = \left(\sum_{|\alpha| \leq k} \|D^\alpha y\|_{L^p(\Omega)}^p\right)^{1/p},$$

where $D^\alpha y$ is the weak derivate of order α. We also find other types of Sobolev spaces such as $W_0^{k,p}(\Omega)$.

Note that when $p = 2$, we can simply write $H^k(\Omega)$ and $H_0^k(\Omega)$ instead of $W^{k,2}(\Omega)$ and $W_0^{k,2}(\Omega)$, respectively (see for example [10]). Furthermore remember that when $k = 1$ and $p = 2$, we have that the space $W^{1,2}(\Omega)$ is better known as $H^1(\Omega)$, since it is a Hilbert space, endowed with the scalar product:

$$(y,v)_{H^1(\Omega)} = \int_\Omega y(x) \cdot v(x)\,dx + \int_\Omega \nabla y(x) \cdot \nabla v(x)\,dx \text{ for all } y,v \in H^1(\Omega),$$

where

$$\nabla y = \left(\frac{\partial y}{\partial x_1}, \frac{\partial y}{\partial x_2}, \frac{\partial y}{\partial x_3}\right),$$

and

$$\nabla v = \left(\frac{\partial v}{\partial x_1}, \frac{\partial v}{\partial x_2}, \frac{\partial v}{\partial x_3}\right).$$

The norm induced by the previous scalar product is given by:

$$\|y\|_{H^1(\Omega)} = \left(\|y\|_{L^2(\Omega)}^2 + \sum_{i=k}^3 \left\|\frac{\partial y}{\partial x_i}\right\|_{L^2(\Omega)}^2\right)^{1/2}.$$

On the other hand, let us denote by $\mathcal{D}(\Omega)$ the space of functions $\varphi : \Omega \longrightarrow \mathbb{R}^3$ of class $C^\infty(\Omega)$ with compact support and by $\mathcal{D}'(\Omega)$ the space of distributions on Ω. Throughout this paper, we will use the standard notations for the Lebesgue and Sobolev spaces, in particular the norm in $L^2(\Omega)$ and the scalar product in $L^2(\Omega)$ will be represented by $\|\cdot\|$ and $(\cdot,\cdot)$ respectively.

Let us define

$$(u,v) := \int_\Omega \sum_{j=1}^3 u_j \cdot v_j\,dx, \quad u = (u_1, u_2, u_3),\ v = (v_1, v_2, v_3) \in L^2(\Omega)^3,$$

$$((u,v)) := \int_\Omega \sum_{j=1}^3 \nabla u_j \cdot \nabla v_j\,dx, \quad u = (u_1, u_2, u_3),\ v = (v_1, v_2, v_3) \in H_0^1(\Omega)^3,$$

and the associated norms are given to from $\mid u \mid^2 := (u,u)$ and $\|u\|^2 := ((u,u))$.

Consider the following notation for the solenoidal Banach spaces H and V, which intrinsically satisfy the condition $\nabla \cdot y = 0$, and which we can represent as:

$$H = \{y \in L^2(\Omega)^3 : \nabla \cdot y = 0 \text{ in } \Omega;\ \gamma_n y = 0 \text{ on } \partial \Omega\},$$

and

$$V = \{y \in H_0^1(\Omega)^3 : \nabla \cdot y = 0 \text{ in } \Omega\}. \tag{2}$$

Here, $\nabla \cdot y$ denotes the divergence of y and γ_n denotes the normal component of the trace operator, where $\gamma_n : y \mapsto n \cdot y \big|_{\partial \Omega} = 0$, here n denotes the external normal to the boundary. These spaces are used very frequently in equations of the dynamics of the stratified fluids and are defined as the closure of Θ in $L^2(\Omega)^3$ and of Θ in $H_0^1(\Omega)^3$, respectively, where

$$\Theta = \{y \in \mathcal{D}(\Omega)^3 : \nabla \cdot y = 0 \text{ in } \Omega\}.$$

It is well-known that H and V are Hilbert spaces with the scalar product $(\cdot, \cdot)$ and $\|\cdot\|$ respectively. Furthermore,

$$V \subset H \equiv H' \subset V',$$

where injections are dense and continuous.

On the other hand, if V is a Banach space with dual space V', then the duality between the spaces V and V' is denoted by $\langle \cdot, \cdot \rangle_{V',V}$ and its associated norm in V' is denoted by $\|\cdot\|_{V'}$.

We introduce the following space of functions y whose derivative y_t exists as an abstract function:

$$W^\alpha([0,T];X) := \{y \in L^2([0,T];X) : y_t \in L^\alpha([0,T];X')\}, \quad 1 \leq \alpha \leq 2,$$

$$W(0,T) := W^2([0,T];X).$$

The spaces defined above are endowed with the following norms:

$$\|y\|_{W^\alpha([0,T];X)} := \left(\|y\|^2_{L^2([0,T];X)} + \|y_t\|^2_{L^\alpha([0,T];X')}\right)^{1/2}$$

$$\|y\|_W := \|y\|_{W^2},$$

are Banach spaces. When X is a Hilbert space, we have that $W^\alpha([0,T];X)$ is a Hilbert space. In particular, the space $W^\alpha([0,T];X)$ is endowed with the following scalar product:

$$(y,v)_{W^\alpha([0,T];X)} = \int_0^T (y(t),v(t))\,dt + \int_0^T (y_t(t),v_t(t))\,dt.$$

In this way, we have the following results for $1 \leq \alpha \leq 2$ (see [10–12]):

$$W^\alpha([0,T];X) \hookrightarrow C([0,T];X) \text{ is continuous,}$$
$$W^\alpha([0,T];H^1(\Omega)^3) \hookrightarrow L^2(\Omega)^3 \text{ is compact,}$$
$$W^\alpha([0,T];H^1(\Omega)^3) \hookrightarrow C([0,T];L^2(\Omega)^3) \text{ is compact.}$$

Now, we defined our set of admissible controls, which denoted by U_{ad}, and its elements are called admissible controls, which satisfy the inequality constraints of our non-linear system given from:

$$U_{ad} = \{u \in L^2(Q_T)^3 : u_{a,i}(x,t) \leq u_i(x,t) \leq u_{b,i}(x,t) \text{ with a.e. on } Q_T \text{ for } i = 1,2,3,4\}. \tag{3}$$

where the control constraints $u_a, u_b \in L^2(Q_T)$ with

$$u_{a,i}(x,t) \leq u_{b,i}(x,t).$$

Remark 1. *Note that our set of admissible controls defined in (3) is a non-empty, convex, and closed subset in $L^2(Q_T)^4$.*

Now, let us recall the following classic result that we will need later to show the existence of optimal controls.

Definition 1 ([6])**.** *Let X be a Banach space and let $J: X \longrightarrow \mathbb{R}$ be a functional. We say that J is weakly lower semicontinuous, if for any sequence $(x_n)_{n \in \mathbb{N}} \subset X$ such that $x_n \rightharpoonup x$ when $n \longrightarrow \infty$ we have that:*

$$J(x) \leq \liminf_{n \to \infty} J(x_n).$$

Formulation of the Optimal Control Problem Associated with the Non-Linear Model

In this part, we will formulate our optimal control problem associated with the partial differential equation described by (1). In order to show the existence of solutions of the non-linear system (1), we represent our model system in a simpler way using the following notation:

$$y(x,t) = \begin{pmatrix} y_1 \\ y_2 \\ y_3 \\ \rho \end{pmatrix} = \begin{pmatrix} y' \\ \rho \end{pmatrix}; \quad \frac{\partial}{\partial t}\begin{pmatrix} y_1 \\ y_2 \\ y_3 \\ \rho \end{pmatrix} = \frac{\partial y}{\partial t} \; ; \; (y' \cdot \nabla)y = \begin{pmatrix} y' \cdot \nabla y_1 \\ y' \cdot \nabla y_2 \\ y' \cdot \nabla y_3 \\ 0 \end{pmatrix} \; ; \; \mu \Delta y = \begin{pmatrix} \mu \Delta y_1 \\ \mu \Delta y_2 \\ \mu \Delta y_3 \\ 0 \end{pmatrix},$$

and

$$My = \begin{pmatrix} 0 \\ 0 \\ g\rho \\ -\dfrac{N^2}{g} y_3 \end{pmatrix} \; ; \; \nabla p = \begin{pmatrix} \dfrac{\partial p}{\partial x_1} \\ \dfrac{\partial p}{\partial x_2} \\ \dfrac{\partial p}{\partial x_3} \\ 0 \end{pmatrix} \; ; \; u = \begin{pmatrix} u_1 \\ u_2 \\ u_3 \\ u_4 \end{pmatrix}.$$

Then, we can rewrite (1) in more compact form as,

$$\begin{cases} \dfrac{\partial y}{\partial t} + (y' \cdot \nabla)y - \mu \Delta y + My + \nabla p = u, & y \in \Omega \times \mathbb{R}, \\ \operatorname{div}(y') = 0, \, x \in \Omega \text{ and } t \geq 0, \\ y(t, \cdot) = 0 \text{ on the boundary of } \Sigma = \partial \Omega \times (0,T), \\ y(0, \cdot) = y_0 \text{ in } \Omega. \end{cases} \tag{4}$$

In this way, we can introduce our energy functional that we want to minimize, which depends on the state and the control (y, u) and that we define by:

$$J(y,u) = \frac{1}{2} \int_0^T \|y - y_d\|_{L^2(\Omega)}^2 \, dt + \frac{\lambda}{2} \int_0^T \|u - u_d\|_{L^2(\Omega)}^2 \, dt,$$

where $y_d \in L^2(\Omega)^4$ is the desired state, $u_d \in L^2(\Omega)^4$ is the desired control (or also called control change) and $\lambda > 0$ is a constant.

Now, we can introduce the functional space given by:

$$\mathbb{V} = \{\varphi(x) = (\varphi_1, \varphi_2, \varphi_3, \varphi_4) : \varphi \in H_0^1(\Omega)^4 : \nabla \varphi' = 0\}, \quad (5)$$

where $\nabla \cdot \varphi' = 0$ denotes the divergence of $\varphi' = (\varphi_1, \varphi_2, \varphi_3)$. The space $\mathbb{V}$ endowed with the inner product and the usual norm of space $H_0^1(\Omega)^4$, the space of all functions $y \in H^1(\Omega)$ with null trace:

$$(y, v)_{H_0^1(\Omega)} := \sum_{|\alpha|=1} (D_x^\alpha y, D_x^\alpha v)_2$$

and

$$\|y\|_{H_0^1(\Omega)} = \sqrt{(y,y)_{H_0^1(\Omega)}} \text{ for all } u, v \in \mathbb{V}.$$

The space given by (5) will be of great importance to us, since through it we can find the functions $y : [0, T] \longmapsto \mathbb{V}$, which are weak solutions of our non-linear problem given by (4).

On the other hand, our space $\mathbb{V}$ is clearly a Banach space with the norm $\|\cdot\|_{H_0^1(\Omega)}$. In this way, it is a Hilbert space. It is also reflexive since $\mathbb{V} \subseteq H_0^1(\Omega)$ is separable.

In summary, we can establish our optimal control problem:

$$\left\{ \text{Minimize } J(y, u) = \frac{1}{2} \int_0^T \|y - y_d\|_{L^2(\Omega)}^2 \, dt + \frac{\lambda}{2} \int_0^T \|u - u_d\|_{L^2(\Omega)}^2 \, dt, \right. \quad (6)$$

subject to the state equations that establish the dependency between the state variable y and the control variable u:

$$\begin{cases} \dfrac{\partial y}{\partial t} + (y' \cdot \nabla)y - \mu \Delta y + My + \nabla p = u \text{ in } Q_T, \\ \text{div}(y') = 0, \text{ in } Q, \\ y(t, \cdot) = 0 \text{ on the boundary of } \Sigma = \partial \Omega \times (0, T), \\ y(0, \cdot) = y_0 \text{ in } \Omega, \\ u \in U_{ad}. \end{cases} \quad (7)$$

Here, $u \in L^2(Q_T)$ is the control, it is an external force that affects the fluid, (for example gravity); $y_0 \in \mathbb{V}$ is a divergence-free vector field in $\mathbb{R}^3$, the kinematic viscosity $\mu > 0$ and U_{ad} represents our set of constraints defined as in (3).

The aim of our control problem is to find a solution $\overline{u} \in L^2(Q_T)$, where $\overline{y}$ is the solution of (7) associated with $\overline{u}$ such that it minimizes our energy functional given by (6).

In this paper, we will show the existence of solutions and establish the use of the first derivative of the energy functional to derive the conditions that the optimal solutions have to satisfy Equations (6) and (7).

3. Weak Formulation for the Non-Linear Problem

In this section, whenever we refer to space $\mathbb{V}$, we will work with the functional space defined by (5), we will also identify $\mathbb{V}^*$ as its dual space and $(\cdot, \cdot)$ and $\|\cdot\|$ will denote the scalar product and the usual norm in $L^2(\Omega)$, respectively.

We are interested in establishing theorems of existence and uniqueness of the solution for our non-linear problem given by (4), for which we first study the existence of a solution in a weaker sense.

First of all, suppose there are functions $y \in C^{2,1}(\Omega \times (0, T))$ and $\nabla p \in C(Q_T)$ classical solutions for our non-linear system of partial differential equations given by (4). Let us show the *weak formulation* for our non-linear problem:

Suppose that y is a solution of (4). Then, multiplying the first equation of (4) by $v \in \mathbb{V}$, we obtain the following:

$$(y_t) \cdot v + (y' \cdot \nabla)y \cdot v - (\mu \Delta y) \cdot v + (My) \cdot v + (\nabla p) \cdot v = u \cdot v.$$

Then, integrating over Ω, we have

$$\int_\Omega (y_t) \cdot v \, dx + \int_\Omega (y' \cdot \nabla)y \cdot v \, dx - \int_\Omega (\mu \Delta y) \cdot v \, dx +$$

$$\int_\Omega (My) \cdot v \, dx + \int_\Omega (\nabla p) \cdot v \, dx = \int_\Omega u \cdot v \, dx,$$

therefore

$$\int_\Omega (y_t) \cdot v \, dx + \int_\Omega (y' \cdot \nabla)y \cdot v \, dx - \mu \int_\Omega (\Delta y) \cdot v \, dx +$$
$$\int_\Omega (My) \cdot v \, dx + \int_\Omega (\nabla p) \cdot v \, dx = \int_\Omega u \cdot v \, dx, \tag{8}$$

then, applying Green's Theorem in the third term of the previous equation, we obtain

$$\int_\Omega (y_t) \cdot v \, dx + \int_\Omega (y' \cdot \nabla)y \cdot v \, dx - \mu \left[\int_{\partial \Omega} \frac{\partial y}{\partial \eta} v \, d\theta - \int_\Omega \nabla y \cdot \nabla v \, dx \right] +$$

$$+ \int_\Omega (My) \cdot v \, dx + \int_\Omega (\nabla p) \cdot v \, dx = \int_\Omega u \cdot v \, dx,$$

thus, we have

$$\int_\Omega (y_t) \cdot v \, dx + \int_\Omega (y' \cdot \nabla)y \cdot v \, dx - \mu \int_{\partial \Omega} \frac{\partial y}{\partial \eta} v \, d\theta + \mu \int_\Omega \nabla y \cdot \nabla v \, dx +$$

$$+ \int_\Omega (My) \cdot v \, dx + \int_\Omega (\nabla p) \cdot v \, dx = \int_\Omega u \cdot v \, dx,$$

Keeping in mind the boundary condition $y\big|_{\partial \Gamma_1} = 0$ and div $(y') = 0$, we obtain the following:

$$\int_\Omega (y_t) \cdot v \, dx + \int_\Omega (y' \cdot \nabla)y \cdot v \, dx - \mu \int_{\partial \Omega} \frac{\partial y}{\partial \eta} v \, d\theta +$$

$$+ \mu \int_\Omega \nabla y \cdot \nabla v \, dx + \int_\Omega (My) \cdot v \, dx = \int_\Omega u \cdot v \, dx,$$

then

$$\int_\Omega (y_t) \cdot v \, dx + \int_\Omega (y' \cdot \nabla)y \cdot v \, dx + \mu \int_\Omega \nabla y \cdot \nabla v \, dx + \int_\Omega (My) \cdot v \, dx = \int_\Omega u \cdot v \, dx. \tag{9}$$

Now, (9) can be rewritten as

$$(y_t, v)_2 + ((y' \cdot \nabla)y, v)_2 + \mu((\nabla y, \nabla v))_2 + (My, v)_2 = (u, v)_2. \tag{10}$$

Next, we introduce the following bilinear and trilinear form for our weak formulation of the (10), where $a(\cdot, \cdot) : H_0^1(\Omega)^3 \times H_0^1(\Omega)^3 \longrightarrow \mathbb{R}$ and $b(\cdot, \cdot, \cdot) : \mathbb{V} \times \mathbb{V} \times \mathbb{V} \longrightarrow \mathbb{R}$ are defined:

$$a((y,v)) = \int_\Omega \nabla y \cdot \nabla v \tag{11}$$

and

$$b(y,v,w) := (y' \cdot \nabla v, w)_2 = \sum_{i,j=1}^3 \int_\Omega y'_i \frac{\partial v_j}{\partial x_i} w_j \, dx \text{ for all } y,v,w \in \mathbb{V}. \tag{12}$$

Then, replacing identities (11) and (12) in (10), we obtain the following:

$$(y_t, v)_2 + ((y' \cdot \nabla)y, v)_2 + \mu((\nabla y, \nabla v))_2 + (My, v)_2 = (u, v)_2$$

$$(y_t, v)_2 + b(y, y, v) + \mu a((y, v)) + (My, v)_2 = (u, v)_2.$$

In summary, we have

$$(y_t, v)_2 + b(y, y, v) + \mu a((y, v)) + (My, v)_2 = (u, v)_2. \tag{13}$$

Equation (13) suggests the following weak formulation for our non-linear system given in (4), and which we express thus:

For every $u \in L^2([0,T]; \mathbb{V}')$ and $y_0 \in \mathbb{V}$, we can find a solution $y \in L^2([0,T], \mathbb{V})$ with $y_t \in L^2([0,T]; \mathbb{V}')$ such that:

$$\begin{cases} \frac{d}{dt}(y,v)_2 + \mu a((y,v))_2 + b(y,y,v) + (My,v)_2 = (u,v)_2 \text{ for all } v \in \mathbb{V} \text{ a.e. } t \in (0,T) \\ y(0) = y_0, \end{cases} \tag{14}$$

where the term

$$b(y, v, w) = (y' \cdot \nabla v, w)_2$$
$$= \int_\Omega (y' \cdot \nabla) v \cdot w \, dx$$
$$= \sum_{i,j=1}^3 \int_\Omega y'_i \frac{\partial v_j}{\partial x_i} w_j \, dx \text{ for all } y, v, w \in \mathbb{V}. \tag{15}$$

corresponds to the non-linear term of our system (4).

We call the expression (14) the variational formulation (or weak) for our non-linear system given in (4).

On the other hand, let us see some properties with respect to the non-linear operator defined in (15), which can be found in [8]: For every $(y, v, w) \in \mathbb{V}$, we have that:

1. $b(y, v, w) = -b(y, w, v)$ if $y \cdot n = 0$ on Γ.
2. $b(y, v, v) = 0$ if $y \cdot n = 0$ on Γ for all $u, v \in \mathbb{V}$.

As a consequence, we have the following lemma.

Lemma 1 ([8,13]). *If $n = 3$, then*

$$|b(y,v,w)| \leq \begin{cases} C \mid y \mid^{1/4} \cdot \|y\|^{3/4} \cdot \|v\| \cdot \mid w \mid^{1/4} \cdot \|w\|^{3/4} \\ C\|y\| \cdot \|v\| \cdot \|w\| \text{ for all } y, v, w \in \mathbb{V}, \end{cases} \tag{16}$$

and in particular,

$$b(y,v,w) \leq C \mid y \mid^{1/2} \cdot \|y\|^{3/2} \cdot \|v\| \text{ for all } y, v \in \mathbb{V}.$$

In this way, we can introduce our definition of a weak solution given from (14) as we will see below.

Existence and Uniqueness of Weak Solutions

Let us introduce the definition of a weak solution.

Definition 2. *Given $u \in L^2([0,T]; \mathbb{V}')$ and $y_0 \in \mathbb{V}$, say that y is a weak solution to the problem (4) on the interval $(0,T)$ if:*

$$\begin{cases} y \in C([0,T]; \mathbb{V}), \dfrac{dy}{dt} \in L^2([0,T], \mathbb{V}), \\ (y_t(t), v)_2 + \mu a((y(t), v))_2 + (My(t), v)_2 + b(y(t), y(t), v) = (u(t), v)_2 \\ \text{for all } v \in \mathbb{V} \text{ a.e. } t \in (0,T), \\ y(0) = y_0. \end{cases} \quad (17)$$

For our purposes, we want to give an equivalent formulation as an equation in functional spaces. For this, we can introduce a linear and continuous operator $A : L^2([0,T]; \mathbb{V}) \longrightarrow L^2([0,T]; \mathbb{V}')$ such that for all $y, v \in L^2([0,T]; \mathbb{V})$ we have the following:

$$\begin{aligned} \langle Ay, v \rangle_{L^2([0,T]; \mathbb{V}'), L^2([0,T]; \mathbb{V})} &= \int_0^T \langle Ay(t), v(t) \rangle_{\mathbb{V}', \mathbb{V}} \, dt \\ &= \int_0^T (y(t), v(t)) \, dt \\ &= \int_0^T \nabla y(t) \cdot \nabla v(t) \, dt, \end{aligned} \quad (18)$$

and we define a non-linear operator $B : W^\alpha([0,T]; \mathbb{V}) \longrightarrow L^2([0,T]; \mathbb{V}')$ such that for all $y \in W^\alpha([0,T]; \mathbb{V}), w \in L^2([0,T]; \mathbb{V})$ we have

$$\begin{aligned} \langle B(y), w \rangle_{L^2([0,T]; \mathbb{V}'), L^2([0,T]; \mathbb{V}))} &= \int_0^T \langle B(y)(t), w(t) \rangle_{\mathbb{V}', \mathbb{V}} \, dt \\ &= \int_0^T b(y(t), y(t), w(t)) \, dt. \end{aligned} \quad (19)$$

The operator B is a bounded mapping from $W^\alpha([0,T]; \mathbb{V})$ to $L^2([0,T]; \mathbb{V}')$, that is, it holds $\|B(y)\|_{L^2([0,T];\mathbb{V}')} \leq c\|y\|^2_{W^\alpha([0,T];\mathbb{V})}$ for every $y \in W^\alpha([0,T];\mathbb{V})$.

Now, with the above notations, we can establish an equivalent formulation for our definition (17) in terms of the following functional differential equation.

Definition 3. *Let $u \in L^2([0,T]; \mathbb{V}')$ and $y_0 \in \mathbb{V}$ be given. A function $y \in W^\alpha([0,T]; \mathbb{V})$ is called a weak solution to the problem (4) on the interval $(0,T)$ if it fulfills:*

$$\begin{cases} y_t + \mu Ay + B(y) + M(y) = u \in L^2([0,T]; \mathbb{V}'), \\ y(0) = y_0 \in \mathbb{V}. \end{cases}$$

Denote by A the stokes operator, with domain $D(A) = (H^2(D))^3 \cap \mathbb{V}$, defined by $Av = -\mathbb{P}(\Delta v)$, for all $v \in D(A)$, where $\mathbb{P}$ is the orthogonal projection that from $L^2(D)^3$ to H and the set

$$a(y, v) = \int_\Omega \nabla y \cdot \nabla v \, dx \text{ for all } y, v \in \mathbb{V},$$

or equivalently

$$(Ay, v) = a(y, v) \text{ for all } y, v \in \mathbb{V}.$$

The Stokes operator A is self-attached on H, with $A \in L(\mathbb{V}, \mathbb{V}')$, where $\mathbb{V}'$ is the dual of $\mathbb{V}$ with the norm denoted by $\|\cdot\|_{\mathbb{V}'}$ and

$$(Ay, y) = \|y\|^2 \text{ for all } y \in \mathbb{V}.$$

Now, we can also equivalently formulate our control problem given in (6) and (7) using the operators defined in (18) and (19):

$$\left\{ \text{Minimize } J(y, u) = \frac{1}{2} \int_0^T \|y - y_d\|_{L^2(\Omega)}^2 \, dt + \frac{\lambda}{2} \int_0^T \|u - u_d\|_{L^2(\Omega)}^2 \, dt, \right. \tag{20}$$

subject to the state equations

$$\begin{cases} y_t + \mu A y + B(y) + M(y) = u \in L^2([0, T]; \mathbb{V}'), \\ y(0) = y_0 \in \mathbb{V}. \end{cases} \tag{21}$$

and the control of restrictions

$$u \in U_{ad}. \tag{22}$$

In this part, we will see how we can reduce our given energy functional (6). Sometimes it is convenient to work with the reduced functional since it allows us to better establish the study on the existence of the optimal values for our optimal control problem given in (6) and (7).

We can rewrite our optimal control problem as an optimization problem only in terms of u, as we will see below: we define the control to state mapping denoted by Y, which associates an element $u \in U_{ad} \subset L^2([0, T]; L^2(\Omega)^4)$ with an element $y \in W^\alpha([0, T]; \mathbb{V})$ and which is the solution of (4).

The control to state mapping for the optimal control problem (6) and (7) is given as follows:

$$\begin{aligned} Y : L^2([0, T]; L^2(\Omega)^4) &\longrightarrow W^\alpha([0, T]; \mathbb{V}) \\ u &\longmapsto Y(u) := y_u, \end{aligned} \tag{23}$$

where y_u is the unique solution of (17).

Remark 2.
1. Note that if we replace $y = Y(u)$ in our energy functional given in (6), then our functional J would be expressed in terms of the control variable u, which we will denote by Ψ:

$$J(u) := J(Y(u), u) = \Psi(u), \tag{24}$$

where we have that

$$\Psi(u) = \frac{1}{2} \int_0^T \|Y(u) - y_d\|_{L^2(\Omega)}^2 \, dt + \frac{\lambda}{2} \int_0^T \|u - u_d\|_{L^2(\Omega)}^2 \, dt,$$

and furthermore, Ψ is minimized on the set

$$U_{ad} = \{u \in L^2(\Omega_T) : u_{a,i}(x, t) \leq u_i(x, t) \leq u_{b,i}(x, t) \text{ a.e. on } \Omega_T \text{ for } i = 1, 2, 3, 4\}, \tag{25}$$

where the term $\Psi(u)$ will be called the reduced energy functional. In our context, Y is the non-linear solution mapping associated with (21).

2. The minimization of J subject to the state Equation (21) is equivalent to minimizing Ψ over all admissible controls.

In order to understand the proof of the following theorem, which is one of the main results of this work, we give the proof in several stages. The main idea of the proof is the following. First, we use the Faedo–Galerkin method to find out approximate solutions of (4). Then, using some auxiliary estimations, we show the convergence of these approximations to the solution of the model (4).

Theorem 1. *For any $y_0 \in \mathbb{V}$, $T > 0$ and $u \in L^2([0,T]; \mathbb{V}')$ given, the problem (4) has a unique weak solution y on the interval $(0, T)$.*

Proof. Stage 1: Existence of the approximate solution.

Note that $\mathbb{V}$ defined by (5) is a reflexive and separable Hilbert space. Then, by a classical result of functional analysis, there is an orthonormal and dense subset $(z_i)_{i \in \mathbb{N}}$ of $\mathbb{V}$.

Let us considerer the finite dimensional subspace

$$Z_m = \mathrm{span}\{z_1, z_2, z_3, \ldots, z_m\} \subseteq \mathbb{V}, \quad \forall m \in \mathbb{N}.$$

Restricting to the space Z_m, we solve the system of equations given from (17):

$$\begin{cases} \text{Let us find } y_m(x,t) = \sum_{i=1}^{m} \alpha_{im}(t) z_i(x) \text{ such that} \\ (y_m'(t), z_j) + \mu((y_m(t), z_j)) + b(y_m(t), y_m(t), z_j) + (My_m(t), z_j) = \langle u(t), z_j \rangle, \\ t \in [0, T] \,;\, j = 1, 2, 3, \ldots, m, \\ y_m(0) = y_{0m}. \end{cases} \quad (26)$$

Here, y_{0m} is the orthogonal projection of the initial data $y_0 \in \mathbb{V}$ on the subspace $V_m = \mathrm{span}\{z_1, z_2, z_3, \ldots, z_m\}$.

We can observe that (26) is in fact a Cauchy initial value problem for a non-linear system of ordinary differential equations. Indeed, in the unknowns $\alpha_{im}(t)$, the system can be written as

$$\sum_{i=1}^{m} (z_i, z_j) \alpha_{im}' + \mu \sum_{i=1}^{m} ((z_i, z_j)) \alpha_{im} + \sum_{i,k=1}^{m} b(z_i, z_k, z_j) \alpha_{im} \alpha_{km} + \sum_{i=1}^{m} (Mz_i, z_j) \alpha_{im} = \langle u(t), z_j \rangle.$$

Now, due to the smoothness of the coefficients, we can use a classical result from the theory of ordinary differential equations, and ensure that there exists a unique classical solution y_m defined on a maximal interval $[0, t_m]$ with $0 < t_m \leq T$. For the convergence, we need to show that $t_m = T$ for all m. In that way, the interval of existence of solutions will not change when m goes to infinity. If $t_m < T$, then

$$\limsup_{t \to t_m} \| y_m(t) \| = +\infty. \quad (27)$$

In the following stage, we prove that $(y_m(t))_{m \in \mathbb{N}}$ is bounded on $[0, T]$ by a constant independent of t and m. Then, the solution is defined in $[0, T]$ for all m.

Stage 2: Estimates for the approximate solution.

Next, we show that $(y_m)_{m \in \mathbb{N}}$ is uniformly bounded in $L^2([0, T]; \mathbb{V})$. Indeed, multiplying equation (26) by $\alpha_{jm}(t)$ and summing from $j = 1$ to m, we obtain

$$(y_m'(t), y_m(t)) + \mu((y_m(t), y_m(t))) + b(y_m(t), y_m(t), y_m(t)) + (My_m(t), y_m(t)) = \langle u(t), y_m(t) \rangle.$$

Using the Cauchy–Schwarz inequality and keeping in mind that $b(y(t), y(t), y(t)) = 0$ for almost all $t \in [0, T]$, we obtain

$$\frac{1}{2}\frac{d}{dt}\mid y_m(t)\mid^2 +\mu\parallel y_m(t)\parallel^2 = \langle u(t), y_m(t)\rangle - (My_m(t), y_m(t))$$
$$\leq \mid \langle u(t), y_m(t)\rangle - (My_m(t), y_m(t)) \mid$$
$$\leq \mid u(t), y_m(t) \mid + \mid My_m(t), y_m(t) \mid$$
$$\leq \parallel u(t) \parallel_{L^2([0,T],\mathbb{V}')} \parallel y_m(t) \parallel + \mid My_m(t) \parallel y_m(t) \mid$$
$$\leq \parallel u(t) \parallel_{L^2([0,T],\mathbb{V}')} \parallel y_m(t) \parallel + \parallel M \parallel \mid y_m(t) \parallel y_m(t) \mid.$$

Therefore, we obtain

$$\frac{d}{dt}\mid y_m(t)\mid^2 +\mu\parallel y_m(t)\parallel^2 \leq \frac{\parallel u(t)\parallel^2}{2} + \frac{\mid y_m(t)\mid^2}{2} + \parallel M \parallel \mid y_m(t) \mid^2. \tag{28}$$

The last inequality implies that

$$\frac{d}{dt}\mid y_m(t)\mid^2 \leq \mid u(t)\mid^2 + c_0 \mid y_m(t)\mid^2, \quad c_0 = \max\{1, \parallel M \parallel\}.$$

Integrating on both sides of the previous expression and using the Grönwall's inequality, we deduce that

$$\mid y_m(t)\mid^2 - \mid y_m(0)\mid^2 \leq \mid u\mid^2 t + c_0 \int_0^t \mid y_m(t)\mid^2 dt$$
$$\mid y_m(t)\mid^2 \leq \mid y_m(0)\mid^2 + \mid u\mid^2 t + c_0 \int_0^t \mid y_m(t)\mid^2 dt$$
$$\mid y_m(t)\mid^2 \leq \left(\mid y_0\mid^2 + \mid u\mid^2 t\right) e^{\int_0^t c_0 \, dt}$$
$$\mid y_m(t)\mid^2 \leq \left(\mid y_0\mid^2 + \mid u\mid^2 t\right) e^{c_0 t}.$$

It follows that

$$\sup_{t\in[0,\,t_m]} \mid y_m(t)\mid^2 \leq \left(\mid y_0\mid^2 + \mid u\mid^2 t\right) e^{c_0 t}. \tag{29}$$

This tell us, that $t_m = T$ for all m. Moreover, $(y_m)_{m\in\mathbb{N}}$ is uniformly bounded in $L^\infty([0,T];H)$.

On other hand, integrating from 0 to T on both sides of Equation (28) and using (29), we obtain

$$\parallel y_m(T) \parallel^2 + \mu \int_0^T \parallel y_m(t) \parallel^2 dt \leq \left(\mid y_0\mid^2 + \mid u\mid^2 T + c_0(\mid y_0\mid^2 + \mid u\mid^2 T)e^{c_0 T}\right),$$

therefore,

$$\mu \int_0^T \parallel y_m(t) \parallel^2 dt \leq \left(\mid y_0\mid^2 + \mid u\mid^2 T + c_0(\mid y_0\mid^2 + \mid u\mid^2 T)e^{c_0 T}\right).$$

Consequently, $(y_m)_{m\in\mathbb{N}}$ is uniformly bounded in $L^2([0,T];\mathbb{V})$.

Stage 3: Estimates for the derivative of approximate solution.

Now, we prove that the derivative $y'_m(t)$ is uniformly bounded in $L^2([0,T];\mathbb{V})$. Indeed, multiplying (26) by $\alpha'_{jm}(t)$ and summing from $j=1$ to m, we obtain

$$\mid y'_m(t)\mid^2 + \mu((y_m(t), y'_m(t))) + b(y_m(t), y_m(t), y'_m(t)) + ((My_m(t), y'_m(t))) = \langle u(t), y'_m(t)\rangle.$$

After integrate the last equation, we obtain

$$\int_0^t |y'_m(t)|^2 \, dt + \mu \int_0^t ((y_m(t), y'_m(t)) \, dt + \int_0^t ((My_m(t), y'_m(t))) \, dt +$$
$$+ \int_0^t b(y_m(t), y_m(t), y'_m(t)) \, dt = \int_0^t \langle u(t), y'_m(t) \rangle dt.$$

Therefore

$$\int_0^t |y'_m(t)|^2 \, dt + \mu \int_0^t ((y_m(t), y'_m(t)) \, dt + \int_0^t ((My_m(t), y'_m(t))) \, dt$$
$$= \int_0^t \langle u(t), y'_m(t) \rangle dt - \int_0^t b(y_m(t), y_m(t), y'_m(t)) \, dt.$$

Taking into account the Cauchy's and Ladyzhenskaya's inequalities, we have that

$$\int_0^t |y'_m(t)|^2 \, dt + \frac{\mu}{2} \int_0^t ((y_m(t), y'_m(t))) \, dt + \int_0^t ((My_m(t), y'_m(t))) \, dt =$$
$$= \int_0^t \langle u(t), y'_m(t) \rangle \, dt - \int_0^t b(y_m(t), y'_m(t), y_m(t)) \, dt$$
$$\leq \| u(t) \|^2_{L^2([0,T];\mathbb{V}')} \| y'_m(t) \|_{L^2([0,T];\mathbb{V})} + \int_0^t |y_m(t)|^2_{L^4([0,T];\mathbb{V})} |\nabla y'_m(t)| \, dt$$
$$\leq \frac{1}{\alpha^2} \| u(t) \|^2_{L^2([0,T];\mathbb{V}')} + \frac{\alpha^2}{4} \| y'_m(t) \|^2_{L^2([0,T];\mathbb{V})}$$
$$+ c \int_0^t |y_m(t)|^{1/2} |\nabla y_m(t)|^{3/2} \ast |\nabla y'_m(t)| \, dt$$
$$\leq \frac{1}{\alpha^2} \| u(t) \|^2_{L^2([0,T];\mathbb{V}')} + \frac{\alpha^2}{4} \| y'_m(t) \|^2_{L^2([0,T];\mathbb{V})} + c \int_0^t |\nabla y_m(t)| |\nabla y'_m(t)| \, dt$$
$$\leq \frac{1}{\alpha^2} \| u(t) \|^2_{L^2([0,T];\mathbb{V}')} + \frac{\alpha^2}{4} \| y'_m(t) \|^2_{L^2([0,T];\mathbb{V})}$$
$$+ c \left(\int_0^t |\nabla y_m(t)|^2 \, dt \right)^{1/2} \left(\int_0^t |\nabla y'_m(t)|^2 \, dt \right)^{1/2}$$
$$\leq \frac{1}{\alpha^2} \| u(t) \|^2_{L^2([0,T];\mathbb{V}')} + \frac{\alpha^2}{4} \| y'_m(t) \|^2_{L^2([0,T];\mathbb{V})}$$
$$+ c \| y_m(t) \|^2_{L^2([0,T];\mathbb{V})} + \frac{\alpha^2}{4} \| y'_m(t) \|^2_{L^2([0,T];\mathbb{V})}.$$

In summary, we have the following:

$$2 \int_0^t |y'_m(t)|^2 \, dt + \mu \int_0^t ((y_m(t), y'_m(t))) \, dt + \int_0^t ((My_m(t), y'_m(t))) \, dt$$
$$\leq \frac{2}{\alpha^2} \| u(t) \|^2_{L^2([0,T];\mathbb{V}')} + c \| y_m(t) \|^2_{L^2([0,T];\mathbb{V})} \text{ for all } t \in [0,T].$$

In this way, due to the fact that $y_m(t)$ is uniformly bounded in $L^\infty([0,T];\mathbb{V})$, it follows that $y'_m(t)$ is uniformly bounded in $L^2([0,T];\mathbb{V})$.

Stage 4: Extraction of subsequence and convergence to the solution.

We can extract a subsequence of $(y_m)_{m\in\mathbb{N}}$ that converges (in an appropriate sense) to a function y and then go to the limit in the approximate problem given by (26) as follows:

Since $(y_m)_{m\in\mathbb{N}}$ is uniformly bounded in $L^2([0,T];\mathbb{V}) \cap L^\infty([0,T];H)$, then there is a subsequence (which we will denote in the same way) $(y_m)_{m\in\mathbb{N}}$ such that

$$\begin{cases} y_m \rightharpoonup y \text{ weak in } L^2([0,T];\mathbb{V}) \\ y_m \rightharpoonup y \text{ weak-* in } L^\infty([0,T];H) \\ \frac{\partial y_m}{\partial t} \rightharpoonup \frac{\partial y}{\partial t} \text{ weakly in } L^2([0,T];\mathbb{V}). \end{cases} \quad (30)$$

Now, note that $\mathbb{V} \hookrightarrow H$ with dense and continuous injections.

Stage 5: Existence of solutions.

Let us take a function $\eta \in \mathcal{D}(0,T)$. In Equation (26), we multiply by η, and integrate over the interval $(0,T)$. Then we obtain,

$$-\int_0^T (y_m(t), \eta'(t)z_j)\, dt + \mu \int_0^T ((y_m(t), \eta(t)z_j)) + \int_0^T b(y_m(t), y_m(t), z_j\eta(t))\, dt$$
$$+ \int_0^T ((My_m(t), z_j\eta(t))) = \int_0^T (u(t), z_j\eta(t))\, dt.$$

Consequently, we have that,

$$-\int_0^T (y(t), \eta'(t)z_j)\, dt + \mu \int_0^T ((y(t), \eta(t)z_j)) + \int_0^T b(y(t), y(t), \eta(t)z_j)\, dt$$
$$+ \int_0^T ((My(t), \eta(t)z_j)) = \int_0^T (u(t), \eta(t)z_j)\, dt,$$

or equivalently

$$\int_0^T (y'(t), \eta(t)z_j)\, dt + \mu \int_0^T ((y(t), \eta(t)z_j)) + \int_0^T b(y(t), y(t), \eta(t)z_j)\, dt$$
$$+ \int_0^T ((My(t), \eta(t)z_j)) = \int_0^T (u(t), \eta(t)z_j)\, dt.$$

This equality is true by linearity and by density for all $v \in \mathbb{V}$. Thus, we have that y verifies the equation given by (17).

Now, let us show that $y(0) = y_0$. Since y is a weak solution of (4), taking $\eta \in C^\infty([0,T])$ with $\eta(T) = 0$, for all $v \in \mathbb{V}$ we have that:

$$-\int_0^T (y(t), \eta'(t)v)\, dt + \mu \int_0^T ((y(t), \eta(t)v)) + \int_0^T b(y(t), y(t), \eta(t)v)\, dt$$
$$+ \int_0^T ((My(t), \eta(t)v)) = (u_0, \eta(0)v) + \int_0^T (u(t), \eta(t)v)\, dt.$$

On the other hand,

$$\frac{d}{dt} \langle y, \eta(v) \rangle = \langle y_t, \eta(v) \rangle + \langle y, \eta_t(v) \rangle,$$

we can integrate from 0 a T and we obtain the following:

$$\langle y(t), \eta(t)(v) \rangle - \langle y(0), \eta(0) \rangle = \int_0^T [\langle y_t, \eta(v) \rangle + \langle y, \eta_t(v) \rangle]\, dt$$
$$= \int_0^T \langle y_t, \eta(v) \rangle\, dt + \int_0^T \langle y, \eta_t(v) \rangle\, dt.$$

Therefore,

$$\int_0^T \langle y, \eta_t(v) \rangle\, dt = \langle y(t), \eta(t)(v) \rangle - \langle y(0), \eta(0) \rangle - \int_0^T \langle y_t, \eta(v) \rangle\, dt.$$

Thus, if η is such that $\eta(T) = 0$, it follows:

$$\int_0^T \langle y, \eta_t(v) \rangle\, dt = -\langle y(0), \eta(0)v \rangle - \int_0^T \langle y_t, \eta(v) \rangle\, dt.$$

Thus, we obtain that

$$\eta(0)(y_0 - y(0), v) = 0 \text{ for all } \eta \in C^\infty([0,T]), v \in \mathbb{V}.$$

Taking $\eta(0) = 1$, obtain that $y(0) = y_0 \in \mathbb{V}$.

Stage 6: Continuity and uniqueness of the weak solution.

Let us show that $y : [0, T] \longmapsto \mathbb{V}$ is continuous. Indeed, note that the non-linear operator $B(y)$ is defined by (19), now since $y_t = u - \mu A y - B(y)$, in this way, by the Lemma (1) it follows that $B(y) \in L^2([0, T]; \mathbb{V}')$ and also u, Ay, $My \in L^2([0, T]; \mathbb{V}')$, therefore, $y_t \in L^2([0, T]; \mathbb{V}')$, thus $y \in C([0, T]; \mathbb{V})$.

Now, suppose that there exist two weak solutions $y_1(t), y_2(t)$ for the equations in the dynamics of the stratified fluids given by (4), with the initials values $y_{0_1}, y_{0_2} \in \mathbb{V}$. Let us denote by $y(t) = y_1(t) - y_2(t)$, then $y(t)$ satisfies $y_t(t) \in L^2([0, T]; \mathbb{V}')$, and for every test function δ, we have the following:

$$\langle y_t, \delta \rangle + \mu(\nabla y, \nabla \delta) + (My, \delta) + b(y_1, y_1, \delta) - b(y_2, y_2, \delta) = 0.$$

In this way, taking $\delta = y$, it follows that:

$$\frac{1}{2}\frac{d}{dt} \mid y(t) \mid^2 + \mu \mid \nabla y(t) \mid^2 + \mid My(t) \mid^2 + b(y_1(t), y_1(t), y(t)) - b(y_2(t), y_2(t), y(t)) = 0.$$

Now, adding and subtracting $b(y_1(t), y_2(t), y(t))$ and having in mind that $b(y_1(t), y(t), y(t)) = 0$, we obtain the following:

$$\frac{d}{dt} \mid y(t) \mid^2 + \mid My(t) \mid^2 + 2\mu \mid \nabla y(t) \mid^2 = 2(-b(y_1(t), y_1(t), y(t)) + b(y_2(t), y_2(t), y(t)))$$

$$= -2b(y(t), y_2(t), y(t))$$

$$= -2 \sum_{i,j=1}^{3} \int_{\Omega} y^i \frac{\partial y_2^j}{\partial t^i} y^j \, dt$$

$$\leq 2 \sum_{i,j=1}^{3} \left(\int_{\Omega} \mid y^i \mid^4 dt \right)^{1/4} \left(\int_{\Omega} \mid \nabla y_2^j \mid^2 dt \right)^{1/2} \left(\int_{\Omega} \mid y^j \mid^4 dt \right)^{1/4}$$

$$\leq 2 \mid \nabla y_2(t) \mid \| y(t) \|_4^2$$

$$\leq 2c \mid \nabla y_2(t) \mid \mid y(t) \mid^{1/2} \mid \nabla y(t) \mid^{3/2}$$

$$\leq c \mid y(t) \mid^{1/2} \mid \nabla y(t) \mid^{3/2}$$

$$\leq c(\mu)(\mid y(t) \mid^{1/2})^4 + 2\mu(\mid \nabla y(t) \mid^{3/2})^{4/3}$$

$$\leq c \mid y(t) \mid^2 + 2\mu \mid \nabla y(t) \mid^2.$$

In summary, we have that

$$\frac{d}{dt} \mid y(t) \mid^2 + \mid My(t) \mid^2 + 2\mu \mid \nabla y(t) \mid^2 \leq c \mid y(t) \mid^2 + 2\mu \mid \nabla y(t) \mid^2.$$

This implies that

$$\frac{d}{dt} \mid y(t) \mid^2 + \mid My(t) \mid^2 < c \mid y(t) \mid^2.$$

Now, since $y_2(t) \in L^2([0, T]; \mathbb{V})$, we can apply Gronwall's Lemma. Using the fact that $y(0) = 0$, it follows

$$\mid y(t) \mid^2 \leq 0 \text{ for all } t \in [0, T],$$

thus, $y_1 = y_2$, as we wanted to prove. □

4. Study of the Existence of Solutions for Our Optimal Control Problem

In this section, we will show the existence of optimal controls for our non-linear system given by (7).

Let us show that our optimal control problem formulated in (6) and (7) has a solution in U_{ad}. To prove this fact, we need the following result associated with the non-linear operator.

Lemma 2 ([14]). *Assume that y_n converges to y in $W^\alpha([0,T];\mathbb{V})$ weakly for $1 \leq \alpha \leq 2$. Then, for any $v \in L^2([0,T];\mathbb{V})$,*

$$\langle B(y_n), v \rangle_{L^2([0,T];\mathbb{V}'), L^2([0,T];\mathbb{V})} \longrightarrow \langle B(y), v \rangle_{L^2([0,T];\mathbb{V}'), L^2([0,T];\mathbb{V})} \text{ as } n \longrightarrow \infty.$$

Now, with the following result, we want to show that our optimal control problem formulated by (6) and (7) has a solution in U_{ad}.

Theorem 2. *The optimal control problem given by (6) and (7) admits an optimal solution $\overline{u} \in U_{ad}$ with associated state $\overline{y} \in W^\alpha([0,T];\mathbb{V})$ for $1 \leq \alpha \leq 2$.*

Proof. Note that the set of admissible controls defined by (3) is non-empty, convex, and closed in $L^2(\Omega)^4$. Then, for every control $u \in L^2(\Omega)^4$, applying Theorem 1, there is a unique weak solution of the state Equations (20) and (21). Therefore, we have that $J(y,u) \geq 0$ for every admissible pair (y,u).

Hence, there exists the infimum of J over all admissible controls and states that such:

$$J(y_n, u_n) = \int_\Omega \|y_n - y_d\|^2 \, dt + \lambda \int_\Omega \|u_n - u_d\|^2 \, dt,$$

then,

$$\begin{aligned}
\|u_n\|^2 &= \|(u_n - u_d) + u_d\|^2 \\
&\leq (\|u_n - u_d\| + \|u_d\|)^2 \\
&= \|u_n - u_d\|^2 + 2\|u_d\| \cdot \|u_n - u_d\| + \|u_d\|^2 \\
&\leq \|u_n - u_d\|^2 + \|u_d\|^2 + \|u_n - u_d\|^2 + \|u_d\|^2 \\
&= 2\|u_n - u_d\|^2 + 2\|u_d\|^2,
\end{aligned}$$

now it follows that

$$\|u_n\|_{L^2([0,T];\mathbb{V})} < \infty \implies \int_0^T \|u_n(x,t)\|^2 \, dt \leq 2\int_0^T \|u_n - u_d\|^2 \, dt + 2\|u_d\|^2 T$$
$$\leq J(u_n, u_n) + 2\|u_d\|^2 T$$
$$< \infty.$$

In summary, we have that:

$$0 \leq \overline{J} = \inf_{(y,u) \text{ admisible}} J(y,u)$$
$$< \infty.$$

On the other hand, there is a sequence $(y_n, u_n)_{n \in \mathbb{N}}$ of admissible pairs such that $J(y_n, u_n) \longrightarrow \overline{J}$ as $n \longrightarrow +\infty$.

First, we will show that $(u_n)_{n \in \mathbb{N}}$ and $(y_n)_{n \in \mathbb{N}}$ are bounded sequences in $L^2(\Omega)^4$ and $W^\alpha([0,T];\mathbb{V})$, respectively.

From the convergence, we see that the set $(J(y_n, u_n))_{n \in \mathbb{N}}$ is bounded, this implies that the set $(u_n)_{n \in \mathbb{N}}$ is bounded in $L^2(\Omega)^4$.

Now, we need to show that $(y_n)_{n \in \mathbb{N}}$ and $(y_{nt})_{n \in \mathbb{N}}$ are bounded in $L^2([0,T];\mathbb{V})$. Indeed,

$$\begin{cases} y_{nt}(t) + \mu A y_n(t) + M y_n(t) + B(y_n(t)) = u_n(t) & \text{in } L^2([0,T];\mathbb{V}') \\ y_n(0) = y_0 & \text{in } \mathbb{V}. \end{cases} \quad (31)$$

Since $y_n(t) \in L^2([0,T]; \mathbb{V})$, we multiply (31) by $\chi_{(0,t)} y_n(t)$, where $\chi_{(0,t)}$ is the characteristic function on the interval $(0,t)$ and applying the identity $b(y_n(t), y_n(t), y_n(t)) = 0$, we get

$$\int_0^t (y_{nt}(t), y_n(t))\, dt + \mu \int_0^t \|y_n(t)\|^2\, dt + \int_0^t ((M(y_n(t), y_n(t)))\, dt = \int_0^t \langle u_n(t), y_n(t)\rangle\, dt, \tag{32}$$

The right-hand side can be estimated by

$$\left| \int_0^t (u_n(t), y_n(t))\, dt \right| \leq \int_0^t |u_n(t)| \cdot |y_n(t)|\, dt$$

$$\leq C \int_0^t \|y_n(t)\| \cdot |u_n(t)|\, dt \tag{33}$$

$$\leq \frac{\mu}{2} \int_0^t \|y_n(t)\|^2\, dt + \frac{C^2}{2\mu} \int_0^t |u_n(t)|^2\, dt,$$

where C only depends on Ω.

Then, applying the integration in parts to (32) and (33) implies that:

$$|y_n(t)|^2 + \mu \int_0^t \|y_n(t)\|^2\, dt + \int_0^t ((M(y_n(t), y_n(t))))\, dt \leq |y_n(0)|^2 + \frac{C^2}{\mu} \int_0^t |u_n(t)|^2\, dt$$

$$\leq |y_0|^2 + \frac{C^2}{\mu} \|u_n\|_{L^2(\Omega)^4}.$$

Since $(u_n)_{n \in \mathbb{N}}$ is bounded in $L^2(\Omega)^4$ and $(y_n)_{n \in \mathbb{N}}$ is bounded in $L^\infty([0,T]; H)$ and $L^\infty([0,T]; V)$, it follows that $(y_n)_{n \in \mathbb{N}}$ is bounded in $L^2([0,T]; V)$.

Now, multiplying (31) by $y_{nt} \in L^2([0,T]; V)$, we obtain the following:

$$\|y_{nt}\|^2_{L^2(\Omega)^4} + \mu \int_0^T ((y_n(t), y_{nt}(t)))\, dt + \int_0^T (M(y_n(t), y_{nt}(t))\, dt +$$

$$+ \int_0^T b(y_n(t), y_n(t), y_{nt}(t))\, dt = \int_0^T (u_n(t), y_{nt}(t))\, dt. \tag{34}$$

Thus

$$\|y_{nt}\|^2_{L^2(\Omega)^4} + \mu \int_0^T ((y_n(t), y_{nt}(t)))\, dt + \int_0^T (M(y_n(t), y_{nt}(t))\, dt$$

$$= \int_0^T (u_n(t), y_{nt}(t))\, dt - \int_0^T b(y_n(t), y_n(t), y_{nt}(t))\, dt.$$

On the side right, we have the following estimate:

$$\left| \int_0^T (u_n(t), y_{nt}(t))\, dt \right| \leq \int_0^T \left(\frac{|u_n(t)|^2}{4} + |y_{nt}(t)|^2 \right) dt$$

$$= \frac{1}{4} \|u_n\|^2_{L^2(\Omega)^4} + \|y_{nt}\|^2_{L^2(\Omega)^4}.$$

Note that

$$\mu \int_0^T ((y_n(t), y_{nt}(t)))\, dt = \frac{\mu}{2}\left(\|y_n(T)\|^2 - \|y_0\|^2 \right).$$

Then, since $(y_n)_{n \in \mathbb{N}}$ is bounded in $L^\infty([0,T]; H)$ and $L^\infty([0,T]; V)$, it follows that

$$\left| \int_0^T b(y_n(t), y_n(t), y_{nt}(t))\, dt \right| \leq C \int_0^T |y_n(t)|^{1/2} \cdot \|y_n(t)\|^{3/2} \cdot \|y_{nt}(t)\|\, dt$$

$$\leq C \int_0^T \|y_{nt}(t)\|\, dt.$$

Therefore, from Equation (34), we have

$$\frac{\mu}{2}\|y_n(T)\|^2 + \int_0^t ((M(y_n(t), y_n(t))) \, dt + C \int_0^T \|y_{nt}(t)\| \, dt \leq \frac{\mu}{2}\|y_0\|^2 + \frac{1}{4}\|u_n\|^2_{L^2(\Omega)^4}.$$

Since $(u_n)_{n \in \mathbb{N}}$ is bounded in $L^2(\Omega)^4$, we can ensure that $(y_{nt})_{n \in \mathbb{N}}$ is bounded in $L^2([0,T];V)$. Thus, it follows that $(y_n)_{n \in \mathbb{N}}$ is bounded in $W^\alpha([0,T];V)$.

Then, we can extract a subsequence $(y'_n, u'_n)_{n \in \mathbb{N}}$ converging weakly in the space $W^\alpha([0,T];V) \times L^2(\Omega)^4$ to some limit $(\bar{y}, \bar{u})$.

Now, let us show that $(\bar{y}, \bar{u})$ is an admissible pair, that is, it satisfies the state equations given by (21). Indeed, note that the set of admissible controls U_{ad} is non-empty, convex, and closed in $L^2(\Omega)^3$, so it is weakly closed. Therefore, $\bar{u}$ is admissible, that is, $\bar{u} \in U_{ad}$, and $\bar{y}$ is the state associated with $\bar{u}$.

Then, let us show that the pair $(\bar{y}, \bar{u})$ satisfies the state equations given by (21), that is, for every $v \in L^2([0,T];V)$, we have the following convergences:

$$\langle y_{n't}, v \rangle_{L^2([0,T];V'), L^2([0,T];V)} \longrightarrow \langle \bar{y}_t, v \rangle_{L^2([0,T];V'), L^2([0,T];V)},$$
$$\langle Ay_{n'}, v \rangle_{L^2([0,T];V'), L^2([0,T];V)} \longrightarrow \langle A\bar{y}, v \rangle_{L^2([0,T];V'), L^2([0,T];V)},$$
$$\langle Ay_{n't}, v \rangle_{L^2([0,T];V'), L^2([0,T];V)} \longrightarrow \langle A\bar{y}_{n't}, v \rangle_{L^2([0,T];V'), L^2([0,T];V)},$$
$$\langle u_{n'}, v \rangle_{L^2([0,T];V'), L^2([0,T];V)} \longrightarrow \langle \bar{u}, v \rangle_{L^2([0,T];V'), L^2([0,T];V)},$$

as $n' \longrightarrow \infty$.

Then, according to Lemma 2, we obtain the convergence of the non-linear term from:

$$\langle B(y_{n'}), v \rangle_{L^2([0,T];V'), L^2([0,T];V)} \longrightarrow \langle B(\bar{y}, v) \rangle_{L^2([0,T];V'), L^2([0,T];V)} \text{ as } n' \longrightarrow +\infty.$$

Consequently, all the terms in the weak formulation of the state equation converge, and

$$\langle \bar{y}_t + \mu A\bar{y} + B(\bar{y}) + M(\bar{y}) - \bar{u}, v \rangle_{L^2([0,T];V'), L^2([0,T];V)} = 0,$$

is fulfilled for all $v \in L^2([0,T];V)$.

Moreover, since the imbedding $W^\alpha([0,T];V) \hookrightarrow C([0,T];V)$ is continuous, then the mapping $w \longmapsto w(0)$ is linear and continuous from $W^\alpha([0,T];V)$ to V, hence, we have that $y_n(0)$ converges weakly to $\bar{y}(0)$.

By the construction of the proof, we have that $y_0 = y_n(0)$ for all n, hence, it holds $\bar{y}(0) = y_0$.

Finally, it remains to show $\bar{J} = J(\bar{y}, \bar{u}) = J(v)$. Remember that our energy functional is given by (20), therefore we have that $J = J(v)$ is a convex functional. Moreover, $J(v)$ is continuous on $W^\alpha([0,T];V) \times L^2(\Omega)^4$, thus by Definition 1 we have that $J = J(v)$ is weakly lower semicontinuous, that is,

$$J(\bar{y}, \bar{u}) \leq \liminf J(y'_n, u'_n) = \bar{J}.$$

Now, since $(\bar{y}, \bar{u})$ is an admissible pair, and $\bar{J}$ is the infimum over all admissible pairs, then it follows that $\bar{J} = \bar{J}(\bar{y}, \bar{u})$.

Thus, we have that $(\bar{y}, \bar{u})$ is a pair of optimal controls. □

5. Optimality Condition

In this section, we will show that the optimal solution must satisfy the first-order necessary optimality condition associated with our optimal control problem given in (6).

We will study the case in which the Gâteaux derivative of the energy functional vanishes. We obtain a possible candidate solution for our optimal control, that is, if the Gâteaux derivative of our functional exists, then the optimal solution must satisfy the first-order necessary condition.

The first-order necessary condition allows conclusions to be drawn that have to do with the form and characterization of control problems.

In this part, we will establish the first-order necessary optimization condition associated with our optimal control problem given in (6). This condition will be necessary for local optimization since it is of vital importance in many aspects, that is, from the first-order necessary conditions, we can establish the candidates to be optimal controls by numerical approximations in such a way that the approximate solutions allow us to solve the first-order optimization system at a discrete level and this would be additional work that could be studied later as future research work.

Now, we can show that the optimal solution must satisfy the first-order necessary condition associated with our problem given in (20). This is performed directly using the Gâteaux derivative of our functional $\Psi(u)$. In fact, for every $h \in L^2([0,T]; L^2(\Omega)^4)$ and for every $\alpha \in \mathbb{R}$, we have that

$$\Psi(\bar{u} + \alpha h) \geq \Psi(\bar{u}),$$

due to the very definition of $\bar{u}$. In particular, we have that

$$\forall \alpha > 0, \quad \frac{\Psi(\bar{u} + \alpha h) - \Psi(\bar{u})}{\alpha} \geq 0,$$

and

$$\forall \alpha < 0, \quad \frac{\Psi(\bar{u} + \alpha h) - \Psi(\bar{u})}{\alpha} \leq 0,$$

which implies that the derivative at the point $\alpha \in \mathbb{R}$ of the function $\alpha \longmapsto \Psi(\bar{u} + \alpha h)$, is precisely the Gâteaux derivative of Ψ in the direction of h at the point $\bar{u}$ vanishes for every $h \in L^2([0,T]; L^2(\Omega)^4)$.

Before stating our main result, let us recall the following result:

Theorem 3 ([8]). *Let y_0 be in $\mathbb{V}$; the mapping $u \longmapsto y_u$ from $L^2([0,T]; L^2(\Omega)^4)$ to $W^\alpha([0,T]; \mathbb{V})$, is Gâteaux differentiable $((Y'(u)) \cdot h_1)$ in every direction h_1 in $L^2([0,T]; L^2(\Omega)^4)$. Furthermore, $(Y'(u)) \cdot h_1 = \sigma(h_1)$ is the solution of the problem given by*

$$\begin{cases} \dfrac{d\sigma}{dt} + \mu A \sigma + B'(y_u) \cdot \sigma + M\sigma = h_1 \text{ in } Q_T, \\ \sigma \in V, \\ \sigma(0) = 0 \text{ in } \Omega; \end{cases} \quad (35)$$

we also have that $\sigma \in L^\infty(0,T;V)) \cap L^2(0,T,(H^2(\Omega))^4)$ and $\|B'(y_u)\sigma\|_{L^2(J_1(\Omega))'} < c\|y_u\|\|\sigma\|$.

Let us introduce the definition of locally optimal control.

Definition 4 (locally optimal control). *A control $\bar{u} \in U_{ad}$ is said to be locally optimal in $L^2(\Omega)^3$ if there is a constant $\beta > 0$ such that*

$$J(\bar{y}, \bar{u}) \leq J(y, u),$$

holds for all $u \in U_{ad}$ with $\|\bar{u} - u\|_{L^2(\Omega)^4} \leq \beta$. Here $\bar{y}$ and y denote the state of the system associated with $\bar{u}$ and u, respectively, that is, $\bar{y} = Y(\bar{u})$ and $y = Y(u)$.

The first-order necessary optimization conditions are in many references, but for the related optimization conditions for optimal control problems with elliptic and parabolic partial differential equations (see [6,7,9]), they were the main references that helped us a lot, studying optimal control problems, as well as the study of stratified fluids (see [15–17]).

Now, let us show our main result of this section and show the first-order necessary optimization condition for our control problem given in (6).

Theorem 4. *Let U be a real Banach space, and let $U_{ad} \subset L^2(\Omega)^4$ be a non-empty, convex, and closed set in $L^2(\Omega)^4$ and the functional $\Psi : U \longrightarrow \mathbb{R}$ be Gâteaux differentiable on U_{ad}. Let $\overline{u} \in U_{ad}$ be a solution of the problem*

$$\min_{u \in U_{ad}} \Psi(u). \tag{36}$$

Then the following optimality condition

$$\Psi'(\overline{u})(u - \overline{u}) \geqslant 0 \tag{37}$$

holds for all $u \in U_{ad}$. If, additionally, $\overline{u} \in U_{ad}$ solves the variational inequality above and Ψ is convex, then $\overline{u}$ is the unique solution of (36).

Proof. Let $u \in U_{ad}$ arbitrary. Consider a convex linear combination given by:

$$u(t) = \overline{u} + t(u - \overline{u}) \tag{38}$$

for any $t \in [0, 1]$.

Now since U_{ad} is non-empty, convex, and closed in $L^2(\Omega)^3$, then we have that $u(t) = \overline{u} + t(u - \overline{u}) \in U_{ad}$ for all $t \in [0, 1]$. Then, from the optimality of $\overline{u}$, we have that

$$\Psi(\overline{u}) \leq \Psi(u(t)) \quad \forall t \in [0, 1]. \tag{39}$$

Then, inserting (38) into (39) we obtain:

$$\Psi(\overline{u}) \leq \Psi(\overline{u} + t(u - \overline{u}))$$
$$0 \leq \Psi(\overline{u} + t(u - \overline{u})) - \Psi(\overline{u}),$$

We can rewrite the last inequality by:

$$\Psi(\overline{u} + t(u - \overline{u})) - \Psi(\overline{u}) \geq 0 \quad \forall t \in [0, 1],$$

thus, it follows that

$$\lim_{t \to 0^+} \frac{\Psi(\overline{u} + t(u - \overline{u})) - \Psi(\overline{u})}{t} \geq 0.$$

Now, using the fact that Ψ is Gâteaux differentiable on U_{ad}, and taking the limit as $t \longrightarrow 0$, we obtain

$$\Psi'(\overline{u})(u - \overline{u}) \geq 0.$$

On the other hand, let $u \in U_{ad}$ be arbitrary and let $\overline{u} \in U_{ad}$ be a solution of Equation (37). Since Ψ is convex, then we have that:

$$\Psi(u) - \Psi(\overline{u}) \geq \Psi'(\overline{u})(u - \overline{u}) \quad \forall u \in U_{ad}. \tag{40}$$

In fact, for all $t \in [0, 1]$, it follows

$$\Psi(\overline{u} + t(u - \overline{u})) \leq (1 - t)\Psi(\overline{u}) + t\Psi(u),$$

hence,

$$\Psi(u) - \Psi(\overline{u}) = \frac{(1-t)\Psi(\overline{u}) + t\Psi(u) - \Psi(\overline{u})}{t}$$
$$\geq \frac{\Psi(\overline{u} + t(u - \overline{u})) - \Psi(\overline{u})}{t}$$
$$\geq \Psi'(\overline{u})(u - \overline{u}) \quad (t \longrightarrow 0^+).$$

Then, from Equations (37) and (40), we obtain that

$$\Psi(u) - \Psi(\overline{u}) \geq \Psi'(\overline{u})(u - \overline{u})$$
$$\geq 0 \quad \forall u \in U_{ad}.$$

Therefore, we have that $\overline{u}$ is an optimal solution. □

In order to characterize optimal solutions, we introduce the adjoint problem to the equations, which describes the non-linear motion in the dynamics of viscous and incompressible stratified fluids in $\mathbb{R}^3$.

Theorem 5 (Necessary Condition). *Let $\overline{u}$ be a locally optimal control for (20) with associated state $\overline{y} = Y(\overline{u})$. Then there exists a unique solution $\overline{\eta} \in V$, which is the weak solution of the adjoint equation*

$$\begin{cases} -\overline{\eta}_t + \mu A\overline{\eta} + B'(\overline{y})^*\overline{\eta} + M\overline{\eta} = (\widehat{y} - y_d) & \text{with } x \in \Omega, \ t > 0, \\ \nabla \cdot \overline{\eta} = 0, & \text{with } x \in \Omega, \ t > 0, \\ \overline{\eta}(x,t) = 0, & \text{with } x \in \partial\Omega, \ t > 0, \\ \overline{\eta}(T) = 0 & \text{with } x \in \Omega. \end{cases} \quad (41)$$

Moreover, the following inequality

$$\int_0^T \int (\overline{\eta} + \lambda(\overline{u} - u_d)) \cdot (u - \overline{u}) \, dx \, dt \geq 0, \text{ for all } u \in U_{ad} \subset L^2(Q_T)^3, \quad (42)$$

is satisfied.

Proof. First of all, let us work with our reduced energy functional Ψ given in (24), which is given by:

$$J(u) := J(Y(u), u) = \Psi(u),$$

where we have that

$$\Psi(u) = \frac{1}{2} \int_0^T \|Y(u) - y_d\|_{L^2(\Omega)}^2 \, dt + \frac{\lambda}{2} \int_0^T \|u - u_d\|_{L^2(\Omega)}^2 \, dt. \quad (43)$$

By Banach space optimization principles, we know that the variational inequality

$$\Psi'(\overline{u})(u - \overline{u}) \geq 0, \text{ for all } u \in U_{ad}$$

is a necessary condition for local optimality of $\overline{u}$. It remains to compute Ψ' and to derive the adjoint system. Let us write Ψ in the form given by (43).

The first derivative Ψ' at $\overline{u}$ is characterized by

$$\Psi'(\overline{u})(u - \overline{u}) = \int_0^T \int_\Omega (y - y_d) \cdot Y'(u)(u - \overline{u}) \, dx \, dt + \int_0^T \int_\Omega \lambda(u - u_d) \cdot (u - \overline{u}) \, dx dt$$
$$= \int_0^T (y - y_d, \sigma)_{L^2(\Omega)} \, dx \, dt + \int_0^T (\lambda(u - u_d), (u - \overline{u}))_{L^2(\Omega)} \, dx \, dt \text{ for all } u \in U_{ad},$$

where $y = Y(u)$ and $\sigma = Y'(\overline{u})(u - \overline{u})$ denote the weak solution of the equation given by (35). Let $\overline{\eta}$ be a test function. Now, multiplying by $\overline{\eta}$ in the weak formulation of (35) and integrating over Ω, we obtain

$$(\sigma_t, \overline{\eta}) + \mu A(\sigma, \overline{\eta}) + b(\sigma, \overline{\sigma}, \overline{\eta}) + b(\overline{\sigma}, \sigma, \overline{\eta}) + (M\sigma, \overline{\eta}) = (u - \overline{u}, \overline{\eta}), \tag{44}$$

Now, in the same way we can introduce σ in the weak formulation of the equation given by (41) and integrate over Ω and we obtain the following

$$(\eta_t, \sigma) + \mu A(\eta, \sigma) + b(\eta, \overline{\eta}, \sigma) + b(\overline{\eta}, \eta, \sigma) + (M\eta, \sigma) = (\overline{y} - y_d, \sigma). \tag{45}$$

From Equations (44) and (45), it follows that

$$\begin{aligned}(u - \overline{u}, \overline{\eta})_{L^2(\Omega)} &= (\overline{y} - y_d, \sigma)_{L^2(\Omega)} = (\overline{y} - y_d, Y'(u)(u - \overline{u}))_{L^2(\Omega)} \\ &= (Y'(u)^*(\overline{y} - y_d), (u - \overline{u}))_{L^2(\Omega)} \\ &= (Y'(u)^*(Y(u) - y_d), (u - \overline{u}))_{L^2(\Omega)}.\end{aligned}$$

Thus, we have that

$$\overline{\eta} = (Y'(\overline{u})^*(\overline{y} - y_d)) = (Y'(\overline{u})^*(Y(\overline{u}) - y_d)).$$

Therefore, it follows that

$$\int_0^T \int (\overline{\eta} + \lambda(\overline{u} - u_d)) \cdot (u - \overline{u}) \, dx \, dt$$
$$= \int_0^T (\overline{\eta} + \lambda(\overline{u} - u_d), u - \overline{u}) \, dx \, dt \geq 0, \quad \text{for all } u \in U_{ad},$$

where $\overline{\eta}$ is the solution for the system (41). □

Author Contributions: Conceptualization, T.C. and H.C., methodology E.A. and T.C., writing—original draft preparation, H.C., investigation, T.C. and H.C., supervision, E.A. and T.C. The authors contributed equally to this work. All authors have read and agreed to the published version of the manuscript.

Funding: There is no external funding for this research.

Institutional Review Board Statement: Not applicable.

Informed Consent Statement: Not applicable.

Data Availability Statement: Not applicable.

Conflicts of Interest: The authors declare no conflict of interest.

References

1. Giniatoulline, A.; Castro, T. On the Existence and Uniqueness of Solutions for Nonlinear System Modeling Three-Dimensional Viscous Stratified Flows. *J. Appl. Math. Phys.* **2014**, *2*, 528–539. [CrossRef]
2. Cushman-Roisin, B.; Beckers, J.M. *Introduction to Geophysical Fluid Dynamics*, 2nd ed.; International Geophysics Series; Elsevier/Academic Press: Amsterdam, The Netherlands, 2011; Volume 101, p. xviii+828.
3. Kundu, P.K.; Cohen, I.M.; Dowling, D. *Fluid Mechanics*, 5th ed.; Elsevier/Academic Press: Berlin, Germany, 2012.
4. Landau, L.D.; Lifshits, E.M. *Fluid Mechanics*; Landau, L.D., Lifshitz, E.M., Eds.; Pergamon Press: Oxford, UK, 1959; Volume 11.
5. Casas, E. An optimal control problem governed by the evolution Navier-Stokes equations. In *Optimal Control of Viscous Flow*; SIAM: Philadelphia, PA, USA, 1998; pp. 79–95.
6. Tröltzsch, F. *Optimal Control of Partial Differential Equations: Theory, Methods, and Applications*; Graduate Studies in Mathematics, American Mathematical Soc.: Providence, RI, USA, 2010; Volume 112.
7. Trélat, E. *Contrôle Optimal: Théorie & Applications*; Vuibert: Paris, France, 2005.
8. Temam, R. *Navier-Stokes Equations: Theory and Numerical Analysis*; American Mathematical Soc.: Providence, RI, USA, 2001; Volume 343.

9. Evans, L.C. *Partial Differential Equations*; *Graduate Studies in Mathematics*; American Mathematical Society: Providence, RI, USA, 1998; Volume 19, p. xviii+662.
10. Adams, R.A.; Fournier, J.J.F. *Sobolev Spaces*, 2nd ed.; Pure and Applied Mathematics (Amsterdam); Elsevier/Academic Press: Amsterdam, The Netherlands, 2003; Volume 140, p. xiv+305.
11. Robinson, J.C. *Infinite-Dimensional Dynamical Systems: An Introduction to Dissipative Parabolic PDEs and the Theory of Global Attractors*; Cambridge University Press: Cambridge, UK, 2001; Volume 28.
12. Simon, J. Compact sets in the space $L^p(0,T;B)$. *Ann. Mat. Pura Appl.* **1987**, *146*, 65–96. [CrossRef]
13. Hinze, M.; Pinnau, R.; Ulbrich, M.; Ulbrich, S. *Optimization with PDE Constraints*; Mathematical Modelling: Theory and Applications; Springer Science & Business Media: Berlin/Heidelberg, Germany, 2009; Volume 23.
14. Anh, C.T.; Trang, P.T. Pull-back attractors for three-dimensional Navier-Stokes-Voigt equations in some unbounded domains. *Proc. Roy. Soc. Edinb. Sect. A* **2013**, *143*, 223–251. [CrossRef]
15. Borthagaray, J.P. Flujo de fluídos Estratificados. Master's Thesis, Facultad de Ingeniería, Universidad de la República, Montevideo, Uruguay, 2012. Available online: https://www.colibri.udelar.edu.uy/jspui/bitstream/20.500.12008/24191/1/Bor12.pdf (accessed on 1 October 2021).
16. Castro, T. Problemas Lineales y no Lineales en la dinámica de Fluidos Estraticados en Dominios Acotados. Ph.D. Thesis, Departamento de Matemáticas, Universidad de los Andes, Bogotá, Colombia, 2014.
17. Sritharan, S.S. *Optimal Control of Viscous Flow*; SIAM: Philadelphia, PA, USA, 1998.

Article

Analysis of Solutions, Asymptotic and Exact Profiles to an Eyring–Powell Fluid Modell

José Luis Díaz [1,*], Saeed Ur Rahman [2], Juan Carlos Sánchez Rodríguez [1], María Antonia Simón Rodríguez [1], Guillermo Filippone Capllonch [1] and Antonio Herrero Hernández [1]

[1] Escuela Politécnica Superior, Universidad Francisco de Vitoria, Ctra. Pozuelo-Majadahonda Km 1800, Pozuelo de Alarcón, 28223 Madrid, Spain; juancarlos.sanchez@ufv.es (J.C.S.R.); mariaantonia.simon@ufv.es (M.A.S.R.); jguillermo.filippone@ufv.es (G.F.C.); antonio.herrero@ufv.es (A.H.H.)

[2] Department of Mathematics, COMSATS University Islamabad, Abbottabad Campus, Abbottabad 22060, Pakistan; saeed@cuiatd.edu.pk

* Correspondence: joseluis.diaz@ufv.es

Abstract: The aim of this article was to provide analytical and numerical approaches to a one-dimensional Eyring–Powell flow. First of all, the regularity, existence, and uniqueness of the solutions were explored making use of a variational weak formulation. Then, the Eyring–Powell equation was transformed into the travelling wave domain, where analytical solutions were obtained supported by the geometric perturbation theory. Such analytical solutions were validated with a numerical exercise. The main finding reported is the existence of a particular travelling wave speed $a = 1.212$ for which the analytical solution is close to the actual numerical solution with an accumulative error of $<10^{-3}$.

Keywords: travelling waves; Eyring–Powell; geometric perturbation; nonlinear reaction–diffusion; unsteady flow

MSC: 35Q35; 35B65; 76D05

1. Introduction

The Eyring–Powell flow is a type of non-Newtonian fluid of paramount relevance in industrial areas, manufacturing, and biological technology. Some trivial examples of non-Newtonian fluids are given by bubbles, boiling, plastic foam processing, columns, toothpaste, mud, honey, and custard. Non-Newtonian fluids are further classified into different classes by virtue of their rheological characteristic conditions. The Eyring–Powell fluid is one such subclass of non-Newtonian fluids with particular features linked with the kinetic theory of liquids. In their seminal paper, Metzner and Otto [1] considered a non-Newtonian fluid focused on the relationship between the speed of flow and shear rate. In 1982, Rajagopal [2] considered the incompressible, unidirectional, and unsteady conditions of a second-grade fluid to obtain solutions for a flow between two rigid plates in which one suddenly starts moving. Later on, with the help of Gupta [3], they established the exact solution for the same kind of fluid between porous plates. These cited seminal works have attracted the attention of the scientific community, leading to further research paths with the same topical background in non-Newtonian fluids. Eldabe et al. [4] obtained results applicable in the field of medicine and the study of blood flow, analysing the effect of coupling forces on an unstable non-Newtonian flow of MHD between two parallel fixed porous plates under a uniform external magnetic field. Another study, carried out by Shao and Lo [5], modelled the hydrodynamics of incompressible particles (SPHs) to simulate Newtonian and non-Newtonian flows with free surfaces. The authors were able to verify the proper functioning of the model in problems such as dam breaks in 2D. Another example of outstanding interest in this regard was the study carried out by Fetecau [6].

Citation: Díaz, J.L.; Rahman, S.U.; Sánchez Rodríguez, J.C.; Simón Rodríguez, M.A.; Filippone Capllonch, G.; Herrero Hernández, A. Analysis of Solutions, Asymptotic and Exact Profiles to an Eyring–Powell Fluid Modell. *Mathematics* 2022, 10, 660. https://doi.org/10.3390/math10040660

Academic Editor: Patricia J. Y. Wong

Received: 20 January 2022
Accepted: 17 February 2022
Published: 20 February 2022

Publisher's Note: MDPI stays neutral with regard to jurisdictional claims in published maps and institutional affiliations.

Copyright: © 2022 by the authors. Licensee MDPI, Basel, Switzerland. This article is an open access article distributed under the terms and conditions of the Creative Commons Attribution (CC BY) license (https://creativecommons.org/licenses/by/4.0/).

Here, solutions were established for unidirectional transient flows of non-Newtonian fluids in pipe-like domains.

Under particular rheological properties describing a non-Newtonian fluid, further applications have been accounted for by the theory of magnetohydrodynamics (MHD). Akbar [7] established the solution for a flow of a two-dimensional fluid under the effect of a magnetic field over stretching surfaces. Hina [8] analysed the heat transfer for the magnetohydrodynamic flow of the Eyring–Powell fluid. Later, Bhatti et al. [9] considered the same MHD fluid over permeable stretching surfaces. In this direction, other relevant studies can be considered (refer to [10–15]).

Further relevant topics in applied sciences involving Eyring–Powell fluids can be mentioned. In [16], the authors analysed the characteristics of the flow of Eyring–Powell nanofluids through a rotating disk subject to various physical phenomena such as a sliding flow and a magnetic field together with homogeneous and heterogeneous reactions. To this end, the proposed equations were solved by a numerical method based on the Runge–Kutta–Fehlberg method of 4th–5th order. Furthermore, in [17], the authors developed a computational technique for a three-dimensional Eyring–Powell fluid with activation energy on a stretched sheet with sliding effects. The resulting nonlinear system of PDEs was transformed into a nonlinear system of ODEs, and a shooting method was explored accordingly. The analysis in [18] discussed the flow and heat transfer of the Eyring–Powell MHD fluid in an infinite circular pipe. The explored solutions of different viscous terms were calculated numerically with the help of an iterative technique.

Note that in all the previously cited references, attention was mainly set on the numerical schemes in search of particular solutions. Analytical conceptions remain within the scope of dimensional analysis.

Further analytical approaches can be found in [19], where a homotopy approach was employed to construct solutions for a boundary layer with natural convection on a permeable vertical plate with thermal radiation. Afterwards, the differential quadrature method (DQM) was used to validate solutions for different parametrical cases involving the local Nusselt number and the local Sherwood number. In [20], the authors used the ADM-Padé approach to study analytical solutions for the deflection and pull-in instability of nanocantilever electromechanical switches, showing the remarkable accuracy compared with the numerical results. The authors claimed the possibility of extending their results to solve a wide range of instability problems. Furthermore, in [21], the authors studied a viscoelastic nanofluid with optimisation techniques subject to the proposal of a certain solution that was progressively optimised. To account for further analytical approaches, in [22], perturbation solutions were obtained for low-Reynolds–Eyring–Powell flow to obtain velocity, temperature, concentration, and stream functions.

After having cited some paramount studies involving analytical conceptions, it shall be noted that in the present study, the intention was to go deeper into the advances of the theory of PDEs to construct profiles of solutions. Unlike the previously cited studies, solutions were explored within the theory of travelling waves. Such a theory was firstly introduced by Kolmogorov, Petrovskii, and Piskunov [23], in combustion theory, and by Fisher [24], to predict the interaction of genes. The main question, introduced by the mentioned authors, was related to the search for an appropriate travelling wave speed for which the analytical travelling wave profile converges to the actual profile (solution of the actual problem, not converted into the travelling domain). Both the travelling profile and the actual one were shown to have the same exponential behaviour. This spirit was kept in our present analysis: indeed, one question to answer is related to the search for an appropriate travelling wave speed for which the analytically obtained solution converges to the actual one (obtained by numerical means) with a certain error tolerance. This was the main target of our analysis, but previously, the regularity, existence, and uniqueness of the solutions were shown. Later, the geometric perturbation theory was employed to support the construction of the analytical profiles of the solutions. These obtained profiles were validated afterwards via a numerical exercise.

2. Mathematical Model

We consider an incompressible, unsteady, and one-dimensional electrically conducting Eyring–Powell fluid. Under these assumptions, the velocity field is given by $\mathbf{V} = (u_1(y), 0, 0)$, where $u_1(y)$ refers to the first velocity component. Note that the proposed problem refers to an open geometry not shaped by dedicated containers or stretched by boundary conditions. The continuity and constitutive equations for an Eyring–Powell fluid are generally given by (refer to [25,26] for an additional discussion on the Eyring–Powell governing equations):

$$div\mathbf{V} = 0, \tag{1}$$

and:

$$\rho_f \frac{d\mathbf{V}}{dt} = div\mathbf{A} + \mathbf{J} \times \mathbf{B}, \tag{2}$$

where ρ_f refers to the density, $\mathbf{J}$ is the current density, $\mathbf{B}$ is the magnetic field, which can be split into $\mathbf{B} = \mathbf{B}_0 + \mathbf{b}$ where $\mathbf{B}_0$ and $\mathbf{b}$ are the imposed and induced magnetic fields, respectively, and $\mathbf{A}$ is given by:

$$\mathbf{A} = -p\mathbf{I} + \tau_{ij}, \tag{3}$$

$$div\mathbf{B} = 0, \quad curl\mathbf{B} = \mu_1 \mathbf{j}, \quad curl\mathbf{E} = -\frac{\partial \mathbf{B}}{\partial t} \tag{4}$$

$$\mathbf{J} = \sigma(\mathbf{E} + \mathbf{V} \times \mathbf{B}), \tag{5}$$

where p is the pressure field, $\mathbf{I}$ is the identity tensor, μ_1 is the magnetic permeability, $\mathbf{E}$ is the electric field, σ is the electric conductivity, and τ_{ij} is the shear stress tensor of an Eyring–Powell fluid [11,13] given by:

$$\tau_{ij} = \mu \frac{\partial u_i}{\partial x_j} + \frac{1}{\beta} \sinh^{-1}\left(\frac{1}{d_1} \frac{\partial u_i}{\partial x_j}\right), \tag{6}$$

where μ is the dynamic viscosity and β and d_1 are characteristic constants of the Powell-Eyring model. Consider that $\sinh^{-1}\left(\frac{1}{d_1} \frac{\partial u_i}{\partial x_j}\right) \cong \frac{1}{d_1} \frac{\partial u_i}{\partial x_j} - \frac{1}{6}\left(\frac{1}{d_1} \frac{\partial u_i}{\partial x_j}\right)^3$, $\left|\frac{1}{d_1} \frac{\partial u_i}{\partial x_j}\right| \leq 1$. The governing equation, in the absence of an induced magnetic field, can be written as:

$$\frac{\partial u_1}{\partial t} = -\frac{1}{\rho}\frac{dP}{dx} + \left(v + \frac{1}{\beta d_1 \rho_f}\right)\frac{\partial^2 u_1}{\partial y^2} - \frac{1}{2\beta d_1^3 \rho_f}\left(\frac{\partial u_1}{\partial y}\right)^2 \frac{\partial^2 u_1}{\partial y^2} - \frac{\sigma B_0^2 u_1}{\rho_f}. \tag{7}$$

where $v = \frac{\mu}{\rho_f}$ is the kinematic viscosity. After differentiation in (7) with x:

$$-\frac{1}{\rho}\frac{d^2 P}{dx^2} = 0, \quad -\frac{1}{\rho}\frac{dP}{dx} = A_1.$$

Using the value of $-\frac{1}{\rho}\frac{dP}{dx}$ in (7), we obtain:

$$\frac{\partial u_1}{\partial t} = A_1 + \left(v + \frac{1}{\beta d_1 \rho_f}\right)\frac{\partial^2 u_1}{\partial y^2} - \frac{1}{2\beta d_1^3 \rho_f}\left(\frac{\partial u_1}{\partial y}\right)^2 \frac{\partial^2 u_1}{\partial y^2} - \frac{\sigma B_0^2 u_1}{\rho_f}. \tag{8}$$

with the following initial condition:

$$u_1(y, 0) = u_0(y) \in L^1_{loc}(R) \cap L^\infty(R). \tag{9}$$

3. Preliminaries

The proposed Eyring–Powell model in (8) is expressed making use of a weak formulation to support the analysis of the regularity, existence, and uniqueness of the solutions.

Definition 1. Consider a test function $\phi_2 \in C^\infty(R)$ defined in $(0, T)$, such that for $0 < \tau < t < T$, the following weak formulation of (8) holds:

$$\int_R u_1(t)\phi_2(t)dy = \int_R u_1(\tau)\phi_2(\tau)dy + \int_\tau^t \int_R u_1 \frac{\partial \phi_2}{\partial s} dyds$$

$$+ A_1 \int_\tau^t \int_R \phi_2 dyds + \left(v + \frac{1}{\beta d_1 \rho_f}\right) \int_\tau^t \int_R u_1 \frac{\partial^2 \phi_1}{\partial y^2} dyds$$

$$+ \frac{1}{6\beta d_1^3 \rho_f} \int_\tau^t \int_R \left(\frac{\partial u_1}{\partial y}\right)^3 \frac{\partial \phi_2}{\partial y} dyds - \frac{\sigma B_0^2}{\rho_f} \int_\tau^t \int_R u_1 \phi_2 dyds.$$

In addition, the following definition holds:

Definition 2. Given a finite spatial location r_0, admit a ball B_r centred in r_0 and with radius $r \gg r_0$. In the proximity of the borders ∂B_r and for $0 < s < \tau < t < T$, the following equation is defined:

$$u_1 \frac{\partial \phi_2}{\partial s} + A_1 \phi_2 + \left(v + \frac{1}{\beta d_1 \rho_f}\right) u_1 \frac{\partial^2 \phi_2}{\partial y^2} + \frac{1}{6\beta d_1^3 \rho_f}\left(\frac{\partial u}{\partial y}\right)^3 \frac{\partial \phi_2}{\partial y} - \frac{\sigma B_0^2}{\rho_f} u_1 \phi_2 = 0, \quad (10)$$

in $B_r \times (0, T)$, with the following boundary and initial conditions:

$$0 < \frac{\partial \phi_2}{\partial y} = \phi_2 \ll 1,$$

and:

$$u_1(y, 0) = u_0(y) \in L^1_{loc}(R) \cap L^\infty(R).$$

4. Existence and Uniqueness Analysis

The following theorem aims to show the existence and bounds of the solutions:

Theorem 1. Given $u_0(y) \in L^1_{loc}(R) \cap L^\infty(R)$, then the solution is bounded for all $(y, t) \in B_r \times [\tau, T)$ with $r \gg 1$.

Proof. Consider a certain value $\eta \in R^+$ such that the following cut-off function is defined (see [27,28]):

$$\psi_\eta \in C_0^\infty(y, t), \qquad 0 \leq \psi_\eta \leq 1,$$

$$\psi_\eta = 1 \text{ in } B_{r-\eta}, \quad \psi_\eta = 0 \text{ in } R - B_{r-\eta},$$

so that:

$$\left|\frac{\partial \psi_\eta}{\partial \eta}\right| = \frac{B_a}{\eta},$$

where B_a is a suitable constant. Multiplying (10) by ψ_η and integrating in $B_r \times [\tau, T)$, we obtain:

$$\int_\tau^t \int_{B_r} u_1 \frac{\partial \phi_2}{\partial s} \psi_\eta dyds + A_1 \int_\tau^t \int_{B_r} \phi_2 \psi_\eta dyds + \left(v + \frac{1}{\beta d_1 \rho_f}\right) \int_\tau^t \int_{B_r} u_1 \frac{\partial^2 \phi_2}{\partial y^2} \psi_\eta dyds$$

$$+ \frac{1}{6\beta d_1^3 \rho_f} \int_\tau^t \int_{B_r} \left(\frac{\partial u_1}{\partial y}\right)^3 \frac{\partial \phi_2}{\partial y} \psi_\eta dyds - \frac{\sigma B_0^2}{\rho_f} \int_\tau^t \int_{B_r} u_1 \phi_2 \psi_\eta dyds = 0. \quad (11)$$

Now, admit an arbitrary $m > 1$ and some large $r_0 > 1$ [27,28]:

$$\int_\tau^t u_1 ds \leq \int_\tau^t u_1^m ds \leq D_1(\tau) r^{\frac{2m}{m-1}}.$$

Considering the spatial variable y close to ∂B_r, it can be assumed that $y \sim r$. Then, for $m = 2$, it holds that:

$$\int_\tau^t u_1 ds \leq D_1(\tau) r^4, \quad \int_\tau^t \left(\frac{\partial u_1}{\partial y}\right)^3 ds \leq 64\, D_1^3(\tau) r^9.$$

The integral for the diffusion term reads:

$$\left(v + \frac{1}{\beta d_1 \rho_f}\right) \int_\tau^t \int_{B_r} u_1 \frac{\partial^2 \phi_2}{\partial y^2} \psi_\eta dy ds$$

$$\leq \left(v + \frac{1}{\beta d_1 \rho_f}\right) \int_{B_r} D_1(\tau) r^2 \frac{\partial^2 \phi_2}{\partial y^2} \psi_\eta dy$$

$$= \left(v + \frac{1}{\beta d_1 \rho_f}\right) D_1(\tau) r^2 \left(\left(\frac{\partial \phi_2}{\partial y} \psi_\eta\right)_{\partial B_r} - \int_{B_r} \frac{\partial \phi_2}{\partial y} \frac{\partial \psi_\eta}{\partial y} dy\right).$$

As $r \gg 1$ and taking ϕ_2 sufficiently small such that $\frac{\partial \phi_2}{\partial y} \psi_\eta \ll 1$ over ∂B_r, the following holds:

$$\left(v + \frac{1}{\beta d_1 \rho_f}\right) \int_\tau^t \int_{B_r} u_1 \frac{\partial^2 \phi_2}{\partial y^2} \psi_\eta dy ds$$

$$= -\left(v + \frac{1}{\beta d_1 \rho_f}\right) \int_{B_r} D_1(\tau) r^2 \frac{\partial \phi_2}{\partial y} \frac{\partial \psi_\eta}{\partial y} dy$$

$$\leq \left(v + \frac{1}{\beta d_1 \rho_f}\right) D_1(\tau) \int_{B_r} r^2 \frac{\partial \phi_2}{\partial y} \frac{B_a}{\eta} dy$$

$$= \left(v + \frac{1}{\beta d_1 \rho_f}\right) B_a D_1(\tau) \int_{B_r} r \frac{\partial \phi_2}{\partial y} dy,$$

and:

$$\frac{1}{6\beta d_1^3 \rho_f} \int_\tau^t \int_{B_r} \left(\frac{\partial u_1}{\partial y}\right)^3 \frac{\partial \phi_2}{\partial y} \psi_\eta dy ds \leq \frac{32}{3\beta d_1^3 \rho_f} \int_{B_r} D_1^3(\tau) r^9 \frac{\partial \phi_2}{\partial y} \psi_\eta dy.$$

Now:

$$\frac{1}{6\beta d_1^3 \rho_f} \int_\tau^t \int_{B_r} \left(\frac{\partial u_1}{\partial y}\right)^3 \frac{\partial \phi_2}{\partial y} \psi_\eta dy ds \leq -\frac{32}{3\beta d_1^3 \rho_f} \int_{B_r} D_1^3(\tau) r^9 \phi_2 \frac{\partial \psi_\eta}{\partial y} dy$$

$$\leq \frac{32}{3\beta d_1^3 \rho_f} \int_{B_r} D_1^3(\tau) r^9 \phi_2 \frac{B_a}{\eta} dy$$

$$= \frac{32 D_1^3(\tau)}{3\beta d_1^3 \rho_f} \int_{B_r} r^8 \phi_2 dy. \qquad (12)$$

Using the expressions (12) and (12) in (11), the following holds:

$$\int_\tau^t \int_{B_r} u_1 \frac{\partial \phi_2}{\partial s} \psi_\eta dy ds + A_1 \int_\tau^t \int_{B_r} \phi_2 \psi_\eta dy ds \le \left(v + \frac{1}{\beta d_1 \rho_f} \right) B_a D_1(\tau) \int_{B_r} r \frac{\partial \phi_2}{\partial y} dy$$

$$+ \frac{32 B_a D_1^3(\tau)}{3\beta d_1^3 \rho_f} \int_{B_r} r^8 \phi_2 dy + \frac{\sigma B_0^2}{\rho_f} \int_\tau^t \int_{B_r} u_1 \phi_2 \psi_\eta dy ds. \tag{13}$$

Next, consider a test function ϕ_2 of the form:

$$\phi_2(r,s) = e^{-ks} \left(1 + r^2\right)^{-a}. \tag{14}$$

We can choose a in such a way that (13) is convergent; therefore:

$$\left(v + \frac{1}{\beta d_1 \rho_f} \right) B_a B_1(\tau) \int_{B_r} r \frac{\partial \phi_2}{\partial y} dy +$$

$$\frac{32 B_a D_1^3(\tau)}{3\beta d_1^3 \rho_f} \int_{B_r} r^8 \phi_2 dy + \frac{\sigma B_0^2 B_1(\tau)}{\rho_f} \int_{B_r} r^2 \phi_2 \psi_\eta dy$$

$$\le 2a \left(v + \frac{1}{\beta d_1 \rho_f} \right) B_a B_1(\tau) \int_{B_r} e^{-ks} r^{-2a} dr \tag{15}$$

$$+ \frac{32 B_a D_1^3(\tau)}{3\beta d_1^3 \rho_f} \int_{B_r} r^{8-2a} \phi_2 dr + \frac{\sigma B_0^2 B_1(\tau)}{\rho_f} \int_{B_r} e^{-ks} r^{2-2a} dr.$$

For $a > 4$ and $r \to \infty$, the following holds:

$$\left(v + \frac{1}{\beta d_1 \rho_f} \right) B_a B_1(\tau) \int_{B_r} r \frac{\partial \phi_2}{\partial y} dy + \frac{\sigma B_0^2 B_1(\tau)}{\rho_f} \int_{B_r} r^2 \phi_2 \psi_\eta dy \le 0. \tag{16}$$

Putting (16) into (13):

$$\int_\tau^t \int_{B_r} u_1 \frac{\partial \phi_2}{\partial s} \psi_\eta dy ds + A_1 \int_\tau^t \int_{B_r} \phi_2 \psi_\eta dy ds \le 0. \tag{17}$$

As both integrals are finite in $\tau < s < t < T$, it is possible to conclude the theorem principles related to the bound of the solutions in $R \times (0, T)$. □

The next intention is to show the boundness of $\frac{\partial u_1}{\partial y}$.

Theorem 2. *Given $u_1(y)$ as the solution of (8), then $\frac{\partial u_1}{\partial y}$ is bounded for $(y, t) \in R \times (0, T)$.*

Proof. Multiplying the equation (8) by u_1 and using integration by parts:

$$\frac{d}{dt} \int_R |u_1|^2 dy = A_1 \int_R u_1 dy - \left(v + \frac{1}{\beta d_1 \rho_f} \right) \int_R \left(\frac{\partial u_1}{\partial y} \right)^2 dy$$

$$+ \frac{1}{6\beta d_1^3 \rho_f} \int_R \left(\frac{\partial u_1}{\partial y} \right)^4 dy - \frac{\sigma B_0^2}{\rho_f} \int_R |u_1|^2 dy,$$

which implies that:

$$\int_R \left(\frac{\partial u_1}{\partial y}\right)^2 \left(\frac{1}{6\beta d_1^3 \rho_f}\left(\frac{\partial u_1}{\partial y}\right)^2 - \left(v + \frac{1}{\beta d_1 \rho_f}\right)\right) dy = \frac{d}{dt}\int_R |u_1|^2 dy$$

$$- A_1 \int_R u_1 dy - \frac{\sigma B_0^2}{\rho_f}\int_R |u_1|^2 dy.$$

After integration on both sides:

$$\int_0^t \int_R \left(\frac{\partial u_1}{\partial y}\right)^2 \left(\frac{1}{6\beta d_1^3 \rho_f}\left(\frac{\partial u_1}{\partial y}\right)^2 - \left(v + \frac{1}{\beta d_1 \rho_f}\right)\right) dyds = \int_R |u_1(y,t)|^2 dy$$

$$- \int_R |u_0(y)|^2 dy - A_1 \int_0^t \int_R u_1 dyds - \frac{\sigma B_0^2}{\rho_f}\int_0^t \int_R |u_1|^2 dyds. \quad (18)$$

From Theorem (1), the right-hand side of (18) is bounded; therefore, we can choose A_2 such that:

$$\int_0^t \int_R \left(\frac{\partial u_1}{\partial y}\right)^2 \left(\frac{1}{6\beta d_1^3 \rho_f}\left(\frac{\partial u_1}{\partial y}\right)^2 - \left(v + \frac{1}{\beta d_1 \rho_f}\right)\right) dyds \leq A_2, \quad (19)$$

which permits concluding that $\frac{\partial u_1}{\partial y}$ is bounded in $R \times (0,t)$ where we can admit $t = T$. □

The next intention is to show the uniqueness of the solution.

Theorem 3. *Let us admit $u_1 > 0$ as a minimal solution and $\hat{u}_1$ as a maximal solution for (8) in $R \times (0,T)$, then u_1 coincides with the maximal solution $\hat{u}_1$, i.e., the solution is unique.*

Proof. Consider $\hat{u}_1$ to be the maximal solution of (8) in $R \times (0,T)$ given by:

$$\hat{u}_1(y,0) = u_0(y) + \epsilon, \quad (20)$$

with $\epsilon > 0$ arbitrarily small. In addition, let us define the minimal solution:

$$u_1(y,0) = u_0(y).$$

The maximal and minimal solutions satisfy the following equations:

$$\frac{\partial \hat{u}_1}{\partial t} = A_1 + \left(v + \frac{1}{\beta d_1 \rho_f}\right)\frac{\partial^2 \hat{u}_1}{\partial y^2} - \frac{1}{2\beta d_1^3 \rho_f}\left(\frac{\partial \hat{u}_1}{\partial y}\right)^2 \frac{\partial^2 \hat{u}_1}{\partial y^2} - \frac{\sigma B_0^2 \hat{u}_1}{\rho_f}, \quad (21)$$

$$\frac{\partial u_1}{\partial t} = A_1 + \left(v + \frac{1}{\beta d_1 \rho_f}\right)\frac{\partial^2 u_1}{\partial y^2} - \frac{1}{2\beta d_1^3 \rho_f}\left(\frac{\partial u_1}{\partial y}\right)^2 \frac{\partial^2 u_1}{\partial y^2} - \frac{\sigma B_0^2 u_1}{\rho_f}. \quad (22)$$

For every test function $\phi_2 \in C^\infty(R)$ and upon subtraction, the following expressions hold:

$$0 \le \int_R (\hat{u}_1 - u_1)\phi_2(t)dy = \int_0^t\int_R (\hat{u}_1 - u_1)\frac{\partial \phi_2}{\partial s}dyds$$

$$+ \left(v + \frac{1}{\beta d_1 \rho_f}\right)\int_0^t\int_R (\hat{u}_1 - u_1)\frac{\partial^2 \phi_2}{\partial y^2}dyds$$

$$+ \frac{1}{6\beta d_1^3 \rho_f}\int_0^t\int_R \left(\left(\frac{\partial \hat{u}_1}{\partial y}\right)^3 - \left(\frac{\partial u_1}{\partial y}\right)^3\right)\frac{\partial^2 \phi_2}{\partial y^2}dyds - \frac{\sigma B_0^2}{\rho_f}\int_0^t\int_R (\hat{u}_1 - u_1)\phi dyds$$

$$\le \int_0^t\int_R (\hat{u}_1 - u_1)\frac{\partial \phi_2}{\partial s}dyds + \left(v + \frac{1}{\beta d_1 \rho_f}\right)\int_0^t\int_R (\hat{u}_1 - u_1)\frac{\partial^2 \phi_2}{\partial y^2}dyds$$

$$+ \frac{1}{6\beta d_1^3 \rho_f}\int_0^t\int_R \left(\frac{\partial \hat{u}_1}{\partial y} - \frac{\partial u_1}{\partial y}\right)\left(\left(\frac{\partial \hat{u}_1}{\partial y}\right)^2 + \frac{\partial \hat{u}_1}{\partial y}\frac{\partial u_1}{\partial y} + \left(\frac{\partial u_1}{\partial y}\right)^2\right)\frac{\partial \phi_2}{\partial y}dyds$$

$$- \frac{\sigma B_0^2}{\rho_f}\int_0^t\int_R (\hat{u}_1 - u_1)\phi dyds \tag{23}$$

Based on Theorem 2's results, we can choose A_3 such that $A_3 = \sup\{\frac{\partial \hat{u}_1}{\partial y}, \frac{\partial u_1}{\partial y}\}$, so that the following holds:

$$\int_R (\hat{u}_1 - u_1)\phi_2(t)dy \le \int_0^t\int_R (\hat{u}_1 - u_1)\frac{\partial \phi_2}{\partial s}dyds + \left(v + \frac{1}{\beta d_1 \rho_f}\right)\int_0^t\int_R (\hat{u}_1 - u_1)\frac{\partial^2 \phi_2}{\partial y^2}dyds$$

$$+ \frac{A_3}{6\beta d_1^3 \rho_f}\int_0^t\int_R \left(\frac{\partial \hat{u}_1}{\partial y} - \frac{\partial u_1}{\partial y}\right)\frac{\partial \phi_2}{\partial y}dyds - \frac{\sigma B_0^2}{\rho_f}\int_0^t\int_R (\hat{u}_1 - u_1)\phi dyds$$

$$= \int_0^t\int_R (\widehat{u_1} - u_1)\frac{\partial \phi_2}{\partial s}dyds + \left(v + \frac{1}{\beta d_1 \rho_f} - \frac{A_3}{6\beta d_1^3 \rho_f}\right)\int_0^t\int_R (\widehat{u_1} - u_1)\frac{\partial^2 \phi_2}{\partial y^2}dyds \tag{24}$$

$$- \frac{\sigma B_0^2}{\rho_f}\int_0^t\int_R (\hat{u}_1 - u_1)\phi dyds. \tag{25}$$

Now, consider the test function given by:

$$\phi_2(|y|, s) = e^{A_4(T-s)}\left(1 + |y|^2\right)^{-b}, \tag{26}$$

where A_4 and b are constants. Making the differentiation of ϕ_2 with regards to s and y, the following holds:

$$\frac{\partial \phi_2}{\partial s} = -A_4\phi_2(|y|, s), \quad \frac{\partial^2 \phi_2}{\partial y^2} \le A_5(b)\phi_2(|y|, s),$$

then:

$$(\hat{u}_1 - u_1)\frac{\partial \phi_2}{\partial s} + \left(v + \frac{1}{\beta d_1 \rho_f} - \frac{A_3}{6\beta d_1^3 \rho_f}\right)(\hat{u}_1 - u_1)\frac{\partial^2 \phi_2}{\partial y^2} - \frac{\sigma B_0^2}{\rho_f}(\hat{u}_1 - u_1)\phi_2$$

$$\le -A_4\phi_2(\hat{u}_1 - u_1) + \left(v + \frac{1}{\beta d_1 \rho_f} - \frac{A_3}{6\beta d_1^3 \rho_f}\right)A_5(b)\phi_2(\hat{u}_1 - u_1) - \frac{\sigma B_0^2}{\rho_f}(\hat{u}_1 - u_1)\phi_2$$

$$= \left(-A_4 + \left(v + \frac{1}{\beta d_1 \rho_f} - \frac{A_3}{6\beta d_1^3 \rho_f}\right)A_5(b) - \frac{\sigma B_0^2}{\rho_f}\right)(\hat{u}_1 - u_1)\phi_2. \tag{27}$$

Using (27) in (24), we obtain:

$$\int_R (\hat{u}_1 - u_1)\phi_2(t)dy \leq \left(-A_4 + \left(v + \frac{1}{\beta d_1 \rho_f} - \frac{A_3}{6\beta d_1^3 \rho_f}\right) A_5(b) - \frac{\sigma B_0^2}{\rho_f}\right)$$
$$\times \int_0^t \int_R (\hat{u}_1 - u_1)\phi_2 dy ds \leq \left|-A_4 + \left(v + \frac{1}{\beta d_1 \rho_f} - \frac{A_3}{6\beta d_1^3 \rho_f}\right) A_5(b) - \frac{\sigma B_0^2}{\rho_f}\right| \quad (28)$$
$$\times \int_0^t \int_R (\hat{u}_1 - u_1)\phi_2 dy ds.$$

Making the differentiation with regard to t:

$$\frac{d}{dt}\int_R (\hat{u}_1 - u_1)\phi_2(t)dy \leq \left|-A_4 + \left(v + \frac{1}{\beta d_1 \rho_f} - \frac{A_3}{6\beta d_1^3 \rho_f}\right) A_5(b) - \frac{\sigma B_0^2}{\rho_f}\right|$$
$$\times \int_R (\hat{u}_1 - u_1)\phi_2(t)dy. \quad (29)$$

Now, let us define:

$$h(t) = \int_R (\hat{u}_1 - u_1)\phi_2(t)dy. \quad (30)$$

Putting (30) into (29), the following holds:

$$\frac{dh}{dt} \leq \left|-A_4 + \left(v + \frac{1}{\beta d_1 \rho_f} - \frac{A_3}{6\beta d_1^3 \rho_f}\right) A_5(b) - \frac{\sigma B_0^2}{\rho_f}\right| h(t), \quad (31)$$

with:

$$h(0) = \epsilon \to 0.$$

After solving (31) by standard means, we obtain $h(t) = 0$, i.e., $\hat{u}_1 = u_1$, which shows the uniqueness of the solutions, as was intended to be proven. □

5. Travelling Waves' Existence and Regularity

The travelling wave profiles are described as $u_1(y,t) = k(\zeta)$, where $\zeta = y - at \in R$, a refers to the travelling wave speed and $k : R \to (0, \infty)$ belongs to $L^\infty(R)$.

The equation (8) is transformed into the travelling wave domain as follows:

$$-ak'(\zeta) = A_1 + \left(v + \frac{1}{\beta d_1 \rho_f}\right)k''(\zeta) - \frac{1}{2\beta d_1^3 \rho_f}(k'(\zeta))^2 k''(\zeta) - \frac{\sigma B_0^2}{\rho_f}k(\zeta). \quad (32)$$

with $k'(\zeta) < 0$ in the hypothesis of a purely decreasing travelling wave (this assumption is further discussed later). Now, let us consider the following new variables:

$$X = k(\zeta), \quad Y = k'(\zeta), \quad (33)$$

such that the following system holds:

$$\begin{aligned} X' &= Y, \\ Y' &= \frac{2\beta d_1^3 \rho_f}{2v\beta d_1^3 \rho_f + 2d_1^2 - Y^2}\left(-aY - A_1 + \frac{\sigma B_0^2}{\rho_f}X\right). \end{aligned} \quad (34)$$

To analyse the suggested system in the proximity of the critical point, admit $X' = 0$ and $Y' = 0$, yielding:

$$X = \frac{A_1 \rho_f}{\sigma B_0^2}.$$

Therefore, $\left(\frac{A_1 \rho_f}{\sigma B_0^2}, 0\right)$ represents the system critical point.

Our intention in the coming sections was to make use of the geometric perturbation theory to characterise the existing critical point and to explore solution orbits close to such a critical point.

5.1. Geometric Perturbation Theory

In this section, we use the singular geometric perturbation theory to show the asymptotic behaviour of an appropriately defined manifold close to the critical point. Afterwards, the obtained results are used to derive a dedicated travelling wave profile.

For this purpose, admit the following manifold as:

$$N_0 = \left\{ X, Y \, / \, X' = Y; \, Y' = \frac{2 \beta d_1^3 \rho_f}{2 v \beta d_1^3 \rho_f + 2 d_1^2 - Y^2} \left(-aY - A_1 + \frac{\sigma B_0^2}{\rho_f} X \right) \right\}, \quad (35)$$

with critical point $\left(\frac{A_1 \rho_f}{\sigma B_0^2}, 0\right)$. The perturbed manifold N_ϵ close to N_0 in the critical point $\left(\frac{A_1 \rho_f}{\sigma B_0^2}, 0\right)$ is defined as:

$$N_\epsilon = \left\{ X, Y \, / \, X' = \epsilon Y; \, Y' = F\epsilon \left(X - \frac{A_1 \rho_f}{\sigma B_0^2} \right) \right\}, \quad (36)$$

where ϵ denotes a perturbation parameter close to equilibrium $(X_1, 0)$ and F is a suitable constant, which is found after root factorisation. Firstly, admit $X_3 = X - \frac{A_1 \rho_f}{\sigma B_0^2}$. Our intention was to apply the Fenichel invariant manifold theorem [29] as formulated in [30]. For this purpose, we have to show that N_0 is a normally hyperbolic manifold, i.e., the eigenvalues of N_0 in the linearised frame close to the critical point, and transversal to the tangent space, have non-zero real part. This is shown based on the following equivalent flow associated with N_0:

$$\begin{pmatrix} X_3' \\ Y' \end{pmatrix} = \begin{pmatrix} 0 & \epsilon \\ F\epsilon & 0 \end{pmatrix} \begin{pmatrix} X_3 \\ Y \end{pmatrix}.$$

The associated eigenvalues are both real $\left(\pm\sqrt{F\epsilon}\right)$, which shows that N_0 is a hyperbolic manifold. Now, we want to show that the manifold N_ϵ is locally invariant under the flow (34), so that the manifold N_0 can be shown as an asymptotic approach to N_ϵ and vice versa. On this basis, we consider the functions:

$$\psi_1 = \epsilon Y,$$
$$\psi_2 = F\epsilon X_3,$$

which are $C^i(R \times [0, \delta))$, $i > 0$, in the proximity of the critical point $\left(\frac{A_1 \rho_f}{\sigma B_0^2}, 0\right)$. In this case, δ is determined based on the following flows that are considered to be measurable a.e. in R:

$$\left\| \psi_1^{M_0} - \psi_1^{M_\epsilon} \right\| \leq F\epsilon \|X_3\| \leq \delta \epsilon.$$

Since the solutions are bounded, we conclude that $\delta = F\|X_3\|$ is finite; therefore, the distance between the manifolds holds the normal hyperbolic condition for $\delta \in (0, \infty)$ and ϵ sufficiently small close to the critical point $\left(\frac{A_1 \rho_f}{\sigma B_0^2}, 0\right)$.

5.2. Travelling Waves' Profiles

Based on the normal hyperbolic condition shown for the manifold N_0 under the flow (34), asymptotic TW profiles can be obtained. For this purpose, let us consider firstly (34) such that the following family of trajectories in the phase plane (X, Y) holds:

$$\frac{dY}{dX} = \frac{2\beta d_1^3 \rho_f}{\left(2\nu\beta d_1^3 \rho_f + 2d_1^2 - Y^2\right) Y} \left(-aY - A_1 + \frac{\sigma B_0^2}{\rho_f} X\right) = H(X, Y). \tag{37}$$

As $H(X, Y)$ is continuous and is changing the sign character if we take X sufficiently large and sufficiently small, it is possible to conclude the existence of a critical trajectory of the form:

$$-aX' - A_1 + \frac{\sigma B_0^2}{\rho_f} X = 0,$$

which implies that:

$$X' = \frac{\sigma B_0^2}{a \rho_f} \left(X - \frac{A_1 \rho_f}{\sigma B_0^2}\right). \tag{38}$$

Solving (38), we obtain:

$$X = \frac{A_1 \rho_f}{\sigma B_0^2} + e^{\frac{\sigma B_0^2}{a \rho_f} \zeta}.$$

After using the value of X, we obtain:

$$k(\zeta) = \frac{A_1 \rho_f}{\sigma B_0^2} + e^{\frac{\sigma B_0^2}{a \rho_f} \zeta},$$

which implies that:

$$u_1(y, t) = \frac{A_1 \rho_f}{\sigma B_0^2} + e^{\frac{\sigma B_0^2}{a \rho_f} (y - at)}.$$

This last expression shows the existence of an exponential profile along the travelling wave frame. This is not a trivial result for the nonlinear reaction under the Eyring Powell fluid.

Note that the solution holds by the symmetry ($\zeta \to -\zeta$) of travelling wave profiles. It suffices to admit $\zeta = y + at$, so that:

$$k(\zeta) = \frac{A_1 \rho_f}{\sigma B_0^2} + e^{-\frac{\sigma B_0^2}{a \rho_f} \zeta}, \quad u_1(y, t) = \frac{A_1 \rho_f}{\sigma B_0^2} + e^{-\frac{\sigma B_0^2}{a \rho_f} (y + at)}. \tag{39}$$

Now, it is the aim to show that the defined supporting manifold N_ϵ preserves the exponential behaviour close to the critical points. For this purpose, the expression (36) is re-written as:

$$\frac{dY}{dX} = \frac{F}{Y} \left(X - \frac{A_1 \rho_f}{\sigma B_0^2}\right). \tag{40}$$

After solving (40):

$$Y = F \left(X - \frac{A_1 \rho_f}{\sigma B_0^2}\right). \tag{41}$$

From the expression (36), the equation (41) becomes:

$$X' = F\epsilon\left(X - \frac{A_1\rho_f}{\sigma B_0^2}\right). \tag{42}$$

After solving (42), we have:

$$X = \frac{A_1\rho_f}{\sigma B_0^2} + e^{F\epsilon\zeta}. \tag{43}$$

From (33), the expression (43) becomes:

$$k(\zeta) = \frac{A_1\rho_f}{\sigma B_0^2} + e^{F\epsilon\zeta}, \quad u_1(y,t) = \frac{A_1\rho_f}{\sigma B_0^2} + e^{F\epsilon(y-at)}.$$

This last expression permits showing the conservation of the exponential profile close to the critical points defined by the asymptotic manifolds N_ϵ.

6. Numerical Validation Assessments

The aim in this section is to develop a numerical simulation to determine an appropriate travelling wave velocity (a) for which the approximated analytical solution (39) and the exact one, obtained numerically, in (34) behave similarly. This exercise can be seen as a validation process of the obtained analytical paths presented in the previous sections. This validation was explored for certain combinations of the fluid properties. Note that other combinations do not have an impact on the analytical ending in the exponential kind of solutions.

The numerical exploration was performed as per the following principles:

- The solver bvp4c in MATLAB was employed. This solver is based on a Runge–Kutta implicit approach with interpolant extensions [31]. The bvp4c collocation method requires specifying pseudo-boundary conditions. In this case, the left boundary is considered positive, $k(\zeta \to -\infty) = 1$, and the right boundary is given by the null critical state, $k(\zeta \to \infty) = 0$. As the intention was to determine the exact coincidence along the profiles for which the exponential tail is given, the solutions were translated into the zero state by the standard vertical translation;
- The integration domain was assumed as $(-200, 200)$, sufficiently large so as to hinder any potential effect of the pseudo-boundary conditions imposed by the collocation method involved in the bvp4c solver;
- The domain was split into 100,000 nodes with an absolute error of 10^{-5} during the computation;
- An absolute error criterion was considered to stop the exploration criteria. The travelling wave speed for which both solutions, the numerically exact one and the analytical approach, were sufficiently close with an absolute error of $<10^{-3}$, named as the critical a^*. For this particular speed, The analytical solution in (39) can be regarded as a valid solution to the problem (34);
- The associated fluid constants in (34) were as one. The travelling wave speed a was the parameter used in the search for an analytical profile matching the error tolerance. In addition and with no loss of generality, $A_1 = 0$. Note that this particular selection of constant values did not impact the ending conclusions, i.e., on the existence of an analytical exponential profile matching the exact solution for a certain value in the travelling wave speed.

The results are compiled in Figures 1–3. The existence of a critical travelling wave speed $a^* = 1.212$ for which the analytical solution in (39) is close to the numerically exact one of (34) with an accumulative error of $<10^{-3}$ was concluded. This numerical exploration permits accounting for the validation of the analytical exponential profile obtained.

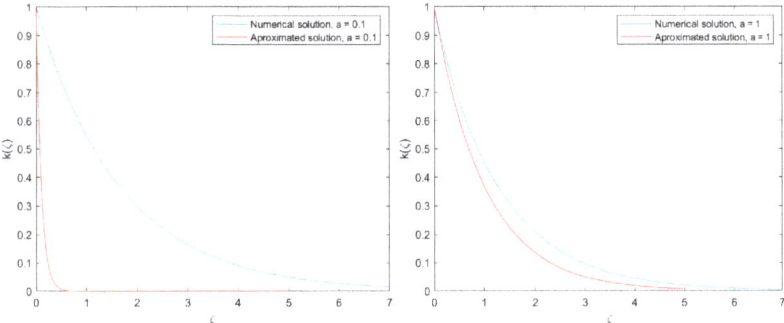

Figure 1. $a = 0.1$ (**left**), $a = 1$ (**right**). The blue line is the exact numerical profile of the set of Equations (34). The red line is the analytical solution obtained in (39) up to $\zeta = 5$ (beyond such values, it is required to change the scale). Solutions on the left are provided for $a = 1$ and solutions on the right for $a = 1.5$. For increasing values of the travelling speed, the solutions behave similarly in their exponential tail.

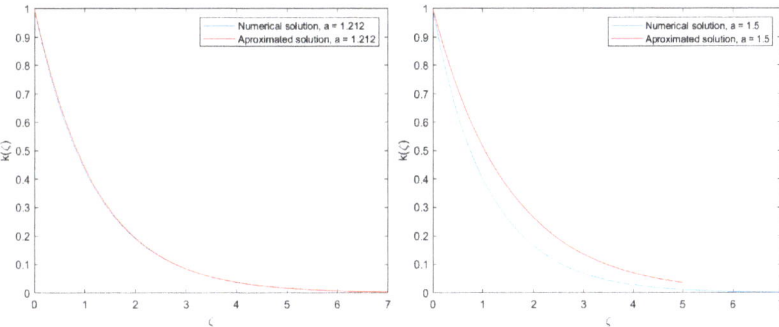

Figure 2. $a = 1.212$ (**left**), $a = 1.5$ (**right**). The blue line is the exact numerical profile of the set of Equations (34). The red line is the analytical solution obtained in (39). The approximated solution and the exact profile closely match an accumulative error (as the integration of the difference of both solutions) of $< 10^{-3}$ for $a = 1.212$. Solutions on the right are given for $a = 1.5$. The approximated solution is above the numerical one.

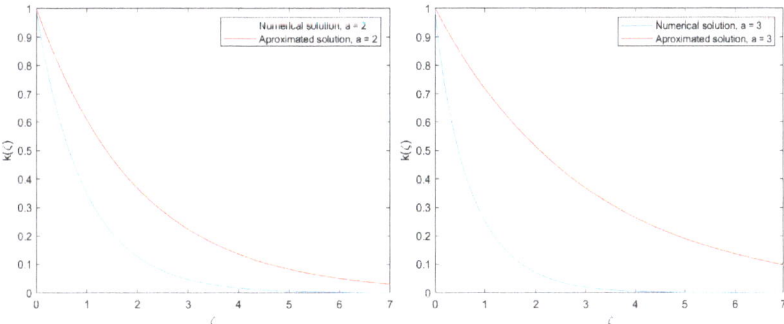

Figure 3. $a = 2$ (**left**), $a = 3$ (**right**). The blue line is the exact numerical profile of the set of Equations (34). The red line is the analytical solution obtained in (39). Solutions on the left are provided for $a = 2$ and solutions on the right for $a = 3$. Note that for increasing values of the travelling wave speed, both profiles diverge.

7. Conclusions

The presented analysis in this article permitted accounting for the regularity, existence, and uniqueness of solutions to an Eyring–Powell fluid flow. Solutions were explored in the travelling wave domain, and asymptotic approaches were provided making use of the singular geometric perturbation theory. Afterwards, the obtained analytical solution was validated for a certain combination of fluid constants and making use of a numerical exercise. The existence of a travelling wave speed of $a = 1.212$ for which the analytical solution is close to the actual numerical solution with an accumulative error of $<10^{-3}$ was concluded. The existence of an exponential travelling wave tail together with a certain minimizing error critical speed constituted the main novelty reported by the present study.

Author Contributions: Conceptualisation, J.L.D.; methodology, J.L.D. and S.U.R.; validation, J.L.D.; formal analysis, J.L.D., S.U.R., J.C.S.R., M.A.S.R., G.F.C. and A.H.H.; investigation, J.L.D., S.U.R., J.C.S.R., M.A.S.R., G.F.C. and A.H.H.; resources, J.L.D.; data curation, J.L.D.; writing—original draft preparation, J.L.D., S.U.R., J.C.S.R., M.A.S.R., G.F.C. and A.H.H.; writing—review and editing, J.L.D., S.U.R., J.C.S.R., M.A.S.R., G.F.C. and A.H.H.; supervision, J.L.D.; project administration, J.L.D.; funding acquisition, J.L.D. All authors have read and agreed to the published version of the manuscript.

Funding: This research was funded by the University Francisco de Victoria School of Engineering.

Data Availability Statement: This research has no associated data.

Conflicts of Interest: The authors declare no conflict of interest.

References

1. Metzner, A.; Otto, R. Agitation of non-Newtonian fluids. *AIChE J.* **1957**, *3*, 3–10. [CrossRef]
2. Rajagopal, K. A note on unsteady unidirectional flows of a non-Newtonian fluid. *Int. J. Non Linear Mech.* **1982**, *17*, 369–373. [CrossRef]
3. Rajagopal, K.; Gupta, A. An exact solution for the flow of a nonNewtonian fluid past an infinite porous plate. *Meccanica* **1984**, *19*, 158–160. [CrossRef]
4. Eldabe, N.; Hassan, A.; Mohamed, M.A. Effect of couple stresses on the MHD of a non-Newtonian unsteady flow between two parallel porous plates. *Z. Naturforschung A* **2003**, *58*, 204–210. [CrossRef]
5. Shao, S.; Lo, E.Y. Incompressible SPH method for simulating Newtonian and non-Newtonian flows with a free surface. *Adv. Water Resour.* **2003**, *26*, 787–800. [CrossRef]
6. Fetecau, C. Analytical solutions for non-Newtonian fluid flows in pipe-like domains. *Int. J. Non-Linear Mech.* **2004**, *39*, 225–231. [CrossRef]
7. Akbar, N.S.; Ebaid, A.; Khan, Z. Numerical analysis of magnetic field effects on Eyring–Powell fluid flow towards a stretching sheet. *J. Magn. Magn. Mater.* **2015**, *382*, 355-358. [CrossRef]
8. Hina, S. MHD peristaltic transport of Eyring–Powell fluid with heat/mass transfer, wall properties and slip conditions. *J. Magnetism. Magn. Mater.* **2016**, *404*, 148–158. [CrossRef]
9. Bhatti, M.; Abbas, T.; Rashidi, M.; Ali, M.; Yang, Z. Entropy generation on MHD Eyring–Powell nanofluid through a permeable stretching surface. *Entropy* **2016**, *18*, 224. [CrossRef]
10. Ara, A.; Khan, N.A.; Khan, H.; Sultan, F. Radiation effect on boundary layer flow of an Eyring–Powell fluid over an exponentially shrinking sheet. *Ain Shams Eng. J.* **2004**, *5*, 1337–1342. [CrossRef]
11. Hayat, T.; Iqbal, Z.; Qasim, M.; Obaidat, S. Steady flow of an Eyring–Powell fluid over a moving surface with convective boundary conditions. *Int. J. Heat Mass Transfer.* **2012**, *55*, 1817–1822. [CrossRef]
12. Hayat, T.; Awais, M.; Asghar, S. Radiactive effects in a three dimensional flow of MHD Eyring–Powell fluid. *J. Egypt Math. Soc.* **2013**, *21*, 379–384. [CrossRef]
13. Jalil, M.; Asghar, S.; Imran, S.M. Self similar solutions for the flow and heat transfer of Powell-Eyring fluid over a moving surface in parallel free stream. *Int. J. Heat Mass Transf.* **2013**, *65*, 73–79. [CrossRef]
14. Khan, J.A.; Mustafa, M.; Hayat, T.; Farooq, M.A.; Alsaedi, A.; Liao, S.J. On model for three-dimensional flow of nanofluid: An application to solar energy. *J. Mol. Liq.* **2014**, *194*, 41–47. [CrossRef]
15. Riaz, A.; Ellahi, R.; Sait, S.M. Role of hybrid nanoparticles in thermal performance of peristaltic flow of Eyring–Powell fluid model. *J. Therm. Anal. Calorim.* **2021**, *143*, 1021–1035. [CrossRef]
16. Gholinia, M.; Hosseinzadeh, K.; Mehrzadi, H.; Ganji, D.D.; Ranjbar, A.A. Investigation of MHD Eyring–Powell fluid flow over a rotating disk under effect of homogeneous–heterogeneous reactions. *Case Stud. Therm. Eng.* **2019**, *13*, 100356. [CrossRef]
17. Umar, M.; Akhtar, R.; Sabir, Z.; Wahab, H.A.; Zhiyu, Z.; Imran, A.; Shoaib, M.; Raja, M.A.Z. Numerical treatment for the three-dimensional Eyring–Powell fluid flow over a stretching sheet with velocity slip and activation energy. *Adv. Math. Phys.* **2019**, *2019*, 9860471. [CrossRef]

18. Nazeer, M.; Ahmad, F.; Saeed, M.; Saleem, A.; Naveed, S.; Akram, Z. Numerical solution for flow of a Eyring–Powell fluid in a pipe with prescribed surface temperature. *J. Braz. Soc. Mech. Sci. Eng.* **2019**, *41*, 1–10. [CrossRef]
19. Talebizadeh, P.; Moghimi, M.A.; Kimiaeifar, A.; Ameri, M. Numerical and analytical solutions for natural convection flow with thermal radiation and mass transfer past a moving vertical porous plate by DQM and HAM. *Int. J. Comput. Methods* **2011**, *8*, 611–631. [CrossRef]
20. Noghrehabadi, A.; Ghalambaz, M.; Ghanbarzadeh, A. A new approach to the electrostatic pull-in instability of nanocantilever actuators using the ADM–Padé technique. *Comput. Math. Appl.* **2012**, *64*, 2806–2815. [CrossRef]
21. Noghrehabadi, A.; Mirzaei, R.; Ghalambaz, M.; Chamkha, A.; Ghanbarzadeh, A. Boundary layer flow heat and mass transfer study of Sakiadis flow of viscoelastic nanofluids using hybrid neural network-particle swarm optimization (HNNPSO). *Therm. Sci. Eng. Prog.* **2017**, *4*, 150–159. [CrossRef]
22. Hayat, T.; Tanveer, A.; Yasmin, H.; Alsaadi, F. Simultaneous effects of Hall current and thermal deposition in peristaltic transport of Eyring–Powell fluid. *Int. J. Biomath.* **2015**, *8*, 1550024. [CrossRef]
23. Kolmogorov, A.N.; Petrovskii, I.G.; Piskunov, N.S. Study of the diffusion equation with growth of the quantity of matter and its application to a biological problem. *Byull. Moskov. Gos. Univ.* **1937**, *1*, 1-25.
24. Fisher, R.A. The advance of advantageous genes. *Ann. Eugen.* **1937**, *7*, 355–369. [CrossRef]
25. Bilal, M.; Ashbar, S. Flow and heat transfer analysis of Eyring–Powell fluid over stratified sheet with mixed convection. *J. Egypt. Math. Soc.* **2020**, *28*, 40. [CrossRef]
26. Ramzan, M.; Bilal, M.; Kanwal, S.; Chung, J.D. Effects of variable thermal conductivity and nonlinear thermal radiation past an Eyring–Powell nanofluid flow with chemical reaction. *Commun. Theor. Phys.* **2017**, *67*, 723–731. [CrossRef]
27. Pablo, A.D. Estudio de una Ecuación de Reacción—Difusión. Ph.D. Thesis, Universidad Autónoma de Madrid, Madrid, Spain, 1989.
28. Pablo, A.D.; Vázquez, J.L. Travelling waves and finite propagation in a reaction–diffusion Equation. *J Differ. Equ.* **1991**, *93*, 19-61. [CrossRef]
29. Fenichel, N. Persistence and smoothness of invariant manifolds for flows. *Indiana Univ. Math. J.* **1971**, *21*, 193–226. [CrossRef]
30. Jones, C.K.R. *Geometric Singular Perturbation Theory in Dynamical Systems*; Springer: Berlin/Heidelberg, Germany, 1995.
31. Enright, H.; Muir, P.H. *A Runge-Kutta Type Boundary Value ODE Solver with Defect Control*; Teh. Rep. 267/93; University of Toronto, Dept. of Computer Sciences: Toronto, ON, Canada, 1993.

Article

Parameter–Elliptic Fourier Multipliers Systems and Generation of Analytic and C^∞ Semigroups

Bienvenido Barraza Martínez [†], Jonathan González Ospino [†], Rogelio Grau Acuña [†] and Jairo Hernández Monzón [*,†]

Departamento de Matemáticas y Estadística, Universidad del Norte, Barranquilla 081007, Colombia; bbarraza@uninorte.edu.co (B.B.M.); gjonathan@uninorte.edu.co (J.G.O.); graur@uninorte.edu.co (R.G.A.)
* Correspondence: jahernan@uninorte.edu.co
† These authors contributed equally to this work.

Abstract: We consider Fourier multiplier systems on $\mathbb{R}^n$ with components belonging to the standard Hörmander class $S_{1,0}^m(\mathbb{R}^n)$, but with limited regularity. Using a notion of parameter-ellipticity with respect to a subsector $\Lambda \subset \mathbb{C}$ (introduced by Denk, Saal, and Seiler) we show the generation of both C^∞ semigroups and analytic semigroups (in a particular case) on the Sobolev spaces $W_p^k(\mathbb{R}^n, \mathbb{C}^q)$ with $k \in \mathbb{N}_0$, $1 \leq p < \infty$ and $q \in \mathbb{N}$. For the proofs, we modify and improve a crucial estimate from Denk, Saal and Seiler, on the inverse matrix of the symbol (see Lemma 2). As examples, we apply the theory to solve the heat equation, a linear thermoelastic plate equation, a structurally damped plate equation, and a generalized plate equation, all in the whole space, in the frame of Sobolev spaces.

Keywords: C^∞-semigroups; analytic semigroups; Fourier multipliers; Λ-ellipticity

MSC: 35J48; 35S05; 35S30; 47D03; 47D06

1. Introduction

Elliptic systems of partial differential equations were introduced in 1955 by A. Douglis and L. Nirenberg in [1]. Then, in 1973, R. Kramer formulated and solved in [2] several Cauchy problems for systems of partial differential equations which are elliptic in the sense given by Douglis and Nirenberg in [1]. In the same year, A. Koževnikov, in his study in [3] about spectral asymptotics for elliptic pseudodifferential systems with the structure of Douglis–Nirenberg, introduced an algebraic condition on the symbol (called the parameter–ellipticity condition) which permitted him to prove the similarity of the system satisfying this condition to an almost diagonal system up to a symbol of order $-\infty$, but he did not consider questions of equation solvability for those operators. In 2009, R. Denk, J. Saal and J. Seiler considered in [4] pseudodifferential Douglis–Nirenberg systems on $\mathbb{R}^n$ with components belonging to the standard Hörmander class $S_{1,\delta}^*(\mathbb{R}^n \times \mathbb{R}^n)$, $0 \leq \delta < 1$. They introduced the formulation of parameter–ellipticity with respect to a subsector $\Lambda \subset \mathbb{C}$, which is motivated by a notion of parameter–ellipticity introduced by Denk, Menniken, and Volevich in [5] and connected with the so-called Newton polygon associated with the system. They showed that their formulation of ellipticity is equivalent to the given by Koževnikov in [3] and that this condition implies the existence of a bounded H_∞-calculus for their pseudodifferential systems in suitable scales of Sobolev spaces with $1 < p < \infty$, hence of L_p-maximal regularity. Furthermore, it is known that the maximal regularity implies the generation of an analytic semigroup, however the reverse implication is false.

In this paper, we will consider certain Fourier multiplier systems on $\mathbb{R}^n$, similar but not necessarily with the exact structure of a Douglis–Nirenberg system, with components belonging to the standard Hörmander class $S_{1,0}^m(\mathbb{R}^n)$, but with limited regularity (see Definition 2), and using the notion of parameter-ellipticity with respect to a subsector $\Lambda \subset \mathbb{C}$ given in [4], we will establish (in Theorem 1) the generation of C^∞ semigroups and analytic semigroups (in a particular case) on the Sobolev spaces $W_p^k(\mathbb{R}^n, \mathbb{C}^q)$ with $k \in \mathbb{N}_0$ and $1 \le p < \infty$ giving a direct proof. For this direct proof of our main result we use the approach based on oscillatory integrals and kernel estimates for them (as in [6]), taking advantage of the fact that the associated symbols to the pseudodifferential operators are matrices valued and the entries of these matrices are symbols of order greater than $1/2$ and are independent of the spatial variable. An application to non-autonomous pseudodifferential Cauchy problems gives the existence and uniqueness of a classical solution (see Theorem 2). As examples, we apply the theory to solve the heat equation, a linear thermoelastic plate equation, a structurally damped plate equation, and a generalized plate equation, all in the whole space, in suitable Sobolev spaces (see Section 5). Other applications of the theory of semigroups and its generalizations address the control and stablility theory for mechanical systems or the controllability of fractional evolution equations or inclusions (see [7–14] and the conclusions in Section 6).

The paper is organized as follows: In Section 2 we present the definition of our system of Fourier multipliers, which are defined in terms of suitable oscillatory integrals. Following [4], we give in Section 3 the notion of Λ ellipticity for this system of Fourier multipliers, with respect to a sector Λ of the complex plane. In order to allow that the correspondent estimate in the definition of Λ ellipticity for the characteristic polynomial of the matrix symbol of our system of Fourier multipliers hold for all values of the symbol variable ξ in $\mathbb{R}^n$, we consider a perturbation of the system by a constant, following again the ideas given in [4] (see Remark 2). Section 4 is the core of the paper. There we obtain the main result of the paper about generation, under suitable hypothesis, of C^∞ semigroups and analytic semigroups for a Sobolev space realization of the perturbed operator associated to a Λ-elliptic system (Theorem 1). We also present in that section, existence and uniqueness results for non-autonomous Cauchy problems based on the obtained results about generation of semigroups (Theorem 2 and corollary 2). In Section 5, as examples and as already mentioned above, the heat equation, a linear thermoelastic plate equation, a structurally damped plate equation, and a generalized plate equation are considered. Finally, in the conclusions in Section 6, we summarize the results obtained in the paper and point out some possible future scope of this work.

2. Fourier Multiplier Systems

In the following, for $n \in \mathbb{N}$, ρ_n denotes the smallest even integer greater than n, E represents an arbitary Banach space, $\mathcal{L}(E)$ the space of linear and continuous maps of E into E, $\mathcal{S}(\mathbb{R}^n, E)$ the Schwartz space of rapidly decreasing functions and $C_b^\infty(\mathbb{R}^n, E)$ the space of all functions $u : \mathbb{R}^n \to E$ such that $\partial^\alpha u$ is bounded and continuous on $\mathbb{R}^n$ for all $\alpha \in \mathbb{N}_0^n$. $W_p^k(\mathbb{R}^n, E)$, for $k \in \mathbb{N}_0$ and $1 \le p \le \infty$, are the usual Sobolev spaces equipped with their standard norm and it is well konwn that $\mathcal{S}(\mathbb{R}^n, E) \subset C_b^\infty(\mathbb{R}^n, E) \cap W_p^k(\mathbb{R}^n, E)$ and that $\mathcal{S}(\mathbb{R}^n, E)$ is dense in $W_p^k(\mathbb{R}^n, E)$ if $1 \le p < \infty$. Also we will use the following notations throughout the paper: $D_{\xi_j} := -i\partial_{\xi_j}$, $\langle\xi\rangle := (1+|\xi|^2)^{1/2}$, $\langle\xi, t\rangle := (1+|\xi|^2+|t|^2)^{1/2}$ and $|\xi, t| := (|\xi|^2+|t|^2)^{1/2}$, for $\xi \in \mathbb{R}^n$ and $t \in \mathbb{R}$.

For the following definition, see Equation (1) in [6].

Definition 1. *Let $m \in \mathbb{R}$ and $\rho \in \mathbb{N}_0$.*

(a) The symbol class $S^{m,\rho}(\mathbb{R}^n, \mathcal{L}(E)) := S_{1,0}^{m,\rho}(\mathbb{R}^n, \mathcal{L}(E))$ consists of all functions $a : \mathbb{R}^n \to \mathcal{L}(E)$ of class C^ρ with the property that for each $\alpha \in \mathbb{N}_0^n$ with $|\alpha| \le \rho$, there exists a positive constant C_α such that

$$\left\|\partial_\xi^\alpha a(\xi)\right\|_{\mathcal{L}(E)} \le C_\alpha \langle\xi\rangle^{m-|\alpha|} \text{ for all } \xi \in \mathbb{R}^n.$$

(b) In $S^{m,\rho}(\mathbb{R}^n, \mathcal{L}(E))$ we define the norm

$$\|a\|_{S^{m,\rho}} := \max_{|\alpha| \le \rho} \sup_{\xi \in \mathbb{R}^n} \langle\xi\rangle^{|\alpha|-m} \left\|\partial_\xi^\alpha a(\xi)\right\|_{\mathcal{L}(E)}.$$

(c) For $a \in S^{m,\rho}(\mathbb{R}^n, \mathcal{L}(E))$ with $\rho \geq \rho_n$, the Fourier multiplier operator $a(D)$ is defined by

$$[a(D)u](x) := \mathrm{Os}-\iint e^{i\xi \cdot \eta} a(\xi) u(x-\eta) \frac{d(\xi,\eta)}{(2\pi)^n} \tag{1}$$

for all $x \in \mathbb{R}^n$ and $u \in C_b^\infty(\mathbb{R}^n, E)$, where the symbol $\mathrm{Os}-\iint$ stands for oscillatory integrals.

In the case that $E = \mathbb{C}^q$, $q \in \mathbb{N}$, we identify $\mathcal{L}(\mathbb{C}^q)$ with $\mathbb{C}^{q \times q}$, $\mathbb{C}^{1 \times 1}$ with $\mathbb{C}$ and we write $S^{m,\rho}(\mathbb{R}^n)$ instead of $S^{m,\rho}(\mathbb{R}^n, \mathbb{C})$.

Remark 1. (a) *The definition and some properties of the oscillatory integrals can be found in [15] for the scalar case and in [16] (Appendix A) for the vector valued case.*

(b) *For $\rho \geq \rho_n$, Lemma A.4 and Remark A.5 in [16] imply that the oscillatory integral in (1) exists. Moreover, due to Lemma A.6 in [16] we have that $a(D) \in \mathcal{L}(C_b^\infty(\mathbb{R}^n, E))$.*

(c) *Fourier multipliers with limited regularity symbols were also studied in [17,18].*

Definition 2 (Compare with [4] (Definition 2.3)). *The Fourier multipliers system we will consider in this paper is a $q \times q$-matrix of Fourier multipliers*

$$A(D) = \big(a_{ij}(D)\big)_{1 \leq i,j \leq q}$$

such that

$$a_{ij} \in S^{r_{ij},\rho}(\mathbb{R}^n),$$

where $r_{ij} \in \mathbb{R}$, $r_i := r_{ii} \geq 0$, for all $i,j = 1,...,q$, and $\rho \in \mathbb{N}$ is such that $\rho \geq \rho_n$.

3. Λ-Elliptic Fourier Multipliers Systems

From now on we fix θ, with $0 < \theta < \pi$, and let $\Lambda(\theta)$ denote the closed subsector of the complex plane $\mathbb{C}$, given by

$$\Lambda := \Lambda(\theta) := \left\{ re^{i\gamma} : r \geq 0, \theta \leq \gamma \leq 2\pi - \theta \right\}.$$

For the following definition we refer to [4] (Definition 3.1).

Definition 3. *Let $A(D)$ be a Fourier multipliers system (as in Definition 2). We say that $A(D)$ is Λ-elliptic (or $\Lambda(\theta)$-elliptic to highlight the angle), if there exist constants $C > 0$ and $R \geq 0$ such that*

$$|p(\xi;\lambda)| \geq C (\langle \xi \rangle^{r_1} + |\lambda|) \cdots (\langle \xi \rangle^{r_q} + |\lambda|)$$

for all $(\xi,\lambda) \in \mathbb{R}^n \times \Lambda$ with $|\xi| \geq R$, where $p(\xi;\lambda) := \det(A(\xi) - \lambda)$.

Remark 2. *Let $A(D)$ be a Λ-elliptic Fourier multipliers system. Due to Lemma 3.4 in [4], there exists a constant $\alpha_0 \geq 0$ such that*

$$|\det(A_{\alpha_0}(\xi) - \lambda)| \geq C(\langle \xi \rangle^{r_1} + |\lambda|) \cdots (\langle \xi \rangle^{r_q} + |\lambda|) \quad \forall \xi \in \mathbb{R}^n \text{ and } \lambda \in \Lambda,$$

where $A_{\alpha_0}(\xi) := A(\xi) + \alpha_0$, i.e., $A_{\alpha_0}(D)$ is Λ-elliptic with $R = 0$.

Lemma 1 ([4], Lemma 3.5). *Let $A(D)$ be Λ-elliptic and*

$$\big(g_{ij}(\xi;\lambda)\big)_{1 \leq i,j \leq q} := (A_{\alpha_0}(\xi) - \lambda)^{-1}.$$

Then,

$$\left|\partial_\xi^\alpha g_{ij}(\xi;\lambda)\right| \leq C_\alpha \left(\langle\xi\rangle^{r_i} + |\lambda|\right)^{-1} \left(\langle\xi\rangle^{r_j} + |\lambda|\right)^{-1} \langle\xi\rangle^{r_{ij}-|\alpha|}, \quad (i \neq j)$$

$$\left|\partial_\xi^\alpha g_{ii}(\xi;\lambda)\right| \leq C_\alpha \left(\langle\xi\rangle^{r_i} + |\lambda|\right)^{-1} \langle\xi\rangle^{-|\alpha|}$$

for all $\alpha \in \mathbb{N}_0^n$, being the estimates uniform in $(\xi,\lambda) \in \mathbb{R}^n \times \Lambda$.

Following the ideas of the proof of this lemma in [4], we note that the condition $r_1 \geq \cdots \geq r_q \geq 0$ given there, is not necessary for the estimates above. However, we get another crucial estimate under the following additional assumption about the orders of the symbols in the system:

$$\sum_{j=1}^{k} r_{i_j \pi(i_j)} = \sum_{j=1}^{k} r_{i_j} \qquad (2)$$

for all subsets of indices $\{i_1, \ldots, i_k\} \subset \{1, \ldots, q\}$ and all bijections $\pi : \{i_1, \ldots, i_k\} \to \{i_1, \ldots, i_k\}$.

The crucial estimate we mentioned above is given in the following lemma.

Lemma 2. *Let $A(D)$ be Λ-elliptic,*

$$\left(g_{ij}(\xi;\lambda)\right)_{1 \leq i,j \leq q} := \left(A_{\alpha_0}(\xi) - \lambda\right)^{-1},$$

and suppose that the assumption (2) holds. Then, for all $i = 1, \ldots, q$, $\alpha \in \mathbb{N}_0^n$ with $0 < |\alpha| \leq \rho$, and $(\xi, \lambda) \in \mathbb{R}^n \times \Lambda$, we have

$$\left|\partial_\xi^\alpha g_{ii}(\xi;\lambda)\right| \leq C_\alpha \sum_{j=1}^{q} \left(\langle\xi\rangle^{r_i} + |\lambda|\right)^{-1} \left(\langle\xi\rangle^{r_j} + |\lambda|\right)^{-1} \langle\xi\rangle^{r_j - |\alpha|} \qquad (3)$$

for some constant C_α.

Proof. Let $i \in \{1, \ldots, q\}$ be fixed. It should first be noted that

$$g_{ii}(\xi;\lambda) = \frac{1}{\det(A_{\alpha_0}(\xi) - \lambda)} \mathrm{Cof}_{(i,i)}\left(A_{\alpha_0}(\xi) - \lambda\right),$$

where $\mathrm{Cof}_{(i,i)}\left(A_{\alpha_0}(\xi) - \lambda\right)$ is the cofactor (i,i) of $A_{\alpha_0}(\xi) - \lambda$, that is, the determinant of the matrix obtained by removing the i-th row and i-th column of this matrix. With the convention $\prod_{l=k}^{m}(\cdots)_l := 1$ if $k > m$, which we will use from now on in this proof, we have that $\mathrm{Cof}_{(i,i)}\left(A_{\alpha_0}(\xi) - \lambda\right)$ is a linear combination of terms

$$\left(\prod_{l=1}^{k}(a_{i_l i_l} + \alpha_0 - \lambda)\right) \prod_{l=k+1}^{q-1} a_{i_l \pi(i_l)},$$

where $\{i_1, \ldots, i_{q-1}\} = \{1, \ldots, q\} \setminus \{i\}$, $0 \leq k \leq q-1$, and $\pi : \{i_1, \ldots, i_{q-1}\} \to \{i_1, \ldots, i_{q-1}\}$ is a bijection which have $\{i_1, \ldots, i_k\}$ as its set of fixed points. Therefore $\{i_{k+1}, \ldots, i_{q-1}\} = \{\pi(i_{k+1}), \ldots, \pi(i_{q-1})\}$ and, in virtue of assumption (2), it holds

$$r_{i_{k+1}\pi(i_{k+1})} + \cdots + r_{i_{q-1}\pi(i_{q-1})} = r_{i_{k+1}} + \cdots + r_{i_{q-1}}. \qquad (4)$$

If $\alpha \in \mathbb{N}_0^n$ with $0 < |\alpha| \leq \rho$, the Leibniz' formula implies that $\partial_\xi^\alpha g_{ii}$ is a linear combination of terms

$$\partial^\beta\left(\frac{1}{p_0}\right)\underbrace{\left(\prod_{l=1}^k \partial^{\gamma_l}(a_{i_l i_l} + \alpha_0 - \lambda)\right)\prod_{l=k+1}^{q-1}\partial^{\gamma_l}a_{i_l\pi(i_l)}}_{=:H}, \quad (5)$$

where $\beta, \gamma_1, \ldots, \gamma_{q-1} \in \mathbb{N}_0^n$ with $\beta + \gamma_1 + \cdots + \gamma_{q-1} = \alpha$, $k \in \{0, 1, \ldots, q\}$, and $p_0 = p_0(\xi, \lambda) := \det(A_{\alpha_0}(\xi) - \lambda)$. Note that the term $a_{ii} + \alpha_0 - \lambda$ is not in H (see (5)), and also we can estimate $|\partial^{\gamma_l}(a_{i_l i_l} + \alpha_0 - \lambda)|$ from above by $\langle\xi\rangle^{r_{i_l}} + |\lambda|$ if $\gamma_l = 0$ and by $\langle\xi\rangle^{r_{i_l} - |\gamma_l|}$ if $\gamma_l \neq 0$.

If $\beta = 0$, then $\gamma_j \neq 0$ for some $j = 1, \ldots, q-1$. Therefore, the term related to $a_{i_j i_j}$ which appears in H is equal to $\partial^{\gamma_j} a_{i_j i_j}$, and then, due to the Λ-ellipticity condition (together with Remark 2) and (4), the expression (5) can be estimated from above by $\left(\langle\xi\rangle^{r_i} + |\lambda|\right)^{-1}\left(\langle\xi\rangle^{r_{i_j}} + |\lambda|\right)^{-1}\langle\xi\rangle^{r_{i_j} - |\alpha|}$.

In order to consider the case $\beta \neq 0$, we will prove first that for each $\alpha \in \mathbb{N}_0^n$, $0 < |\alpha| \leq \rho$, there exists $C > 0$ such that

$$|\partial^\alpha p_0(\xi, \lambda)| \leq C\left(\sum_{j=1}^q \left(\prod_{\substack{i=1\\i\neq j}}^q(\langle\xi\rangle^{r_i} + |\lambda|)\right)\langle\xi\rangle^{r_j}\right)\langle\xi\rangle^{-|\alpha|} \quad (6)$$

for all $\xi \in \mathbb{R}^n$ and $\lambda \in \Lambda$. Let $\mathcal{Z} := \{1, \ldots, q\}$. Note that p_0 is a linear combination of terms of the form

$$\left(\prod_{l=1}^k(a_{i_l i_l} + \alpha_0 - \lambda)\right)\prod_{l=k+1}^q a_{i_l\pi(i_l)} \quad (k = 0, \ldots, q),$$

where $\pi : \mathcal{Z} \to \mathcal{Z}$ is a bijection with fixed points $i_1, \ldots, i_k$, and therefore $\{i_{k+1}, \ldots, i_q\} = \{\pi(i_{k+1}), \ldots, \pi(i_q)\}$ which, again due to the assumption (2), yields

$$r_{i_{k+1}\pi(i_{k+1})} + \cdots + r_{i_q\pi(i_q)} = r_{k+1} + \cdots + r_q. \quad (7)$$

Indeed, if $\mathcal{P}_k$, $k = 0, 1, \ldots, q$, denotes the set of all bijections $\pi : \mathcal{Z} \to \mathcal{Z}$ with exactly k fixed points, then p_0 can be written as

$$p_0 = \sum_{k=0}^{q-1}\sum_{\substack{\pi\in\mathcal{P}_k\\i_1<\cdots<i_k\\i_{k+1}<\cdots<i_q}}\pm\left(\prod_{l=1}^k(a_{i_l i_l} + \alpha_0 - \lambda)\right)\prod_{l=k+1}^q a_{i_l\pi(i_l)},$$

where in each summand, $i_1, \ldots, i_k$ are the fixed points of π.

If $\alpha \in \mathbb{N}_0^n$, $0 < |\alpha| \leq \rho$, then

$$\partial^\alpha p_0 = \sum_{k=0}^{q-1}\sum_{\substack{\pi\in\mathcal{P}_k\\i_1<\cdots<i_k\\i_{k+1}<\cdots<i_q}}\sum_{\substack{\alpha_1,\ldots,\alpha_q\in\mathbb{N}_0^n\\\alpha_1+\cdots+\alpha_q=\alpha}}C_{\alpha_1\ldots\alpha_q}\underbrace{\left(\prod_{l=1}^k\partial^{\alpha_l}(a_{i_l i_l} + \alpha_0 - \lambda)\right)\prod_{l=k+1}^q\partial^{\alpha_l}a_{i_l\pi(i_l)}}_{=:Q_k}.$$

Now,

$$|\partial^{\alpha_l}(a_{i_l i_l} + \alpha_0 - \lambda)| \leq C\begin{cases}\langle\xi\rangle^{r_{i_l}} + |\lambda|, & \alpha_l = 0,\\ \langle\xi\rangle^{r_{i_l}}\langle\xi\rangle^{-|\alpha_l|}, & \alpha_l \neq 0,\end{cases}$$

and

$$|\partial^{\alpha_l}a_{i_l\pi(i_l)}| \leq C\langle\xi\rangle^{r_{i_l\pi(i_l)}}\langle\xi\rangle^{-|\alpha_l|}.$$

Since $\alpha \neq 0$, $\alpha_j \neq 0$ for some j and, therefore, taking (7) in account, it holds

$$|Q_k| \leq C \Big(\prod_{\substack{l=1 \\ l \neq j}}^{q} (\langle \xi \rangle^{r_{i_l}} + |\lambda|) \Big) \langle \xi \rangle^{r_{i_j} - |\alpha|}.$$

Then, we have

$$|\partial^\alpha p_0| \leq \overline{C} \sum_{k=0}^{q-1} \sum_{\pi \in \mathcal{P}_k} \sum_{j=1}^{q} \Big(\prod_{\substack{l=1 \\ l \neq j}}^{q} (\langle \xi \rangle^{r_{i_l}} + |\lambda|) \Big) \langle \xi \rangle^{r_{i_j}} \langle \xi \rangle^{-|\alpha|}$$

$$\leq \hat{C} \Big(\sum_{j=1}^{q} \Big(\prod_{\substack{i=1 \\ i \neq j}}^{q} (\langle \xi \rangle^{r_i} + |\lambda|) \Big) \langle \xi \rangle^{r_j} \Big) \langle \xi \rangle^{-|\alpha|},$$

which shows (6). Thus, we can estimate $\partial^\beta (1/p_0)$ for $\beta \neq 0$. Indeed, if $\beta \neq 0$ it holds that (see [19], Lemma 10.4, p. 74)

$$\partial^\beta \Big(\frac{1}{p_0} \Big) = \sum_{k=1}^{|\beta|} \sum_{\substack{\beta_1, \dots, \beta_k \in \mathbb{N}_0^n \setminus \{0\} \\ \beta_1 + \dots + \beta_k = \beta}} C_{\beta_1 \dots \beta_k} \frac{(\partial^{\beta_1} p_0) \cdots (\partial^{\beta_k} p_0)}{p_0^{1+k}}.$$

Due to (6) and the Λ-ellipticity condition we obtain

$$\Big| \partial^\beta \Big(\frac{1}{p_0} \Big) \Big| \leq C_\beta \sum_{k=1}^{|\beta|} \sum_{\substack{\beta_1, \dots, \beta_k \in \mathbb{N}_0^n \setminus \{0\} \\ \beta_1 + \dots + \beta_k = \beta}} \frac{\Big(\sum_{j=1}^{q} \Big(\prod_{\substack{i=1 \\ i \neq j}}^{q} (\langle \xi \rangle^{r_i} + |\lambda|) \Big) \langle \xi \rangle^{r_j} \Big)^k \langle \xi \rangle^{-|\beta|}}{|p_0|^{1+k}}$$

$$\leq \hat{C}_\beta \sum_{k=1}^{|\beta|} \frac{\Big(\sum_{j=1}^{q} \Big(\prod_{\substack{i=1 \\ i \neq j}}^{q} (\langle \xi \rangle^{r_i} + |\lambda|)^k \Big) \langle \xi \rangle^{k r_j} \Big) \langle \xi \rangle^{-|\beta|}}{\prod_{i=1}^{q} (\langle \xi \rangle^{r_i} + |\lambda|)^{1+k}}$$

$$= \frac{\hat{C}_\beta}{\prod_{i=1}^{q} (\langle \xi \rangle^{r_i} + |\lambda|)} \sum_{k=1}^{|\beta|} \sum_{j=1}^{q} \frac{\langle \xi \rangle^{k r_j} \langle \xi \rangle^{-|\beta|}}{(\langle \xi \rangle^{r_j} + |\lambda|)^k}$$

$$= \frac{\hat{C}_\beta}{\prod_{i=1}^{q} (\langle \xi \rangle^{r_i} + |\lambda|)} \sum_{k=1}^{|\beta|} \sum_{j=1}^{q} \Big(\frac{\langle \xi \rangle^{r_j}}{\langle \xi \rangle^{r_j} + |\lambda|} \Big)^{k-1} \frac{\langle \xi \rangle^{r_j} \langle \xi \rangle^{-|\beta|}}{\langle \xi \rangle^{r_j} + |\lambda|}$$

$$\leq \frac{C_\beta^*}{\prod_{i=1}^{q} (\langle \xi \rangle^{r_i} + |\lambda|)} \Big(\sum_{j=1}^{q} \frac{\langle \xi \rangle^{r_j}}{\langle \xi \rangle^{r_j} + |\lambda|} \Big) \langle \xi \rangle^{-|\beta|}.$$

Now, since

$$|H| \leq \Big(\prod_{\substack{l=1 \\ l \neq i}}^{q} (\langle \xi \rangle^{r_l} + |\lambda|) \Big) \langle \xi \rangle^{-|\gamma_1 + \dots + \gamma_{q-1}|},$$

if $0 < |\beta| \leq \rho$, we can estimate (5) from above by

$$\frac{C_\beta^*}{\prod_{i=1}^q (\langle\xi\rangle^{r_i} + |\lambda|)} \Big(\sum_{j=1}^q \frac{\langle\xi\rangle^{r_j}}{\langle\xi\rangle^{r_j} + |\lambda|}\Big)\Big(\prod_{\substack{l=1\\l\neq i}}^q (\langle\xi\rangle^{r_l} + |\lambda|)\Big)\langle\xi\rangle^{-|\alpha|}$$

$$= C_\beta^* \sum_{j=1}^q \frac{\langle\xi\rangle^{r_j - |\alpha|}}{\big(\langle\xi\rangle^{r_i} + |\lambda|\big)\big(\langle\xi\rangle^{r_j} + |\lambda|\big)}.$$

With the estimates from above for (5), in both cases $\beta = 0$ and $\beta \neq 0$, we obtain the estimate (3) for $0 < |\alpha| \leq \rho$ and $(\xi, \lambda) \in \mathbb{R}^n \times \Lambda$. □

Under the assumption (2) on the order of the symbols in the system, Lemma 1, estimate (3), and the equivalence

$$\langle\xi\rangle^r + |\lambda| \sim \left\langle \xi, |\lambda|^{1/r}\right\rangle^r \quad (r \geq 0),$$

lead to the following assertion.

Corollary 1. *Let $A(D)$ be Λ-elliptic,*

$$b_\lambda(\cdot) := (A_{\alpha_0}(\cdot) - \lambda)^{-1} = \big(g_{ij}(\cdot; \lambda)\big)_{1 \leq i,j \leq q'}$$

and suppose that the assumption (2) holds. Then for each $i, j = 1, \ldots, q$, we have

$$(b_\lambda(\cdot))_{ij} = g_{ij}(\cdot; \lambda) \in S^{-r_{ji}, \rho}(\mathbb{R}^n, \mathcal{L}(\mathbb{C}^q)), \quad \forall \lambda \in \Lambda$$

with

$$|g_{ii}(\xi; \lambda)| \leq C \left\langle \xi, |\lambda|^{1/r_i}\right\rangle^{-r_i}, \quad (i = 1, \ldots, q)$$

$$\left|\partial_\xi^\alpha g_{ii}(\xi; \lambda)\right| \leq C_\alpha \sum_{j=1}^q \left\langle \xi, |\lambda|^{1/r_i}\right\rangle^{-r_i} \left\langle \xi, |\lambda|^{1/r_j}\right\rangle^{-r_j} \langle\xi\rangle^{r_j - |\alpha|}, \quad ((i, \alpha) \in \mathcal{Z}_1)$$

$$\left|\partial_\xi^\alpha g_{ij}(\xi; \lambda)\right| \leq C \left\langle \xi, |\lambda|^{1/r_i}\right\rangle^{-r_i} \left\langle \xi, |\lambda|^{1/r_j}\right\rangle^{-r_j} \langle\xi\rangle^{r_{ij} - |\alpha|}, \quad ((i, j, \alpha) \in \mathcal{Z}_2)$$

for all $(\xi, \lambda) \in \mathbb{R}^n \times \Lambda$, where C is a positive constant independent on α, ξ and λ, $\mathcal{Z}_1 := \{(i, \alpha) : 1 \leq i \leq q, 0 < |\alpha| \leq \rho\}$, and $\mathcal{Z}_2 := \{(i, j, \alpha) : 1 \leq i, j \leq q, i \neq j, |\alpha| \leq \rho\}$.

4. Generation of Analytic and C^∞-Semigroups

In this section, under the assumption (2) on the order of the symbols, we will prove the main result of this paper (Theorem 1). For that we will need to estimate the norm $\|b_\lambda(D)u\|_{W_p^k(\mathbb{R}^n, \mathbb{C}^q)}$.

Let $A(D)$ be Λ-elliptic with $r_{ij} > 0$, $\rho \geq \rho_n$, and suppose that the assumption (2) holds. Then, note that $r_{ij} + r_{ji} = r_i + r_j$ for $i, j = 1, \ldots, q$. Moreover, let $r^+ := \max_{1 \leq i \leq q}\{r_i\}$, $r_- := \min_{1 \leq i,j \leq q}\{r_{ij}\}$, $\omega \geq 1$ and

$$\Lambda_\omega := \Lambda(\theta)_\omega := \{\lambda \in \Lambda = \Lambda(\theta) : |\lambda| \geq \omega\}.$$

Note that for b_λ, as in corollary 1, $u \in C_b^\infty(\mathbb{R}^n, \mathbb{C}^q) \cap W_p^k(\mathbb{R}^n, \mathbb{C}^q)$ and $\beta \in \mathbb{N}_0^n$, we have

$$\partial_x^\beta(b_\lambda(D)u)(x) = \text{Os} - \iint e^{i\xi\cdot\eta} b_\lambda(\xi)(\partial_x^\beta u)(x-\eta)\frac{d(\xi,\eta)}{(2\pi)^n}$$
$$= \lim_{\varepsilon\searrow 0}\int_{\mathbb{R}^n} K_\varepsilon(\eta,\lambda)(\partial_x^\beta u)(x-\eta)d\eta \qquad (8)$$

with

$$K_\varepsilon(\eta,\lambda) := \int_{\mathbb{R}^n} e^{i\xi\cdot\eta}\chi_\varepsilon(\xi,\eta;\lambda)b_\lambda(\xi)\frac{d\xi}{(2\pi)^n}, \qquad (9)$$

and

$$\chi_\varepsilon(\xi,\eta;\lambda) := \chi_\varepsilon(\xi;\lambda)\psi_\varepsilon(\eta)$$

for $\xi,\eta \in \mathbb{R}^n$, $0 < \varepsilon < 1$, where ψ is a function in $\mathcal{S}(\mathbb{R}^n)$ with $\psi(0) = 1$, $\psi_\varepsilon(\eta) := \psi(\varepsilon\eta)$, $\chi_\varepsilon(\xi;\lambda) := \varphi_\varepsilon((|\xi|^2 + |\lambda|^{2/r^+})^{1/2})$ with $\varphi_\varepsilon(x) := \varphi(\varepsilon x)$ for $x \in \mathbb{R}$ and $\varphi \in \mathcal{S}(\mathbb{R})$ satisfies $\varphi(0) = 1$.

It was proven in [20] (p. 845) that for $\alpha \in \mathbb{N}_0^n$, there exists a constant $C_\alpha > 0$ such that for all $\xi \in \mathbb{R}^n$ and $\lambda \in \Lambda_\omega$,

$$\left|\partial_\xi^\alpha \chi_\varepsilon(\xi;\lambda)\right| \leq C_\alpha (|\xi|^2 + |\lambda|^{2/r^+})^{-|\alpha|/2} \qquad (0 < \varepsilon < 1).$$

Now, due to

$$\frac{\omega^{2/r^+}+1}{\omega^{2/r^+}}(|\xi|^2 + |\lambda|^{2/r^+}) \geq \frac{1}{\omega^{2/r^+}}(\omega^{2/r^+}|\xi|^2 + \omega^{2/r^+}|\lambda|^{2/r^+} + |\lambda|^{2/r^+})$$
$$\geq |\xi|^2 + |\lambda|^{2/r^+} + 1,$$

we have

$$\left|\partial_\xi^\alpha \chi_\varepsilon(\xi;\lambda)\right| \leq \overline{C}_\alpha \left\langle \xi, |\lambda|^{1/r^+} \right\rangle^{-|\alpha|} \qquad (0 < \varepsilon < 1). \qquad (10)$$

We will obtain some estimate for K_ε with help of (10) and the following lemma and remark.

Lemma 3 ([15], Lemma 6.3). *Let $\chi \in \mathcal{S}(\mathbb{R}^n)$ with $\chi(0) = 1$. Then:*
(a) $\chi(\varepsilon x) \xrightarrow[\varepsilon\searrow 0]{} 1$ *uniformly on all compact subset of $\mathbb{R}^n$.*
(b) $\partial_x^\alpha \chi(\varepsilon x) \xrightarrow[\varepsilon\searrow 0]{} 0$ *uniformly on $\mathbb{R}^n$, if $\alpha \neq 0$.*
(c) *For all $\alpha \in \mathbb{N}_0^n$, there exists some $C_\alpha > 0$, independent on $0 < \varepsilon < 1$, such that*

$$|\partial_x^\alpha \chi(\varepsilon x)| \leq C_\alpha \langle x \rangle^{-(|\alpha|-\sigma)} \text{ for all } x \in \mathbb{R}^n \text{ and } 0 \leq \sigma \leq |\alpha|.$$

Remark 3. *Note that, if $\frac{1}{2} < r_-$, then for all $\frac{1}{2} \leq \delta < r_-$, we obtain*

$$1 < \delta + r_{ij} \leq r_{ji} + r_{ij} = r_i + r_j \text{ (for all } i,j\text{),}$$

and

$$\left\langle |\lambda|^{1/r^+}\xi, |\lambda|^{1/r_i}\right\rangle^{-r_i} \leq \frac{1}{(|\lambda|^{2/r^+}|\xi|^2 + |\lambda|^{2/r_i})^{r_i/2}}$$
$$\leq \frac{1}{(|\lambda|^{2/r^+}|\xi|^2 + |\lambda|^{2/r^+})^{r_i/2}}$$
$$= |\lambda|^{-r_i/r^+}\langle \xi \rangle^{-r_i} \qquad (11)$$

for all $\xi \in \mathbb{R}^n$ and $\lambda \in \Lambda_\omega$. Moreover, $\sigma := \frac{r_-}{r^+} \in (1/2r^+, 1]$ and $\mu := |\lambda|^{1/r^+}$, with $\lambda \in \Lambda_\omega$, satisfies

$$\mu^{-r_{ij}} = \frac{1}{|\lambda|^{r_{ij}/r^+}} \leq \frac{1}{|\lambda|^\sigma} \quad \text{for all } i,j.$$

Now, we will establish a key lemma for the generation of analytic semigroup. In the lemma, σ and μ are as in Remark 3.

Lemma 4. *Let $\frac{1}{2} \leq \delta < \min\{1, r_-\}$ and K_ε as in (9). Then:*

(a) *There exists a constant $C > 0$ such that for all $\varepsilon \in (0,1)$, $\eta \in \mathbb{R}^n$ and $\lambda \in \Lambda_\omega$ it holds*

$$(1 + |\mu\eta|)|\mu\eta|^n \|K_\varepsilon(\eta, \lambda)\|_{\mathcal{L}(\mathbb{C}^q)} \leq \frac{C}{|\lambda|^\sigma} \mu^n |\mu\eta|^\delta. \tag{12}$$

(b) *There exists a strongly measurable function $K : \mathbb{R}^n \times \Lambda_\omega \to \mathcal{L}(\mathbb{C}^q)$ with $K_\varepsilon(\eta, \lambda) \to K(\eta, \lambda)$ ($\varepsilon \searrow 0$) pointwise, and the estimate (12) holds with K_ε being replaced by K. In consequence there exists a constant $M > 0$, independent on λ, such that*

$$\|K(\cdot, \lambda)\|_{L^1(\mathbb{R}^n, \mathcal{L}(\mathbb{C}^q))} \leq \frac{M}{|\lambda|^\sigma} \quad \forall \lambda \in \Lambda_\omega. \tag{13}$$

Proof. (a) First, note that with the change $\xi \mapsto \mu\xi$ we obtain

$$K_\varepsilon(\eta, \lambda) = \mu^n \int_{\mathbb{R}^n} e^{i\mu\xi \cdot \eta} \chi_\varepsilon(\mu\xi, \eta; \lambda) b_\lambda(\mu\xi) \frac{d\xi}{(2\pi)^n}.$$

Note also that, for $\alpha \in \mathbb{N}_0^n$ with $0 < |\alpha| \leq \rho$, it holds

$$\int_{\mathbb{R}^n} D_\xi^\alpha (\chi_\varepsilon(\mu\xi, \eta; \lambda) b_\lambda(\mu\xi)) \frac{d\xi}{(2\pi)^n} = 0.$$

With this, $|e^{i\mu\xi \cdot \eta} - 1| \leq 2|\mu\xi|^\delta |\eta|^\delta$ for all $\xi, \eta \in \mathbb{R}^n$ and $\delta \in (0,1)$, partial integration, Leibniz rule, (10), corollary 1, Lemma 3, and Remark 3, we obtain for all $\alpha \in \mathbb{N}_0^n$ with $|\alpha| = n + l$, $l = 0, 1$, and $\frac{1}{2} \leq \delta < \min\{1, r_-\}$, that

$$\begin{aligned}
&\|(\mu\eta)^\alpha K_\varepsilon(\eta,\lambda)\|_{\mathcal{L}(\mathbb{C}^q)} \\
&= \left\| \mu^n \int_{\mathbb{R}^n} e^{i\mu\xi\cdot\eta} D_\xi^\alpha(\chi_\varepsilon(\mu\xi,\eta;\lambda) b_\lambda(\mu\xi)) \frac{d\xi}{(2\pi)^n} \right\|_{\mathcal{L}(\mathbb{C}^q)} \\
&= \left\| \mu^n \int_{\mathbb{R}^n} (e^{i\mu\xi\cdot\eta}-1)\psi(\varepsilon\eta) D_\xi^\alpha(\chi_\varepsilon(\mu\xi;\lambda) b_\lambda(\mu\xi)) \frac{d\xi}{(2\pi)^n} \right\|_{\mathcal{L}(\mathbb{C}^q)} \\
&\leq \mu^n \int_{\mathbb{R}^n} 2|\mu\xi|^\delta |\eta|^\delta |\psi(\varepsilon\eta)| \sum_{\gamma\leq\alpha} C_{\gamma\alpha} |D_\xi^{\alpha-\gamma}(\chi_\varepsilon(\mu\xi;\lambda))| \|\partial_\xi^\gamma(b_\lambda(\mu\xi))\|_{\mathcal{L}(\mathbb{C}^q)} d\xi \\
&\leq 2\mu^n |\mu\eta|^\delta \int_{\mathbb{R}^n} |\xi|^\delta \sum_{\gamma\leq\alpha} C_{\gamma\alpha} \mu^{|\alpha|} C_{\alpha-\gamma} \langle\mu\xi,\mu\rangle^{|\gamma|-|\alpha|} \|(\partial_\xi^\gamma b_\lambda)(\mu\xi)\|_{\mathcal{L}(\mathbb{C}^q)} d\xi \\
&\leq 2\mu^n |\mu\eta|^\delta \int_{\mathbb{R}^n} |\xi|^\delta \sum_{i,j} \sum_{\gamma\leq\alpha} \overline{C}_{\gamma\alpha} \mu^{|\alpha|} C_{\alpha-\gamma} \langle\mu\xi,\mu\rangle^{|\gamma|-|\alpha|} |(\partial_\xi^\gamma g_{ij}(\xi;\lambda))(\mu\xi)| d\xi \\
&\leq C\mu^n |\mu\eta|^\delta \int_{\mathbb{R}^n} |\xi|^\delta \Big[\sum_{i=1}^q \widehat{C}_{0\alpha} \mu^{|\alpha|} \langle\mu\xi,\mu\rangle^{-|\alpha|} \langle\mu\xi,|\lambda|^{1/r_i}\rangle^{-r_i} \\
&\quad + \sum_{j=1}^q \sum_{\mathcal{Z}_1} \widehat{C}_\alpha \mu^{|\alpha|} \langle\mu\xi,\mu\rangle^{|\gamma|-|\alpha|} \langle\mu\xi\rangle^{r_j-|\gamma|} \langle\mu\xi,|\lambda|^{1/r_i}\rangle^{-r_i} \langle\mu\xi,|\lambda|^{1/r_j}\rangle^{-r_j} \\
&\quad + \sum_{\mathcal{Z}_2} \widehat{C}_{\gamma\alpha} \mu^{|\alpha|} \langle\mu\xi,\mu\rangle^{|\gamma|-|\alpha|} \langle\mu\xi\rangle^{r_{ij}-|\gamma|} \langle\mu\xi,|\lambda|^{1/r_i}\rangle^{-r_i} \langle\mu\xi,|\lambda|^{1/r_j}\rangle^{-r_j} \Big] d\xi \\
&\stackrel{(11)}{\leq} C\mu^n |\mu\eta|^\delta \int_{\mathbb{R}^n} |\xi|^\delta \Big[\sum_{i=1}^q \widehat{C}_{0\alpha} \mu^{|\alpha|} |\mu\xi,\mu|^{-|\alpha|} \mu^{-r_i} \langle\xi\rangle^{-r_i} \\
&\quad + \sum_{j=1}^q \sum_{\mathcal{Z}_1} \widehat{C}_\alpha \mu^{|\alpha|} \langle\mu\xi\rangle^{r_j-|\alpha|} \mu^{-r_i} \langle\xi\rangle^{-r_i} \mu^{-r_j} \langle\xi\rangle^{-r_j} \\
&\quad + \sum_{\mathcal{Z}_2} \widehat{C}_{\gamma\alpha} \mu^{|\alpha|} \langle\mu\xi\rangle^{r_{ij}-|\alpha|} \mu^{-r_i} \langle\xi\rangle^{-r_i} \mu^{-r_j} \langle\xi\rangle^{-r_j} \Big] d\xi \\
&\leq \overline{C} \mu^n |\mu\eta|^\delta \Big[\frac{1}{|\lambda|^\sigma} \sum_{i=1}^q \underbrace{\int_{\mathbb{R}^n} \langle\xi\rangle^{-(r_i+n+l-\delta)} d\xi}_{=:c_{il}<\infty} \\
&\quad + \sum_{i,j=1}^q \underbrace{\int_{\mathbb{R}^n} \mu^{n+l-r_i-r_j} |\xi|^\delta \langle\mu\xi\rangle^{r_{ij}-(n+l)} \langle\xi\rangle^{-r_i-r_j} d\xi}_{=:I_{ijl}} \Big].
\end{aligned}$$

Let $\Omega_1 := \{\xi \in \mathbb{R}^n : |\xi| < 1\}$, $\Omega_2 := \mathbb{R}^n \setminus \Omega_1$ and

$$I_{ijl}^{(k)} := \int_{\Omega_k} \mu^{n+l-r_i-r_j} |\xi|^\delta \langle\mu\xi\rangle^{r_{ij}-(n+l)} \langle\xi\rangle^{-r_i-r_j} d\xi$$

for $k = 1, 2$. Since $I_{ijl} = I_{ijl}^{(1)} + I_{ijl}^{(2)}$, we will estimate $I_{ijl}^{(k)}$. We consider two cases: Case 1. If $r_{ij} \leq n + l$ for some i, j, it holds

$$I_{ijl}^{(1)} \leq \int_{\Omega_1} \mu^{n+l-r_i-r_j}|\xi|^\delta \mu^{r_{ij}-(n+l)}|\xi|^{r_{ij}-(n+l)}d\xi$$

$$= \mu^{-r_{ji}}\int_{\Omega_1}|\xi|^{\delta+r_{ij}-(n+l)}d\xi \leq \frac{C}{|\lambda|^\sigma},$$

since $\frac{1}{2} \leq \delta < r_{ij}$ (thus $\delta + r_{ij} > 1$). Furthermore,

$$I_{ijl}^{(2)} \leq \int_{\Omega_2} \mu^{n+l-r_i-r_j}|\xi|^\delta \mu^{r_{ij}-(n+l)}|\xi|^{r_{ij}-(n+l)}|\xi|^{-r_i-r_j}d\xi$$

$$= \mu^{-r_{ji}}\int_{\Omega_2}|\xi|^{\delta-r_{ji}-n-l}d\xi \leq \frac{C}{|\lambda|^\sigma},$$

due to $\delta < r_{ji} + l$ for $l = 0, 1$. Therefore,

$$I_{ijl} \leq \frac{\widehat{C}}{|\lambda|^\sigma} \qquad (l = 0, 1). \tag{14}$$

Case 2. Suppose $r_{ij} > n+l$ for some i, j. Since $\mu \geq 1$, then we get

$$I_{ijl}^{(1)} \leq \int_{\Omega_1} \mu^{n+l-r_i-r_j}|\xi|^\delta \left(1 + \mu^2|\xi|^2\right)^{\frac{r_{ij}-(n+l)}{2}} d\xi$$

$$\leq \int_{\Omega_1} \mu^{n+l-r_i-r_j}|\xi|^\delta 2^{\frac{r_{ij}-n-l}{2}} \mu^{r_{ij}-n-l}d\xi$$

$$= 2^{\frac{r_{ij}-n-l}{2}} \mu^{-r_{ji}}\int_{\Omega_1}|\xi|^\delta d\xi \leq \frac{C}{|\lambda|^\sigma}.$$

Moreover,

$$I_{ijl}^{(2)} = \int_{\Omega_2} \mu^{n+l-r_i-r_j}|\xi|^\delta \left(1 + \mu^2|\xi|^2\right)^{\frac{r_{ij}-(n+l)}{2}} \langle\xi\rangle^{-r_i-r_j}d\xi$$

$$\leq \int_{\Omega_2} \mu^{n+l-r_i-r_j}|\xi|^\delta |\xi|^{r_{ij}-(n+l)}\left(1 + \mu^2\right)^{\frac{r_{ij}-(n+l)}{2}}|\xi|^{-r_i-r_j}d\xi$$

$$\leq \int_{\Omega_2} \mu^{n+l-r_i-r_j}|\xi|^{\delta-r_{ji}-(n+l)} 2^{\frac{r_{ij}-n-l}{2}} \mu^{r_{ij}-n-l}d\xi$$

$$= 2^{\frac{r_{ij}-n-l}{2}} \mu^{-r_{ji}}\int_{\Omega_2}|\xi|^{\delta-r_{ji}-n-l}d\xi \leq \frac{C}{|\lambda|^\sigma}.$$

Thus, (14) holds too. In consequence

$$\|(\mu\eta)^\alpha K_\varepsilon(\eta,\lambda)\|_{\mathcal{L}(\mathbb{C}^q)} \leq \frac{C}{|\lambda|^\sigma}\mu^n|\mu\eta|^\delta$$

for all $\eta \in \mathbb{R}^n, \lambda \in \Lambda_\omega, \alpha \in \mathbb{N}_0^n$ with $|\alpha| = n+l, l = 0, 1, \varepsilon \in (0,1)$ and $\frac{1}{2} \leq \delta < \min\{1, r_-\}$. Therefore, we have

$$|\mu\eta|^{n+l} \|K_\varepsilon(\eta, \lambda)\|_{\mathcal{L}(\mathbb{C}^q)} \leq n^{\frac{n+l}{2}} \sum_{|\alpha|=n+l} \|(\mu\eta)^\alpha K_\varepsilon(\eta, \lambda)\|_{\mathcal{L}(\mathbb{C}^q)} \leq \frac{C}{|\lambda|^\sigma} \mu^n |\mu\eta|^\delta.$$

Adding these inequalities for $l = 0$ and $l = 1$, we obtain the assertion (a).

(b) Let $\varepsilon, \varepsilon' \in (0,1), \eta \in \mathbb{R}^n$ and $\lambda \in \Lambda_\omega$. From the proof of (a) we see that

$$(\mu\eta)^\alpha (K_\varepsilon(\eta, \lambda) - K_{\varepsilon'}(\eta, \lambda))$$
$$= \mu^n \int_{\mathbb{R}^n} (e^{i\mu\xi\cdot\eta} - 1) D_\xi^\alpha [(\chi_\varepsilon(\mu\xi, \eta; \lambda) - \chi_{\varepsilon'}(\mu\xi, \eta; \lambda)) b_\lambda(\mu\xi)] \frac{d\xi}{(2\pi)^n}. \quad (15)$$

From Lemma 3 we know that $D_\xi^\gamma (\chi_\varepsilon(\mu\xi, \eta; \lambda) - \chi_{\varepsilon'}(\mu\xi, \eta; \lambda)) \longrightarrow 0 \; (\varepsilon, \varepsilon' \searrow 0)$ for all $\gamma \in \mathbb{N}_0^n$ and all ξ, η. Therefore the integrand in (15) converges pointwise to zero for $\varepsilon, \varepsilon' \searrow 0$. Furthermore, in the same way of the proof of part (a) we have that

$$\left\|(e^{i\mu\xi\cdot\eta} - 1) D_\xi^\alpha [(\chi_\varepsilon(\mu\xi, \eta; \lambda) - \chi_{\varepsilon'}(\mu\xi, \eta; \lambda)) b_\lambda(\mu\xi)]\right\|_{\mathcal{L}(\mathbb{C}^q)}$$
$$\leq C|\mu\eta|^\delta \Bigg[\frac{1}{|\lambda|^\sigma} \sum_{i=1}^q \langle \xi \rangle^{-(r_i + n + l - \delta)}$$
$$+ \sum_{i,j=1}^q \mu^{n+l-r_i-r_j} |\xi|^\delta \langle \mu\xi \rangle^{r_{ij} - (n+l)} \langle \xi \rangle^{-r_i - r_j}\Bigg] \in L^1(\mathbb{R}_\xi^n).$$

Hence, by dominated convergence we get for fixed $(\eta, \lambda) \in (\mathbb{R}^n \setminus \{0\}) \times \Lambda_\omega$ that $\|K_\varepsilon(\eta, \lambda) - K_{\varepsilon'}(\eta, \lambda)\|_{\mathcal{L}(\mathbb{C}^q)} \longrightarrow 0 \; (\varepsilon, \varepsilon' \searrow 0)$. Therefore there exists a strongly measurable function $K : \mathbb{R}^n \times \Lambda_\omega \to \mathcal{L}(\mathbb{C}^q)$ with $K_\varepsilon(\eta, \lambda) \to K(\eta, \lambda) \; (\varepsilon \searrow 0)$ pointwise a.e. Then, inequality (12) holds for $K(\eta, \lambda)$ instead of $K_\varepsilon(\eta, \lambda)$ and in consequence (13) is true due to

$$\int_{\mathbb{R}^n} \frac{\mu^n |\mu\eta|^{\delta - n}}{1 + |\mu\eta|} d\eta < \infty.$$

□

Proposition 1. *Let $A(D)$ be Λ-elliptic with $\rho \geq \rho_n$, $\frac{1}{2} < r_-$ and let $b_\lambda(\cdot) := (A_{\alpha_0}(\cdot) - \lambda)^{-1}$ for all $\lambda \in \Lambda_\omega$. If $k \in \mathbb{N}_0$ and $1 \leq p < \infty$, then $b_\lambda(D) \in \mathcal{L}\left(W_p^k(\mathbb{R}^n, \mathbb{C}^q)\right)$ with*

$$\|b_\lambda(D)\|_{\mathcal{L}(W_p^k(\mathbb{R}^n, \mathbb{C}^q))} \leq \frac{M}{|\lambda|^\sigma} \quad \forall \lambda \in \Lambda_\omega,$$

where the constant $M > 0$ is independent on λ and σ.

Proof. Let $\beta \in \mathbb{N}_0^n$ with $|\beta| \leq k, \lambda \in \Lambda_\omega, u \in C_b^\infty(\mathbb{R}^n, \mathbb{C}^q) \cap W_p^k(\mathbb{R}^n, \mathbb{C}^q)$ and $x \in \mathbb{R}^n$. Then (see (8))

$$\partial_x^\beta (b_\lambda(D) u)(x) = \lim_{\varepsilon \searrow 0} \int_{\mathbb{R}^n} K_\varepsilon(\eta, \lambda) (\partial_x^\beta u)(x - \eta) d\eta \quad (16)$$

with K_ε as in (9). From (16), Lemma 4 and dominated convergence, we get

$$\partial_x^\beta (b_\lambda(D) u)(x) = \int_{\mathbb{R}^n} K(\eta, \lambda) (\partial_x^\beta u)(x - \eta) d\eta = (K(\cdot, \lambda) * (\partial_x^\beta u))(x),$$

where $*$ stands for the standard convolution. Since $\partial_x^\beta u \in L^p(\mathbb{R}^n, \mathbb{C}^q)$, we have $K(\cdot, \lambda) * (\partial_x^\beta u) \in L^1(\mathbb{R}^n, \mathbb{C}^q)$ and

$$\left\|\partial_x^\beta(b_\lambda(D)u)\right\|_{L^p(\mathbb{R}^n, \mathbb{C}^q)} \leq \|K(\cdot, \lambda)\|_{L^1(\mathbb{R}^n, L(\mathbb{C}^q))} \|\partial_x^\beta u\|_{L^p(\mathbb{R}^n, \mathbb{C}^q)}$$
$$\leq \frac{M}{|\lambda|^\sigma} \|u\|_{W_p^k(\mathbb{R}^n, \mathbb{C}^q)}$$

due to Lemma 4 (b). This implies that

$$\|b_\lambda(D)u\|_{W_p^k(\mathbb{R}^n, \mathbb{C}^q)} \leq \frac{\widetilde{M}}{|\lambda|^\sigma} \|u\|_{W_p^k(\mathbb{R}^n, \mathbb{C}^q)} \qquad (17)$$

for all $u \in C_b^\infty(\mathbb{R}^n, \mathbb{C}^q) \cap W_p^k(\mathbb{R}^n, \mathbb{C}^q)$ and $\lambda \in \Lambda_\omega$. Because of $1 \leq p < \infty$, $\mathcal{S}(\mathbb{R}^n, \mathbb{C}^q)$ is dense in $W_p^k(\mathbb{R}^n, \mathbb{C}^q)$ which gives $b_\lambda(D) \in \mathcal{L}\left(W_p^k(\mathbb{R}^n, \mathbb{C}^q)\right)$ and the estimate on its norm. □

For $k \in \mathbb{N}_0$ and $1 \leq p < \infty$, we define the $W_p^k(\mathbb{R}^n, \mathbb{C}^q)$-realization $A_{\alpha_0, k}$ of the system $A_{\alpha_0}(D)$ as the unbounded operator given by

$$D(A_{\alpha_0, k}) := \left\{ u \in W_p^k(\mathbb{R}^n, \mathbb{C}^q) : A_{\alpha_0}(D)u \in W_p^k(\mathbb{R}^n, \mathbb{C}^q) \right\},$$
$$A_{\alpha_0, k} u := A_{\alpha_0}(D)u \text{ for } u \in D(A_{\alpha_0, k}).$$

Now we are able to show the main result of this paper. We recall that $\rho \geq \rho_n$, $\frac{1}{2} < r_-$ and $\sigma = \frac{r_-}{r^+} \in (\frac{1}{2r^+}, 1]$.

Theorem 1. *Let $A(D)$ be $\Lambda(\theta)$-elliptic with $0 < \theta < \pi/2$ and $\vartheta := \pi - \theta$. Let $k \in \mathbb{N}_0$, $1 \leq p < \infty$ and $A_{\alpha_0, k}$ be the $W_p^k(\mathbb{R}^n, \mathbb{C}^q)$-realization of $A_{\alpha_0}(D)$. Then, for the resolvent set $\rho(-A_{\alpha_0, k})$ of $-A_{\alpha_0, k}$ we have $\rho(-A_{\alpha_0, k}) \supset \Sigma_{\vartheta, \omega} := \{\lambda \in \mathbb{C} : |\lambda| \geq \omega \text{ and } |\arg \lambda| \leq \vartheta\}$ and*

$$\left\|(\lambda + A_{\alpha_0, k})^{-1}\right\|_{\mathcal{L}\left(W_p^k(\mathbb{R}^n, \mathbb{C}^q)\right)} \leq \frac{M}{|\lambda|^\sigma} \qquad (\lambda \in \Sigma_{\vartheta, \omega}). \qquad (18)$$

for some constant $M > 0$. Therefore, $-A_{\alpha_0, k} : W_p^k(\mathbb{R}^n, \mathbb{C}^q) \supset D(A_{\alpha_0, k}) \to W_p^k(\mathbb{R}^n, \mathbb{C}^q)$ generates an infinitely differentiable semigroup on $W_p^k(\mathbb{R}^n, \mathbb{C}^q)$, which is analytic and strongly continuous if $\sigma = 1$ (i.e., $r_1 = \cdots = r_q = r_-$).

Remark 4. *The semigroup is given by $(e^{-\tau A_{\alpha_0, k}})_{\tau \geq 0}$ with $e^{-0 A_{\alpha_0, k}} := I$ and*

$$e^{-\tau A_{\alpha_0, k}} := \frac{1}{2\pi i} \int_\Gamma e^{-\tau \lambda} (\lambda I - A_{\alpha_0, k})^{-1} d\lambda \quad (\tau > 0),$$

where $\Gamma : \lambda = \omega + iy$, $-\infty < y < \infty$ stands for a lying in $\rho(-A_{\alpha_0, k})$ path, and $[t \mapsto e^{-\tau A_{\alpha_0, k}}] \in C^\infty((0, \infty); \mathcal{L}(W_p^k(\mathbb{R}^n, \mathbb{C}^q)))$. See [21, Theorem 3.4, Ch. 1] for a reference. Further results about differential and analytical properties of semigroups of operators can be found also in [22] and in the references therein.

Proof of Theorem 1. Because of the density of $\mathcal{S}(\mathbb{R}^n, \mathbb{C}^q)$ in $W_p^k(\mathbb{R}^n, \mathbb{C}^q)$ and

$$(A_{\alpha_0, k} - \widetilde{\lambda}) b_{\widetilde{\lambda}}(D) u = b_{\widetilde{\lambda}}(D) (A_{\alpha_0, k} - \widetilde{\lambda}) u = u$$

for all $u \in \mathcal{S}(\mathbb{R}^n, \mathbb{C}^q)$ and $\widetilde{\lambda} \in \Lambda(\theta)_\omega$, it follows from (17) that $\Lambda(\theta)_\omega \subset \rho(A_{\alpha_0, k})$ and $b_{\widetilde{\lambda}}(D) = (A_{\alpha_0, k} - \widetilde{\lambda})^{-1}$ in $W_p^k(\mathbb{R}^n, \mathbb{C}^q)$. Now, if $\lambda \in \Sigma_{\vartheta, \omega}$, then $\widetilde{\lambda} := -\lambda \in \Lambda(\theta)_\omega$. Therefore we have

$$(\lambda + A_{\alpha_0, k}) b_{-\lambda}(D) u = b_{-\lambda}(D) (\lambda + A_{\alpha_0, k}) u = u$$

for all $u \in \mathcal{S}(\mathbb{R}^n, \mathbb{C}^q)$ and $\lambda \in \Sigma_{\theta,\omega}$. It follows that $\Sigma_{\theta,\omega} \subset \rho(-A_{\alpha_0,k})$ and $b_{-\lambda}(D) = (\lambda + A_{\alpha_0,k})^{-1}$ for $\lambda \in \Sigma_{\theta,\omega}$. Then (18) follows from Proposition 1. □

The above result on the generation of semigroup in $W_p^k(\mathbb{R}^n, \mathbb{C}^q)$ allow us to solve non-autonomous Cauchy problems, based on an abstract result in [23], Chapter IV. For this, let $T > 0$ and assume $\mathcal{A} = \{A(t, D) : t \in [0, T]\}$ to be a uniformly bounded family of Λ-elliptic systems. For $k \in \mathbb{N}_0$ and $1 \le p < \infty$, we denote by $A_k(t)$ the $W_p^k(\mathbb{R}^n, \mathbb{C}^q)$-realization of $A(t, D)$. Then, we study the Cauchy problem

$$\begin{cases} \partial_t u(t) + A_k(t)u(t) = f(t), & t \in (0, T], \\ u(0) = u_0. \end{cases} \tag{19}$$

A function $u \in C^1\left((0, T], W_p^k(\mathbb{R}^n, \mathbb{C}^q)\right) \cap C\left([0, T], W_p^k(\mathbb{R}^n, \mathbb{C}^q)\right)$ is called a classical solution of (19), if $u(t) \in D(A_k(t))$ for all $t \in (0, T]$, $\partial_t u(t) + A_k(t)u(t) = f(t)$ for all $t \in (0, T]$ and $u(0) = u_0$.

Using Theorem 1 and the abstract result on Cauchy problems given in Theorem 2.5.1 of Chapter IV in [23], we obtain, in the same way to the proof of Theorem 4.3 in [6], the following result.

Theorem 2. *Let $\mathcal{A} = \{A(t, D) : t \in [0, T]\}$ be a uniformly bounded family of $\Lambda(\theta)$-elliptic systems, $0 < \theta < \pi/2$, with symbols $(a_{ij}(t, \xi))_{1 \le i,j \le q}$ for all $t \in [0, T]$, such that $[t \mapsto a_{ij}(t, \cdot)] \in C^\alpha([0, T], S^{r_{ij},p}(\mathbb{R}^n))$ for all $i, j = 1, \ldots, q$ and some $\alpha \in (0, 1)$, with $r_1 = \cdots = r_q = r_- > 1/2$. Furthermore, suppose that there exists $\alpha_0 \in \mathbb{R}$ such that $A_{\alpha_0}(t, D) := A(t, D) + \alpha_0$ is $\Lambda(\theta)$-elliptic, $0 < \theta < \pi/2$, with the same constant C and $R = 0$, for all $t \in [0, T]$ (see Definition 3 and Remark 2). Moreover, let $k \in \mathbb{N}_0$, $1 \le p < \infty$ and $\varepsilon \in (0, 1)$. Then, for every $u_0 \in W_p^k(\mathbb{R}^n, \mathbb{C}^q)$ and $f \in C^\varepsilon\left([0, T], W_p^k(\mathbb{R}^n, \mathbb{C}^q)\right)$, the Cauchy problem*

$$\begin{cases} \partial_t v(t) + A_{\alpha_0,k}(t)v(t) = e^{-\alpha_0 t} f(t), & t \in (0, T], \\ v(0) = u_0. \end{cases} \tag{20}$$

has a unique classical solution, where $A_{\alpha_0,k}(t)$ is the $W_p^k(\mathbb{R}^n, \mathbb{C}^q)$-realization of $A_{\alpha_0}(t, D)$.

Corollary 2. *Suppose that the same hypothesis from Theorem 2 hold. Then, there exists a unique classical solution of problem (19).*

Proof. First note that $A_{\alpha_0,k}(t) = A_k(t) + \alpha_0$. Now, let $v(t)$, $t \in [0, T]$, be the classical solution of problem (20) and set $u(t) := e^{\alpha_0 t} v(t)$ for $t \in [0, T]$. Then u is the unique classical solution of problem (19). □

Remark 5. *If $-A_{\alpha_0,k}(t)$, $t \in [0, T]$, generates only an infinitely differentible semigroup on $W_p^k(\mathbb{R}^n, \mathbb{C}^q)$ and, $A_{\alpha_0,k}(\cdot)^{-1}$ is strongly continuously differentiable on $[0, T]$ and satisfies some additional conditions, Theorems 4.3, 4.4, and Remark 4.5 in [24] imply the existence and uniqueness of a strict solution of (20), and therefore of (19), for each $u_0 \in W_p^k(\mathbb{R}^n, \mathbb{C}^q)$. Such strict solution is taken in sense of Definition 1.1 in [24].*

Remark 6. *(i) With the method used in this paper some better assertions could be obtained, for instance maximal L^p-regularity or the existence of a H_∞-calculus as in [4].*

(ii) Using some ideas from [4], one could change the basic space $W_p^k(\mathbb{R}^n, \mathbb{C}^q)$ by $\prod_{i=1}^q W_p^{k-l_i}(\mathbb{R}^n)$ for some suitable integers l_i, $i = 1, \ldots, q$. Thus one could obtain similar result as in Theorem 1, but under weaker assumption on the structure of the system. This remark will be useful for the analysis, in a forthcoming paper, of the generalized thermoelastic plate equations with fractional damping.

5. Examples

In this section, we will consider some examples where we could apply our results. Initially, as a naive example, we consider the Cauchy problem associated to the n-dimensional linear heat equation in the whole space. That is

$$\begin{cases} u_t(x,t) - \alpha \Delta u(x,t) = 0 & (x \in \mathbb{R}^n, t > 0), \\ u(x,0) = u_0(x) & (x \in \mathbb{R}^n), \end{cases} \tag{21}$$

where $\alpha > 0$ is related to the thermal diffusivity and $u(x,t)$ represents the temperature in point x at time t. The differential equation in (21) can be written in the form

$$u_t - A(D)u = 0,$$

where

$$A(\xi) = -\alpha |\xi|^2, \quad \xi \in \mathbb{R}^n.$$

Note that in this case $r_1 = 2 > 1/2$ and therefore the condition (2) holds trivially. Let define

$$A_-(\xi) := -A(\xi).$$

Now, for all $\lambda \in \Lambda(\theta)$ with $0 < \theta < \pi/2$, and all $|\xi| \geq \frac{1}{\sqrt{3}}$, it can be shown that

$$|\det(\lambda - A_-(\xi))| = |\lambda - \alpha |\xi|^2| \geq M(\langle \xi \rangle^2 + |\lambda|).$$

Then $A(D)$ is $\Lambda(\theta)$-elliptic and we can apply corollary 2 to solve problem (21).

Consider now the thermoelastic plate equations on $\mathbb{R}^n$ given by

$$\begin{cases} v_{tt} + \Delta^2 v + \Delta \theta = 0, \\ \theta_t - \Delta \theta - \Delta v_t = 0 \end{cases} \tag{22}$$

together with the initial conditions

$$v(0, \cdot) = v_0, \quad v_t(0, \cdot) = v_1, \quad \theta(0, \cdot) = \theta_0.$$

The equations in (22) were derived in [25], where v denotes a mechanical variable representing the vertical displacement of the plate, while θ denotes a thermal variable describing the temperature relative to a constant reference temperature $\bar{\theta}$.

Using the substitution $u = (\theta, v_t, -\Delta v)^\top$, the system (22) can be written as

$$u_t - A(D)u = 0, \tag{23}$$

where

$$A(\xi) := \begin{pmatrix} -|\xi|^2 & -|\xi|^2 & 0 \\ |\xi|^2 & 0 & -|\xi|^2 \\ 0 & |\xi|^2 & 0 \end{pmatrix}. \tag{24}$$

Note that in this case, $r_{ij} = 2 > 1/2$ for all $i,j = 1,2,3$, and assumption (2) holds. Now, we define

$$A_-(\xi) := -A(\xi) \tag{25}$$

and consider the determinant of $\lambda - A_-(\xi)$, which is given by:

$$\det(\lambda - A_-(\xi)) = \lambda^3 - |\xi|^2 \lambda^2 + 2|\xi|^4 \lambda - |\xi|^6.$$

It is easy to see that

$$\det(\lambda - A_-(\xi)) = |\xi|^6 p\left(\frac{\lambda}{|\xi|^2}\right), \qquad (26)$$

where

$$p(t) = t^3 - t^2 + 2t - 1.$$

Since $p(0) < 0$, $p(1) > 0$ and $p'(t) > 0$ for all $t \in \mathbb{R}$, there exists a unique real number $\alpha \in (0,1)$ such that $p(\alpha) = 0$. Now, since p is a polynomial with real coefficients, there exist positive constants β and γ, such that

$$p(t) = (t - \lambda_1)(t - \lambda_2)(t - \lambda_3) \qquad (27)$$

with $\lambda_1 = \alpha$, $\lambda_2 = \beta + \gamma i$ and $\lambda_3 = \overline{\lambda_2}$. In particular, we get $\lambda_1 + \lambda_2 + \lambda_3 = 1$, and therefore $\beta = \frac{1-\alpha}{2} > 0$. Hence, according to (26) and (27), it follows that

$$\det(\lambda - A_-(\xi)) = \left(\lambda - |\xi|^2 \lambda_1\right)\left(\lambda - |\xi|^2 \lambda_2\right)\left(\lambda - |\xi|^2 \lambda_3\right). \qquad (28)$$

By inequality (2.7) in [26], there exists $\frac{\pi}{2} < \vartheta_0 < \pi$ such that

$$\left|\lambda \lambda_j^{-1} + |\xi|^2\right| \geq C(|\lambda| + |\xi|^2) \quad (j = 1,2,3) \quad \forall \lambda \in -\Lambda(\vartheta_0) \text{ and } \xi \in \mathbb{R}^n, \qquad (29)$$

where $-\Lambda(\vartheta_0) := \{-\lambda : \lambda \in \Lambda(\vartheta_0)\}$. Hence, for all $\lambda \in \Lambda(\vartheta_0)$ and $|\xi| \geq \frac{1}{\sqrt{3}}$, we have

$$\begin{aligned}
\left|\lambda - |\xi|^2 \lambda_j\right| &= |\lambda_j|\left|(-\lambda)\lambda_j^{-1} + |\xi|^2\right| \\
&\geq c|\lambda_j|(|\lambda| + |\xi|^2) \\
&\geq C(|\lambda| + \langle\xi\rangle^2)
\end{aligned} \qquad (30)$$

for $j = 1, 2, 3$. Note that $2^r |\xi|^r \geq \langle\xi\rangle^r$ if $|\xi| \geq \frac{1}{\sqrt{3}}$ and $r \geq 0$.

Proposition 2. *Let $A_-(\xi)$ be defined as in (25). Then $A_-(D)$ is $\Lambda(\vartheta)$-elliptic with $0 < \vartheta < \pi/2$.*

Proof. This follows from (28)–(30). □

Theorem 3. *Let $T > 0$, $\varepsilon \in (0,1)$, $k \in \mathbb{N}_0$, $1 \leq p < \infty$, $A(D)$ be defined by (23) and (24) and let A_k be the $W_p^k(\mathbb{R}^n, \mathbb{C}^3)$-realization of $A(D)$. Then, for each $u_0 \in W_p^k(\mathbb{R}^n, \mathbb{C}^3)$ and $f \in C^\varepsilon([0,T], W_p^k(\mathbb{R}^n, \mathbb{C}^3))$ the Cauchy problem*

$$\begin{cases} \partial_t u(t) + A_k u(t) = f(t), & t \in (0,T], \\ u(0) = u_0. \end{cases}$$

has a unique classical solution.

Proof. It follows from Proposition 2 and corollary 2. □

Now, as a third example, we consider the lineal structurally damped plate equation on $\mathbb{R}^n$

$$v_{tt} + \Delta^2 v - \rho \Delta v_t = f, \qquad (31)$$

together with initial conditions

$$v(0, \cdot) = v_0, \quad v_t(0, \cdot) = v_1.$$

Here, $\rho > 0$ is a fixed parameter. A description of this equation can be found in [27] and the references therein.

Using the substitution $u = (v_t, -\Delta v)^\top$ and $F = (f, 0)^T$, the Equation (31) can be written as
$$u_t - \mathscr{A}(D)u = F,$$
where
$$\mathscr{A}(\xi) := \begin{pmatrix} -\rho|\xi|^2 & -|\xi|^2 \\ |\xi|^2 & 0 \end{pmatrix}.$$

Note again that $r_{ij} = 2 > 1/2$ for all $i, j \in \{1, 2\}$, and assumption (2) holds. Now, we define $\mathscr{A}_-(\xi) := -\mathscr{A}(\xi)$ and consider the determinant of $\lambda - \mathscr{A}_-(\xi)$, which is given by
$$\det(\lambda - \mathscr{A}_-(\xi)) = \lambda^2 - \rho|\xi|^2 \lambda + |\xi|^4.$$

Note that $\det(\lambda_\pm - \mathscr{A}_-(\xi)) = 0$ if only if $\lambda_\pm = |\xi|^2 \left(\dfrac{\rho}{2} \pm \dfrac{\sqrt{\rho^2 - 4}}{2} \right) =: |\xi|^2 z_\pm$. If $\xi \neq 0$, then $\lambda_\pm > 0$ for $\rho \geq 2$ and $\lambda_\pm \in \mathbb{C}$ (with $\operatorname{Re} z_+ > 0$ and $z_- = \overline{z_+}$) for $0 < \rho < 2$. Therefore, $\det(\lambda - \mathscr{A}_-(\xi)) = (\lambda - |\xi|^2 z_+)(\lambda - |\xi|^2 z_-)$ and in consequence
$$|\det(\lambda - \mathscr{A}_-(\xi))| \geq C(\langle \xi \rangle^2 + |\lambda|)(\langle \xi \rangle^2 + |\lambda|) \quad \forall \lambda \in \Lambda(\pi/2) \text{ and } |\xi| \geq 1/\sqrt{3}.$$

In consequence, $\mathscr{A}_-(D)$ is $\Lambda(\theta)$-elliptic with $0 < \theta < \pi/2$. Using the same arguments as in the previous example, we have that the Cauchy problem associated with (31) has a unique classical solution.

As a last example we consider a generalized plate equation in $\mathbb{R}^n$ with intermediated damping. Let $\alpha, \rho > 0$, $\beta \in [0, 1]$ and $L := (-\Delta)^\alpha$. Then the associated symbol of L is $p(\xi) = |\xi|^{2\alpha}$, $\xi \in \mathbb{R}^n$. The generalized plate equation in $\mathbb{R}^n$ with intermediated damping is given by
$$u_{tt} + Lu + \rho L^\beta u_t = 0 \tag{32}$$
together with the initial conditions
$$u(0, \cdot) = u_0, \quad u_t(0, \cdot) = u_1. \tag{33}$$

The generalized thermoelastic plate equation has been introduced in [28], a plate equation with intermediate damping was studied in [29] and a plate equation with intermediate rotational force and damping in [30]. For the particular case $\alpha = 2$, (32) models the equation of a plate with: (i) frictional damping if $\beta = 0$, (ii) structural damping if $\beta = 1/2$ and (iii) Kelvin-Voigt damping if $\beta = 1$.

If $U := \left(u_t, L^{1/2} u \right)$, the equation (32) can equivalently be written as
$$U_t + \widetilde{A}(D)U = 0, \qquad \widetilde{A}(\xi) := \begin{bmatrix} \rho|\xi|^{2\alpha\beta} & |\xi|^\alpha \\ -|\xi|^\alpha & 0 \end{bmatrix}.$$

Now, let $\chi(\xi)$ be an arbitrary 0-excision function and $A(\xi) := \chi(\xi)\widetilde{A}(\xi)$. In the following we will omit without loss of generality the factor $\chi(\xi)$ in the definition of $A(\xi)$ and we will assume that $\rho = 1$.

Using the ideas of the proof of Lemma 6.1 in [4] we obtain the following lemma.

Lemma 5. *Assume that the parameters $\alpha > 0$ and $\beta \in (0, 1)$ satisfy the conditions*
$$\alpha > \frac{1}{2} \quad \wedge \quad \frac{1}{4\alpha} < \beta < 1 - \frac{1}{4\alpha}.$$

Then, for the the following choice of orders:

$$r_1 = 2\alpha\beta, r_2 = 2\alpha(1-\beta) \text{ and } r_{12} = r_{21} = \alpha,$$

$A(D)$ *is $\Lambda(\theta)$-elliptic for any $0 < \theta < \pi$.*

Under the hypotheses of the previous lemma we have that

$$r_+ = \begin{cases} 2\alpha(1-\beta), & 0 < \beta < \frac{1}{2}, \\ \alpha, & \beta = \frac{1}{2}, \\ 2\alpha\beta. & \frac{1}{2} < \beta < 1, \end{cases} \quad r_- = \begin{cases} 2\alpha\beta, & 0 < \beta < \frac{1}{2}, \\ \alpha, & \beta = \frac{1}{2}, \\ 2\alpha(1-\beta), & \frac{1}{2} < \beta < 1, \end{cases} \text{ and }$$

$$\sigma = \frac{r_-}{r_+} = \begin{cases} \frac{\beta}{1-\beta}, & 0 < \beta < \frac{1}{2}, \\ 1, & \beta = \frac{1}{2}, \\ \frac{1-\beta}{\beta}, & \frac{1}{2} < \beta < 1. \end{cases}$$

Consequently, we can apply corollary 2 and Remark 5 to solve problem (32) and (33).

6. Conclusions

In this article, we have proved that the additive inverse of a suitable Sobolev space realization of a Λ-elliptic Fourier multipliers system (in the sense of the Definition 3) generates an infinitely differentiable semigroup on such Sobolev space, and that under certain additional conditions, it generates an analytic semigroup on the same Sobolev space (see Theorem 1). We emphasize again in these conclusions that the proof of the generation of semigroups was done directly using an approach based on oscillatory integrals and non trivial kernel estimates for them. With the results about generation of semigroups we addressed the analysis of some application problems in Section 5 using well-known statements for the existence and uniqueness of solutions for abstract evolution equations. Now, regarding the possible future scope of this work, we recall Remark 6: using techniques similar to those in this paper, questions about maximal L^p-regularity, the existence of a H_∞-calculus, the improvement of the basic spaces, and the weakening of the assumptions for the structure of the system of Fourier multipliers, would be addressed in a forthcoming paper. In the other direction, it is interesting to study assumptions, under which Λ-elliptic Fourier multipliers systems generate Cosine families of operators in some appropriate functional or distributional spaces, to consider control problems for fractional evolution inclusions or equations following ideas from, for example [9,11–14].

Author Contributions: Conceptualization, B.B.M. and J.H.M.; Formal analysis, B.B.M., J.G.O., R.G.A. and J.H.M.; Funding acquisition, B.B.M. and J.H.M.; Investigation, B.B.M., J.G.O., R.G.A. and J.H.M.; Supervision, B.B.M., J.G.O., R.G.A. and J.H.M.; Writing—original draft, B.B.M., J.G.O. and R.G.A.; Writing—review and editing, J.H.M. All authors have read and agreed to the published version of the manuscript.

Funding: This research was funded by MINCIENCIAS-COLOMBIA (formerly COLCIENCIAS) grant number 121571250194.

Data Availability Statement: Not applicable.

Conflicts of Interest: The authors declare no conflict of interest.

References

1. Douglis, A.; Nirenberg, L. Interior estimates for elliptic systems of partial differential equations. *Comm. Pure Appl. Math.* **1955**, *8*, 503–538. [CrossRef]
2. Kramer, R. The Cauchy problem for Douglis-Nirenberg elliptic systems of partial differential equations. *Trans. Amarican Math. Soc.* **1973**, *182*, 211–225. [CrossRef]
3. Kozhevnikov, A. Spectral problems for pseudo-differential systems elliptic in the Douglis-Nirenberg sense and their applications. *Math. USSR Sb.* **1973**, *21*, 63–90. [CrossRef]
4. Denk, R.; Saal, J.; Seiler, J. Bounded H_∞-calculus for pseudodifferential Douglis-Nirenberg systems of mild regularity. *Math. Nachr.* **2009**, *282*, 386–407. [CrossRef]
5. Denk, R.; Mennicken, R.; Volevich, L. The Newton Polygon and elliptic problems with parameter. *Math. Nachr.* **1998**, *192*, 125–157. [CrossRef]
6. Barraza Martínez, B.; Denk, R.; Hernández Monzón, J. Analytic semigroups of pseudodifferential operators on vector-valued sobolev spaces. *Bull. Braz. Math. Soc. New Ser.* **2014**, *45*, 197–242. [CrossRef]
7. Barraza Martínez, B.; Denk, R.; Hernández Monzón, J.; Kammerlander, F.; Nendel, M. Regularity and asymptotic behavior for a damped plate–membrane transmission problem. *J. Math. Anal. Appl.* **2019**, *474*, 1082–1103. [CrossRef]
8. Barraza Martínez, B.; Denk, R.; González Ospino, J.; Hernández Monzón, J.; Rau, S. Long time asymptotics for a coupled thermoelastic plate-membrane system. *Math. Meth. Appl. Sci.* **2021**, *44*, 12881–12908. [CrossRef]
9. Kavitha, K.; Vijayakumar, V.; Udhayakumar, R.; Sakthivel, N.; Sooppy Nisar, K. A note on approximate controllability of the Hilfer fractional neutral differential inclusions with infinite delay. *Math. Meth. Appl. Sci.* **2021**, *44*, 4428–4447. [CrossRef]
10. Lasiecka, I.; Triggiani, R. *Control Theory for Partial Differential Equations: Continuous and Approximation Theories I, Abstract Parabolic Systems*; Encyclopedia of Mathematics and its Applications 74; Cambridge University Press: Cambridge, UK, 2000.
11. Mohan Raja, M.; Vijayakumar, V.; Udhayakumar, R. A new approach on approximate controllability of fractional evolution inclusions of order $1 < r < 2$ with infinite delay. *Chaos Solitons Fractals. Nonlinear Sci. Nonequilibrium Complex Phenom.* **2020**, *141*, 110343.
12. Patel, R.; Shukla, A.; Jadon, S.S. Existence and optimal control problem for semilinear fractional order (1,2] control system. *Math. Meth. Appl. Sci.* **2020**, 1–12. [CrossRef]
13. Shukla, A.; Sukavanam, N.; Pandey, D.N.; Arora, U. Approximate Controllability of Second-Order Semilinear Control System. *Circuits Syst Signal Process* **2016**, *35*, 3339–3354. [CrossRef]
14. Vijayakumar, V.; Panda, S.K.; Nisar, K.S.; Baskonus, H.M. Results on approximate controllability results for second-order Sobolev-type impulsive neutraldifferential evolution inclusions with infinite delay. *Numer. Methods Partial. Differ. Eq.* **2021**, *37*, 1200–1221. [CrossRef]
15. Kumano-go, H. *Pseudo-Differential Operators*; MIT Press: Cambridge, MA, USA, 1981.
16. Barraza Martínez, B.; Denk, R.; Hernández Monzón, J. Pseudodifferential operators with non-regular operator-valued symbols. *Manuscr. Math.* **2014**, *144*, 349–372. [CrossRef]
17. Amann, H. Operator-Valued Fourier Multipliers, Vector-Valued Besov Spaces, and Applications. *Math. Nachrichten* **1997**, *186*, 5–56. [CrossRef]
18. Girardi, M.; Weis, L. Operator–valued Fourier multiplier theorems on Besov spaces. *Math. Nachrichten* **2003**, *251*, 34–51. [CrossRef]
19. Wong, M.W. *Partial Differential Equations*; Topics in Fourier Analysis; CRC Press: Boca Raton, FL, USA, 2014.
20. Barraza Martínez, B.; Denk, R.; Hernández Monzón, J.; Nau, T. Generation of Semigroups for Vector-Valued Pseudodifferential Operators on the Torus. *J. Fourier. Anal. Appl.* **2016**, *22*, 823–853. [CrossRef]
21. Krein, S.G. *Linear Differential Equations in Banach Spaces*; Translations of Mathematical Monographs; American Mathematical Society: Providence, RI, USA, 1972; Volume 29.
22. Kostić, M. Differential and Analytical Properties of Semigroups of Operators. *Integral Equations Oper. Theory* **2010**, *67*, 499–557. [CrossRef]
23. Amann, H. *Linear and Quasilinear Parabolic Problems*; Birkhäuser Verlag: Basel, Switzerland, 1995; Volumen I.
24. Yagi, A. Parabolic Evolution Equations in which the coefficients are the Generators of Infinitely Diffetentiable Semigroups. *Funkc. Ekvacioj* **1989**, *32*, 107–124.
25. Lagnese, J. *Boundary Stabilization of Thin Plates*; SIAM Studies in Applied Mathematics, 10; Society for Industrial and Applied Mathematics: Philadelphia, PA, USA, 1989.
26. Denk, R.; Shibata, Y. Maximal regularity for the thermoelastic plate equations with free boundary conditions. *J. Evol. Equ.* **2017**, *17*, 215–261. [CrossRef]
27. Denk, R.; Schnaubelt, R. A structurally damped plate equation with Dirichlet-Neumann boundary conditions. *J. Differ. Equ.* **2015**, *259*, 1323–1353. [CrossRef]
28. Muñoz Rivera, J.E.; Racke, R. Large solutions and smoothing properties for nonlinear thermoelastic systems. *J. Differ. Equ.* **1996**, *127*, 454–483. [CrossRef]
29. Bravo, J.C.V.; Oquendo, H.P.; Rivera, J.E.M. Optimal decay rates for Kirchhoff plates with intermediate damping. *TEMA Tend. Mat. Appl. Comput.* **2020**, *21*, 261–269. [CrossRef]
30. Tebou, L. Regularity and stability for a plate model involving fractional rotational forces and damping. *Z. Angew. Math. Phys.* **2021**, *72*, 158. [CrossRef]

Article

Effects of the Wiener Process on the Solutions of the Stochastic Fractional Zakharov System

Farah M. Al-Askar [1], Wael W. Mohammed [2,3,*], Mohammad Alshammari [2] and M. El-Morshedy [4,5]

[1] Department of Mathematical Science, Collage of Science, Princess Nourah Bint, Abdulrahman University, P.O. Box 84428, Riyadh 11671, Saudi Arabia; famalaskar@pnu.edu.sa
[2] Department of Mathematics, Faculty of Science, University of Ha'il, Ha'il 2440, Saudi Arabia; dar.alshammari@uoh.edu.sa
[3] Department of Mathematics, Faculty of Science, Mansoura University, Mansoura 35516, Egypt
[4] Department of Mathematics, College of Science and Humanities in Al-Kharj, Prince Sattam Bin Abdulaziz University, Al-Kharj 11942, Saudi Arabia; m.elmorshedy@psau.edu.sa
[5] Department of Statistics and Computer Science, Faculty of Science, Mansoura University, Mansoura 35516, Egypt
* Correspondence: wael.mohammed@mans.edu.eg

Citation: Al-Askar, F.M.; Mohammed, W.W.; Alshammari, M.; El-Morshedy, M. Effects of the Wiener Process on the Solutions of the Stochastic Fractional Zakharov System. *Mathematics* 2022, 10, 1194. https://doi.org/10.3390/math10071194

Academic Editor: Patricia J. Y. Wong

Received: 16 March 2022
Accepted: 2 April 2022
Published: 6 April 2022

Publisher's Note: MDPI stays neutral with regard to jurisdictional claims in published maps and institutional affiliations.

Copyright: © 2022 by the authors. Licensee MDPI, Basel, Switzerland. This article is an open access article distributed under the terms and conditions of the Creative Commons Attribution (CC BY) license (https://creativecommons.org/licenses/by/4.0/).

Abstract: We consider in this article the stochastic fractional Zakharov system derived by the multiplicative Wiener process in the Stratonovich sense. We utilize two distinct methods, the Riccati–Bernoulli sub-ODE method and Jacobi elliptic function method, to obtain new rational, trigonometric, hyperbolic, and elliptic stochastic solutions. The acquired solutions are helpful in explaining certain fascinating physical phenomena due to the importance of the Zakharov system in the theory of turbulence for plasma waves. In order to show the influence of the multiplicative Wiener process on the exact solutions of the Zakharov system, we employ the MATLAB tools to plot our figures to introduce a number of 2D and 3D graphs. We establish that the multiplicative Wiener process stabilizes the solutions of the Zakharov system around zero.

Keywords: fractional Zakharov system; stochastic Zakharov system; Riccati–Bernoulli sub-ODE method; Jacobi elliptic function method

MSC: 60H15; 60H10; 35A20; 83C15; 35Q51

1. Introduction

In 1972, Zakharov [1] developed the Zakharov system. It is a group of coupled nonlinear wave equations that explains the interaction of high-frequency Langmuir (dispersive) and low-frequency ion-acoustic (roughly nondispersive) waves. In one dimension, the Zakharov system can be authored as

$$\begin{aligned} v_{tt} - v_{xx} + (|u|^2)_{xx} &= 0, \\ iu_t + u_{xx} + 2uv &= 0, \end{aligned} \quad (1)$$

where $v : \Omega \times \mathbb{R}^+ \to \mathbb{R}$ denotes the plasma density as determined by its equilibrium value, and $u : \Omega \times \mathbb{R}^+ \to \mathbb{C}$ denotes the high-frequency electric field's envelope. The Zakharov system is similar to nonlinear Schrödinger equations and significant in plasma turbulence theory. As a result, the Zakharov system has piqued the interest of many physicists and mathematicians, and has been extensively studied both theoretically and numerically [2–6]. To solve system problems (1), researchers have used a variety of methods. For example, Song et al. [7] introduced unbounded wave solutions, kink wave solutions, and periodic wave solutions by utilizing bifurcation theory method. Wang and Li [8] used the extended F-expansion method to obtain periodic wave solutions. Javidi et al. [9] applied the variational iteration technique to obtain solitary wave solutions. Taghizadeh et al. [10] obtained some exact solutions using infinite series method. Hong et al. [11] obtained a few new doubly periodic solutions utilizing the Jacobian elliptic function expansion method.

In recent years, the fractional derivatives are utilized to describe numerous physical phenomena in engineering applications, signal processing, electromagnetic theory, finance, physics, mathematical biology, and various scientific studies, see for instance [12–17]. For instance, the fractional derivative is utilized in control theory, controller tuning, optics, seismic wave analysis, dynamical system, signal processing, and viscoelasticity.

On the other hand, the benefits of taking random effects into consideration in predicting, simulating, analyzing and modeling complex phenomena has been extensively distinguished in biology, engineering, physics, geophysical, chemistry, climate dynamics, and other fields [18–21]. Stochastic partial differential equations (SPDEs) are suitable mathematical equations for complicated systems subject to noise or random influences. Normally, random influences can be thought of as a simple estimate of turbulence in fluids. Therefore, we have to generalize the Zakharov system by taking into account more elements due to some important effects such as ion nonlinearities and transit-time damping.

To achieve a higher level of qualitative agreement, we consider here the following stochastic fractional-space Zakharov system (SFSZS) with multiplicative noise in the Stratonovich sense:

$$iu_t + \mathbb{T}^\alpha_{xx} u + 2uv + i\sigma u \circ \mathcal{W}_t = 0, \quad (2)$$

$$v_{tt} - \mathbb{T}^\alpha_{xx} v + \mathbb{T}^\alpha_{xx}(|u|^2) = 0, \quad (3)$$

where $\mathbb{T}^\alpha$ is the conformable fractional derivative (CFD) [22], $\mathcal{W}(t)$ is standard Wiener process (SWP).

In [23,24], the stochastic dissipative Zakharov system are obtained by utilizing the global-random attractors provided with normal topology, while in [25], the uniqueness and existence of solutions of the Zakharov system with stochastic term are obtained by applying the method of Galerkin approximation.

The novelty of this paper is to construct the exact fractional stochastic solutions of the SFSZS (2)–(3). This study is the first one to obtain the exact solutions of the SFSZS (2)–(3). We use two distinct methods including the Jacobi elliptic function and the Riccati–Bernoulli sub-ODE to achieve a wide range of solutions, including hyperbolic, trigonometric, rational, and elliptic functions. Besides that, we employ Matlab tools to plot 3D and 2D graphs for some of the analytical solutions developed in this study to check the effect of the Wiener process on the solutions of SFSZS (2)–(3).

The following is how the paper is arranged. In Section 2, we define the CFD and Wiener process and we state some features about them. To obtain the wave equation of SFSZS (2)–(3), we use a suitable wave transformation in Section 3. In Section 4, we apply two different methods to construct the exact solutions of SFSZS (2)–(3). In Section 5, we study the effect of the SWP on the obtained solutions. Finally, we present the paper's conclusion.

2. Preliminaries

In this section, we introduce some definitions and features for CFD, which are reported in [22] and SWP.

Definition 1. *Assume* $f : (0, \infty) \to \mathbb{R}$; *hence, the CFD of* f *of order* α *is defined as*

$$\mathbb{T}^\alpha_x f(x) = \lim_{h \to 0} \frac{f(x + hx^{1-\alpha}) - f(x)}{h}.$$

Theorem 1. *Let* $f, g : (0, \infty) \to \mathbb{R}$ *be differentiable, and also* α *differentiable functions; then, the next rule holds:*

$$\mathbb{T}^\alpha_x (f \circ g)(x) = x^{1-\alpha} g'(x) f'(g(x)).$$

Let us state some properties of the CFD:

1. $\mathbb{T}_x^\alpha[af(x)+bg(x)] = a\mathbb{T}_x^\alpha f(x) + b\mathbb{T}_x^\alpha g(x)$, $a,b \in \mathbb{R}$,
2. $\mathbb{T}_x^\alpha[C] = 0$, C is a constant,
3. $\mathbb{T}_x^\alpha[x^\hbar] = \hbar x^{\hbar-\alpha}$, $\hbar \in \mathbb{R}$,
4. $\mathbb{T}_x^\alpha g(x) = x^{1-\alpha}\frac{dg}{dx}$,

In the next definition, we define standard Wiener process $\mathcal{W}(t)$:

Definition 2. *stochastic process $\{\mathcal{W}(t)\}_{t\geq 0}$ is called a Wiener process if it satisfies*

1. $\mathcal{W}(0) = 0$,
2. $\mathcal{W}(t)$, $t \geq 0$ is continuous function of t,
3. For $t_1 < t_2$, $\mathcal{W}(t_1) - \mathcal{W}(t_2)$ is independent,
4. $\mathcal{W}(t_2) - \mathcal{W}(t_1)$ has a Gaussian distribution with mean 0 and variance $t_2 - t_1$.

We know the stochastic integral $\int_0^t \Theta d\mathcal{W}$ may be interpreted in a variety of ways [26]. The Stratonovich and Itô interpretations of a stochastic integral are widely used. The stochastic integral is Itô (denoted by $\int_0^t \Theta d\mathcal{W}$) when it is evaluated at the left-end, while a Stratonovich stochastic integral (denoted by $\int_0^t \Theta \circ d\mathcal{W}$) is one that is calculated at the midpoint. The next is the relationship between the Stratonovich and Itô integral:

$$\int_0^t \Theta(\tau, Z_\tau) d\mathcal{W}(\tau) = \int_0^t \Theta(\tau, Z_\tau) \circ d\mathcal{W}(\tau) - \frac{1}{2}\int_0^t \Theta(\tau, Z_\tau)\frac{\partial \Theta(\tau, Z_\tau)}{\partial z}d\tau, \quad (4)$$

where Θ is supposed to be sufficiently regular and $\{Z_t, t \geq 0\}$ is a stochastic process.

3. Wave Equation for SFSZS

To acquire the wave equation for the SFSZS (2)–(3), the next wave transformation is applied:

$$u(x,t) = \varphi(\mu)e^{(i\theta - \sigma\mathcal{W}(t) - \sigma^2 t)}, \quad \mu = k(\frac{1}{\alpha}x^\alpha - \lambda t) \text{ and } \theta = \frac{\lambda}{2\alpha}x^\alpha + \rho t, \quad (5)$$

where φ is a deterministic function and k, λ, ρ are nonzero constants. Plugging Equation (5) into Equation (2) and using

$$\begin{aligned}
\frac{du}{dt} &= (-\lambda k\varphi' + i\rho\varphi - \sigma\varphi\mathcal{W}_t - \frac{1}{2}\sigma^2\varphi)e^{(i\theta - \sigma\mathcal{W}(t) - \sigma^2 t)}, \\
&= (-\lambda k\varphi' + i\rho\varphi - \sigma\varphi \circ \mathcal{W}_t)e^{(i\theta - \sigma\mathcal{W}(t) - \sigma^2 t)}, \\
\mathbb{T}_{xx}^\alpha &= (k^2\varphi'' + i\lambda k\varphi' - \frac{1}{4}\lambda^2\varphi)e^{(i\theta - \sigma\mathcal{W}(t) - \sigma^2 t)},
\end{aligned} \quad (6)$$

where we used (4). We obtain, for the real part,

$$k^2\varphi'' - (\frac{1}{4}\lambda^2 + \rho)\varphi + 2\varphi v = 0. \quad (7)$$

Now, we suppose

$$v(x,t) = \psi(\mu),$$

where ψ is real deterministic function, to obtain

$$v_t = -\lambda k\psi', \quad v_{tt} = \lambda^2 k^2\psi'', \quad \mathbb{T}_{xx}^\alpha v = k^2\psi''. \quad (8)$$

Substituting Equation (8) into Equation (3), we attain

$$(\lambda^2 - 1)\psi'' + (\varphi^2)''e^{(-2\sigma\mathcal{W}(t) - 2\sigma^2 t)} = 0. \quad (9)$$

Taking expectation $\mathbb{E}(\cdot)$ on both sides, we have

$$(\lambda^2 - 1)\psi'' + (\varphi^2)'' e^{-2\sigma^2 t} \mathbb{E}(e^{-2\sigma \mathcal{W}(t)}) = 0. \tag{10}$$

Since $\mathcal{W}(t)$ is standard Gaussian process; hence, $\mathbb{E}(e^{\hbar \mathcal{W}(t)}) = e^{\frac{\hbar^2}{2}t}$ for any real constant $\hbar$. Now, Equation (10) has the form

$$(\lambda^2 - 1)\psi'' + (\varphi^2)'' = 0, \tag{11}$$

Integrating Equation (11) twice and putting the constants of integration equal zero yields

$$(\lambda^2 - 1)\psi + \varphi^2 = 0. \tag{12}$$

Hence, Equation (12) becomes

$$\psi = \frac{-\varphi^2}{(\lambda^2 - 1)}. \tag{13}$$

Putting Equation (13) into Equation (7), we obtain the next wave equation

$$\varphi'' - \gamma_1 \varphi^3 - \gamma_2 \varphi = 0, \tag{14}$$

where

$$\gamma_1 = \frac{2}{k^2(\lambda^2 - 1)} \quad \text{and} \quad \gamma_2 = \frac{1}{4k^2}(\lambda^2 + 4\rho). \tag{15}$$

4. The Analytical Solutions of the SFSZS

To find the solutions of Equation (14), we utilize two different methods: Riccati–Bernoulli sub-ODE [27] and the Jacobi elliptic function method [28]. Therefore, we acquire the analytical solutions of the SFSZS (2)–(3).

4.1. Riccati–Bernoulli Sub-ODE Method

Assume the following Riccati–Bernoulli equation:

$$\varphi' = \hbar_1 \varphi^2 + \hbar_2 \varphi + \hbar_3, \tag{16}$$

where $\hbar_1, \hbar_2, \hbar_3$ are undefined constants and $\varphi = \varphi(\mu)$.

Differentiating Equation (16) with respect to μ, we obtain

$$\varphi'' = 2\hbar_1 \varphi \varphi' + \hbar_2 \varphi',$$

and using Equation (16) yields

$$\varphi'' = 2\hbar_1^2 \varphi^3 + 3\hbar_1 \hbar_2 \varphi^2 + (2\hbar_1 \hbar_3 + \hbar_2^2)\varphi + \hbar_2 \hbar_3. \tag{17}$$

Substituting (17) into (14), we have

$$(2\hbar_1^2 - \gamma_1)\varphi^3 + 3\hbar_1 \hbar_2 \varphi^2 + (2\hbar_1 \hbar_3 + \hbar_2^2 - \gamma_2)\varphi + \hbar_2 \hbar_3 = 0.$$

Equating each coefficient of $\varphi^i (i = 0, 1, 2, 3)$ to zero, we achieve the next algebraic equations

$$\hbar_2 \hbar_3 = 0,$$

$$(2\hbar_1 \hbar_3 + \hbar_2^2 - \gamma_2) = 0,$$

$$3\hbar_1 \hbar_2 = 0,$$

$$2\hbar_1^2 - \gamma_1 = 0.$$

When the above equations are solved, the result is

$$\hbar_1 = \pm\sqrt{\frac{1}{2}\gamma_1}, \quad \hbar_2 = 0, \quad \hbar_3 = \frac{\gamma_2}{2\hbar_1} = \pm\frac{\gamma_2}{\sqrt{2\gamma_1}}. \tag{18}$$

There are numerous solutions to the Riccati–Bernoulli Equation (16) depending on $\hbar_1$ and $\hbar_3$.

First case: If $\frac{\hbar_3}{\hbar_1} = 0$, then Riccati–Bernoulli Equation (16) has the solution

$$\varphi(\mu) = \frac{-1}{\hbar_1 \mu + C}.$$

Hence, the SFSZS (2)–(3) has the analytical solutions

$$u(x,t) = \varphi(\mu)e^{(i\theta - \sigma W(t) - \sigma^2 t)} = \frac{-1}{\hbar_1(\frac{k}{\alpha}x^\alpha - k\lambda t) + C}e^{(i\theta - \sigma W(t) - \sigma^2 t)}, \tag{19}$$

$$v(x,t) = \frac{-\varphi^2}{(\lambda^2 - 1)} = \frac{-1}{(\lambda^2 - 1)\left(\hbar_1(\frac{k}{\alpha}x^\alpha - k\lambda t) + C\right)^2}. \tag{20}$$

Second case: If $\frac{\hbar_3}{\hbar_1} > 0$, then the Riccati–Bernoulli equation (16) has the solution

$$\varphi(\mu) = \sqrt{\frac{\hbar_3}{\hbar_1}} \tan\left(\sqrt{\frac{\hbar_3}{\hbar_1}}(\hbar_1 \mu + C)\right),$$

or

$$\varphi(\mu) = -\sqrt{\frac{\hbar_3}{\hbar_1}} \cot\left(\sqrt{\frac{\hbar_3}{\hbar_1}}(\hbar_1 \mu + C)\right).$$

Therefore, SFSZSs (2)–(3) have the following solutions:

$$u(x,t) = e^{(i\theta - \sigma W(t) - \sigma^2 t)} \sqrt{\frac{\hbar_3}{\hbar_1}} \tan\left(\sqrt{\frac{\hbar_3}{\hbar_1}}(\hbar_1(\frac{k}{\alpha}x^\alpha - k\lambda t) + C)\right), \tag{21}$$

$$v(x,t) = \frac{-\hbar_3}{(\lambda^2 - 1)\hbar_1} \tan^2\left(\sqrt{\frac{\hbar_3}{\hbar_1}}(\hbar_1(\frac{k}{\alpha}x^\alpha - k\lambda t) + C)\right), \tag{22}$$

or

$$u(x,t) = -e^{(i\theta - \sigma W(t) - \sigma^2 t)} \sqrt{\frac{\hbar_3}{\hbar_1}} \cot\left(\sqrt{\frac{\hbar_3}{\hbar_1}}(\hbar_1(\frac{k}{\alpha}x^\alpha - k\lambda t) + C)\right), \tag{23}$$

$$v(x,t) = \frac{-\hbar_3}{(\lambda^2 - 1)\hbar_1} \cot^2\left(\sqrt{\frac{\hbar_3}{\hbar_1}}(\hbar_1(\frac{k}{\alpha}x^\alpha - k\lambda t) + C)\right), \tag{24}$$

respectively.

Third case: If $\frac{\hbar_3}{\hbar_1} < 0$ and $|\varphi| < \sqrt{-\frac{\hbar_3}{\hbar_1}}$, then Riccati–Bernoulli Equation (16) has the solution

$$\varphi(\mu) = -\sqrt{\frac{-\hbar_3}{\hbar_1}} \tanh\left(\sqrt{\frac{-\hbar_3}{\hbar_1}}(\hbar_1 \mu + C)\right).$$

Thus, the SFSZS (2)–(3) have the following analytical solutions:

$$u(x,t) = -e^{(i\theta - \sigma W(t) - \sigma^2 t)} \sqrt{\frac{-\hbar_3}{\hbar_1}} \tanh\left(\sqrt{\frac{-\hbar_3}{\hbar_1}}(\hbar_1(\frac{k}{\alpha}x^\alpha - k\lambda t) + C)\right), \tag{25}$$

$$v(x,t) = \frac{-\hbar_3}{(\lambda^2 - 1)\hbar_1} \tanh^2\left(\sqrt{\frac{-\hbar_3}{\hbar_1}}(\hbar_1(\frac{k}{\alpha}x^\alpha - k\lambda t) + C)\right). \tag{26}$$

Fourth case: If $\frac{\hbar_3}{\hbar_1} < 0$ and $\varphi^2 > \frac{-\hbar_3}{\hbar_1}$, then Riccati–Bernoulli Equation (16) has the solution

$$\varphi(\mu) = -\sqrt{\frac{-\hbar_3}{\hbar_1}} \coth\left(\sqrt{\frac{-\hbar_3}{\hbar_1}}(\hbar_1 \mu + C)\right).$$

Consequently, the analytical solutions of the SFSZS (2)–(3) are

$$u(x,t) = -e^{(i\theta - \sigma W(t) - \sigma^2 t)} \sqrt{\frac{-\hbar_3}{\hbar_1}} \coth\left(\sqrt{\frac{\hbar_3}{\hbar_1}}(\hbar_1(\frac{k}{\alpha}x^\alpha - k\lambda t) + C)\right), \quad (27)$$

$$v(x,t) = \frac{-\hbar_3}{(\lambda^2 - 1)\hbar_1} \coth^2\left(\sqrt{\frac{\hbar_3}{\hbar_1}}(\hbar_1(\frac{k}{\alpha}x^\alpha - k\lambda t) + C)\right), \quad (28)$$

where $\hbar_1$ and $\hbar_2$ are defined in Equation (18).

4.2. The Jacobi Elliptic Function Method

Assuming that the solutions to Equation (14) are of the form

$$\varphi(\mu) = a + b sn(\delta \mu), \quad (29)$$

where $sn(\delta \mu) = sn(\delta \mu, m)$, for $0 < m < 1$, is the Jacobi elliptic sine function and a, b, δ are unknown constants. Differentiate Equation (29) two times and we have

$$\varphi''(\mu) = -(m^2 + 1)b\delta^2 sn(\delta \mu) + 2m^2 b \delta^2 sn^3(\delta \mu). \quad (30)$$

Substituting Equations (29) and (30) into Equation (14), we attain

$$(2m^2 b \delta^2 - \gamma_1 b^3)sn^3(\delta \mu) - 3\gamma_1 ab^2 sn^2(\delta \mu)$$

$$-[(m^2 + 1)b\delta^2 + 3\gamma_1 a^2 b + \gamma_2 b]sn(\delta \mu) - (\gamma_1 a^3 + a\gamma_2) = 0.$$

Setting each coefficient of $[sn(\delta \mu)]^n$ ($n = 0, 1, 2, 3$) equal to zero, we attain

$$\gamma_1 a^3 + a \gamma_2 = 0,$$

$$(m^2 + 1)b\delta^2 + 3\gamma_1 a^2 b + \gamma_2 b = 0,$$

$$3\gamma_1 ab^2 sn^2 = 0,$$

and

$$2m^2 b \delta^2 - \gamma_1 b^3 = 0.$$

Solving the above equations, we have

$$a = 0, \ b = \pm\sqrt{\frac{-2m^2 \gamma_2}{(m^2 + 1)\gamma_1}}, \ \delta^2 = \frac{-\gamma_2}{(m^2 + 1)}.$$

Hence, the solution of Equation (14), by using (29), has the form

$$\varphi(\mu) = \pm\sqrt{\frac{-2m^2 \gamma_2}{(m^2 + 1)\gamma_1}} sn(\sqrt{\frac{-\gamma_2}{(m^2 + 1)}}\mu).$$

Therefore, the analytical solutions of the SFSZS (2)–(3) are

$$u(x,t) = \pm\sqrt{\frac{-2m^2 \gamma_2}{(m^2 + 1)\gamma_1}} sn\left(\sqrt{\frac{-\gamma_2}{(m^2 + 1)}}(\frac{k}{\alpha}x^\alpha - k\lambda t)\right) e^{(i\theta - \sigma W(t) - \sigma^2 t)}, \quad (31)$$

$$v(x,t) = \frac{k^2 m^2 \gamma_2}{(m^2+1)} sn^2\left(\sqrt{\frac{-\gamma_2}{(m^2+1)}}(\frac{k}{\alpha}x^\alpha - k\lambda t)\right), \qquad (32)$$

for $\gamma_2 < 0$ and $\gamma_1 > 0$. When $m \to 1$, the solutions (31)–(32) transfer into

$$u(x,t) = \pm\sqrt{\frac{-\gamma_2}{\gamma_1}} \tanh\left(\sqrt{\frac{-\gamma_2}{2}}(\frac{k}{\alpha}x^\alpha - k\lambda t)\right) e^{(i\theta - \sigma W(t) - \sigma^2 t)}, \qquad (33)$$

$$v(x,t) = -\frac{k^2 \gamma_2}{2} \tanh^2\left(\sqrt{\frac{-\gamma_2}{2}}(\frac{k}{\alpha}x^\alpha - k\lambda t)\right). \qquad (34)$$

Analogously, we can replace sn in (29) by cn and dn in order to obtain the solutions of Equation (14), respectively, as follows:

$$\varphi(\mu) = \pm\sqrt{\frac{-2m^2 \gamma_2}{(2m^2-1)\gamma_1}} cn(\frac{-\gamma_2}{(2m^2-1)}\mu),$$

and

$$\varphi(\mu) = \pm\sqrt{\frac{2m^2 \gamma_2}{(2-m^2)\gamma_1}} dn(\frac{-\gamma_2}{(2-m^2)}\mu).$$

Consequently, the solutions of the SFSZS (2)–(3) have the following forms:

$$u(x,t) = \pm\sqrt{\frac{-2m^2 \gamma_2}{(2m^2-1)\gamma_1}} cn\left(\sqrt{\frac{-\gamma_2}{(2m^2-1)}}(\frac{k}{\alpha}x^\alpha - k\lambda t)\right) e^{(i\theta - \sigma W(t) - \sigma^2 t)}, \qquad (35)$$

$$v(x,t) = \frac{k^2 m^2 \gamma_2}{(2m^2-1)} cn^2\left(\sqrt{\frac{-\gamma_2}{(2m^2-1)}}(\frac{k}{\alpha}x^\alpha - k\lambda t)\right), \qquad (36)$$

for $\frac{\gamma_2}{(2m^2-1)} < 0, \gamma_1 > 0$, and

$$u(x,t) = \pm\sqrt{\frac{-2m^2 \gamma_2}{(2m^2-1)\gamma_1}} dn\left(\sqrt{\frac{-\gamma_2}{(2m^2-1)}}(\frac{k}{\alpha}x^\alpha - k\lambda t)\right) e^{(i\theta - \sigma W(t) - \sigma^2 t)}, \qquad (37)$$

$$v(x,t) = \frac{k^2 m^2 \gamma_2}{(2-m^2)} dn^2\left(\sqrt{\frac{-\gamma_2}{(2-m^2)}}(\frac{k}{\alpha}x^\alpha - k\lambda t)\right), \qquad (38)$$

for $\gamma_2 < 0, \gamma_1 > 0$, respectively. When $m \to 1$, the solutions (35)–(36) and (37)–(38) transfer into

$$u(x,t) = \pm\sqrt{\frac{-2\gamma_2}{\gamma_1}} \text{sech}\left(\sqrt{-\gamma_2}(\frac{k}{\alpha}x^\alpha - k\lambda t)\right) e^{(i\theta - \sigma W(t) - \sigma^2 t)}, \qquad (39)$$

$$v(x,t) = k^2 m^2 \gamma_2 \text{sech}^2\left(\sqrt{-\gamma_2}(\frac{k}{\alpha}x^\alpha - k\lambda t)\right), \qquad (40)$$

for $\gamma_2 < 0, \gamma_1 > 0$.

5. The Influence of Noise on SFSZS Solutions

The influence of the noise on the analytical solution of the SFSZS (2)–(3) is addressed here. Fix the parameters $k = 1, \rho = 1, m = 0.5$, and $\lambda = 3$. We introduce a number of simulations for various values of σ (noise intensity) and α (fractional derivative order). We employ the MATLAB tools to plot our figures. In Figures 1 and 2, if $\sigma = 0$, we see that the surface fluctuates for different values of α:

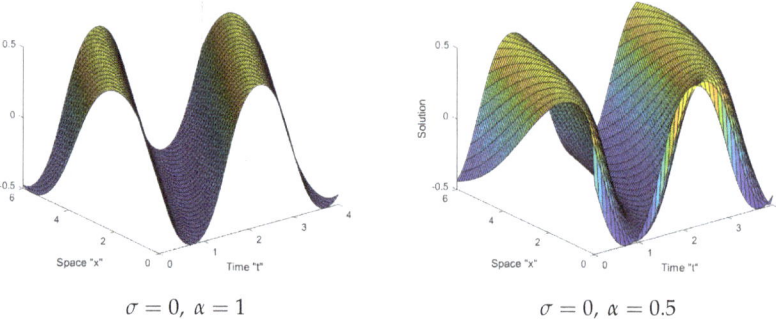

Figure 1. 3D graphs of the solution (31).

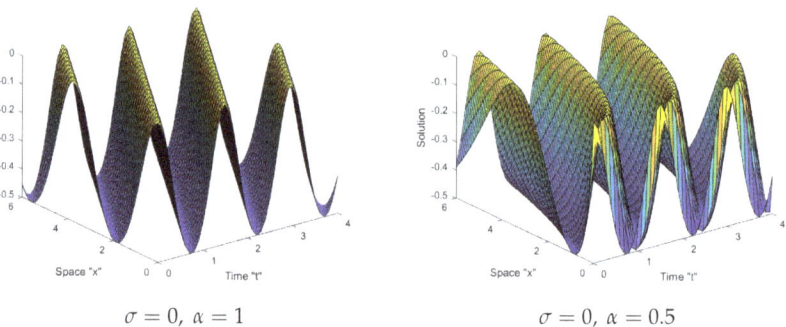

Figure 2. 3D graphs of the solution (32).

In the following Figures 3–5, we can see that after minor transit patterns, the surface becomes considerably flattered when noise is included and its strength is increased $\sigma = 1, 2$.

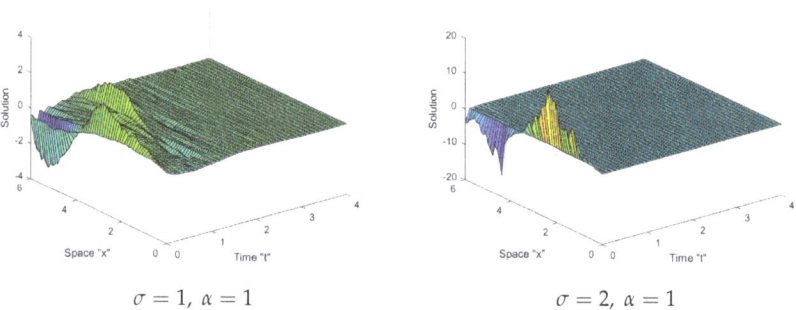

Figure 3. 3D graphs of the solution (31) with $\alpha = 1$.

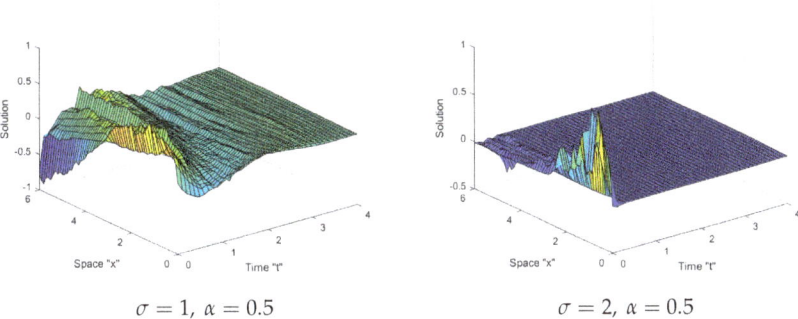

$\sigma = 1, \alpha = 0.5$ $\sigma = 2, \alpha = 0.5$

Figure 4. 3D graphs of the equation (31) with $\alpha = 0.5$.

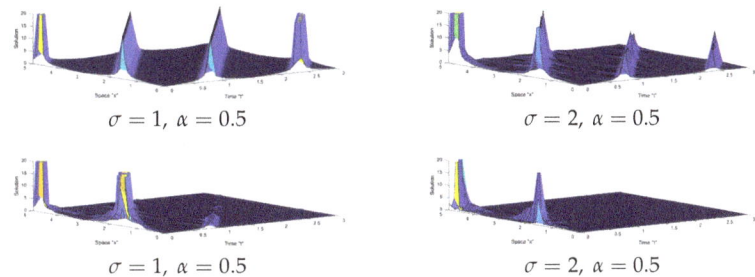

$\sigma = 1, \alpha = 0.5$ $\sigma = 2, \alpha = 0.5$

$\sigma = 1, \alpha = 0.5$ $\sigma = 2, \alpha = 0.5$

Figure 5. 3D graphs of the equation (21) with $\alpha = 1$.

In Figure 6, we introduce 2D plots of the u in (31) with $\sigma = 0, 0.5, 1, 2$ and $\alpha = 1$, which emphasize the results above.

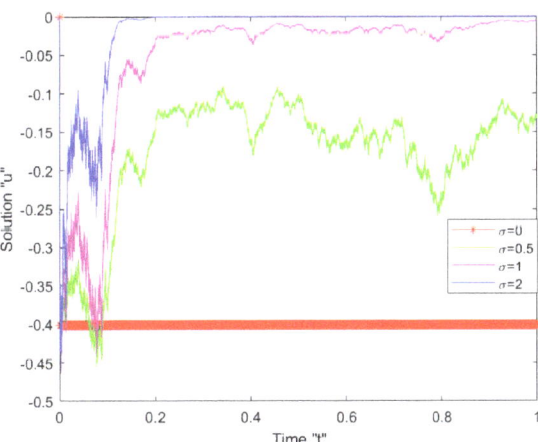

Figure 6. 2D graphs of the u in (31).

From Figures 1–6, we deduce the following:

1. The surface expands as the fractional order α increases;
2. Multiplicative Wiener process stabilizes the solutions of SFSBE around zero.

6. Conclusions

In this article, we provided a wide range of exact solutions of the stochastic fractional Zakharov system (2)–(3). We applied two different methods such as the Riccati–Bernoulli sub-ODE method and Jacobi elliptic function method to attain rational, trigonometric, hyperbolic, and elliptic stochastic fractional solutions. Such solutions are critical for comprehending certain essential, fundamental, complex phenomena. The solutions obtained will be extremely useful for further studies such as fiber applications, spatial plasma, quasi particle theory, coastal water motion, and industrial research. Finally, the effect of multiplicative Wiener process on the exact solution of Zakharov system (2)–(3) is demonstrated. In future research, we can address the fractional-time Zakharov system (2)–(3) with multidimensional multiplicative noise.

Author Contributions: Conceptualization, F.M.A.-A., W.W.M., M.A. and M.E.-M.; methodology, F.M.A.-A. and W.W.M.; software, W.W.M. and M.E.-M.; formal analysis, F.M.A.-A., W.W.M., M.A. and M.E.-M.; investigation, F.M.A.-A. and W.W.M.; resources, F.M.A.-A., W.W.M., M.A. and M.E.-M.; data curation, F.M.A.-A. and W.W.M.; writing—original draft preparation, F.M.A.-A., W.W.M., M.A. and M.E.-M.; writing—review and editing, F.M.A.-A. and W.W.M.; visualization, F.M.A.-A. and W.W.M. All authors have read and agreed to the published version of the manuscript.

Funding: This research received no external funding.

Institutional Review Board Statement: Not applicable.

Informed Consent Statement: Not applicable.

Data Availability Statement: Not applicable.

Acknowledgments: Princess Nourah bint Abdulrahman University Researchers Supporting Project number (PNURSP2022R273), Princess Nourah bint Abdulrahman University, Riyadh, Saudi Arabia.

Conflicts of Interest: The authors declare no conflict of interest.

References

1. Zakharov, V.E. Collapse of Langmuir waves. *Sov. J. Exper. Theor. Phys.* **1972**, *35*, 908–914.
2. Goubet, O.; Moise, I. Attractors for dissipative Zakharov equations. *Nonlinear Anal. TMA* **1998**, *31*, 823–847. [CrossRef]
3. Guo, B. On the IBVP for some more extensive Zakharov equations. *J. Math.* **1987**, *7*, 269–275.
4. Li, Y. On the initial boundary value problems for two dimensional systems of Zakharov equations and of complex-Schrödinger-real-Boussinesq equations. *J. Partial Diff. Equ.* **1992**, *5*, 81–93.
5. Masselin, V. A result on the blow-up rate for the Zakharov equations in dimension 3. *SIAM J. Math. Anal.* **2001**, *33*, 440–447. [CrossRef]
6. Guo, B.; Sheng, L. The global existence and uniqueness of classical solutions of periodic initial boundary problems of Zakharov equations. *Acta Math. Appl. Sin.* **1982**, *5*, 310–324.
7. Song, M.; Liu, Z. Traveling wave solutions for the generalized Zakharov equations. *Math. Probl. Eng.* **2012**, *2012*, 747295. [CrossRef]
8. Wang, M.L.; Li, X.Z. Extended F-expansion method and periodic wave solutions for the generalized Zakharov equations. *Phys. Lett. A* **2005**, *343*, 48–54. [CrossRef]
9. Javidi, M.; Golbabai, A. Construction of a solitary wave solution for the generalized Zakharov equation by a variational iteration method. *Comput. Math. Appl.* **2007**, *54*, 1003–1009. [CrossRef]
10. Taghizadeh, N.; Mirzaadsh, M.; Farahrooz, F. Exact solutions of the generalized-Zakharov (GZ) equation by the infinite series method. *Appl. Appl. Math.* **2010**, *5*, 621–628.
11. Hong, B.; Lu, D.; Sun, F. The extended Jacobi Elliptic Functions expansion method and new exact solutions for the Zakharov equations. *World J. Model. Simul.* **2009**, *5*, 216–224.
12. Yuste, S.B.; Acedo, L.; Lindenberg, K. Reaction front in an $A + B \to C$ reaction–subdiffusion process. *Phys. Rev. E* **2004**, *69*, 036126. [CrossRef] [PubMed]
13. Mohammed, W.W.; Iqbal, N. Impact of the same degenerate additive noise on a coupled system of fractional space diffusion equations. *Fractals* **2022**, *30*, 2240033. [CrossRef]
14. Iqbal, N.; Yasmin, H.; Ali, A.; Bariq, A.; Al-Sawalha, M.M.; Mohammed, W.W. Numerical Methods for Fractional-Order Fornberg-Whitham Equations in the Sense of Atangana-Baleanu Derivative. *J. Funct. Spaces* **2021**, *2021*, 2197247. [CrossRef]
15. Mohammed, W.W. Approximate solutions for stochastic time-fractional reaction–diffusion equations with multiplicative noise. *Math. Methods Appl. Sci.* **2021**, *44*, 2140–2157. [CrossRef]

16. Iqbal, N.; Wu, R.; Mohammed, W.W. Pattern formation induced by fractional cross-diffusion in a 3-species food chain model with harvesting. *Math. Comput. Simul.* **2021**, *188*, 102–119. [CrossRef]
17. Barkai, E.; Metzler, R.; Klafter, J. From continuous time random walks to the fractional Fokker–Planck equation. *Phys. Rev.* **2000**, *61*, 132–138. [CrossRef]
18. Arnold, L. *Random Dynamical Systems*; Springer: Berlin, Germany, 1998.
19. Weinan, E.; Li, X.; Vanden-Eijnden, E. *Some Recent Progress in Multiscale Modeling, Multiscale Modeling and Simulation*; Lect. Notes in Computer Science Engineering; Springer: Berlin, Germany, 2004; Volume 39, pp. 3–21.
20. Mohammed, W.W.; Blömker, D. Fast diffusion limit for reaction-diffusion systems with stochastic Neumann boundary conditions. *SIAM J. Math. Anal.* **2016**, *48*, 3547–3578. [CrossRef]
21. Mohammed, W.W. Modulation Equation for the Stochastic Swift–Hohenberg Equation with Cubic and Quintic Nonlinearities on the Real Line. *Mathematics* **2020**, *6*, 1217. [CrossRef]
22. Khalil, R.; Al Horani, M.; Yousef, A.; Sababheh, M. A new definition of fractional derivative. *J. Comput. Appl. Math.* **2014**, *264*, 65–70. [CrossRef]
23. Guo, B.; Lv, Y.; Yang, X. Dynamics of Stochastic Zakharov Equations. *J. Math. Phys.* **2009**, *50*, 052703. [CrossRef]
24. Guo, Y.; Guo, B.; Li, D. Global random attractors for the stochastic dissipative Zakharov equations. *Acta Math. Appl. Sin.* **2014**, *30*, 289–304. [CrossRef]
25. Guo, Y.F.G.B.; Li, D. Asymptotic behavior of stochastic dissipative quantum Zakharov equations. *Stoch. Dyn.* **2013**, *13*, 1250016. [CrossRef]
26. Kloeden, P.E.; Platen, E. *Numerical Solution of Stochastic Differential Equations*; Springer: New York, NY, USA, 1995.
27. Yang, X.F.; Deng, Z.C.; Wei, Y. A Riccati-Bernoulli sub-ODE method for nonlinear partial differential equations and its application. *Adv. Diff. Equ.* **2015**, *1*, 117–133. [CrossRef]
28. Fan, E.; Zhang, J. Applications of the Jacobi elliptic function method to special-type nonlinear equations. *Phys. Lett. A* **2002**, *305*, 383–392. [CrossRef]

Article

$gL1$ Scheme for Solving a Class of Generalized Time-Fractional Diffusion Equations

Xuhao Li [1] and Patricia J. Y. Wong [2,*]

[1] School of Mathematical Sciences, Anhui University, Hefei 230601, China; lixh@ahu.edu.cn
[2] School of Electrical and Electronic Engineering, Nanyang Technological University, Singapore 639798, Singapore
* Correspondence: ejywong@ntu.edu.sg

Abstract: In this paper, a numerical scheme based on a general temporal mesh is constructed for a generalized time-fractional diffusion problem of order α. The main idea involves the generalized linear interpolation and so we term the numerical scheme the $gL1$ **scheme**. The stability and convergence of the numerical scheme are analyzed using the energy method. It is proven that the temporal convergence order is $(2-\alpha)$ for a general temporal mesh. Simulation is carried out to verify the efficiency of the proposed numerical scheme.

Keywords: generalized fractional derivative; time-diffusion problem; generalized linear interpolation; numerical scheme

MSC: 65M12; 65N12

1. Introduction

The fractional model has been shown to be a powerful tool in modeling various memory process in applications [1,2], such as diffusion process in a porous media. The essence of this tool lies in fractional derivative (or integral) which is an extension of integer derivative (or integral). Many well known mathematicians such as Euler, Lagrange, Liouville, Riemann, Grüwald, Letnikov and Caputo have devoted their efforts to fractional calculus and have made great contributions to this topic. The extension from integer derivative (or integral) to fractional derivative (or integral) may not be unique due to the different techniques applied. To unify the different approaches, Agrawal [3] has proposed some *generalized* fractional operators which may unify some well known fractional operators such as Caputo, Riemann-Louville and Hadamard. The generalized fractional operators incorporate a scale function $z(t)$ and a weight function $w(t)$. With these two functions, many equations can be written in a general form and thus can be solved in an elegant way as shown in [3]. Moreover, by choosing different $z(t)$ and $w(t)$, one can readily obtain the well known fractional operators.

The generalized fractional operators naturally lead to *generalized* fractional problems. As in the fractional situation, the analytical solutions may not be easily derived and hence the corresponding numerical solutions are both necessary and useful in applications. In fact, some pioneer works have been done on the numerical treatment of certain generalized fractional problems [4–10]. In the earlier papers [8–10], the convergence of the numerical scheme is established using the Lax–Richtmyer theorem but the order of convergence is not explicitly given. Inspired by [11,12], some generalized weighted shifted Grünwald-Letnikov (gWSGL) type approximations [4–6] and generalized Alikhanov's approximation [7] were recently proposed, which improve the accuracy of previous work. In fact, the convergence order of these methods are shown to be $O(\tau_z^2)$ (or higher) based on a particular choice of the temporal mesh that closely depends on the scale function $z(t)$. It is noteworthy that

the higher convergence order comes at the expense of more computations and restrictions in reality.

In this paper, we shall consider a generalized time-fractional diffusion problem that is more general than that in [9]. As one of the pioneer numerical treatments for generalized time-fractional diffusion problems, the authors in [9] first present analytical solution of a generalized time-fractional problem involving second order spatial derivative. Then, based on a uniform temporal mesh, they construct a numerical scheme by finite difference method. The stability of the numerical scheme is investigated via an estimate of the inverse of the coefficient matrix, and the convergence then follows from the Lax–Richtmyer theorem without giving explicit convergence order. Different from the work of [9], we aim to derive a numerical scheme based on a more general temporal mesh than [9] and give the convergence order of the proposed scheme explicitly using energy method. Our major contributions in this paper are as follows:

- We consider a problem involving an operator $\mathcal{L}$ and propose a numerical scheme based on a general temporal mesh using generalized linear interpolation.
- We establish the stability and convergence of the proposed scheme, which is based on a general temporal mesh, via energy method. The analysis in the context of general temporal mesh is not trivial.

We consider the following generalized time-fractional diffusion equation with weight function $w(t) \equiv 1$

$$\begin{cases} {}^C_0 D^\alpha_{t;[z(t),1]} u(x,t) = \mathcal{L}u(x,t) + f(x,t), & (x,t) \in (0,1) \times (0,1) \\ u(x,0) = \psi(x), & x \in [0,1] \\ u(0,t) = \phi_1(t), \quad u(1,t) = \phi_2(t), & t \in (0,1] \end{cases} \tag{1}$$

where $\mathcal{L}$ is a linear operator defined by

$$\mathcal{L}u(x,t) = (p(x,t)u_x(x,t))_x - q(x,t)u(x,t),$$

with $p(x,t) \geq p_0 > 0$ and $q(x,t) \geq 0$, ${}^C_0 D^\alpha_{t;[z(t),1]} u(x,t)$ $(0 < \alpha < 1)$ is the generalized Caputo fractional derivative given by

$$ {}^C_0 D^\alpha_{t;[z(t),1]} u(x,t) = \frac{1}{\Gamma(1-\alpha)} \int_0^t \frac{1}{[z(t)-z(s)]^\alpha} \frac{\partial u(x,s)}{\partial s} ds, \tag{2}$$

and $\phi_1(t), \phi_2(t), \psi(x), f(x,t)$ are given functions that are sufficiently smooth. We remark that (i) a generalized fractional problem of type (1) with any weight function $w(t)$ (not necessarily 1) can be converted to (1) by a simple formula $u(x,t) = w(t)v(x,t)$ (see [4–7]); and (ii) the generalized fractional equation considered in [9] is a special case of (1) when $p(x,t) \equiv 1$ and $q(x,t) \equiv 0$.

The plan of the paper is as follows. In Section 2, we shall develop a numerical scheme for the problem (1) based on a more general temporal mesh than [9]. Then, the stability as well as the convergence of the proposed numerical scheme will be established rigorously using energy method in Section 3. In Section 4, we carry out experiments to verify as well as to demonstrate the efficiency of the proposed numerical scheme. Finally, a brief conclusion is given in Section 5.

2. Numerical Scheme

In this section, we shall derive a numerical scheme for the problem (1) using the key idea of *generalized linear interpolation*. To begin, let

$$\Delta : 0 = t_0 < t_1 < \cdots < t_{N-1} < t_N = 1 \text{ and } \Delta' : 0 = x_0 < x_1 < \cdots < x_{M-1} < x_M = 1$$

be *any* mesh in the temporal dimension and a uniform mesh in the spatial dimension with step size $h = \frac{1}{M}$, respectively. Throughout, assume that the scale function $z(t)$ is a strictly increasing function. Let $Z : t \to z(t)$ be a map from $[0,1]$ to $[z(0), z(1)]$. Denote $z(t_n) = z_n$. Moreover, denote by U_j^n the exact solution of (1) at (x_j, t_n), and by u_j^n an approximation of U_j^n.

$$L_{j,k-1}(z(t)) = \frac{z(t) - z_{k-1}}{z_k - z_{k-1}} u_j^k + \frac{z(t) - z_k}{z_{k-1} - z_k} u_j^{k-1}. \tag{3}$$

Note that $L_{j,k-1}(z(t))$ is a *generalized linear polynomial* of $z(t)$ and it will be used to approximate $u(x_j, t)$ over the interval $[t_{k-1}, t_k]$ in (2). Indeed, we derive the following approximation scheme at (x_j, t_n)

$$\begin{aligned}
{}_0^C D^\alpha_{t;[z(t),1]} u(x_j, t_n) &= \frac{1}{\Gamma(2-\alpha)} \sum_{k=1}^n \int_{t_{k-1}}^{t_k} \frac{1}{[z(t_n) - z(s)]^\alpha} \frac{\partial u(x,s)}{\partial s} ds \\
&\approx \frac{1}{\Gamma(2-\alpha)} \sum_{k=1}^n \int_{t_{k-1}}^{t_k} \frac{1}{[z(t_n) - z(s)]^\alpha} \left[L_{j,k-1}(z(s)) \right]' ds \\
&= \frac{1}{\Gamma(2-\alpha)} \sum_{k=1}^n \int_{t_{k-1}}^{t_k} \frac{1}{[z(t_n) - z(s)]^\alpha} \frac{u_j^k - u_j^{k-1}}{z_k - z_{k-1}} z'(s) ds \\
&= \mu \left[\omega_z^0 u_j^n - \sum_{k=1}^{n-1} \left(\omega_z^{n-k-1} - \omega_z^{n-k} \right) u_j^k - \omega_z^{n-1} u_j^0 \right] := gL1[u(x_j, t_n)],
\end{aligned} \tag{4}$$

where $\mu = \frac{1}{\Gamma(2-\alpha)}$ and the coefficients

$$\omega_z^{n-k-1} = \frac{(z_n - z_k)^{1-\alpha} - (z_n - z_{k+1})^{1-\alpha}}{z_{k+1} - z_k}, \quad 0 \le k \le n-1. \tag{5}$$

We shall call (4) the **gL1 approximation** of the generalized Caputo fractional derivative.

Remark 1.
(a) Note that (4) is derived for any temporal mesh Δ and this is an extension of [9] which considers uniform temporal mesh. Moreover, the technique used to obtain (4) involves generalized linear interpolation whereas in [9] finite difference is used to approximate the derivatives in the integrand of the fractional derivative.
(b) The Formula (4) is also different from the nonuniform L1 formula in [13] since a scale function $z(t)$ such that $z_j \ne z_i, i \ne j$ is considered.

To proceed further, we shall investigate the accuracy of the gL1 approximation (4) and the properties of the coefficients ω_z^k which are both vital in subsequent analysis. For the former one, we introduce the following definition

Definition 1 ([14]). *Given the mesh $\Delta : 0 = t_0 < t_1 < \cdots < t_{N-1} < t_N = 1$, denote $z(t_k) = z_k$. The mesh*

$$\Delta_z : z(0) = z_0 < z_1 < \cdots < z_{N-1} < z_N = z(1)$$

is said to be quasi uniform if

$$\frac{\tau_{z,\max}}{\tau_{z,\min}} \le \rho,$$

where $\tau_{z,\max} = \max_{1 \le k \le N} |z_k - z_{k-1}|$, $\tau_{z,\min} = \min_{1 \le k \le N} |z_k - z_{k-1}|$ and $\rho > 0$ is a constant.

Theorem 1 (**gL1 approximation**). *Assume that for any fixed $x = x_j$, $u(x_j, Z^{-1}(z)) = g(z) \in C^2[z(0), z(1)]$. Suppose that the mesh $\Delta_z : z(0) = z_0 < z_1 < \cdots < z_{N-1} < z_N = z(1)$ is quasi uniform. Then, we have for any fixed $\alpha \in (0,1)$,*

$${}_0^C D^\alpha_{t;[z(t),1]} u(x_j, t_n) = gL1[u(x_j, t_n)] + O(\tau_{z,\max}^{2-\alpha}). \tag{6}$$

Proof. From (4) we see that the error term R_j^n satisfies

$$_0^C D_{t;[z(t),1]}^\alpha u(x_j, t_n) = gL1[u(x_j, t_n)] + R_j^n,$$

and

$$R_j^n = \frac{1}{\Gamma(1-\alpha)} \sum_{k=1}^n \int_{t_{k-1}}^{t_k} [z(t_n) - z(s)]^{-\alpha} \left\{ \frac{\partial u(x_j, s)}{\partial s} - [L_{j,k-1}(z(s))]' \right\} ds.$$

Noting that $L_{j,k-1}(z(t_k)) = u_j^k = u(x_j, t_k)$ and the relation $Z^{-1}(z) = t$, after applying integration by parts, we get

$$R_j^n = -\frac{\alpha}{\Gamma(1-\alpha)} \sum_{k=1}^n \int_{z_{k-1}}^{z_k} (z_n - z)^{-\alpha-1} \left[u(x_j, Z^{-1}(z)) - L_{j,k-1}(z) \right] dz. \tag{7}$$

Since $u(x_j, Z^{-1}(z)) = g(z) \in C^2[z(0), z(1)]$, it is well known that

$$u(x_j, Z^{-1}(z)) - L_{j,k-1}(z) = (z - z_{k-1})(z - z_k) \frac{g_{zz}(\xi_k)}{2}, \qquad z_{k-1} < \xi_k < z_k. \tag{8}$$

Denote $M_g = \max_{z(0) \leq z \leq z(1)} |g_{zz}(z)|$. Upon substituting (8) into (7), we find

$$|R_j^n| \leq \frac{\alpha M_g}{2\Gamma(1-\alpha)} \sum_{k=1}^n \int_{z_{k-1}}^{z_k} (z_n - z)^{-\alpha-1}(z - z_{k-1})(z_k - z) dz$$

$$= \frac{M_g}{2\Gamma(2-\alpha)} \left[\sum_{k=1}^{n-1} \int_{z_{k-1}}^{z_k} (z_n - z)^{-\alpha-1}(z - z_{k-1})(z_k - z) dz + \int_{z_{n-1}}^{z_n} \frac{z - z_{n-1}}{(z_n - z)^\alpha} dz \right]$$

$$\leq \frac{M_g}{2\Gamma(2-\alpha)} \left[\sum_{k=1}^{n-1} \frac{(z_k - z_{k-1})^2}{4} \int_{z_{k-1}}^{z_k} (z_n - z)^{-\alpha-1} dz + \frac{(z_n - z_{n-1})^{2-\alpha}}{1-\alpha} \right].$$

This further gives

$$|R_j^n| \leq \frac{M_g}{2\Gamma(2-\alpha)} \left[\frac{\tau_{z,\max}^2}{4} \int_{z_0}^{z_{n-1}} (z_n - z)^{-\alpha-1} dz + \frac{\tau_{z,\max}^{2-\alpha}}{1-\alpha} \right]$$

$$= \frac{M_g}{2\Gamma(2-\alpha)} \left[\frac{\tau_{z,\max}^2}{4\alpha} \left((z_n - z_{n-1})^{-\alpha} - (z_n - z_0)^{-\alpha}\right) + \frac{\tau_{z,\max}^{2-\alpha}}{1-\alpha} \right]$$

$$\leq \frac{M_g}{2\Gamma(2-\alpha)} \left[\frac{\tau_{z,\max}^2}{4\alpha} (z_n - z_{n-1})^{-\alpha} + \frac{\tau_{z,\max}^{2-\alpha}}{1-\alpha} \right]$$

$$\leq \frac{M_g}{2\Gamma(2-\alpha)} \left[\frac{\rho^\alpha}{4\alpha} + \frac{1}{1-\alpha} \right] \tau_{z,\max}^{2-\alpha}.$$

Hence, for any fixed $\alpha \in (0,1)$, we get

$$|R_j^n| = O(\tau_{z,\max}^{2-\alpha}).$$

This completes the proof. □

Remark 2. *There is some relation between the commonly used uniform mesh of t and the quasi uniform mesh of $z(t)$.*

(a) *For finite intervals of t, say $t \in [0,1]$, in practice the partition of $[0,1]$ always results in finite number of subintervals, so we are able to find a constant ρ such that $\frac{\tau_{z,\max}}{\tau_{z,\min}} \leq \rho$. Hence, it is clear that any general mesh of t yields a quasi uniform mesh of $z(t)$. In particular, we can say that for finite intervals, the commonly used uniform mesh of t is a special case of the quasi uniform mesh of $z(t)$.*

(b) For infinite intervals of t, in general the uniform mesh of t may not yield the quasi uniform mesh of $z(t)$. However, if $0 < c < |z'(t)| < C$ for all t in the infinite interval, then the uniform mesh of t will give the quasi uniform mesh of $z(t)$, and so we can conclude here that the uniform mesh of t is a special case of the quasi uniform mesh of $z(t)$.

Our next result gives the properties of the coefficients ω_z^k in (5) that is vital in subsequent analysis.

Lemma 1. *For fixed n, we have*

$$\omega_z^{n-k-1} \geq (1-\alpha)(z_n - z_k)^{-\alpha} > 0, \qquad 0 \leq k \leq n-1 \tag{9}$$
$$\omega_z^{n-k-1} \geq \omega_z^{n-k}, \qquad 0 \leq k \leq n-1. \tag{10}$$

Proof. Let $F(z) = (z_n - z)^{1-\alpha}$. Applying mean value theorem and noting the Definition (5), we get

$$F'(\xi) = -(1-\alpha)(z_n - \xi)^{-\alpha} = \frac{F(z_{k+1}) - F(z_k)}{z_{k+1} - z_k} = -\omega_z^{n-k-1}, \qquad z_k \leq \xi \leq z_{k+1}$$

i.e.,

$$\omega_z^{n-k-1} = (1-\alpha)(z_n - \xi)^{-\alpha}, \qquad z_k \leq \xi \leq z_{k+1}. \tag{11}$$

Since $(z_n - \cdot)^{-\alpha}$ is an increasing function, (11) immediately leads to (9) and (10). □

We are now ready to construct a numerical scheme for the generalized time-fractional diffusion Equation (1). Discretizing (1) at (x_j, t_n) and using the approximation (4) together with finite difference method in the spatial dimension yields

$$\begin{cases} \mu \left[\omega_z^0 u_j^n - \sum_{k=1}^{n-1} \left(\omega_z^{n-k-1} - \omega_z^{n-k} \right) u_j^k - \omega_z^{n-1} u_j^0 \right] = \Lambda u_j^n + f_j^n, & 1 \leq j \leq M-1 \\ u_j^0 = \psi(x_j), & 1 \leq j \leq M-1 \\ u_0^n = \phi_1(t_n), \quad u_M^n = \phi_1(t_n), & 0 \leq n \leq N \end{cases} \tag{12}$$

where $\mu = \frac{1}{\Gamma(2-\alpha)}$ and Λ is an operator given by

$$\Lambda u_j^n = \delta_x(p\delta_x u)_j^n - q_j^n u_j^n,$$

with

$$\delta_x(p\delta_x u)_j^n = \frac{1}{h}\left(p_{j+\frac{1}{2}}^n \delta_x u_{j+\frac{1}{2}}^n - p_{j-\frac{1}{2}}^n \delta_x u_{j-\frac{1}{2}}^n \right),$$

$p_{j+\frac{1}{2}}^n = p(x_{j+\frac{1}{2}}, t_n), q_j^n = q(x_j, t_n)$ and $\delta_x u_{j+\frac{1}{2}}^n = \left(u_{j+1}^n - u_j^n \right)/h$. We shall call (12) the *gL1 scheme* of the generalized time-fractional diffusion Equation (1).

Remark 3. *It is easy to verify that the coefficient matrix of the system (12) is strictly diagonally dominated. Therefore, it is uniquely solvable.*

3. Theoretical Results

In this section, we shall analyze the stability as well as the convergence of the numerical scheme (12). To begin, let $U_h = \{u = (u_0, u_1, \cdots, u_M) | u_0 = u_M = 0\}$ and for any $u, v \in U_h$, define

$$\delta_x u_{j+\frac{1}{2}} = \frac{1}{h}(u_{j+1} - u_j), \qquad \delta_x u_j = \frac{1}{h}\left(u_{j+\frac{1}{2}} - u_{j-\frac{1}{2}} \right), \qquad \delta_x^2 u_j = \frac{1}{h}\left(\delta_x u_{j+\frac{1}{2}} - \delta_x u_{j-\frac{1}{2}} \right)$$

and

$$(u,v) = h\sum_{j=1}^{M-1} u_j v_j, \quad |u|_1 = \sqrt{h\sum_{j=0}^{M-1} \left(\delta_x u_{j+\frac{1}{2}}\right)^2}, \quad \|u\|_\infty = \max_{1\leq j\leq M-1} |u_j|. \tag{13}$$

Obviously, $\|\cdot\| = \sqrt{(\cdot,\cdot)}$ is a norm defined over the space U_h.

Next, we shall present three lemmas that will be used later to establish the stability and convergence results. The first one gives a relation between $|u|_1$ and $\|u\|_\infty$.

Lemma 2 ([15]). *For any $u \in U_h$, we have the inequality $\|u\|_\infty \leq \frac{1}{2}|u|_1$.*

The next lemma is from [16] which reveals a relation between $|u|_1$ and $\|u\|$.

Lemma 3 (Discrete Poincare inequality [16]). *Suppose that $u \in U_h$, then*

$$\frac{2}{h}\sin\left(\frac{\pi h}{2}\right)\|u\| \leq |u|_1. \tag{14}$$

Remark 4. *If $h < 1$ which is the case in our method, from the fact $\sin\left(\frac{\pi}{2}h\right) \geq h$, the inequality (14) yields $|u|_1 \geq 2\|u\|$ that will be used in subsequent analysis.*

The last lemma gives an explicit expression of $-(\Lambda u, u)$.

Lemma 4. *For any $u \in U_h$, we have*

$$-(\Lambda u, u) = h\sum_{j=0}^{M-1} p_{j+\frac{1}{2}}\left(\delta_x u_{j+\frac{1}{2}}\right)^2 + h\sum_{j=1}^{M-1} q_j u_j^2.$$

Proof. Using the definition in (13), it is found that

$$\begin{aligned}
-(\Lambda u, u) &= -h\sum_{j=1}^{M-1}[\delta_x(p\delta_x u)_j - q_j u_j]u_j = -h\sum_{j=1}^{M-1}[\delta_x(p\delta_x u)_j]u_j + h\sum_{j=1}^{M-1} q_j(u_j)^2 \\
&= -\sum_{j=1}^{M-1}\left(p_{j+\frac{1}{2}}\delta_x u_{j+\frac{1}{2}} - p_{j-\frac{1}{2}}\delta_x u_{j-\frac{1}{2}}\right)u_j + h\sum_{j=1}^{M-1} q_j(u_j)^2 \\
&= -\sum_{j=1}^{M-1} p_{j+\frac{1}{2}} u_j \delta_x u_{j+\frac{1}{2}} + \sum_{j=1}^{M-1} p_{j-\frac{1}{2}} u_j \delta_x u_{j-\frac{1}{2}} + h\sum_{j=1}^{M-1} q_j(u_j)^2 \\
&= \sum_{j=0}^{M-1} p_{j+\frac{1}{2}}(u_{j+1} - u_j)\delta_x u_{j+\frac{1}{2}} + h\sum_{j=1}^{M-1} q_j(u_j)^2,
\end{aligned}$$

where we have used $u_0 = u_M = 0$ in the last equality. The result is immediate from the above equation. □

Remark 5. *Since $p(x,t) \geq p_0 > 0$ and $q(x,t) \geq 0$, it is clear from Lemma 4 that $-(\Lambda u, u) \geq p_0|u|_1^2$ for any $u \in U_h$.*

Now, let us present the stability and convergence of the numerical scheme (12). To this aim, we shall first consider (12) with zero boundary conditions.

Theorem 2. Let $\{u_j^n, 1 \leq j \leq M-1, 1 \leq n \leq N\}$ be the solution of the system (12) with zero boundary conditions. Then, we have

$$\|u^n\|^2 + \frac{p_0}{\omega_z^0 \mu}|u^n|_1^2 \leq E, \quad 1 \leq n \leq N \tag{15}$$

where $\mu = \frac{1}{\Gamma(2-\alpha)}, \omega_z^0 = (z_n - z_{n-1})^{-\alpha}, p_0 > 0$ and

$$E = \|u^0\|^2 + \frac{\Gamma(1-\alpha)(z(1) - z(0))^\alpha}{4p_0} \max_{1 \leq n \leq N} \|f^n\|^2.$$

Proof. Multiplying both sides of the first equation of (12) by $-u_j^n$ and summing j from 1 to $(M-1)$ gives

$$-\mu \left[\omega_z^0 u_j^n - \sum_{k=1}^{n-1}\left(\omega_z^{n-k-1} - \omega_z^{n-k}\right) u_j^k - \omega_z^{n-1} u_j^0\right] = -(\Lambda u^n, u^n) - (f^n, u^n),$$

which is rearranged to

$$\mu \omega_z^0 (u^n, u^n) - (\Lambda u^n, u^n) = \mu \sum_{k=1}^{n-1}\left(\omega_z^{n-k-1} - \omega_z^{n-k}\right)(u^k, u^n) + \mu \omega_z^{n-1}(u^0, u^n) + (f^n, u^n). \tag{16}$$

Since we consider zero boundary conditions here, it is obvious that $u^n \in U_h$. Therefore, using Remark 5, we get a lower bound for the left side of (16) below

$$\mu \omega_z^0 (u^n, u^n) - (\Lambda u^n, u^n) \geq \mu \omega_z^0 \|u^n\|^2 + p_0 |u^n|_1^2.$$

Noting (10) in Lemma 1 and using $xy \leq \frac{1}{2}(x^2 + y^2)$, an upper bound for the first two terms on the right side of (16) is found as follows

$$\mu \sum_{k=1}^{n-1}\left(\omega_z^{n-k-1} - \omega_z^{n-k}\right)(u^k, u^n) + \mu \omega_z^{n-1}(u^0, u^n)$$

$$\leq \frac{\mu}{2}\left[\sum_{k=1}^{n-1}\left(\omega_z^{n-k-1} - \omega_z^{n-k}\right)(u^k, u^k) + \omega_z^{n-1}(u^0, u^0)\right] + \frac{\mu}{2}\omega_z^0(u^n, u^n)$$

$$= \frac{\mu}{2}\left[\sum_{k=1}^{n-1}\left(\omega_z^{n-k-1} - \omega_z^{n-k}\right)\|u^k\|^2 + \omega_z^{n-1}\|u^0\|^2\right] + \frac{\mu}{2}\omega_z^0 \|u^n\|^2.$$

For the third term on the right side of (16), the Young's inequality gives the following upper bound

$$(f^n, u^n) \leq \frac{\|f^n\|^2}{4\epsilon} + \epsilon \|u^n\|^2, \quad \forall \epsilon > 0.$$

Upon substituting the above upper and lower bounds into (16), we immediately get

$$\frac{\mu}{2}\omega_z^0\|u^n\|^2 + p_0|u^n|_1^2 - \epsilon\|u^n\|^2 \leq \frac{\mu}{2}\left[\sum_{k=1}^{n-1}\left(\omega_z^{n-k-1} - \omega_z^{n-k}\right)\|u^k\|^2 + \omega_z^{n-1}\|u^0\|^2\right] + \frac{1}{4\epsilon}\|f^n\|^2. \tag{17}$$

Next, using Lemma 3 and noting Remark 4, we have $|u^n|_1 \geq 2\|u^n\|$. Then, with $\epsilon = 2p_0$, the left side of (17) gives the following lower bound

$$\frac{\mu}{2}\omega_z^0\|u^n\|^2 + p_0|u^n|_1^2 - \epsilon\|u^n\|^2 \geq \frac{\mu}{2}\omega_z^0\|u^n\|^2 + \left(p_0 - \frac{\epsilon}{4}\right)|u^n|_1^2 = \frac{\mu}{2}\omega_z^0\|u^n\|^2 + \frac{p_0}{2}|u^n|_1^2.$$

Substituting the above into (17) leads to

$$\omega_z^0 \|u^n\|^2 + \frac{p_0}{\mu}|u^n|_1^2 \leq \sum_{k=1}^{n-1}\left(\omega_z^{n-k-1} - \omega_z^{n-k}\right)\|u^k\|^2 + \omega_z^{n-1}\left(\|u^0\|^2 + \frac{1}{4p_0 \mu \omega_z^{n-1}}\|f^n\|^2\right). \tag{18}$$

Further, from (9) we see that $\omega_z^{n-1} \geq (1-\alpha)(z_n - z_0)^{-\alpha} > 0$ and hence

$$\frac{1}{\omega_z^{n-1}} \leq \frac{(z_n - z_0)^\alpha}{1-\alpha} \leq \frac{(z(1) - z(0))^\alpha}{1-\alpha}.$$

Using the above inequality and $\mu = \frac{1}{\Gamma(2-\alpha)}$ in (18), we find

$$\omega_z^0\left(\|u^n\|^2 + \frac{p_0}{\omega_z^0 \mu}|u^n|_1^2\right) \leq \sum_{k=1}^{n-1}\left(\omega_z^{n-k-1} - \omega_z^{n-k}\right)\|u^k\|^2 + \omega_z^{n-1} E,$$

where E is defined in the theorem. Noting (10), the above inequality readily leads to

$$\omega_z^0\left(\|u^n\|^2 + \frac{p_0}{\omega_z^0 \mu}|u^n|_1^2\right) \leq \sum_{k=1}^{n-1}\left(\omega_z^{n-k-1} - \omega_z^{n-k}\right)\left[\|u^k\|^2 + \frac{p_0(z_k - z_{k-1})^\alpha}{\mu}|u^k|_1^2\right] + \omega_z^{n-1} E,$$

or equivalently

$$\omega_z^0\left[\|u^n\|^2 + \frac{p_0(z_n - z_{n-1})^\alpha}{\mu}|u^n|_1^2\right]$$
$$\leq \sum_{k=1}^{n-1}\left(\omega_z^{n-k-1} - \omega_z^{n-k}\right)\left[\|u^k\|^2 + \frac{p_0(z_k - z_{k-1})^\alpha}{\mu}|u^k|_1^2\right] + \omega_z^{n-1} E. \quad (19)$$

Now, we shall show by mathematical induction that

$$\|u^n\|^2 + \frac{p_0(z_n - z_{n-1})^\alpha}{\mu}|u^n|_1^2 \leq E, \qquad 1 \leq n \leq N. \quad (20)$$

In fact, let $n = 1$ in (19) and we get

$$\omega_z^0\left[\|u^1\|^2 + \frac{p_0(z_1 - z_0)^\alpha}{\mu}|u^1|_1^2\right] \leq \omega_z^0 E,$$

which implies that (20) holds for $n = 1$. Suppose that (20) is true up to $(n-1)$. Then, from (19), we have

$$\omega_z^0\left[\|u^n\|^2 + \frac{p_0(z_n - z_{n-1})^\alpha}{\mu}|u^n|_1^2\right]$$
$$\leq \sum_{k=1}^{n-1}\left(\omega_z^{n-k-1} - \omega_z^{n-k}\right)\left[\|u^k\|^2 + \frac{p_0(z_k - z_{k-1})^\alpha}{\mu}|u^k|_1^2\right] + \omega_z^{n-1} E$$
$$\leq \sum_{k=1}^{n-1}\left(\omega_z^{n-k-1} - \omega_z^{n-k}\right) E + \omega_z^{n-1} E = \omega_z^0 E,$$

which immediately gives (20), or equivalently (15). This completes the proof. □

Remark 6 (Stability). *Using a similar argument as in [4–7], it can readily be deduced from Theorem 2 that the numerical scheme (12) is robust (or stable) with respect to the initial data $\psi(x)$ and the non-homogeneous data $f(x,t)$.*

We are now ready to establish the convergence of the proposed scheme (12).

Theorem 3 (Convergence). *Assume that $u(x, Z^{-1}(z)) = \bar{u}(x,z) \in C^{4,2}([0,1] \times [z(0), z(1)])$. Suppose that the mesh $\Delta_z : z(0) = z_0 < z_1 < \cdots < z_{N-1} < z_N = z(1)$ is quasi uniform. Let $\{U_j^n = u(x_j, t_n)\}$ be the exact solution of the problem (1), $\{u_j^n\}$ be the numerical solution obtained from the scheme (12) and $e_j^n = U_j^n - u_j^n$ be the error at (x_j, t_n). Then, we have*

$$\|e^n\|^2 + c(\alpha,z)|e^n|_1^2 \leq \left[O(\tau_{z,\max}^{2-\alpha} + h^2)\right]^2, \quad 1 \leq n \leq N \tag{21}$$

where $c(\alpha,z) = \frac{p_0}{\omega_z^0 \mu}$.

Proof. Since $\{U_j^n\}$ is the exact solution of (1), it is clear that

$$\begin{cases} \mu\left[\omega_z^0 U_j^n - \sum_{k=1}^{n-1}\left(\omega_z^{n-k-1} - \omega_z^{n-k}\right)U_j^k - \omega_z^{n-1}U_j^0\right] = \Lambda U_j^n + f_j^n + T_j^n, & 1 \leq j \leq M-1 \\ U_j^0 = \psi(x_j), & 1 \leq j \leq M-1 \\ U_0^n = \phi_1(t_n), \quad U_M^n = \phi_1(t_n), & 0 \leq n \leq N \end{cases} \tag{22}$$

where T_j^n is the local truncation error of the j-th equation.

Noting (6) in Theorem 1, and using Taylor expansion at $x = x_j$ in (22), we find that

$$T_j^n = O(\tau_{z,\max}^{2-\alpha} + h^2), \quad 1 \leq j \leq M-1, 1 \leq n \leq N. \tag{23}$$

Next, from (12) and (22) it is obvious that $\{e_j^n\}$ is the solution of the system

$$\begin{cases} \mu\left[\omega_z^0 e_j^n - \sum_{k=1}^{n-1}\left(\omega_z^{n-k-1} - \omega_z^{n-k}\right)e_j^k - \omega_z^{n-1}e_j^0\right] = \Lambda e_j^n + T_j^n, & 1 \leq j \leq M-1 \\ e_j^0 = 0, & 1 \leq j \leq M-1 \\ e_0^n = e_M^n = 0, & 0 \leq n \leq N. \end{cases} \tag{24}$$

Hence, $e^n \in U_h$. Finally, applying Theorem 2 to (24) and noting $e_j^0 = 0$, we obtain for $1 \leq n \leq N$,

$$\|e^n\|^2 + c(\alpha,z)|e^n|_1^2 \leq \frac{\Gamma(1-\alpha)(z(1)-z(0))^\alpha}{4p_0} \max_{1 \leq n \leq N} \|T^n\|^2 = \left[O(\tau_{z,\max}^{2-\alpha} + h^2)\right]^2 \tag{25}$$

which completes the proof. □

Remark 7. *From Theorem 3, it is easily seen that*

$$\|e^n\| = O(\tau_{z,\max}^{2-\alpha} + h^2).$$

Hence, the temporal convergence order in the norm $\|\cdot\|$ is $(2-\alpha)$, which is optimal. On the other hand, the convergence order in $\|\cdot\|_\infty$ is not optimal. In fact, from Lemma 2, (21) and the properties of quasi uniform mesh, we get

$$\|e^n\|_\infty \leq \frac{1}{2}|e^n|_1 \leq \sqrt{\frac{(z_n - z_{n-1})^{-\alpha}}{4p_0\Gamma(2-\alpha)}} O(\tau_{z,\max}^{2-\alpha} + h^2)$$

$$\leq \sqrt{\frac{\tau_{\min,z}^{\alpha}}{4p_0\Gamma(2-\alpha)}} O(\tau_{z,\max}^{2-\alpha} + h^2) = O(\tau_{z,\max}^{2-\frac{3}{2}\alpha} + h^2).$$

Remark 8. *Theorem 3 is an extension of the work [9] in the sense that*

- *the problem (1) involves an operator $\mathcal{L}$ and is more general than the problem considered in [9];*
- *we consider a general temporal mesh which is quasi uniform in terms of the scale function $z(t)$, in view of Remark 2 this is more general than the uniform temporal mesh considered in [9];*
- *(21) and Remark 7 give the explicit convergence order of the proposed scheme (12), while convergence is proven without giving the explicit convergence order in [9].*

4. Numerical Simulation

In this section, we shall use two examples to demonstrate the efficacy of the proposed numerical scheme (12) and to verify the theoretical result in Remark 7. To be specific, we shall

- compute errors at $t = 1$ using

$$e(N, h) = \|e^N\| \, (\text{or} \|e^N\|_\infty)$$

as well as the corresponding temporal and spatial convergence orders by

$$\text{TCO} = \log_2 \frac{e(N, h)}{e(2N, h)} \quad \text{and} \quad \text{SCO} = \log_2 \frac{e(N, h)}{e(N, h/2)},$$

respectively;
- demonstrate that the proposed numerical scheme (12) works well for three types of temporal meshes, namely
    - **Uniform**: uniform mesh with respect to t;
    - **Graded**: graded mesh [17,18] with $t_j = Z^{-1}\left((z(1) - z(0))\left(\frac{j}{N}\right)^r + z(0)\right)$, $0 \leq j \leq N$ (let $r = \frac{2-\alpha}{\alpha}$ in the experiment to get optimal accuracy, refer to [17,18] for details);
    - **Uniform$_z$**: uniform mesh with respect to $z(t)$.

In view of Remark 2, we note that all the above types of temporal meshes are particular cases of quasi uniform mesh of $z(t)$.

Clearly, the exact solution is required to compute $e(N, h)$. When the exact solution is not available (which is commonly encountered in applications), we shall use 'approximate' exact solution, which is obtained by the numerical scheme (12) with sufficiently small mesh sizes (e.g., $M = N = 2000$ in our experiments), as 'exact' solution to compute errors. This is reasonable as the numerical scheme (12) is convergent.

Example 1 ([6,7,9]). *Consider the generalized time-fractional diffusion equation*

$$\begin{cases} {}_0^C D^\alpha_{t;[z(t),1]} u(x,t) = u_{xx}(x,t) + f(x,t), & (x,t) \in (0,1) \times (0,1) \\ u(x,0) = \sin(\pi x), & x \in [0,1] \\ u(0,t) = 0, \quad u(1,t) = 0, & t \in (0,1] \end{cases} \quad (26)$$

where $0 < \alpha < 1$, $z(t)$ is a strictly increasing scale function and

$$f(x,t) = \frac{2}{\Gamma(2.15)}(x^2 - x)t^{1.15} + \pi^2 \sin(\pi x) - 2t^2.$$

Note that when $z(t) = t$ and $\alpha = 0.85$, the exact solution of Equation (26) is

$$u(x,t) = \sin(\pi x) + x(x-1)t^2.$$

In this example, $p(x,t) \equiv 1$ and $q(x,t) \equiv 0$. Let us start with $\alpha = 0.85$ and $z(t) = t, t^{0.5}, t^2$. Applying the numerical scheme (12) with fixed $h = \frac{1}{512}$ and varied N, we compute the errors and temporal convergence orders for three types of temporal meshes—Uniform, Graded, Uniform$_z$. The results are displayed in Table 1. From the table, it is easily seen that the experimental temporal convergence orders ($\approx$1.15) are consistent with the theoretical ones ($=2 - \alpha$) for various scale functions $z(t)$ and different types of temporal meshes. It is a pleasant surprise that the numerical performance in terms of maximum norm is better than the theoretical result in Remark 7.

Next, we investigate the performance of the proposed numerical scheme for different values of α and scale functions $z(t)$. Here, we use the uniform mesh of t (Uniform) and compute $\|e^N\|$.

- In Table 2, we fix $h = \frac{1}{512}$ and let N vary. It is observed that the temporal convergence order is $(2 - \alpha)$ which is consistent with the theoretical one.
- In Table 3, we fix $N = 2000$ and let h vary to investigate the spatial convergence. Obviously, the scheme (12) achieves second order spatial convergence order which is the same as that stated in Remark 7.

Table 1. (Example 1) Temporal convergence order when $\alpha = 0.85, h = \frac{1}{512}$.

$z(t)$	N	Uniform Mesh				Graded Mesh				Uniform$_z$ Mesh			
		$\|e^N\|_\infty$		$\|e^N\|$		$\|e^N\|_\infty$		$\|e^N\|$		$\|e^N\|_\infty$		$\|e^N\|$	
t	16	8.55×10^{-4}	-	6.07×10^{-4}	-	1.15×10^{-3}	-	8.17×10^{-4}	-	-	-	-	-
	32	3.84×10^{-4}	1.15	2.73×10^{-4}	1.15	5.22×10^{-4}	1.14	3.71×10^{-4}	1.14	-	-	-	-
	64	1.71×10^{-4}	1.16	1.22×10^{-4}	1.16	2.34×10^{-4}	1.16	1.66×10^{-4}	1.16	-	-	-	-
	128	7.55×10^{-5}	1.18	5.36×10^{-5}	1.18	1.03×10^{-4}	1.18	7.33×10^{-5}	1.18	-	-	-	-
$t^{0.5}$	16	1.86×10^{-3}	-	1.32×10^{-3}	-	4.87×10^{-3}	-	3.46×10^{-3}	-	3.61×10^{-3}	-	2.56×10^{-3}	-
	32	8.38×10^{-4}	1.15	5.95×10^{-4}	1.15	2.27×10^{-3}	1.10	1.61×10^{-3}	1.10	1.66×10^{-3}	1.12	1.18×10^{-3}	1.12
	64	3.74×10^{-4}	1.16	2.66×10^{-4}	1.16	1.03×10^{-3}	1.13	7.35×10^{-4}	1.13	7.51×10^{-4}	1.14	5.34×10^{-4}	1.14
	128	1.65×10^{-4}	1.18	1.17×10^{-4}	1.18	4.60×10^{-4}	1.17	3.27×10^{-4}	1.17	3.33×10^{-4}	1.17	2.37×10^{-4}	1.17
t^2	16	2.66×10^{-5}	-	1.88×10^{-5}	-	1.50×10^{-5}	-	1.06×10^{-5}	-	5.68×10^{-6}	-	4.02×10^{-6}	-
	32	1.22×10^{-5}	1.12	8.66×10^{-6}	1.12	6.86×10^{-6}	1.12	4.86×10^{-6}	1.12	2.49×10^{-6}	1.19	1.76×10^{-6}	1.19
	64	5.52×10^{-6}	1.15	3.90×10^{-6}	1.15	3.08×10^{-6}	1.15	2.18×10^{-6}	1.15	1.07×10^{-6}	1.23	7.55×10^{-7}	1.23
	128	2.44×10^{-6}	1.18	1.73×10^{-6}	1.18	1.36×10^{-6}	1.18	9.63×10^{-7}	1.18	4.50×10^{-7}	1.24	3.19×10^{-7}	1.24

Table 2. (Example 1) Temporal convergence order for various α when $h = \frac{1}{512}$.

$z(t)$	N	$\alpha = 0.2$		$\alpha = 0.5$		$\alpha = 0.8$	
$t^{0.5}$	8	1.2119×10^{-4}	-	6.4821×10^{-4}	-	2.3862×10^{-3}	-
	16	3.6868×10^{-5}	1.72	2.3301×10^{-4}	1.48	1.0446×10^{-3}	1.19
	32	1.1124×10^{-5}	1.73	8.3262×10^{-5}	1.48	4.5475×10^{-4}	1.20
	64	3.3301×10^{-6}	1.74	2.9572×10^{-5}	1.49	1.9656×10^{-4}	1.21
t^2	8	3.6792×10^{-6}	-	7.9954×10^{-6}	-	2.7299×10^{-5}	-
	16	1.1025×10^{-6}	1.74	2.8681×10^{-6}	1.48	1.2814×10^{-5}	1.09
	32	3.2908×10^{-7}	1.74	1.0251×10^{-6}	1.48	5.7126×10^{-6}	1.17
	64	9.7656×10^{-8}	1.75	3.6452×10^{-7}	1.49	2.4954×10^{-6}	1.19

Table 3. (Example 1) Spatial convergence order for various α when $N = 2000$.

$z(t)$	h	$\alpha = 0.2$		$\alpha = 0.5$		$\alpha = 0.8$	
$t^{0.5}$	$\frac{1}{10}$	5.3034×10^{-3}	-	5.5169×10^{-3}	-	5.7900×10^{-3}	-
	$\frac{1}{20}$	1.3214×10^{-3}	2.00	1.3746×10^{-3}	2.00	1.4425×10^{-3}	2.01
	$\frac{1}{40}$	3.2999×10^{-4}	2.00	3.4325×10^{-4}	2.00	3.6020×10^{-4}	2.00
	$\frac{1}{80}$	8.2382×10^{-5}	2.00	8.5692×10^{-5}	2.00	8.9924×10^{-5}	2.00
t^2	$\frac{1}{10}$	5.2701×10^{-3}	-	5.4177×10^{-3}	-	5.6052×10^{-3}	-
	$\frac{1}{20}$	1.3131×10^{-3}	2.00	1.3497×10^{-3}	2.01	1.3961×10^{-3}	2.01
	$\frac{1}{40}$	3.2791×10^{-4}	2.00	3.3704×10^{-4}	2.00	3.4862×10^{-4}	2.00
	$\frac{1}{80}$	8.1862×10^{-5}	2.00	8.4140×10^{-5}	2.00	8.7030×10^{-5}	2.00

Our next example is modified from an example in [19] and it involves a general operator $\mathcal{L}$.

Example 2 ([19]). *Consider the generalized time-fractional diffusion equation*

$$\begin{cases} {}^{C}_{0}D^{\alpha}_{t;[z(t),1]}u(x,t) = \mathcal{L}u + f(x,t), & (x,t) \in (0,1) \times (0,1) \\ u(x,0) = \sin(\pi x), & x \in [0,1] \\ u(0,t) = 0, \quad u(1,t) = 0, & t \in (0,1] \end{cases} \quad (27)$$

where $\mathcal{L}u = \partial_x(p(x,t)\partial_x u) - q(x,t)u$,

$$p(x,t) = 2 - \cos(xt), \qquad q(x,t) = 1 - \sin(xt)$$

and

$$f(x,t) = \left[\frac{\Gamma(4+\alpha)}{6}t^3 + \frac{2}{\Gamma(3-\alpha)}t^{2-\alpha} + \left(t^{3+\alpha} + t^2 + 1\right)\left(\pi^2 p(x,t) + q(x,t)\right)\right]\sin(\pi x)$$
$$- \pi\left(t^{4+\alpha} + t^3 + t\right)\sin(xt)\cos(\pi x).$$

When $z(t) = t$, *the exact solution of (27) is*

$$u(x,t) = \sin(\pi x)(t^{3+\alpha} + t^2 + 1).$$

First, consider (27) when $\alpha = 0.5$. With fixed $h = \frac{1}{2000}$, we shall apply the numerical scheme (12) and compute the errors $\|e^N\|$, $\|e^N\|_\infty$ and temporal convergence orders. The results are presented in Table 4, and it is clear that the numerical scheme (12) works well for different types of temporal meshes as well as for a wide range of problems (i.e., different $z(t)$). The experimental temporal convergence orders in $\|\cdot\|$ (≈ 1.5) agree with the theoretical ones ($=2 - \alpha$), while once again it is a pleasant surprise that the numerical performance in terms of maximum norm is better than the theoretical result in Remark 7.

Next, we investigate the temporal convergence and spatial convergence of the numerical scheme (12) for different values of α and scale functions $z(t)$. Here, we use the uniform mesh of t and compute $\|e^N\|$. The results are presented in Tables 5 and 6. We observe that the experimental temporal/spatial convergence orders are consistent with the theoretical result.

Table 4. (Example 2) Temporal convergence order when $\alpha = 0.5$, $h = \frac{1}{2000}$.

$z(t)$	N	Uniform Mesh				Graded Mesh				Uniform$_z$ Mesh			
		$\|e^N\|_\infty$		$\|e^N\|$		$\|e^N\|_\infty$		$\|e^N\|$		$\|e^N\|_\infty$		$\|e^N\|$	
t	40	7.02×10^{-4}	-	4.93×10^{-4}	-	3.13×10^{-3}	-	2.20×10^{-3}	-	-	-	-	-
	80	2.53×10^{-4}	1.47	1.78×10^{-4}	1.47	1.18×10^{-3}	1.41	8.26×10^{-4}	1.41	-	-	-	-
	160	8.94×10^{-5}	1.50	6.28×10^{-5}	1.50	4.27×10^{-4}	1.46	3.00×10^{-4}	1.46	-	-	-	-
	320	3.06×10^{-5}	1.55	2.15×10^{-5}	1.55	1.49×10^{-4}	1.52	1.04×10^{-4}	1.52	-	-	-	-
$t^{0.5}$	40	1.15×10^{-3}	-	8.05×10^{-4}	-	1.25×10^{-2}	-	8.80×10^{-3}	-	2.92×10^{-3}	-	2.05×10^{-3}	-
	80	4.12×10^{-4}	1.48	2.89×10^{-4}	1.48	4.91×10^{-3}	1.35	3.45×10^{-3}	1.35	1.07×10^{-3}	1.44	7.55×10^{-4}	1.44
	160	1.46×10^{-4}	1.50	1.02×10^{-4}	1.50	1.83×10^{-3}	1.42	1.29×10^{-3}	1.42	3.86×10^{-4}	1.48	2.71×10^{-4}	1.48
	320	4.97×10^{-5}	1.55	3.49×10^{-5}	1.55	6.47×10^{-4}	1.50	4.55×10^{-4}	1.50	1.33×10^{-4}	1.53	9.36×10^{-5}	1.53
t^2	40	2.56×10^{-4}	-	1.80×10^{-4}	-	4.48×10^{-4}	-	3.15×10^{-4}	-	1.03×10^{-4}	-	7.22×10^{-5}	-
	80	9.26×10^{-5}	1.47	6.50×10^{-5}	1.47	1.64×10^{-4}	1.45	1.15×10^{-4}	1.45	3.64×10^{-5}	1.50	2.55×10^{-5}	1.50
	160	3.28×10^{-5}	1.50	2.31×10^{-5}	1.50	5.86×10^{-5}	1.48	4.12×10^{-5}	1.48	1.27×10^{-5}	1.51	8.94×10^{-6}	1.51
	320	1.12×10^{-5}	1.55	7.90×10^{-6}	1.55	2.02×10^{-5}	1.54	1.42×10^{-5}	1.54	4.32×10^{-6}	1.56	3.04×10^{-6}	1.56

Table 5. (Example 2) Temporal convergence order for various α when $h = \frac{1}{2000}$.

$z(t)$	N	$\alpha = 0.2$		$\alpha = 0.5$		$\alpha = 0.8$	
$t^{0.5}$	10	8.7309×10^{-4}	-	5.9471×10^{-3}	-	2.5396×10^{-2}	-
	20	2.7332×10^{-4}	1.68	2.2093×10^{-3}	1.43	1.1397×10^{-2}	1.16
	40	8.3985×10^{-5}	1.70	8.0538×10^{-4}	1.46	5.0256×10^{-3}	1.18
	80	2.5426×10^{-5}	1.72	2.8938×10^{-4}	1.48	2.1831×10^{-3}	1.20
t^2	10	2.0452×10^{-4}	-	1.3063×10^{-3}	-	5.1492×10^{-3}	-
	20	6.5603×10^{-5}	1.64	4.9048×10^{-4}	1.41	2.3170×10^{-3}	1.15
	40	2.0515×10^{-5}	1.68	1.8006×10^{-4}	1.45	1.0227×10^{-3}	1.18
	80	6.2940×10^{-6}	1.70	6.5018×10^{-5}	1.47	4.4443×10^{-4}	1.20

Table 6. (Example 2) Spatial convergence order for various α when $N = 2000$.

$z(t)$	h	$\alpha = 0.2$		$\alpha = 0.5$		$\alpha = 0.8$	
$t^{0.5}$	$\frac{1}{10}$	1.3899×10^{-2}	-	1.3094×10^{-2}	-	1.1890×10^{-2}	-
	$\frac{1}{20}$	3.4684×10^{-3}	2.00	3.2680×10^{-3}	2.00	2.9682×10^{-3}	2.00
	$\frac{1}{40}$	8.6645×10^{-4}	2.00	8.1642×10^{-4}	2.00	7.4155×10^{-4}	2.00
	$\frac{1}{80}$	2.1633×10^{-4}	2.00	2.0384×10^{-4}	2.00	1.8515×10^{-4}	2.00
t^2	$\frac{1}{10}$	1.4330×10^{-2}	-	1.4555×10^{-2}	-	1.4952×10^{-2}	-
	$\frac{1}{20}$	3.5756×10^{-3}	2.00	3.6316×10^{-3}	2.00	3.7304×10^{-3}	2.00
	$\frac{1}{40}$	8.9322×10^{-4}	2.00	9.0719×10^{-4}	2.00	9.3187×10^{-4}	2.00
	$\frac{1}{80}$	2.2301×10^{-4}	2.00	2.2650×10^{-4}	2.00	2.3266×10^{-4}	2.00

5. Conclusions

In this paper, we derive a numerical scheme based on a general temporal mesh for the generalized time-fractional diffusion problem. The main idea involves the generalized linear interpolation. The stability and convergence of the proposed numerical scheme is established rigorously using energy method. More importantly, it is shown that the global convergence order is $O(\tau_{z,\max}^{2-\alpha} + h^2)$ that extends the previous work [9]. For future work, we plan to investigate (i) the validity of the proposed scheme for nonsmooth data; (ii) high order methods based on general temporal mesh and spatial mesh for generalized fractional problems with smooth as well as nonsmooth data. We believe this will make the numerical scheme more applicable in reality.

Author Contributions: Formal analysis, X.L. and P.J.Y.W.; Investigation, X.L. and P.J.Y.W.; writing—original draft, X.L. and P.J.Y.W.; writing—review and editing, X.L. and P.J.Y.W. All authors have read and agreed to the published version of the manuscript.

Funding: This research received no external funding.

Institutional Review Board Statement: Not applicable.

Informed Consent Statement: Not applicable.

Data Availability Statement: Not applicable.

Conflicts of Interest: The authors declare no conflict of interest.

References

1. Diethelm, K. *The Analysis of Fractional Differential Equations*; Springer Science & Business Media: Berlin/Heidelberg, Germany, 2010.
2. Podlubny, I. *Fractional Differential Equations*; Academic Press: San Diego, CA, USA, 1999.
3. Agrawal, O.P. Some generalized fractional calculus operators and their applications in integral equations. *Fract. Calc. Appl. Anal.* **2012**, *15*, 700–711. [CrossRef]

4. Ding, Q.; Wong, P.J.Y. A higher order numerical scheme for generalized fractional diffusion equations. *Int. J. Numer. Methods Fluids* **2020**, *92*, 1866–1889. [CrossRef]
5. Ding, Q.; Wong, P.J.Y. A new approximation for the generalized fractional derivative and its application to generalized fractional diffusion equation. *Numer. Methods Partial Differ. Equ.* **2021**, *37*, 643–673. [CrossRef]
6. Li, X.; Wong, P.J.Y. A gWSGL numerical scheme for generalized fractional sub-diffusion problems. *Commun. Nonlinear Sci. Numer. Simul.* **2020**, *82*, 104991. [CrossRef]
7. Li, X.; Wong, P.J.Y. Generalized Alikhanov's approximation and numerical treatment of generalized fractional sub-diffusion equations. *Commun. Nonlinear Sci. Numer. Simul.* **2021**, *97*, 105719. [CrossRef]
8. Xu, Y.; Agrawal, O.P. Numerical solutions and analysis of diffusion for new generalized fractional Burgers equation. *Fract. Calc. Appl. Anal.* **2013**, *16*, 709–736. [CrossRef]
9. Xu, Y.; He, Z.; Agrawal, O.P. Numerical and analytical solutions of new generalized fractional diffusion equation. *Comput. Math. Appl.* **2013**, *66*, 2019–2029. [CrossRef]
10. Xu, Y.; He, Z.; Xu, Q. Numerical solutions of fractional advection-diffusion equations with a kind of new generalized fractional derivative. *Int. J. Comput. Math.* **2014**, *91*, 588–600. [CrossRef]
11. Alikhanov, A.A. A new difference scheme for the time fractional diffusion equation. *J. Comput. Phys.* **2015**, *280*, 424–438. [CrossRef]
12. Tian, W.; Zhou, H.; Deng, W. A class of second order difference approximations for solving space fractional diffusion equations. *Math. Comp.* **2015**, *84*, 1703–1727. [CrossRef]
13. Liao, H.-L.; Li, D.; Zhang, J. Sharp error estimate of the nonuniform L1 formula for linear reaction-subdiffusion equations. *SIAM J. Numer. Anal.* **2018**, *56*, 1112–1133. [CrossRef]
14. Chen, L. Introduction to Finite Element Methods. Available online: https://www.math.uci.edu/chenlong/226/Ch2FEM.pdf (accessed on 6 February 2022).
15. Li, X.; Wong, P.J.Y. A higher order non-polynomial spline method for fractional sub-diffusion problems. *J. Comput. Phys.* **2017**, *328*, 47–65. [CrossRef]
16. Omrani, K.; Abidi, F.; Achouri, T.; Khiari, N. A new conservative finite difference scheme for the Rosenau equation. *Appl. Math. Comput.* **2008**, *201*, 35–43. [CrossRef]
17. Kopteva, N. Error analysis of the L1 method on graded and uniform meshes for a fractional-derivative problem in two and three dimensions. *Math. Comp.* **2019**, *88*, 2135–2155. [CrossRef]
18. Stynes, M.; O'Riordan, E.; Gracia, J.L. Error analysis of a finite difference method on graded meshes for a time-fractional diffusion equation. *SIAM J. Numer. Anal.* **2017**, *55*, 1057–1079. [CrossRef]
19. Alikhanov, A.A.; Huang, C. A high-order L2 type difference scheme for the time-fractional diffusion equation. *Appl. Math. Comput.* **2021**, *411*, 126545. [CrossRef]

Article

To Solve Forward and Backward Nonlocal Wave Problems with Pascal Bases Automatically Satisfying the Specified Conditions

Chein-Shan Liu [1], Chih-Wen Chang [2], Yung-Wei Chen [3] and Jian-Hung Shen [3,*]

[1] Center of Excellence for Ocean Engineering, National Taiwan Ocean University, Keelung 202301, Taiwan
[2] Department of Mechanical Engineering, National United University, Miaoli 360301, Taiwan
[3] Department of Marine Engineering, National Taiwan Ocean University, Keelung 202301, Taiwan
* Correspondence: 20666006@email.ntou.edu.tw; Tel.: +886-2-24622192 (ext. 7133)

Abstract: In this paper, the numerical solutions of the backward and forward non-homogeneous wave problems are derived to address the nonlocal boundary conditions. When boundary conditions are not set on the boundaries, numerical instability occurs, and the solution may have a significant boundary error. For this reason, it is challenging to solve such nonlinear problems by conventional numerical methods. First, we derive a nonlocal boundary shape function (NLBSF) from incorporating the Pascal triangle as free functions; hence, the new, two-parameter Pascal bases are created to automatically satisfy the specified conditions for the solution. To satisfy the wave equation in the domain by the collocation method, the solution of the forward nonlocal wave problem can be quickly obtained with high precision. For the backward nonlocal wave problem, we construct the corresponding NLBSF and Pascal bases, which exactly implement two final time conditions, a left-boundary condition and a nonlocal boundary condition; in addition, the numerical method for the backward nonlocal wave problem under two-side, nonlocal boundary conditions is also developed. Nine numerical examples, including forward and backward problems, are tested, demonstrating that this scheme is more effective and stable. Even for boundary conditions with a large noise at final time, the solution recovered in the entire domain for the backward nonlocal wave problem is accurate and stable. The accuracy and efficiency of the method are validated by comparing the estimation results with the existing literature.

Keywords: backward nonlocal wave equation; Pascal bases automatically satisfying specified conditions; integral boundary condition; nonlocal boundary shape function

MSC: 35L70

1. Introduction

Integral-type, nonlocal boundary conditions (BCs) are an interesting area of a fast-developing differential equations theory. These problems arise in various fields of physics, mechanics, biology, biotechnology, etc. Nonlocal BCs may come up when the value of the solution on the boundary is connected with the values inside the domain. Theoretical and numerical investigation of this kind of problem is actually valuable, and much attention is given to it in the scientific literature [1–6]. Different, nonlocal BCs are also discussed in partial differential equations (PDEs), for example, Dehghan [7] proposed the numerical solution of several finite difference methods for the one-dimensional, non-classic boundary value problem. Saadatmandi and Dehghan [8] developed a numerical technique based on the shifted Legendre tau technique to demonstrate its validity and applicability for the hyperbolic partial differential equation with an integral condition. Dehghan and Saadatmandi [9] used the variational iteration method for solving the one-dimensional wave equation with classical and integral boundary conditions; this method changed the wave equation with nonlocal BCs into a direct problem. For forward problems, some solutions using theory and numerical methods for the nonlocal problems of the 1D wave equation were studied in [10–12].

As pointed out by Ames and Straughan [13], the backward wave problem has pivotal applications in optimal control theory and geophysics. The backward wave problem is an ill-posed problem, which has been studied in [14–20]. Especially when we consider the backward wave problem under nonlocal boundary conditions, the resulting problem is highly ill-posed, and the numerical method must be designed specifically to overcome the ill-posed property of the backward problem. The idea of a nonlocal boundary shape function (NLBSF) was first developed in [21] to solve the nonlocal, parabolic-type PDE, but has not yet been applied to hyperbolic-type PDE in the literature. We employ the NLBSF to resolve the nonlocal wave problem.

In this paper, we subject the wave equation to an unconventional right-boundary condition which includes an integral term over the spatial domain. In this situation, we encounter a nonlocal wave problem, the solution to which might suffer a large boundary error, since the BC is not given on a boundary. For this reason, it is hard to use the conventional numerical method to tackle this sort of problem. It is important in the field of numerical simulations of nonlocal wave problems to reduce the boundary error so that the error in the entire domain can be reduced. To guarantee the fulfilment of the nonlocal BC, a novel method with the Pascal bases automatically satisfying the specified conditions is pursued in the paper.

Sequentially, the forward wave problem of a one-dimensional wave equation under a nonlocal BC on the right-end is described in Section 2, wherein we construct the so-called NLBSF with the help of the nonlocal shape functions derived. The NLBSF satisfies all the conditions specified for the forward nonlocal wave problem with a free function involved. In Section 3, we develop a numerical method with two-parameter Pascal bases to solve the forward nonlocal wave problem. The bases satisfying all conditions are obtained by taking the Pascal polynomials for the free function. Four testing examples of the forward nonlocal wave problem are presented in Section 4, the high accuracy of which can be appreciated. In Section 5, we develop a numerical method with two-parameter Pascal bases relying on the Pascal polynomials to solve the backward nonlocal wave problem. The bases satisfying all the conditions are specified for the backward nonlocal wave problem. Three testing examples with a large noise being imposed on the final time data of the backward nonlocal wave problem are exhibited in Section 6, the robustness and high accuracy of which can be observed. In Section 7, the method of NLBSF is extended to solve the backward nonlocal wave problem under two-side nonlocal BCs. The conclusions are drawn in Section 8.

2. A Nonlocal Wave Problem

The one-dimensional wave equation is equipped with a nonlocal condition:

$$u_{tt}(x,t) - u_{xx}(x,t) = F(x,t), (x,t) \in \Omega := \left\{ (x,t) \big| 0 < x < l,\ 0 < t \leq t_f \right\}, \quad (1)$$

$$u(x,0) = f(x),\ u_t(x,0) = g(x), \quad (2)$$

$$u(0,t) = p(t),\ \int_0^l u(x,t)dx = q(t), \quad (3)$$

where $f(x)$ and $g(x)$ are initial conditions, $F(x,t)$ is the given function, $q(t)$ and $p(t)$ are boundary conditions and the last condition is different from the conventional boundary condition on the right end. The data $f(x)$, $g(x)$, $q(t)$ and $p(t)$ must satisfy

$$\int_0^l f(x)dx = q(0),\ \int_0^l g(x)dx = \dot{q}(0), \quad (4)$$

$$f(0) = p(0),\ g(0) = \dot{p}(0), \quad (5)$$

which are compatibility conditions derived from Equation (3) with $t = 0$ and Equation (2).

We first derive two main results to satisfy the specified conditions (2) and (3) and then use them to solve Equation (1) to Equation (3).

Theorem 1. *The function*

$$E^0(x,t) = w(x,t) - s_1(x)[w(0,t) - p(t)] - s_2(x)\left[\int_0^l w(x,t)dx - q(t)\right], \tag{6}$$

$\forall\, w(x,t) \in C^1(\Omega)$ *satisfies the conditions in Equation (3), where the nonlocal shape functions*

$$s_1(x) = 1 - \frac{2x}{l}, \quad s_2(x) = 1 - \frac{2x}{l^2} \tag{7}$$

are derived from

$$s_1(0) = 1, \quad \int_0^l s_1(x)dx = 0, \quad s_2(0) = 0, \quad \int_0^l s_2(x)dx = 1. \tag{8}$$

Proof. Inserting $x = 0$ into Equation (6) and taking Equation (8) into account generates

$$\begin{aligned} E^0(0,t) &= w(0,t) - s_1(0)[w(0,t) - p(t)] - s_2(0)\left[\int_0^l w(x,t)dx - q(t)\right] \\ &= w(0,t) - [w(0,t) - p(t)] = p(t). \end{aligned} \tag{9}$$

Then, we prove

$$\int_0^l E^0(x,t)dx = q(t), \tag{10}$$

by inserting Equation (6) for $E^0(x,t)$,

$$\begin{aligned} \int_0^l E^0(x,t)dx &= \int_0^l w(x,t)dx - \int_0^l s_1(x)dx[w(0,t) - p(t)] \\ &\quad - \int_0^l s_2(x)dx\left[\int_0^l w(x,t)dx - q(t)\right], \end{aligned} \tag{11}$$

which, taking Equation (8) into account, yields

$$\int_0^l E^0(x,t)dx = \int_0^l w(x,t)dx - \left[\int_0^l w(x,t)dx - q(t)\right] = q(t). \tag{12}$$

Hence, this theorem is proved. □

Notice that the nonlocal shape functions $s_1(x)$ and $s_2(x)$ were used by Dehghan and Saadatmandi [9] to transform Equation (1) to Equation (3) into a problem with a homogeneous boundary condition and a nonlocal condition for a new variable. Here, we give a different approach.

For $E^0(x,t)$, we have the following compatibility conditions:

$$\int_0^l E^0(x,0)dx = \int_0^l f(x)dx, \quad \int_0^l E_t^0(x,0)dx = \int_0^l g(x)dx. \tag{13}$$

It follows from Equation (12) that

$$\int_0^l E^0(x,0)dx = q(0), \quad \int_0^l E_t^0(x,0)dx = \dot{q}(0). \tag{14}$$

Upon comparing them with Equations (4) and (13), they are verified. It follows from Equations (9) and (5) that

$$E^0(0,0) = p(0) = f(0), \quad E_t^0(0,0) = \dot{p}(0) = g(0). \tag{15}$$

Now, we prove that there exists a function $E(x,t)$ which satisfies the specified conditions (2) and (3).

Theorem 2. *The function*

$$E(x,t) = E^0(x,t) - \left(1-t^2\right)\left[E^0(x,0) - f(x)\right] - t\left[E_t^0(x,0) - g(x)\right] \quad (16)$$

satisfies the conditions (2) and (3).

Proof. We first prove

$$E(x,0) = f(x), \quad E_t(x,0) = g(x). \quad (17)$$

Inserting $t=0$ into Equation (16), we have

$$E(x,0) = E^0(x,0) - \left[E^0(x,0) - f(x)\right] = f(x). \quad (18)$$

Differentiating Equation (16) to t and inserting $t=0$, one has

$$\begin{aligned} E_t(x,0) &= \left\{E_t^0(x,t) + 2t\left[E^0(x,0) - f(x)\right] - \left[E_t^0(x,0) - g(x)\right]\right\}\big|_{t=0} \\ &= E_t^0(x,0) - \left[E_t^0(x,0) - g(x)\right] = g(x). \end{aligned} \quad (19)$$

Then, we prove

$$E(0,t) = p(t), \quad \int_0^l E(x,t)dx = q(t). \quad (20)$$

Inserting $x=0$ into Equation (16) and using Equation (9) and the compatibility conditions $E^0(0,0) = f(0)$ and $E_t^0(0,0) = g(0)$ in Equation (15) yields

$$E(0,t) = E^0(0,t) - \left(1-t^2\right)\left[E^0(0,0) - f(0)\right] - t\left[E_t^0(0,0) - g(0)\right] = E^0(0,t) = p(t). \quad (21)$$

It follows from Equation (16) that

$$\begin{aligned} \int_0^l E(x,t)dx &= \int_0^l E^0(x,t)dx - \left(1-t^2\right)\int_0^l \left[E^0(x,0) - f(x)\right]dx \\ &\quad - t\int_0^l \left[E_t^0(x,0) - g(x)\right]dx, \end{aligned} \quad (22)$$

which, with the aid of Equations (12) and (13), becomes

$$\int_0^l E(x,t)dx = \int_0^l E^0(x,t)dx = q(t). \quad (23)$$

Consequently, this theorem is proved. □

3. Numerical Method for Forward Nonlocal Wave Problem

Let

$$w_{ij}(x,t) := x^{i-j}t^{j-1}, \quad i=1,\ldots, \; j=1,\ldots,i, \quad (24)$$

be the Pascal triangle in terms of x and t [22]. We can reconstruct $w_{ij}(x,t)$ to be the Pascal bases for $u(x,t)$ in Equation (1) to Equation (3) based on Theorem 2.

Theorem 3. *For the Pascal polynomial $w_{ij}(x,t)$ and*

$$E_{ij}^0(x,t) = w_{ij}(x,t) - s_1(x)\left[w_{ij}(0,t) - p(t)\right] - s_2(x)\left[\frac{l^{i-j+1}}{i-j+1}t^{j-1} - q(t)\right], \quad (25)$$

the two-parameter functions

$$E_{ij}(x,t) = E_{ij}^0(x,t) - \left(1-t^2\right)\left[E_{ij}^0(x,0) - f(x)\right] - t\left[E_{ij,t}^0(x,0) - g(x)\right] \quad (26)$$

are Pascal bases to match Equations (2) and (3).

Proof. In Theorem 2, $E(x,t)$ replaced by $E_{ij}(x,t)$ and $E^0(x,t)$ by $E_{ij}^0(x,t)$, inserting $w_{ij}(x,t)$ for $w(x,t)$ into Equation (6) and integrating $\int_0^l x^{i-j}t^{j-1}dx$ out, this theorem is proved. □

The two-parameter functions $E_{ij}(x,t)$ in Equation (26) are called the Pascal bases, which are used to solve the forward nonlocal wave Equation (1) to Equation (3) by

$$u(x,t) = \sum_{j=1}^{m}\sum_{k=1}^{j} a_{jk}s_{jk}E_{jk}(x,t), \quad (27)$$

where a_{jk} are subjected to

$$\sum_{j=1}^{m}\sum_{k=1}^{j} a_{jk} = 1, \quad (28)$$

such that $u(x,t)$ fulfills Equations (2) and (3).

Inserting Equation (27) into Equation (1) and including Equation (28), we determine a_{jk} by

$$\sum_{j=1}^{m}\sum_{k=1}^{j} a_{jk}s_{jk}\left[E_{jk,tt}(x_i,y_j) - E_{jk,xx}(x_i,y_j)\right] = F(x_i,t_j), \quad (29)$$

where n_1 and n_2 are the grid numbers in the spatial and time direction $x_i = i(l/n_1 + 1)$, $t_j = j(t_f/n_2)$ and $N = n_1 \times n_2$. Consequently, the $N+1$ linear Equations (28) and (29) are written as a matrix-vector form:

$$\mathbf{Aa} = \mathbf{b}, \quad (30)$$

where $\mathbf{A}$ is the coefficient matrix, $\mathbf{b}$ is given source term and $\mathbf{a}$ is the vector form of a_{jk}. Let s_k be the kth component of the vectorization of s_{jk} which has multiple scales given in [23] by

$$s_k = \frac{R_0}{\|\mathbf{a}_k\|}, \quad (31)$$

where $\mathbf{a}_k$ denotes the kth column of $\mathbf{A}$, and R_0 is a characteristic length which can increase numerical stability and accuracy. Solving the linear system (30), we can obtain a_{jk} and then $u(x,y)$ is calculated from Equation (27).

4. Examples for Forward Nonlocal Wave Problem

Example 1. *Consider the exact solution as follows:*

$$u(x,t) = x^2 + 2t - 3x^2t - x^4 + \sin(2\pi t). \quad (32)$$

The data $F(x,t), f(x), g(x), q(t)$ and $p(t)$ can be obtained

$$F(x,t) = u_{tt}(x,t) - u_{xx}(x,t) = 12x^2 - 2 + 6t - 4\pi^2\sin(2\pi t), \quad (33)$$

$$\begin{aligned}&f(x) = x^2 - x^4, \quad g(x) = 2 + 2\pi - 3x^2, \\ &p(t) = 2t + \sin(2\pi t), \quad q(t) = \tfrac{l^3}{3} - \tfrac{l^5}{5} + (2l - l^3)t + l\sin(2\pi t).\end{aligned} \quad (34)$$

We take $l = 1$, $t_f = 1$, $m = 5$, $R_0 = 0.1$ and $N = 5 \times 5$. Figure 1 shows an absolute maximum error (ME) of $u(x,t)$ with respect to t. When the convergence criteria $\varepsilon = 10^{-10}$, the total iteration number of the conjugate gradient method (CGM) is 10. Figure 2 displays ME(u) with respect to x at $t_f = 1$. We can observe that the solution is very accurate with ME $= 1.45 \times 10^{-13}$. In paper [24], by using the boundary consistent method for the usual wave equation with the Dirichlet boundary conditions, ME $= 2.01 \times 10^{-8}$ and is much larger than 1.45×10^{-13}. The current solution is much more accurate than that in [24].

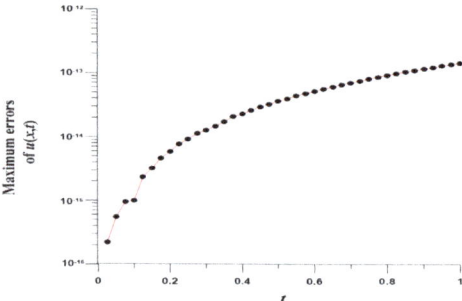

Figure 1. For Example 1: ME(u) versus t.

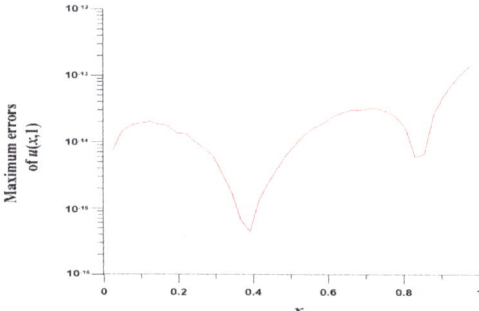

Figure 2. For Example 1: ME(u) versus x at $t_f = 1$.

Example 2. *In order to further display the accuracy of the presented method we consider the exact solution as follows:*

$$u(x,t) = \exp(x + \sin t). \tag{35}$$

Then, $F(x,t), f(x), g(x), q(t)$ and $p(t)$ can be expressed as follows:

$$F(x,t) = u_{tt}(x,t) - u_{xx}(x,t) = \left(\cos^2 t - \sin t - 1\right)\exp(x + \sin t). \tag{36}$$

$$f(x) = g(x) = e^x,$$
$$p(t) = \exp(\sin t), \quad q(t) = \left(e^l - 1\right)\exp(\sin t). \tag{37}$$

We take $l = 1$, $t_f = 1$, $m = 14$, $R_0 = 0.1$ and $N = 12 \times 12$. When the convergence criteria $\varepsilon = 10^{-9}$, the total iteration number of the CGM is 7200, and ME $= 2.93 \times 10^{-8}$. Further, when the iteration number is stopped at the 2000 step, the MEs of $u(x,t)$ are plotted versus t in Figure 3. The ME(u) with respect to x at $t_f = 1$ is shown in Figure 4. Obviously, the solution is quite accurate with ME $= 4.54 \times 10^{-8}$. When considering the same setting as above and $l = 8$, in Figure 5, the solid line displays ME(u) with respect to x, where ME $= 4.56 \times 10^{-1}$, and max $u(x,t)$ is 5689.34. Therefore, the solution of this method is acceptable.

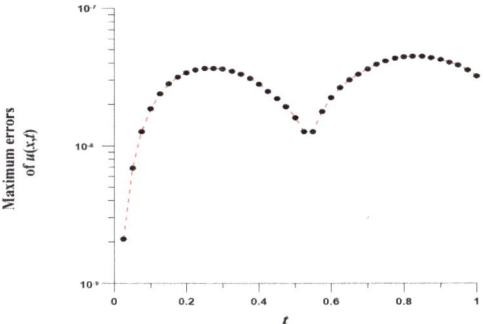

Figure 3. For Example 2: ME(u) versus t in the time interval.

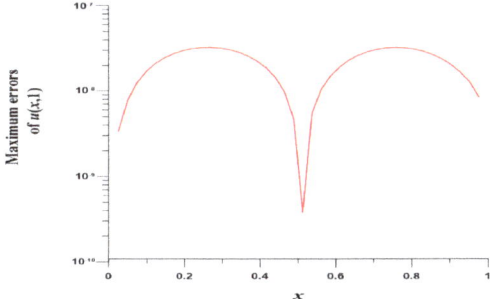

Figure 4. For Example 2 with l = 1: ME(u) versus x at $t_f = 1$.

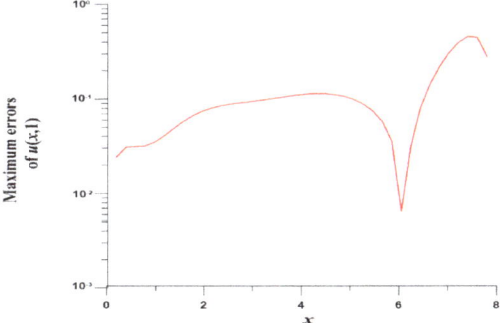

Figure 5. For Example 2 with l = 8: ME(u) versus x at $t_f = 1$.

Example 3 . *This example is for the linear Klein–Gordon equation:*

$$u_{tt}(x,t) - u_{xx}(x,t) + 3u(x,t) = 0, \quad (x,t) \in \Omega. \tag{38}$$

We set the exact solution as follows:

$$u(x,t) = \sin(x - 2t). \tag{39}$$

Then, $f(x)$, $g(x)$, $q(t)$ and $p(t)$ can be expressed as follows:

$$f(x) = \sin x, \quad g(x) = -2\cos x,$$
$$p(t) = -\sin 2t, \quad q(t) = \cos 2t - \cos(l - 2t). \tag{40}$$

We take $l = 1, t_f = 1, m = 11, R_0 = 0.1$ and $N = 20 \times 20$. When convergence criteria $\varepsilon = 10^{-10}$, the total iteration number (TIN) of the CGM is 1221, and ME $= 7.27 \times 10^{-8}$. Further, when the iteration number is at the 1000 step, the MEs of $u(x,t)$ are plotted versus t and x, as shown in Figures 6 and 7. Obviously, the solution is quite accurate with ME $= 5.06 \times 10^{-8}$. For the different convergence criteria, the convergence results are shown in Table 1. Hence, this method can quickly obtain solutions without using higher-order polynomials or strict convergence conditions.

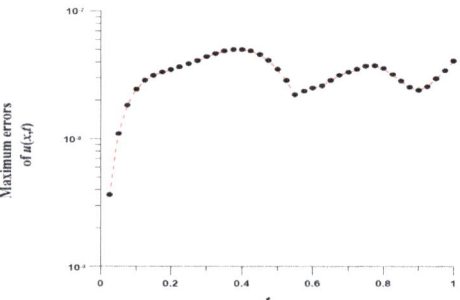

Figure 6. For Example 3: ME(u) versus t in the time interval.

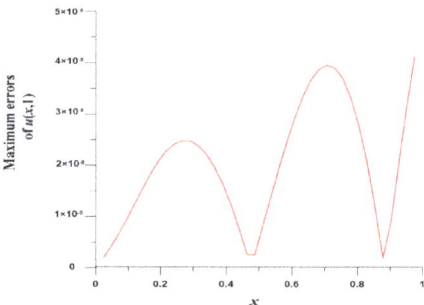

Figure 7. For Example 3: ME(u) versus x at $t_f = 1$.

Table 1. The iteration number and ME under the different convergence criteria.

ε	TIN	ME
10^{-8}	328	1.28×10^{-7}
10^{-10}	1221	7.27×10^{-8}
10^{-12}	9959	7.33×10^{-8}

Example 4. *This example is given in [8];*

$$u(x,t) = \cos(\pi x)\sin(\pi t) \tag{41}$$

is the exact solution.

$$f(x) = 0, \quad g(x) = \pi\cos(\pi x),$$
$$p(t) = \sin(\pi t), \quad q(t) = 0. \tag{42}$$

Instead of the Pascal polynomials, for this example, we take

$$w_{ij}(x,t) = \cos(i\pi x)\sin(j\pi t), \quad 1 \leq i,j \leq m.$$

We take $l = 1$, $t_f = 0.5$, $m = 5$, $R_0 = 1$ and $N = 5 \times 5$. In this case, we use the Gaussian elimination to solve the linear system. Figure 8 displays the MEs of $u(x,t)$ versus t, which are highly accurate with ME $= 7.77 \times 10^{-16}$ and are much more accurate than [8]. Figure 9 displays ME(u) with respect to x at $t_f = 0.5$.

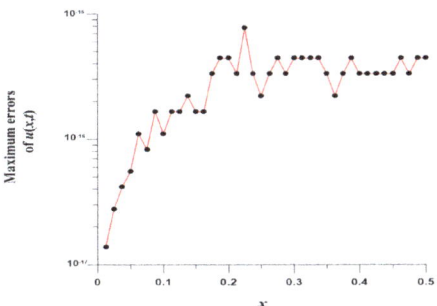

Figure 8. For Example 4: ME(u) versus t in the time interval.

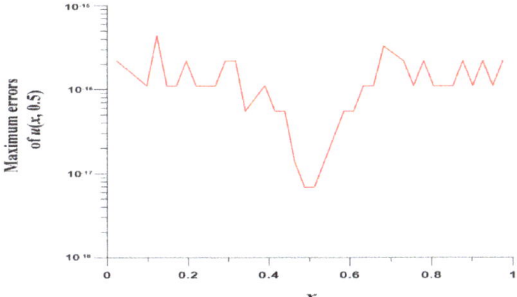

Figure 9. For Example 4: ME(u) versus x at $t_f = 0.5$.

5. Numerical Method for Backward Nonlocal Wave Problem

We consider the backward nonlocal wave problem and replace Equation (2) by the final time conditions:

$$u\left(x,t_f\right) = h(x), \quad u_t\left(x,t_f\right) = r(x). \tag{43}$$

The data $h(x)$, $r(x)$, $q(t)$ and $p(t)$ satisfy

$$\int_0^l h(x)dx = q\left(t_f\right), \quad \int_0^l r(x)dx = \dot{q}\left(t_f\right), \tag{44}$$

$$h(0) = p\left(t_f\right), \quad r(0) = \dot{p}\left(t_f\right), \tag{45}$$

which are available from Equation (3) with $t = t_f$ and using Equation (43).

For the backward nonlocal wave problem, Theorem 2 is modified as follows.

Theorem 4. *The following NLBSF:*

$$E(x,t) = E^0(x,t) - \left[1 + \left(t - t_f\right)^2\right]\left[E^0\left(x,t_f\right) - h(x)\right] - \left(t - t_f\right)\left[E_t^0\left(x,t_f\right) - r(x)\right] \tag{46}$$

satisfies the conditions (43) and (3), where $E^0(x,t)$ is still given by Equation (6).

Proof. Inserting $t = t_f$ into Equation (46), we have

$$E(x, t_f) = E^0(x, t_f) - \left[E^0(x, t_f) - h(x)\right] = h(x). \tag{47}$$

Differentiating Equation (46) to t and inserting $t = t_f$, one has

$$\begin{aligned} E_t(x, t_f) &= \left\{ E_t^0(x,t) - 2(t-t_f)\left[E^0(x,t_f) - h(x)\right] - \left[E_t^0(x,t_f) - r(x)\right]\right\}\Big|_{t=t_f} \\ &= E_t^0(x,t_f) - \left[E_t^0(x,t_f) - r(x)\right] = r(x). \end{aligned} \tag{48}$$

Next, we prove the compatibility conditions for $E^0(x,t)$:

$$\int_0^l E^0(x,t_f)dx = \int_0^l h(x)dx, \quad \int_0^l E_t^0(x,t_f)dx = \int_0^l r(x)dx, \tag{49}$$

It follows from Equation (12) that

$$\int_0^l E^0(x,t_f)dx = q(t_f), \quad \int_0^l E_t^0(x,t_f)dx = \dot{q}(t_f). \tag{50}$$

Upon comparing them to Equation (44), we can derive Equation (49). Similarly, it follows from Equations (9) and (45) that

$$E^0(0,t_f) = p(t_f) = h(0), \quad E_t^0(0,t_f) = \dot{p}(t_f) = r(0). \tag{51}$$

Finally, we prove that $E(x,t)$ satisfies

$$E(0,t) = p(t), \quad \int_0^l E(x,t)dx = q(t). \tag{52}$$

Inserting $x = 0$ into Equation (46) and using Equation (9) and the compatibility conditions $E^0(0, t_f) = h(0)$ and $E_t^0(0, t_f) = r(0)$ in Equation (51), one has

$$\begin{aligned} E(0,t) &= E^0(0,t) - \left[1 + (t-t_f)^2\right]\left[E^0(0,t_f) - h(0)\right] - (t-t_f)\left[E_t^0(0,t_f) - r(0)\right] \\ &= E^0(0,t) = p(t). \end{aligned} \tag{53}$$

From Equation (46) it follows that

$$\begin{aligned} \int_0^l E(x,t)dx = \int_0^l E^0(x,t)dx &- \left[1 + (t-t_f)^2\right]\int_0^l \left[E^0(x,t_f) - h(x)\right]dx \\ &- (t-t_f)\int_0^l \left[E_t^0(x,t_f) - r(x)\right]dx, \end{aligned} \tag{54}$$

which, with the aid of Equations (12) and (49), becomes

$$\int_0^l E(x,t)dx = \int_0^l E^0(x,t)dx = q(t). \tag{55}$$

The proof is ended. □

Replacing $E(x,t)$ and $E^0(x,t)$ in Theorem 4 by $E_{ij}(x,t)$ and $E_{ij}^0(x,t)$, respectively, Theorem 3 is still applicable for the backward nonlocal wave problem but with

$$E_{ij}(x,t) = E_{ij}^0(x,t) - \left[1 + \left(t - t_f\right)^2\right]\left[E_{ij}^0\left(x, t_f\right) - h(x)\right] - \left(t - t_f\right)\left[E_{ij,t}^0\left(x, t_f\right) - r(x)\right], \quad (56)$$

which automatically satisfies the conditions (43) and (3),

To solve the backward nonlocal wave problem in Equations (1), (43) and (3), we take

$$u(x,t) = \sum_{j=1}^{m}\sum_{k=1}^{j} c_{jk}s_{jk}E_{jk}(x,t), \quad (57)$$

where

$$\sum_{j=1}^{m}\sum_{k=1}^{j} c_{jk} = 1. \quad (58)$$

Other procedures are similar to that in Section 3.

6. Numerical Examples for Backward Nonlocal Wave Problem

To test the backward nonlocal wave problem, we add a noise s on

$$\hat{h}(x) = h(x) + sR, \quad \hat{r}(x) = r(x) + sR, \quad (59)$$

where R is a random number. We fix $s = 0.1$ for all testing examples given below.

Example 5. *For Example 1, we consider the final time conditions:*

$$h(x) = x^2 + \left(2 - 3x^2\right)t_f - x^4 + \sin\left(2\pi t_f\right), \quad r(x) = 2 - 3x^2 + 2\pi\cos\left(2\pi t_f\right). \quad (60)$$

If no noise is added, i.e., $s = 0$ under $l = 1$, $t_f = 1$, $m = 5$, $R_0 = 0.1$, TIN = 500 and $N = 10 \times 10$, $u(x,t)$ is very accurate with ME $= 9.14 \times 10^{-13}$, which is slightly worse than 1.45×10^{-13} for the forward wave problem, as presented in Example 1.

Under $l = 1$, $t_f = 1$, $m = 5$, $R_0 = 0.1$, TIN = 500 and $N = 5 \times 5$, the solution is obtained very quickly. In Figure 10, the dashed line shows the ME of $u(x,t)$ with respect to x, of which ME $= 3.04 \times 10^{-3}$, where max $u(x,t)$ is 1.9988. Then, we take $t_f = 10$ and $N = 20 \times 20$, and other parameters remain the same. In Figure 10, the solid line displays ME(u) with respect to x, where ME $= 4.81 \times 10^{-3}$, and max $u(x,t)$ is 19.98. Hence, the method can obtain a stable and accurate solution with $O\left(10^{-3}\right)$ even for the final time with noise disturbance.

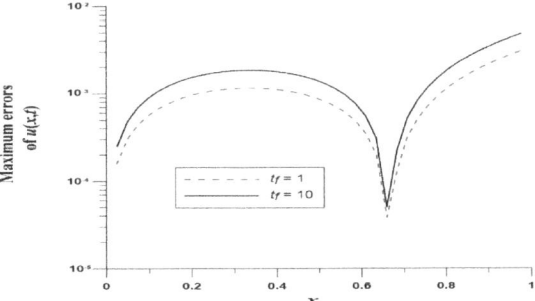

Figure 10. For Example 5 of the backward nonlocal wave problem: ME(u) versus x with different final times.

Example 6. *Then, we consider*

$$h(x) = \exp(x + \sin t_f), \quad r(x) = \cos t_f \exp(x + \sin t_f). \quad (61)$$

Other data are given in Example 2.

We take $l = 2$, $t_f = 3$, $m = 12$, $R_0 = 0.1$, TIN = 2000 and $N = 15 \times 15$. In Figure 11, the MEs of $u(x,t)$ are plotted versus x. Although under a large noise with $s = 0.1$, the solution is with ME $= 3.29 \times 10^{-2}$, where max $u(x,t)$ is 19.13.

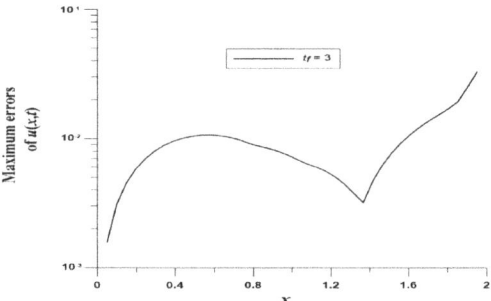

Figure 11. For Example 6 of the backward nonlocal wave problem: ME(u) versus x in the spatial interval.

Example 7. *According to Example 3, we consider the backward nonlocal wave problem for the linear Klein–Gordon equation with the final time data:*

$$h(x) = \sin(x - 2t_f), \quad r(x) = -2\cos\left(x - 2t_f\right). \quad (62)$$

Under $l = 1$, $t_f = 2$, $m = 15$, $R_0 = 0.1$, TIN = 2000 and $N = 15 \times 15$, in Figure 12, the solid line displays the ME of $u(x,t)$ with respect to x, of which ME $= 4.03 \times 10^{-3}$, and max $u(x,t)$ is 1. Then, we take $t_f = 4$ and $N = 25 \times 25$, and other parameters remain the same. In Figure 12, the dashed line shows ME(u) with respect to x, where ME $= 2.73 \times 10^{-3}$.

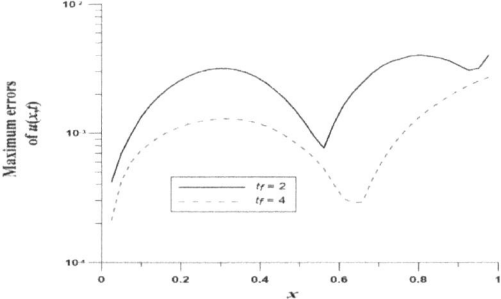

Figure 12. For Example 7 of the backward nonlocal wave problem of the Klein–Gordon equation: ME(u) versus x with different final times.

When we extend the domain to $l = 3$ and $t_f = 4$, ME increases to 8.52×10^{-2}. However, we can take $R_0 = 0.001$ and $N = 30 \times 30$ and reduce ME to 6.16×10^{-2}. Therefore, it can be seen that increasing the grid number N and decreasing the characteristic length R_0 can increase the numerical accuracy.

7. Complex Two-Side Nonlocal BCs

The method presented in Section 5 is easily tailored to account for the backward nonlocal wave problem under complex two-side, nonlocal BCs:

$$u_{tt}(x,t) - u_{xx}(x,t) = F(x,t), \quad (x,t) \in \Omega, \tag{63}$$

$$u\left(x, t_f\right) = h(x), \quad u_t\left(x, t_f\right) = r(x), \tag{64}$$

$$a_1 u(0,t) + a_2 u_x(0,t) + \int_0^l a_3(x) u(x,t) dx = p(t), \tag{65}$$

$$b_1 u(l,t) + b_2 u_x(l,t) + \int_0^l b_3(x) u(x,t) dx = q(t). \tag{66}$$

The key function $E^0(x,t)$ in Theorem 1 is modified to

$$\begin{aligned}E^0(x,t) = w(x,t) &- s_1(x)\left[a_1 w(0,t) + a_2 w_x(0,t) + \int_0^l a_3(x) w(x,t) dx - p(t)\right] \\ &- s_2(x)\left[b_1 w(l,t) + b_2 w_x(l,t) + \int_0^l b_3(x) w(x,t) dx - q(t)\right],\end{aligned} \tag{67}$$

where the nonlocal shape functions are derived from

$$\begin{aligned} a_1 s_1(0) + a_2 s_1'(0) + \int_0^l a_3(x) s_1(x) dx = 1, \\ b_1 s_1(l) + b_2 s_1'(l) + \int_0^l b_3(x) s_1(x) dx = 0, \end{aligned} \tag{68}$$

$$\begin{aligned} a_1 s_2(0) + a_2 s_2'(0) + \int_0^l a_3(x) s_2(x) dx = 0, \\ b_1 s_2(l) + b_2 s_2'(l) + \int_0^l b_3(x) s_2(x) dx = 1. \end{aligned} \tag{69}$$

Inserting Equation (67) and $w(x,t) = x^{i-j} t^{j-1}$ into Equation (46), we can generate the Pascal bases

$$E_{ij}(x,t) = E^0(x,t) - \left[1 + \left(t - t_f\right)^2\right]\left[E^0\left(x, t_f\right) - h(x)\right] - \left(t - t_f\right)\left[E_t^0\left(x, t_f\right) - r(x)\right], \tag{70}$$

$$\begin{aligned}E^0(x,t) = x^{i-j} t^{j-1} &- s_1(x)\left[a_1 x^{i-j} t^{j-1}\big|_{x=0} + a_2(i-j) x^{i-j-1} t^{j-1}\big|_{x=0}\right] \\ &- s_1(x)\left[\int_0^l a_3(x) x^{i-j} t^{j-1} dx - p(t)\right] \\ &- s_2(x)\left[b_1 x^{i-j} t^{j-1}\big|_{x=l} + b_2(i-j) x^{i-j-1} t^{j-1}\big|_{x=l} + \int_0^l b_3(x) x^{i-j} t^{j-1} dx - q(t)\right].\end{aligned} \tag{71}$$

Example 8. *As an extension of Example 7, we consider the backward nonlocal wave problem for the linear Klein–Gordon equation with the final time data and two-side nonlocal BCs:*

$$h(x) = \sin\left(x - 2t_f\right), \quad r(x) = -2\cos\left(x - 2t_f\right), \tag{72}$$

$$u(0,t) + u_x(0,t) + \int_0^l u(x,t) dx = p(t), \quad u(l,t) + \int_0^l x u(x,t) dx = q(t), \tag{73}$$

where

$$p(t) = (2 - \cos l)\cos(2t) - (1 + \sin l)\sin(2t), \tag{74}$$

$$q(t) = \sin(l - 2t) + (\sin l - l \cos l)\cos(2t) + (1 - \cos l - l \sin l)\sin(2t). \tag{75}$$

For this problem, we can derive

$$s_1(x) = \frac{12l + 4l^3 - (12 + 6l^2)x}{l^4 + 4l^3 + 12l - 12}, \quad s_2(x) = \frac{12(1+l)x - 12 + 6l^2}{l^4 + 4l^3 + 12l - 12}. \tag{76}$$

Under $l = 4, t_f = 1$, $m = 20, R_0 = 1$, TIN = 2000 and $N = 30 \times 30$, in Figure 13, the solid line displays ME(u) with respect to x, of which ME $= 2.36 \times 10^{-3}$. If $t_f = 2$, we obtain ME $= 7.02 \times 10^{-3}$, the results of which are shown in Figure 13 by a dashed line. As the figure shows, this method still yields a stable solution even if the computation time increases.

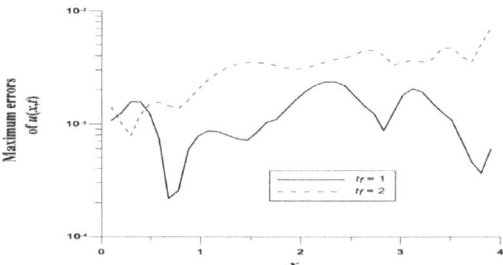

Figure 13. For Example 8 of the backward nonlocal wave problem of the Klein–Gordon equation under two-side nonlocal BCs: ME(u) versus x with different final times.

Example 9. Let
$$u_{tt}(x,t) - u_{xx}(x,t) - 3u(x,t) = 0, \quad (x,t) \in \Omega, \tag{77}$$

$$h(x) = \exp\left(x - 2t_f\right), \quad r(x) = -2\exp\left(x - 2t_f\right), \tag{78}$$

$$u(0,t) - u_x(0,t) + \int_0^l xu(x,t)dx = p(t), \quad u_x(l,t) + \int_0^l u(x,t)dx = q(t), \tag{79}$$

where
$$p(t) = e^{-2t}\left(le^l - e^l + 1\right), \quad q(t) = e^{-2t}\left(2e^l - 1\right), \tag{80}$$

and $u(x,t) = \exp(x - 2t)$ is the exact solution.

For this problem, we can derive
$$s_1(x) = \frac{12 + 6l^2 - 12lx}{12 + 18l + 6l^2 - l^3}, \quad s_2(x) = \frac{12 - 4l^2 + (12 + 6l)x}{12 + 18l + 6l^2 - l^3}. \tag{81}$$

Under $l = 3$, $m = 10$, $R_0 = 1$, TIN = 2000 and $N = 20 \times 20$, in Figure 14, the solid line displays ME(u) with respect to x for $t_f = 0.5$, of which ME $= 3.92 \times 10^{-3}$, and the dashed line displays ME(u) with respect to x for $t_f = 1$, of which ME $= 4.94 \times 10^{-2}$. Notice max(u) = 17.76. When considering $m = 20$, $l = 5$ and $t_f = 1$, ME(u) with respect to x is shown in Figure 15, where ME $= 3.292 \times 10^{-1}$, and max $u(x,t)$ is 124.97. The result shows that the solution of this method is acceptable. Hence, we successfully apply the NLBSF to resolve the wave problem with two-side nonlocal BCs, especially for the backward problem in time.

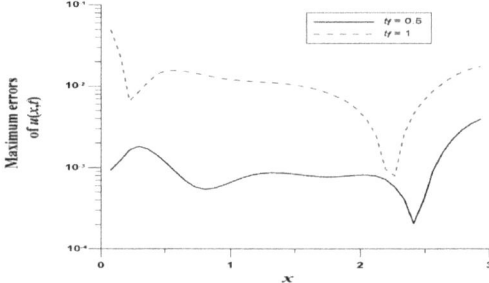

Figure 14. For Example 9 of the backward nonlocal wave problem under two-side nonlocal BCs: ME(u) versus x with different final times.

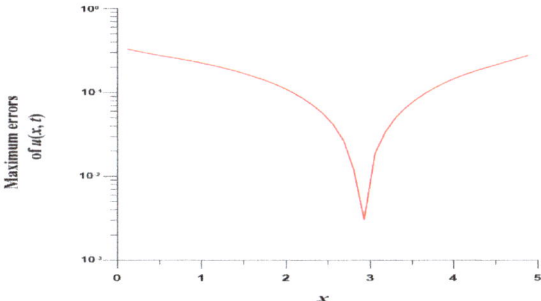

Figure 15. For Example 9 of the backward nonlocal wave problem under two-side nonlocal BCs: ME(u) versus x in the spatial interval.

8. Conclusions

In this paper, the numerical solutions of the backward and forward non-homogeneous wave problems with nonlocal boundary conditions were developed. When boundary conditions are not set on the boundaries, the solution may have a large boundary error. For this reason, it is difficult to solve such nonlinear problems by conventional numerical methods, especially when addressing the backward nonlocal wave problem. To reduce the boundary error and increase numerical accuracy by the NLBSF method, we let the free function be the Pascal triangle and then the solution was a weighted superposition of the complete Pascal bases. These basis functions automatically satisfy a left-boundary condition, a nonlocal right-boundary condition and two initial conditions for the forward nonlocal wave problem or two final time conditions for the backward nonlocal wave problem. We gave four examples for the forward nonlocal wave problem to support that the nonlocal wave equation can be solved quickly and accurately. For the backward nonlocal wave problem with one-side or two-side nonlocal boundary conditions, we recovered accurate solutions in the entire domain; even a large time span and large noise were taken into account. From the nine examples, the results demonstrate that the presented method is more effective and stable than conventional numerical schemes. Hence, it can be concluded that the proposed method for the forward or backward problems in time is accurate, stable, effective and robust for addressing boundary conditions with noise level effects.

Author Contributions: C.-S.L. contributed to the conception and supervision of the work (conceptualization, resources, methodology, writing—original draft), collected and analyzed the data and interpreted the results. C.-W.C. contributed to the conception of the work (project administration, software). Y.-W.C. contributed to the writing, design and validation of the work (writing—editing, validating and visualizing the data) and the funding acquisition. J.-H.S. contributed to the writing and supervision of the work (writing—review and editing, software, project administration). All authors have read and agreed to the published version of the manuscript.

Funding: The third authors would like to thank the Ministry of Science and Technology, Taiwan, for their financial support (grant number MOST 111-2221-E-019-048).

Institutional Review Board Statement: Not applicable.

Informed Consent Statement: Not applicable.

Data Availability Statement: Not applicable.

Conflicts of Interest: The authors declare that there are no conflict of interest regarding the publication of this paper.

References

1. Goodrich, C.S. On a nonlocal BVP with nonlinear boundary conditions. *Results Math.* **2013**, *63*, 1351–1364. [CrossRef]
2. Webb, J.R.L.; Infante, G. Positive solutions of nonlocal boundary value problems involving integral conditions. *NoDEA-Nonlinear Differ. Equ. Appl.* **2008**, *15*, 45–67. [CrossRef]

3. Ahmad, B.; Alsaedi, A.; Alghamdi, B.S. Analytic approximation of solutions of the forced Duffing equation with integral boundary conditions. *Nonlinear Anal. Real World Appl.* **2008**, *9*, 1727–1740. [CrossRef]
4. Boucherif, A. Second-order boundary value problems with integral boundary conditions. *Nonlinear Anal. Theory Methods Appl.* **2009**, *70*, 364–371. [CrossRef]
5. Dehghan, M. Numerical solution of a non-local boundary value problem with Neumann's boundary conditions. *Commun. Numer. Methods Eng.* **2003**, *19*, 1–12. [CrossRef]
6. Chen, Z.; Jiang, W.; Du, H. A new reproducing kernel method for Duffing equations. *Int. J. Comput. Math.* **2021**, *98*, 2341–2354. [CrossRef]
7. Dehghan, M. On the solution of an initial-boundary value problem that combines Neumann and integral condition for the wave equation. *Numer. Meth. Part Differ. Equ.* **2005**, *21*, 24–40. [CrossRef]
8. Saadatmandi, A.; Dehghan, M. Numerical solution of the one-dimensional wave equation with an integral condition. *Numer. Meth. Part Differ. Equ.* **2007**, *23*, 282–292. [CrossRef]
9. Dehghan, M.; Saadatmandi, A. Variational iteration method for solving the wave equation subject to an integral conservation condition. *Chaos Solitons Fractals* **2009**, *41*, 1448–1453. [CrossRef]
10. Beilin, S.A. Existence of solutions for one-dimensional wave equations with nonlocal conditions. *Electron. J. Differ. Equ.* **2001**, *76*, 1–8.
11. Pulkina, L.S. A nonlocal problem with integral conditions for hyperbolic equations. *Electron. J. Differ. Equ.* **1999**, *45*, 1–8. [CrossRef]
12. Gordeziani, D.G.; Avalishvili, G.A. On the constructing of solutions of the nonlocal initial boundary value problems for one-dimensional medium oscillation equations. *Mat. Modelirovanie* **2000**, *12*, 94–103.
13. Ames, K.A.; Straughan, B. *Non-Standard and Improperly Posed Problems*; Academic Press: New York, NY, USA, 1997.
14. Dunninger, D.R.; Zachmanoglou, E.C. The condition for uniqueness of solutions of the Dirichlet problem for the wave equation in coordinate rectangles. *J. Math. Anal. Appl.* **1967**, *20*, 17–21. [CrossRef]
15. Abdul-Latif, A.I.; Diaz, J.B. Dirichlet, Neumann, and mixed boundary value problems for the wave equation $u_{xx} - u_{yy} = 0$ for a rectangle. *Appl. Anal.* **1971**, *1*, 1–12. [CrossRef]
16. Papi Frosali, G. On the stability of the Dirichlet problem for the vibrating string equation. *Ann. Sc. Norm. Super. Pisa—Cl. Sci.* **1979**, *6*, 719–728.
17. Levine, H.A.; Vessella, S.; Payne, L.E. Stabilization and regularization for solutions of an ill posed problem for the wave equation. *Math. Meth. Appl. Sci.* **1985**, *7*, 202–209. [CrossRef]
18. Vakhania, N.N. On boundary value problems for the hyperbolic case. *J. Complex.* **1994**, *10*, 341–355. [CrossRef]
19. Kabanikhin, S.I.; Bektemesov, M.A.; Nurseitov, D.B.; Krivorotko, O.I.; Alimova, A.N. An optimization method in the Dirichlet problem for the wave equation. *J. Inverse Ill-Posed Probl.* **2012**, *20*, 193–211. [CrossRef]
20. Lesnic, D. The decomposition method for forward and backward time-dependent problems. *J. Comput. Appl. Math.* **2002**, *147*, 27–39. [CrossRef]
21. Liu, C.S.; Chang, J.R. Solving a nonlinear heat equation with nonlocal boundary conditions by a method of nonlocal boundary shape functions. *Numer. Heat Tranf. B-Fundam.* **2021**, *80*, 1–13. [CrossRef]
22. Liu, C.S.; Young, D.L. A multiple-scale Pascal polynomial for 2D Stokes and inverse Cauchy–Stokes problems. *J. Comput. Phys.* **2016**, *312*, 1–13. [CrossRef]
23. Liu, C.S. A two-side equilibration method to reduce the condition number of an ill-posed linear system. *CMES-Comp. Model. Eng. Sci.* **2013**, *91*, 17–42.
24. Liu, C.S.; Wang, F. Overcoming the near boundary error in the solution of non-homogeneous wave equation by a boundary consistent method. *Eur. Phys. J. Plus.* **2020**, *135*, 5. [CrossRef]

Article

Parameter Uniform Numerical Method for Singularly Perturbed 2D Parabolic PDE with Shift in Space

V. Subburayan [1] and S. Natesan [2,*]

[1] Department of Mathematics, College of Engineering and Technology, SRM Institute of Science and Technology, Kattankulathur 603203, Tamilnadu, India
[2] Department of Mathematics, Indian Institute of Technology, Guwahati 781039, Assam, India
* Correspondence: natesan@iitg.ac.in

Abstract: Singularly perturbed 2D parabolic delay differential equations with the discontinuous source term and convection coefficient are taken into consideration in this paper. For the time derivative, we use the fractional implicit Euler method, followed by the fitted finite difference method with bilinear interpolation for locally one-dimensional problems. The proposed method is shown to be almost first-order convergent in the spatial direction and first-order convergent in the temporal direction. Theoretical results are illustrated with numerical examples.

Keywords: delay differential equations; 2D parabolic equations; fractional step method; convection diffusion problems

MSC: 34K26; 35B25; 65M22; 65M50; 65N22

Citation: Subburayan, V.; Natesan, S. Parameter Uniform Numerical Method for Singularly Perturbed 2D Parabolic PDE with Shift in Space. *Mathematics* **2022**, *10*, 3310. https://doi.org/10.3390/math10183310

Academic Editors: Patricia J. Y. Wong and Luigi Rodino

Received: 10 August 2022
Accepted: 8 September 2022
Published: 12 September 2022

Publisher's Note: MDPI stays neutral with regard to jurisdictional claims in published maps and institutional affiliations.

Copyright: © 2022 by the authors. Licensee MDPI, Basel, Switzerland. This article is an open access article distributed under the terms and conditions of the Creative Commons Attribution (CC BY) license (https://creativecommons.org/licenses/by/4.0/).

1. Introduction

Differential equations with small or large parameters can be used to describe a variety of applied practical problems, including the theory of boundary layers. For example, the shock waves occurring in gas motions, edge effects when elastic plates deform, etc. These mathematical problems are very difficult (or even impossible) to solve exactly, so approximate solutions are necessary. It is possible to obtain an approximation of the solution through perturbation methods. Basically, these methods aim to solve a simpler problem (as a first approximation) and systematically improve the approximate solution.

When using finite difference or finite element methods on equally spaced grids and allowing the perturbation parameter tend to zero, boundary layers produce inaccurate numerical solutions. The most popular method for overcoming this difficulty is to construct uniformly valid numerical methods on layers adapted to the mesh. There are several uniformly valid methods available in the literature, for instance, to cite a few (see Refs. [1,2] and the references therein). As pointed out in Ref. [3], the direct discretization of the singularly perturbed 2D parabolic differential equations leads to a pentadiagonal linear system of equations. This problem is exceedingly complex to solve computationally. We use the fractional step method in order to reduce the computation cost. At each time level, the fractional step method leads to the tridiagonal system of algebraic equations. Several types of research have been conducted recently on the fractional step method, such as Refs. [4–6] and the references therein.

Singularly perturbed delay differential equations (SPDDEs) are a class of perturbation problems with at least one delay or deviating argument. This type of problem occurs frequently in the modelling of various types of physical and biological problems. For example, the neuronal variability and its theoretical analysis have been modelled as delay parabolic equations [7,8]. Asymptotic analyses for 1D stationery SPDDEs have been well studied by Lange and Miura [9]. Several numerical methods for SPDDEs of 1D stationery problems have been reported in the literature, such as Refs. [10–13] and the reference therein. The numerical method for 1D parabolic equations was initiated by Ref. [14] and it gained the interest of many researchers. Das and Natesan [15] presented computing techniques for solving 2D time SPDDEs. Ref. [16] presented some applications and existence results for partial delay differential equations. The modelling of option pricing, to generalize the celebrated Black–Scholes equation with suitable weight, led to the 2D parabolic differential equations with space shift [17]. We consider discontinuous convection and source terms in 2D parabolic SPDDEs in this article, as mentioned in the abstract. This problem exhibits interior layers at $x = d_x$ and $y = d_y$ and, due to the presents of the shift in space, the boundary layers occurs at $x = 1$ and $y = 1$. The existence results pertaining to the parabolic equation with discontinuous coefficients are addressed in Ref. [18]. The method presented in this article is a combination of the layers adopted technique and linear interpolations. The interpolation term takes care of the delay arguments. The proposed method is validated theoretically and numerically to be uniformly convergent in both space and time by considering some numerical examples.

The constant C is generic positive, that is, it is independent of the perturbation parameter as well as the discretization parameters N and M throughout the paper. For convenience, it is assumed that the number of mesh points in the spatial domains Ω_x and Ω_y are same, that is, N and the index set $\mathcal{I}_{N_0} = \{1, 2, 3, \cdots, N_0\}$ for any positive integer N_0. It is conventional to assume for the convection coefficient problem that $\varepsilon \leq CN^{-1}$ for practical purposes. Further, to measure the error bounds and derivative bounds, we use the following norm $\|\psi\|_D = \sup_{\mathbf{x} \in D} \|\psi(\mathbf{x})\|$, $\mathbf{x} = (x, y)$.

The article is organized as follows: the problem is considered in Section 2. The fractional implicit Euler method for time derivative and locally 1D problems are presented in Section 3. In the same section, the stability results and derivative estimates of the locally one-dimensional problems are presented. Section 4 presents the numerical method for the considered problem. The discretizations incurred by the errors are estimated in Section 5. Numerical validations through some test example problems are done in Section 6. Finally, in Section 7, some concluding remarks are made.

2. Statement of Continuous Problem

Motivated by the works of Refs. [7,17], we consider the following two-dimensional singularly perturbed parabolic differential equations: We find u such that

$$\mathfrak{L}u := u_t - \varepsilon \Delta u + \nabla u \cdot \bar{p}(\mathbf{x}) + q(\mathbf{x})u(\mathbf{x} - \mathbf{d}, t) = g(\mathbf{x}, t), \ (\mathbf{x}, t) \in \mathfrak{D}^* \times (0, T], \quad (1)$$

$$u(\mathbf{x}, 0) = u_0(\mathbf{x}), \ \mathbf{x} \in \mathfrak{D}, \quad (2)$$

$$u(\mathbf{x}, t) = 0, \text{ on } \partial \mathfrak{D} \times [0, T], \quad (3)$$

$$u(\mathbf{x}, t) = 0, \text{ on } [-d_x, 0] \times [-d_y, 1] \times [0, T] \cup [-d_x, 1] \times [-d_y, 0] \times [0, T], \quad (4)$$

where $\mathbf{x} = (x, y)$, $\mathbf{d} = (d_x, d_y)$, $\Omega_x = (0, 1) = \Omega_y$, $\mathfrak{D} = \Omega_x \times \Omega_y$, $\mathfrak{D}^* = \Omega_x^* \times \Omega_y^*$, $\Omega_\nu^* = \Omega_\nu^- \cup \Omega_\nu^+$, $\Omega_\nu^- = (0, d_\nu)$, $\Omega_\nu^+ = (d_\nu, 1)$, $\nu = x, y$, the functions u_0, q are sufficiently differentiable and bonded on $\overline{\mathfrak{D}}$, p_1, p_2, g_1, g_2 are sufficiently differentiable and bounded on their respective domains $\mathfrak{D}^*$, $\mathfrak{D}^* \times [0, T]$. In addition, we assume that,

$u_x(d_x^-, y, t) = u_x(d_x^+, y, t)$, $u_y(x, d_y^-, t) = u_y(x, d_y^+, t)$,

$\bar{p}(\mathbf{x}) = (p_1(\mathbf{x}), p_2(\mathbf{x}))^T$, $\nabla u = (u_x, u_y)$,

$p_1^+ \geq p_1(\mathbf{x}) \geq p_1^- > 0$, $\mathbf{x} \in \Omega_x^- \times \Omega_y^*$, $p_1^+ \geq -p_1(\mathbf{x}) \geq p_1^- > 0$, $\mathbf{x} \in \Omega_x^+ \times \Omega_y^*$,

$p_2^+ \geq p_2(\mathbf{x}) \geq p_2^- > 0$, $\mathbf{x} \in \Omega_x^* \times \Omega_y^-$, $p_2^+ \geq -p_2(\mathbf{x}) \geq p_2^- > 0$, $\mathbf{x} \in \Omega_x^* \times \Omega_y^+$,

$|p_1(d_x^-, y) - p_1(d_x^+, y)| < \infty$, $|p_2(x, d_y^-) - p_2(x, d_y^+)| < \infty$,

$q(\mathbf{x}) = q_1(\mathbf{x}) + q_2(\mathbf{x})$, $0 \geq q_1, q_2 \geq \beta$, $g(\mathbf{x}, t) = g_1(\mathbf{x}, t) + g_2(\mathbf{x}, t)$.

Let $\mathcal{L}_x := -\varepsilon\frac{\partial^2}{\partial x^2} + p_1(\mathbf{x})\frac{\partial}{\partial x} + q_1(\mathbf{x})I_\mathbf{d}$ and $\mathcal{L}_y := -\varepsilon\frac{\partial^2}{\partial y^2} + p_2(\mathbf{x})\frac{\partial}{\partial y} + q_2(\mathbf{x})I_\mathbf{d}$ be two differential operators, $I_\mathbf{d} u(\mathbf{x}, t) = u(\mathbf{x} - \mathbf{d}, t)$, then the differential operator $\mathcal{L}$ defined in (1) can be written as $\mathcal{L} := \frac{\partial}{\partial t} + \mathcal{L}_x + \mathcal{L}_y$.

3. Time Domain Discretization and Stability Analysis

3.1. Discretization of Time Domain

The time domain $[0, T]$ is discretized uniformly with step length $h_t = T/M$, where M is a positive integer. Then we have the uniform mesh in the temporal direction $\overline{\Omega}_t^M = \{t_k = k \times h_t\}_{k=0}^M$.

3.2. An Alternating Direction Implicit Method

Let us assume that $\hat{u}^0(\mathbf{x}) = u_0(\mathbf{x})$, $\mathbf{x} \in \overline{\mathcal{D}}$. Now, we discretize the IBVP (1)–(3) using the fractional implicit Euler method and obtain the following semidiscrete scheme on the time levels $n = 0, 1, \cdots, M - 1$:

let $y \in \Omega_y$, then

$$\begin{cases} \mathcal{D}_x \hat{u}^{n+\frac{1}{2}} = \hat{u}^n + h_t g_1(x, y, t_{n+1}), \; x \in \Omega_x^*, \\ \hat{u}^{n+\frac{1}{2}}(0, y) = 0 = \hat{u}^{n+\frac{1}{2}}(1, y), \\ \hat{u}_x^{n+\frac{1}{2}}(d_x^-, y) = \hat{u}_x^{n+\frac{1}{2}}(d_x^+, y), \end{cases} \quad (5)$$

let $x \in \Omega_x$, then

$$\begin{cases} \mathcal{D}_y \hat{u}^{n+1} = \hat{u}^{n+\frac{1}{2}} + h_t g_2(x, y, t_{n+1}), \; y \in \Omega_y^* \\ \hat{u}^{n+1}(x, 0) = 0 = \hat{u}^{n+1}(x, 1), \\ \hat{u}_y^{n+1}(x, d_y^-) = \hat{u}_y^{n+1}(x, d_y^+), \end{cases} \quad (6)$$

where $\hat{u}^n(x, y)$ is the exact solution of u at the time level $t = t_n$, $\mathcal{D}_x := I + h_t \mathcal{L}_x$ and $\mathcal{D}_y := I + h_t \mathcal{L}_y$.

If the exact solution of the problem (1) is known at $t = t_n$, then we have the following semi-discrete scheme: let $y \in \Omega_y$, then

$$\begin{cases} \mathcal{D}_x \overline{u}^{n+\frac{1}{2}} = u(x, y, t_n) + h_t g_1(x, y, t_{n+1}), \; x \in \Omega_x^*, \\ \overline{u}^{n+\frac{1}{2}}(0, y) = \overline{u}^{n+\frac{1}{2}}(1, y) = 0, \\ \overline{u}_x^{n+\frac{1}{2}}(d_x^-, y) = \overline{u}_x^{n+\frac{1}{2}}(d_x^+, y), \end{cases} \quad (7)$$

let $x \in \Omega_x$, then

$$\begin{cases} \mathcal{D}_y \overline{u}^{n+1} = \overline{u}^{n+\frac{1}{2}} + h_t g_2(x, y, t_{n+1}), \; y \in \Omega_y^*, \\ \overline{u}^{n+1}(x, 0) = \overline{u}^{n+1}(x, 1) = 0, \\ \overline{u}_y^{n+1}(x, d_y^-) = \overline{u}_y^{n+1}(x, d_y^+). \end{cases} \quad (8)$$

Solving the problem (1)–(4) is more computationally expensive than solving lower-dimensional problems. As a result, we used the ADI scheme to divide the two-dimensional problem into two sets of one-dimensional problems in order to decrease the computing cost and to have an efficient numerical solution.

3.3. Stability Results and Derivative Estimates

This section presents the maximum principles for the above-mentioned locally one dimensional problems. Further, with regard to the applications of the maximum principle, we estimate the solution derivative bounds and local and global truncation errors in the temporal direction.

The test functions

$$s(x) = \begin{cases} x+1, & x \in [x, d_x], \\ d_x \dfrac{d_x - x}{1 - d_x} + d_x + 1, & x \in [d_x, 1] \end{cases} \quad \text{and} \quad s(y) = \begin{cases} y+1, & y \in [0, d_y], \\ d_y \dfrac{d_y - y}{1 - d_y} + d_y + 1, & y \in [d_y, 1] \end{cases}$$

are used in the following lemmas and sections.

Lemma 1. *Let $\psi \in C^0(\overline{\Omega}_x) \cap C^2(\Omega_x^*)$ be a function satisfying $\psi(x) \geq 0$, $x = 0, 1$, $\mathfrak{D}_x \psi(x) \geq 0$, $x \in \Omega_x^*$ and $\psi'(d_x-) - \psi'(d_x+) \geq 0$, then $\psi(x) \geq 0$, $x \in \overline{\Omega}_x$.*

Proof. The proof is by construction and similar to Refs. [12,13]. It is shown that $\mathfrak{D}_x s(x) > 0$, $x \neq d_x$ and $s'(d_x^-) - s'(d_x^+) \geq 0$. By using the argument given by Ref. [12], Theorem 3.1, one can prove this lemma. □

Similar to the above lemma and using the test function $s(y)$, we can prove the following lemma.

Lemma 2. *Let $\psi \in C^0(\overline{\Omega}_y) \cap C^2(\Omega_y^*)$ be a function satisfies $\psi(y) \geq 0$, $y = 0, 1$, $\mathfrak{D}_y \psi(y) \geq 0$, $y \in \Omega_y^*$ and $\psi'(d_y-) - \psi'(d_y+) \geq 0$, then $\psi(y) \geq 0$, $x \in \overline{\Omega}_y$.*

One can prove that the solutions of (5) and (6) are stable and unique if they exist. Further, they are bounded from Lemmas 1 and 2.

Lemma 3. *Assume that $\left|\dfrac{\partial^i u}{\partial t^i}\right| \leq C$, $0 \leq i \leq 3$. Then $\|e_n\| \leq C h_t^2$ where $u(t_n) = \overline{u}^n(x, y) + e_n$, $u(t_n) = u(x, y, t_n)$. In addition, $\sup_{n \leq T/h_t} \|E_n\|_\infty \leq C h_t$, where the global error $E_n = u(t_n) - \hat{u}^n$.*

Proof. The proof is similar to that of Refs. [4,6]. For that, one can express

$$u(t_{n-1}) = \mathfrak{D}_x[\mathfrak{D}_y u(t_n) - h_t g_2(x, y, t_n)] - h_t g_1(x, y, t_n) + O(h_t^2)$$

$$u(t_{n-1}) = \mathfrak{D}_x[\mathfrak{D}_y \overline{u}(t_n) - h_t g_2(x, y, t_n)] - h_t g_1(x, y, t_n),$$

$$\mathfrak{D}_x \mathfrak{D}_y e_n = O(h_t^2).$$

First by the application of Lemma 1 then by Lemma 2, we have $|e_n| \leq C h_t^2$. To prove the second part, consider

$$E_n = e_n + \overline{u}^n - \hat{u}^n,$$

$$\mathfrak{D}_y(\overline{u}^n - \hat{u}^n) = \overline{u}^{(n-1)+\frac{1}{2}} - \hat{u}^{(n-1)+\frac{1}{2}}, \quad \mathfrak{D}_x(\overline{u}^{(n-1)+\frac{1}{2}} - \hat{u}^{(n-1)+\frac{1}{2}}) = E_{n-1},$$

$$\overline{u}^n - \hat{u}^n = \mathfrak{D}_y^{-1} \mathfrak{D}_x^{-1} E_{n-1},$$

making use of the arguments given in Ref. [4], we have $|E_n| \leq C h_t$, which concludes the proof. □

From the above lemma, we can conclude that the semidiscretization process is uniformly convergent of order $O(h_t)$. In the rest of the sections it is assumed that, $d_x = 0.5 = d_y$.

Let the solution $\hat{u}^{n+\frac{1}{2}}$ be decomposed as $\hat{u}^{n+\frac{1}{2}} = v^{n+\frac{1}{2}} + w^{n+\frac{1}{2}}$ for obtaining the sharp bounds on the derivatives. Further, let the decomposition of the regular component be $v^{n+\frac{1}{2}} = \sum_{k=0}^{2} \varepsilon^k v_k^{n+\frac{1}{2}}$, leading the desired bounds on the derivatives. The functions $v_k^{n+\frac{1}{2}}$, $k = 0, 1, 2$, $w^{n+\frac{1}{2}}$ satisfy the following problems:

$$\begin{cases} v_0^{n+\frac{1}{2}} + h_t \left(p_1(\mathbf{x}) \frac{d}{dx} v_0^{n+\frac{1}{2}} + q_1(\mathbf{x}) I_\mathbf{d} v_0^{n+\frac{1}{2}} \right) = v_0^n + h_t g_1(t_{n+1}), \; x \in \Omega_x^*, \\ v_0^{n+\frac{1}{2}}(x) = \hat{u}^{n+\frac{1}{2}}(x), \; x \in [-d_x, 0], \; v_0^{n+\frac{1}{2}}(1) = \hat{u}^{n+\frac{1}{2}}(1), \end{cases} \quad (9)$$

$$\begin{cases} v_1^{n+\frac{1}{2}} + h_t \left(p_1(\mathbf{x}) \frac{d}{dx} v_1^{n+\frac{1}{2}} + q_1(\mathbf{x}) I_\mathbf{d} v_1^{n+\frac{1}{2}} \right) = v_1^n + h_t \frac{d^2}{dx^2} \left(v_0^{n+\frac{1}{2}} \right), \; x \in \Omega_x^*, \\ v_1^{n+\frac{1}{2}}(x) = 0, \; x \in [-d_x, 0], \; v_1^{n+\frac{1}{2}}(1) = 0, \end{cases} \quad (10)$$

$$\begin{cases} \mathfrak{D}_x v_2^{n+\frac{1}{2}} = v_2^n + h_t \frac{d^2}{dx^2} \left(v_1^{n+\frac{1}{2}} \right), \; x \in \Omega_x^*, \\ v_2^{n+\frac{1}{2}}(x) = 0, \; x \in [-d_x, 0], \; v_2^{n+\frac{1}{2}}(1) = 0, \\ \frac{d}{dx} v_2^{n+\frac{1}{2}}(d_x^-) = \frac{d}{dx} v_2^{n+\frac{1}{2}}(d_x^+), \end{cases} \quad (11)$$

and the functions $v^{n+\frac{1}{2}}$ and $w^{n+\frac{1}{2}}$ satisfy the following boundary-value problems (BVPs):

$$\begin{cases} \mathfrak{D}_x v^{n+\frac{1}{2}} = v^n + h_t g_1(t_{n+1}), \; x \in \Omega_x^*, \\ v^{n+\frac{1}{2}}(x) = \hat{u}^{n+\frac{1}{2}}(x), \; x \in [-d_x, 0], \; v^{n+\frac{1}{2}}(1) = \hat{u}^{n+\frac{1}{2}}(1), \\ \left[v^{n+\frac{1}{2}}(d_x) \right] = \sum_{k=0}^{2} [v_k^{n+\frac{1}{2}}(d_x)], \; \left[\frac{d}{dx} v^{n+\frac{1}{2}}(d_x) \right] = \sum_{k=0}^{1} \varepsilon^k \left[\frac{d}{dx} v_k^{n+\frac{1}{2}}(d_x) \right], \end{cases} \quad (12)$$

and

$$\begin{cases} \mathfrak{D}_x w^{n+\frac{1}{2}} = w^n, \; x \in \Omega_x^*, \\ w^{n+\frac{1}{2}}(x) = 0, \; x \in [-d_x, 0], \; w^{n+\frac{1}{2}}(1) = 0, \\ \left[w^{n+\frac{1}{2}}(d_x) \right] = -\left[v^{n+\frac{1}{2}}(d_x) \right], \; \left[\frac{d}{dx} w^{n+\frac{1}{2}}(d_x) \right] = -\left[\frac{d}{dx} v^{n+\frac{1}{2}}(d_x) \right], \end{cases} \quad (13)$$

where the square bracket operation denotes the jump discontinuity $[\alpha(\zeta)] = \alpha(\zeta^+) - \alpha(\zeta^-)$. It is assumed that $v^0 = \hat{u}^0$, $w^0 = 0$.

Theorem 1. *Let $\hat{u}^{n+\frac{1}{2}}$ be the solution of the problem (5) and let k be a nonnegative integer, then the regular and singular components satisfy the following bounds on the derivatives*

$$\left\| \frac{d^k v^{n+\frac{1}{2}}}{dx^k} \right\|_{\Omega^*} \leq C(\varepsilon^{-k+2} + 1), \; 0 \leq k \leq 3,$$

$$\left| \frac{d^k w^{n+\frac{1}{2}}(x)}{dx^k} \right| \leq C \varepsilon^{-k} \begin{cases} \exp\left(\frac{p_1^-(x - d_x)}{\varepsilon} \right), \; x \in \Omega_x^-, & 0 \leq k \leq 3, \\ \exp\left(\frac{p_1^-(d_x - x)}{\varepsilon} \right) + \varepsilon \exp\left(\frac{p_1^-(x - 1)}{\varepsilon} \right), \; x \in \Omega_x^+. \end{cases}$$

Proof. We show that by integrating the differential Equations (9)–(11), and using the argument presented in Refs. [13,19], and Lemma 1, we have $\|v^{n+\frac{1}{2}}\| \leq C$. Successive differentiation of Equations (9)–(11), we have $\|\frac{d^k}{dx^k}v^{n+\frac{1}{2}}\| \leq C(\varepsilon^{2-k}+1)$. From the Lemma 1, we see that $\hat{u}^{n+\frac{1}{2}}$ and $v^{n+\frac{1}{2}}$ are bounded, hence $w^{n+\frac{1}{2}}$. Let us assume that $|w^{n+\frac{1}{2}}(d_x)| \leq \gamma$. Now define the barrier functions

$$\phi^{\pm}(x) = C\gamma \exp\left(\frac{p_1^-(x-d_x)}{\varepsilon}\right) \pm w^{n+\frac{1}{2}}, \; x \in \Omega_x^-.$$

It is easy to show that $\phi^{\pm}(0) \geq 0$, $\phi^{\pm}(d_x) \geq 0$ and $\mathfrak{D}_x\phi^{\pm}(x) \geq 0$ on Ω_x^-. From the results of Ref. [19], we have $|w^{n+\frac{1}{2}}(x)| \leq C \exp\left(\frac{p_1^-(x-d_x)}{\varepsilon}\right)$, $x \in \Omega_x^-$. Using the following barrier functions

$$\psi^{\pm} = C\gamma(\varepsilon + \exp\left(\frac{p_1^-(d_x-x)}{\varepsilon}\right) - \varepsilon \exp\left(\frac{p_1^-(x-1)}{\varepsilon}\right)) \pm w^{n+\frac{1}{2}}, \; x \in \Omega_x^+$$

we prove that $|w^{n+\frac{1}{2}}(x)| \leq C\left(\exp\left(\frac{p_1^-(d_x-x)}{\varepsilon}\right) + \varepsilon \exp\left(\frac{p_1^-(x-1)}{\varepsilon}\right)\right)$, $x \in \Omega_x^+$. Further the successive differentiation's leads the desired results. □

In a similar manner, one can decompose $\hat{u}^{n+1}$ as $v^{n+1} + w^{n+1} = \hat{u}^{n+1}$ and v^{n+1}, w^{n+1} satisfy the following BVPs:

$$\begin{cases} \mathfrak{D}_y v^{n+1} = v^{n+\frac{1}{2}} + h_t g_2(t_{n+1}), \; y \in \Omega_y^*, \\ v^{n+1}(y) = \hat{u}^{n+1}(y), \; y \in [-d_y, 0], \; v^{n+1}(1) = \hat{u}^{n+1}(1), \\ [v^{n+1}(d_y)] = \sum_{k=0}^{1} \varepsilon^k \left[v_k^{n+1}(d_y)\right], \; \left[\frac{d}{dy}v^{n+1}(d_y)\right] = \sum_{k=0}^{1} \varepsilon^k \left[\frac{d}{dy}v_k^{n+1}(d_y)\right], \end{cases} \quad (14)$$

$$\begin{cases} \mathfrak{D}_y w^{n+1} = w^{n+\frac{1}{2}}, \; y \in \Omega_y^*, \\ w^{n+1}(y) = 0, \; y \in [-d_y, 0], \; w^{n+1}(1) = 0, \\ [w^{n+1}(d_y)] = -[v^{n+1}(d_y)], \; \left[\frac{d}{dy}w^{n+1}(d_y)\right] = -\left[\frac{d}{dy}v^{n+1}(d_y)\right] \end{cases} \quad (15)$$

and we have the following result.

Theorem 2. *Let $\hat{u}^{n+1}$ be the solution to the problem (6), then its regular and singular components satisfy the following bounds on the derivatives*

$$\left\|\frac{d^k v^{n+1}}{dy^k}\right\|_{\Omega^*} \leq C(1 + \varepsilon^{2-k}), \; k = 0, 1, 2, 3,$$

$$\left|\frac{d^k w^{n+1}(x)}{dy^k}\right| \leq C \begin{cases} \varepsilon^{-k} \exp\left(\frac{p_2^-(y-d_y)}{\varepsilon}\right), \; y \in \Omega_y^-, & k = 0, 1, 2, 3, \\ \varepsilon^{-k} \exp\left(\frac{p_2^-(d_y-y)}{\varepsilon}\right) + \varepsilon^{-k+1} \exp\left(\frac{p_2^-(y-1)}{\varepsilon}\right), \; y \in \Omega_y^+. \end{cases}$$

4. Discrete Problem

4.1. Spatial Domain Discretization

From Theorems 1 and 2, we observe that the IBVP (1)–(3) exhibits twin interior layers along the lines (d_x, y), $y \in \Omega_y$ and (x, d_y), $x \in \Omega_x$ and weak boundary layers along $x = 1$ and $y = 1$. Let N be the number of mesh points in both spatial x and y directions.

As the mesh defined in Ref. [13], we define the mesh points in both x and y directions, which is given in the following: let $\tau_{1,x} = \min\{\frac{d_x}{2}, \frac{2}{p_1}\varepsilon \ln N\}$, $\tau_{2,x} = \min\{\frac{1-d_x}{4}, \frac{2}{p_1}\varepsilon \ln N\}$, $\tau_{1,y} = \min\{\frac{d_y}{2}, \frac{2}{p_2}\varepsilon \ln N\}$ and $\tau_{2,y} = \min\{\frac{1-d_y}{4}, \frac{2}{p_2}\varepsilon \ln N\}$. Using the transition parameters $\tau_{i,\nu}$, $i=1,2$, $\nu = x,y$, we partitioned the domains $\overline{\Omega}_x$ and $\overline{\Omega}_y$ as follows:

$$\overline{\Omega}_x = \cup_{i=1}^{5}\Omega_{i,x}, \ \Omega_{1,x} = [0, d_x - \tau_{1,x}], \ \Omega_{2,x} = [d_x - \tau_{1,x}, d_x], \ \Omega_{3,x} = [d_x, d_x + \tau_{2,x}],$$
$$\Omega_{4,x} = [d_x + \tau_{2,x}, 1 - \tau_{2,x}], \Omega_{5,x} = [1 - \tau_{2,x}, 1],$$
$$\overline{\Omega}_y = \cup_{i=1}^{5}\Omega_{i,y}, \ \Omega_{1,y} = [0, d_y - \tau_{1,y}], \ \Omega_{2,y} = [d_y - \tau_{1,y}, d_y], \ \Omega_{3,y} = [d_y, d_y + \tau_{2,y}],$$
$$\Omega_{4,y} = [d_y + \tau_{2,y}, 1 - \tau_{2,y}], \Omega_{5,y} = [1 - \tau_{2,y}, 1].$$

On each sub-domains $\Omega_{i,x}$, $i = 1, 2, 3, 4, 5$, respectively, we place $\frac{N}{4}, \frac{N}{4}, \frac{N}{8}, \frac{N}{4}, \frac{N}{8}$ mesh points with mesh sizes $\frac{4(d_x - \tau_{1,x})}{N}, \frac{4\tau_{1,x}}{N}, \frac{8\tau_{2,x}}{N}, \frac{4(1 - 2\tau_{2,x} - d_x)}{N}, \frac{8\tau_{2,x}}{N}$. In the same manner the mesh points in $\Omega_{i,y}$, $i = 1, 2, 3, 4, 5$ are defined. Now let us denote the mesh sizes to be $h_x(i) = x_i - x_{i-1}$, $i \in \mathcal{I}_N$ and $h_y(i) = y_i - y_{i-1}$, $i \in \mathcal{I}_N$ and define the mesh $\overline{\Omega}_x^N = \{x_i\}_{i=0}^{i=N}$, $x_0 = 0$, $x_i = x_{i-1} + h_x(i)$, $i \in \mathcal{I}_N$ and $\overline{\Omega}_y^N = \{y_i\}_{i=0}^{i=N}$, $y_0 = 0$, $y_i = y_{i-1} + h_y(i)$, $i \in \mathcal{I}_N$. The mesh distribution is depicted in the Figure 1.

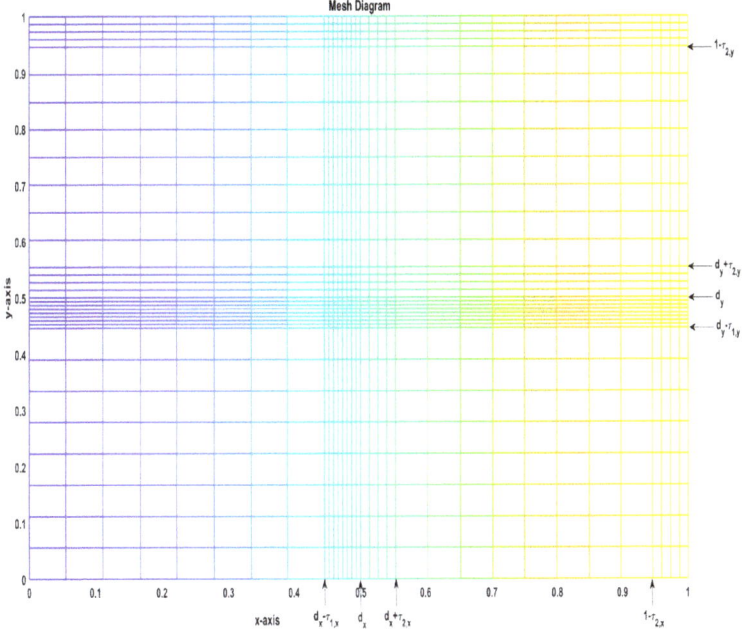

Figure 1. Mesh points distribution.

4.2. The Finite Difference Schemes

On the meshes $\overline{\Omega}_x^N$ and $\overline{\Omega}_y^N$, we define the following finite difference schemes.

fix $y = y_j$,

$$\mathfrak{D}_x^N U_{i,j}^{n+\frac{1}{2}} := \begin{cases} U_{i,j}^{n+\frac{1}{2}} + (-\varepsilon\delta_x^2 U_{i,j}^{n+\frac{1}{2}} + p_{1_{i,j}} D_x^- U_{i,j}^{n+\frac{1}{2}} + q_{1_{i,j}} I_{\mathbf{d}}^N U_{i,j}^{n+\frac{1}{2}})h_t = U_{i,j}^n \\ \qquad + h_t g_1(x_i, y_j, t_{n+1}), i \in \mathcal{I}_{\frac{N}{2}-1}, \\ D_x^- U_{N/2,j}^{n+\frac{1}{2}} = D_x^+ U_{N/2,j}^{n+\frac{1}{2}}, \qquad i = \frac{N}{2}, \\ U_{i,j}^{n+\frac{1}{2}} + (-\varepsilon\delta_x^2 U_{i,j}^{n+\frac{1}{2}} + p_{1_{i,j}} D_x^+ U_{i,j}^{n+\frac{1}{2}} + q_{1_{i,j}} I_{\mathbf{d}}^N U_{i,j}^{n+\frac{1}{2}})h_t = U_{i,j}^n \\ \qquad + h_t g_1(x_i, y_j, t_{n+1}), i \in \mathcal{I}_{N-1} \setminus \mathcal{I}_{\frac{N}{2}}, \end{cases} \qquad (16)$$

$U_{0,j}^{n+\frac{1}{2}} = \hat{u}^{n+\frac{1}{2}}(0, y_j);\; U_{N,j}^{n+\frac{1}{2}} = \hat{u}^{n+\frac{1}{2}}(1, y_j),$

fix $x = x_i$,

$$\mathfrak{D}_y^N U_{i,j}^{n+1} := \begin{cases} U_{i,j}^{n+1} + (-\varepsilon\delta_y^2 U_{i,j}^{n+1} + p_{2_{i,j}} D_y^- U_{i,j}^{n+1} + q_{2_{i,j}} I_{\mathbf{d}}^N U_{i,j}^{n+1})h_t = U_{i,j}^{n+\frac{1}{2}} \\ \qquad + h_t g_2(x_i, y_j, t_{n+1}), j \in \mathcal{I}_{\frac{N}{2}-1} \\ D_y^- U_{i,N/2}^{n+1} = D_y^+ U_{i,N/2}^{n+1}, \qquad j = \frac{N}{2}, \\ U_{i,j}^{n+1} + (-\varepsilon\delta_y^2 U_{i,j}^{n+1} + p_{2_{i,j}} D_y^+ U_{i,j}^{n+1} + q_{2_{i,j}} I_{\mathbf{d}}^N U_{i,j}^{n+1})h_t = U_{i,j}^{n+\frac{1}{2}} \\ \qquad + h_t g_2(x_i, y_j, t_{n+1}), j \in \mathcal{I}_{N-1} \setminus \mathcal{I}_{\frac{N}{2}}, \end{cases} \qquad (17)$$

$U_{0,j}^{n+1} = \hat{u}^{n+1}(x_i, 0);\; U_{i,N}^{n+1} = \hat{u}^{n+1}(x_i, 1),$

where δ_ζ^2, D_ζ^- and D_ζ^+, $\zeta = x, y$ are the standard finite difference operators,

$$I_{\mathbf{d}}^N U_{i,j}^{n+\frac{1}{2}} = \begin{cases} 0, & i \in \mathcal{I}_{\frac{N}{2}-1}, \\ U_{\eta,\xi}^{n+\frac{1}{2}} l_{\eta,x}(x_i - d_x) l_{\xi,y}(y_j - d_y) + U_{\eta+1,\xi}^{n+\frac{1}{2}} l_{\eta+1,x}(x_i - d_x) l_{\xi,y}(y_j - d_y) \\ + U_{\eta,\xi+1}^{n+\frac{1}{2}} l_{\eta,x}(x_i - d_x) l_{\xi+1,y}(y_j - d_y) \\ + U_{\eta+1,\xi+1}^{n+\frac{1}{2}} l_{\eta+1,x}(x_i - d_x) l_{\xi+1,y}(y_j - d_y), & i \in \mathcal{I}_{N-1} \setminus \mathcal{I}_{\frac{N}{2}} \end{cases}$$

$$I_{\mathbf{d}}^N U_{i,j}^{n+1} = \begin{cases} 0, & j \in \mathcal{I}_{\frac{N}{2}-1}, \\ U_{\eta,\xi}^{n+1} l_{\eta,x}(x_i - d_x) l_{\xi,y}(y_j - d_y) + U_{\eta+1,\xi}^{n+1} l_{\eta+1,x}(x_i - d_x) l_{\xi,y}(y_j - d_y) \\ + U_{\eta,\xi+1}^{n+1} l_{\eta,x}(x_i - d_x) l_{\xi+1,y}(y_j - d_y) \\ + U_{\eta+1,\xi+1}^{n+1} l_{\eta+1,x}(x_i - d_x) l_{\xi+1,y}(y_j - d_y), & j \in \mathcal{I}_{N-1} \setminus \mathcal{I}_{\frac{N}{2}}, \end{cases}$$

$l_{\eta,x}(x_i - d_x) = \dfrac{x_{\eta+1} - (x_i - d_x)}{h_x(\eta+1)}, l_{\eta+1,x}(x_i - d_x) = \dfrac{(x_i - d_x) - x_\eta}{h_x(\eta+1)},$

$l_{\xi,y}(y_j - d_y) = \dfrac{y_{\xi+1} - (y_j - d_y)}{h_y(\xi+1)}, l_{\xi+1,y}(y_j - d_y) = \dfrac{(y_j - d_y) - y_\xi}{h_y(\xi+1)}$, $x_\eta, x_{\eta+1}, y_\xi, y_{\xi+1}$ are the nodal points such that $x_i - d_x \in [x_\eta, x_{\eta+1}]$ and $y_j - d_y \in [y_\xi, y_{\xi+1}]$. The above two difference operators $\mathfrak{D}_x^N$ and $\mathfrak{D}_y^N$ satisfy the following discrete maximum principles.

Note: Let us denote the difference operators $D_x^* = \begin{cases} D_x^-, & i < \frac{N}{2}, \\ D_x^+, & i > \frac{N}{2}, \end{cases}$ and $D_y^* = \begin{cases} D_y^-, & j < \frac{N}{2}, \\ D_y^+, & j > \frac{N}{2}. \end{cases}$
In the following we use the above difference operators. Further, the test functions
$$s(x_i) = \begin{cases} x_i + 1, & i \leq N/2, \\ d_x \dfrac{d_x - x_i}{1 - d_x} + d_x + 1, & i > N/2, \end{cases} \text{ and } s(y_j) = \begin{cases} y_j + 1, & j \leq N/2, \\ d_y \dfrac{d_y - y_j}{1 - d_y} + d_y + 1, & j > N/2, \end{cases}$$
are also used.

4.3. Discrete Stability Results

Lemma 4. *Let the mesh function be $\Psi_{i,j}$, satisfies $\Psi_{0,j} \geq 0$, $\Psi_{N,j} \geq 0$, $\mathfrak{D}_x^N \Psi_{i,j} \geq 0$ and $[D_x^+ - D_x^-]\Psi_{N/2,j} \leq 0$, then $\Psi_{i,j} \geq 0$ for all i.*

Proof. Making use of the test mesh function $s(x_i)$ and the arguments given in Ref. [13], Lemma 6.1, the lemma can be proved. □

Lemma 5. *Let the mesh function be $\Psi_{i,j}$, satisfies $\Psi_{i,0} \geq 0$, $\Psi_{i,N} \geq 0$, $\mathfrak{D}_y^N \Psi_{i,j} \geq 0$ and $[D_y^+ - D_y^-]\Psi_{i,N/2} \leq 0$, then $\Psi_{i,j} \geq 0$ for all j.*

Using the above two Lemmas 4 and 5, we can have the following discrete stability results.

Lemma 6. *Let $U_{i,j}^{n+\frac{1}{2}}$ be a numerical solution defined by (16), then*
$$|U_{i,j}^{n+\frac{1}{2}}| \leq C \max \left\{ |U_{0,j}^{n+\frac{1}{2}}|, |U_{N,j}^{n+\frac{1}{2}}|, \sup_i |\mathfrak{D}_x^N U_{i,j}^{n+\frac{1}{2}}| \right\}, \quad \text{for all } i.$$

Lemma 7. *Let $U_{i,j}^{n+1}$ be a numerical solution defined by (17), then*
$$|U_{i,j}^{n+1}| \leq C \max \left\{ |U_{i,0}^{n+1}|, |U_{i,N}^{n+1}|, \sup_j |\mathfrak{D}_y^N U_{i,j}^{n+1}| \right\}, \quad \text{for all } j.$$

Remark 1. *From Lemmas 6 and 7, we can see that, the numerical solutions defined in (16) and (17) are stable. Further, by the results of Ref. [20], the matrices associated with the difference schemes (16) and (17) are M-matrices.*

5. Error Computation

Analogous to the continuous solution, the numerical solution is decomposed into smooth and singular components. The solution $U^{n+\frac{1}{2}}$ is decomposed as $U^{n+\frac{1}{2}} = V^{n+\frac{1}{2}} + W^{n+\frac{1}{2}}$ satisfy the following difference equations:

$$\begin{cases} \mathfrak{D}_x^N V_{i,j}^{n+\frac{1}{2}} - V_{i,j}^n + h_l g_1(x_i, y_j, t_{n+1}), & i \in \mathcal{I}_N \setminus \{N, \frac{N}{2}, 0\}, \\ D_x^+ V_{N/2,j}^{n+\frac{1}{2}} - D_x^- V_{N/2,j}^{n+\frac{1}{2}} = \left[v^{n+\frac{1}{2}'}(d_x) \right], \; V_{0,j}^{n+\frac{1}{2}} = 0, \; V_{N,j}^{n+\frac{1}{2}} = 0, \end{cases} \quad (18)$$

$$\begin{cases} \mathfrak{D}_x^N W_{i,j}^{n+\frac{1}{2}} = W_{i,j}^n, & i \in \mathcal{I}_N \setminus \{N, \frac{N}{2}, 0\}, \\ D_x^+ W_{N/2,j}^{n+\frac{1}{2}} - D_x^- W_{N/2,j}^{n+\frac{1}{2}} = -\left[v^{n+\frac{1}{2}'}(d_x) \right], \; W_{0,j}^{n+\frac{1}{2}} = 0, \; W_{N,j}^{n+\frac{1}{2}} = 0. \end{cases} \quad (19)$$

Similarly, the solution U^{n+1} is decomposed as $U^{n+1} = V^{n+1} + W^{n+1}$ and they satisfy the following difference equations:

$$\begin{cases} \mathfrak{D}_y^N V_{i,j}^{n+1} = V_{i,j}^{n+\frac{1}{2}} + h_t g_2(x_i, y_j, t_{n+1}), \ j \in \mathcal{I}_N \setminus \{N, \frac{N}{2}, 0\}, \\ D_y^+ V_{i,N/2}^{n+1} - D_y^- V_{i,N/2}^{n+1} = \left[v^{n+1'}(d_y)\right], \ V_{i,0}^{n+1} = 0, \ V_{i,N}^{n+1} = 0, \end{cases} \quad (20)$$

$$\begin{cases} \mathfrak{D}_y^N W_{i,j}^{n+1} = W_{i,j}^{n+\frac{1}{2}}, \ j \in \mathcal{I}_N \setminus \{N, \frac{N}{2}, 0\}, \\ D_y^+ W_{i,N/2}^{n+1} - D_y^- W_{i,N/2}^{n+1} = -\left[v^{n+1'}(d_y)\right], \ W_{i,0}^{n+1} = 0, \ W_{i,N}^{n+1} = 0. \end{cases} \quad (21)$$

Note: The error estimate in each time level is proved in the following way:

Step 1: First we estimate the absolute difference of U and V;
Step 2: We estimate the error bound of the regular component, that is $|v - V|$;
Step 3: To estimate the error bound of the singular component $|w - W|$ in the entire domain, first we estimate in the outer region and then using the estimate of $|U - V|$, we estimate $|w - W|$ in the inner layer region;
Step 4: Using the triangle inequality, we estimate the error bound of the numerical solution in each time level.

Lemma 8. *Let $U_{i,j}^{\frac{1}{2}}$ and $V_{i,j}^{\frac{1}{2}}$ be numerical solutions of (16) and (18), respectively, when $n = 0$, then*

$$|U_{i,j}^{\frac{1}{2}} - V_{i,j}^{\frac{1}{2}}| \leq C \begin{cases} N^{-1}, & i \in \mathcal{I}_{\frac{N}{4}}, \\ \zeta + N^{-1}, & i \in \mathcal{I}_{\frac{5N}{8}} \setminus \mathcal{I}_{\frac{N}{4}}, \\ N^{-1}, & i \in \mathcal{I}_{N-1} \setminus \mathcal{I}_{\frac{5N}{8}}, \end{cases}$$

ζ is constant.

Proof. Fix j. Let us consider the mesh function

$$\Psi^{\pm}(x_i) = C[N^{-1}s(x_i) + \psi(x_i)] \pm [U_{i,j}^{\frac{1}{2}} - V_{i,j}^{\frac{1}{2}}], \ \forall i,$$

where $\zeta = \max_{\frac{N}{4}+1 \leq i,j \leq \frac{5N}{8}-1} |U_{i,j}^{\frac{1}{2}} - V_{i,j}^{\frac{1}{2}}|$, and

$$\psi(x_i) = \begin{cases} \left(\dfrac{x_i - (d_x - \tau_{1,x})}{\tau_{1,x}}\right)\zeta, & i \in \mathcal{I}_{\frac{N}{2}} \setminus \mathcal{I}_{\frac{N}{4}} \\ \left(1 + \dfrac{d_x - x_i}{\tau_{2,x}}\right)\zeta, & i \in \mathcal{I}_{\frac{5N}{8}-1} \setminus \mathcal{I}_{\frac{N}{2}} \\ 0, & \text{otherwise.} \end{cases}$$

It is easy to show that $\Psi^{\pm}(x_i) \geq 0, \ i = 0, N$, and by the arguments of [13], we have

$$\mathfrak{D}_x^N \Psi^{\pm}(x_i) = \mathfrak{D}_x^N(CN^{-1}s(x_i) + \psi(x_i)) \pm \mathfrak{D}_x^N(U_{i,j}^{\frac{1}{2}} - V_{i,j}^{\frac{1}{2}}) \geq 0, \ i \neq \frac{N}{2},$$

$$(D_x^+ - D_x^-)\Psi^{\pm}(x_{\frac{N}{2}}) \leq 0, \ i = \frac{N}{2}.$$

By the Lemma 4, we have $\Psi^{\pm}(x_i) \geq 0$. Hence the proof of the lemma. □

Lemma 9. *Let $v^{\frac{1}{2}}$ and $V^{\frac{1}{2}}$ be two solutions of (12) and (18), respectively, the $|v^{\frac{1}{2}}(x_i,y) - V^{\frac{1}{2}}_{i,y}| \leq CN^{-1}, \forall i.$*

Proof. Now, we see that

$$\mathfrak{D}^N_x(v^{\frac{1}{2}}(x_i,y) - V^{\frac{1}{2}}_{i,y}) = \mathfrak{D}^N_x v^{\frac{1}{2}}(x_i,y) - \mathfrak{D}^N_x V^{\frac{1}{2}}_{i,y} = \mathfrak{D}^N_x v^{\frac{1}{2}}(x_i,y) - \mathfrak{D}_x v^{\frac{1}{2}}(x_i,y)$$

$$= h_t \left[-\varepsilon \left(\delta_x^2 - \frac{d^2}{dx^2} \right) + p_{1_{i,j}}\left(D_x^* - \frac{d}{dx} \right) + q_{1_{i,j}}[I_\mathbf{d}^N - I_\mathbf{d}] \right] v^{\frac{1}{2}}(x_i,y),$$

from the results given in Refs. [2,21,22], we have $|\mathfrak{D}^N_x(v^{\frac{1}{2}}(x_i,y) - V^{\frac{1}{2}}_{i,y})| \leq Ch_t N^{-1}$. Using the following barrier function

$$\psi^\pm(x_i) = CN^{-1}s(x_i) \pm (v^{\frac{1}{2}}(x_i,y) - V^{\frac{1}{2}}_{i,y}),$$

we can see that $\psi^\pm(x_i) \geq 0$, $i = 0, N$, $\mathfrak{D}^N_x \psi^\pm(x_i) \geq 0$ and $(D_x^+ - D_x^-)\psi^\pm(x_{\frac{N}{2}}) \leq 0$. From the Lemma 4, we have the desired result. □

Lemma 10. *Let $w^{\frac{1}{2}}$ and $W^{\frac{1}{2}}$ be the solutions of (13) and (19), respectively, then $|w^{\frac{1}{2}}(x_i,y) - W^{\frac{1}{2}}_{i,y}| \leq CN^{-1}\ln N, \forall i.$*

Proof. By the triangle inequality, Theorem 1, Lemmas 8 and 9, we have

$$|\hat{u}^{\frac{1}{2}}(x_i,y) - U^{\frac{1}{2}}_{i,y}| \leq |U^{\frac{1}{2}}_{i,y} - V^{\frac{1}{2}}_{i,y}| + |v^{\frac{1}{2}}(x_i,y) - V^{\frac{1}{2}}_{i,y}| + |\hat{u}^{\frac{1}{2}}(x_i,y) - v^{\frac{1}{2}}(x_i,y)|$$

$$\leq CN^{-1} + C \begin{cases} \exp\left(\dfrac{p_1^-(x_i - d_x)}{\varepsilon}\right), & i \in \mathcal{I}_{\frac{N}{2}}, \\ \varepsilon \exp\left(\dfrac{p_1^-(x_i - 1)}{\varepsilon}\right) + \exp\left(\dfrac{p_1^-(d_x - x_i)}{\varepsilon}\right), & i \in \mathcal{I}_N - \mathcal{I}_{\frac{N}{2}}, \end{cases}$$

$$+ C \begin{cases} N^{-1}, & i \in \mathcal{I}_{\frac{N}{4}}, \\ \zeta + N^{-1}, & i \in \mathcal{I}_{\frac{5N}{8}-1} \setminus \mathcal{I}_{\frac{N}{4}}, \\ N^{-1}, & i \in \mathcal{I}_N \setminus \mathcal{I}_{\frac{5N}{8}-1} \end{cases}$$

$$\leq C \begin{cases} N^{-1}, & i \in \mathcal{I}_{\frac{N}{4}}, \\ \zeta + N^{-1} + \exp\left(\dfrac{p_1^-(x_i - d_x)}{\varepsilon}\right), & i \in \mathcal{I}_{\frac{N}{2}} \setminus \mathcal{I}_{\frac{N}{4}}, \\ \zeta + N^{-1} + \exp\left(\dfrac{p_1^-(d_x - x_i)}{\varepsilon}\right), & i \in \mathcal{I}_{\frac{5N}{8}-1} \setminus \mathcal{I}_{\frac{N}{2}}, \\ N^{-1}, & i \in \mathcal{I}_N \setminus \mathcal{I}_{\frac{5N}{8}-1}, \end{cases}$$

where $\zeta = \max_{\frac{N}{4}+1 \leq i,j \leq \frac{5N}{8}-1} |U^{\frac{1}{2}}_{i,j} - V^{\frac{1}{2}}_{i,j}|$. Hence $|\hat{u}^{\frac{1}{2}}(x_i,y) - U^{\frac{1}{2}}_{i,y}| \leq CN^{-1}$, $i = 0, 1, \cdots, \frac{N}{4}$, $\frac{5N}{8}, \cdots, N$. Therefore $|w^{\frac{1}{2}}(x_i,y) - W^{\frac{1}{2}}_{i,y}| \leq CN^{-1}, i = 0, 1, \cdots, \frac{N}{4}, \frac{5N}{8}, \cdots, N$. To prove the result inside the inner region, we consider the following mesh function

$$\psi^\pm(x_i) = CN^{-1}\phi(x_i) \pm (w^{\frac{1}{2}} - W^{\frac{1}{2}}), \ x_i \in (d_x - \tau_{1,x}, d_x) \cup (d_x, d_x + \tau_{2,x}) \cap \overline{\Omega}^N_x,$$

where $\phi(x_i) = \begin{cases} (1+x_i) + \frac{\tau_x}{\varepsilon^2}(x_i - (d_x - \tau_{1,x})), & x_i \in [d_x - \tau_{1,x}, d_x) \cap \overline{\Omega}_x^N, \\ \left(1 + d_x + d_x \frac{d_x - x_i}{1 - d_x}\right) + \frac{\tau_x}{\varepsilon^2}(d_x + \tau_{2,x} - x_i), & x_i \in [d_x, d_x + \tau_{2,x}] \cap \overline{\Omega}_x^N, \end{cases}$

$\tau_x = \min\{\tau_{1,x}, \tau_{2,x}\}$. Then we have, $\psi^{\pm}(x_i) \geq 0$, $i = \frac{N}{4}, \frac{5N}{8}$. Further $|\mathfrak{D}_x^N(w^{\frac{1}{2}} - W^{\frac{1}{2}})| \leq C_1 h_t \varepsilon^{-2} N^{-1}$, $i = \frac{N}{4}+1, \cdots, \frac{N}{2}-1, \frac{N}{2}+1, \cdots, \frac{5N}{8}$. Now,

$$\mathfrak{D}_x^N \psi^{\pm}(x_i) = CN^{-1} \mathfrak{D}_x^N \phi(x_i) \pm \mathfrak{D}_x^N(w^{\frac{1}{2}} - W^{\frac{1}{2}}), \ x_i \in (d_x - \tau_{1,x}, d_x) \cup (d_x, d_x + \tau_{2,x}) \cap \overline{\Omega}_x^N$$

$$\geq CN^{-1} \begin{cases} 1 + h_t p_1^- + \frac{\tau_x}{\varepsilon^2} h_t p_1^-, & x_i \in (d_x - \tau_{1,x}, d_x) \cap \overline{\Omega}_x^N \\ 1 + h_t(p_1^- \frac{d_x}{1-d_x} + \beta_1) + \frac{\tau_x}{\varepsilon^2} h_t(p_1^- + \beta_1), & x_i \in (d_x, d_x + \tau_{2,x}) \cap \overline{\Omega}_x^N \end{cases}$$

$$\mp C_1 h_t \varepsilon^{-2} N^{-1} \geq 0$$

for a suitable choice of $C > 0$. At the point $x_{N/2}$, we have $(D_x^+ - D_x^-)\psi^{\pm}(x_{N/2}) \leq 0$. From the Lemma 4, we have $|w^{\frac{1}{2}} - W^{\frac{1}{2}}| \leq CN^{-1} \ln N$, $i = \frac{N}{4}, \cdots, \frac{5N}{8}$. Therefore $|w^{\frac{1}{2}}(x_i, y) - W_{i,y}^{\frac{1}{2}}| \leq CN^{-1} \ln N$, $\forall i$. □

Lemma 11. Let $\hat{u}^{\frac{1}{2}}$ and $U^{\frac{1}{2}}$ be the solution of (5) and (16), respectively, then $\|\hat{u}^{\frac{1}{2}} - U^{\frac{1}{2}}\| \leq CN^{-1} \ln N$.

Proof. The proof follows from the above two lemmas. □

Lemma 12. Let v^1, w^1, $\hat{u}^1$, V^1, W^1, and U^1 be the solutions of (14), (15), (6), (20), (21), and (17), respectively, then

$$\|v^1 - V^1\| \leq CN^{-1}, \ \|w^1 - W^1\| \leq CN^{-1} \ln N,$$

$$\|\hat{u}^1 - U^1\| \leq CN^{-1} \ln N.$$

Proof. We see that, $\hat{u}^1(x, 0) = U_{x,0}^1$ and $\hat{u}^1(x, 1) = U_{x,N}^1$.

Similar to the proof of Lemma 8, we can prove the following,

$$|U^1 - V^1| \leq C \begin{cases} N^{-1}, & i,j \in \mathcal{I}_{\frac{N}{4}}, \\ \zeta + N^{-1}, & i,j \in \mathcal{I}_{\frac{5N}{8}} \setminus \mathcal{I}_{\frac{N}{4}}, \\ N^{-1}, & i,j \in \mathcal{I}_{N-1} \setminus \mathcal{I}_{\frac{5N}{8}} \end{cases}, \ \zeta = \max_{\frac{N}{4}+1 \leq i,j \leq \frac{5N}{8}-1} |U_{i,j}^1 - V_{i,j}^1|.$$

Let v^1 and V^1 be the solutions of (14) and (20), then similar to Lemma 9, we have

$$\mathfrak{D}_y^N(v^1(x, y_j) - V_{x,j}^1) = \mathfrak{D}_y^N v^1(x, y_j) - \mathfrak{D}_y^N V_{x,j}^1 = \mathfrak{D}_y^N v^1(x, y_j) - \mathfrak{D}_y v^1(x, y_j)$$

$$= h_t \left[-\varepsilon \left(\delta_y^2 - \frac{d^2}{dy^2} \right) + p_{2_{i,j}} \left(D_y^* - \frac{d}{dy} \right) + q_{2_{i,j}} [I_d^N - I_d] \right] v^1(x, y_j),$$

and $|\mathfrak{D}_y^N(v^1(x,y_j) - V_{x,j}^1)| \leq Ch_t N^{-1}$. Then by a suitable barrier function one can prove that $\|v^1 - V^1\| \leq CN^{-1}$. Similar to the Lemma 11, we estimate $\|w^1 - W^1\|$,

$$|\hat{u}^1(x,y_j) - U_{x,j}^1| \leq |U_{x,j}^1 - V_{x,j}^1| + |v^1(x,y_j) - V_{x,j}^1| + |\hat{u}^1(x,y_j) - v(x,y_j)|$$

$$\leq C \begin{cases} N^{-1}, & i,j \in \mathcal{I}_{\frac{N}{4}}, \\ \zeta + N^{-1} + \exp\left(\frac{p_2^-(y_j - d_y)}{\varepsilon}\right), & i,j \in \mathcal{I}_{\frac{N}{2}} \setminus \mathcal{I}_{\frac{N}{4}}, \\ \zeta + N^{-1} + \exp\left(\frac{p_2^-(d_y - y_j)}{\varepsilon}\right), & i,j \in \mathcal{I}_{\frac{5N}{8}} \setminus \mathcal{I}_{\frac{N}{2}}, \\ N^{-1}, & i,j \in \mathcal{I}_N \setminus \mathcal{I}_{\frac{5N}{8}}. \end{cases}$$

Hence $|\hat{u}^1(x,y_j) - U_{x,j}^1| \leq CN^{-1}$, $j = 0, 1, \cdots, \frac{N}{4}, \frac{5N}{8}, \cdots, N$ and $|w^1(x,y_j) - W_{x,j}^1| \leq CN^{-1}, j = 0, 1, \cdots, \frac{N}{4}, \frac{5N}{8}, \cdots, N$. Using the barrier function

$$\psi^{\pm}(y_j) = CN^{-1}\phi(y_j) \pm (w^1 - W^1), \; y_j \in (d_y - \tau_{1,y}, d_y) \cup (d_y, d_y + \tau_{2,y}) \cap \overline{\Omega}_y^N,$$

where $\phi(y_j) = \begin{cases} (1 + y_j) + \frac{\tau_y}{\varepsilon^2}(y_j - (d_y - \tau_{1,y})), & y_j \in [d_y - \tau_{1,y}, d_y) \cap \overline{\Omega}_y^N, \\ \left(1 + d_y + d_y \frac{d_y - y_j}{1 - d_y}\right) + \frac{\tau_y}{\varepsilon^2}(d_y + \tau_{2,y} - y_j), & y_j \in [d_y, d_y + \tau_{2,y}] \cap \overline{\Omega}_y^N, \end{cases}$

$\tau_y = \min\{\tau_{1,y}, \tau_{2,y}\}$ we prove that $\|w^1 - W^1\| \leq CN^{-1} \ln N, j = \frac{N}{4} + 1, \cdots, \frac{5N}{8} - 1$. Hence the proof. □

Theorem 3. Let $\hat{u}^{n+\frac{1}{2}}, \hat{u}^{n+1}, U_{i,j}^{n+\frac{1}{2}}$ and $U_{i,j}^{n+1}$ be the solutions of (5), (6), (16), and (17), respectively, then

$$\|\hat{u}^{n+\frac{1}{2}} - U^{n+\frac{1}{2}}\| \leq CN^{-1} \ln N, \quad \text{and} \quad \|\hat{u}^{n+1} - U^{n+1}\| \leq CN^{-1} \ln N.$$

Proof. We prove the theorem on each time level $t = t_n$. We know that $\hat{u}^{n+\frac{1}{2}}(0,y) - U_{0,y}^{n+\frac{1}{2}} = 0$, $\hat{u}^{n+\frac{1}{2}}(1,y) - U_{N,y}^{n+\frac{1}{2}} = 0$, $\hat{u}^{n+1}(x,0) - U_{x,0}^{n+1} = 0$ and $\hat{u}^{n+1}(x,1) - U_{x,N}^{n+1} = 0$.

$$\mathfrak{D}_x^N(U^{n+\frac{1}{2}} - V^{n+\frac{1}{2}}) = \mathfrak{D}_x^N U^{n+\frac{1}{2}} - \mathfrak{D}_x^N V^{n+\frac{1}{2}} = U^n - V^n,$$

$$\|\mathfrak{D}_x^N(U^{n+\frac{1}{2}} - V^{n+\frac{1}{2}})\| \leq C \begin{cases} N^{-1}, & i,j \in \mathcal{I}_{\frac{N}{4}}, \\ \zeta + N^{-1}, & i,j \in \mathcal{I}_{\frac{5N}{8}} \setminus \mathcal{I}_{\frac{N}{4}}, \\ N^{-1}, & i,j \in \mathcal{I}_{N-1} \setminus \mathcal{I}_{\frac{5N}{8}}, \end{cases}$$

$$\mathfrak{D}_y^N(U^{n+1} - V^{n+1}) = \mathfrak{D}_y^N U^{n+1} - \mathfrak{D}_y^N V^{n+1} = U^{n+\frac{1}{2}} - V^{n+\frac{1}{2}},$$

$$\|\mathfrak{D}_x^N(U^{n+1} - V^{n+1})\| \leq C \begin{cases} N^{-1}, & i,j \in \mathcal{I}_{\frac{N}{4}}, \\ \zeta + N^{-1}, & i,j \in \mathcal{I}_{\frac{5N}{8}} \setminus \mathcal{I}_{\frac{N}{4}}, \\ N^{-1}, & i,j \in \mathcal{I}_{N-1} \setminus \mathcal{I}_{\frac{5N}{8}}, \end{cases}$$

$$\zeta = \max_n \max_{\frac{N}{4}+1 \leq i,j \leq \frac{5N}{8}-1} |U_{i,j}^n - V_{i,j}^n|,$$

with the successive applications of Lemmas 6 and 7 and the iteration in n, we prove that

$$\|U^\mu - V^\mu\| \leq C \begin{cases} N^{-1}, & i,j \in \mathcal{I}_{\frac{N}{4}}, \\ \zeta + N^{-1}, & i,j \in \mathcal{I}_{\frac{5N}{8}} \setminus \mathcal{I}_{\frac{N}{4}}, \\ N^{-1}, & i,j \in \mathcal{I}_{N-1} \setminus \mathcal{I}_{\frac{5N}{8}}, \end{cases} \quad \mu = n+1 \ \& \ \mu = n+\frac{1}{2}.$$

Using the following barrier functions

$$\Psi_1^\pm(x_i) = CN^{-1}s(x_i) \pm [v^{n+\frac{1}{2}}(x_i, y_j) - V_{i,j}^{n+\frac{1}{2}}], \ \forall i,$$

$$\Psi_2^\pm(y_j) = CN^{-1}s(y_j) \pm [v^{n+1}(x_i, y_j) - V_{i,j}^{n+1}], \ \forall j,$$

and from Lemmas 6 and 7, we can prove that

$$\|v^{n+\frac{1}{2}} - V^{n+\frac{1}{2}}\| \leq CN^{-1}, \ \|v^{n+1} - V^{n+1}\| \leq CN^{-1}.$$

It is observed that $|w^\mu(x_i, y_j) - W_{i,j}^\mu| \leq CN^{-1}$, $\mu = n + \frac{1}{2}, n+1$, $i,j = 0, 1, \cdots, \frac{N}{4}$, $\frac{5N}{8}, \cdots, N$. Using the following barrier functions

$$\Phi_1^\pm(x_i) = CN^{-1}\phi_1(x_i) \pm (w^{n+\frac{1}{2}} - W^{n+\frac{1}{2}}), \ x_i \in [\Omega_{2,x} \cup \Omega_{3,x}] \cap \overline{\Omega}_x^N,$$

$$\Phi_2^\pm(y_j) = CN^{-1}\phi_2(y_j) \pm (w^{n+1} - W^{n+1}), \ y_j \in [\Omega_{2,y} \cup \Omega_{3,y}] \cap \overline{\Omega}_y^N,$$

where $\phi_1(x_i) = \begin{cases} (1+x_i) + \frac{\tau_x}{\varepsilon^2}(x_i - (d_x - \tau_{1,x})), & x_i \in \Omega_{2,x} \cap \overline{\Omega}_x^N, \\ \left(1 + d_x + d_x \frac{d_x - x_i}{1 - d_x}\right) + \frac{\tau_x}{\varepsilon^2}(d_x + \tau_{2,x} - x_i), & x_i \in \Omega_{3,x} \cap \overline{\Omega}_x^N, \end{cases}$

$\phi_2(y_j) = \begin{cases} (1+y_j) + \frac{\tau_y}{\varepsilon^2}(y_j - (d_y - \tau_{1,y})), & y_j \in \Omega_{2,y} \cap \overline{\Omega}_y^N, \\ \left(1 + d_y + d_y \frac{d_y - y_j}{1 - d_y}\right) + \frac{\tau_y}{\varepsilon^2}(d_y + \tau_{2,y} - y_j), & y_j \in \Omega_{3,y} \cap \overline{\Omega}_y^N, \end{cases}$

$\tau_\mu = \min\{\tau_{1,\mu}, \tau_{2,\mu}\}$, $\mu = x, y$ we prove that $|w^\mu(x_i, y_j) - W_{i,j}^\mu| \leq CN^{-1}$, $\mu = n + \frac{1}{2}, n+1$, and $i, j = \frac{N}{4} + 1, \cdots, \frac{5N}{8} - 1$. By the triangle inequality, we have the desired results. □

Theorem 4. *Let $u(x_i, y_j, t_n)$ and $U_{i,j}^n$ be the solutions of (1) and (17), then*

$$\|u - U\| \leq C(h_t + N^{-1}\ln N).$$

Proof. The error can be obtained from the following

$$u(x_i, y_j, t_n) - U_{i,j}^n = \hat{u}^n(x_i, y_j) - U_{i,j}^n + u(x_i, y_j, t_n) - \overline{u}^n(x_i, y_j) + \overline{u}^n(x_i, y_j) - \hat{u}^n(x_i, y_j)$$

$$\|u(t_n) - U^n\| \leq \|\overline{u}^n - \hat{u}^n\| + \|\hat{u}^n - U^n\| + \|u(t_n) - \overline{u}^n\|.$$

From Lemma 3, Theorem 3 and Ref. [6], Theorem 1, we have

$$\|u(t_n) - U^n\| \leq \|u(t_n) - \overline{u}^n\| + \|\overline{u}^n - \hat{u}^n\| + \|\hat{u}^n - U^n\| \leq Ch_t + CN^{-1}\ln N,$$

which completes the proof. □

6. Numerical Validation

Two examples are presented in this section to validate the theoretical results presented in this article. The exact analytical solutions to the test problems are unknown, therefore we use the double mesh principle to calculate the maximum point-wise error and computational order of convergence. For fixed M, we define

$$E_\varepsilon^N = \max_{i,j} |\ U_{i,j}^N(h_x, h_y, h_t) - U_{i,j}^N(\frac{h_x}{2}, \frac{h_y}{2}, \frac{h_t}{2})\ |,\ 0 \leq i,j \leq N$$

$$D_{x,y}^N = \max_\varepsilon E_\varepsilon^N,\ \rho^N = \log_2\left(\frac{D_{x,y}^N}{D_{x,y}^{2N}}\right),$$

where $U_{i,j}^N(h_x, h_y, h_t)$ and $U_{i,j}^N(\frac{h_x}{2}, \frac{h_y}{2}, \frac{h_t}{2})$ are the numerical solutions at the node (x_i, y_j, t_n) with mesh sizes (h_x, h_y, h_t) and $(\frac{h_x}{2}, \frac{h_y}{2}, \frac{h_t}{2})$, respectively, $D_{x,y}^N$ is maximum over ε for fixed N.

Example 1. *Consider the 2D parabolic PDE (1) with discontinuous source and convection coefficients with the following data:*

$$\frac{\partial u}{\partial t} - \varepsilon \Delta u + \bar{p}(\mathbf{x}) \cdot \nabla u + q(\mathbf{x}) u(\mathbf{x} - \mathbf{d}, t) = g(\mathbf{x}, t),\ (\mathbf{x}, t) \in \mathfrak{D}^* \times (0, T]$$

$$p_1(\mathbf{x}) = \begin{cases} 1 + x(1-x),\ x \in (0, d_x),\ \forall y, \\ -(1 + x(1-x)),\ x \in (d_x, 1), \end{cases} \quad p_2(\mathbf{x}) = \begin{cases} 1 + y(1-y),\ y \in (0, d_y),\ \forall x, \\ -(1 + x(1-x)),\ y \in (d_y, 1), \end{cases}$$

$$q_1(\mathbf{x}) = -0.5 - x(1-x),\ q_2(\mathbf{x}) = -0.5 - y(1-y),\ d_x = 0.5 = d_y,$$

$$g_1(\mathbf{x}, t) = \begin{cases} -x^2 y(1-x)(1-y)^2 \exp\left(t^2 - \frac{xy}{1 + x^2 + y^2}\right),\ x \in (0, d_x), \\ xy(1-x)^2(1-y) exp\left(t^2 - \frac{x^2 y^2}{1 + x^2 - y^2}\right),\ x \in (d_x, 1), \end{cases}$$

$$g_2(\mathbf{x}, t) = \begin{cases} -x^3 y^2,\ y \in (0, d_y), \\ (1-x)^5 \sqrt{1-y},\ y \in (d_y, 1), \end{cases} \quad u_0 = \frac{xy(1-x)(1-y)}{1 + x^2 + y^2}.$$

Table 1 presents the maximum pointwise error and the order of convergence corresponding to Example 1. Figures 2 and 3 depict the numerical solution and pointwise maximum error of the problem studied in Example 1, respectively.

Table 1. Maximum error and order of convergence for the Example 1 with $M = 2^7$.

	N Number of Mesh Points in Space Directions				
$\varepsilon \downarrow$	16	32	64	128	256
10^{-1}	5.5196×10^{-3}	3.0933×10^{-3}	1.6543×10^{-3}	8.5850×10^{-4}	4.3790×10^{-4}
	0.83544	0.90292	0.94632	0.97123	-
10^{-3}	2.1762×10^{-2}	1.5092×10^{-2}	1.0563×10^{-2}	7.6976×10^{-3}	5.4021×10^{-3}
	0.52801	0.51484	0.45650	0.51089	-
10^{-5}	2.2373×10^{-2}	1.5657×10^{-2}	1.0944×10^{-2}	8.0343×10^{-3}	5.6554×10^{-3}
	0.51496	0.51669	0.44586	0.50655	-
10^{-7}	2.2379×10^{-2}	1.5663×10^{-2}	1.0948×10^{-2}	8.0378×10^{-3}	5.6580×10^{-3}
	0.51482	0.51668	0.44577	0.50650	-
10^{-9}	2.2379×10^{-2}	1.5663×10^{-2}	1.0948×10^{-2}	8.0378×10^{-3}	5.6580×10^{-3}
	0.51482	0.51668	0.44577	0.50650	-
$D_{x,y}^N$	2.2379×10^{-2}	1.5663×10^{-2}	1.0948×10^{-2}	8.0378×10^{-3}	5.6580×10^{-3}
ρ^N	0.51482	0.51668	0.44577	0.50650	-

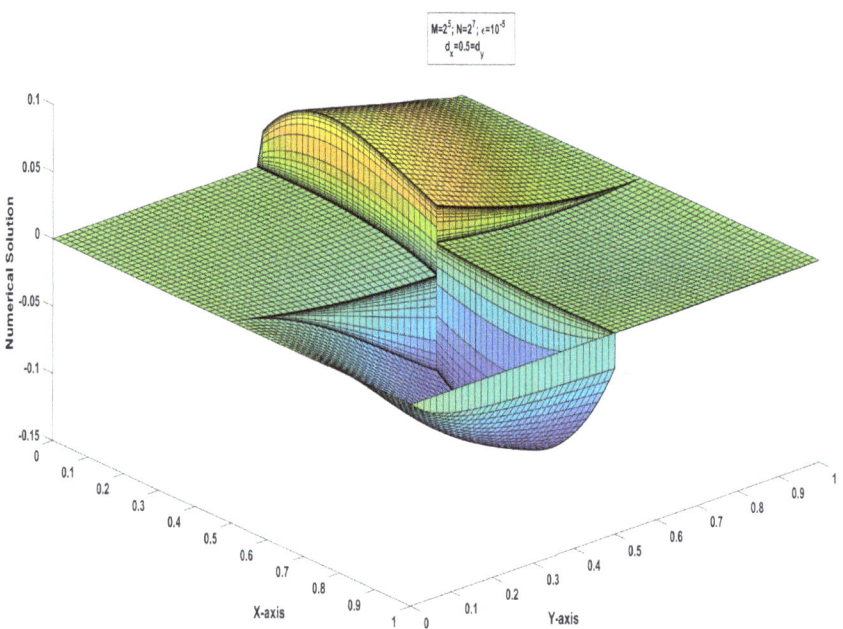

Figure 2. Numerical solution of Example 1 for fixed $M = 2^5$, $N = 2^7$, $\varepsilon = 10^{-5}$.

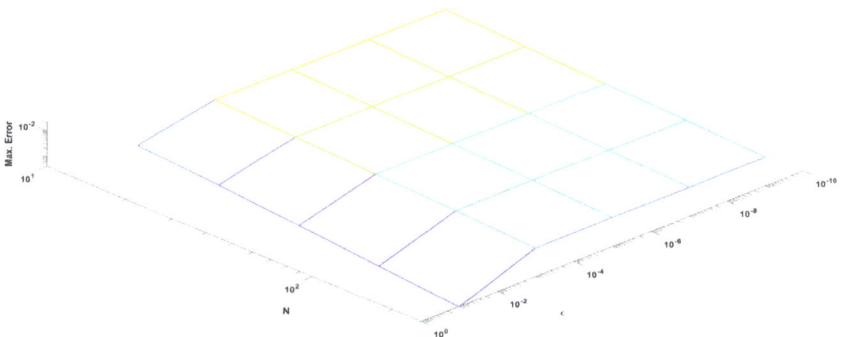

Figure 3. Maximum error of Example 1.

Example 2. *Consider the 2D parabolic PDE (1) with discontinuous source and convection coefficients with the following data:*

$$p_1(\mathbf{x}) = \begin{cases} 1 + x(1-x) + y^2, & x \in (0, d_x), \; \forall y, \\ -(1 + x(1-x) + \exp(-y)), & x \in (d_x, 1), \end{cases} \quad d_x = 0.5, d_y = 0.25$$

$$p_2(\mathbf{x}) = \begin{cases} 1 + y(1-y) + \sqrt{x}, & y \in (0, d_y), \; \forall x, \\ -(1 + y(1-y) + x^2), & y \in (d_y, 1), \end{cases}$$

$$c_1(\mathbf{x}) = -0.5 - x(1-x), \; c_2(\mathbf{x}) = -0.5 - y^2(1-y),$$

$$g_1(\mathbf{x}, t) = \begin{cases} 4txy \exp(x^2 + y^2), & x \in (0, d_x), \\ 4t(1-x)(1-y), & x \in (d_x, 1), \end{cases} \quad g_2(\mathbf{x}, t) = \begin{cases} 4xy \exp(x^2 + y^2), & y \in (0, d_y), \\ 4t(1-x)(1-y), & y \in (d_y, 1), \end{cases}$$

$$u_0 = \frac{xy(1-x)(1-y)}{1 + x^2 + y^2}.$$

The maximum pointwise error and the order of convergence corresponding to Example 2 are given in Table 2. Figures 4 and 5 display the numerical solution and pointwise maximum error of Example 2, respectively.

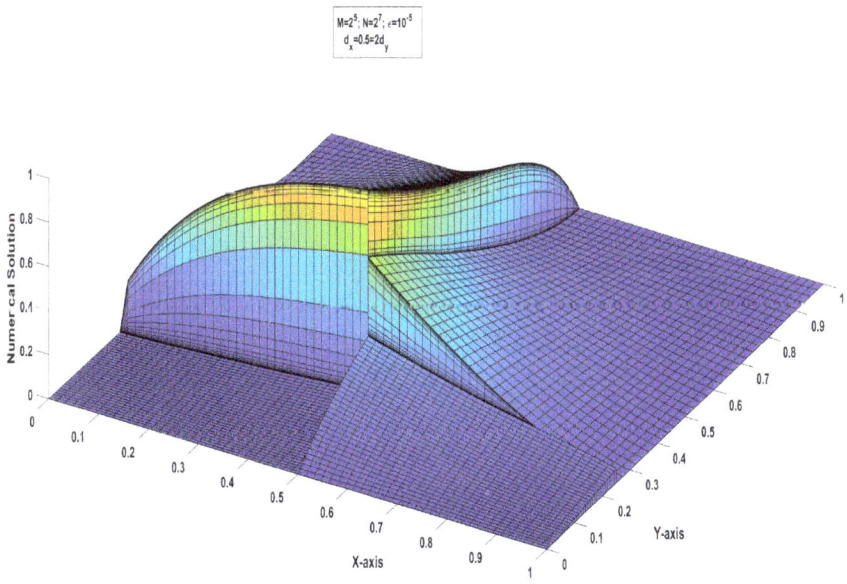

Figure 4. Numerical solution of Example 2 for fixed $M = 2^5$, $N = 2^7$, $\varepsilon = 10^{-5}$.

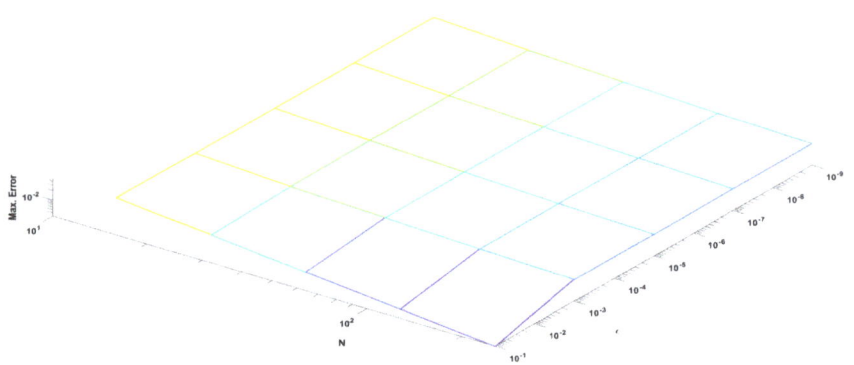

Figure 5. Maximum error of Example 2.

Table 2. Maximum error and order of convergence for the Example 2 with $M = 2^7$.

$\varepsilon \downarrow$	N Number of Mesh Points in Space Directions				
	16	32	64	128	256
10^{-1}	4.6432×10^{-2}	2.4055×10^{-2}	1.2254×10^{-2}	6.1910×10^{-3}	3.1182×10^{-3}
	0.94879	0.97310	0.98498	0.98946	-
10^{-3}	4.3139×10^{-2}	2.9874×10^{-2}	2.3658×10^{-2}	1.8574×10^{-2}	1.5132×10^{-2}
	0.53011	0.33654	0.34909	0.29568	-
10^{-5}	4.4807×10^{-2}	3.1372×10^{-2}	2.3990×10^{-2}	1.8528×10^{-2}	1.5113×10^{-2}
	0.51422	0.38706	0.37270	0.29390	-
10^{-7}	4.4821×10^{-2}	3.1389×10^{-2}	2.3995×10^{-2}	1.8528×10^{-2}	1.5113×10^{-2}
	0.51390	0.38755	0.37302	0.29389	-
10^{-9}	4.4821×10^{-2}	3.1389×10^{-2}	2.3995×10^{-2}	1.8528×10^{-2}	1.5113×10^{-2}
	0.51390	0.38756	0.37302	0.29389	-
$D_{x,y}^N$	4.6432×10^{-2}	3.1389×10^{-2}	2.3995×10^{-2}	1.8574×10^{-2}	1.5132×10^{-2}
ρ^N	0.56483	0.38756	0.36945	0.29568	-

7. Concluding Remarks

This article discusses singularly perturbed 2D parabolic delay differential equations with discontinuous convection coefficients and source terms. As pointed out in Ref. [3], the fractional step method results in low-cost computation for 2D problems. Therefore, we first apply the fractional implicit Euler method for the time derivative. Then the higher dimensional problem is reduced to lower dimensional problems. In fact, we get $2N$ system of uncoupled equations. Each equation is a singularly perturbed differential equation with a discontinuous convection coefficient and source term. As discussed in Ref. [13], we discretized the spatial domains Ω_μ, $\mu = x, y$ in the same manner, such as $\overline{\Omega}_\mu^N$, $\mu = x, y$. On each mesh we apply the difference scheme $\mathfrak{D}_\mu^N U_{i,j}$, $\mu = x, y$. It is proved that the present method is of almost first-order convergence in space and time. Figures 2 and 4 represent the test problems solutions stated in Examples 1 and 2, respectively, we see that, the layers occurs at the points d_x and d_y. Tables 1 and 2 present the maximum pointwise errors of the test example problems. It is also worth noting that when the parameter ε drops, the maximum pointwise error grows and stabilizes. It is assumed that the number of mesh points in the time direction is $M = 128$. From Figures 3 and 5 we see that the maximum pointwise error decreases as N increases. The present method works for the problems with any delay arguments of size $0 << d_\mu \leq 1$, $\mu = x, y$. In Example 1 we assumed that $d_x = 0.5 = d_y$, whereas in Example 2 we assumed that $d_x = 0.5$, $d_y = 0.25$.

Author Contributions: Methodology, V.S.; software, V.S.; formal analysis, S.N.; investigation, S.N.; writing—original draft preparation, V.S.; writing—review and editing, S.N. All authors have read and agreed to the published version of the manuscript.

Funding: This research received no external funding.

Institutional Review Board Statement: Not applicable.

Informed Consent Statement: Not applicable.

Data Availability Statement: Not applicable.

Acknowledgments: The authors are thankful for the DST-SERB for providing the fund under the scheme TARE, File No. TAR/2021/000053. The authors wish to acknowledge the referees for their valuable comments and suggestions, which helped to improve the presentation.

Conflicts of Interest: The authors declare no conflict of interest.

References

1. Roos, H.G.; Stynes, M.; Tobiska, L. *Robust Numerical Methods for Singularly Perturbed Differential Equations*; Springer: Berlin, Germany, 2008.
2. Miller, J.J.H.; O'Riordan, E.; Shishkin, G.I. Fitted Numerical Methods for Singular Perturbation Problems. In *Error Estimates in the Maximum Norm for Linear Problems in One and Two Dimensions*; World Scientific Publishing Co., Pte., Ltd.: Singapore, 2012.
3. Clavero, C.; Jorge, J.C. A fractional step method for 2D parabolic convection–diffusion singularly perturbation problems: Uniform convergence and order reduction. *Numer. Algorithms* **2017**, *75*, 809–826. [CrossRef]
4. Clavero, C.; Jorge, J.C.; Lisbona, F.; Shishkin, G.I. An alternating direction scheme on a nonuniform mesh for reaction–diffusion parabolic problem. *IMA J. Numer. Anal.* **2000** *20*, 263–280. [CrossRef]
5. Mukherjee, K.; Natesan, S. Parameter-uniform fractional step hybrid numerical scheme for 2D singularly perturbed parabolic convection–diffusion problems. *J. Appl. Math. Comput.* **2019**, *60*, 51–86. [CrossRef]
6. Majumdar, A.; Natesan, S. Parameter-uniform numerical method for singularly perturbed 2-D parabolic convection-diffusion problem with interior layers. *Math. Meth. Appl. Sci.* **2022**, *45*, 3039–3057. [CrossRef]
7. Stein, R.B. A theoretical analysis of neuronal variability. *Biol. J.* **1965**, *5*, 173–194 [CrossRef]
8. Musila, M.; Lansky, P. Generalized Stein's model for anatomically complex neurons. *BioSystems* **1991**, *25*, 179–191. [CrossRef]
9. Lange, C.G.; Miura, R.M. Singularly perturbation analysis of boundary-value problems for differential-difference equations. *SIAM J. Appl. Math.* **1982**, *42*, 502–530. [CrossRef]
10. Amiraliyev, G.M.; Cimen, E. Numerical method for a singularly perturbed convection-diffusion problem with delay. *Appl. Math. Comput.* **2010**, *216*, 2351–2359. [CrossRef]
11. Kadalbajoo, M.K.; Sharma, K.K. Numerical treatment of boundary value problems for second order singularly perturbed delay differential equations. *Comput. Appl. Math.* **2005**, *24*, 151–172. [CrossRef]
12. Subburayan, V.; Ramanujam, N. An Initial Value Technique for Singularly Perturbed Convection–Diffusion Problems with a Negative Shift. *J. Optim. Theory Appl.* **2013**, *158*, 234–250. [CrossRef]
13. Subburayan, V. A parameter uniform numerical method for singularly perturbed delay problems with discontinuous convection coefficient. *Arab J. Math. Sci.* **2016**, *22*, 191–206. [CrossRef]
14. Ansari, A.R.; Bakr, S.A.; Shishkin, G.I. A parameter-robust finite difference method for singularly perturbed delay parabolic partial differential equations. *J. Comput. Appl. Math.* **2007**, *205*, 552–566. [CrossRef]
15. Abhishek, D.; Natesan, S. Parameter-uniform numerical method for singularly perturbed 2D delay parabolic convection–diffusion problems on Shishkin mesh. *J. Appl. Math. Comput.* **2019**, *59*, 207–225.
16. Wu, J. *Theory and Applications of Partial Functional Differential Equations*; Springer: New York, NY, USA, 1996.
17. Briani, M.; Chioma, C.; Natalini, R. Convergence of numerical schemes for viscosity solutions to integro-differential degenerate parabolic problems arising in financial theory. *Numer. Math.* **2004**, *98*, 607–646. [CrossRef]
18. Ladyzenskaja, O.A.; Solonnikov, V.A.; Ural'ceva, N.N. *Linear and Quasi-Linear Equations of Parabolic Type*; American Mathematical Soc.: Providence, RI, USA, 1968.
19. Farrell, P.A.; Hegarty, A.F.; Miller, J.J.H.; O'Riordan, E.; Shishkin, G.I. Global maximum norm parameter-uniform numerical method for a singularly perturbed convection-diffusion problem with discontinuous convection coefficient. *Math. Comput. Model.* **2004**, *40*, 1375–1392. [CrossRef]
20. Poole, G.; Boullion, T. A survey on M-Matrices. *SIAM Rev.* **1974**, *16*, 419–427. [CrossRef]
21. Zadorin, A.I. Approaches to constructing two-dimensional interpolation formulas in the presence of boundary layers. *J. Phys. Conf. Ser.* **2022**, *2182*, 2–9. [CrossRef]
22. Süli, E.; Mayers, D.F. *An Introduction to Numerical Analysis*; Cambridge University Press: Cambridge, UK, 2003.

Article

Boundary Feedback Stabilization of Two-Dimensional Shallow Water Equations with Viscosity Term

Ben Mansour Dia [1,*], Mouhamadou Samsidy Goudiaby [2] and Oliver Dorn [3]

[1] College of Petroleum Engineering and Geosciences (CPG), King Fahd University of Petroleum and Minerals (KFUPM), Dhahran 31261, Saudi Arabia
[2] Département de Mathématiques, UFR des Sciences et Technologies, Université Assane Seck de Ziguinchor, Ziguinchor BP 523, Senegal
[3] Department of Mathematics, Alan Turing Building, The University of Manchester, Oxford Rd., Manchester M13 9PL, UK
* Correspondence: ben.dia@kfupm.edu.sa; Tel.: +966-13-860-2908

Abstract: This paper treats a water flow regularization problem by means of local boundary conditions for the two-dimensional viscous shallow water equations. Using an *a-priori* energy estimate of the perturbation state and the Faedo–Galerkin method, we build a stabilizing boundary feedback control law for the volumetric flow in a finite time that is prescribed by the solvability of the associated Cauchy problem. We iterate the same approach to build by cascade a stabilizing feedback control law for infinite time. Thanks to a positive arbitrary time-dependent stabilization function, the control law provides an exponential decay of the energy.

Keywords: shallow water flow; Faedo–Galerkin method; feedback control; PDE's stabilization

MSC: 76D55; 93D15; 65M60; 93B18

1. Introduction

Regularization of free-surface fluid flows is a problem of practical interest for environmental and budgetary purposes in the current situation of climate change that rarefies fresh water sources worldwide. Depending on the specific application, the regularization of fluid flows is performed through control methodologies of the Navier–Stokes equations or a system of partial differential equations derived from them, which describe a particular setting and/or physical properties. Several mechanisms of controlling fluid flows have been designed in the recent past, see [1–5].

Control and stabilization of fluid flows governed by the Navier–Stokes equations have been extensively studied in the literature using various approaches. In the three-dimensional setting, a local stabilization around an unstable stationary state is performed in [6] by means of a feedback control law. In [7], the existence of time-points values of boundary feedback laws is achieved by an optimal control problem to alleviate the high regularity required for the velocity components. One of the widely adopted approaches formulates the associate optimal control problem in infinite dimensional spaces, which gives rise to a Riccati equation [8]. Stabilization of the Navier-Stokes equations from the boundary or from a portion of the boundary is mainly investigated by means of feedback control laws. In addition to the series of papers [9–13], the inclusive examination in [14] lists a number of approaches for control by means of feedback laws. It also discusses the associated challenges, such as start-control, impulse-control and distributed-control laws, which have been studied for the Oseen and Navier-Stokes equations. Recently, global solution as well as an optimality system and a second-order sufficient optimality condition were obtained for the stationary two-dimensional Stokes equations [15,16], while an optimal controllability of a stationary two-dimensional non-Newtonian fluid in a pipeline network is studied in [17].

When the horizontal length scale of the physical domain is much greater than the vertical one, the flow movement can be captured by the water height and the horizontal velocity field. In that particular setting of shallow water flows, great advances have been made in the mechanism of controlling free-surface flow parameters by local boundary conditions, despite the challenges associated with the nonlinearity of the governing equations, see [18,19] for detailed and comprehensive reviews. Global stability of the two-dimensional water flow has been achieved in L^2-norm [20] using the symmetrization of the flux matrices, in H^2-norm [21], by acting on the tangential velocity. The approach of tracking the flow energy through the Riemann invariant variables is adopted in [22,23] in the one-dimensional setting and is explored in [24] for the two-dimensional channel flow. Besides the provided flexibility in practical experiments, the adding of the viscosity influence provides regularizing effects in estimating the flow energy, see [25].

In this paper, we address the stabilization of two-dimensional viscous shallow water around a steady-state, that is, the problem of driving the flow-state variables of viscous incompressible fluid inside a bounded container to a desired steady state. The control law acts on the volumetric flow vector along a portion of the boundary. Due to the challenges inherent in dealing with the nonlinear advection, we alleviate the nonlinearity issues by processing to the linearization around the steady state for small perturbations of the flow state. The resulting system of linear partial differential equations is referred to as the linearized shallow-water model, for which the existence and the uniqueness of solution is addressed by combining some notions of compactness and an a-priori energy estimate using the Faedo-Galerkin method. Subsequently, the stabilization of the nonlinear model around the steady state is rearranged as the stabilization of the linearized model around zero. In a short time, prescribed by the existence of a solution to the Cauchy problem associated with the weak formulation in an Hilbertian basis, the control building process explores only the estimation of the non-viscous energy of the linearized model and relies on a continuous time-dependent stabilization rate. The global-time stabilization result is established by cascading over a sequence of intervals.

The content of this paper is organized as follows: Section 2 introduces the equations governing the flow of a viscous shallow water in a three-dimensional domain with a given bathymetry. In Section 3, we detail the problem setting: we present the steady-state model, discuss the linearization, set the notations and the assumptions of the function spaces, and state the stabilization problem. Section 4 is devoted to the design of the small-time feedback control law. The main result of the stabilization of the linearized shallow-water model through the exponential decay of the energy is presented in Section 5. We conclude by giving some perspective directions of improvement of the presented method in Section 6.

2. 2-D Viscous Shallow-Water Equations

Consider a three-dimensional domain with a non-flat bottom in which a viscous water flows with a free-surface denoted by Ω, a bounded subset of $\mathbb{R}^2$, with boundary $\partial \Omega = \Gamma_1 \cup \Gamma_2$. The SWE (shallow-water equations) are a set of partial differential equations derived by depth integrating the Navier–Stokes equations, see [26–29], with the assumption that the horizontal length scale of the domain is much greater than the vertical one. In the absence of Coriolis, frictional, and wind effects, the 2D viscous SWE with a viscosity coefficient μ in $[m^2 \cdot s^{-1}]$ are given by

$$\begin{cases} \partial_t H + \partial_x(HV_1) + \partial_y(HV_2) = 0 & \text{in } \mathcal{Q}, \\ \partial_t(HV_1) + \partial_x\left(HV_1^2\right) + gH\partial_x(H+\eta) + \partial_y(HV_1V_2) = \mu\Delta(HV_1) & \text{in } \mathcal{Q}, \\ \partial_t(HV_2) + \partial_x(HV_1V_2) + \partial_y\left(HV_2^2\right) + gH\partial_y(H+\eta) = \mu\Delta(HV_2) & \text{in } \mathcal{Q}, \\ (H, V_1, V_2)(0, \cdot, \cdot) = \left(H^0, V_1^0, V_2^0\right)(\cdot, \cdot) & \text{in } \Omega, \\ \text{boundary conditions to be specified,} \end{cases} \quad (1)$$

where $\mathcal{Q} = (0, T) \times \Omega$, $T > 0$ denotes the duration of the study, H the height of the water column, (V_1, V_2) the velocity vector with reference to (Ox, Oy), η the bathymetry describing the bottom elevation, and g is the constant of the acceleration due to the gravity force. The symbol ∂_t designates the time derivative while ∂_x and ∂_y are the space derivatives in the x-direction and y-direction, respectively. The differential operator Δ represents the diffusion field $\Delta = \partial_{xx} + \partial_{yy}$. The triplet (H, V_1, V_2) varies with (t, x, y) and forms the solution of (1) while the bathymetry $\eta(x, y)$ is independent of the time variable because there is no sediment transport. For the unidirectional propagation, an alternative approach to describing the waves at the free surface of shallow water under the influence of gravity is to consider the Korteweg–de Vries equation, see [30], where notions in differential geometry help to establish the existence of global solutions, see [31].

The diffusion effects have been modeled in several ways in the literature. It is shown in [32] that the formulation $\mu H \Delta V_i$ on the right hand side of (1) is not consistent with the primitive form of the equations for the energy norm and an energetically consistent formulation is given therein. This is deeply analyzed through the existence of weak solutions to the SWE in [33], where, by looking for (V_1, V_2) bounded in $L^2(0, T, H^1(\Omega))$, $H \in L^\infty(0, T, L^1(\Omega))$ and $H \log H \in L^\infty(0, T, L^1(\Omega))$ to induce the dissipation, the term HV_i stands as an obstacle for the existence of solutions. That is why there is a constraint of small data to guarantee the existence of time-local weak solutions.

For the diffusion formulation $\mu\Delta(HV_i)$, as used here on the right hand side of (1), the existence of weak solutions and its stability are described in [26]. In that case, the diffusion provides regularizing effects due to an entropic inequality on the height variable H. It is important to notice that the stability result is restricted to the models where capillarity and friction are taken into account. For the 1-D model, a clearer result for the existence of weak global solutions can be elaborated with much less restrictive data [33].

Using the volumetric flow variable vector $\mathbf{Q} = (Q_1, Q_2) = (HV_1, HV_2)$, the system (1) is rewritten for further analysis in the following conservative form:

$$\begin{aligned} \partial_t H + \text{div}\mathbf{Q} &= 0, & \text{in } \mathcal{Q}, \\ \partial_t \mathbf{Q} + \text{div}\mathcal{F}(H, \mathbf{Q}) + gH\nabla(H+\eta) - \mu\Delta\mathbf{Q} &= 0, & \text{in } \mathcal{Q}, \end{aligned} \quad (2)$$

where $\mathbf{Q} = (Q_1, Q_2)^\top$ (the superscript $\top$ is the transpose operator), the matrix $\mathcal{F}(H, \mathbf{Q}) = \mathbf{Q} \cdot \mathbf{Q}^\top / H$, the differential operator ∇ is the gradient field, and $\text{div}(\cdot)$ stands for the divergence operator, $\text{div}(f) = \nabla \cdot f$ for a sufficiently regular vector function. Although the non-conservative formulation, see [20], is known to provide a better mass conservation of the volumetric quantity of water, it does not hold across a shock or a hydraulic jump since velocities do not generate fundamental conservation equations. On the other hand, the conservative formulation (2) supports front discontinuities such as shock waves at a fluid's interface and irregular source terms, and appeals to Riemann solver for numerical resolution, see [22,23,34,35]. Therefore, the conservative form (2) is well-suited for our stabilization problem, which we state in the next section.

3. Statement of the Problem

In this section, we lay out the stabilization problem from the linearization around the steady state to the setting of finding the boundary feedback control law.

3.1. Steady-State, Linearization

The objective of the stabilization is to bring the variables of the flow to a given steady state that is the reference state. In practice, this consists of finding a controller (inflows, outflows) allowing to adjust the flow parameters to keep the flow state variables near this reference state. We denote the steady state by $\bar{U} = (\bar{h}, \bar{q}_1, \bar{q}_2)^\top$ and it is stationary and given by:

$$\begin{aligned} \mathrm{div}\bar{q} &= 0, & \text{in } \Omega, \\ g\bar{h}\nabla(\bar{h}+\eta) - \tfrac{1}{\bar{h}}\mathcal{F}(\bar{h},\bar{q})\cdot\nabla\bar{h} + \tfrac{1}{\bar{h}}(\nabla\bar{q})\cdot\bar{q} - \mu\Delta\bar{q} &= 0 & \text{in } \Omega. \end{aligned} \qquad (3)$$

The hydrodynamical variable vector (H, Q_1, Q_2) is formed by the equilibrium state $(\bar{h}, \bar{q}_1, \bar{q}_2)$ and a perturbation state denoted by (h, q_1, q_2). Hence, the linearization consists of using

$$\begin{aligned} H(t,x,y) &= \bar{h}(x,y) + h(t,x,y), \\ Q_1(t,x,y) &= \bar{q}_1(x,y) + q_1(t,x,y), \\ Q_2(t,x,y) &= \bar{q}_2(x,y) + q_2(t,x,y). \end{aligned} \qquad (4)$$

We proceed to the linearization of the system (2) by replacing the state variables H, Q_1 and Q_2 by their above expressions. In addition, we consider the following assumption $|h| \ll \bar{h}$, $|q_1| \ll |\bar{q}_1|$ and $|q_2| \ll |\bar{q}_2|$ to justify keeping only the first-order terms in the perturbation state because we neglect higher order terms. We denote by

$$\bar{v} = \begin{pmatrix} \bar{v}_1 \\ \bar{v}_2 \end{pmatrix}, \quad \boldsymbol{\alpha}_0 = \begin{pmatrix} \alpha_0^1 \\ \alpha_0^2 \end{pmatrix}, \quad A = \begin{pmatrix} \beta_0^1 & \gamma_0^1 \\ \beta_0^2 & \gamma_0^2 \end{pmatrix}, \quad \text{and} \quad B = \begin{pmatrix} \alpha_1^1 & \alpha_2^1 \\ \alpha_1^2 & \alpha_2^2 \end{pmatrix},$$

where the coefficients are given by:

$$\begin{aligned} \alpha_0^1 &= g\partial_x \bar{h} + g\partial_x \eta, & \alpha_0^2 &= g\partial_y \bar{h} + g\partial_y \eta, \\ \beta_0^1 &= \tfrac{1}{\bar{h}}\left(2\partial_x \bar{q}_1 - 2\bar{v}_1 \partial_x \bar{h} + \partial_y \bar{q}_2 - \bar{v}_2 \partial_y \bar{h}\right), & \beta_0^2 &= \tfrac{1}{\bar{h}}\left(\partial_x \bar{q}_2 - \bar{v}_2 \partial_x \bar{h}\right), \\ \gamma_0^1 &= \tfrac{1}{\bar{h}}\left(\partial_y \bar{q}_1 - \bar{v}_1 \partial_y \bar{h}\right), & \gamma_0^2 &= \tfrac{1}{\bar{h}}\left(2\partial_y \bar{q}_2 - 2\bar{v}_2 \partial_y \bar{h} + \partial_x \bar{q}_1 - \bar{v}_1 \partial_x \bar{h}\right), \\ \alpha_1^1 &= c^2 - \bar{v}_1^2, & \alpha_2^1 &= -\bar{v}_1 \bar{v}_2, \\ \alpha_1^2 &= -\bar{v}_1 \bar{v}_2, & \alpha_2^2 &= c^2 - \bar{v}_2^2. \end{aligned}$$

The constant $c = \sqrt{g\bar{h}}$ is the wave speed at the equilibrium. The linearization gives rise to the model governing the evolution of the residual state. This is the following linearized 2D shallow-water system

$$\begin{aligned} \partial_t h + \mathrm{div}\, q &= 0 & \text{in } \mathcal{Q}, \\ \partial_t q + (\mathrm{div}\, q)\bar{v} + \nabla q \cdot \bar{v} - \mu \Delta q + B \cdot \nabla h + A \cdot q + h\boldsymbol{\alpha}_0 &= 0 & \text{in } \mathcal{Q}, \\ q(t=0) &= q^0 & \text{in } \Omega, \\ h(t=0) &= h^0 & \text{in } \Omega. \end{aligned} \qquad (5)$$

With given initial state (h^0, q^0), the control problem consists of providing suitable boundary conditions $\mathcal{V} = (\mathcal{V}_1, \mathcal{V}_2)$ on a portion of the boundary, Γ_1, so that the state (h, q) converges in time towards $(0,0,0)$ with the assumption that the physical domain is uniformly convex with a Lipschitz boundary. Note that the advection, in the linearized system (5), runs with constant flux matrices depending only on the steady state $\partial_x \mathcal{F}(\bar{U})$ and $\partial_y \mathcal{F}(\bar{U})$. The controlled boundary portion Γ_1 is defined in the next section.

3.2. Notations and Function Spaces

Physically, the domain Ω is a regular (it provides the required smoothness for a Lipschitz boundary) open-bounded subset of $\mathbb{R}^2$ with boundary $\partial\Omega$. We remind the reader that there is no sediment movement; the bathymetry is, therefore, a time-invariant function, see Figure 1.

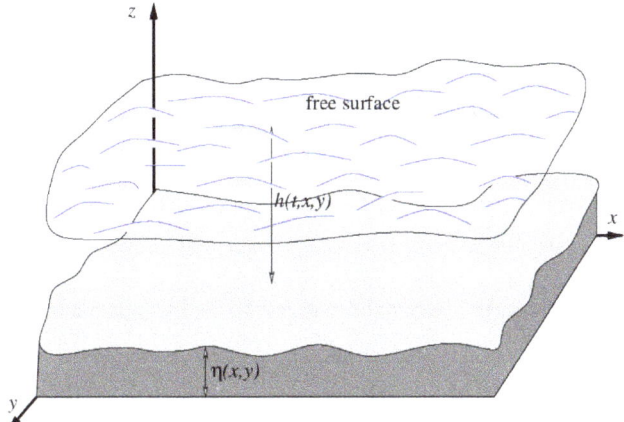

Figure 1. Domain representation.

For the sake of clarity, we specify the following two statements:

(S1) The boundary portion, where the control action is applied, is given by

$$\Gamma_1 = \{(x,y) \in \partial\Omega : 2\bar{v}_1 n_x + \bar{v}_2 n_y < 0 \text{ and } \bar{v}_1 n_x + 2\bar{v}_2 n_y < 0\}.$$

The boundary portion Γ_1 exists (is nonempty) and is included in the boundary portion given by $(\bar{v}_1, \bar{v}_2)^\top \cdot \vec{n} < 0$, where the vector $\vec{n} = (n_x, n_y)^\top$ is the external normal unit vector at the boundary. The uncontrolled boundary portion $\Gamma_2 = \partial\Omega \backslash \Gamma_1$.

(S2) The flux variation is bounded at the boundary $\partial\Omega$. This follows naturally because of the sub-critical flow regime considered here, and is stated for the sake of clarity. It means that the limit when (x,y) tends to the boundary $\partial\Omega$ of the term $\|\nabla q\|_{L^2(\Omega)}$ is bounded, that is,

$$\max\left\{\lim_{(x,y)\to(x_b,y_b)} \|\nabla q(x,y)\|_{L^2(\Omega)} \text{ for } (x_b, y_b) \in \partial\Omega\right\} \text{ is finite.}$$

The regularity of the steady-state $(\bar{h}, \bar{v}_1, \bar{v}_2)$ depends on the nature of the bathymetry η; for instance, $\bar{h}, \bar{v}_1$ and $\bar{v}_2$ are constant if the bathymetry is constant (flat bottom tomography). We, therefore, consider a sufficiently regular bathymetry η, such that $\bar{h}, \bar{v}_1$ and $\bar{v}_2$ are differentiable in Ω: $\bar{h} \in H_0^1(\Omega)$, $\bar{v}_1 \in H^1(\Omega)$ and $\bar{v}_2 \in H^1(\Omega)$.

For $\mathcal{Q} = (0, T) \times \Omega$, we consider the space $L^2(0, T; H^1(\Omega))$. In the same setting, we introduce also the space $L^2\left(0, T; H^1_{\Gamma_1}(\Omega)\right)$, where the Hilbert space $H^1_{\Gamma_1}(\Omega)$ is given by

$$H^1_{\Gamma_1}(\Omega) = \left\{u \in L^2(\Omega) : \nabla u \in L^2(\Omega) \text{ and } u_{|\Gamma_2} = 0\right\}.$$

The space $H^1(\Omega)$ and its subspace $H^1_{\Gamma_1}(\Omega)$ are equipped with the norm $\|\cdot\|_{H^1(\Omega)}$ defined for a function u by $\|u\|^2_{H^1(\Omega)} = \|u\|^2_{L^2(\Omega)} + \|\nabla u\|^2_{L^2(\Omega)}$. In the rest of this paper, we denote by W the space given by $W = L^2\left(0, T; H^1(\Omega)\right) \times L^2\left(0, T; H^1_{\Gamma_1}(\Omega)\right) \times L^2\left(0, T; H^1_{\Gamma_1}(\Omega)\right)$.

3.3. The Stabilization Problem

With the conditions (4), the task of stabilizing the nonlinear state (H, Q_1, Q_2) around the steady state $(\bar{h}, \bar{q}_1, \bar{q}_2)$ is reformulated as a stabilization problem of the perturbation state (h, q) around $(0, 0, 0)$. The objective is to find suitable local boundary conditions on q that take the flow-state variables as quickly as possible to the steady-state equilibrium. We formulate this goal as a stabilization problem in the following way

$$
\begin{aligned}
\partial_t h + \operatorname{div} q &= 0 \text{ in } \mathcal{Q}, \\
\partial_t q + (\operatorname{div} q)\bar{v} + \nabla q \cdot \bar{v} - \mu \Delta q + B \cdot \nabla h + A \cdot q + h\alpha_0 &= 0 \text{ in } \mathcal{Q}, \\
q(t=0) &= q^0 \text{ in } \Omega, \\
h(t=0) &= h^0 \text{ in } \Omega, \\
q &= \mathcal{V} \text{ on } (0, \infty) \times \Gamma_1, \\
q &= 0 \text{ on } (0, \infty) \times \Gamma_2.
\end{aligned} \tag{6}
$$

Concretely, we look for $\mathcal{V}$ such that (h, q) from (6) converges to $(0, 0, 0)$. In that sequel, we state the weak formulation associated with (6) that consists in writing (6) as a system of ordinary differential equations depending only on the variable t by using the Green's formula of integration by parts: for all $(\varphi, \phi, \psi) \in W$, find (h, q_1, q_2) in W satisfying

$$
\int_\Omega \varphi \partial_t h \, d\Omega - \int_\Omega q \nabla \varphi \, d\Omega = -\int_{\Gamma_1} \varphi q \cdot \mathbf{n} \, d\sigma, \tag{7}
$$

$$
\begin{aligned}
&\int_\Omega \partial_t q_1 \phi \, d\Omega + \int_\Omega (\operatorname{div} q \bar{v}_1) \phi \, d\Omega - \int_\Omega q_1 \operatorname{div}(\phi \bar{v}) \, d\Omega + \mu \int_\Omega \nabla q_1 \nabla \phi \, d\Omega - \int_\Omega h \operatorname{div}(\phi B_{1.}) \, d\Omega \\
&+ \int_\Omega \beta_0^1 q_1 \phi \, d\Omega + \int_\Omega \gamma_0^1 q_2 \phi \, d\Omega + \int_\Omega h \alpha_0^1 \phi \, d\Omega \\
&= -\int_{\Gamma_1} (q_1 \phi) \bar{v} \cdot \mathbf{n} \, d\sigma + \mu \int_{\Gamma_1} (\nabla q_1 \cdot \mathbf{n}) \phi \, d\sigma - \int_{\Gamma_1} h \phi (B_{1.} \cdot \mathbf{n}) \, d\sigma,
\end{aligned} \tag{8}
$$

$$
\begin{aligned}
&\int_\Omega \partial_t q_2 \psi \, d\Omega + \int_\Omega (\operatorname{div} q \bar{v}_2) \psi \, d\Omega - \int_\Omega q_2 \operatorname{div}(\psi \bar{v}) \, d\Omega + \mu \int_\Omega \nabla q_2 \nabla \psi \, d\Omega - \int_\Omega h \operatorname{div}(\psi B_{2.}) \, d\Omega \\
&+ \int_\Omega \beta_0^2 q_1 \psi \, d\Omega + \int_\Omega \gamma_0^2 q_2 \psi \, d\Omega + \int_\Omega h \alpha_0^2 \psi \, d\Omega \\
&= -\int_{\Gamma_1} (q_2 \psi) \bar{v} \cdot \mathbf{n} \, d\sigma + \mu \int_{\Gamma_1} (\nabla q_2 \cdot n) \psi \, d\sigma - \int_{\Gamma_1} h \psi (B_{2.} \cdot \mathbf{n}) \, d\sigma.
\end{aligned} \tag{9}
$$

From now, the weak formulation of the stabilization problem (6) refers to (7)–(9), which are obtained by integration by parts of (6) multiplied with the test function (φ, ϕ, ψ).

4. Preliminary Result: Small-Time Control Design

The stabilization problem (6) is constrained by the existence of a solution. In this section, we examine the existence of a solution to the dynamical system resulting from the representation of the weak formulation in an Hilbertian basis and we address the short-time stabilization problem.

Lemma 1 (Existence of small-time weak solutions). *There exists a time T_1 such that the ordinary differential Equations (7)–(9) with the Cauchy condition admit a solution on the time interval $[0, T_1]$.*

The above lemma addresses the existence of local weak solutions. The proof is elaborated in two steps: the first one consists of writing the weak form as a system of differential equations using a Hilbertian basis of finite dimensions of W. The second step deals with the existence of a solution of the resulting system of differential equations thanks to the Cauchy–Peano theorem, see [36,37].

Proof. The existence of a local weak solution is elaborated using the Cauchy–Peano theorem. Let $\{a_i\}_{i\geq 1}$ (respectively, by $\{e_i\}_{i\geq 1}$) denote an Hilbertian basis of the space $H^1(\Omega)$ (respectively, $H^1_{\Gamma_1}(\Omega)$). We consider a positive integer n such that the finite dimensional space $span\{a_i : 1 \leq i \leq n\}$ contains the term h_n^0 of a sequence of functions $(h_n^0)_{n\geq 1}$ that converges toward the initial condition h^0 (respectively, $span\{e_i : 1 \leq i \leq n\}$) containing the terms q^0_{1n} and q^0_{2n} sequences of functions $(q^0_{1n})_{n\geq 1}$ and $(q^0_{2n})_{n\geq 1}$ converging, respectively, to q^0_1 and q^0_2). For a sufficiently large n, the projection of h, q_1 and q_2 allows us to write

$$h \approx \sum_{i=1}^n \alpha_i(t) a_i(x,y), \quad q_1 \approx \sum_{i=1}^n \beta_i(t) e_i(x,y), \quad \text{and} \quad q_2 \approx \sum_{i=1}^n \gamma_i(t) e_i(x,y),$$

where $(\alpha_i(t))_{1\leq i\leq n}$, $(\beta_i(t))_{1\leq i\leq n}$ and $(\gamma_i(t))_{1\leq i\leq n}$ are, respectively, the unknown coordinates of h, q_1 and q_2 at time t. Replacing test functions (φ, ϕ, ψ) by the (a_j, e_j, e_j) for the jth dimension, the weak formulation becomes:

$$\sum_{i=1}^n \partial_t \alpha_i(t) \int_\Omega a_i e_j d\Omega - \sum_{i=1}^n \beta_i(t) \int_\Omega a_i \partial_x e_j d\Omega - \sum_{i=1}^n \gamma_i(t) \int_\Omega g a_i \partial_y e_j d\Omega = -\int_{\Gamma_1} e_j \mathcal{V} \cdot \mathbf{n} d\sigma,$$

$$\sum_{i=1}^n \partial_t \beta_i(t) \int_\Omega e_i e_j d\Omega + \sum_{i=1}^n \beta_i(t) \int_\Omega \bar{v}_1 e_j \partial_x e_i d\Omega + \sum_{i=1}^n \gamma_i(t) \int_\Omega \bar{v}_1 e_j \partial_y e_i d\Omega$$

$$- \sum_{i=1}^n \beta_i(t) \int_\Omega e_i \text{div}(e_j \bar{v}) d\Omega + \sum_{i=1}^n \beta_i(t) \mu \int_\Omega \nabla e_i \nabla e_j d\Omega$$

$$- \sum_{i=1}^n \alpha_i(t) \int_\Omega a_i \text{div}(e_j \mathbf{B}_{1\cdot}) d\Omega + \sum_{i=1}^n \beta_i(t) \int_\Omega A_{11} e_i e_j d\Omega$$

$$+ \sum_{i=1}^n \gamma_i(t) \int_\Omega A_{12} e_i e_j d\Omega + \sum_{i=1}^n \alpha_i(t) \int_\Omega \alpha_0^1 a_i e_j d\Omega$$

$$= -\int_{\Gamma_1} (\mathcal{V}_1 e_j) \bar{v} \cdot \mathbf{n} d\sigma + \mu \sum_{i=1}^n \beta_i(t) \int_{\Gamma_1} (\nabla e_i \cdot \mathbf{n}) e_j d\sigma - \int_{\Gamma_1} h e_j (\mathbf{B}_{1\cdot} \cdot \mathbf{n}) d\sigma,$$

$$\sum_{i=1}^n \partial_t \gamma_i(t) \int_\Omega e_i e_j d\Omega + \sum_{i=1}^n \beta_i(t) \int_\Omega \bar{v}_2 e_j \partial_x e_i d\Omega + \sum_{i=1}^n \gamma_i(t) \int_\Omega \bar{v}_2 e_j \partial_y e_i d\Omega$$

$$- \sum_{i=1}^n \gamma_i(t) \int_\Omega e_i \text{div}(e_j \bar{v}) d\Omega + \sum_{i=1}^n \gamma_i(t) \mu \int_\Omega \nabla e_i \nabla e_j d\Omega$$

$$- \sum_{i=1}^n \alpha_i(t) \int_\Omega a_i \text{div}(e_j \mathbf{B}_{2\cdot}) d\Omega + \sum_{i=1}^n \beta_i(t) \int_\Omega A_{21} e_i e_j d\Omega$$

$$+ \sum_{i=1}^n \gamma_i(t) \int_\Omega A_{22} e_i e_j d\Omega + \sum_{i=1}^n \alpha_i(t) \int_\Omega \alpha_0^2 a_i e_j d\Omega$$

$$= -\int_{\Gamma_1} (\mathcal{V}_2 e_j) \bar{v} \cdot \mathbf{n} d\sigma + \mu \sum_{i=1}^n \gamma_i(t) \int_{\Gamma_1} (\nabla e_i \cdot \mathbf{n}) e_j d\sigma - \int_{\Gamma_1} h e_j (\mathbf{B}_{2\cdot} \cdot \mathbf{n}) d\sigma.$$

Let us introduce the matrices M_k for $k = 1, \cdots, 11$ as well as the vectors m_l for $l = 1, \cdots, 3$ as follows

$$M_{1_{ji}} = \int_\Omega a_i e_j d\Omega, \quad M_{2_{ji}} = \int_\Omega a_i \partial_x e_j d\Omega, \quad M_{3_{ji}} = \int_\Omega a_i \partial_y e_j d\Omega$$

$$M_{4_{ji}} = \int_\Omega e_i e_j d\Omega, \quad M_{5_{ji}} = \int_\Omega \bar{v}_1 e_j \partial_x e_i d\Omega - \int_\Omega e_i \text{div}(e_j \bar{v}) d\Omega + \mu \int_\Omega \nabla e_i \nabla e_j d\Omega + \int_\Omega A_{11} e_i e_j d\Omega,$$

$$M_{6_{ji}} = \int_\Omega \bar{v}_1 e_j \partial_y e_i d\Omega + \int_\Omega A_{12} e_i e_j d\Omega, \quad M_{7_{ji}} = -\int_\Omega e_i \text{div}(e_j B_{1.}) d\Omega + \int_\Omega \alpha_0^1 e_i e_j d\Omega,$$

$$M_{8_{ji}} = \int_\Omega \bar{v}_2 e_j \partial_x e_i d\Omega + \int_\Omega A_{21} e_i e_j d\Omega,$$

$$M_{9_{ji}} = \int_\Omega \bar{v}_2 e_j \partial_y e_i d\Omega - \int_\Omega e_i \text{div}(e_j \bar{v}) d\Omega + \mu \int_\Omega \nabla e_i \nabla e_j d\Omega + \int_\Omega A_{22} e_i e_j d\Omega$$

$$M_{10_{ji}} = -\int_\Omega e_i \text{div}(e_j B_{2.}) d\Omega + \int_\Omega \alpha_0^2 e_i e_j d\Omega, \quad M_{11_{ji}} = \mu \int_{\Gamma_1} (\nabla e_i \cdot \mathbf{n}) e_j d\sigma,$$

and

$$m_{1_j} = -\int_{\Gamma_1} e_j n_x d\sigma, \quad m_{2_j} = -\int_{\Gamma_1} e_j n_y d\sigma, \quad m_{3_j} = -\int_{\Gamma_1} e_j \bar{v} \cdot \mathbf{n} d\sigma,$$

$$m_{4_j} = -\int_{\Gamma_1} h e_j (B_{1.} \cdot \mathbf{n}) d\sigma \quad m_{5_j} = -\int_{\Gamma_1} h e_j (B_{2.} \cdot \mathbf{n}) d\sigma.$$

We now count the n components; this yields the following system of matrix equations

$$\begin{cases} M_1 \partial_t a(t) - M_2 b(t) - M_3 c(t) = \mathcal{V}_1 m_1 + \mathcal{V}_2 m_2, \\ M_4 \partial_t b(t) + M_5 b(t) + M_6 c(t) + M_7 a(t) = \mathcal{V}_1 m_3 + M_{11} b(t) + m_4, \\ M_4 \partial_t c(t) + M_8 b(t) + M_9 c(t) + M_{10} a(t) = \mathcal{V}_2 m_3 + M_{11} c(t) + m_5, \end{cases}$$

where the vectors a, b and c are given by the coordinates of the state variables h, q_1 and q_2, respectively, i.e., $a = (\alpha_1, \cdots, \alpha_n)$, $b = (\beta_1, \cdots, \beta_n)$, and $c = (\gamma_1, \cdots, \gamma_n)$. To introduce the matrices:

$$P_1 = \begin{pmatrix} M_1 & 0 & 0 \\ 0 & M_4 & 0 \\ 0 & 0 & M_4 \end{pmatrix}, \quad P_2 = \begin{pmatrix} 0 & M_2 & M_3 \\ M_7 & M_5 & M_6 \\ M_{10} & M_8 & M_9 \end{pmatrix}, \text{ and } P_3 = \begin{pmatrix} 0 & 0 & 0 \\ 0 & M_{11} & 0 \\ 0 & 0 & M_{11} \end{pmatrix},$$

and the vectors

$$y = \begin{pmatrix} a \\ b \\ c \end{pmatrix}, \quad p_1 = \begin{pmatrix} m_1 \\ m_3 \\ 0 \end{pmatrix}, \quad p_2 = \begin{pmatrix} m_2 \\ 0 \\ m_3 \end{pmatrix} \text{ and } p_3 = \begin{pmatrix} 0 \\ m_4 \\ m_5 \end{pmatrix},$$

we write the weak form of Equations (7)–(9) together as an ordinary differential equation, with the initial condition y_0 associated with (h^0, q^0), in the form

$$\begin{cases} y'(t) = f(t, y), \\ y(t = 0) = y_0, \end{cases} \tag{10}$$

where

$$f(t, y(t)) = -P_1^{-1} P_2 y(t) + P_1^{-1} P_3 y(t) + \mathcal{V}_1(t) P_1^{-1} p_1 + \mathcal{V}_2(t) P_1^{-1} p_2 + P_1^{-1} p_3(t).$$

It remains now to prove the continuity of the functional f. For that, we consider the matrix norm $\|\cdot\|_2$ given by:

$$\|M\|_2 = \sup_{\zeta} \frac{\|M\zeta\|_2}{\|\zeta\|_2}, \quad \text{where } \|\zeta\|_2 = \sqrt{\sum_i^n |\zeta_i|^2}.$$

We have

$$\begin{aligned}
\|f\|_2 &= \left\| -P_1^{-1} P_2 y(t) + P_1^{-1} P_3 y(t) + \mathcal{V}_1(t) P_1^{-1} p_1 + \mathcal{V}_2(t) P_1^{-1} p_2 + P_1^{-1} p_3(t) \right\|_2 \\
&\leq \left\| -P_1^{-1} P_2 y(t) \right\|_2 + \left\| P_1^{-1} P_3 y(t) \right\|_2 + \left\| \mathcal{V}_1(t) P_1^{-1} p_1 \right\|_2 + \left\| \mathcal{V}_2(t) P_1^{-1} p_2 \right\|_2 + \left\| P_1^{-1} p_3(t) \right\|_2.
\end{aligned}$$

Yet, we know that

$$\begin{aligned}
\left\| -P_1^{-1} P_2 y \right\|_2 &= \left\| -P_1^{-1} P_2 (y - y_0 + y_0) \right\|_2 \\
&\leq \left\| -P_1^{-1} P_2 (y - y_0) \right\|_2 + \left\| -P_1^{-1} P_2 y_0 \right\|_2 \\
&\leq \left\| -P_1^{-1} P_2 \right\|_2 (\|y - y_0\|_2 + \|y_0\|_2).
\end{aligned}$$

Similarly, we bound the quantity $\left\| -P_1^{-1} P_3 y \right\|_2$. The terms $\left\| \mathcal{V}_1(t) P_1^{-1} p_1 \right\|_2$ and $\left\| \mathcal{V}_2(t) P_1^{-1} p_2 \right\|_2$ contain the control actions ($\mathcal{V}_1, \mathcal{V}_2$); their majoration follows from the statement (S2). As the perturbation state for the height is supposed to be small compared to $\bar{h}$ and given the definition of the space W, the term $\left\| P_1^{-1} p_3(t) \right\|_2$ is bounded. Therefore, there exists a constant K_1 such that

$$\|f\|_2 \leq K_1. \tag{11}$$

It is clear that $\|y - y_0\|_2 \leq E(0)$ because the control law acts to decrease the initial total energy $E(0)$. Denoting $T_1 = E(0)/K_1$, it yields that f is bounded according to (11). Moreover, f is continuous because it is a composition of a linear function followed by a translation. Therefore, the Cauchy–Peano theorem ensures the existence of solutions to (10) in the time interval $[0, T_1]$. □

The proof below is enough for the infinite dimensional setting in Lemma 1 because for the drift function f satisfying the Lipschitz condition in the variable y, the Cauchy–Picard theorem, see [38], transmits the result from the finite dimensional case to an infinite dimensional case. Yet, the drift f fulfills the Lipschitz condition because of (11) and its affine structure.

4.1. Energy Estimate

Here, we define and estimate the energy of the perturbation state at a time $t \in [0, T_1]$.

Definition 1 (Energy). *For $t \in [0, T_1]$, we consider the energy defined as :*

$$\begin{aligned}
E(t) &= \left\| \sqrt{g\bar{h}} h \right\|_{L^2(\Omega)}^2 + \|q_1\|_{L^2(\Omega)}^2 + \|q_2\|_{L^2(\Omega)}^2 + \mu \int_0^t \|\nabla q(\tau)\|_{L^2(\Omega)}^2 d\tau \\
&= E^1(t) + \mu \int_0^t \|\nabla q(\tau)\|_{L^2(\Omega)}^2 d\tau,
\end{aligned} \tag{12}$$

where $E^1(t)$ is the non-viscous energy and T_1 is the time bound given in Lemma 1.

To establish an estimate on the energy, we replace the test functions (φ, ϕ, ψ) by $(g\bar{h}h, \boldsymbol{q})$ in the variational form (7)–(9), to obtain

$$\frac{1}{2}\int_\Omega g\bar{h}\partial_t h^2\, d\Omega - \int_\Omega g\boldsymbol{q}\cdot\nabla(\bar{h}h)\, d\Omega = -\int_{\Gamma_1} g\bar{h}h\boldsymbol{q}\cdot\mathbf{n}\, d\sigma,$$

$$\frac{1}{2}\int_\Omega \partial_t(q_1^2 + q_2^2)\, d\Omega + \mu\int_\Omega \|\nabla\boldsymbol{q}\|_2^2\, d\Omega + \int_\Omega (\text{div}\boldsymbol{q})\bar{\boldsymbol{v}}\cdot\boldsymbol{q}\, d\Omega - \int_\Omega q_1\text{div}(q_1\bar{\boldsymbol{v}})\, d\Omega$$
$$- \int_\Omega q_2\text{div}(q_2\bar{\boldsymbol{v}})\, d\Omega - \int_\Omega h\text{div}(\boldsymbol{B}\cdot\boldsymbol{q})\, d\Omega + \int_\Omega (\boldsymbol{A}\cdot\boldsymbol{q})\cdot\boldsymbol{q}\, d\Omega + \int_\Omega h\boldsymbol{\alpha}_0\cdot\boldsymbol{q}\, d\Omega$$
$$= -\int_{\Gamma_1}(q_1^2 + q_2^2)\bar{\boldsymbol{v}}\cdot\mathbf{n}\, d\sigma + \mu\int_{\Gamma_1}(q_1\nabla q_1 + q_2\nabla q_2)\cdot\mathbf{n}\, d\sigma - \int_{\Gamma_1} h(\boldsymbol{B}\cdot\boldsymbol{q})\cdot\mathbf{n}\, d\sigma.$$

Adding the two equalities yields

$$\frac{1}{2}\partial_t E^1(t) + \mu\int_\Omega \|\nabla\boldsymbol{q}\|_2^2\, d\Omega = I_1 + I_2 + I_3 + I_4 - \int_{\Gamma_1} g\bar{h}h\boldsymbol{q}\cdot\mathbf{n}\, d\sigma - \int_{\Gamma_1}(q_1^2 + q_2^2)\bar{\boldsymbol{v}}\cdot\mathbf{n}\, d\sigma$$
$$+ \mu\int_{\Gamma_1}(q_1\nabla q_1 + q_2\nabla q_2)\cdot\mathbf{n}\, d\sigma - \int_{\Gamma_1} h(\boldsymbol{B}\cdot\boldsymbol{q})\cdot\mathbf{n}\, d\sigma,$$

where the quantities I_i are given by

$$I_1 = \int_\Omega g\boldsymbol{q}\cdot\nabla(\bar{h}h)\, d\Omega + \int_\Omega h\,\text{div}(\boldsymbol{B}\cdot\boldsymbol{q})\, d\Omega,\quad I_2 = -\int_\Omega \text{div}\boldsymbol{q}\,\bar{\boldsymbol{v}}\cdot\boldsymbol{q}\, d\Omega,$$
$$I_3 = \int_\Omega q_1\text{div}(q_1\bar{\boldsymbol{v}})\, d\Omega + \int_\Omega q_2\text{div}(q_2\bar{\boldsymbol{v}})\, d\Omega,\quad I_4 = -\int_\Omega (\boldsymbol{A}\cdot\boldsymbol{q})\cdot\boldsymbol{q}\, d\Omega - \int_\Omega h\boldsymbol{\alpha}_0\cdot\boldsymbol{q}\, d\Omega.$$

We now investigate how to isolate the nonlinear terms in each I_i with the purpose of having no derivative terms on the boundary. For that, we apply the Green formula in an adaptive manner. Afterward, we take the maximum bound over the steady-state variables, which allows us to obtain a bound estimate for each quantity. For the quantity I_1, it comes that

$$I_1 \leq \max_\Omega\left(\frac{g\|\nabla\bar{h}\|}{\sqrt{\bar{h}}}\right)\int_\Omega \sqrt{\bar{h}}\|h\boldsymbol{q}\|\, d\Omega + \max_\Omega\left(\frac{\bar{v}_1^2}{\sqrt{\bar{h}}}\right)\int_\Omega \sqrt{\bar{h}}|h\partial_x q_1|\, d\Omega$$
$$+ \max_\Omega\left(\frac{|\partial_x\bar{v}_1^2|}{\sqrt{\bar{h}}}\right)\int_\Omega \sqrt{\bar{h}}|hq_1|\, d\Omega + \max_\Omega\left(\frac{\bar{v}_2^2}{\sqrt{\bar{h}}}\right)\int_\Omega \sqrt{\bar{h}}|h\partial_y q_2|\, d\Omega$$
$$+ \max_\Omega\left(\frac{|\partial_y\bar{v}_2^2|}{\sqrt{\bar{h}}}\right)\int_\Omega \sqrt{\bar{h}}|hq_2|\, d\Omega + \max_\Omega\left(\frac{|\bar{v}_1\bar{v}_2|}{\sqrt{\bar{h}}}\right)\int_\Omega \sqrt{\bar{h}}|h\partial_x q_2|\, d\Omega$$
$$+ \max_\Omega\left(\frac{|\partial_x(\bar{v}_1\bar{v}_2)|}{\sqrt{\bar{h}}}\right)\int_\Omega \sqrt{\bar{h}}|hq_2|\, d\Omega + \max_\Omega\left(\frac{|\bar{v}_1\bar{v}_2|}{\sqrt{\bar{h}}}\right)\int_\Omega \sqrt{\bar{h}}|h\partial_y q_1|\, d\Omega$$
$$+ \max_\Omega\left(\frac{|\partial_y(\bar{v}_1\bar{v}_2)|}{\sqrt{\bar{h}}}\right)\int_\Omega \sqrt{\bar{h}}|hq_1|\, d\Omega + \int_{\partial\Omega} g\bar{h}h\boldsymbol{q}\cdot\mathbf{n}\, d\sigma. \quad (13)$$

Similarly, we bound the quantities I_2, I_3, and I_4 as follows

$$I_2 \leq \frac{1}{2}\max_\Omega(|\partial_x\bar{v}_1|)\int_\Omega q_1^2\, d\Omega + \frac{1}{2}\max_\Omega(|\partial_y\bar{v}_2|)\int_\Omega q_2^2\, d\Omega + \max_\Omega(|\bar{v}_1|)\int_\Omega |q_1\partial_y q_2|\, d\Omega$$
$$+ \max_\Omega(|\bar{v}_2|)\int_\Omega |q_2\partial_x q_1|\, d\Omega - \int_{\partial\Omega}\frac{\bar{v}_1}{2}q_1^2 n_x\, d\sigma - \int_{\partial\Omega}\frac{\bar{v}_2}{2}q_2^2 n_y\, d\sigma, \quad (14)$$

$$
\begin{aligned}
I_3 \leq\; & \frac{1}{2}\max_\Omega(|\partial_x\bar{v}_1|)\int_\Omega q_1^2 d\Omega + \max_\Omega(|\partial_x\bar{v}_2|)\int_\Omega |q_1 q_2| d\Omega + \max_\Omega(|\bar{v}_2|)\int_\Omega |q_1 \partial_x q_2| d\Omega \\
& + \max_\Omega(|\partial_y\bar{v}_2|)\int_\Omega |q_1 q_2| d\Omega + \max_\Omega(|\bar{v}_1|)\int_\Omega |q_2 \partial_y q_1| d\Omega + \frac{1}{2}\max_\Omega(|\partial_y\bar{v}_2|)\int_\Omega q_2^2 d\Omega \\
& - \int_{\partial\Omega}\frac{\bar{v}_1}{2}q_1^2 n_x d\sigma - \int_{\partial\Omega}\frac{\bar{v}_2}{2}q_2^2 n_y d\sigma,
\end{aligned} \qquad (15)
$$

and

$$
\begin{aligned}
I_4 \leq\; & \max_\Omega(|\beta_0^1|)\int_\Omega q_1^2 d\Omega + \max_\Omega(|\gamma_0^1 + \beta_0^2|)\int_\Omega |q_1 q_2| d\Omega + \max_\Omega(|\gamma_0^2|)\int_\Omega q_2^2 d\Omega \\
& + \max_\Omega\left(\frac{|\alpha_0^1|}{\sqrt{\bar{h}}}\right)\int_\Omega \sqrt{\bar{h}}|hq_1| d\Omega + \max_\Omega\left(\frac{|\alpha_0^2|}{\sqrt{\bar{h}}}\right)\int_\Omega \sqrt{\bar{h}}|hq_2| d\Omega.
\end{aligned} \qquad (16)
$$

We now apply the Young inequality to separate the nonlinear terms (in the perturbation state) for the upper bound of each of the inequalities (13)–(16). That implies the existence of ε_i for $(i = 1, \cdots, 18)$, such that

$$
\begin{aligned}
\frac{1}{2}\partial_t E^1(t) + \mu\int_\Omega \|\nabla q\|_2^2 d\Omega \leq\; & T_{\text{bord}}(t) + C_h\int_\Omega \bar{h}h^2 d\Omega + C_{q_1}\int_\Omega q_1^2 d\Omega + C_{q_2}\int_\Omega q_2^2 d\Omega \\
& + \left(\varepsilon_2 \max_\Omega\left(\frac{\bar{v}_1^2}{\sqrt{\bar{h}}}\right) + \varepsilon_{11}\max_\Omega(|\bar{v}_2|)\right)\int_\Omega (\partial_x q_1)^2 d\Omega \\
& + \left(\varepsilon_8 \max_\Omega\left(\frac{|\bar{v}_1 \bar{v}_2|}{\sqrt{\bar{h}}}\right) + \varepsilon_{15}\max_\Omega(|\bar{v}_1|)\right)\int_\Omega (\partial_y q_1)^2 d\Omega \\
& + \left(\varepsilon_6 \max_\Omega\left(\frac{|\bar{v}_1 \bar{v}_2|}{\sqrt{\bar{h}}}\right) + \varepsilon_{13}\max_\Omega(|\bar{v}_2|)\right)\int_\Omega (\partial_x q_2)^2 d\Omega \\
& + \left(\varepsilon_4 \max_\Omega\left(\frac{\bar{v}_2^2}{\sqrt{\bar{h}}}\right) + \varepsilon_{10}\max_\Omega(|\bar{v}_1|)\right)\int_\Omega (\partial_y q_2)^2 d\Omega,
\end{aligned}
$$

where

$$
\begin{aligned}
C_h =\; & \frac{1}{\varepsilon_1}\max_\Omega\left(\frac{g\|\nabla\bar{h}\|}{\sqrt{\bar{h}}}\right) + \frac{1}{\varepsilon_2}\max_\Omega\left(\frac{\bar{v}_1^2}{\sqrt{\bar{h}}}\right) + \frac{1}{\varepsilon_3}\max_\Omega\left(\frac{|\partial_x \bar{v}_1^2|}{\sqrt{\bar{h}}}\right) + \frac{1}{\varepsilon_4}\max_\Omega\left(\frac{\bar{v}_2^2}{\sqrt{\bar{h}}}\right); \\
& + \frac{1}{\varepsilon_5}\max_\Omega\left(\frac{|\partial_y \bar{v}_2^2|}{\sqrt{\bar{h}}}\right) + \frac{1}{\varepsilon_6}\max_\Omega\left(\frac{|\bar{v}_1 \bar{v}_2|}{\sqrt{\bar{h}}}\right) + \frac{1}{\varepsilon_7}\max_\Omega\left(\frac{|\partial_x(\bar{v}_1 \bar{v}_2)|}{\sqrt{\bar{h}}}\right) + \frac{1}{\varepsilon_8}\max_\Omega\left(\frac{|\bar{v}_1 \bar{v}_2|}{\sqrt{\bar{h}}}\right) \\
& + \frac{1}{\varepsilon_9}\max_\Omega\left(\frac{|\partial_y(\bar{v}_1 \bar{v}_2)|}{\sqrt{\bar{h}}}\right) + \frac{1}{\varepsilon_{17}}\max_\Omega\left(\frac{|\alpha_0^1|}{\sqrt{\bar{h}}}\right) + \frac{1}{\varepsilon_{18}}\max_\Omega\left(\frac{|\alpha_0^2|}{\sqrt{\bar{h}}}\right),
\end{aligned}
$$

$$
\begin{aligned}
C_{q_1} =\; & \varepsilon_1 \max_\Omega\left(\frac{g\|\nabla\bar{h}\|}{\sqrt{\bar{h}}}\right) + \varepsilon_3 \max_\Omega\left(\frac{|\partial_x \bar{v}_1^2|}{\sqrt{\bar{h}}}\right) + \varepsilon_9 \max_\Omega\left(\frac{|\partial_y(\bar{v}_1 \bar{v}_2)|}{\sqrt{\bar{h}}}\right) + \max_\Omega\left(|\partial_x \bar{v}_1|\right) \\
& + \frac{1}{\varepsilon_{10}}\max_\Omega(|\bar{v}_1|) + \frac{1}{\varepsilon_{12}}\max_\Omega(|\partial_x \bar{v}_2|) + \frac{1}{\varepsilon_{13}}\max_\Omega(|\bar{v}_2|) + \frac{1}{\varepsilon_{14}}\max_\Omega(|\partial_y \bar{v}_1|) + \max_\Omega\left(\beta_0^1\right) \\
& + \frac{1}{\varepsilon_{16}}\max_\Omega\left(|\gamma_0^1 + \beta_0^2|\right) + \varepsilon_{17}\max_\Omega\left(\frac{|\alpha_0^1|}{\sqrt{\bar{h}}}\right),
\end{aligned}
$$

$$
\begin{aligned}
C_{q_2} &= \varepsilon_1 \max_\Omega \left(\frac{g\|\nabla \bar{h}\|}{\sqrt{\bar{h}}} \right) + \varepsilon_5 \max_\Omega \left(\frac{|\partial_y \bar{v}_2^2|}{\sqrt{\bar{h}}} \right) + \varepsilon_7 \max_\Omega \left(\frac{|\partial_x (\bar{v}_1 \bar{v}_2)|}{\sqrt{\bar{h}}} \right) + \max_\Omega \left(|\partial_y \bar{v}_2| \right) \\
&+ \frac{1}{\varepsilon_{11}} \max_\Omega (|\bar{v}_2|) + \varepsilon_{12} \max_\Omega (|\partial_x \bar{v}_2|) + \varepsilon_{14} \max_\Omega (|\partial_y \bar{v}_1|) + \frac{1}{\varepsilon_{15}} \max_\Omega (|\bar{v}_1|) + \max_\Omega \left(|\gamma_0^2| \right) \\
&+ \varepsilon_{16} \max_\Omega \left(|\gamma_0^1 + \beta_0^2| \right) + \varepsilon_{18} \max_\Omega \left(\frac{|\alpha_0^2|}{\sqrt{\bar{h}}} \right),
\end{aligned}
$$

and

$$
\begin{aligned}
T_{\text{bord}}(t) &= -\int_{\Gamma_1} \left(\bar{v}_1 q_1^2 n_x + \bar{v}_2 q_2^2 n_y \right) d\sigma - \int_{\Gamma_1} (q_1^2 + q_2^2) \bar{v} \cdot \mathbf{n} \, d\sigma \\
&+ \mu \int_{\Gamma_1} (q_1 \nabla q_1 + q_2 \nabla q_2) \cdot \mathbf{n} \, d\sigma - \int_{\Gamma_1} h(\mathbf{B} \cdot \mathbf{q}) \cdot \mathbf{n} \, d\sigma.
\end{aligned}
$$

Note that C_h, C_{q_1} and C_{q_2} are constant while T_{bord} is time variable. Let us denote

$$C_m = \max \left(\frac{C_h}{g}, C_{q_1}, C_{q_2} \right)$$

and

$$
C_v = \max \left(\begin{array}{c} \varepsilon_2 \max_\Omega \left(\frac{\bar{v}_1^2}{\sqrt{\bar{h}}} \right) + \varepsilon_{11} \max_\Omega (|\bar{v}_2|), \varepsilon_8 \max_\Omega \left(\frac{|\bar{v}_1 \bar{v}_2|}{\sqrt{\bar{h}}} \right) + \frac{1}{\varepsilon_{15}} \max_\Omega (|\bar{v}_1|), \\ \varepsilon_6 \max_\Omega \left(\frac{|\bar{v}_1 \bar{v}_2|}{\sqrt{\bar{h}}} \right) + \varepsilon_{13} \max_\Omega (|\bar{v}_2|), \varepsilon_4 \max_\Omega \left(\frac{\bar{v}_2^2}{\sqrt{\bar{h}}} \right) + \varepsilon_{10} \max_\Omega (|\bar{v}_1|) \end{array} \right).
$$

Since the ε_i can be chosen arbitrarily, we then take $\varepsilon_2, \varepsilon_4, \varepsilon_6, \varepsilon_8, \varepsilon_{10}, \varepsilon_{11}, \varepsilon_{13}$ and ε_{15} such that $\frac{\mu}{2} \geqslant C_v$. Therefore, it comes that

$$
\begin{aligned}
\partial_t E^1(t) + \frac{\mu}{2} \int_\Omega \|\nabla q\|_2^2 d\Omega &\leqslant T_{\text{bord}}(t) + C_m E^1(t) \\
\partial_t E^1(t) + \frac{\mu}{2} \int_\Omega \|\nabla q\|_2^2 d\Omega &\leqslant T_{\text{bord}}(t) + C_m E^1(t) + C_m \frac{\mu}{2} \int_0^t \int_\Omega \|\nabla q\|_2^2 d\Omega dt.
\end{aligned}
$$

Finally, with (12), the energy E of the stabilization problem (6) satisfies

$$\partial_t E(t) - C_m E(t) \leqslant T_{\text{bord}}(t). \tag{17}$$

4.2. Short-Time Control Building Process

In this section, we address the existence and the design of the boundary feedback control law in the time interval $[0, T_1]$, which stabilizes the perturbation state in the sense that the energy decreases.

Lemma 2. *Let r be a continuous time function for which the integral diverges when t tends to $+\infty$; there exists a nonlinear control law $\mathcal{V}_1 = (u_{1_1}, u_{1_2})$ to set as the boundary condition on Γ_1 such that, for all $t \in [0, T_1]$, the energy E satisfies the following estimate:*

$$E^1(t) + \int_0^t \|\nabla q\|_{L^2(\Omega)}^2 ds \leqslant E^1(0) \exp \left(\int_0^t -r(s) ds \right) \quad \forall t \in [0, T_1]. \tag{18}$$

This lemma is an intermediate result that proves the existence of a boundary control law in the time interval $[0, T_1]$.

Proof. We have shown the existence of a solution in the time interval $[0, T_1]$ in Lemma 1. Let us now consider the energy estimate (17) with $T_{\text{bord}}(t)$ expressed in terms of the control commands

$$T_{\text{bord}}(t) = a_1 u_{1_1}^2(t) + b_1(h) u_{1_1}(t) + a_2 u_{2_1}^2(t) + b_2(h) u_{2_1}(t),$$

where

$$a_1 = -\int_{\Gamma_1} (2\bar{v}_1 n_x + \bar{v}_2 n_y) d\sigma, \quad a_2 = -\int_{\Gamma_1} (\bar{v}_1 n_x + 2\bar{v}_2 n_y) d\sigma,$$

$$b_1(h) = -\int_{\Gamma_1} \left((c^2 - \bar{v}_1^2) n_x - \bar{v}_1 \bar{v}_2 n_y \right) h \, d\sigma + \mu \int_{\Gamma_1} \nabla q_1 \cdot \mathbf{n} \, d\sigma,$$

$$b_2(h) = -\int_{\Gamma_1} \left((c^2 - \bar{v}_1^2) n_y - \bar{v}_1 \bar{v}_2 n_x \right) h \, d\sigma + \mu \int_{\Gamma_1} \nabla q_2 \cdot \mathbf{n} \, d\sigma.$$

The energy estimate can then be written in terms of the control command as follows

$$\frac{1}{2} \partial_t E(t) - C_m E(t) \leqslant a_1 u_{1_1}^2(t) + b_1(h) u_{1_1}(t) + a_2 u_{2_1}^2(t) + b_2(h) u_{2_1}(t).$$

Now we introduce the positive and continuous function r which stands for the stabilization rate. We also denote by F_0 the positive function given by

$$F_0(t) = E(0) \exp\left(-\int_0^t r(s) ds \right)$$

such that

$$a_1 u_{1_1}^2(t) + b_1(h) u_{1_1}(t) + a_2 u_{2_1}^2(t) + b_2(h) u_{2_1}(t) \leqslant \frac{1}{2} \frac{\partial F_0}{\partial t} - C_m F_0. \tag{19}$$

Furthermore, we denote by $G_0 = \frac{1}{2} \partial_t F_0 - C_m F_0$, and we set the following two inequalities

$$a_1 u_{1_1}^2(t) + b_1(h) u_{1_1}(t) - \frac{1}{2} G_0 \leqslant 0 \quad \text{and} \quad a_2 u_{2_1}^2(t) + b_2(h) u_{2_1}(t) - \frac{1}{2} G_0 \leqslant 0,$$

so that the inequality (19) holds. The solutions of the associated second-order polynomials are, respectively,

$$\xi_{1_1} = \frac{-b_1 - \sqrt{b_1^2 + 2a_1 G_0}}{2a_1}, \quad \xi_{1_2} = \frac{-b_1 + \sqrt{b_1^2 + 2a_1 G_0}}{2a_1},$$

$$\xi_{2_1} = \frac{-b_2 - \sqrt{b_2^2 + 2a_2 G_0}}{2a_2}, \quad \xi_{2_2} = \frac{-b_2 + \sqrt{b_2^2 + 2a_2 G_0}}{2a_2},$$

because a_1 and a_2 are negative by construction (see statement (S1)). The coefficients b_1 and b_2 depend on the perturbation height h and on the limit, towards the boundary, of the L^2 norm of the gradient of the perturbation flow; therefore, to guarantee the boundedness of the control command, we define u_{i_1} (for i=1;2) using the following combination

$$u_{i_1} = \max(-\text{sign}(b_i), 0) \xi_{i_1} + \max(\text{sign}(b_i), 0) \xi_{i_2}. \tag{20}$$

The function $sign(x)$ returns the sign of the real x. The control laws defined at (20) guarantee that the boundary condition $\mathcal{V}_1 = (u_{1_1}, u_{2_1})$ is bounded and decreases the energy of the perturbation system thanks to

$$E^1(t) + \int_0^t \|\nabla q\|_{L^2(\Omega)}^2 ds \leq E^1(0) \exp\left(\int_0^t -r(s)ds\right) \quad \forall t \in [0, T_1].$$

$\square$

It is important to note that the control $\mathcal{V}_1$ does not act on the system after the energy reaches $E(T_1)$.

5. Stabilization Result

In this section, we establish the existence and uniqueness of the weak solution of the linearized system (6) equipped with the feedback control law, which is devised by cascade and achieves an exponential convergence of the state variables (h, q) towards $(0, 0, 0)$. We start by the existence of a sequence of intervals by replicating Lemma 1. For that, we adapt the energy definition for all time $t > 0$.

Definition 2 (Energy). *We consider the following definition of the energy:*

$$\begin{aligned}E(t) &= \left\|\sqrt{g\bar{h}}h\right\|_{L^2(\Omega)}^2 + \|q_1\|_{L^2(\Omega)}^2 + \|q_2\|_{L^2(\Omega)}^2 + \mu \int_{T_k}^t \|\nabla q\|_{L^2(\Omega)}^2 d\sigma \quad (21)\\ &= E^1(t) + \mu \int_{T_k}^t \|\nabla q\|_{L^2(\Omega)}^2 d\sigma,\end{aligned}$$

where $E^1(t)$ is the non-viscous energy and T_k is the lower bound of the time interval $[T_k, T_{k+1}]$, which is defined in the next lemma.

Lemma 3. *There exists a sequence of intervals $\left([T_k, T_{k+1}]\right)_{k \geq 0}$ such that*

1. *In each interval $[T_k, T_{k+1}]$, there exists a stabilizing boundary control command $\mathcal{V}_k$*
2. *For all $t \in [T_k, T_{k+1}]$, the energy satisfies*

$$E(t) \leq E^1(0) exp\left(-\int_0^{T_{k+1}} r(s)ds\right). \quad (22)$$

Proof. for the sake of clarity, we proceed by induction to prove Lemma 3.

- Verification for $k = 0$:
  Let $T_0 = 0$; thanks to Lemma 1, it exists T_1 such that the differential Equation (10) admits solutions in the time interval $[T_0, T_1]$. Lemma 2 gives us the existence of a control command $\mathcal{V}_1$ satisfying (22). The Lemma 3 is then true for $k = 0$.
- Suppose that the statement is true till rank k, and let us show it is true at rank $k + 1$:
  The induction hypothesis gives the existence of T_k. We now consider the control problem (6) with initial data $(h(T_k), q(T_k))$. Similarly to the analysis performed in Section 4, it yields the following differential equation

$$\begin{cases} y'(t) = f_k(t, y) \\ y(t = T_k) = y_k. \end{cases} \quad (23)$$

Applying Lemma 1, it comes that $\|f_k\|_2 \leq K_{k+1}$ and $T_{k+1} = E(T_k)/K_k + T_k$ such that (23) has a solution in $[T_k, T_{k+1}]$. Thanks to Lemma 2, it exists a stabilizing control command $\mathcal{V}_{k+1}$, and for all $t \in [T_k, T_{k+1}]$, we have

$$E(t) \leq E^1(T_k) \exp\left(-\int_{T_k}^t r(s)ds\right)$$
$$\leq E(T_k) \exp\left(-\int_{T_k}^t r(s)ds\right).$$

Since $T_k \in [T_{k-1}, T_k]$, we have

$$E(T_k) \leq E^1(T_{k-1}) \exp\left(-\int_{T_{k-1}}^{T_k} r(s)ds\right),$$

which implies that

$$E(t) \leq E^1(T_{k-1}) \exp\left(-\int_{T_{k-1}}^{T_k} r(s)ds\right) \exp\left(-\int_{T_k}^t r(s)ds\right)$$
$$\leq E^1(T_{k-1}) \exp\left(-\int_{T_{k-1}}^t r(s)ds\right)$$
$$\vdots$$
$$\leq E^1(0) \exp\left(-\int_0^t r(s)ds\right).$$

The statement is then true at rank $k+1$, and that proves the Lemma 3. □

We have shown the existence of the sequence of interval $\left([T_k, T_{k+1}]\right)_{k \geq 1}$ and the existence of a boundary control command $\mathcal{V}_k$ in each interval $[T_k, T_{k+1}]$. We can now design the feedback control law for all $t \geq 0$.

Definition 3 (Control law). *The boundary control law $\mathcal{V}$ for the stabilization problem (6) is given by*

$$\mathcal{V}(t) = \sum_{k=0}^{\infty} \mathcal{V}_k(t) \mathbb{1}_{[T_k, T_{k+1}]}(t), \tag{24}$$

where the local control command $\mathcal{V}_k = (u_{1_k}, u_{2_k})$ *is defined in* $[T_k, T_{k+1}]$ *by*

$$u_{i_k} = \max(-\text{sign}(b_i), 0)\xi_{i_1}^k + \max(\text{sign}(b_i), 0)\xi_{i_2}^k \text{ for } i = 1; 2.$$

The quantities $\xi_{i_1}^k$ *and* $\xi_{i_2}^k$ *are solutions of second-order polynomials and are written as*

$$\xi_{1_1}^k = \frac{-b_1 - \sqrt{b_1^2 + 2a_1 G_k}}{2a_1}, \quad \xi_{1_2}^k = \frac{-b_1 + \sqrt{b_1^2 + 2a_1 G_k}}{2a_1},$$

$$\xi_{2_1}^k = \frac{-b_2 - \sqrt{b_2^2 + 2a_2 G_k}}{2a_2}, \quad \xi_{2_2}^k = \frac{-b_2 + \sqrt{b_2^2 + 2a_2 G_k}}{2a_2},$$

where the coefficients a_i and b_i are given in Section 4.2 where the function G_k is defined in the time interval $[T_k, T_{k+1}]$ as follows:

$$G_k(t) = \frac{1}{2}\partial_t F_k(t) - C_m F_k(t), \quad \text{with} \quad F_k(t) = E(T_k) \exp\left(-\int_{T_k}^t r(s)ds\right). \tag{25}$$

The time function r represents the stabilization rate, and C_m is a constant depending on the steady state.

We can now state our main result.

Theorem 1 (main result). *Let r be a continuous time function for which the integral over the interval $[0, t]$ diverges when t tends to $+\infty$. Then, there exists a sequence of intervals $([T_k, T_{k+1}])_{k \geqslant 0}$ such that*

$$\bigcup_{k=0}^{+\infty}]T_k, T_{k+1}] =]0, +\infty[,$$

and the stabilization problem (6) with the boundary conditions (24) admits a unique solution (h, q) for which the energy E decreases according to the following estimate:

$$E(t) \leqslant E^1(0) \exp\left(\int_0^t -r(s)ds\right). \tag{26}$$

The continuity of the functions $x \mapsto \sqrt{x}$ and $x \mapsto x^2$ and of the hydrodynamic water level h imply that the control law $\mathcal{V}$ built by concatenating the stabilizing control commands $\mathcal{V}_k$ is continuous. It is also worth noticing that the control vanishes when the energy reaches zero, and that the sequence of the time intervals is well-defined, i.e.,

$$\bigcup_{k=0}^{+\infty}]T_k, T_{k+1}] =]0, +\infty[.$$

Proof. The proof is performed using the Faedo–Galerkin method. As outlined at the beginning of the proof of Lemma 1, we consider again $\{a_i\}_{1 \leqslant i \leqslant n}$ (respectively, by $\{e_i\}_{1 \leqslant i \leqslant n}$) by a finite Hilbertian basis of the space $H^1(\Omega)$ (respectively $H^1_{\Gamma_1}(\Omega)$). Let $W_n = Vect\{a_1, \cdots, a_n\} \times Vect\{e_1, \cdots, e_n\} \times Vect\{e_1, \cdots, e_n\}$ be the vector space of finite dimension generated by $\{a_i\} \times \{e_{1i}\} \times \{e_i\}$. Let (h_n^0, q_n^0) be a sequence in $W_n(\Omega)$ converging to (h^0, q^0) in $L^2(\Omega)$. The weak form associated with the problem (6) in $W_n(\Omega)$ is given by:

$$\int_\Omega \varphi \partial_t h_n d\Omega - \int_\Omega q_n \nabla \varphi d\Omega = -\int_{\Gamma_1} \varphi q_n \cdot \mathbf{n} d\sigma, \tag{27}$$

$$\int_\Omega \partial_t q_{1_n} \phi \, d\Omega + \int_\Omega (\mathrm{div}\, \boldsymbol{q}_n \bar{v}_1) \phi \, d\Omega - \int_\Omega q_{1_n} \mathrm{div}(\phi \bar{v}) \, d\Omega + \mu \int_\Omega \nabla q_{1_n} \nabla \phi \, d\Omega$$
$$- \int_\Omega h_n \mathrm{div}(\phi \boldsymbol{B}_{1.}) \, d\Omega + \int_\Omega \beta_0^1 q_{1_n} \phi \, d\Omega + \int_\Omega \gamma_0^1 q_{2_n} \phi \, d\Omega + \int_\Omega h_n \alpha_0^1 \phi \, d\Omega$$
$$= - \int_{\Gamma_1} (q_{1_n} \phi) \bar{v} \cdot \mathbf{n} \, d\sigma + \mu \int_{\Gamma_1} (\nabla q_{1_n} \cdot \mathbf{n}) \phi \, d\sigma - \int_{\Gamma_1} h_n \phi (\boldsymbol{B}_{1.} \cdot \mathbf{n}) \, d\sigma, \tag{28}$$

$$\int_\Omega \partial_t q_{2_n} \psi \, d\Omega + \int_\Omega (\mathrm{div}\, \boldsymbol{q}_n \bar{v}_2) \psi \, d\Omega - \int_\Omega q_{2_n} \mathrm{div}(\psi \bar{v}) \, d\Omega + \mu \int_\Omega \nabla q_{2_n} \nabla \psi \, d\Omega$$
$$- \int_\Omega h_n \mathrm{div}(\psi \boldsymbol{B}_{2.}) \, d\Omega + \int_\Omega \beta_0^2 q_{1_n} \psi \, d\Omega + \int_\Omega \gamma_0^2 q_{2_n} \psi \, d\Omega + \int_\Omega h_n \alpha_0^2 \psi \, d\Omega$$
$$= - \int_{\Gamma_1} (q_{2_n} \psi) \bar{v} \cdot \mathbf{n} \, d\sigma + \mu \int_{\Gamma_1} (\nabla q_{2_n} \cdot \mathbf{n}) \psi \, d\sigma - \int_{\Gamma_1} h_n \psi (\boldsymbol{B}_{2.} \cdot \mathbf{n}) \, d\sigma. \tag{29}$$

Referring to the energy estimate, it comes that

$$E_n^1(t) \leq E_n(t) \leq E_n^1(0) \exp\left(\int_0^t -r(s) ds \right) \quad \forall t \in [0,T], \tag{30}$$

with

$$E_n^1(t) = \left\| \sqrt{g\bar{h}} h_n \right\|_{L^2(\Omega)}^2 + \| q_{1_n} \|_{L^2(\Omega)}^2 + \| q_{2_n} \|_{L^2(\Omega)}^2.$$

For $T \geq 0$ to be sufficiently large, and a steady state $\bar{U}$ sufficiently regular, the integration over the time interval $[0, T]$ of (30) gives us the existence of a positive constant $C \geq 0$, such that

$$\| h_n \|_{L^2(0,T,\Omega)}^2 + \| \boldsymbol{q}_n \|_{L^2(0,T,\Omega)}^2 \leq C.$$

This latter inequality implies that $(h_n, \boldsymbol{q}_n)$ is bounded in $L^2(0, T, L^2(\Omega)^3)$, which is a Hilbert space. Therefore, we can extract a sub-sequence, denoted also by $(h_n, \boldsymbol{q}_n)$, converging weakly to the limit $(h, \boldsymbol{q})$ in $L^2(0, T, L^2(\Omega)^3)$. Let us now introduce the following spaces $H_T^1, S_t(T)$ and $S_l(T)$

$$H_T^1 = \left\{ g \in H^1(0,T), \text{ such that } g(T) = 0 \right\},$$
$$S_t(T) = \left\{ \varphi : \varphi(t,x,y) = g_1(t) \sum_{i=1}^{n_0} a_i e_i(x,y), \text{ such that } g_1 \in H_T^1 \text{ and } a_i \in \mathbb{R} \right\},$$
$$S_l(T) = \left\{ f \in H_T^1 \times H^1(\Omega), \text{ such that } f(T,x,y) = 0 \right\}.$$

For the mass equation: the integration over the time interval $[0, T]$ of (27) results in,

$$-\int_0^T (h_n, \partial \varphi)_\Omega dt + (h_n(0,x,y), \varphi(0,x,y))_\Omega - (h_n(T,x,y), \varphi(T,x,y))_\Omega$$
$$- \int_0^T (\boldsymbol{q}_n, \nabla \varphi)_\Omega dt = -\int_0^T \int_{\partial\Omega} \varphi \boldsymbol{q}_n \cdot \mathbf{n} d\sigma dt, \tag{31}$$

where $\varphi \in H^1(\Omega)$. Taking $\varphi \in S_t(T) \times H^1(\Omega)$, that is $\varphi = g_1(t) \sum_{i=1}^{n_0} a_i e_i(x,y) = a_1 e_1(x,y)$, the equality (31) becomes

$$-\int_0^T (h_n, e_1)_\Omega \partial_t g_1(t) dt - (h_n(0,x,y), e_1(0,x,y))_\Omega g_1(0) - \int_0^T (q_k, \nabla e_1)_\Omega g_1(t) dt$$
$$= -\int_0^T \left(g_1(t) v_1(t) \int_{\Gamma_1} e_1 n_x d\sigma \right) dt - \int_0^T \left(g_1(t) v_2(t) \int_{\Gamma_1} e_1 n_y d\sigma \right) dt,$$
$$= -\int_{\Gamma_1} e_1 n_x d\sigma \int_0^T g_1(t) v_1(t) dt - \int_{\Gamma_1} e_1 n_y d\sigma \int_0^T g_1(t) v_2(t) dt.$$

Since $S_t(T)$ is dense in $S_l(T)$, taking the limit when n tends to $+\infty$, we obtain by compactness:

$$-\int_0^T (\tilde{h}, e_1)_\Omega \partial_t g_1(t) dt - (\tilde{h}(0,x,y), e_1(0,x,y))_\Omega g_1(0) - \int_0^T (\tilde{q}, \nabla e_1)_\Omega g_1(t) dt$$
$$= -\int_{\Gamma_1} e_1 n_x d\sigma \int_0^T g_1(t) v_1(t) dt - \int_{\Gamma_1} e_1 n_y d\sigma \int_0^T g_1(t) v_2(t) dt,$$

where e_1 is taken in $H^1(\Omega)$ and g in H_T^1, respectively.

Since $D(0,T) \times D(\Omega) \subset H^1(0,T) \times H^1(\Omega)$ and $L^2(Q) \subset D'(Q)$, we consider from now on the test function $\varphi \in D(Q) \times D(\Omega)$. That allows us to drop the second member in the equation above because if a function belongs to $D(Q)$, it vanishes at the boundary. Subsequently, we can write

$$-(h, \partial_t \varphi)_{(D(0,T) \times D(\Omega))', (D(0,T) \times D(\Omega))} - (q, \nabla \varphi)_{(D(0,T) \times D(\Omega))', (D(0,T) \times D(\Omega))} = 0.$$

Finally, we conclude that, in the distributions sense,

$$\partial_t h + div q = 0.$$

For the first equation of the momentum, we have

$$-(\partial_t q_{1_k}, \psi)_\Omega - (q_{1_k}(0,x,y), \psi(0,x,y))_\Omega + (q_{1_k}(T,x,y), \psi(T,x,y))_\Omega + \int_0^T (\bar{u} div q_k, \psi)_\Omega dt$$
$$- \int_0^T (q_{1_k}, div(\psi \bar{v}))_\Omega dt + \mu \int_0^T (\nabla q_{1_k}, \nabla \psi)_\Omega dt - \int_0^T (h_k, div(\psi B_{1.}))_\Omega dt$$
$$+ \int_0^T \left(\beta_0^1 q_{1_k}, \psi \right)_\Omega dt + \int_0^T \left(\gamma_0^1 q_{2_k}, \psi \right)_\Omega dt + \int_0^T \left(\alpha_0^1 h_k, \psi \right)_\Omega dt \qquad (32)$$
$$= \int_0^T \int_{\Gamma_1} (v_1 \psi) \bar{v} \cdot \mathbf{n} d\sigma dt + \mu \int_0^T \int_{\Gamma_1} (\nabla q_{1_k} \cdot \mathbf{n}) \psi \, d\sigma dt - \int_0^T \int_{\Gamma_1} h_k \psi (B_{1.} \cdot \mathbf{n}) d\sigma dt.$$

Taking $\psi \in S_t(T)$, $\psi = g_2(t)\sum_{i=1}^{n_0} b_i^1 e_i(x,y) = g_2(t)e_2(x,y)$, the relation (32) becomes

$$
\begin{aligned}
-(\partial_t q_{1_k}, \psi)_\Omega &\quad - \quad (q_{1_k}(0,x,y), e_2(0,x,y))_\Omega g_2(0) + \int_0^T (\bar{v}_1 \text{div} q_k, e_2))_\Omega g_2(t)dt \\
&\quad - \int_0^T (q_{1_k}, \text{div}(e_2 \bar{v}))_\Omega g_2(t)dt + \mu \int_0^T (\nabla q_{1_k}, \nabla e_2)_\Omega g_2(t)dt \\
&\quad - \int_0^T (h_k, \text{div}(e_2 \mathbf{B}_{1.}))_\Omega g_2(t)dt + \int_0^T \left(\beta_0^1 q_{1_k}, e_2\right)_\Omega g_2(t)dt \\
&\quad + \int_0^T \left(\gamma_0^1 q_{2_k}, e_2\right)_\Omega g_2(t)dt + \int_0^T \left(\alpha_0^1 h_k, e_2\right)_\Omega g_2(t)dt \\
&= \int_0^T v_1(t) g_2(t)dt \int_{\Gamma_1} e_2 \bar{v} \cdot \mathbf{n} d\sigma + \mu \int_0^T g_2(t) \int_{\Gamma_1} (\nabla q_{1_k} \cdot \mathbf{n}) e_2 \, d\sigma dt \\
&\quad - \int_0^T g_2(t) \int_{\Gamma_1} h_k e_2 (\mathbf{B}_{1.} \cdot \mathbf{n}) \, d\sigma dt.
\end{aligned}
$$

Since the test function is in the space $S_t(T)$ that is dense in $S_l(T)$, by taking the limit, it follows that

$$
\begin{aligned}
-(\partial_t q_1, \psi)_\Omega &\quad - \quad (q_1(0,x,y), e_2(0,x,y))_\Omega g_2(0) + \int_0^T (\bar{v}_1 \text{div} q, e_2))_\Omega g_2(t)dt \\
&\quad - \int_0^T (q_1, \text{div}(e_2 \bar{v}))_\Omega g_2(t)dt + \mu \int_0^T (\nabla q_1, \nabla e_2)_\Omega g_2(t)dt \\
&\quad - \int_0^T (h, \text{div}(e_2 \mathbf{B}_{1.}))_\Omega g_2(t)dt + \int_0^T \left(\beta_0^1 q_1, e_2\right)_\Omega g_2(t)dt \\
&\quad + \int_0^T \left(\gamma_0^1 q_2, e_2\right)_\Omega g_2(t)dt + \int_0^T \left(\alpha_0^1 h, e_2\right)_\Omega g_2(t)dt \\
&= \int_0^T v_1(t) g_2(t)dt \int_{\Gamma_1} e_2 \bar{v} \mathbf{n} d\sigma + \mu \int_0^T g_2(t) \int_{\Gamma_1} (\nabla q_1 \mathbf{n}) e_2 \, d\sigma dt \\
&\quad - \int_0^T g_2(t) \int_{\Gamma_1} h e_2 (\mathbf{B}_{1.} \mathbf{n}) \, d\sigma dt,
\end{aligned}
$$

with $e_2 \in H^1(\Omega)$ and $g_2 \in H_T^1$.

As previously for the mass conservation equation, we obtain in the distributions sense that

$$\partial_t q_1 + \bar{v}_1 \text{div} q + \nabla q_1 \cdot \bar{v} - \mu \Delta q + \mathbf{B}_{1.} \nabla h + \beta_0^1 q_1 + \gamma_0^1 q_2 + \alpha_0^1 h = 0.$$

Following the same process, we establish the existence result for the second equation of the momentum conservation. Since $E(t) \leqslant \liminf_{k \to \infty} E_k(t)$, (26) follows from (30). □

6. Conclusions

We presented a methodology for building a local boundary control law for the exponential stabilization of two-dimensional shallow viscous water flow. The control law acts only on the volumetric flow parameter in a portion of the boundary and is built by cascade over a sequence of intervals that are given by the existence of weak solutions of the perturbation state. The latter state is obtained by neglecting higher orders terms in the linearization. Nevertheless, it is desirable to address the construction of the control law using the nonlinear model directly. A prospective direction toward improving the presented approach, to address in future, is to consider higher order terms in the approximation in the reformulation of the governing equations of around the equilibrium.

Author Contributions: Conceptualization, B.M.D. and O.D.; Formal analysis, B.M.D. and M.S.G.; Funding acquisition, B.M.D.; Methodology, M.S.G. and O.D.; Supervision, O.D.; Writing—original draft, B.M.D.; Writing—review & editing, M.S.G. and O.D. All authors have read and agreed to the published version of the manuscript.

Funding: This research was funded by the CIPR (Center for Integrative Petroleum Research), College of Petroleum Engineering and Geosciences at King Fahd University of Petroleum and Minerals, Startup funds.

Data Availability Statement: Not applicable.

Conflicts of Interest: The authors declare no conflict of interest.

References

1. Aamo, O.M.; Krstic, M. *Flow Control by Feedback: Stabilization and Mixing*, 1st ed.; Springer: London, UK, 2003.
2. Coron, J.-M. *Control and Nonlinearity*; Volume 136 of Mathematical Surveys and Monographs; American Mathematical Society: Providence, RI, USA, 2007.
3. Ito, K.; Ravindran, S.S. Optimal control of thermally convected fluid flows. *SIAM J. Sci. Comput.* **1998**, *19*, 1847–1869. [CrossRef]
4. Koumoutsakos, P.; Mezic, I. *Control of Fluid Flow*; Springer-Verlag: Berlin/Heidelberg, Germany, 2006.
5. Sritharan, S. *Optimal Control of Viscous Flow*; Society for Industrial and Applied Mathematics: Philadelphia, PA, USA, 1998.
6. Raymond J.P. Feedback boundary stabilization of the three-dimensional incompressible Navier-Stokes equations. *J. Math. Pures Appl.* **2007**, *87*, 627–669. [CrossRef]
7. Barbu, V.; Lasiecka, I.; Triggiani, R. Tangential boundary stabilization of Navier-Stokes equations. In *Memoirs of the American Mathematical Society*; No. 852; American Mathematical Society: Providence, RI, USA, 2006.
8. Badra, M. Feedback stabilization of the 2-D and 3-D Navier-Stokes equations based on an extended system. *ESAIM Control Optim. Calc. Var.* **2009**, *15*, 934–968. [CrossRef]
9. Badra, M. Lyapunov function and local feedback boundary stabilization of the Navier-Stokes equations. *SIAM J. Control Optim.* **2009**, *48*, 1797–1830. [CrossRef]
10. Fursikov, A.V. Exact Controllability and Feedback Stabilization from a Boundary for the Navier-Stokes Equations. In *Control of Fluid Flow*; Lecture Notes in Control and Information Sciences; Springer: Berlin/Heidelberg, Germany, 2006; pp. 173–188.
11. Fursikov, A.V. Stabilizability of Two-Dimensional Navier—Stokes Equations with Help of a Boundary Feedback Control. *J. Math. Fluid Mech.* **2001**, *3*, 259–301. [CrossRef]
12. Ngom E.M.D.; Sène A.; Le Roux, D.Y. Boundary stabilization of the Navier-Stokes equations with feedback controller via a Galerkin method. *Evol. Equ. Control Theory* **2014**, *3*, 147–166. [CrossRef]
13. Ravindran, S. Stabilization of Navier-Stokes equations by boundary feedback. *Int. J. Numer. Anal. Model.* **2007**, *4*, 608–624.
14. Fursikov, A.V.; Gorshkov, A.V. Certain questions of feedback stabilization for Navier-Stokes equations. *Evol. Equ. Control Theory* **2012**, *1*, 109–140. [CrossRef]
15. Baranovskii, E.S.; Artemov, M.A. Optimal Control for a Nonlocal Model of Non-Newtonian Fluid Flows. *Mathematics* **2021**, *9*, 275. [CrossRef]
16. Baranovskii, E.S.; Lenes, E.; Mallea-Zepeda, E.; Rodriguez, J.; Vaasquez, L. Control Problem Related to 2D Stokes Equations with Variable Density and Viscosity. *Symmetry* **2021**, *13*, 2050. [CrossRef]
17. Baranovskii, E.S. Feedback optimal control problem for a network model of viscous fluid flows. *Math. Notes* **2022**, *112*, 26–39. [CrossRef]
18. Barbu, V. Stabilization of a plane channel flow by wall normal controllers. *Nonlinear Anal.-Theory Methods Appl.* **2007**, *67*, 2573–2588. [CrossRef]
19. Bastin, G.; Coron, J.-M.; Hayat, A. Feedforward boundary control of 2×2 non-linear hyperbolic systems with application to Saint-Venant equations. *Eur. J. Control* **2021**, *57*, 41–53. [CrossRef]
20. Dia, B.; Oppelstrup, J. Boundary feedback control of 2d shallow water equations. *Int. J. Dyn. Control* **2013**, *1*, 41–53. [CrossRef]
21. Balogh, A.; Liu, W.; Krstić, M. Stability enhancement by boundary control in 2-d channel flow. *IEEE Trans. Autom. Control* **2001**, *46*, 1696–1711. [CrossRef]
22. Goudiaby, M.; Diagne, M.; Dia, B. Solutions to a Riemann problem at a junction. In Proceedings of the CARI (2014), Saint-Louis, Sénégal, 16–23 October 2014; pp. 5–62.
23. Goudiaby, M.S.; Kreiss, G. A Riemann problem at a junction of open canals. *J. Hyperbolic Differ. Equ.* **2013**, *10*, 431–460. [CrossRef]
24. Dia, B.; Oppelstrup, J. Stabilizing local boundary conditions for two-dimensional shallow water equations. *Adv. Mech. Eng.* **2018**, *10*, 1–11. [CrossRef]
25. Fattorini, H.; Sritharan, S. Existence of optimal controls for viscous flow problems. *Proc. R. Soc. A Math. Phys. Eng. Sci.* **1992**, *439*, 81–102.
26. Bresch, D.; Desjardins, B. Existence of global weak solutions for a 2d viscous shallow water equations and convergence to the quasi-geostrophic model. *Commun. Math. Phys.* **2003**, *238*, 211–223. [CrossRef]

27. Bresch, D.; Desjardins, B.; Métivier, G. Recent mathematical results and open problems about shallow water equations. In *Analysis and Simulation of Fluid Dynamics Series in Advances in Mathematical Fluid Mechanics*; Birkhäuser: Basel, Switzerland, 2006; pp. 15–31.
28. Gerbeau, J.; Perthame, B. Derivation of viscous Saint-Venant system for laminar shallow water: Numerical validation. *Discrete Contin. Dyn. Syst. Ser. B* **2001**, *1*, 89–102. [CrossRef]
29. Marche, F. Derivation of a new two-dimensional viscous shallow water model with varying topography, bottom friction and capillary effects. *Eur. J. Mech. B Fluids* **2007**, *26*, 49–63. [CrossRef]
30. Constantin, A.; Escher, J. Global existence and blow-up for a shallow water equation. *Ann. Sc. Norm. Super. Pisa—Cl. Sci. Ser.* **1998**, *4*, 303–328.
31. Constantin, A. Existence of permanent and breaking waves for a shallow water equation: A geometric approach. *Ann. L'Institut Fourier* **2000**, *50*, 321–362. [CrossRef]
32. Gent, P. The energetically consistent shallow water equations. *J. Atmos. Sci.* **1993**, *50*, 1323–1325. [CrossRef]
33. Orenga, P. Un théoréme d'existence de solutions d'un problème de shallow water. *Arch. Rat. Mech. Anal.* **1995**, *130*, 183–204. [CrossRef]
34. Goudiaby, M.S.; Kreiss, G. Existence result for the coupling of shallow water and Borda–Carnot equations with Riemann data. *J. Hyperbolic Differ. Equ.* **2020**, *17*, 185–212. [CrossRef]
35. Audusse, E. Modelisation Hyperbolique et Analyse Numérique pour les éCoulements en Eaux peu Profondes. Ph.D. Thesis, Université Paris 13 Nord, Villetaneuse, France, 2004.
36. Ruohonen, K. An effective Cauchy-Peano existence theorem for unique solutions. *Int. J. Found. Comput. Sci.* **1996**, *7*, 151–160. [CrossRef]
37. Hájek, P.; Johanis, M. On Peano's theorem in Banach spaces. *J. Differ. Equ.* **2009**, *249*, 3342–3351. [CrossRef]
38. Feng, Z.; Li, F.; Lv, Y.; Zhang, S. A note on Cauchy-Lipschitz-Picard theorem. *J. Inequalities Appl.* **2016**, *2016*, 271. [CrossRef]

Article

Kinetics of a Reaction-Diffusion Mtb/SARS-CoV-2 Coinfection Model with Immunity

Ali Algarni [1,*], Afnan D. Al Agha [2], Aisha Fayomi [1] and Hakim Al Garalleh [2]

[1] Department of Statistics, Faculty of Science, King Abdulaziz University, P.O. Box 80203, Jeddah 21589, Saudi Arabia; afayomi@kau.edu.sa
[2] Department of Mathematical Science, College of Engineering, University of Business and Technology, P.O. Box 110200, Jeddah 21361, Saudi Arabia; a.alagha@ubt.edu.sa (A.D.A.A.); h.algaralleh@ubt.edu.sa (H.A.G.)
* Correspondence: ahalgarni@kau.edu.sa

Abstract: The severe acute respiratory syndrome coronavirus 2 (SARS-CoV-2) and Mycobacterium tuberculosis (Mtb) coinfection has been observed in a number of nations and it is connected with severe illness and death. The paper studies a reaction–diffusion within-host Mtb/SARS-CoV-2 coinfection model with immunity. This model explores the connections between uninfected epithelial cells, latently Mtb-infected epithelial cells, productively Mtb-infected epithelial cells, SARS-CoV-2-infected epithelial cells, free Mtb particles, free SARS-CoV-2 virions, and CTLs. The basic properties of the model's solutions are verified. All equilibrium points with the essential conditions for their existence are calculated. The global stability of these equilibria is established by adopting compatible Lyapunov functionals. The theoretical outcomes are enhanced by implementing numerical simulations. It is found that the equilibrium points mirror the single infection and coinfection states of SARS-CoV-2 with Mtb. The threshold conditions that determine the movement from the monoinfection to the coinfection state need to be tested when developing new treatments for coinfected patients. The impact of the diffusion coefficients should be monitored at the beginning of coinfection as it affects the initial distribution of particles in space.

Keywords: tuberculosis; COVID-19; diffusion; coinfection; stability

MSC: 35B35; 37N25; 92D05

1. Introduction

Coronavirus disease 2019 (COVID-19) is a viral disease induced by severe acute respiratory syndrome coronavirus 2 (SARS-CoV-2) and emerged in 2019. Although the number of new cases decreased in the last few months, COVID-19 is continuing its spread around the globe [1]. Following the World Health Organization (WHO) report issued on 1 March 2023, above 758,000,000 affirmed cases and over 6,800,000 deaths have been accounted globally [1]. COVID-19 coinfections with other viral or bacterial diseases are common, which complicates the treatment of COVID-19 [2]. Tuberculosis (TB) is a bacterial infection attributable to Mycobacterium tuberculosis (Mtb). Currently, COVID-19 co-occurring with TB has been declared in a number of nations [3]. As COVID-19 and TB are greatly infectious diseases, understanding Mtb/SARS-CoV-2 coinfection is very crucial for protection and treatment of coinfection.

SARS-CoV-2 is an enveloped RNA virus which is linked with the Betacoronavirus genus [4]. It breaks into the host cell using the angiotensin-converting enzyme 2 (ACE2) receptor [5]. It primarily infects the alveolar epithelial type-II cells of the lungs [6]. Similar to SARS-CoV-2, Mtb infects alveolar epithelial type-II cells through pattern recognition receptors such as toll-like receptors, complement receptors, and CD14 receptors [7]. Thus, the lung is the major infection site for these pathogens. Nevertheless, they can invade cells within different organs [6]. Since SARS-CoV-2 and Mtb infect the same target, this could increase the seriousness of disease in coinfected people [4]. Both pathogens are disseminated through respiratory droplets [2]. The most dominant features of Mtb/SARS-CoV-2 co-occurring are fever, cough, and dyspenea [2]. Risk factors in coinfection include age and comorbidities such as diabetes, HIV, and hypertension [2,3]. The immune response in coinfection includes T cells [8]. Specifically, cytotoxic T lymphocytes (CTLs) work on eliminating infected cells from the body. In the mild cases, the immune response can clear both infections. It has been proposed that Mtb/SARS-CoV-2 patients are at higher risk of death and developing severe disease than SARS-CoV-2 patients without Mtb [2,3,8]. Moreover, some studies reported that SARS-CoV-2 infection may cause latent Mtb to become active in coinfected people [3,4]. Other studies also observed that coinfected patients have low lymphocyte counts [2,8]. Thus, understanding the mechanism of coinfection is very important to evolve treatments for coinfected patients.

Mathematical models have been utilized to assist experimental and medical studies of different infections. These models are partitioned into epidemiological and within-host models. Epidemiological systems consider the interactions between individuals at the population level, while within-host systems explore the interplay between pathogens and cells within the host's body. A variety of COVID-19 epidemiological models (see for example, [9–15]) and within-host models (see for example, [16–18]) have been introduced and investigated. Similarly, TB models have been widely studied as epidemiological models (see for example, [19–22]) and within-host models (see for example, [23–27]). Some coinfection models of COVID-19 with other diseases have been developed. For instance, Pinky and Dobrovolny [28] analyzed a model that tests the impact of SARS-CoV-2 coinfection with the influenza virus. Al Agha and Elaiw [29] established a within-host SARS-CoV-2/malaria model with immune response. Elaiw et al. [30] developed a SARS-CoV-2/HIV coinfection model that takes the latent stage of infected epithelial cells (EPCs) into consideration. Elaiw and Al Agha [31] studied a SARS-CoV-2/cancer system with two immune responses.

Many epidemiological models of TB/COVID-19 coinfection have been proposed (see for example, [32–34]). On the other hand, within-host models are not widely considered. In [35], a within-host coinfection model has been formalized using ordinary differential Equations (ODEs). This work develops a reaction–diffusion within-host Mtb/SARS-CoV-2 coinfection model. It depicts the interplay between uninfected EPCs, latently Mtb-infected EPCs, productively Mtb-infected EPCs, SARS-CoV-2-infected EPCs, Mtb particles, SARS-CoV-2 particles, and CTLs. Additionally, this model is formalized using partial differential Equations (PDEs) which count the nonuniform distribution of cells and pathogens with their ability to move. Thus, PDEs are more realistic than ODEs which assume the spatial distribution homogeneity of cells and particles. Using the developed model, we (i) establish the boundedness and nonnegativity of the solutions, (ii) determine all equilibrium points and find the thresholds, (iii) confirm the global stability of each point, and (iv) use numerical simulations to validate the theoretical observations.

The remaining sections are divided as follows. Section 2 represents the model. Section 3 proves the boundedness and nonnegativity of the solutions. Moreover, it recounts all equilibrium points. Section 4 employs Lyapunov functionals to show the global stability of each point. Section 5 implements numerical simulations. The last section provides the conclusion with upcoming works.

2. A Reaction–Diffusion Mtb/SARS-CoV-2 Coinfection Model

This part describes the model under consideration. In this model, we assume that Mtb and SARS-CoV-2 have the same target, and CTLs kill infected cells at the same rate. The model consists of seven PDEs as follows:

$$\begin{cases} \dfrac{\partial U(x,t)}{\partial t} = D_U \Delta U + \lambda - \eta_1 UB - \eta_2 UV - \epsilon_1 U, \\ \dfrac{\partial L(x,t)}{\partial t} = D_L \Delta L + \eta_1 UB - aL, \\ \dfrac{\partial I^B(x,t)}{\partial t} = D_{I^B} \Delta I^B + aL - \gamma I^B Z - \epsilon_2 I^B, \\ \dfrac{\partial I^V(x,t)}{\partial t} = D_{I^V} \Delta I^V + \eta_2 UV - \gamma I^V Z - \epsilon_3 I^V, \\ \dfrac{\partial B(x,t)}{\partial t} = D_B \Delta B + \mu_1 \epsilon_2 I^B - \epsilon_4 B, \\ \dfrac{\partial V(x,t)}{\partial t} = D_V \Delta V + \mu_2 I^V - \epsilon_5 V, \\ \dfrac{\partial Z(x,t)}{\partial t} = D_Z \Delta Z + \omega I^B Z + \omega I^V Z - \epsilon_6 Z, \end{cases} \quad (1)$$

where the time $t > 0$ and the position $x \in \Psi$. The domain Ψ is bounded and connected with a smooth boundary $\partial \Psi$. The compartments U, L, I^B, I^V, B, V, and Z designate the concentrations of uninfected EPCs, latently Mtb-infected EPCs, productively Mtb-infected EPCs, SARS-CoV-2-infected EPCs, Mtb particles, SARS-CoV-2 particles, and CTLs at (x, t), respectively. Uninfected EPCs are generated at rate λ. Mtb converts healthy EPCs into latently infected cells at rate $\eta_1 UB$, while SARS-CoV-2 infects the same type of cells at rate $\eta_2 UV$. Latently Mtb-infected cells become an active producer at rate aL. Mtb particles are created at a total production rate $\mu_1 \epsilon_2 I^B$. SARS-CoV-2 virions are ejected from SARS-CoV-2-infected cells at rate $\mu_2 I^V$. CTLs remove Mtb and SARS-CoV-2 infected cells at rates $\gamma I^B Z$ and $\gamma I^V Z$, respectively. The corresponding stimulation rates are $\omega I^B Z$ and $\omega I^V Z$, respectively. The compartments U, I^B, I^V, B, V, and Z die at rates $\epsilon_1 U$, $\epsilon_2 I^B$, $\epsilon_3 I^V$, $\epsilon_4 B$, $\epsilon_5 V$, and $\epsilon_6 Z$, respectively. We assume that each compartment K diffuses with a diffusion coefficient D_K. The operator $\Delta = \dfrac{\partial^2}{\partial x^2}$ is the Laplacian operator. We presume that all parameters of model (1) are positive. The initial conditions (ICs) of system (1) are

$$U(x,0) = \nu_1(x), \quad L(x,0) = \nu_2(x), \quad I^B(x,0) = \nu_3(x), \quad I^V(x,0) = \nu_4(x),$$
$$B(x,0) = \nu_5(x), \quad V(x,0) = \nu_6(x), \quad Z(x,0) = \nu_7(x), \quad x \in \Psi, \quad (2)$$

where $\nu_i(x) \geq 0$, $i = 1, 2, \ldots, 7$, are continuous functions in Ψ. The boundary conditions (BCs) of (1) are

$$\frac{\partial U}{\partial \vec{r}} = \frac{\partial L}{\partial \vec{r}} = \frac{\partial I^B}{\partial \vec{r}} = \frac{\partial I^V}{\partial \vec{r}} = \frac{\partial B}{\partial \vec{r}} = \frac{\partial V}{\partial \vec{r}} = \frac{\partial Z}{\partial \vec{r}} = 0, \quad t > 0, \quad x \in \partial \Psi, \quad (3)$$

where $\dfrac{\partial}{\partial \vec{r}}$ is the outward normal derivative on $\partial \Psi$. These Neumann BCs suggest that the boundary is isolated.

In the upcoming parts of the paper and for simplicity, we consider the contraction $K(x,t) \equiv K$ for each compartment K in model (1).

3. Basic Properties

This section certifies that the solutions of system (1)–(3) are unique, nonnegative, and bounded. Additionally, it computes all equilibrium points of model (1).

Let $\mathbb{S} = BUC(\Psi, \mathbb{R}^7)$ be the set of functions that are bounded and continuous from Ψ to $\mathbb{R}^7$. The positive cone $\mathbb{S}_+ = BUC(\Psi, \mathbb{R}^7_+) \subset \mathbb{S}$ forms a partial order on $\mathbb{S}$. Define $\|f\|_{\mathbb{S}} = \sup_{x \in \Psi} |f(x)|$. Consequently, $(\mathbb{S}, \|\cdot\|_{\mathbb{S}})$ is a Banach lattice [36,37].

Theorem 1. *Suppose that $D_U = D_L = D_{I^B} = D_{I^V} = D_Z = D_1$. Then, model (1) with any ICs (2) has a unique, nonnegative, and bounded solution on $\bar{\Psi} \times [0, +\infty)$.*

Proof. For any $\nu = (\nu_1, \nu_2, \nu_3, \nu_4, \nu_5, \nu_6, \nu_7)^T \in \mathbb{S}_+$, we define $P = (P_1, P_2, P_3, P_4, P_5, P_6, P_7)^T :$ $\mathbb{S}_+ \to \mathbb{S}$ by

$$\begin{cases} P_1(\nu)(x) = \lambda - \eta_1 \nu_1(x)\nu_5(x) - \eta_2 \nu_1(x)\nu_6(x) - \epsilon_1 \nu_1(x), \\ P_2(\nu)(x) = \eta_1 \nu_1(x)\nu_5(x) - a\nu_2(x), \\ P_3(\nu)(x) = a\nu_2(x) - \gamma \nu_3(x)\nu_7(x) - \epsilon_2 \nu_3(x), \\ P_4(\nu)(x) = \eta_2 \nu_1(x)\nu_6(x) - \gamma \nu_4(x)\nu_7(x) - \epsilon_3 \nu_4(x), \\ P_5(\nu)(x) = \mu_1 \epsilon_2 \nu_3(x) - \epsilon_4 \nu_5(x), \\ P_6(\nu)(x) = \mu_2 \nu_4(x) - \epsilon_5 \nu_6(x), \\ P_7(\nu)(x) = \omega \nu_3(x)\nu_7(x) + \omega \nu_4(x)\nu_7(x) - \epsilon_6 \nu_7(x). \end{cases}$$

We observe that P is Lipschitz on $\mathbb{S}_+$. Therefore, it is possible to rewrite system (1)–(3) as the abstract DE:

$$\begin{cases} \dfrac{dJ}{dt} = DJ + P(J), \ t > 0, \\ J_0 = \nu \in \mathbb{S}_+, \end{cases}$$

where $J = (U, L, I^B, I^V, B, V, Z)^T$ and $DJ = (D_U \Delta U, D_L \Delta L, D_{I^B} \Delta I^B, D_{I^V} \Delta I^V, D_B \Delta B,$ $D_V \Delta V, D_Z \Delta Z)^T$. We can show that

$$\lim_{h \to 0^+} \frac{1}{h} \text{dist}(\nu + hP(\nu), \mathbb{S}_+) = 0, \ \nu \in \mathbb{S}_+.$$

Hence, for any $\nu \in \mathbb{S}_+$, model (1)–(3) has a unique nonnegative mild solution for the time interval $[0, T_e)$.

To verify the boundedness, we consider the function

$$Y_1(x, t) = U + L + I^V.$$

As $D_U = D_L = D_{I^V} = D_1$, then by utilizing model (1) we obtain

$$\begin{aligned} \frac{\partial Y_1}{\partial t} - D_1 \Delta Y_1 &= \lambda - \epsilon_1 U - aL - \gamma I^V Z - \epsilon_3 I^V \\ &\leq \lambda - \epsilon_1 U - aL - \epsilon_3 I^V \\ &\leq \lambda - \sigma_1 \left[U + L + I^V \right] \\ &= \lambda - \sigma_1 Y_1, \end{aligned}$$

where $\sigma_1 = \min\{a, \epsilon_1, \epsilon_3\}$. Thus, Y_1 satisfies the system

$$\begin{cases} \dfrac{\partial Y_1}{\partial t} - D_1 \Delta Y_1 \leq \lambda - \sigma_1 Y_1, \\ \dfrac{\partial Y_1}{\partial \vec{r}} = 0, \\ Y_1(x, 0) \geq 0. \end{cases}$$

Assume that $\widetilde{Y}_1(t)$ satisfies the system

$$\begin{cases} \dfrac{d\widetilde{Y}_1(t)}{dt} = \lambda - \sigma_1 \widetilde{Y}_1(t), \\ \widetilde{Y}_1(0) = \max_{x \in \Psi} Y_1(x, 0), \end{cases}$$

which implies that $\widetilde{Y}_1(t) \leq \max\left\{\dfrac{\lambda}{\sigma_1}, \max_{x \in \Psi} Y_1(x, 0)\right\}$. In accord with the comparison principle (CP) [38], we obtain $Y_1(x, t) \leq \widetilde{Y}_1(t)$. As a result, we have

$$Y_1(x,t) \leq \max\left\{\frac{\lambda}{\sigma_1}, \max_{x \in \Psi} Y_1(x,0)\right\} := Q_1.$$

This ensures that U, L, and I^V are bounded. From the third equation of (1), we have

$$\begin{aligned}\frac{\partial I^B}{\partial t} - D_{I^B}\Delta I^B &= aL - \gamma I^B Z - \epsilon_2 I^B \\ &\leq aL - \epsilon_2 I^B \\ &\leq aQ_1 - \epsilon_2 I^B.\end{aligned}$$

We can conclude from the CP [38] that

$$I^B \leq \max\left\{\frac{aQ_1}{\epsilon_2}, \max_{x \in \Psi} I^B(x,0)\right\} := Q_2.$$

Thus, I^B is bounded. From the fifth equation of (1), we have

$$\begin{aligned}\frac{\partial B}{\partial t} - D_B\Delta B &= \mu_1\epsilon_2 I^B - \epsilon_4 B \\ &\leq \mu_1\epsilon_2 Q_2 - \epsilon_4 B.\end{aligned}$$

Based on the CP [38], we obtain

$$B \leq \max\left\{\frac{\mu_1\epsilon_2 Q_2}{\epsilon_4}, \max_{x \in \Psi} B(x,0)\right\}.$$

Hence, B is bounded. From the sixth equation of model (1), we obtain

$$\begin{aligned}\frac{\partial V}{\partial t} - D_V\Delta V &= \mu_2 I^V - \epsilon_5 V \\ &\leq \mu_2 Q_1 - \epsilon_5 V.\end{aligned}$$

The CP [38] implies that

$$V \leq \max\left\{\frac{\mu_2 Q_1}{\epsilon_5}, \max_{x \in \Psi} V(x,0)\right\} := Q_3.$$

Thus, V is bounded. Finally, we introduce the function

$$Y_2(x,t) = I^B + I^V + \frac{\gamma}{\omega}Z.$$

Then, we obtain

$$\begin{aligned}\frac{\partial Y_2}{\partial t} - D_1\Delta Y_2 &= aL + \eta_2 UV - \epsilon_2 I^B - \epsilon_3 I^V - \frac{\gamma\epsilon_6}{\omega}Z \\ &\leq aQ_1 + \eta_2 Q_1 Q_3 - \sigma_2 Y_2,\end{aligned}$$

where $\sigma_2 = \min\{\epsilon_2, \epsilon_3, \epsilon_6\}$. By the CP, [38], we obtain

$$Y_2(x,t) \leq \max\left\{\frac{aQ_1 + \eta_2 Q_1 Q_3}{\sigma_2}, \max_{x \in \Psi} Y_2(x,0)\right\}.$$

This implies that Z is bounded. The above results show that all solutions are bounded on $\Psi \times [0, T_e)$, and so solutions are bounded on $\Psi \times [0, +\infty)$. This conclusion is derived from the standard theory for semi-linear parabolic Equations [39]. □

Proposition 1. *The conditions $\mathcal{R}_{0B}$, $\mathcal{R}_{0V}$, $\mathcal{R}_{1B}$, $\mathcal{R}_{1V}$, and σ exist such that system (1) has six equilibrium points:*

(i) The uninfected equilibrium E_0 always exists;
(ii) The Mtb immune-free equilibrium E_1 is defined when $\mathcal{R}_{0B} > 1$;
(iii) The COVID-19 immune-free equilibrium E_2 is defined if $\mathcal{R}_{0V} > 1$;
(iv) The Mtb equilibrium with immunity E_3 exists if $\mathcal{R}_{1B} > 1$;
(v) The COVID-19 equilibrium with immunity E_4 exists if $\mathcal{R}_{1V} > 1$;
(vi) The Mtb/SARS-CoV-2 coinfection equilibrium E_5 exists if $\dfrac{\omega \lambda \eta_2 \mu_2 \epsilon_4}{\epsilon_2 \epsilon_5 [\omega \epsilon_1 \epsilon_4 + \eta_1 \mu_1 \epsilon_2 \epsilon_6]} + 1 > \dfrac{\epsilon_3}{\epsilon_2} + \mathcal{R}_{1B}$, $\dfrac{\omega \lambda \eta_1 \mu_1 \epsilon_2 \epsilon_5}{\epsilon_3 \epsilon_4 [\omega \epsilon_1 \epsilon_5 + \eta_2 \mu_2 \epsilon_6]} + 1 > \dfrac{\epsilon_2}{\epsilon_3} + \mathcal{R}_{1V}$, $\dfrac{\mathcal{R}_{0V}}{\mathcal{R}_{0B}} > 1$, $\epsilon_2 > \epsilon_3$, and $\sigma > 1$.

Proof. The equilibrium points of Equation (1) can be drawn by solving the system:

$$\begin{cases} 0 = \lambda - \eta_1 UB - \eta_2 UV - \epsilon_1 U, \\ 0 = \eta_1 UB - aL, \\ 0 = aL - \gamma I^B Z - \epsilon_2 I^B, \\ 0 = \eta_2 UV - \gamma I^V Z - \epsilon_3 I^V, \\ 0 = \mu_1 \epsilon_2 I^B - \epsilon_4 B, \\ 0 = \mu_2 I^V - \epsilon_5 V, \\ 0 = \omega I^B Z + \omega I^V Z - \epsilon_6 Z. \end{cases}$$

Then, we obtain the following:

(i) The uninfected equilibrium $E_0 = (U_0, 0, 0, 0, 0, 0, 0)$, where $U_0 = \dfrac{\lambda}{\epsilon_1} > 0$. Thus, E_0 always exists.

(ii) The Mtb immune-free equilibrium $E_1 = (U_1, L_1, I_1^B, 0, B_1, 0, 0)$. The components are given as follows:

$$U_1 = \dfrac{\epsilon_4}{\eta_1 \mu_1}, \quad L_1 = \dfrac{\epsilon_1 \epsilon_4}{a \eta_1 \mu_1} (\mathcal{R}_{0B} - 1), \quad I_1^B = \dfrac{\epsilon_1 \epsilon_4}{\eta_1 \mu_1 \epsilon_2} (\mathcal{R}_{0B} - 1), \quad B_1 = \dfrac{\epsilon_1}{\eta_1} (\mathcal{R}_{0B} - 1),$$

where $\mathcal{R}_{0B} = \dfrac{\lambda \eta_1 \mu_1}{\epsilon_1 \epsilon_4}$. We note that U_1 is positive, whilst L_1, I_1^B, and B_1 are positive when $\mathcal{R}_{0B} > 1$. Hence, E_1 exists if $\mathcal{R}_{0B} > 1$. The parameter $\mathcal{R}_{0B}$ appoints the onset of Mtb infection with inactive CTLs.

(iii) The COVID-19 immune-free equilibrium $E_2 = (U_2, 0, 0, I_2^V, 0, V_2, 0)$. Its coordinates are written as follows:

$$U_2 = \dfrac{\epsilon_3 \epsilon_5}{\eta_2 \mu_2}, \quad I_2^V = \dfrac{\epsilon_1 \epsilon_5}{\eta_2 \mu_2} (\mathcal{R}_{0V} - 1), \quad V_2 = \dfrac{\epsilon_1}{\eta_2} (\mathcal{R}_{0V} - 1),$$

where $\mathcal{R}_{0V} = \dfrac{\lambda \eta_2 \mu_2}{\epsilon_1 \epsilon_3 \epsilon_5}$. Thus, $U_2 > 0$, whilst $I_2^V > 0$ and $V_2 > 0$ when $\mathcal{R}_{0V} > 1$. Accordingly, E_2 is defined when $\mathcal{R}_{0V} > 1$. The threshold $\mathcal{R}_{0V}$ locates the start of COVID-19 infection, where the CTL immunity is inactive.

(iv) The Mtb equilibrium with immunity $E_3 = (U_3, L_3, I_3^B, 0, B_3, 0, Z_3)$, where

$$U_3 = \dfrac{\omega \lambda \epsilon_4}{\omega \epsilon_1 \epsilon_4 + \eta_1 \mu_1 \epsilon_2 \epsilon_6}, \quad L_3 = \dfrac{\lambda \eta_1 \mu_1 \epsilon_2 \epsilon_6}{a[\omega \epsilon_1 \epsilon_4 + \eta_1 \mu_1 \epsilon_2 \epsilon_6]}, \quad I_3^B = \dfrac{\epsilon_6}{\omega},$$

$$B_3 = \dfrac{\mu_1 \epsilon_2 \epsilon_6}{\omega \epsilon_4}, \quad Z_3 = \dfrac{\epsilon_2}{\gamma} (\mathcal{R}_{1B} - 1),$$

where $\mathcal{R}_{1B} = \dfrac{\omega \lambda \eta_1 \mu_1}{\omega \epsilon_1 \epsilon_4 + \eta_1 \mu_1 \epsilon_2 \epsilon_6}$. We note that U_3, L_3, I_3^B and B_3 are always positive, while $Z_3 > 0$ if $\mathcal{R}_{1B} > 1$. This implies that E_3 exists if $\mathcal{R}_{1B} > 1$. The threshold $\mathcal{R}_{1B}$ sets the activation of CTLs versus Mtb-infected EPCs.

(v) The COVID-19 equilibrium with immunity $E_4 = (U_4, 0, 0, I_4^V, 0, V_4, Z_4)$. The components are given as

$$U_4 = \frac{\omega \lambda \epsilon_5}{\omega \epsilon_1 \epsilon_5 + \eta_2 \mu_2 \epsilon_6}, \quad I_4^V = \frac{\epsilon_6}{\omega}, \quad V_4 = \frac{\mu_2 \epsilon_6}{\omega \epsilon_5}, \quad Z_4 = \frac{\epsilon_3}{\gamma}(\mathcal{R}_{1V} - 1),$$

where $\mathcal{R}_{1V} = \frac{\omega \lambda \eta_2 \mu_2}{\epsilon_3 [\omega \epsilon_1 \epsilon_5 + \eta_2 \mu_2 \epsilon_6]}$. We see that $U_4, I_4^V, V_4 > 0$, while $Z_4 > 0$ if $\mathcal{R}_{1V} > 1$. Hence, E_4 is defined when $\mathcal{R}_{1V} > 1$. Here, the threshold $\mathcal{R}_{1V}$ defines the stimulation status of CTL immunity versus SARS-CoV-2-infected EPCs.

(vi) The Mtb/SARS-CoV-2 coinfection equilibrium $E_5 = (U_5, L_5, I_5^B, I_5^V, B_5, V_5, Z_5)$. The components are defined as

$$U_5 = \frac{(\epsilon_2 - \epsilon_3)\epsilon_5}{\eta_2 \mu_2 (\sigma - 1)},$$

$$L_5 = \frac{\eta_1 \mu_1 \epsilon_2 \epsilon_3 \epsilon_4 \epsilon_5 (\omega \epsilon_1 \epsilon_5 + \eta_2 \mu_2 \epsilon_6)}{a\omega(\eta_1 \mu_1 \epsilon_2 \epsilon_5 - \eta_2 \mu_2 \epsilon_4)^2}\left[\frac{\omega \lambda \eta_1 \mu_1 \epsilon_2 \epsilon_5}{\epsilon_3 \epsilon_4 (\omega \epsilon_1 \epsilon_5 + \eta_2 \mu_2 \epsilon_6)} + 1 - \frac{\epsilon_2}{\epsilon_3} - \mathcal{R}_{1V}\right],$$

$$I_5^B = \frac{\epsilon_3(\omega \epsilon_1 \epsilon_5 + \eta_2 \mu_2 \epsilon_6)}{\omega(\epsilon_2 - \epsilon_3)\eta_2 \mu_2(\sigma - 1)}\left[\frac{\omega \lambda \eta_1 \mu_1 \epsilon_2 \epsilon_5}{\epsilon_3 \epsilon_4(\omega \epsilon_1 \epsilon_5 + \eta_2 \mu_2 \epsilon_6)} + 1 - \frac{\epsilon_2}{\epsilon_3} - \mathcal{R}_{1V}\right],$$

$$I_5^V = \frac{\epsilon_2 \epsilon_5 (\omega \epsilon_1 \epsilon_4 + \eta_1 \mu_1 \epsilon_2 \epsilon_6)}{\omega(\epsilon_2 - \epsilon_3)\eta_2 \mu_2 \epsilon_4 (\sigma - 1)}\left[\frac{\omega \lambda \eta_2 \mu_2 \epsilon_4}{\epsilon_2 \epsilon_5 (\omega \epsilon_1 \epsilon_4 + \eta_1 \mu_1 \epsilon_2 \epsilon_6)} + 1 - \frac{\epsilon_3}{\epsilon_2} - \mathcal{R}_{1B}\right],$$

$$B_5 = \frac{\mu_1 \epsilon_2 \epsilon_3 (\omega \epsilon_1 \epsilon_5 + \eta_2 \mu_2 \epsilon_6)}{\omega(\epsilon_2 - \epsilon_3)\eta_2 \mu_2 \epsilon_4 (\sigma - 1)}\left[\frac{\omega \lambda \eta_1 \mu_1 \epsilon_2 \epsilon_5}{\epsilon_3 \epsilon_4 (\omega \epsilon_1 \epsilon_5 + \eta_2 \mu_2 \epsilon_6)} + 1 - \frac{\epsilon_2}{\epsilon_3} - \mathcal{R}_{1V}\right],$$

$$V_5 = \frac{\epsilon_2 (\omega \epsilon_1 \epsilon_4 + \eta_1 \mu_1 \epsilon_2 \epsilon_6)}{\omega(\epsilon_2 - \epsilon_3)\eta_2 \epsilon_4 (\sigma - 1)}\left[\frac{\omega \lambda \eta_2 \mu_2 \epsilon_4}{\epsilon_2 \epsilon_5 (\omega \epsilon_1 \epsilon_4 + \eta_1 \mu_1 \epsilon_2 \epsilon_6)} + 1 - \frac{\epsilon_3}{\epsilon_2} - \mathcal{R}_{1B}\right],$$

$$Z_5 = \frac{\eta_1 \mu_1 \epsilon_2 \epsilon_3 \epsilon_5 (\mathcal{R}_{0V}/\mathcal{R}_{0B} - 1)}{\gamma \eta_2 \mu_2 \epsilon_4 (\sigma - 1)},$$

where $\sigma = \frac{\eta_1 \mu_1 \epsilon_2 \epsilon_5}{\eta_2 \mu_2 \epsilon_4}$. We see that L_5, I_5^B, and B_5 are positive if $\frac{\omega \lambda \eta_1 \mu_1 \epsilon_2 \epsilon_5}{\epsilon_3 \epsilon_4 (\omega \epsilon_1 \epsilon_5 + \eta_2 \mu_2 \epsilon_6)} + 1 > \frac{\epsilon_2}{\epsilon_3} + \mathcal{R}_{1V}$, while I_5^V and V_5 are positive if $\frac{\omega \lambda \eta_2 \mu_2 \epsilon_4}{\epsilon_2 \epsilon_5 (\omega \epsilon_1 \epsilon_4 + \eta_1 \mu_1 \epsilon_2 \epsilon_6)} + 1 > \frac{\epsilon_3}{\epsilon_2} + \mathcal{R}_{1B}$, and $Z_5 > 0$ if $\frac{\mathcal{R}_{0V}}{\mathcal{R}_{0B}} > 1$. In addition, we need the two conditions $\epsilon_2 > \epsilon_3$ and $\sigma > 1$. Hence, E_5 exists when the above conditions are met. □

4. Global Properties

This part is aimed to prove the global stability of all equilibria by adopting correct Lyapunov functionals. The construction of these Lyapunov functionals follows the methods presented in [40–42].

We consider a function $\Xi_i(U, L, I^B, I^V, B, V, Z)$ and suppose that χ_i' is the largest invariant subset of $\chi_i = \left\{(U, L, I^B, I^V, B, V, Z) \mid \frac{d\Xi_i}{dt} = 0\right\}, i = 0, 1, \ldots, 5$.

Theorem 2. *The equilibrium E_0 is globally asymptotically stable (GS) if $\mathcal{R}_{0B} \leq 1$ and $\mathcal{R}_{0V} \leq 1$.*

Proof. We opt a Lyapunov functional (LF)

$$\Xi_0(t) = \int_\Psi \tilde{\Xi}_0(x,t) \, dx, \quad \text{where}$$

$$\tilde{\Xi}_0 = U_0\left(\frac{U}{U_0} - 1 - \ln\frac{U}{U_0}\right) + L + I^B + I^V + \frac{1}{\mu_1}B + \frac{\epsilon_3}{\mu_2}V + \frac{\gamma}{\omega}Z.$$

By taking the partial derivative, we obtain

$$\frac{\partial \tilde{\Xi}_0}{\partial t} = \left(1 - \frac{U_0}{U}\right)\left(D_U \Delta U + \lambda - \eta_1 UB - \eta_2 UV - \epsilon_1 U\right) + D_L \Delta L + \eta_1 UB - aL + D_{I^B} \Delta I^B$$

$$+ aL - \gamma I^B Z - \epsilon_2 I^B + D_{I^V} \Delta I^V + \eta_2 UV - \gamma I^V Z - \epsilon_3 I^V + \frac{1}{\mu_1}\left(D_B \Delta B + \mu_1 \epsilon_2 I^B - \epsilon_4 B\right)$$

$$+ \frac{\epsilon_3}{\mu_2}\left(D_V \Delta V + \mu_2 I^V - \epsilon_5 V\right) + \frac{\gamma}{\omega}\left(D_Z \Delta Z + \omega I^B Z + \omega I^V Z - \epsilon_6 Z\right)$$

$$= \left(1 - \frac{U_0}{U}\right)(\lambda - \epsilon_1 U) + \left(\eta_1 U_0 - \frac{\epsilon_4}{\mu_1}\right)B + \left(\eta_2 U_0 - \frac{\epsilon_3 \epsilon_5}{\mu_2}\right)V - \frac{\gamma \epsilon_6}{\omega}Z + \left(1 - \frac{U_0}{U}\right)D_U \Delta U$$

$$+ D_L \Delta L + D_{I^B} \Delta I^B + D_{I^V} \Delta I^V + \frac{1}{\mu_1} D_B \Delta B + \frac{\epsilon_3}{\mu_2} D_V \Delta V + \frac{\gamma}{\omega} D_Z \Delta Z.$$

The derivative $\frac{d\Xi_0}{dt}$ is given by

$$\frac{d\Xi_0}{dt} = -\epsilon_1 \int_\Psi \frac{(U - U_0)^2}{U} dx + \frac{\epsilon_4}{\mu_1}(\mathcal{R}_{0B} - 1)\int_\Psi B\, dx + \frac{\epsilon_3 \epsilon_5}{\mu_2}(\mathcal{R}_{0V} - 1)\int_\Psi V\, dx - \frac{\gamma \epsilon_6}{\omega}\int_\Psi Z\, dx$$

$$+ D_U \int_\Psi \left(1 - \frac{U_0}{U}\right)\Delta U\, dx + D_L \int_\Psi \Delta L\, dx + D_{I^B}\int_\Psi \Delta I^B\, dx + D_{I^V}\int_\Psi \Delta I^V\, dx \quad (4)$$

$$+ \frac{1}{\mu_1}D_B \int_\Psi \Delta B\, dx + \frac{\epsilon_3}{\mu_2}D_V \int_\Psi \Delta V\, dx + \frac{\gamma}{\omega}D_Z \int_\Psi \Delta Z\, dx.$$

Based on the Divergence theorem and Neumann BCs, we obtain

$$0 = \int_{\partial\Psi} \nabla\Phi \cdot \vec{r}\, dx = \int_\Psi \text{div}(\nabla\Phi)\, dx = \int_\Psi \Delta\Phi\, dx,$$

$$0 = \int_{\partial\Psi} \frac{1}{\Phi}\nabla\Phi \cdot \vec{r}\, dx = \int_\Psi \text{div}(\frac{1}{\Phi}\nabla\Phi)\, dx = \int_\Psi \left[\frac{\Delta\Phi}{\Phi} - \frac{\|\nabla\Phi\|^2}{\Phi^2}\right]dx, \quad \text{for } \Phi \in \{U, L, I^B, I^V, B, V, Z\}. \quad (5)$$

As a result, the derivative in (4) is altered to

$$\frac{d\Xi_0}{dt} = -\epsilon_1 \int_\Psi \frac{(U - U_0)^2}{U} dx + \frac{\epsilon_4}{\mu_1}(\mathcal{R}_{0B} - 1)\int_\Psi B\, dx + \frac{\epsilon_3 \epsilon_5}{\mu_2}(\mathcal{R}_{0V} - 1)\int_\Psi V\, dx - \frac{\gamma \epsilon_6}{\omega}\int_\Psi Z\, dx$$

$$- D_U U_0 \int_\Psi \frac{\|\nabla U\|^2}{U^2} dx.$$

We see that $\frac{d\Xi_0}{dt} \leq 0$ if $\mathcal{R}_{0B} \leq 1$ and $\mathcal{R}_{0V} \leq 1$. Furthermore, $\frac{d\Xi_0}{dt} = 0$ if $U = U_0$ and $B = V = Z = 0$. The solutions approach χ_0' that has $B = V = 0$. Thus, $\frac{\partial B}{\partial t} = 0$ and $\frac{\partial V}{\partial t} = 0$. According to the fifth and sixth equations of system (1), we acquire $I^B = I^V = 0$. Therefore, $\frac{\partial I^B}{\partial t} = 0$ and the third equation of (1) gives $L = 0$. Consequently, $\chi_0' = \{E_0\}$ and in compliance with LaSalle's invariance principle (LIP) [43], the point E_0 is GS if $\mathcal{R}_{0B} \leq 1$ and $\mathcal{R}_{0V} \leq 1$. □

Theorem 3. Let $\mathcal{R}_{0B} > 1$. Then, the equilibrium E_1 is GS if $\frac{\mathcal{R}_{0V}}{\mathcal{R}_{0B}} \leq 1$ with $\mathcal{R}_{1B} \leq 1$.

Proof. We adopt an LF

$$\Xi_1(t) = \int_\Psi \tilde{\Xi}_1(x,t)\, dx, \quad \text{where}$$

$$\tilde{\Xi}_1 = U_1\left(\frac{U}{U_1} - 1 - \ln\frac{U}{U_1}\right) + L_1\left(\frac{L}{L_1} - 1 - \ln\frac{L}{L_1}\right) + I_1^B\left(\frac{I^B}{I_1^B} - 1 - \ln\frac{I^B}{I_1^B}\right) + I^V$$

$$+ \frac{1}{\mu_1}B_1\left(\frac{B}{B_1} - 1 - \ln\frac{B}{B_1}\right) + \frac{\epsilon_3}{\mu_2}V + \frac{\gamma}{\omega}Z.$$

By calculating the partial derivative, we obtain

$$
\begin{aligned}
\frac{\partial \widetilde{\Xi}_1}{\partial t} &= \left(1 - \frac{U_1}{U}\right)\left(D_U \Delta U + \lambda - \eta_1 UB - \eta_2 UV - \epsilon_1 U\right) + \left(1 - \frac{L_1}{L}\right)\left(D_L \Delta L + \eta_1 UB - aL\right) \\
&+ \left(1 - \frac{I_1^B}{I^B}\right)\left(D_{I^B} \Delta I^B + aL - \gamma I^B Z - \epsilon_2 I^B\right) + D_{I^V} \Delta I^V + \eta_2 UV - \gamma I^V Z - \epsilon_3 I^V \\
&+ \frac{1}{\mu_1}\left(1 - \frac{B_1}{B}\right)\left(D_B \Delta B + \mu_1 \epsilon_2 I^B - \epsilon_4 B\right) + \frac{\epsilon_3}{\mu_2}\left(D_V \Delta V + \mu_2 I^V - \epsilon_5 V\right) \\
&+ \frac{\gamma}{\omega}\left(D_Z \Delta Z + \omega I^B Z + \omega I^V Z - \epsilon_6 Z\right).
\end{aligned}
\quad (6)
$$

By employing the equilibrium conditions at E_1, we obtain

$$
\begin{cases}
\lambda = \eta_1 U_1 B_1 + \epsilon_1 U_1, \\
\eta_1 U_1 B_1 = aL_1, \\
aL_1 = \epsilon_2 I_1^B, \\
\epsilon_2 I_1^B = \frac{\epsilon_4}{\mu_1} B_1.
\end{cases}
$$

Hence, the derivative in (6) can be simplified to

$$
\begin{aligned}
\frac{\partial \widetilde{\Xi}_1}{\partial t} &= \left(1 - \frac{U_1}{U}\right)(\epsilon_1 U_1 - \epsilon_1 U) + \eta_1 U_1 B_1 \left(4 - \frac{U_1}{U} - \frac{UL_1 B}{U_1 L B_1} - \frac{L I_1^B}{L_1 I^B} - \frac{I^B B_1}{I_1^B B}\right) + \left(\eta_2 U_1 - \frac{\epsilon_3 \epsilon_5}{\mu_2}\right) V \\
&+ \left(\gamma I_1^B - \frac{\gamma \epsilon_6}{\omega}\right) Z + \left(1 - \frac{U_1}{U}\right) D_U \Delta U + \left(1 - \frac{L_1}{L}\right) D_L \Delta L + \left(1 - \frac{I_1^B}{I^B}\right) D_{I^B} \Delta I^B \\
&+ D_{I^V} \Delta I^V + \frac{1}{\mu_1}\left(1 - \frac{B_1}{B}\right) D_B \Delta B + \frac{\epsilon_3}{\mu_2} D_V \Delta V + \frac{\gamma}{\omega} D_Z \Delta Z.
\end{aligned}
$$

By using (5), $\dfrac{d\Xi_1}{dt}$ is given by

$$
\begin{aligned}
\frac{d\Xi_1}{dt} &= -\epsilon_1 \int_\Psi \frac{(U-U_1)^2}{U}\,dx + \eta_1 U_1 B_1 \int_\Psi \left(4 - \frac{U_1}{U} - \frac{UL_1 B}{U_1 L B_1} - \frac{L I_1^B}{L_1 I^B} - \frac{I^B B_1}{I_1^B B}\right) dx + \frac{\epsilon_3 \epsilon_5}{\mu_2}\left(\frac{\mathcal{R}_{0V}}{\mathcal{R}_{0B}} - 1\right) \int_\Psi V\,dx \\
&+ \frac{\gamma(\omega \epsilon_1 \epsilon_4 + \eta_1 \mu_1 \epsilon_2 \epsilon_6)}{\omega \eta_1 \mu_1 \epsilon_2}(\mathcal{R}_{1B} - 1) \int_\Psi Z\,dx - D_U U_1 \int_\Psi \frac{\|\nabla U\|^2}{U^2}\,dx - D_L L_1 \int_\Psi \frac{\|\nabla L\|^2}{L^2}\,dx \\
&- D_{I^B} I_1^B \int_\Psi \frac{\|\nabla I^B\|^2}{I^{B^2}}\,dx - \frac{D_B B_1}{\mu_1} \int_\Psi \frac{\|\nabla B\|^2}{B^2}\,dx.
\end{aligned}
$$

In this situation, $\dfrac{d\Xi_1}{dt} \leq 0$ if $\dfrac{\mathcal{R}_{0V}}{\mathcal{R}_{0B}} \leq 1$ and $\mathcal{R}_{1B} \leq 1$. In addition, $\dfrac{d\Xi_1}{dt} = 0$ when $U = U_1$, $L = L_1$, $I^B = I_1^B$, $B = B_1$, while $V = Z = 0$. The solutions tend to χ_1' with $V = 0$ and therefore $\dfrac{\partial V}{\partial t} = 0$. The sixth equation of (1) yields $I^V = 0$. Hence, $\chi_1' = \{E_1\}$ and E_1 is GS when $\mathcal{R}_{0B} > 1$, $\dfrac{\mathcal{R}_{0V}}{\mathcal{R}_{0B}} \leq 1$ and $\mathcal{R}_{1B} \leq 1$ according to LIP [43]. □

Theorem 4. *Let $\mathcal{R}_{0V} > 1$. The equilibrium E_2 is GS if $\dfrac{\mathcal{R}_{0B}}{\mathcal{R}_{0V}} \leq 1$ and $\mathcal{R}_{1V} \leq 1$.*

Proof. We pick an LF

$$
\Xi_2(t) = \int_\Psi \widetilde{\Xi}_2(x,t)\,dx, \quad \text{where}
$$

$$\tilde{\Xi}_2 = U_2\left(\frac{U}{U_2} - 1 - \ln\frac{U}{U_2}\right) + L + I^B + I_2^V\left(\frac{I^V}{I_2^V} - 1 - \ln\frac{I^V}{I_2^V}\right) + \frac{1}{\mu_1}B + \frac{\epsilon_3}{\mu_2}V_2\left(\frac{V}{V_2} - 1 - \ln\frac{V}{V_2}\right) + \frac{\gamma}{\omega}Z.$$

Then, $\frac{\partial \tilde{\Xi}_2}{\partial t}$ is computed as

$$\begin{aligned}\frac{\partial \tilde{\Xi}_2}{\partial t} =& \left(1 - \frac{U_2}{U}\right)\left(D_U \Delta U + \lambda - \eta_1 UB - \eta_2 UV - \epsilon_1 U\right) + D_L \Delta L + \eta_1 UB - aL + D_{I^B}\Delta I^B + aL \\ & - \gamma I^B Z - \epsilon_2 I^B + \left(1 - \frac{I_2^V}{I^V}\right)\left(D_{I^V}\Delta I^V + \eta_2 UV - \gamma I^V Z - \epsilon_3 I^V\right) + \frac{1}{\mu_1}\left(D_B \Delta B + \mu_1 \epsilon_2 I^B - \epsilon_4 B\right) \\ & + \frac{\epsilon_3}{\mu_2}\left(1 - \frac{V_2}{V}\right)\left(D_V \Delta V + \mu_2 I^V - \epsilon_5 V\right) + \frac{\gamma}{\omega}\left(D_Z \Delta Z + \omega I^B Z + \omega I^V Z - \epsilon_6 Z\right).\end{aligned} \quad (7)$$

By considering the equilibrium conditions at E_2

$$\begin{cases} \lambda = \eta_2 U_2 V_2 + \epsilon_1 U_2, \\ \eta_2 U_2 V_2 = \epsilon_3 I_2^V, \\ \epsilon_3 I_2^V = \frac{\epsilon_3 \epsilon_5}{\mu_2}V_2, \end{cases}$$

the derivative in (7) becomes

$$\begin{aligned}\frac{\partial \tilde{\Xi}_2}{\partial t} =& \left(1 - \frac{U_2}{U}\right)(\epsilon_1 U_2 - \epsilon_1 U) + \eta_2 U_2 V_2\left(3 - \frac{U_2}{U} - \frac{UI_2^V V}{U_2 I^V V_2} - \frac{I^V V_2}{I_2^V V}\right) + \left(\eta_1 U_2 - \frac{\epsilon_4}{\mu_1}\right)B \\ & + \left(\gamma I_2^V - \frac{\gamma \epsilon_6}{\omega}\right)Z + \left(1 - \frac{U_2}{U}\right)D_U \Delta U + D_L \Delta L + D_{I^B}\Delta I^B + \left(1 - \frac{I_2^V}{I^V}\right)D_{I^V}\Delta I^V \\ & + \frac{1}{\mu_1}D_B \Delta B + \frac{\epsilon_3}{\mu_2}\left(1 - \frac{V_2}{V}\right)D_V \Delta V + \frac{\gamma}{\omega}D_Z \Delta Z.\end{aligned}$$

By using (5), the derivative of $\Xi_2(t)$ is expressed as

$$\begin{aligned}\frac{d\Xi_2}{dt} =& -\epsilon_1 \int_\Psi \frac{(U - U_2)^2}{U}dx + \eta_2 U_2 V_2 \int_\Psi \left(3 - \frac{U_2}{U} - \frac{UI_2^V V}{U_2 I^V V_2} - \frac{I^V V_2}{I_2^V V}\right)dx + \frac{\epsilon_4}{\mu_1}\left(\frac{\mathcal{R}_{0B}}{\mathcal{R}_{0V}} - 1\right)\int_\Psi B\,dx \\ & + \frac{\gamma(\omega \epsilon_1 \epsilon_5 + \eta_2 \mu_2 \epsilon_6)}{\omega \eta_2 \mu_2}(\mathcal{R}_{1V} - 1)\int_\Psi Z\,dx - D_U U_2 \int_\Psi \frac{\|\nabla U\|^2}{U^2}dx \\ & - D_{I^V}I_2^V \int_\Psi \frac{\|\nabla I^V\|^2}{I^{V2}}dx - \frac{D_V V_2 \epsilon_3}{\mu_2}\int_\Psi \frac{\|\nabla V\|^2}{V^2}dx.\end{aligned}$$

We note that $\frac{d\Xi_2}{dt} \leq 0$ if $\frac{\mathcal{R}_{0B}}{\mathcal{R}_{0V}} \leq 1$, and $\mathcal{R}_{1V} \leq 1$. Moreover, $\frac{d\Xi_2}{dt} = 0$ when $U = U_2$, $I^V = I_2^V$, $V = V_2$ and $B = Z = 0$. The solutions approach χ_2', which has an element with $B = 0$ and hence $\frac{\partial B}{\partial t} = 0$. From the fifth equation of (1), we have $I^B = 0$. Consequently, $\frac{\partial I^B}{\partial t} = 0$ and thus $L = 0$ according to the third equation of (1). Thereupon, $\chi_2' = \{E_2\}$ and E_2 is GS when $\mathcal{R}_{0V} > 1$, $\frac{\mathcal{R}_{0B}}{\mathcal{R}_{0V}} \leq 1$ and $\mathcal{R}_{1V} \leq 1$ as attributed to LIP [43]. □

Theorem 5. *Assume that $\mathcal{R}_{1B} > 1$. Then, the equilibrium E_3 is GS if* $\frac{\lambda \omega \eta_2 \mu_2 \epsilon_4}{\epsilon_2 \epsilon_5 [\omega \epsilon_1 \epsilon_4 + \eta_1 \mu_1 \epsilon_2 \epsilon_6]} +$
$1 \leq \frac{\epsilon_3}{\epsilon_2} + \mathcal{R}_{1B}.$

Proof. We pick an LF
$$\Xi_3(t) = \int_\Psi \widetilde{\Xi}_3(x,t)\,dx, \quad \text{where}$$

$$\begin{aligned}\widetilde{\Xi}_3 =& U_3\left(\frac{U}{U_3} - 1 - \ln\frac{U}{U_3}\right) + L_3\left(\frac{L}{L_3} - 1 - \ln\frac{L}{L_3}\right) + I_3^B\left(\frac{I^B}{I_3^B} - 1 - \ln\frac{I^B}{I_3^B}\right) + I^V \\ &+ \left(\frac{1}{\mu_1} + \frac{\gamma Z_3}{\mu_1 \epsilon_2}\right) B_3\left(\frac{B}{B_3} - 1 - \ln\frac{B}{B_3}\right) + \left(\frac{\epsilon_3}{\mu_2} + \frac{\gamma Z_3}{\mu_2}\right)V + \frac{\gamma}{\omega}Z_3\left(\frac{Z}{Z_3} - 1 - \ln\frac{Z}{Z_3}\right).\end{aligned}$$

Then, $\dfrac{\partial \widetilde{\Xi}_3}{\partial t}$ is written as

$$\begin{aligned}\frac{\partial \widetilde{\Xi}_3}{\partial t} =& \left(1 - \frac{U_3}{U}\right)\left(D_U \Delta U + \lambda - \eta_1 UB - \eta_2 UV - \epsilon_1 U\right) + \left(1 - \frac{L_3}{L}\right)\left(D_L \Delta L + \eta_1 UB - aL\right) \\ &+ \left(1 - \frac{I_3^B}{I^B}\right)\left(D_{I^B}\Delta I^B + aL - \gamma I^B Z - \epsilon_2 I^B\right) + D_{I^V}\Delta I^V + \eta_2 UV - \gamma I^V Z - \epsilon_3 I^V \\ &+ \left(\frac{1}{\mu_1} + \frac{\gamma Z_3}{\mu_1 \epsilon_2}\right)\left(1 - \frac{B_3}{B}\right)\left(D_B \Delta B + \mu_1 \epsilon_2 I^B - \epsilon_4 B\right) + \left(\frac{\epsilon_3}{\mu_2} + \frac{\gamma Z_3}{\mu_2}\right)\left(D_V \Delta V + \mu_2 I^V - \epsilon_5 V\right) \\ &+ \frac{\gamma}{\omega}\left(1 - \frac{Z_3}{Z}\right)\left(D_Z \Delta Z + \omega I^B Z + \omega I^V Z - \epsilon_6 Z\right).\end{aligned} \quad (8)$$

By utilizing the equilibrium requirements at E_3 to add the terms of Equation (8)

$$\begin{cases} \lambda = \eta_1 U_3 B_3 + \epsilon_1 U_3, \\ \eta_1 U_3 B_3 = aL_3, \\ aL_3 = \gamma I_3^B Z_3 + \epsilon_2 I_3^B, \\ \epsilon_2 I_3^B = \dfrac{\epsilon_4}{\mu_1} B_3, \\ \gamma I_3^B Z_3 = \dfrac{\gamma \epsilon_6}{\omega} Z_3, \end{cases}$$

we obtain

$$\begin{aligned}\frac{\partial \widetilde{\Xi}_3}{\partial t} =& \left(1 - \frac{U_3}{U}\right)(\epsilon_1 U_3 - \epsilon_1 U) + \eta_1 U_3 B_3\left(4 - \frac{U_3}{U} - \frac{UL_3 B}{U_3 L B_3} - \frac{L I_3^B}{L_3 I^B} - \frac{I^B B_3}{I_3^B B}\right) \\ &+ \left(\eta_2 U_3 - \frac{\epsilon_3 \epsilon_5}{\mu_2} - \frac{\gamma \epsilon_5 Z_3}{\mu_2}\right)V + \left(1 - \frac{U_3}{U}\right)D_U \Delta U + \left(1 - \frac{L_3}{L}\right)D_L \Delta L + \left(1 - \frac{I_3^B}{I^B}\right)D_{I^B}\Delta I^B \\ &+ D_{I^V}\Delta I^V + \left(\frac{1}{\mu_1} + \frac{\gamma Z_3}{\mu_1 \epsilon_2}\right)\left(1 - \frac{B_3}{B}\right)D_B \Delta B + \left(\frac{\epsilon_3}{\mu_2} + \frac{\gamma Z_3}{\mu_2}\right)D_V \Delta V \\ &+ \frac{\gamma}{\omega}\left(1 - \frac{Z_3}{Z}\right)D_Z \Delta Z.\end{aligned}$$

By using (5), the derivative of $\Xi_3(t)$ is presented as

$$\begin{aligned}\frac{d\Xi_3}{dt} =& -\epsilon_1 \int_\Psi \frac{(U - U_3)^2}{U}\,dx + \eta_1 U_3 B_3 \int_\Psi \left(4 - \frac{U_3}{U} - \frac{UL_3 B}{U_3 L B_3} - \frac{L I_3^B}{L_3 I^B} - \frac{I^B B_3}{I_3^B B}\right)dx \\ &+ \frac{\epsilon_2 \epsilon_5}{\mu_2}\left(\frac{\lambda \omega \eta_2 \mu_2 \epsilon_4}{\epsilon_2 \epsilon_5 [\omega \epsilon_1 \epsilon_4 + \eta_1 \mu_1 \epsilon_2 \epsilon_6]} + 1 - \frac{\epsilon_3}{\epsilon_2} - \mathcal{R}_{1B}\right)\int_\Psi V\,dx - D_U U_3 \int_\Psi \frac{\|\nabla U\|^2}{U^2}\,dx \\ &- D_L L_3 \int_\Psi \frac{\|\nabla L\|^2}{L^2}\,dx - D_{I^B} I_3^B \int_\Psi \frac{\|\nabla I^B\|^2}{I^{B^2}}\,dx - D_B B_3\left(\frac{1}{\mu_1} + \frac{\gamma Z_3}{\mu_1 \epsilon_2}\right)\int_\Psi \frac{\|\nabla B\|^2}{B^2}\,dx \\ &- \frac{\gamma D_Z Z_3}{\omega}\int_\Psi \frac{\|\nabla Z\|^2}{Z^2}\,dx.\end{aligned}$$

We see that $\frac{d\Xi_3}{dt} \leq 0$ if $\frac{\lambda\omega\eta_2\mu_2\epsilon_4}{\epsilon_2\epsilon_5[\omega\epsilon_1\epsilon_4 + \eta_1\mu_1\epsilon_2\epsilon_6]} + 1 \leq \frac{\epsilon_3}{\epsilon_2} + \mathcal{R}_{1B}$. In addition, it is possible to show that $\frac{d\Xi_3}{dt} = 0$ when $(U, L, I^B, I^V, B, V, Z) = (U_3, L_3, I_3^B, 0, B_3, 0, Z_3)$. Then, $\chi'_3 = \{E_3\}$ and in reference to LIP [43], E_3 is GS when $\mathcal{R}_{1B} > 1$ and $\frac{\lambda\omega\eta_2\mu_2\epsilon_4}{\epsilon_2\epsilon_5[\omega\epsilon_1\epsilon_4 + \eta_1\mu_1\epsilon_2\epsilon_6]} + 1 \leq \frac{\epsilon_3}{\epsilon_2} + \mathcal{R}_{1B}$. □

Theorem 6. *Let $\mathcal{R}_{1V} > 1$. Thereupon, the equilibrium E_4 is GS if $\frac{\lambda\omega\eta_1\mu_1\epsilon_2\epsilon_5}{\epsilon_3\epsilon_4[\omega\epsilon_1\epsilon_5 + \eta_2\mu_2\epsilon_6]} + 1 \leq \frac{\epsilon_2}{\epsilon_3} + \mathcal{R}_{1V}$.*

Proof. We nominate an LF

$$\Xi_4(t) = \int_\Psi \widetilde{\Xi}_4(x,t)\,dx, \quad \text{where}$$

$$\begin{aligned}\widetilde{\Xi}_4 =& U_4\left(\frac{U}{U_4} - 1 - \ln\frac{U}{U_4}\right) + L + I^B + I_4^V\left(\frac{I^V}{I_4^V} - 1 - \ln\frac{I^V}{I_4^V}\right) + \left(\frac{1}{\mu_1} + \frac{\gamma Z_4}{\mu_1\epsilon_2}\right)B \\ &+ \left(\frac{\epsilon_3}{\mu_2} + \frac{\gamma Z_4}{\mu_2}\right)V_4\left(\frac{V}{V_4} - 1 - \ln\frac{V}{V_4}\right) + \frac{\gamma}{\omega}Z_4\left(\frac{Z}{Z_4} - 1 - \ln\frac{Z}{Z_4}\right).\end{aligned}$$

By computing the partial derivative, we obtain

$$\begin{aligned}\frac{\partial \Xi_4}{\partial t} =& \left(1 - \frac{U_4}{U}\right)\left(D_U\Delta U + \lambda - \eta_1 UB - \eta_2 UV - \epsilon_1 U\right) + D_L\Delta L + \eta_1 UB - aL + D_{I^B}\Delta I^B + aL \\ &- \gamma I^B Z - \epsilon_2 I^B + \left(1 - \frac{I_4^V}{I^V}\right)\left(D_{I^V}\Delta I^V + \eta_2 UV - \gamma I^V Z - \epsilon_3 I^V\right) \\ &+ \left(\frac{1}{\mu_1} + \frac{\gamma Z_4}{\mu_1\epsilon_2}\right)\left(D_B\Delta B + \mu_1\epsilon_2 I^B - \epsilon_4 B\right) + \left(\frac{\epsilon_3}{\mu_2} + \frac{\gamma Z_4}{\mu_2}\right)\left(1 - \frac{V_4}{V}\right)\left(D_V\Delta V + \mu_2 I^V - \epsilon_5 V\right) \\ &+ \frac{\gamma}{\omega}\left(1 - \frac{Z_4}{Z}\right)\left(D_Z\Delta Z + \omega I^B Z + \omega I^V Z - \epsilon_6 Z\right).\end{aligned} \quad (9)$$

By considering the equilibrium conditions at E_4

$$\begin{cases}\lambda = \eta_2 U_4 V_4 + \epsilon_1 U_4, \\ \eta_2 U_4 V_4 = \gamma I_4^V Z_4 + \epsilon_3 I_4^V, \\ \epsilon_3 I_4^V = \frac{\epsilon_3\epsilon_5}{\mu_2}V_4, \\ \gamma I_4^V Z_4 = \frac{\gamma\epsilon_6}{\omega}Z_4,\end{cases}$$

the derivative in (9) is transformed to

$$\begin{aligned}\frac{\partial \Xi_4}{\partial t} =& \left(1 - \frac{U_4}{U}\right)(\epsilon_1 U_4 - \epsilon_1 U) + \eta_2 U_4 V_4\left(3 - \frac{U_4}{U} - \frac{UI_4^V V}{U_4 I^V V_4} - \frac{I^V V_4}{I_4^V V}\right) + \left(\eta_1 U_4 - \frac{\epsilon_4}{\mu_1} - \frac{\gamma\epsilon_4 Z_4}{\mu_1\epsilon_2}\right)B \\ &+ \left(1 - \frac{U_4}{U}\right)D_U\Delta U + D_L\Delta L + D_{I^B}\Delta I^B + \left(1 - \frac{I_4^V}{I^V}\right)D_{I^V}\Delta I^V + \left(\frac{1}{\mu_1} + \frac{\gamma Z_4}{\mu_1\epsilon_2}\right)D_B\Delta B \\ &+ \left(\frac{\epsilon_3}{\mu_2} + \frac{\gamma Z_4}{\mu_2}\right)\left(1 - \frac{V_4}{V}\right)D_V\Delta V + \frac{\gamma}{\omega}\left(1 - \frac{Z_4}{Z}\right)D_Z\Delta Z.\end{aligned}$$

By using (5), the derivative of $\Xi_4(t)$ has the form

$$\frac{d\Xi_4}{dt} = -\epsilon_1 \int_\Psi \frac{(U-U_4)^2}{U}\,dx + \eta_2 U_4 V_4 \int_\Psi \left(3 - \frac{U_4}{U} - \frac{U I_4^V V}{U_4 I^V V_4} - \frac{I^V V_4}{I_4^V V}\right) dx$$
$$+ \frac{\epsilon_3 \epsilon_4}{\mu_1 \epsilon_2}\left(\frac{\lambda \omega \eta_1 \mu_1 \epsilon_2 \epsilon_5}{\epsilon_3 \epsilon_4[\omega\epsilon_1\epsilon_5 + \eta_2\mu_2\epsilon_6]} + 1 - \frac{\epsilon_2}{\epsilon_3} - \mathcal{R}_{1V}\right) \int_\Psi B\,dx - D_U U_4 \int_\Psi \frac{\|\nabla U\|^2}{U^2}\,dx$$
$$- D_{IV} I_4^V \int_\Psi \frac{\|\nabla I^V\|^2}{I^{V2}}\,dx - D_V V_4 \left(\frac{\epsilon_3}{\mu_2} + \frac{\gamma Z_4}{\mu_2}\right)\int_\Psi \frac{\|\nabla V\|^2}{V^2}\,dx - \frac{\gamma D_Z Z_4}{\omega}\int_\Psi \frac{\|\nabla Z\|^2}{Z^2}\,dx.$$

It follows that $\frac{d\Xi_4}{dt} \leq 0$ if $\frac{\lambda \omega \eta_1 \mu_1 \epsilon_2 \epsilon_5}{\epsilon_3 \epsilon_4[\omega\epsilon_1\epsilon_5 + \eta_2\mu_2\epsilon_6]} + 1 \leq \frac{\epsilon_2}{\epsilon_3} + \mathcal{R}_{1V}$. In addition, $\frac{d\Xi_4}{dt} = 0$ when $(U, L, I^B, I^V, B, V, Z) = (U_4, 0, 0, I_4^V, 0, V_4, Z_4)$. Hence, $\chi_4' = \{E_4\}$ and E_4 is GS if $\mathcal{R}_{1V} > 1$ and $\frac{\lambda \omega \eta_1 \mu_1 \epsilon_2 \epsilon_5}{\epsilon_3 \epsilon_4[\omega\epsilon_1\epsilon_5 + \eta_2\mu_2\epsilon_6]} + 1 \leq \frac{\epsilon_2}{\epsilon_3} + \mathcal{R}_{1V}$ based on LIP [43]. □

Theorem 7. *Suppose that* $\frac{\lambda \omega \eta_2 \mu_2 \epsilon_4}{\epsilon_2 \epsilon_5[\omega\epsilon_1\epsilon_4 + \eta_1\mu_1\epsilon_2\epsilon_6]} + 1 > \frac{\epsilon_3}{\epsilon_2} + \mathcal{R}_{1B}$, $\frac{\lambda \omega \eta_1 \mu_1 \epsilon_2 \epsilon_5}{\epsilon_3 \epsilon_4[\omega\epsilon_1\epsilon_5 + \eta_2\mu_2\epsilon_6]} + 1 > \frac{\epsilon_2}{\epsilon_3} + \mathcal{R}_{1V}$, $\frac{\mathcal{R}_{0V}}{\mathcal{R}_{0B}} > 1$, $\epsilon_2 > \epsilon_3$, *and* $\sigma > 1$. *Then, the equilibrium* E_5 *is GS.*

Proof. We start with an LF
$$\Xi_5(t) = \int_\Psi \tilde{\Xi}_5(x,t)\,dx, \quad \text{where}$$

$$\tilde{\Xi}_5 = U_5\left(\frac{U}{U_5} - 1 - \ln\frac{U}{U_5}\right) + L_5\left(\frac{L}{L_5} - 1 - \ln\frac{L}{L_5}\right) + I_5^B\left(\frac{I^B}{I_5^B} - 1 - \ln\frac{I^B}{I_5^B}\right) + I_5^V\left(\frac{I^V}{I_5^V} - 1 - \ln\frac{I^V}{I_5^V}\right)$$
$$+ \left(\frac{1}{\mu_1} + \frac{\gamma Z_5}{\mu_1 \epsilon_2}\right) B_5\left(\frac{B}{B_5} - 1 - \ln\frac{B}{B_5}\right) + \left(\frac{\epsilon_3}{\mu_2} + \frac{\gamma Z_5}{\mu_2}\right) V_5\left(\frac{V}{V_5} - 1 - \ln\frac{V}{V_5}\right)$$
$$+ \frac{\gamma}{\omega} Z_5\left(\frac{Z}{Z_5} - 1 - \ln\frac{Z}{Z_5}\right).$$

By computing the partial derivative, we obtain

$$\frac{\partial \Xi_5}{\partial t} = \left(1 - \frac{U_5}{U}\right)\left(D_U \Delta U + \lambda - \eta_1 UB - \eta_2 UV - \epsilon_1 U\right) + \left(1 - \frac{L_5}{L}\right)\left(D_L \Delta L + \eta_1 UB - aL\right)$$
$$+ \left(1 - \frac{I_5^B}{I^B}\right)\left(D_{I^B}\Delta I^B + aL - \gamma I^B Z - \epsilon_2 I^B\right) + \left(1 - \frac{I_5^V}{I^V}\right)\left(D_{I^V}\Delta I^V + \eta_2 UV - \gamma I^V Z - \epsilon_3 I^V\right)$$
$$+ \left(\frac{1}{\mu_1} + \frac{\gamma Z_5}{\mu_1 \epsilon_2}\right)\left(1 - \frac{B_5}{B}\right)\left(D_B \Delta B + \mu_1 \epsilon_2 I^B - \epsilon_4 B\right)$$
$$+ \left(\frac{\epsilon_3}{\mu_2} + \frac{\gamma Z_5}{\mu_2}\right)\left(1 - \frac{V_5}{V}\right)\left(D_V \Delta V + \mu_2 I^V - \epsilon_5 V\right)$$
$$+ \frac{\gamma}{\omega}\left(1 - \frac{Z_5}{Z}\right)\left(D_Z \Delta Z + \omega I^B Z + \omega I^V Z - \epsilon_6 Z\right).$$

At equilibrium, the following conditions are satisfied:
$$\begin{cases} \lambda = \eta_1 U_5 B_5 + \eta_2 U_5 V_5 + \epsilon_1 U_5, \\ \eta_1 U_5 B_5 = aL_5, \\ aL_5 = \gamma I_5^B Z_5 + \epsilon_2 I_5^B, \\ \eta_2 U_5 V_5 = \gamma I_5^V Z_5 + \epsilon_3 I_5^V, \\ \epsilon_2 I_5^B = \frac{\epsilon_4}{\mu_1} B_5, \\ \epsilon_3 I_5^V = \frac{\epsilon_3 \epsilon_5}{\mu_2} V_5, \\ \gamma I_5^B Z_5 + \gamma I_5^V Z_5 = \frac{\gamma \epsilon_6}{\omega} Z_5. \end{cases}$$

By using the above conditions with (5), the time derivative of $\Xi_5(t)$ is written as

$$\frac{d\Xi_5}{dt} = -\epsilon_1 \int_\Psi \frac{(U-U_5)^2}{U} dx + \eta_1 U_5 B_5 \int_\Psi \left(4 - \frac{U_5}{U} - \frac{UL_5B}{U_5LB_5} - \frac{LI_5^B}{L_5I^B} - \frac{I^B B_5}{I_5^B B}\right) dx$$

$$+ \eta_2 U_5 V_5 \int_\Psi \left(3 - \frac{U_5}{U} - \frac{UI_5^V V}{U_5 I^V V_5} - \frac{I^V V_5}{I_5^V V}\right) dx - D_U U_5 \int_\Psi \frac{\|\nabla U\|^2}{U^2} dx - D_L L_5 \int_\Psi \frac{\|\nabla L\|^2}{L^2} dx$$

$$- D_{I^B} I_5^B \int_\Psi \frac{\|\nabla I^B\|^2}{I^{B^2}} dx - D_{I^V} I_5^V \int_\Psi \frac{\|\nabla I^V\|^2}{I^{V^2}} dx - D_B B_5 \left(\frac{1}{\mu_1} + \frac{\gamma Z_5}{\mu_1 \epsilon_2}\right) \int_\Psi \frac{\|\nabla B\|^2}{B^2} dx$$

$$- D_V V_5 \left(\frac{\epsilon_3}{\mu_2} + \frac{\gamma Z_5}{\mu_2}\right) \int_\Psi \frac{\|\nabla V\|^2}{V^2} dx - \frac{\gamma D_Z Z_5}{\omega} \int_\Psi \frac{\|\nabla Z\|^2}{Z^2} dx.$$

Thus, $\frac{d\Xi_5}{dt} \leq 0$ and $\frac{d\Xi_5}{dt} = 0$ when $(U, L, I^B, I^V, B, V, Z) = (U_5, L_5, I_5^B, I_5^V, B_5, V_5, Z_5)$. This implies that $\chi_5' = \{E_5\}$ and E_5 is GS when it exists in regard to LIP [43]. □

5. Numerical Simulations

In this part, we implement numerical simulations using MATLB PDE solver (pdepe) to validate the theoretical observations attained in the previous parts. This solver solves initial boundary value problems for systems of PDEs in one spatial variable x and time t. The domain of x is provided as $\Psi = [0,2]$ with step sizes $\Delta x = 0.02$ and $\Delta t = 0.1$. The ICs of system (1) are determined as the following:

$U(x,0) = 10^5(1 + 0.2\cos^2(\pi x))$, $L(x,0) = 10^4(1 + 0.2\cos^2(\pi x))$, $I^B(x,0) = 10^3(1 + 0.2\cos^2(\pi x))$,
$I^V(x,0) = 10^3(1 + 0.2\cos^2(\pi x))$, $B(x,0) = 500(1 + 0.2\cos^2(\pi x))$, $V(x,0) = 500(1 + 0.2\cos^2(\pi x))$,
$Z(x,0) = 0.1(1 + 0.2\cos^2(\pi x))$.

To present the global stability of the equilibria of system (1), the results are divided into six cases. In each case, we change the values of η_1, η_2, and ω while keeping all other values as shown in Table 1. These cases are stated as follows:

(i) We choose $\eta_1 = 2.5 \times 10^{-9}$, $\eta_2 = 1 \times 10^{-11}$, and $\omega = 8 \times 10^{-3}$. This gives $\mathcal{R}_{0B} = 0.1923 < 1$ and $\mathcal{R}_{0V} = 0.4667 < 1$. This indicates that $E_0 = (4 \times 10^5, 0, 0, 0, 0, 0, 0)$ is GS (Figure 1), which comes to an agreement with Theorem 2. This case simulates the condition of an individual with no Mtb and SARS-CoV-2 infections.

(ii) We select $\eta_1 = 2.5 \times 10^{-7}$, $\eta_2 = 1 \times 10^{-11}$, and $\omega = 8 \times 10^{-7}$ to obtain $\mathcal{R}_{0B} = 19.2308 > 1$, $\frac{\mathcal{R}_{0V}}{\mathcal{R}_{0B}} = 0.0243 < 1$, and $\mathcal{R}_{1B} = 0.0638 < 1$. The result agrees with Theorem 3 that the equilibrium $E_1 = (20,800, 9480, 7584, 0, 729,231, 0, 0)$ is GS (Figure 2). In this situation, the patient has Mtb monoinfection and the CTL immunity is inefficient.

(iii) We take $\eta_1 = 2.5 \times 10^{-9}$, $\eta_2 = 1 \times 10^{-9}$, and $\omega = 1 \times 10^{-8}$. We obtain $\mathcal{R}_{0V} = 46.6667 > 1$, $\frac{\mathcal{R}_{0B}}{\mathcal{R}_{0V}} = 0.0041 < 1$, and $\mathcal{R}_{1V} = 0.04 < 1$. These conditions implicate the global stability of $E_2 = (8571.43, 0, 0, 391,429, 0, 4.56667 \times 10^8, 0)$, which harmonizes with Theorem 4 (Figure 3). In this case, the patient has SARS-CoV-2 monoinfection in the absence of CTLs.

(iv) We choose $\eta_1 = 2.5 \times 10^{-7}$, $\eta_2 = 1 \times 10^{-11}$, and $\omega = 1 \times 10^{-4}$. This gives $\mathcal{R}_{1B} = 5.6497 > 1$ and $\frac{\lambda \omega \eta_2 \mu_2 \epsilon_4}{\epsilon_2 \epsilon_5 [\omega \epsilon_1 \epsilon_4 + \eta_1 \mu_1 \epsilon_2 \epsilon_6]} + 1 = 1.0027 < 5.6497 = \frac{\epsilon_3}{\epsilon_2} + \mathcal{R}_{1B}$. This implies that the equilibrium $E_3 = (117,514, 7062.15, 1000, 0, 96,153.8, 0, 4.64972)$ is GS (Figure 4), which comes to an agreement with Theorem 5. Here, the CTL immunity is turned on to exterminate the Mtb infection. Consequently, the densities of Mtb-infected cells and Mtb particles decrease, whilst the density of healthy cells increases.

(v) We consider $\eta_1 = 2.5 \times 10^{-9}$, $\eta_2 = 1 \times 10^{-9}$, and $\omega = 1 \times 10^{-6}$. Thus, we obtain $\mathcal{R}_{1V} = 3.6842 > 1$ and $\dfrac{\lambda \omega \eta_1 \mu_1 \epsilon_2 \epsilon_5}{\epsilon_3 \epsilon_4 [\omega \epsilon_1 \epsilon_5 + \eta_2 \mu_2 \epsilon_6]} + 1 = 1.7591 < 53.6842 = \dfrac{\epsilon_2}{\epsilon_3} + \mathcal{R}_{1V}$. In favor of Theorem 6, $E_4 = (31{,}578.9, 0, 0, 1 \times 10^5, 0, 1.16667 \times 10^8, 0.05368)$ is GS (Figure 5). This case mimics the condition of a COVID-19 patient with active CTLs which work on removing SARS-CoV-2-infected cells.

(vi) We choose $\eta_1 = 2 \times 10^{-7}$, $\eta_2 = 1 \times 10^{-9}$, and $\omega = 2 \times 10^{-6}$. These values give $\dfrac{\lambda \omega \eta_2 \mu_2 \epsilon_4}{\epsilon_2 \epsilon_5 [\omega \epsilon_1 \epsilon_4 + \eta_1 \mu_1 \epsilon_2 \epsilon_6]} + 1 = 1.0096 > 0.1784 = \dfrac{\epsilon_3}{\epsilon_2} + \mathcal{R}_{1B}$, $\dfrac{\lambda \omega \eta_1 \mu_1 \epsilon_2 \epsilon_5}{\epsilon_3 \epsilon_4 [\omega \epsilon_1 \epsilon_5 + \eta_2 \mu_2 \epsilon_6]} + 1 = 113.5704 > 56.8293 = \dfrac{\epsilon_2}{\epsilon_3} + \mathcal{R}_{1V}$, $\dfrac{\mathcal{R}_{0V}}{\mathcal{R}_{0B}} = 3.0333 > 1$, and $\sigma = 16.4835 > 1$. This implies the global stability of $E_5 = (27{,}125.6, 5712.6, 4380.44, 45{,}619.6, 421{,}196, 5.322 \times 10^7, 0.043)$, which is compatible with Theorem 7 (Figure 6). In this situation, the person has SARS-CoV-2/Mtb coinfection with robust CTL immunity.

5.1. The Movement from the Monoinfection to the Coinfection State

From the results above, we see that increasing the infection rate of EPCs by SARS-CoV-2, η_2, forces the system to move from Mtb monoinfection state to SARS-CoV-2/Mtb coinfection state. In other words, E_3 loses its stability and E_5 becomes GS. Similarly, increasing the infection rate by Mtb, η_1, pushes the system from SARS-CoV-2 monoinfection state to the coinfection state. In this case, E_4 loses its stability and E_5 becomes GS. Therefore, the values of these parameters need to be controlled as they have a powerful effect in converting the system from the monoinfection zone to the coinfection zone.

5.2. The Impact of the Diffusion Coefficients On Coinfection

To test the impact of the diffusion coefficients in model (1) on the behavior of the solutions, we change the values of the coefficients considered in case (vi) to $D_U = D_L = D_{I^B} = D_{I^V} = D_B = D_V = D_Z = 1 \times 10^{-5}$. We observe from Figure 7 that the effect of this change appears at the initial times, while the final solutions are not affected. Thus, the diffusion coefficients do not affect the robustness of the global stability of the solutions. Therefore, the impact of these coefficients should be monitored at the beginning of coinfection as it affects the distribution of particles in space.

Table 1. Parameters' values of system (1).

Parameter	Value	Source
λ	4×10^3	[44]
η_1	Varied	–
η_2	Varied	–
a	0.4	[24]
γ	0.5	[23]
μ_1	100	[25]
μ_2	700	[44]
ω	Varied	–
ϵ_1	0.01	[44]
ϵ_2	0.5	[25]
ϵ_3	0.01	[44]
ϵ_4	0.52	[27]
ϵ_5	0.6	[16]
ϵ_6	0.1	[44]
D_U	0.1	Assumed
D_L	0.1	Assumed
D_{I^B}	0.1	Assumed
D_{I^V}	0.1	Assumed
D_B	0.2	Assumed
D_V	0.2	Assumed
D_Z	0.1	Assumed

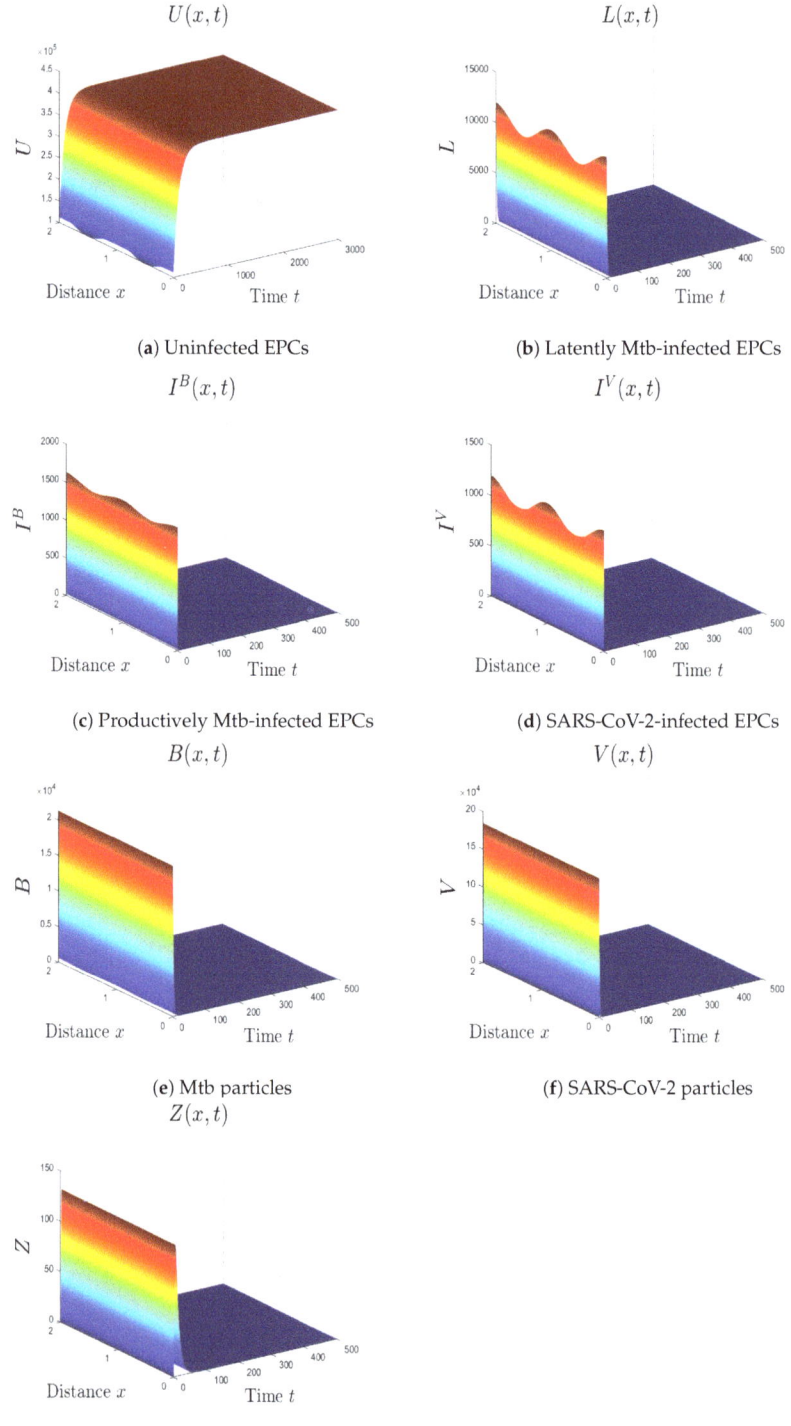

Figure 1. The numerical results of system (1) for $\eta_1 = 2.5 \times 10^{-9}$, $\eta_2 = 1 \times 10^{-11}$, and $\omega = 8 \times 10^{-3}$. The uninfected equilibrium $E_0 = (4 \times 10^5, 0, 0, 0, 0, 0, 0)$ is GS.

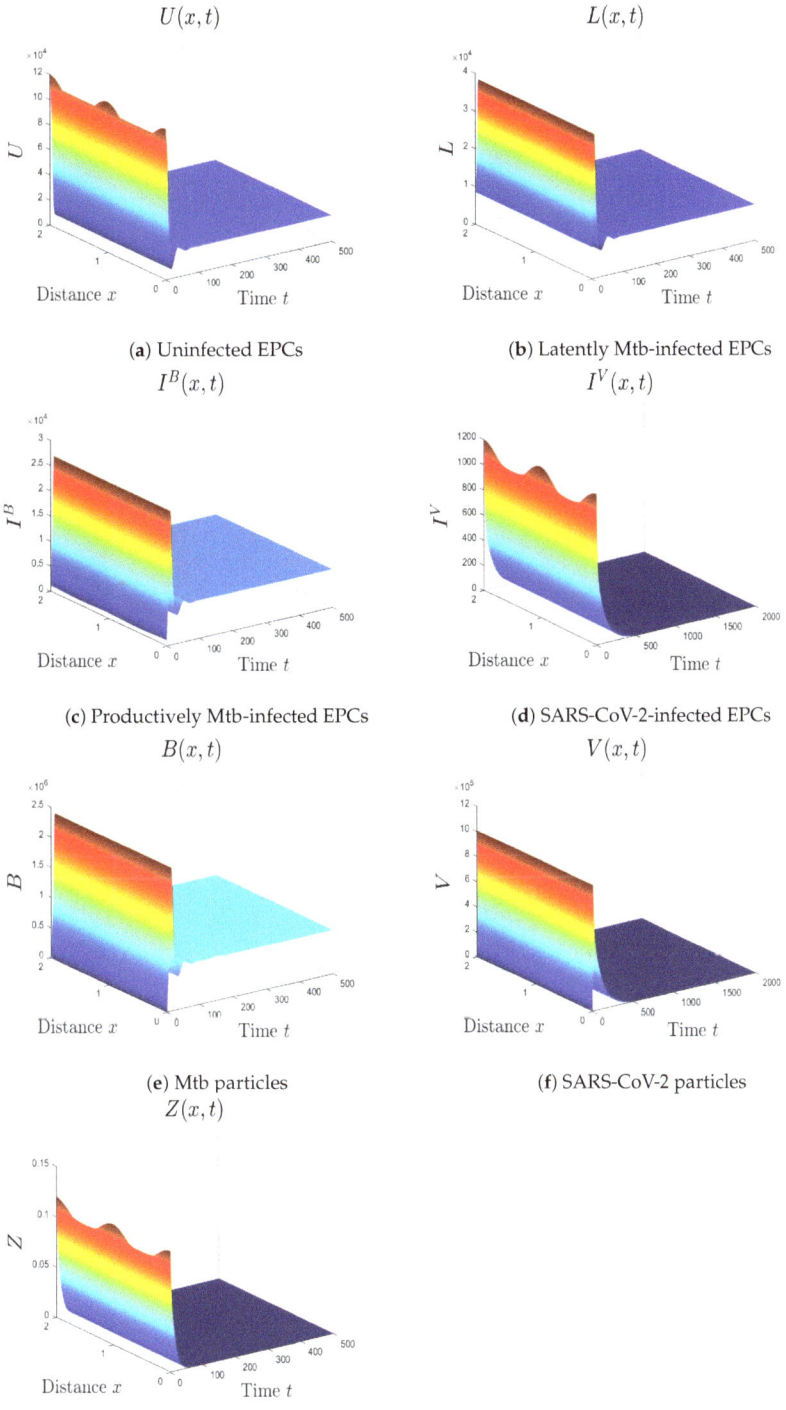

Figure 2. The numerical results of system (1) for $\eta_1 = 2.5 \times 10^{-7}$, $\eta_2 = 1 \times 10^{-11}$, and $\omega = 8 \times 10^{-7}$. The equilibrium $E_1 = (20{,}800, 9480, 7584, 0, 729{,}231, 0, 0)$ is GS.

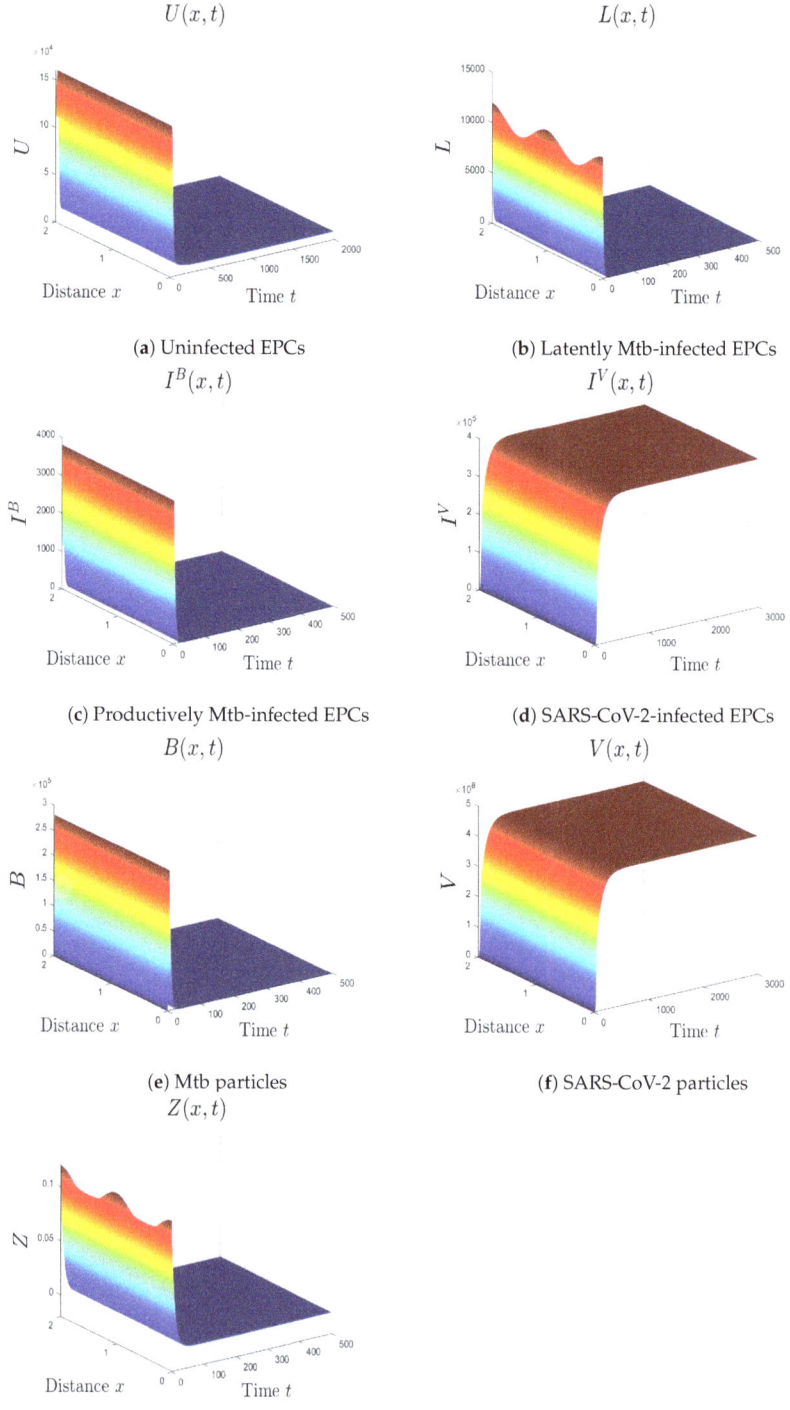

Figure 3. The numerical results of system (1) for $\eta_1 = 2.5 \times 10^{-9}$, $\eta_2 = 1 \times 10^{-9}$, and $\omega = 1 \times 10^{-8}$. The equilibrium $E_2 = (8571.43, 0, 0, 391{,}429, 0, 4.56667 \times 10^8, 0)$ is GS.

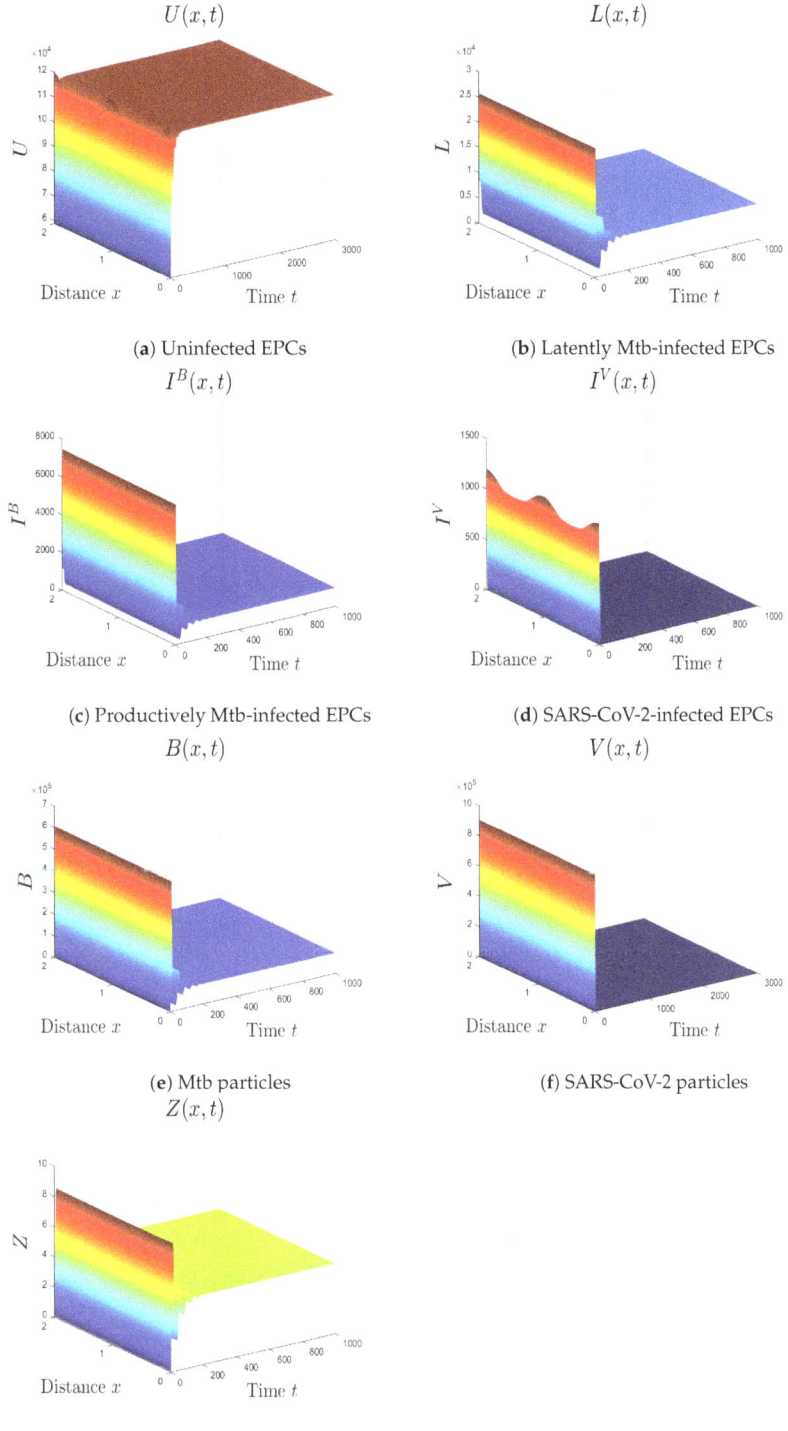

Figure 4. The numerical results of system (1) for $\eta_1 = 2.5 \times 10^{-7}$, $\eta_2 = 1 \times 10^{-11}$, and $\omega = 1 \times 10^{-4}$. The equilibrium $E_3 = (117,514, 7062.15, 1000, 0, 96,153.8, 0, 4.64972)$ is GS.

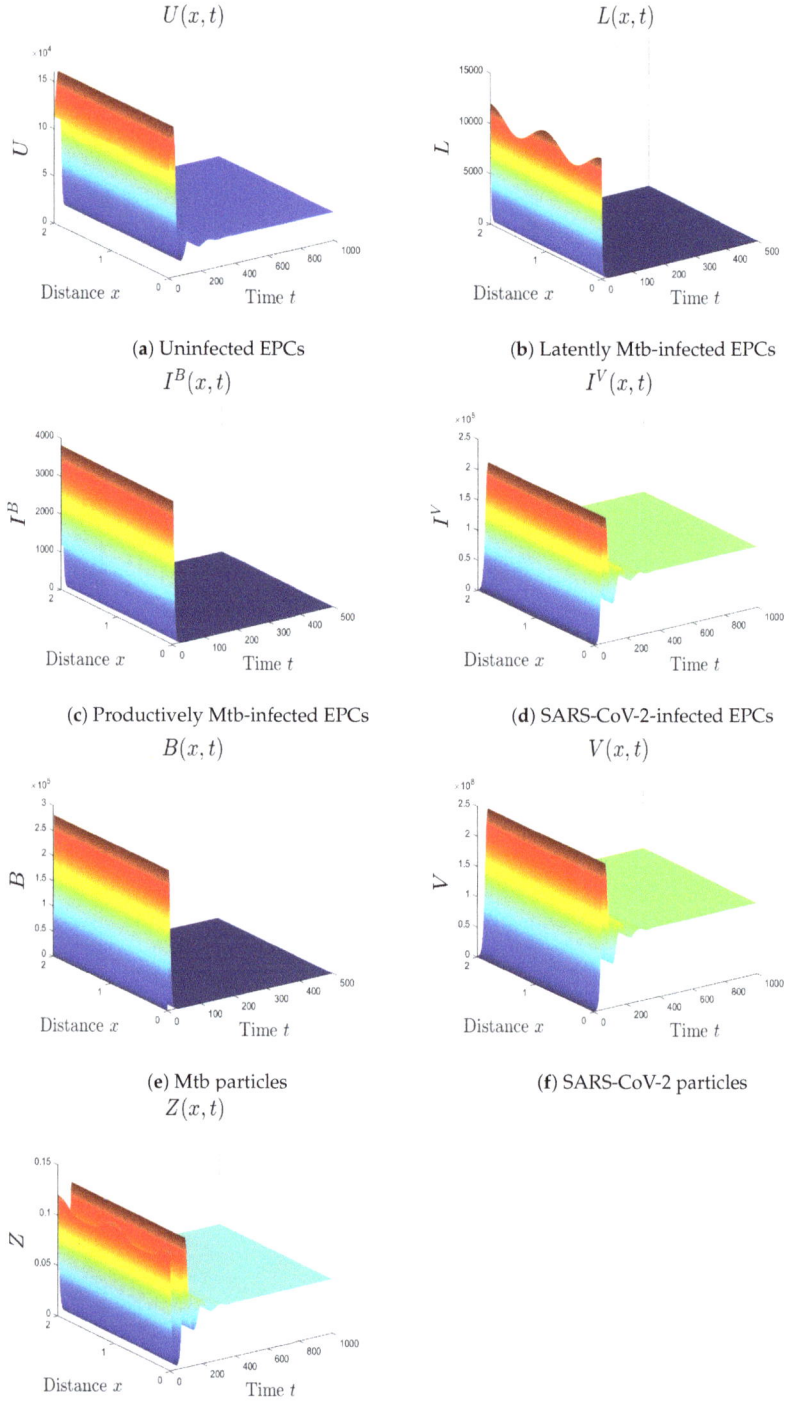

Figure 5. The numerical results of system (1) for $\eta_1 = 2.5 \times 10^{-9}$, $\eta_2 = 1 \times 10^{-9}$, and $\omega = 1 \times 10^{-6}$. The equilibrium $E_4 = (31{,}578.9, 0, 0, 1 \times 10^5, 0, 1.16667 \times 10^8, 0.0536842)$ is GS.

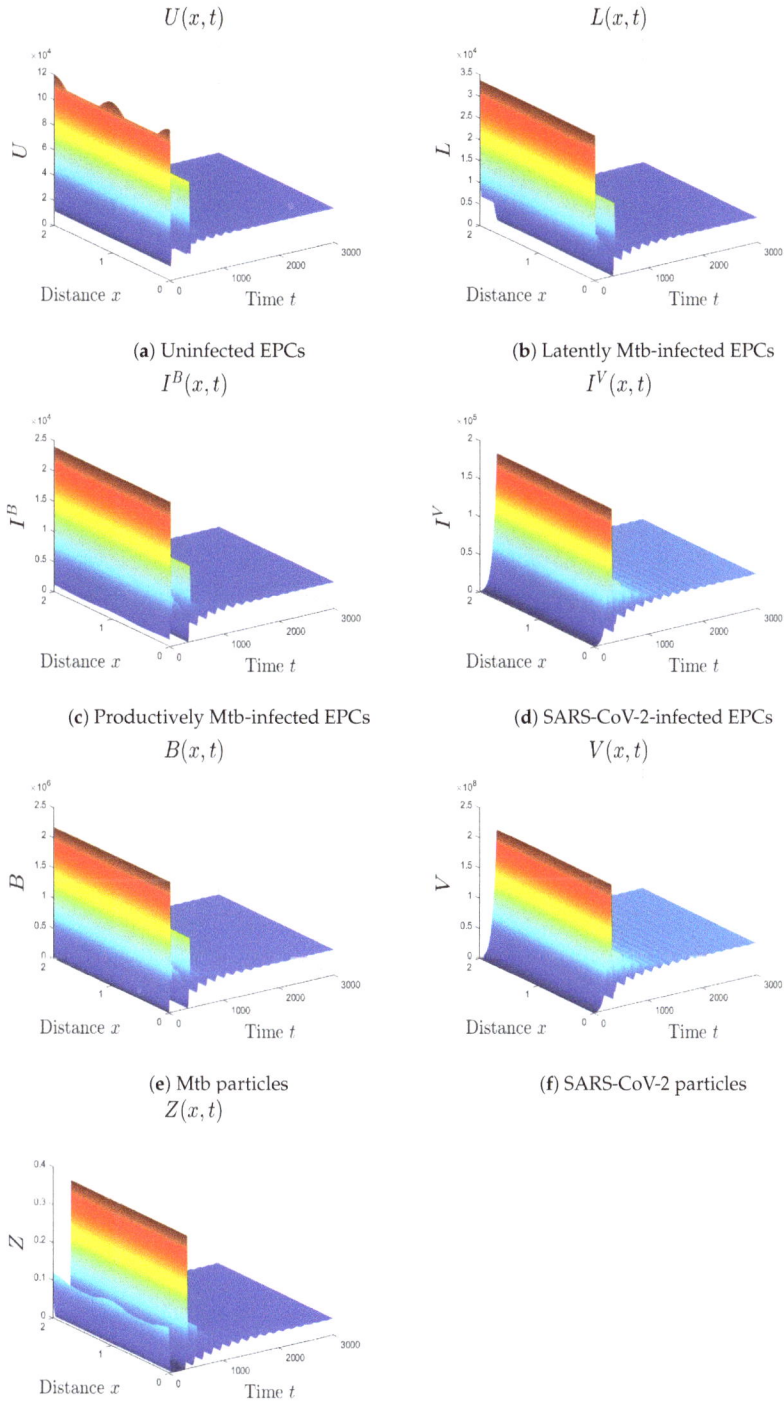

Figure 6. The numerical results of system (1) for $\eta_1 = 2 \times 10^{-7}$, $\eta_2 = 1 \times 10^{-9}$, and $\omega = 2 \times 10^{-6}$. The equilibrium $E_5 = (27{,}125.6, 5712.6, 4380.44, 45{,}619.6, 421{,}196, 5.322 \times 10^7, 0.043)$ is GS.

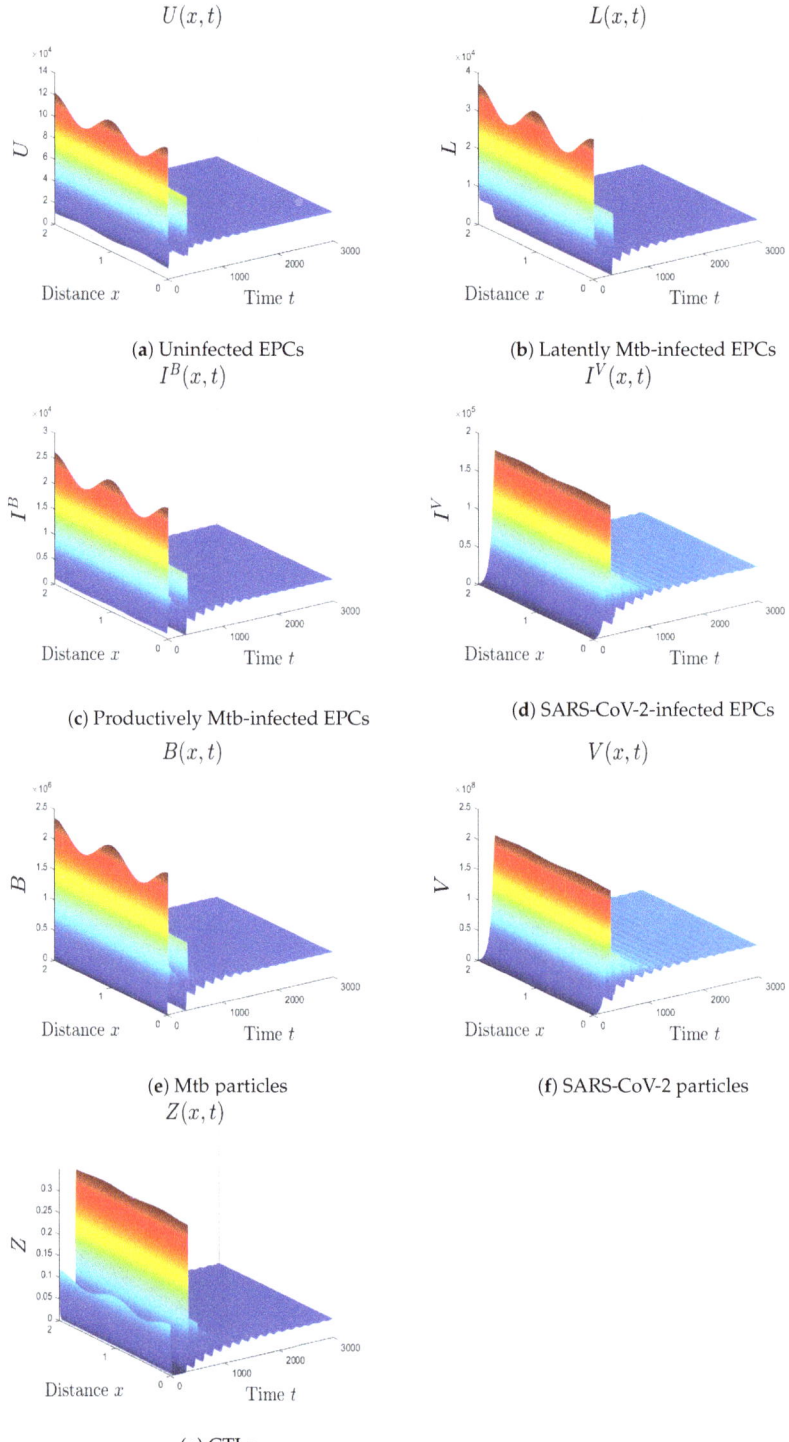

Figure 7. The impact of changing the diffusion coefficients in case (vi) to 1×10^{-5}. The initial distributions of the solutions are affected, while the global stability is not affected.

6. Conclusions and Future Works

There is an emerging evidence that the COVID-19 patients who have Mtb are more likely to develop acute disease and die [2,3,8]. Therefore, understanding Mtb/SARS-CoV-2 coinfection is critical to treat this group of patients. Here, we introduced a reaction–diffusion within-host Mtb/SARS-CoV-2 model. It counts the connections between uninfected EPCs, latently Mtb-infected EPCs, productively Mtb-infected EPCs, SARS-CoV-2-infected EPCs, Mtb particles, SARS-CoV-2 virions, and CTLs. It owns six equilibrium points as the following:

(i) The uninfected equilibrium E_0 constantly exists. It is GS if $\mathcal{R}_{0B} \leq 1$ and $\mathcal{R}_{0V} \leq 1$. This equilibrium imitates the status of a healthy individual with negative SARS-CoV-2 and Mtb tests.

(ii) The Mtb immune-free equilibrium E_1 is marked if $\mathcal{R}_{0B} > 1$, while it is GS if $\dfrac{\mathcal{R}_{0V}}{\mathcal{R}_{0B}} \leq 1$ and $\mathcal{R}_{1B} \leq 1$. The patient here suffers from Mtb monoinfection, where the CTL immunity has not yet been activated.

(iii) The COVID-19 immune-free equilibrium E_2 occurs when $\mathcal{R}_{0V} > 1$. It is GS if $\dfrac{\mathcal{R}_{0B}}{\mathcal{R}_{0V}} \leq 1$ and $\mathcal{R}_{1V} \leq 1$. Here, the patient has SARS-CoV-2 monoinfection with inefficient CTLs.

(iv) The Mtb equilibrium with immunity E_3 exists if $\mathcal{R}_{1B} > 1$, while it is GS if $\dfrac{\lambda \omega \eta_2 \mu_2 \epsilon_4}{\epsilon_2 \epsilon_5 [\omega \epsilon_1 \epsilon_4 + \eta_1 \mu_1 \epsilon_2 \epsilon_6]} + 1 \leq \dfrac{\epsilon_3}{\epsilon_2} + \mathcal{R}_{1B}$. In this condition, the CTL immunity is stimulated to eliminate Mtb infection.

(v) The COVID-19 equilibrium with immunity E_4 exists if $\mathcal{R}_{1V} > 1$, and it is GS if $\dfrac{\lambda \omega \eta_1 \mu_1 \epsilon_2 \epsilon_5}{\epsilon_3 \epsilon_4 [\omega \epsilon_1 \epsilon_5 + \eta_2 \mu_2 \epsilon_6]} + 1 \leq \dfrac{\epsilon_2}{\epsilon_3} + \mathcal{R}_{1V}$. This simulates the case of an individual with COVID-19 infection and active CTL immunity.

(vi) The Mtb/SARS-CoV-2 coinfection equilibrium E_5 exists and it is GS if $\dfrac{\omega \lambda \eta_2 \mu_2 \epsilon_4}{\epsilon_2 \epsilon_5 [\omega \epsilon_1 \epsilon_4 + \eta_1 \mu_1 \epsilon_2 \epsilon_6]} + 1 > \dfrac{\epsilon_3}{\epsilon_2} + \mathcal{R}_{1B}$, $\dfrac{\omega \lambda \eta_1 \mu_1 \epsilon_2 \epsilon_5}{\epsilon_3 \epsilon_4 [\omega \epsilon_1 \epsilon_5 + \eta_2 \mu_2 \epsilon_6]} + 1 > \dfrac{\epsilon_2}{\epsilon_3} + \mathcal{R}_{1V}$, $\dfrac{\mathcal{R}_{0V}}{\mathcal{R}_{0B}} > 1$, $\epsilon_2 > \epsilon_3$, and $\sigma > 1$. Here, the patient with a single infection becomes infected with both SARS-CoV-2 and Mtb.

We found that the numerical computations are quite congruous with the theoretical contributions. The equilibrium points reflect three states: the healthy state, the monoinfection state, and the coinfection state. The threshold parameters defined in Proposition 1 determine the locomotion between these states. Thus, the values of parameters in model (1) should be selected with caution. In addition, the global stability of the solutions of model (1) is robust against the values of the diffusion coefficients. However, the initial distributions of particles are affected by the selection of these values. Thus, it should be monitored as it may affect the initial status of the coinfected patients. In fact, Mtb/SARS-CoV-2 coinfection is a disease that needs to be further investigated and requires more awareness in high-TB burden regions such as India, Indonesia, and China [2]. Understanding the dynamics of coinfection will help develop new treatments, find better ways to treat coinfected patients, or recommend preventive measures for coinfected patients. The main limitation of this work is that we did not acquire real data to estimate the values of parameters in system (1). We gathered the values from SARS-CoV-2 monoinfection models or Mtb monoinfection models. Furthermore, we proved the boundedness only for the case when $D_U = D_L = D_{I^B} = D_{I^V} = D_Z$. In addition, we assumed that CTLs kill infected cells at the same rate constant. Therefore, this work could be polished by (i) utilizing real data to obtain an estimation of the values of parameters in system (1) when the data on coinfection become available, (ii) proving the boundedness for different diffusion coefficients, (iii) analyzing the model with different killing rates of CTLs, (iv) counting the time delays inherent in the latent stage or other responses, (v) adding the role of antibodies in eliminating SARS-CoV-2 or Mtb particles, (vi) using fractional derivatives to study model (1) [45,46], (vii) performing a sensitivity analysis for the threshold parameters to identify the most sensitive parameters in the model [47], (viii) considering mutations that can generate more aggressive variants of

SARS-CoV-2 and their effect on coinfection dynamics [48], and (ix) developing a multiscale model to connect within-host dynamics with between-hosts dynamics and gain a better comprehension of the coinfection mechanism.

Author Contributions: Conceptualization, A.A., A.F. and H.A.G.; Methodology, A.A., A.D.A.A., A.F. and H.A.G.; Formal analysis, A.D.A.A.; Investigation, A.A. and A.F.; Writing—original draft, A.D.A.A.; Writing—review & editing, A.D.A.A. and H.A.G. All authors have read and agreed to the published version of the manuscript.

Funding: This project was funded by the Deanship Scientific Research (DSR), King Abdulaziz University, Jeddah, under the Grant No. (IFPIP:699-130-1443).

Data Availability Statement: The data that support the findings of this study are available from the corresponding author upon reasonable request.

Acknowledgments: This project was funded by the Deanship Scientific Research (DSR), King Abdulaziz University, Jeddah, under the Grant No. (IFPIP:699-130-1443). The authors acknowledge with thanks DSR for technical and financial support.

Conflicts of Interest: The authors declare no conflict of interest.

References

1. Coronavirus Disease (COVID-19), Weekly Epidemiological Update (12 October 2022), World Health Organization (WHO). 2022. Available online: https://www.who.int/publications/m/item/weekly-epidemiological-update-on-covid-19---1-march-2023 (accessed on 1 January 2023).
2. Song, W.; Zhao, J.; Zhang, Q.; Liu, S.; Zhu, X.; An, Q.Q.; Xu, T.T.; Li, S.J.; Liu, J.Y.; Tao, N.N.; et al. COVID-19 and Tuberculosis coinfection: An overview of case reports/case series and meta-analysis. *Front. Med.* **2021**, *8*, 657006. [CrossRef] [PubMed]
3. Shah, T.; Shah, Z.; Yasmeen, N.; Baloch, Z.; Xia, X. Pathogenesis of SARS-CoV-2 and Mycobacterium tuberculosis coinfection. *Front. Immunol.* **2022**, *13*, 909011. [CrossRef] [PubMed]
4. Luke, E.; Swafford, K.; Shirazi, G.; Venketaraman, V. TB and COVID-19: An exploration of the characteristics and resulting complications of co-infection. *Front. Biosci.* **2022**, *14*, 6. [CrossRef] [PubMed]
5. Gatechompol, S.; Avihingsanon, A.; Putcharoen, O.; Ruxrungtham, K.; Kuritzkes, D.R. COVID-19 and HIV infection co-pandemics and their impact: A review of the literature. *AIDS Res. Ther.* **2021**, *18*, 28. [CrossRef] [PubMed]
6. Shariq, M.; Sheikh, J.; Quadir, N.; Sharma, N.; Hasnain, S.; Ehtesham, N. COVID-19 and tuberculosis: The double whammy of respiratory pathogens. *Eur. Respir. Rev.* **2022**, *31*, 210264. [CrossRef]
7. Tapela, K.; Olwal, C.O.; Quaye, O. Parallels in the pathogenesis of SARS-CoV-2 and M. tuberculosis: A synergistic or antagonistic alliance? *Future Microbiol.* **2020**, *15*, 1691–1695. [CrossRef] [PubMed]
8. Petrone, L.; Petruccioli, E.; Vanini, V.; Cuzzi, G.; Gualano, G.; Vittozzi, P.; Nicastri, E.; Maffongelli, G.; Grifoni, A.; Sette, A.; et al. Coinfection of tuberculosis and COVID-19 limits the ability to in vitro respond to SARS-CoV-2. *Int. J. Infect. Dis.* **2021**, *113*, S82–S87. [CrossRef]
9. Liang, K. Mathematical model of infection kinetics and its analysis for COVID-19, SARS and MERS. *Infect. Genet. Evol.* **2020**, *82*, 104306. [CrossRef] [PubMed]
10. Krishna, M.V. Mathematical modelling on diffusion and control of COVID–19. *Infect. Dis. Model.* **2020**, *5*, 588–597. [CrossRef]
11. Ivorra, B.; Ferrández, M.R.; Vela-Pérez, M.; Ramos, A.M. Mathematical modeling of the spread of the coronavirus disease 2019 (COVID-19) taking into account the undetected infections. The case of China. *Commun. Nonlinear Sci. Numer. Simul.* **2020**, *88*, 105303. [CrossRef]
12. Yang, C.; Wang, J. A mathematical model for the novel coronavirus epidemic in Wuhan, China. *Math. Biosci. Eng.* **2020**, *17*, 2708–2724. [CrossRef] [PubMed]
13. Krishna, M.V.; Prakash, J. Mathematical modelling on phase based transmissibility of Coronavirus. *Infect. Dis. Model.* **2020**, *5*, 375–385. [CrossRef] [PubMed]
14. Rajagopal, K.; Hasanzadeh, N.; Parastesh, F.; Hamarash, I.I.; Jafari, S.; Hussain, I. A fractional-order model for the novel coronavirus (COVID-19) outbreak. *Nonlinear Dyn.* **2020**, *101*, 711–718. [CrossRef] [PubMed]
15. Chen, T.M.; Rui, J.; Wang, Q.P.; Zhao, Z.Y.; Cui, J.A.; Yin, L. A mathematical model for simulating the phase-based transmissibility of a novel coronavirus. *Infect. Dis. Poverty* **2020**, *9*, 24. [CrossRef]
16. Almocera, A.S.; Quiroz, G.; Hernandez-Vargas, E.A. Stability analysis in COVID-19 within-host model with immune response. *Commun. Nonlinear Sci. Numer.* **2020**, *95*, 105584. [CrossRef]
17. Hernandez-Vargas, E.A.; Velasco-Hernandez, J.X. In-host mathematical modeling of COVID-19 in humans. *Annu. Control* **2020**, *50*, 448–456. [CrossRef]
18. Li, C.; Xu, J.; Liu, J.; Zhou, Y. The within-host viral kinetics of SARS-CoV-2. *Math. Biosci. Eng.* **2020**, *17*, 2853–2861. [CrossRef]
19. Blower, S.M.; Mclean, A.R.; Porco, T.C.; Small, P.M.; Hopewell, P.C.; Sanchez, M.A.; Moss, A.R. The intrinsic transmission dynamics of tuberculosis epidemics. *Nat. Med.* **1995**, *1*, 815–821. [CrossRef]

20. Castillo-Chavez, C.; Feng, Z. To treat or not to treat: The case of tuberculosis. *J. Math. Biol.* **1997**, *35*, 629–656. [CrossRef]
21. Feng, Z.; Castillo-Chavez, C.; Capurro, A. A model for tuberculosis with exogenous reinfection. *Theor. Popul. Biol.* **2000**, *57*, 235–247. [CrossRef]
22. Castillo-Chavez, C.; Song, B. Dynamical models of tuberculosis and their applications. *Math. Biosci. Eng.* **2004**, *1*, 361–404. [CrossRef] [PubMed]
23. Du, Y.; Wu, J.; Heffernan, J. A simple in-host model for Mycobacterium tuberculosis that captures all infection outcomes. *Math. Popul. Stud.* **2017**, *24*, 37–63. [CrossRef]
24. He, D.; Wang, Q.; Lo, W. Mathematical analysis of macrophage-bacteria interaction in tuberculosis infection. *Discret. Contin. Dyn. Syst. Ser. B* **2018**, *23*, 3387–3413. [CrossRef]
25. Yao, M.; Zhang, Y.; Wang, W. Bifurcation analysis for an in-host Mycobacterium tuberculosis model. *Discret. Contin. Dyn. Syst. Ser. B* **2021**, *26*, 2299–2322. [CrossRef]
26. Zhang, W. Analysis of an in-host tuberculosis model for disease control. *Appl. Math. Lett.* **2020**, *99*, 105983. [CrossRef]
27. Ibargüen-Mondragón, E.; Esteva, L.; Burbano-Rosero, E. Mathematical model for the growth of Mycobacterium tuberculosis in the granuloma. *Math. Biosci. Eng.* **2018**, *15*, 407–428. [PubMed]
28. Pinky, L.; Dobrovolny, H.M. SARS-CoV-2 coinfections: Could influenza and the common cold be beneficial? *J. Med. Virol.* **2020**, *92*, 2623–2630. [CrossRef]
29. Agha, A.D.A.; Elaiw, A.M. Global dynamics of SARS-CoV-2/malaria model with antibody immune response. *Math. Biosci. Eng.* **2022**, *19*, 8380–8410. [CrossRef]
30. Elaiw, A.M.; Agha, A.D.A.; Azoz, S.A.; Ramadan, E. Global analysis of within-host SARS-CoV-2/HIV coinfection model with latency. *Eur. Phys. J. Plus* **2022**, *137*, 174. [CrossRef]
31. Elaiw, A.M.; Agha, A.D.A. Global dynamics of SARS-CoV-2/cancer model with immune responses. *Appl. Math. Comput.* **2021**, *408*, 126364. [CrossRef]
32. Mekonen, K.; Balcha, S.; Obsu, L.; Hassen, A. Mathematical modeling and analysis of TB and COVID-19 coinfection. *J. Appl. Math.* **2022**, *2022*, 2449710. [CrossRef]
33. Bandekar, S.; Ghosh, M. A co-infection model on TB—COVID-19 with optimal control and sensitivity analysis. *Math. Comput. Simul.* **2022**, *200*, 1–31. [CrossRef] [PubMed]
34. Marimuthu, Y.; Nagappa, B.; Sharma, N.; Basu, S.; Chopra, K. COVID-19 and tuberculosis: A mathematical model based forecasting in Delhi, India. *Indian J. Tuberc.* **2020**, *67*, 177–181. [CrossRef] [PubMed]
35. Elaiw, A.M.; Agha, A.D.A. Analysis of the in-host dynamics of tuberculosis and SARS-CoV-2 coinfection. *Mathematics* **2023**, *11*, 1104. [CrossRef]
36. Zhang, Y.; Xu, Z. Dynamics of a diffusive HBV model with delayed Beddington-DeAngelis response. *Nonlinear Anal. Real World Appl.* **2014**, *15*, 118–139. [CrossRef]
37. Xu, Z.; Xu, Y. Stability of a $CD4^+$ T cell viral infection model with diffusion. *Int. J. Biomath.* **2018**, *11*, 1–16. [CrossRef]
38. Protter, M.H.; Weinberger, H.F. *Maximum Principles in Differential Equations*; Prentic Hall: Englewood Cliffs, NJ, USA, 1967.
39. Henry, D. *Geometric Theory of Semilinear Parabolic Equations*; Springer: New York, NY, USA, 1993.
40. Korobeinikov, A. Global properties of basic virus dynamics models. *Bull. Math. Biol.* **2004**, *66*, 879–883. [CrossRef]
41. Roy, P.; Roy, A.; Khailov, E.; Basir, F.A.; Grigorieva, E. A model of the optimal immunotherapy of psoriasis by introducing IL-10 and IL-22 inhibitor. *J. Biol. Syst.* **2020**, *28*, 609–639. [CrossRef]
42. Cao, X.; Roy, S.; Basir, F.A.; Roy, P. Global dynamics of HIV infection with two disease transmission routes—A mathematical model. *Commun. Math. Biol. Neurosci.* **2020**, *2020*, 8.
43. Khalil, H.K. *Nonlinear Systems*; Prentice-Hall: Hoboken, NJ, USA, 1996.
44. Sumi, T.; Harada, K. Immune response to SARS-CoV-2 in severe disease and long COVID-19. *iScience* **2022**, *25*, 104723. [CrossRef]
45. Ain, Q.T.; Chu, Y. On fractal fractional hepatitis B epidemic model with modified vaccination effects. *Fractals* **2022**, 1–18. [CrossRef]
46. Ain, Q.T.; Anjum, N.; Din, A.; Zeb, A.; Djilali, S.; Khan, Z. On the analysis of Caputo fractional order dynamics of Middle East Lungs Coronavirus (MERS-CoV) model. *Alex. Eng. J.* **2022**, *61*, 5123–5131.
47. Elaiw, A.M.; Agha, A.D.A. Global stability of a reaction-diffusion malaria/COVID-19 coinfection dynamics model. *Mathematics* **2022**, *10*, 4390. [CrossRef]
48. Bellomo, N.; Burini, D.; Outada, N. Multiscale models of Covid-19 with mutations and variants. *Netw. Heterog. Media* **2022**, *17*, 293–310. [CrossRef]

Disclaimer/Publisher's Note: The statements, opinions and data contained in all publications are solely those of the individual author(s) and contributor(s) and not of MDPI and/or the editor(s). MDPI and/or the editor(s) disclaim responsibility for any injury to people or property resulting from any ideas, methods, instructions or products referred to in the content.

Article

Streamline Diffusion Finite Element Method for Singularly Perturbed 1D-Parabolic Convection Diffusion Differential Equations with Line Discontinuous Source

R. Soundararajan [1,2], V. Subburayan [2,*] and Patricia J. Y. Wong [3]

[1] Department of Mathematics, RKM Vivekananda College (Autonomous), Mylapore, Chennai 600004, India; soundararajan.rajendran@gmail.com or rsoundar@rkmvc.ac.in or rr2867@srmist.edu.in

[2] Department of Mathematics, Faculty of Engineering and Technology, SRM Institute of Science and Technology, Kattankulathur 603203, India

[3] School of Electrical and Electronic Engineering, Nanyang Technological University, 50 Nanyang Avenue, Singapore 639798, Singapore; ejywong@ntu.edu.sg

* Correspondence: suburayan123@gmail.com or subburav@srmist.edu.in

Abstract: This article presents a study on singularly perturbed 1D parabolic Dirichlet's type differential equations with discontinuous source terms on an interior line. The time derivative is discretized using the Euler backward method, followed by the application of the streamline–diffusion finite element method (SDFEM) to solve locally one-dimensional stationary problems on a Shishkin mesh. Our proposed method is shown to achieve first-order convergence in time and second-order convergence in space. Our proposed method offers several advantages over existing techniques, including more accurate approximations of the solution on the boundary layer region, better efficiency, and robustness in dealing with discontinuous line source terms. The numerical examples presented in this paper demonstrate the effectiveness and efficiency of our method, which has practical applications in various fields, such as engineering and applied mathematics. Overall, our proposed method provides an effective and efficient solution to the challenging problem of solving singularly perturbed parabolic differential equations with discontinuous line source terms, making it a valuable tool for researchers and practitioners in various domains.

Keywords: singularly perturbed problem; parabolic differential equation; convection–diffusion problem; line discontinuous source term; streamline–diffusion finite element method; Shishkin mesh; uniformly convergent

MSC: 34K26; 35B25; 65M22; 65M50; 65N22

Citation: Soundararajan, R.; Subburayan, V.; Wong, P. J.Y. Streamline Finite Element Method for Singularly Perturbed 1D-Parabolic Convection Diffusion Differential Equations with Line Discontinuous Source. *Mathematics* 2023, 11, 2034. https://doi.org/10.3390/math11092034

Academic Editor: Gabriel Eduard Vilcu

Received: 22 March 2023
Revised: 21 April 2023
Accepted: 24 April 2023
Published: 25 April 2023

Copyright: © 2023 by the authors. Licensee MDPI, Basel, Switzerland. This article is an open access article distributed under the terms and conditions of the Creative Commons Attribution (CC BY) license (https://creativecommons.org/licenses/by/4.0/).

1. Introduction

In the literature, there are several articles available that deal with the numerical solution of singularly perturbed 1D parabolic differential equations with sufficiently smooth data functions, see [1–5]. Such problems, but with non-smooth data functions, can be seen in [6–8]. In [9], Clavero considered a numerical scheme with two small parameters in both the convection and diffusion terms. In [10], Gracia and O'Riordan considered a singularly perturbed reaction–diffusion parabolic problem with an initial condition that was not smooth. In [11], Clavero and Jorge considered 1D singularly perturbed parabolic convection diffusion systems and used a splitting uniformly convergent method. In [12], Yao Cheng, Yanjie Mei and H G Roos considered the local discontinuous Glerkin method for time dependent singularly perturbed convection diffusion problems on layer adapted meshes.

While there have been several studies on solving parabolic differential equations with various boundary conditions, such as Dirichlet and Neumann conditions, the problem of nonlinear parabolic stochastic differential equations with nonlinear Robin conditions remains an active area of research. For instance, the recent article, [13], discusses Well-Posedness for Nonlinear Parabolic Stochastic Differential Equations with Nonlinear Robin Conditions which provides a rigorous analysis of the mathematical properties of this problem. In this study, we focus on the related, but distinct, problem of numerically solving 1D singularly perturbed parabolic differential equations with discontinuous source terms on an interior line.

This type of problem has a regular boundary layer at $x = 1$ (boundary point) as the parameter ε tends to zero [14]. As a layer near the boundary exists, conventional discretization techniques, such as Finite Difference Methods (FDMs) or Finite Element Methods (FEMs), cannot yield an accurate solution, unless the mesh is highly refined [14]. Therefore, it is essential that any method proposed must employ a layer-adapted mesh to achieve uniform accuracy. Mukherjee and Natesan [15] developed a hybrid finite difference approach that converges uniformly for singularly perturbed 1D parabolic initial-boundary value problems (IBVPs) on the piecewise uniform Shishkin mesh. Similarly, Das et al. [16] proposed a numerical technique on the Bakhvalov-Shishkin mesh to solve 2D delay parabolic IBVPs. Hughes and Brooks [17] introduced the Streamline–diffusion finite element method (SDFEM), which is widely recognized as an effective technique for obtaining the numerical solutions of convection-dominated flow problems. Later, Roos and Zarin [18] applied SDFEM on the Shishkin mesh to solve a singularly perturbed two-point boundary value problem with a non-smooth source function.

The main focus of this paper was to investigate the numerical treatment of 1D singularly perturbed parabolic Dirichlet's differential equations with discontinuous source terms on an interior line. This problem contains an interior layer at $x = z$ due to the presence of line discontinuities. The authors propose a method that first uses the backward Euler method to discretize the time derivative, followed by applying SDFEM on the Shishkin mesh to solve the locally one-dimensional stationary problem. In [19], Ghiocel Groza and Nicolae Pop considered a numerical scheme for the locally one-dimensional stationary boundary value problem. Various numerical examples were used to validate the suggested method, both theoretically and numerically, and it demonstrated uniform convergence in both space and time.

The paper is organized as follows: Section 2 presents the statement of the problem, the temporal discretization, derivative estimates and stability findings of locally 1D problems. In Sections 3 and 4, the weak formulation and the numerical scheme for solving our problem are described. In Section 5, the error estimate for the SDFEM method is provided, while Section 6 offers numerical validation through various test examples. Finally, Section 7 provides some concluding remarks.

2. Continuous Problem and Stability Analysis

2.1. Statement of Continuous Problem

Inspired by the work of [20], the following singularly perturbed 1D parabolic differential equation is investigated in this paper.

Find a function u such that

$$\mathfrak{M}u := u_t - \varepsilon u_{xx} + a(x)u_x + b(x)u = \delta(x-z)g(t) + f(x,t), \ (x,t) \in \Omega^* \times (0,T], \quad (1)$$

$$u(x,0) = u_0(x), \ x \in \Omega, \quad (2)$$

$$u(0,t) = 0 = u(1,t), \ t \in [0,T], \quad (3)$$

where $0 < \varepsilon \ll 1$ is a very small positive parameter, $\Omega^* = \Omega_- \cup \Omega_+$, $\Omega_- = (0,z)$, $\Omega_+ = (z,1)$, $\overline{\Omega} = [0,1]$, the functions $a(x) \geq \alpha > 0$, $b(x) > \beta > 0$, $g(t), f(x,t)$ and $u_0(x)$ are sufficiently differentiable and bounded in their respective domains, $\delta(x-z)$ is the delta function, and T is some fixed positive time.

In [18], Roos and Zarin used the SDFEM method to solve a two-point boundary value problem with a point source function, which exhibits singular perturbation and requires a layer adaptive mesh like Shishkin mesh. In their model, there was only one interior layer at a single point. However, in our problem, which involves time evolution, we have an interior layer along a line source. Thus, we need to accurately capture the numerical solution along this line source.

In the paper, the positive constant C is used to denote a generic constant that is not dependent on the perturbation parameter ε, or the discretization parameters, such as N or M. For practical purposes, the accepted convention is to assume $\varepsilon \leq CN^{-1}$ for the convection coefficient problem. Additionally, the authors use the supremum norm $|\psi|_D = \sup_{\mathbf{x} \in D} |\psi(\mathbf{x})|$ to measure the error and derivative bounds.

2.2. Time Domain Discretization and Locally 1D Problems

We introduce equidistant meshes in the time domain $[0, T]$ with time step Δt, such that $\Omega_t^M = \{t_i = i\Delta t\}_{i=0}^M$, $\Delta t = \frac{T}{M}$, where M represents the number of mesh elements in the time direction. Now, discretizing the time derivative by means of the Euler fractional method on uniform mesh, we obtain the following ordinary differential equation for every time step t_n in the set Ω_t^M, where n ranges from 1 to M:

$$(I + \Delta t L)\tilde{u}^n = \tilde{u}^{n-1} + \Delta t[f(x, t_n) + \delta(x - z)g(t_n)], \ x \in \Omega^* \quad (4)$$

$$\tilde{u}^n(0) = 0 = \tilde{u}^n(1), \quad (5)$$

where the differential operator $L = -\varepsilon \frac{d^2}{dx^2} + a(x)\frac{d}{dx} + b(x)$ and $\tilde{u}^n$ is the solution of (4) and (5). Note that $\tilde{u}^0(x) = 0 = u_0(x)$, $x \in \overline{\Omega}$.

To achieve the stability of the scheme given by (4) and (5), one can easily prove that the operator $\mathcal{Q} = (I + \Delta t L)$ satisfies the maximum principle:

$$\|\mathcal{Q}^{-1}\|_\infty \leq \frac{1}{1 + \beta \Delta t}. \quad (6)$$

We can rewrite the semi-discretized problem (4) and (5) as:

$$\begin{cases} L^*\tilde{u}^n := -\varepsilon \frac{d^2 \tilde{u}^n(x)}{d^2 x} + a(x)\frac{d\tilde{u}^n(x)}{dx} + c(x)\tilde{u}^n(x) = g^n(x), \ x \in \Omega^*, \\ \tilde{u}^n(0) = 0 = \tilde{u}^n(1) \end{cases} \quad (7)$$

where $c(x) = b(x) + \frac{1}{\Delta t}$ and $g^n(x) = \frac{1}{\Delta t}\tilde{u}^{n-1} + \{f(x, t_n) + \delta(x - z)g(t_n)\}$. The above scheme (7) is an ordinary differential equation in space variable x for each time step t_n.

2.3. Maximum Principle and Derivative Estimates

Lemma 1 (Maximum Principle). *Suppose that there exists a function ζ, belonging to the set $C^0(\overline{\Omega}) \cap C^2(\Omega^*)$, that satisfies the following conditions: $\zeta(x) \geq 0$ for $x = 0, 1$, $L^*\zeta(x) \geq 0$ for all $x \in \Omega^*$ and $\zeta'(z^-) - \zeta'(z^+) \geq 0$ Then, it can be concluded that $\zeta(x) \geq 0$ for all $x \in \overline{\Omega}$.*

Proof. The method of proof for the lemma is comparable to the one used in (Lemma 2 in [21]). □

Lemma 2. *Suppose $\tilde{u}^n$ is the solution of problem (7) and is decomposed as $\tilde{u}^n = r + s$. Then, the derivatives of the regular components satisfy*

$$\left\|\frac{d^l r(x)}{dx^l}\right\|_{\Omega^*} \leq C(1 + \varepsilon^{-l+2}), \ l = 0, 1, 2, 3, \quad (8)$$

and, the derivatives of the singular components satisfy

$$\left|\frac{d^l s(x)}{dx^l}\right| \leq C\varepsilon^{-l} \begin{cases} \exp\left(\frac{\alpha(x-z)}{\varepsilon}\right), & x \in \Omega_-, \; l = 0,1,2,3, \\ \exp\left(\frac{\alpha(x-1)}{\varepsilon}\right), & x \in \Omega_+. \end{cases} \qquad (9)$$

Proof. A similar strategy to the one used in (Theorem 9.1 in [22]) is employed for the proof. □

2.4. Truncation Error

Lemma 3. *Assume that,* $\left|\frac{\partial^i u}{\partial t^i}\right| \leq C$, $i = 0,1,2,3$, *then* $\|e_n\|_\infty \leq C\Delta t^2$ *and* $\|E_n\|_\infty \leq C\Delta t$, *where* $e_n = u(x,t_n) - \tilde{u}^n$ *and* $E_n = \sum_{j=1}^n e_j$.

Proof. As $\tilde{u}^n$ is the solution of (4) and (5), we have

$$(I + \Delta t L)\tilde{u}^n - \Delta t\{f(x,t_n) + \delta(x-z)g(t_n)\} = u^{n-1}. \qquad (10)$$

By means of Taylor expansion, we have

$$u(x,t_{n-1}) = u(x,t_n) - \Delta t \frac{\partial u}{\partial t}(x,t_n) + O(\Delta t^2). \qquad (11)$$

From Equation (1) and if the solution of (1) is smooth enough, we have

$$\frac{\partial u}{\partial t}(x,t_n) = \{f(x,t_n) + \delta(x-z)g(t_n)\} - Lu^n. \qquad (12)$$

From (10)–(12), we have

$$(I + \Delta t L)e_n = O(\Delta t^2), \quad e_n(0) = e_n(1) = 0.$$

From this, we have $\|e_n\| \leq C(\Delta t)^2$ by using the stability result in (6).

The stability result and consistency property of (4) and (5) together implies $\|E_n\| \leq C\Delta t$. □

3. Weak Formulation

The standard weak formulation of problem (7) for a fixed n is given as follows. Find $\tilde{u}^n \in V = H_0^1(\overline{\Omega})$, such that

$$B(\tilde{u}^n, v) = g^n(v), \quad \forall v \in V,$$

where

$$B(y,v) = \varepsilon(y',v') + (ay' + cy, v)$$

$$g^n(v) = (g^n, v).$$

Here, $(.\,,.)$ represents the inner product in $L_2(\Omega^*)$.
Consider the mesh in space as $\overline{\Omega}_x^N = \{x_0, x_1, \ldots, x_N\}$, where N is some positive integer. We define a mesh that includes the point z as one of its nodes. Let ϕ_i be the basis for the finite-dimensional subspace V_h of piece-wise linear polynomials. The basis is given by

$$\phi_i(x) = \begin{cases} \frac{x - x_{i-1}}{h_i} & x_{i-1} \leq x \leq x_i, \\ \frac{x_{i+1} - x}{h_{i+1}} & x_i \leq x \leq x_{i+1}, \\ 0 & \text{otherwise}, \end{cases}$$

where $h_i = x_i - x_{i-1}$ and $i \in \{1,2,\ldots,N\}$. We use this basis to ensure that z is one of the mesh points.

The standard Galerkin method is given as follows: find $\tilde{u}_h^n \in V_h \subset V = H_0^1(\overline{\Omega})$ such that

$$B_h(\tilde{u}_h^n, v_h) = g_h^n(v_h), \quad \forall v_h \in V_h.$$

4. Streamline Diffusion Finite Element Formulation

The streamline diffusion weak formulation for the problem (7) is to find $\tilde{u}_h^n \in V_h \subset V = H_0^1(\overline{\Omega})$, such that

$$B_h(\tilde{u}_h^n, v_h) = g_h^n(v_h), \quad \forall v \in V_h, \tag{13}$$

where

$$B_h(y, w) = \varepsilon(y', w') + (ay' + cy, w) + \sum_{i=1}^{N} \int_{x_{i-1}}^{x_i} \delta_i(-\varepsilon y'' + ay' + cy) aw' dx,$$

$$g_h^n(w) = (g^n, w) + \sum_{i=1}^{N} \int_{x_{i-1}}^{x_i} \delta_i g^n(x) a(x) w' dx.$$

The parameter, known as the Streamline–diffusion (SD) parameter, denoted as δ_i, is decided later.

The SDFEM's relevant difference scheme is presented below.

$$L_{SD}^N := -\varepsilon[D^+ u_i - D^- u_i] + \alpha_i D^- u_i + \beta_i D^+ u_i + \gamma_i u_i = g_h(\phi_i), \tag{14}$$

where the symbols D^+ and D^- are given by the following:

$$D^+ u_i = \frac{u_{i+1} - u_i}{h_{i+1}}, \quad D^- u_i = \frac{u_i - u_{i-1}}{h_i},$$

and

$$\alpha_i = \int_{x_{i-1}}^{x_i} a(x)\phi_i dx - h_i \int_{x_{i-1}}^{x_i} c(x)\phi_{i-1}\phi_i dx + \frac{\delta_i}{h_i} \int_{x_{i-1}}^{x_i} a(x)^2 dx$$
$$- \delta_i \int_{x_{i-1}}^{x_i} a(x)c(x)\phi_{i-1} dx,$$

$$\beta_i = \int_{x_i}^{x_{i+1}} a(x)\phi_i dx + h_{i+1} \int_{x_i}^{x_{i+1}} c(x)\phi_{i+1}\phi_i dx - \frac{\delta_{i+1}}{h_{i+i}} \int_{x_i}^{x_{i+1}} a(x)^2 dx$$
$$- \delta_{i+1} \int_{x_i}^{x_{i+1}} a(x)c(x)\phi_{i+1} dx,$$

$$\gamma_i = \int_{x_{i-1}}^{x_{i+1}} c(x)\phi_i dx + \frac{\delta_i}{h_i} \int_{x_{i-1}}^{x_i} a(x)c(x) dx - \frac{\delta_{i+1}}{h_{i+1}} \int_{x_i}^{x_{i+1}} a(x)c(x) dx.$$

The standard Galerkin method is effective for step lengths that are sufficiently small. If this condition is not met, the method can be stabilized by utilizing the characteristics of an M-matrix. To satisfy this condition, the streamline–diffusion parameter δ_i can be determined such that the matrix resulting from the associated difference scheme (14) transforms into an M-matrix, as outlined below:

$$[-\alpha_i]_{\delta_i=0} \leq \varepsilon,$$

This can be written as $\overline{C}_i h_i \leq \overline{A}_i + \varepsilon$, where $\overline{A}_i = \int_{x_{i-1}}^{x_i} a(x)\phi_i dx$ and $\overline{C}_i = \int_{x_{i-1}}^{x_i} c(x)\phi_{i-1}\phi_i dx$. If this condition is not met, α_i is set to zero for $i \in \{1, 2, \ldots, N\}$ to achieve an M-matrix, which results in the following:

$$\delta_i = \frac{(h_i \overline{C}_i - \overline{A}_i)h_i}{\overline{A^2}_i - h_i \overline{AC}_i}$$

where, $\overline{A^2}_i = \int_{x_{i-1}}^{x_i}(a(x))^2 dx$ and $\overline{AC}_i = \int_{x_{i-1}}^{x_i} a(x)c(x)\phi_{i-1} dx$. If we summarize the above conditions, then we obtain

$$\delta_i = \begin{cases} 0, & if \ \overline{C}_i h_i \leq \overline{A}_i + \varepsilon \\ \frac{(h_i \overline{C}_i - \overline{A}_i) h_i}{\overline{A}^2_i - h_i \overline{AC}_i}, & otherwise. \end{cases} \quad (15)$$

As a result, it is evident that $\delta_i = O(h_i)$. By choosing v_h as ϕ_i as well as $\tilde{u}_h = (\tilde{u}_h^n(x_1), \tilde{u}_h^n(x_2), \ldots, \tilde{u}_h^n(x_N)) \in R^N$, we obtain the linear system of algebraic equations associated with the SDFEM scheme

$$K \tilde{u}_h = g_h,$$

where K represents a tridiagonal matrix $K = (k_{ij})$ and $g_h = g_h^n(\phi_i)$. Upon computing the coefficients,

$$k_{i,i-1} = -\varepsilon h_i^{-1} - h_i^{-1} \int_{x_{i-1}}^{x_i} a(x)\phi_i dx + \int_{x_{i-1}}^{x_i} c(x)\phi_{i-1}\phi_i dx - \delta_i h_i^{-2} \int_{x_{i-1}}^{x_i} a(x)^2 dx$$
$$+ \delta_i h_i^{-1} \int_{x_{i-1}}^{x_i} a(x)c(x)\phi_{i-1} dx,$$

$$k_{i,i} = \varepsilon h_i^{-1} + \varepsilon h_{i+1}^{-1} + h_i^{-1} \int_{x_{i-1}}^{x_i} a(x)\phi_i dx - h_{i+1}^{-1} \int_{x_i}^{x_{i+1}} c(x)\phi_i dx + \int_{x_{i-1}}^{x_i} c(x)\phi_i^2 dx$$
$$+ \int_{x_i}^{x_{i+1}} c(x)\phi_i^2 dx + \delta_i h_i^{-2} \int_{x_{i-1}}^{x_i} a(x)^2 dx$$
$$+ \delta_{i+1} h_{i+1}^{-2} \int_{x_i}^{x_{i+1}} a(x)^2 dx + \delta_i h_i^{-1} \int_{x_{i-1}}^{x_i} a(x)c(x)\phi_i dx - \delta_{i+1} h_{i+1}^{-1} \int_{x_i}^{x_{i+1}} a(x)c(x)\phi_i dx$$

$$k_{i,i+1} = -\varepsilon h_{i+1}^{-1} + h_{i+1}^{-1} \int_{x_i}^{x_{i+1}} a(x)\phi_i dx + \int_{x_i}^{x_{i+1}} c(x)\phi_{i+1}\phi_i dx$$
$$- \delta_{i+1} h_{i+1}^{-2} \int_{x_i}^{x_{i+1}} a(x)^2 dx - \delta_{i+1} h_{i+1}^{-1} \int_{x_i}^{x_{i+1}} a(x)c(x)\phi_{i+1} dx.$$

Remark 1. *We defined the SD parameter using the procedure given in [23]. Realistically, the conventional Galerkin method satisfies the criterion that defines an M-matrix for almost all 1D problems. In such a situation, the Galerkin method and the SDFEM both yield almost identical outcomes.*

Remark 2. *Generally, the conventional Galerkin method is analogous to the central finite difference approach. However, in regions where convection is dominant, applying a central finite difference approximation to the convective term may lead to oscillations [14]. In such instances, the SDFEM is a superior alternative.*

4.1. Discrete Green's Function and Stability

To establish the $(l_\infty, w_{-1,\infty})$ stability of the SDFEM, we introduce the discrete Green's function. The i-th discrete Green's function, denoted as $\lambda^i \in V_h$, is determined by solving the following problem:

$$\begin{cases} B_h(\phi_j, \lambda^i) = \delta_{ij}, \\ \lambda^i(0) = \lambda^i(1) = 0, \end{cases} \quad (16)$$

where δ_{ij} denotes the Kronecker delta. Additional details on these and related concepts can be found in references such as [24–26].

Lemma 4 ([25]). *If $\lambda^i = \sum_{j=1}^N \lambda_j^i \phi_j$, then the discrete Green's function exhibits the following conditions:*

(1) $\lambda_j^i \geq 0, \ i, j \in \{1, 2, \ldots, N\}$,
(2) $0 \leq \lambda_1^i < \ldots < \lambda_i^i > \lambda_{i+1}^i \ldots > \lambda_N^i$.

Lemma 5. *If we denote $c_0 = \min_i \{c_i\}, i = 1, 2, \ldots, N$ where $c_i = k_{i+1,i} - k_{i,i+1}$ and $\lambda^i = \sum_{j=1}^N \lambda_j^i \phi_j$, then $\lambda_i^i \leq c_0^{-1}$.*

Proof. From (16), for any $v_h \in V_h$, we have
$$B_h(v_h, \lambda^i) = v_h(x_i).$$
Considering $v_h = \sum_{j=1}^{i} \phi_j$, one can derive
$$\sum_{j=1}^{N} \sum_{k=1}^{j} k_{j,k} \lambda_j^i = 1.$$
Expanding, we obtain
$$(k_{1,1} + k_{1,2})\lambda_1^i + \sum_{j=2}^{i}(k_{j,j-1} + k_{j,j} + k_{j,j+1})\lambda_j^i +$$
$$k_{i+1,i}(\lambda_{i+1}^i - \lambda_i^i) + \lambda_i^i(k_{i+1,i} - k_{i,i+1}) = 1.$$
K is an M-matrix implying $(k_{i,i-1} + k_{i,i} + k_{i,i+1}) \geq 0$, for $i \in \{2, \ldots, N-1\}$. Now, by means of Lemma 4 and $k_{1,1} > k_{1,2}$ (property), we have
$$\lambda_i^i(k_{i+1,i} - k_{i,i+1}) \leq 1.$$
This implies that
$$\lambda_i^i \leq \frac{1}{(k_{i+1,i} - k_{i,i+1})} = c_i^{-1}.$$
So, we conclude that $\lambda_i^i \leq c_0^{-1}$. □

Lemma 6 ([25]). *The SDFEM, equipped with the streamline–diffusion parameter specified in Equation (15), is uniformly stable in the $(l_\infty, w_{-1,\infty})$ norm, as demonstrated by the following result:*
$$\|v_h\|_\infty \leq \frac{2}{c_0} \max_j \left| \sum_{k=j}^{N} (Kv_h)_k \right|, \quad \forall v_h \in V_h, \ j = 1, \ldots, N.$$

4.2. Shishkin Type Mesh

We used a general type mesh introduced in [27] with adapted layers at the points $x = z$ and $x = 1$. Let N be a positive even integer greater than 4 and $\sigma_1 = \min\{\frac{z}{2}, \frac{\tau_0}{\alpha}\varepsilon \ln N\}$, $\sigma_2 = \min\{\frac{1-z}{2}, \frac{\tau_0}{\alpha}\varepsilon \ln N\}$, $\tau_0 \geq 2$. Here, we considered $\sigma_1 = \sigma_2 = \frac{\tau_0}{\alpha}\varepsilon \ln N$. Let $\Omega_s = (0, z - \sigma_1) \cup (z, 1 - \sigma_2)$ and $\Omega_0 = (z - \sigma_1, z) \cup (1 - \sigma_2, 1)$. On Ω_s and Ω_0, the mesh is equidistant and graded respectively. The transition points are chosen to be
$$x_{\frac{N}{4}} = z - \sigma_1, \quad x_{\frac{N}{2}} = z, \quad x_{\frac{3N}{4}} = 1 - \sigma_2.$$
We chose two mesh generating functions φ_1 and φ_2 for the particular layers:
$$\varphi_1(\tfrac{1}{4}) = \ln N, \quad \varphi_1(\tfrac{1}{2}) = 0,$$
$$\varphi_2(\tfrac{3}{4}) = \ln N, \quad \varphi_2(1) = 0.$$
The nodes of the Shishkin mesh (S-mesh) are as follows:
$$x_i = \begin{cases} \frac{4i}{N}(z - \sigma_1) & i = 0, \ldots, \frac{N}{4}, \\ z - \frac{\tau_0}{\alpha}\varepsilon \varphi_1(t_i) & i = \frac{N}{4} + 1, \ldots, \frac{N}{2}, \\ z + \frac{4(1-z-\sigma_2)(i - \frac{N}{2})}{N} & i = \frac{N}{2} + 1, \ldots, \frac{3N}{4}, \\ -\frac{\tau_0}{\alpha}\varepsilon \varphi_2(t_i) + 1 & i = \frac{3N}{4} + 1, \ldots, N, \end{cases} \quad (17)$$

where $t_i = \frac{i}{N}$, $\varphi_i = -\ln \psi_i$ for $i = 1, 2$, $\psi_1(t) = \exp(-(2-4t)\ln N)$ and $\psi_2(t) = \exp(-(4-4t)\ln N)$ on Shishkin mesh (S-mesh).

$\max_i |\psi_i'|$, $i = 1, 2$ plays a part in error analysis as we see in the upcoming section. we have $\max |\psi'| \leq C \ln N$ in the S-mesh. Assuming that the mesh generating function φ_i, for $i = 1, 2$, obeys the following:

$$\max\{|\varphi_i'|\} \leq NC_0, \ for \ i = 1, 2. \tag{18}$$

We observe that on the coarse part Ω_s, the following holds for the S-mesh:

$$h_i N \leq C. \tag{19}$$

On the layer part it is true that on the S-mesh,

$$h_i \leq C\varepsilon \frac{\ln N}{N} \tag{20}$$

and, by the assumption (18), we obtain

$$\frac{h_i}{\varepsilon} \leq CN^{-1} \max |\varphi'| \leq C. \tag{21}$$

5. Error Estimations

The error at each time level t_n, where $1 \leq n \leq M - 1$, can be expressed as the difference between $\tilde{u}^n(x_i)$ and $\tilde{u}_h^n(x_i)$ for all $x_i \in \Omega^*$. Another way to represent this error is by utilizing the linear interpolant $\tilde{u}_I^n$ of $\tilde{u}^n$ as follows:

$$e(x_i) = (\tilde{u}^n - \tilde{u}_h^n)(x_i) = (\tilde{u}^n - \tilde{u}_I^n)(x_i) + (\tilde{u}_I^n - \tilde{u}_h^n)(x_i)$$
$$= e^I + e^D.$$

The errors of interpolation and discretization are denoted by e^I and e^D, respectively. In this section, we begin by deriving an estimate for the upper bound of the discretization error, based on the error caused by interpolation. Following that, we estimate the upper bound of the interpolation error.

The discretization error is given by

$$e^D = (\tilde{u}_I^n - \tilde{u}_h^n)(x) = \sum_{i=0}^{N} e_i \phi_i. \tag{22}$$

By means of the orthogonality property, we have

$$B_h(\tilde{u}^n - \tilde{u}_h^n, v_h) = 0, \ \forall v_h \in V_h.$$

Using the above property, we obtain

$$B_h(e^D, \phi_i) = B_h(\tilde{u}_I^n - \tilde{u}_h^n, \phi_i)$$
$$= B_h(\tilde{u}_I^n - \tilde{u}^n, \phi_i), \ i \in \{1, 2, \ldots, N-1\}.$$

Therefore, the equation for error is

$$\begin{cases} B_h(e^D, \phi_i) = B_h(\tilde{u}_I^n - \tilde{u}^n, \phi_i), \ i \in \{1, 2, \ldots, N-1\}, \\ e_0^D = 0, \ e_N^D = 0. \end{cases} \tag{23}$$

The following lemma gives the explicit expression for $B_h(\tilde{u}_I^n - \tilde{u}^n, \phi_i)$.

Lemma 7. *The error Equation (23) involves the bilinear form $B_h(\tilde{u}_I^n - \tilde{u}^n, \phi_i)$, which can be explicitly expressed as follows:*

$$B_h(\tilde{u}_I^n - \tilde{u}^n, \phi_i) = O_i + (P_i + P_{i+1}) + (Q_i - Q_{i+1}) + (R_i - R_{i+1}) + (S_i - S_{i+1}),$$

where

$$O_i = \int_{x_{i-1}}^{x_{i+1}} a'(x)(\tilde{u}_I^n - \tilde{u}^n)\phi_i dx, \tag{24}$$

$$P_i = \int_{x_{i-1}}^{x_i} c(x)(\tilde{u}_I^n - \tilde{u}^n)\phi_i dx, \tag{25}$$

$$Q_i = \frac{\delta_i}{h_i}\int_{x_{i-1}}^{x_i} (a(x)c(x)(\tilde{u}_I^n - \tilde{u}^n) + a(x)^2(\tilde{u}_I^n - \tilde{u}^n)')dx, \tag{26}$$

$$R_i = -\varepsilon\delta_i h_i^{-1}\int_{x_{i-1}}^{x_i} a(x)(\tilde{u}_I^n - \tilde{u}^n)'' dx, \tag{27}$$

$$S_i = h_i^{-1}\int_{x_{i-1}}^{x_i} a(x)(\tilde{u}_I^n - \tilde{u}^n)dx. \tag{28}$$

Proof. One can prove the required results by a simple calculation. □

Lemma 8. *Assume that $a(x) \in W^{2,1}$, then the following estimates are true:*

(i) $\sum_{i=1}^{N} |O_i| \leq c_1\|\tilde{u}^n - \tilde{u}_I^n\|_\infty$, (ii) $\sum_{i=1}^{N} |P_i| \leq c_2\|\tilde{u}^n - \tilde{u}_I^n\|_\infty$,

(iii) $\|Q_i\|_\infty \leq c_3\|\tilde{u}^n - \tilde{u}_I^n\|_\infty$, (iv) $\|R_i\|_\infty \leq c_4\|\tilde{u}^n - \tilde{u}_I^n\|_\infty$,

(v) $\|S_i\|_\infty \leq c_5\|\tilde{u}^n - \tilde{u}_I^n\|_\infty$.

Proof. We prove this Lemma sequentially:

(i). From (24), we know that

$$O_i = \int_{x_{i-1}}^{x_{i+1}} a'(x)(\tilde{u}_I^n - \tilde{u}^n)\phi_i dx.$$

Now, taking all the intervals and summing up, we have

$$\sum_{i=1}^{N} |O_i| \leq \|\tilde{u}_I^n - \tilde{u}^n\|_\infty \sum_{i=1}^{N}\int_{x_{i-1}}^{x_{i+1}} a'(x)dx$$
$$\leq \|\tilde{u}_I^n - \tilde{u}^n\|_\infty |a(x)|_{1,1}$$
$$= c_1\|\tilde{u}_I^n - \tilde{u}^n\|_\infty.$$

(ii). From Equation (25), we have

$$P_i = \int_{x_{i-1}}^{x_i} c(x)(\tilde{u}_I^n - \tilde{u}^n)\phi_i dx.$$

If we conduct a summation over all intervals, and derive

$$\sum_{i=1}^{N} |P_i| \leq \|\tilde{u}_I^n - \tilde{u}^n\|_\infty \|a(x)\|_\infty h_i$$
$$= c_2\|\tilde{u}_I^n - \tilde{u}^n\|_\infty.$$

(iii). From Equation (26), we have

$$Q_i = \frac{\delta_i}{h_i} \int_{x_{i-1}}^{x_i} (a(x)c(x)(\tilde{u}_I^n - \tilde{u}^n) + a(x)^2(\tilde{u}_I^n - \tilde{u}^n)')dx.$$

If the inequality $\overline{C}_i h_i \leq \overline{A}_i + \varepsilon$ holds, then $\delta_i = 0$ and, as a result, $r_i = 0$. On the other hand, if the condition is not satisfied, then we have $\delta_i \neq 0$. In this scenario, it can be observed that $\delta_i = O(h_i)$, we obtain

$$|Q_i| \leq C\|a(x)\|_\infty \|\tilde{u}_I^n - \tilde{u}^n\|_\infty (\|c(x)\|_\infty h_i - 2|a(x)|_{1,1})$$
$$= c_3 \|\tilde{u}_I^n - \tilde{u}^n\|_\infty.$$

(iv). From Equation (27), we have

$$R_i = -\frac{\varepsilon \delta_i}{h_i} \int_{x_{i-1}}^{x_i} a(x)(\tilde{u}_I^n - \tilde{u}^n)''dx,$$

and, here also we have $r_i = 0$ when $\overline{C}_i h_i \leq \overline{A}_i + \varepsilon$, and if it is not true, we have

$$|R_i| \leq C|a(x)|_{2,1} \|\tilde{u}_I^n - \tilde{u}^n\|_\infty$$
$$= c_4 \|\tilde{u}_I^n - \tilde{u}^n\|_\infty.$$

(v). Now, finally from Equation (28), we have

$$S_i = \frac{1}{h_i} \int_{x_{i-1}}^{x_i} a(x)(\tilde{u}_I^n - \tilde{u}^n)dx.$$

Simplifying this, we obtain

$$|S_i| \leq \|a(x)\|_\infty \|\tilde{u}_I^n - \tilde{u}^n\|_\infty$$
$$= c_5 \|\tilde{u}_I^n - \tilde{u}^n\|_\infty.$$

□

Lemma 9. *Consider the problem (7) and let $\tilde{u}^n$ be the exact solution to this problem. Furthermore, let $\tilde{u}_I^n$ denote the interpolant of $\tilde{u}^n$ on a given grid and let $\tilde{u}_h^n$ represent the approximate solution at the time level t_n. Then, It follows that*

$$\|\tilde{u}^n - \tilde{u}_h^n\|_\infty \leq C \|\tilde{u}_I^n - \tilde{u}^n\|_\infty.$$

Proof. Using Lemmas 6 and 8, we have

$$\|\tilde{u}_I^n - \tilde{u}_h^n\|_\infty \leq C \max_{i \in \{1,\ldots,N\}} \left| \sum_{j=i}^{N} (K(\tilde{u}_I^n - \tilde{u}_h^n))_j \right|$$

$$= C \max_{i \in \{1,\ldots,N\}} \left| \sum_{j=i}^{N} B_h(\tilde{u}_I^n - \tilde{u}^n, \phi_j) \right|$$

$$\leq C \left(\left| \sum_{i=1}^{N} O_i \right| + 2 \left| \sum_{i=1}^{N} P_i \right| + \max_{i \in \{1,\ldots,N\}} (Q_i - Q_N) + \max_{i \in \{1,\ldots,N\}} (R_i - R_N) \right)$$
$$+ C \max_{i \in \{1,\ldots,N\}} (S_i - S_N)$$

$$\leq C \left(\sum_{i=1}^{N} |O_i| + 2 \sum_{i=1}^{N} |P_i| + 2(\|Q_i\|_\infty + \|R_i\|_\infty + \|S_i\|_\infty) \right)$$

$$\leq C \|\tilde{u}_I^n - \tilde{u}^n\|_\infty.$$

This implies that the discretization error e^D given in (22) is bounded in terms of the interpolation error e^I. By applying the triangle inequality, we establish the following inequality:

$$\|\tilde{u}^n - \tilde{u}^n_h\|_\infty \leq C |\tilde{u}^n_I - \tilde{u}^n\|_\infty.$$

Therefore, we have successfully demonstrated the validity of this inequality. □

We now proceed to estimate the upper bound of the interpolation error for the S-mesh.

Theorem 1. *Let $\tilde{u}^n$ be the classical solution of the problem (7), $\tilde{u}^n_I$ be its interpolant on a Shishkin mesh with the grid points x_i as in (17) and $\varepsilon \leq \frac{C}{N}$. Then, the following holds:*

$$\|\tilde{u}^n_I - \tilde{u}^n\|_\infty \leq \begin{cases} C(N^{-1} \ln N)^2, & x \in \Omega_0, \\ CN^{-2}, & x \in \Omega_s. \end{cases}$$

Proof. We perform a separate analysis of the error due to interpolation on the domain Ω_- as well as Ω_+.

First, consider x in the domain Ω_-. Let $\tilde{u}^n_1(x)$ be the solution to the problem:

$$\begin{cases} L^* \tilde{u}^n_1(x) = g^n(x), & x \in \Omega_- = (0, z), \\ \tilde{u}^0(0) = 0, \ \tilde{u}^0(z) = d. \end{cases}$$

For now, assume that d is a constant. Then, the solution $\tilde{u}^n_1(x)$ exists and we can decompose it as a sum of two functions r_1 and s_1, where r_1 and s_1 satisfy bounds (8) and (9). Then, we can write

$$\tilde{u}^n_1(x) - \tilde{u}^n_{1,I}(x) = r_1(x) - r_{1,I}(x) + s_1(x) - s_{1,I}(x).$$

By means of classical theory, and from (19) and (8), we have the following estimate for the interpolation error $r_1(x) - r_{1,I}(x)$ on the regular part:

$$|r_1(x) - r_{1,I}(x)| \leq Ch_i^2 \max_{x_{i-1} \leq x \leq x_i} |r''_1| \leq Ch_i^2 \leq CN^{-2}.$$

For the interpolation error $r_1(x) - r_{1,I}(x)$ in the layer part, one can derive:

$$|r_1(x) - r_{1,I}(x)| < C\varepsilon^2 (N^{-1} \ln N)^2 \exp\left(\frac{-2\alpha}{\tau_0 \varepsilon}(x_{i-1} - z)\right)$$

$$\leq C(N^{-1} \ln N)^2.$$

The above expression is obtained by utilizing the inequality (20), selecting the transition point σ_1, and assuming the condition $\varepsilon \leq \frac{C}{N}$ holds. Now, for the interpolation error $s_1(x) - s_{1,I}(x)$ on the regular part, we have

$$|s_1(x) - s_{1,I}(x)| \leq 2|s_1(x)| \leq C \max_{x_{i-1} \leq x \leq x_i} \exp\left(-\frac{\alpha}{\varepsilon}(z - x)\right)$$

$$\leq C \exp\left(-\frac{\alpha}{\varepsilon} \sigma_1\right)$$

$$= CN^{-\tau_0}.$$

Regarding the interpolation error for the layer component, i.e., $s_1(x) - s_{1,I}(x)$, we apply the classical theory to obtain the following:

$$|s_1(x) - s_{1,I}(x)| \leq Ch_i^2 \max_{x_{i-1} \leq x \leq x_i} |s''_1|$$

$$\leq C(N^{-1} \ln N)^2 \max_{x_{i-1} \leq x \leq x_i} \exp\left(\frac{-\alpha}{\varepsilon}(z - x)\right)$$

$$\leq C(N^{-1} \ln N)^2.$$

Here, we used the inequality (20), the first inequality of (9) and (21). Similarly, we can prove the case $x \in \Omega_+$. □

Theorem 2. *Suppose that $u(x,t)$ represents the classical solution of problem (1)–(3), $\tilde{u}_h^n(x)$ represents the numerical solution of the SDFEM scheme (fully discrete) (13) at the nth time step t_n. Under the conditions of Lemma 3 and Theorem 1, we have the error estimate as follows:*

$$\|\tilde{u}_h^n(x) - u(x,t_n)\|_\infty \leq \begin{cases} C((N^{-1}\ln N)^2 + \Delta t), & x \in \Omega_0, \\ C(N^{-2} + \Delta t), & x \in \Omega_s. \end{cases}$$

Proof. We can prove this error estimate by combining the results from Lemma 3 and Theorem 1. □

6. Numerical Validation

In order to demonstrate the accuracy of the theoretical findings, we provide two illustrative examples in this section. We employed the double mesh principle to estimate the errors and their convergence rates for the test problems, as the exact solutions are unknown. The principle involves obtaining the numerical solution $Y^{2N,k/2}(x_i^n, t_i)$ on a grid $\Omega_x^{2N} \times \Omega_t^{2M}$, where the spatial direction is divided into $2N$ intervals, while the temporal direction is divided into $2M$ intervals. The mesh $\Omega_x^{2N} \times \Omega_t^{2M}$ is obtained by dividing each segment of the previous mesh $\Omega_x^N \times \Omega_t^M$, where the spatial direction is divided into N intervals, while the temporal direction is divided into M intervals, in two equal parts. Subsequently, we estimate the maximum point-wise error and convergence rate for each ε.

$$E_\varepsilon^{N,k} = \max_{i,n} \left| Y^{N,k}(x_i^n, t_n) - Y^{2N,k/2}(x_i^n, t_n) \right|,$$

$$D_x^{N,k} = \max_\varepsilon E_\varepsilon^{N,k}, \ r^{N,k} = \log_2\left(\frac{D_x^{N,k}}{D_x^{2N,k/2}}\right).$$

Example 1. *We examined the one-dimensional parabolic partial differential equation with a line source, described by Equations (1)–(3). The given data for this problem were as follows:*

$$u(x,0) = 0, \ x \in \Omega = (0,1),$$
$$u(0,t) = 0, \ u(1,t) = 0, \ t \in [0,1],$$
$$a(x) = x+5; \ b(x) = 1; \ f(x,t) = x+t; \ g(t) = 1; \ z = \frac{1}{2}.$$

In Table 1, we list the order of convergence and the maximum point-wise error corresponding to Example 1. When M=50, the CPU run time for the error given in the table was 7.6844×10^2 s. Additionally, Figure 1 shows the spatial profile of the solution of the problem described in Example 1 at different times t, for a fixed value of ε and is a visual representation of the solution with a strong boundary layer at $x = 1$, where the solution changed rapidly over a very small distance. This boundary layer arose due to the strong boundary condition $\tilde{u}_h^n(1,t) = 0$, which forced the solution to approach the value zero very quickly. The figure also shows the location of a strong interior layer at $x = \frac{1}{2}$, which caused a localized increase in the solution, which arose due to the line source term at the line $x = \frac{1}{2}$. Figure 2 shows the corresponding point-wise maximum error, that is, the maximum error decreased as N increased, irrespective of ε.

Table 1. Maximum error and order of convergence for Example 1 with the number $M = 50,100$.

ε ↓	M ↓	2^6	2^7	2^8	2^9	2^{10}	2^{11}	2^{12}
2^{-6}	50	1.0843×10^{-1}	3.1740×10^{-2}	1.2410×10^{-2}	4.0043×10^{-3}	1.2979×10^{-3}	3.6024×10^{-4}	1.0865×10^{-4}
	100	1.0286×10^{-1}	2.6681×10^{-2}	1.0315×10^{-2}	3.7978×10^{-3}	1.5062×10^{-3}	6.2557×10^{-4}	2.6478×10^{-4}
2^{-7}	50	1.1120×10^{-1}	2.8842×10^{-2}	1.1237×10^{-2}	3.5721×10^{-3}	1.1214×10^{-3}	3.9296×10^{-4}	1.6141×10^{-4}
	100	1.0748×10^{-1}	2.8066×10^{-2}	1.1374×10^{-2}	4.6676×10^{-3}	1.8575×10^{-3}	8.9909×10^{-4}	4.2970×10^{-4}
2^{-8}	50	1.1289×10^{-1}	2.7113×10^{-2}	1.0495×10^{-2}	3.2872×10^{-3}	1.2105×10^{-3}	4.5429×10^{-4}	1.9634×10^{-4}
	100	1.1002×10^{-1}	2.9689×10^{-2}	1.2033×10^{-2}	5.0398×10^{-3}	2.4171×10^{-3}	1.1748×10^{-3}	5.8837×10^{-4}
2^{-9}	50	1.1361×10^{-1}	2.6175×10^{-2}	1.0085×10^{-2}	3.2652×10^{-3}	1.2404×10^{-3}	5.0069×10^{-4}	2.1944×10^{-4}
	100	1.1175×10^{-1}	3.0602×10^{-2}	1.2410×10^{-2}	5.3361×10^{-3}	2.5656×10^{-3}	1.3340×10^{-3}	6.5985×10^{-4}
2^{-10}	50	1.1395×10^{-1}	2.5686×10^{-2}	9.8700×10^{-3}	3.3070×10^{-3}	1.2620×10^{-3}	5.1495×10^{-4}	2.3576×10^{-4}
	100	1.1263×10^{-1}	3.1082×10^{-2}	1.2609×10^{-2}	5.5213×10^{-3}	2.6932×10^{-3}	1.3756×10^{-3}	7.0938×10^{-4}
2^{-11}	50	1.1411×10^{-1}	2.5438×10^{-2}	9.7602×10^{-3}	3.3285×10^{-3}	1.2731×10^{-3}	5.2436×10^{-4}	2.4101×10^{-4}
	100	1.1307×10^{-1}	3.1327×10^{-2}	1.2711×10^{-2}	5.6167×10^{-3}	2.7588×10^{-3}	1.4141×10^{-3}	7.2555×10^{-4}
2^{-12}	50	1.1418×10^{-1}	2.5312×10^{-2}	9.7046×10^{-3}	3.3393×10^{-3}	1.2787×10^{-3}	5.2911×10^{-4}	2.4429×10^{-4}
	100	1.1329×10^{-1}	3.1451×10^{-2}	1.2763×10^{-2}	5.6650×10^{-3}	2.7921×10^{-3}	1.4321×10^{-3}	7.3508×10^{-4}
2^{-13}	50	1.1422×10^{-1}	2.5249×10^{-2}	9.6767×10^{-3}	3.3448×10^{-3}	1.2815×10^{-3}	5.3150×10^{-4}	2.4594×10^{-4}
	100	1.1340×10^{-1}	3.1514×10^{-2}	1.2789×10^{-2}	5.6894×10^{-3}	2.8088×10^{-3}	1.4416×10^{-3}	7.3966×10^{-4}
2^{-14}	50	1.1424×10^{-1}	2.5217×10^{-2}	9.6627×10^{-3}	3.3475×10^{-3}	1.2829×10^{-3}	5.3270×10^{-4}	2.4679×10^{-4}
	100	1.1345×10^{-1}	3.1545×10^{-2}	1.2803×10^{-2}	5.7016×10^{-3}	2.8172×10^{-3}	1.4469×10^{-3}	7.4190×10^{-4}
2^{-15}	50	1.1425×10^{-1}	2.5201×10^{-2}	9.6557×10^{-3}	3.3489×10^{-3}	1.2836×10^{-3}	5.3330×10^{-4}	2.4725×10^{-4}
	100	1.1348×10^{-1}	3.1561×10^{-2}	1.2809×10^{-2}	5.7077×10^{-3}	2.8214×10^{-3}	1.4496×10^{-3}	7.4301×10^{-4}
$D_x^{N,k}$	50	1.1425×10^{-1}	3.1740×10^{-2}	1.2410×10^{-2}	4.0043×10^{-3}	1.2979×10^{-3}	5.3330×10^{-4}	2.4725×10^{-4}
	100	1.1348×10^{-1}	3.1561×10^{-2}	1.2809×10^{-2}	5.7077×10^{-3}	2.8214×10^{-3}	1.4496×10^{-3}	7.4301×10^{-4}
$r^{N,k}$	50	1.8478×10^0	1.3548×10^0	1.6319×10^0	1.6253×10^0	1.2832×10^0	1.1089×10^0	-
	100	1.8462×10^0	1.3010×10^0	1.1662×10^0	1.0165×10^0	9.6076×10^{-1}	9.6419×10^{-1}	-

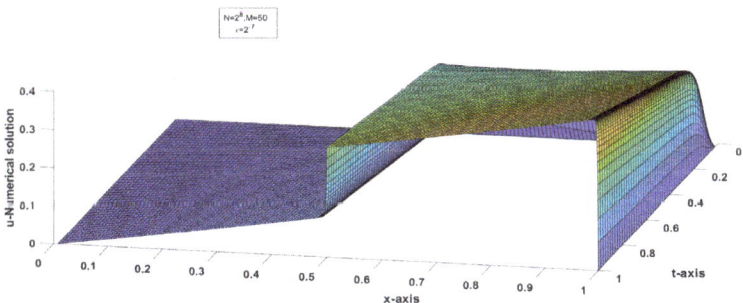

Figure 1. Numerical solution of Example 1.

Example 2. *We examined another one-dimensional parabolic partial differential equation with a line source, described by Equations (1)–(3). The given data for this problem were as follows:*

$$u(x,0) = 0, \ x \in \Omega = (0,1),$$
$$u(0,t) = 0, \ u(1,t) = 0, \ t \in [0,1],$$
$$a(x) = \frac{5+x}{5+3x^2} + e^{-1/x^2}; \ b(x) = 1; \ f(x,t) = e^{-\frac{1}{x}} + \sqrt{t}; \ g(t) = 1; \ z = \frac{1}{2}.$$

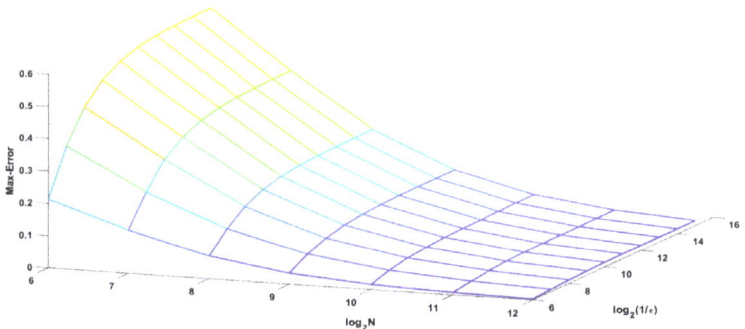

Figure 2. Maximum error of Example 1, when $M = 50$.

Table 2 presents the maximum point-wise error and the associated convergence rate for Example 2, when $M = 50$. The CPU run time for the error given in the table was 7.8426×10^2 s. Additionally, as illustrated in Example 1, the graphs of numerical solution and point-wise maximum error of the problem are illustrated in Figures 3 and 4, respectively.

Table 2. Maximum error and order of convergence for Example 2 with the number $M = 50,100$.

ε	M	N (Number of Grid Points)						
$\downarrow$	$\downarrow$	2^6	2^7	2^8	2^9	2^{10}	2^{11}	2^{12}
2^{-6}	50	2.1266×10^{-1}	1.3349×10^{-1}	7.0424×10^{-2}	3.3712×10^{-2}	1.5223×10^{-2}	7.1724×10^{-3}	3.4900×10^{-3}
	100	2.8109×10^{-1}	2.2380×10^{-1}	1.3696×10^{-1}	7.0987×10^{-2}	3.3312×10^{-2}	1.5960×10^{-2}	7.8452×10^{-3}
2^{-7}	50	3.5020×10^{-1}	2.2511×10^{-1}	1.2890×10^{-1}	6.7146×10^{-2}	3.3507×10^{-2}	1.6344×10^{-2}	7.8856×10^{-3}
	100	4.5196×10^{-1}	3.8586×10^{-1}	2.6099×10^{-1}	1.4770×10^{-1}	7.6575×10^{-2}	3.8040×10^{-2}	1.8516×10^{-2}
2^{-8}	50	4.4469×10^{-1}	3.0061×10^{-1}	1.7211×10^{-1}	9.0480×10^{-2}	4.6009×10^{-2}	2.3068×10^{-2}	1.1432×10^{-2}
	100	5.8200×10^{-1}	5.2658×10^{-1}	3.6716×10^{-1}	2.1077×10^{-1}	1.1126×10^{-1}	5.6420×10^{-2}	2.8120×10^{-2}
2^{-9}	50	5.0400×10^{-1}	3.4278×10^{-1}	1.9902×10^{-1}	1.0568×10^{-1}	5.3720×10^{-2}	2.7130×10^{-2}	1.3529×10^{-2}
	100	6.6504×10^{-1}	6.0947×10^{-1}	4.3599×10^{-1}	2.5668×10^{-1}	1.3564×10^{-1}	6.9369×10^{-2}	3.4832×10^{-2}
2^{-10}	50	5.3763×10^{-1}	3.6934×10^{-1}	2.1445×10^{-1}	1.1366×10^{-1}	5.8382×10^{-2}	2.9379×10^{-2}	1.4749×10^{-2}
	100	7.1658×10^{-1}	6.5915×10^{-1}	4.7996×10^{-1}	2.8410×10^{-1}	1.5157×10^{-1}	7.7503×10^{-2}	3.8981×10^{-2}
2^{-11}	50	5.5558×10^{-1}	3.8344×10^{-1}	2.2246×10^{-1}	1.1819×10^{-1}	6.0637×10^{-2}	3.0661×10^{-2}	1.5383×10^{-2}
	100	7.4477×10^{-1}	6.8558×10^{-1}	5.0407×10^{-1}	3.0050×10^{-1}	1.6044×10^{-1}	8.2210×10^{-2}	4.1429×10^{-2}
2^{-12}	50	5.6486×10^{-1}	3.9071×10^{-1}	2.2677×10^{-1}	1.2054×10^{-1}	6.1870×10^{-2}	3.1290×10^{-2}	1.5730×10^{-2}
	100	7.6104×10^{-1}	6.9976×10^{-1}	5.1666×10^{-1}	3.0910×10^{-1}	1.6535×10^{-1}	8.4716×10^{-2}	4.2767×10^{-2}
2^{-13}	50	5.6958×10^{-1}	3.9441×10^{-1}	2.2904×10^{-1}	1.2175×10^{-1}	6.2500×10^{-2}	3.1619×10^{-2}	1.5897×10^{-2}
	100	7.6927×10^{-1}	7.0691×10^{-1}	5.2310×10^{-1}	3.1350×10^{-1}	1.6788×10^{-1}	8.6049×10^{-2}	4.3442×10^{-2}
2^{-14}	50	5.7196×10^{-1}	3.9627×10^{-1}	2.3017×10^{-1}	1.2236×10^{-1}	6.2816×10^{-2}	3.1785×10^{-2}	1.5984×10^{-2}
	100	7.7341×10^{-1}	7.1050×10^{-1}	5.2636×10^{-1}	3.1573×10^{-1}	1.6915×10^{-1}	8.6729×10^{-2}	4.3793×10^{-2}
2^{-15}	50	5.7315×10^{-1}	3.9720×10^{-1}	2.3074×10^{-1}	1.2267×10^{-1}	6.2975×10^{-2}	3.1868×10^{-2}	1.6027×10^{-2}
	100	7.7548×10^{-1}	7.1230×10^{-1}	5.2803×10^{-1}	3.1685×10^{-1}	1.6980×10^{-1}	8.7074×10^{-2}	4.3971×10^{-2}
$D_x^{N,k}$	50	5.7315×10^{-1}	3.9720×10^{-1}	2.3074×10^{-1}	1.2267×10^{-1}	6.2975×10^{-2}	3.1868×10^{-2}	1.6027×10^{-2}
	100	7.7548×10^{-1}	7.1230×10^{-1}	5.2803×10^{-1}	3.1685×10^{-1}	1.6980×10^{-1}	8.7074×10^{-2}	4.3971×10^{-2}
$r^{N,k}$	50	5.2904×10^{-1}	7.8358×10^{-1}	9.1156×10^{-1}	9.6189×10^{-1}	9.8265×10^{-1}	9.9160×10^{-1}	-
	100	1.2260×10^{-1}	4.3187×10^{-1}	7.3683×10^{-1}	8.9999×10^{-1}	9.6349×10^{-1}	9.8568×10^{-1}	-

From the above two Examples, 1 and 2, we see that the solutions of the problems exhibited an interior layer at $x = \frac{1}{2}$ and a boundary layer at $x = 1$.

Note: For the numerical computation, a system with the following configuration i7 processor, 8.00 GB RAM was used.

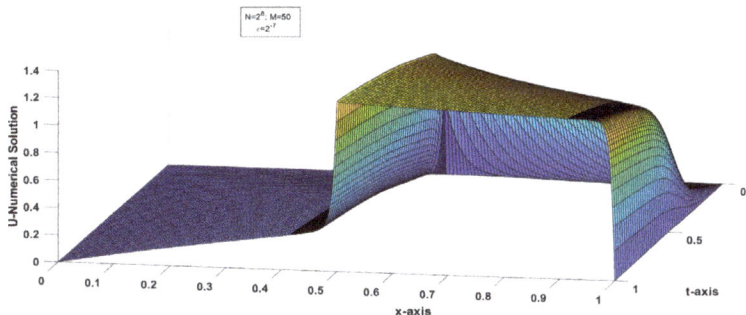

Figure 3. Numerical solution of Example 2.

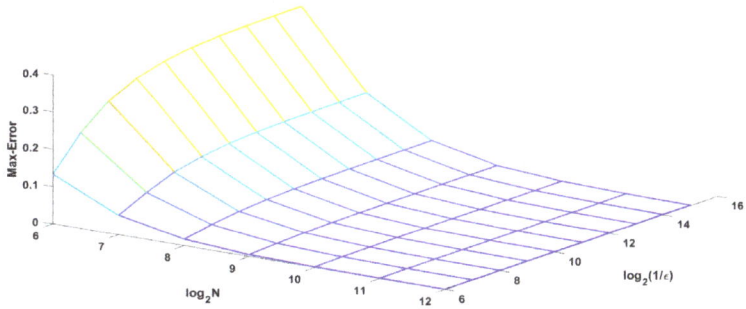

Figure 4. Maximum error of Example 2, when $M = 50$.

7. Conclusions

In this study, we analyzed 1D parabolic equations that were singularly perturbed and contained a discontinuous source term on an interior line. Our objective was to discretize the time derivative using the Euler backward method and apply SDFEM to the locally one-dimensional stationary problems on Shishkin mesh. We aimed to determine the accuracy order of the spatial arrangement and evaluate test problems in terms of their maximum pointwise errors.

Our results showed that the accuracy order of the spatial arrangement was of second order nature, but, due to the presence of the first-order term Δt in the error bound, the overall accuracy order was limited to first-order accuracy. These findings are presented as Theorems 1 and 2. Examples 1 and 2 represent the test problems, and Figures 1 and 3 depict their solutions. The layer occurred at the interior line $x = z$ and boundary line $x = 1$, which is evident from these figures. Figures 2 and 4 represent the convergence of the numerical solutions, that is, they illustrate that a higher value of N corresponded to a lower maximum pointwise error.

We evaluated the test problems in terms of their maximum pointwise errors, presented in Tables 1 and 2. From the tables we see that the computational order of convergence was almost one, but Theorem 2 showed second-order convergence in space and first-order convergence in time. This was due to the first-order term in the final result. Our results demonstrated that the maximum pointwise error stabilized as parameter ϵ decreased and decreased as parameter N increased.

It is worth noting that the results for SDFEM for ordinary differential equations, together with discontinuous source terms, are already available in the literature, as in, for example, [18], and, for the parabolic PDE without source line, in [3]. However, our results in this paper extend SDFEM to a parabolic PDE with a line source term, which is a significant contribution to the field. The error estimates are presented using the above-defined norm.

In summary, our study successfully achieved the objective of extending SDFEM to a parabolic PDE with a line source term. We determined the accuracy order of the spatial arrangement, evaluated the test problems in terms of their maximum pointwise errors, and demonstrated the stability of the maximum pointwise error as the parameter ϵ decreases.

Author Contributions: Methodology, R.S., V.S.; software, R.S., V.S.; formal analysis, R.S., V.S.; investigation, R.S., V.S.; writing—original draft preparation, R.S., V.S., P.J.Y.W.; writing—review and editing, R.S., V.S., P.J.Y.W. All authors have read and agreed to the published version of the manuscript.

Funding: This research received no external funding.

Data Availability Statement: Not applicable.

Conflicts of Interest: The authors declare no conflict of interest.

References

1. Das, P. A higher order difference method for singularly perturbed parabolic partial differential equations. *J. Differ. Equ. Appl.* **2018**, *24*, 452–477. [CrossRef]
2. Clavero, C.; Gracia, J.L.; Jorge, J.C. High-order numerical methods for one-dimensional parabolic singularly perturbed problems with regular layers. *Numer. Methods Partial. Differ. Equ.* **2005**, *21*, 149–169. [CrossRef]
3. Avijit, D.; Natesan, S. SDFEM for singularly perturbed parabolic initial-boundary-value problems on equidistributed grids. *Calcolo* **2020**, *57*, 23 . [CrossRef]
4. Yuzbasi, S.; Sahin, N. Numerical solutions of singularly perturbed one-dimensional parabolic convection–diffusion problems by the Bessel collocation method. *Appl. Math. Comput.* **2013**, *220*, 305–315.
5. Izadi, M.; Yuzbasi, S. A hybrid approximation scheme for 1-D singularly perturbed parabolic convection-diffusion problems. *Math. Commun.* **2022**, *27*, 47–62.
6. O'Riordana, E.; Shishkin, G.I. Singularly perturbed parabolic problems with non-smooth data. *J. Comput. Appl. Math.* **2004**, *166*, 233–245. [CrossRef]
7. Chandru, M.; Das, P.; Ramos, H. Numerical treatment of two-parameter singularly perturbed parabolic convection diffusion problems with non-smooth data. *Math. Methods Appl. Sci.* **2018**, *41*, 5359–5387. [CrossRef]
8. Bullo, T.A.; Degla, G.A.; Duressa, G.F. Uniformly convergent higher-order finite difference scheme for singularly perturbed parabolic problems with non-smooth data. *J. Appl. Math. Comput. Mech.* **2021**, *20*, 5–16. [CrossRef]
9. Clavero, C.; Gracia, J.L.; Shishkin, G.I.; Shishkina, L.P. An efficient numerical scheme for 1D parabolic singularly perturbed problems with an interior and boundary layers. *J. Comput. Appl. Math.* **2017**, *318*, 634–645. [CrossRef]
10. Gracia, J.L.; O'Riordan, E. A singularly perturbed parabolic problem with a layer in the initial condition. *Appl. Math. Comput.* **2012**, *219*, 498–510. [CrossRef]
11. Clavero, C.; Jorge, J.C. A splitting uniformly convergent method for one-dimensional parabolic singularly perturbed convection-diffusion systems. *Appl. Numer. Math.* **2023**, *183*, 317–332. [CrossRef]
12. Cheng, Y.; Mei, Y.; Roos, H.-G. The local discontinuous Galerkin method on layer-adapted meshes for time-dependent singularly perturbed convection-diffusion problems. *Comput. Math. Appl.* **2022**, *117*, 245–256. [CrossRef]
13. Mohammed, M. Well-Posedness for Nonlinear Parabolic Stochastic Differential Equations with Nonlinear Robin Conditions. *Symmetry* **2022**, *18*, 1722. [CrossRef]
14. Roos, H.G.; Stynes, M.; Tobiska, L. *Robust Numerical Methods for Singularly Perturbed Differential Equations*, 2nd ed.; Springer: Berlin/Heidelberg, Germany, 2008.
15. Mukherjee, K.; Natesan, S. Parameter-uniform hybrid numerical scheme for time-dependent convection-dominated initial-boundary-value problems. *Computing* **2009**, *84*, 209–230. [CrossRef]
16. Das, A.; Natesan, S. Uniformly convergent numerical method for singularly perturbed 2D delay parabolic convection–difusion problems on Bakhvalov–Shishkin mesh. *Int. J. Math. Model. Numer. Optim* **2018**, *8*, 305–330.
17. Hughes, T.J.R.; Brooks, A.N. A multidimensional upwind scheme with no crosswind difusion. *Finite Elem. Methods Convect. Domin. Flows* **1979**, *34*, 19–35 .
18. Roos, H.G.; Zarin, H. The streamline-difusion method for a convection–difusion problem with a point source. *J. Comput. Appl. Math.* **2003**, *150*, 109–128. [CrossRef]
19. Ghiocel Groza, H.; Pop, N. A Numerical Method for Solving of the Boundary Value Problems for Ordinary Differential Equations. *Result Math.* **2009**, *53*, 295–302. [CrossRef]
20. Brayanov, I.A. Numerical solution of a two-dimensional singularly perturbed reaction-diffusion problem with discontinuous coefficients. *Appl. Math. Comput.* **2006**, *182*, 631–643. [CrossRef]

21. Farrell, P.A.; Hegarty, A.F.; Miller, J.J.H.; O'Riordan, E.; Shishkin, G.I. Global Maximum Norm Parameter-Uniform Numerical Method for a Singularly Perturbed Convection-Diffusion Problem with Discontinuous Convection Coefficient. *Math. Comput. Model.* **2004**, *40*, 1375–1392. [CrossRef]
22. Miller, J.J.H.; O'Riordan, E.; Shishkin, G.I. *Fitted Numerical Methods for Singularly Perturbation Problems*, Revised ed.; World Scientific: Singapore, 1996.
23. Roos, H.G.; Uzelac, Z. The SDFEM for a convection–difusion problem with two small parameters. *Comput. Methods Appl. Math.* **2003**, *3*, 443–458. [CrossRef]
24. Andreev, V.B. The Green function and a priori estimates of solutions of monotone three-point singularly perturbed fnite-difference schemes. *Differ. Equ.* **2001**, *37*, 923–933. [CrossRef]
25. Chen, L.; Xu, J. An optimal streamline difusion fnite element method for a singularly perturbed problem. *Comput. Methods Am. Math.* **2005**, *383*, 191–201.
26. Liu, L.L.; Leng, H.; Long, G. Analysis of the SDFEM for singularly perturbed diferential-difference equations. *Calcolo* **2018**, *55*, 23. [CrossRef]
27. Roos, H.G.; LinB, T. Sufficient conditions for uniform convergence on layer-adapted grids. *Computing* **1999**, *63*, 27–45. [CrossRef]

Disclaimer/Publisher's Note: The statements, opinions and data contained in all publications are solely those of the individual author(s) and contributor(s) and not of MDPI and/or the editor(s). MDPI and/or the editor(s) disclaim responsibility for any injury to people or property resulting from any ideas, methods, instructions or products referred to in the content.

Article

Analytical Solutions to the Chavy-Waddy–Kolokolnikov Model of Bacterial Aggregates in Phototaxis by Three Integration Schemes

Alejandro León-Ramírez [1], Oswaldo González-Gaxiola [2,*] and Guillermo Chacón-Acosta [2]

[1] Postgraduate Studies in Natural Sciences and Engineering, Universidad Autónoma Metropolitana-Cuajimalpa, Vasco de Quiroga 4871, Mexico City 05348, Mexico; alejandro.leon@cua.uam.mx
[2] Applied Mathematics and Systems Department, Universidad Autonoma Metropolitana–Cuajimalpa, Vasco de Quiroga 4871, Mexico City 05348, Mexico; gchacon@cua.uam.mx
* Correspondence: ogonzalez@cua.uam.mx

Abstract: In this work, we find analytical solutions to the Chavy-Waddy–Kolokolnikov equation, a continuum approximation for modeling aggregate formation in bacteria moving toward the light, also known as phototaxis. We used three methods to obtain the solutions, the generalized Kudryashov method, the $e^{-R(\xi)}$-expansion, and exponential function methods, all of them being very efficient for finding traveling wave-like solutions. Findings can be classified into the case where the nonlinear term can be considered a small perturbation of the linear case and the regime of instability and pattern formation. Standing waves and traveling fronts were also found among the physically interesting cases, in addition to recovering stationary spike-like solutions.

Keywords: diffusion equations; traveling waves; phototaxis; bacterial motion; biological aggregation

MSC: 35Q92; 35K55; 92B05

1. Introduction

Bacteria have evolved various mechanisms to adapt and survive in their environments, such as migrating towards regions with higher nutrient concentrations or better living conditions. Chemotaxis is a common adaptation where bacteria sense and respond to chemical gradients, moving towards a region with a higher concentration of a particular substance. Another adaptation is phototaxis, which involves the movement of photosynthetic, motile organisms towards light. Both chemotaxis and phototaxis play important roles in evolutionary and ecological processes. Chemotaxis has been extensively studied in biology and mathematics, with the Keller–Segel equation being one of the earliest and most well-known models [1]. This equation consists of a reaction–diffusion–advection-like equation for bacterial density containing a function for chemotactic sensitivity, another function for the production and death of individuals, and a cross-diffusion term that couples with the concentration of the chemical signal that has its kinetics [2]. On the other hand, from a biological perspective, it has been verified that for the successful realization of phototaxia, the presence of both photoreceptors and pili is crucial, as they play a key role in facilitating its progression [3], which proved to be fundamental in agent model simulations [4]. From mathematical modeling, there is a series of papers, where D. Levy et al. [5–10] proposed some models to describe how phototaxis bacteria behave based on some basic features extracted from observations and experiments. The tools range from stochastic equations, particle models, kinetic models, to master equations in terms of probabilities and partial differential equations (PDEs). Group dynamics is a crucial feature in this system and was encoded through an internal degree of freedom called excitation [6,9]. Some models show additional internal variables involved with excitation, such as rotation; it was found that the sensitivity to perform phototaxis decreases if there is no rotation of the colony [11]. Among Levy's papers, there are two relevant PDE models, the first being a reaction–diffusion equation system for bacterial concentration, excitation, and substrate memory derived as a continuous limit of a stochastic model [5,6]. This resembles the chemotactic model, which has also been adapted to analyze phototaxis [12,13]. The second model involves local interactions by means of a proposed system of master equations for the probability of finding bacteria in a particular state. Such a system includes reaction–diffusion, persistence, and sticking terms [9,10]. From the latter, Chavy-Waddy and Kolokolnikov (CWK) proposed a simplified system of equations for the probability that the bacteria move and obtained a fourth-order nonlinear partial differential equation, only depending on one parameter that combines the probabilities of moving to either side, staying, or changing direction according to the sensing distance [14]. The resulting model is of swarming type for bacterial aggregation, like the Cahn–Hillard equation [15]. The stationary solution coincides with a state of particle aggregation, for which Taranets and Chugunova [16] studied the rate of convergence and the existence of non-negative solutions. Recently, the physical characteristics of the bacteria, such as their shape and the way the flaps work, are also being explored for increasingly accurate models of phototaxis [17]. The CWK equation includes a reverse diffusion term, a fourth-order term related to a long-range effect term, and a nonlinear term with a unique parameter that considers the aggregate extent and whose value determines the instability region for structure formation.

In this paper, we solve the CWK equation for propagating non-deformable pulses, employing three generalizations of Kudryashov's method. The Kudryashov method is highly efficient for finding exact solutions to nonlinear differential equations. It has a wide range of applications, from physics, engineering, mathematics, and biology. Particularly in biology, it was used to delve into nonlinear phenomena, such as the study of HIV-1 infection [18], population dynamics [19], etc. These methods are suitable for describing soliton-like traveling wave solutions that have a clear biophysical interpretation in the present model.

The article's structure is the following. We present the CWK phototaxis model that will be solved in Section 2. Section 3 provides an overview of the methods employed, including the solutions found in each case and some graphical representations of important cases. In Section 4, we highlight the importance of our solutions and discuss the overall results. We also present five appendices with the largest expressions and additional results. Our findings provide a collection of exact solutions for studying phototaxis from the reduced CWK one-dimensional model.

2. Mathematical 1D Model of Aggregation in Bacterial Colonies

As mentioned previously, Chavy-Waddy and Kolokolnikov proposed in [14] a nonlinear parabolic fourth-order partial differential equation for modeling the movement of phototaxic bacterial aggregates using the random models proposed by Levy et al. The CWK formula is as follows:

$$u_t = -u_{xx} - u_{xxxx} + \alpha \left(\frac{u_x u_{xx}}{u} \right)_x. \tag{1}$$

The first two right-hand terms are similar to reverse diffusion and a long-range term. Reverse diffusion occurs when transport is towards zones where the concentration gradient is high, opposite to what happens in diffusion. This is the case, for instance, in the Cahn–Hilliard equation for the phase separation process [15,20]. The fourth-order term is sometimes associated with long-range terms where the influence of distant neighbors on the concentration at a given point is considered [21,22]. Both terms balance each other; while the inverse diffusion destabilizes the system, the fourth-order term stabilizes the higher Fourier modes. The third term is the one containing the nonlinearity and the only parameter of the model, α, which controls the size of the aggregate and is given by

$$\alpha = \frac{c(2d+1)(d+1)^2}{(c[1+d(d^2+2d+3)]-2a)}, \quad (2)$$

where the constants are given in terms of the simplified Levy's master equation [9]. a is the jump rate at which the bacterium moves, preserving its orientation, c is the rate at which it moves after switching to a new orientation, and d is the bacterium's sensing radius. The model given by Equation (1) is similar to the swarming models of biological aggregation based on attraction–repulsion forces [23,24]. However, it is a way simpler since it only involves a single equation with stationary finger-like solutions, as found in the experiments. The stationary finger-like solution found in [14] is as follows:

$$u(x,t) = A\left[\text{sech}\left(\frac{\sqrt{\alpha-1}}{2}x\right)\right]^{\frac{2}{\alpha-1}}, \quad (3)$$

where A is a real normalization constant, and only depends on the value of α. We note that $\alpha = 1$ is a particular value; indeed, in [14], it is shown that $\alpha > 1$ is necessary to obtain the steady state since it is obtained in the unstable regime when $c > 2a/d$, where patterns can occur; see Appendix A. Some extreme cases satisfy this condition when the motion rate after changing orientation becomes very large $c \to \infty$. If the bacterium stops without changing orientation $a = 0$, one obtains $\alpha \geq [(1+d)^2(1+2d)]/[1+d(3+2d+d^2)]$. From this, three cases follow depending on the value of the sensitivity distance. If $d = 1$, then $\alpha \geq 12/7$; if $d \to \infty$, then $\alpha \geq 2$; if $d = 0$, then $\alpha \geq 1$. In all these cases, the unstable threshold is fulfilled in general when $\alpha > 1$.

The simplest case is when $\alpha = 0$, where Equation (1) reduces to $u_t = -u_{xx} - u_{xxxx}$, which only has a contribution to the flux due to inverse diffusion and long-range terms. It is a linear equation that conventional methods can solve; nonetheless, the methods used in this paper also give additional solutions, so we will present them for the sake of completeness. Appendix B presents the solutions of the case $\alpha = 0$ by the method of separation of variables and comparison with some of the solutions obtained here. The nonlinear equation is not straightforward to solve by the usual methods, so for non-zero α cases, solutions are obtained by the methods explored herein and include two regimes, $0 < \alpha < 1$ and $\alpha > 1$, being the most relevant cases.

Finding the stationary solution of Equation (1) is accomplished in [14] by reducing the order of the equation and then studying the orbits of the system, which involves the following transformation $u(x,t) = e^{v(x,t)}$, and Equation (1) becomes

$$v_t = -v_x^2 - v_{xx} - v_{xxxx} + (4\alpha-6)v_x^2 v_{xx} + (\alpha-4)v_x v_{xxx} + (\alpha-3)v_{xx}^2 + (\alpha-1)v_x^4. \quad (4)$$

In this equation, there seem to be four particular values of α. However, when changing to $z = v_x$, the corresponding equation has only two characteristic values for $\alpha = 1, 3$. Indeed, for $\alpha = 3$, the equation for z can be easily integrated, as found in [16], where they also analyze the stability of some stationary state families of the CWK equation. Moreover, time-dependent solutions were presented, giving their convergence rate to the stationary case.

In the next section, we will present some stationary and time-dependent solution families, each obtained with the so-called Kudryashov method. Since Equation (1) is of the parabolic type, and it is well known that parabolic equations admit traveling wave-like solutions as in [25,26], we expect that the CWK equation also admits soliton-like solutions suitable to be found with the Kudryashov method. To do so, we use Equation (4) and make the following variable change $\xi = x - \omega t$, under the assumption of traveling-wave-like solutions, resulting in the following:

$$\omega v_\xi - v_\xi^2 - v_{\xi\xi} - v_{\xi\xi\xi\xi} + (4\alpha-6)v_\xi^2 v_{\xi\xi} + (\alpha-4)v_\xi v_{\xi\xi\xi} + (\alpha-3)v_{\xi\xi}^2 + (\alpha-1)v_\xi^4 = 0, \quad (5)$$

where ω is the constant wave velocity. Lastly, we substitute $\phi(\xi) = v_\xi$ to obtain a simplified version of Equation (5):

$$\omega\phi - \phi^2 - \phi_\xi - \phi_{\xi\xi\xi} + (4\alpha - 6)\phi^2\phi_\xi + (\alpha - 4)\phi\phi_{\xi\xi} + (\alpha - 3)(\phi_\xi)^2 + (\alpha - 1)\phi^4 = 0. \quad (6)$$

We will present in the next section the methods used to solve Equation (6), and hence Equation (1), and the collection of families that each technique will produce.

3. Methods and Solutions

In this section, we will describe briefly each of the proposed methods, their application, and the families of solutions obtained by means of them.

3.1. Brief Description of the Generalized Kudryashov Method

The purpose of this section is to present the algorithm of the generalized Kudryashov method for finding exact solutions of nonlinear evolution equations, such as Equation (6), consisting of the following steps:

Step 1: We assume the exact solutions to Equation (6) can be formulated as follows:

$$\phi(\xi) = \frac{\sum_{i=0}^{N} a_i Q^i(\xi)}{\sum_{j=0}^{M} b_j Q^j(\xi)}, \quad (7)$$

where a_i and b_j are arbitrary constants with $a_N \neq 0$, $b_M \neq 0$, and the function $Q(\xi)$ satisfies the next differential equation [27]:

$$Q_\xi = Q^2 - Q. \quad (8)$$

The relation between integers N and M can be established by considering the homogeneous balance between the higher-order derivatives and the nonlinear factors in Equation (6). In our case, $N = 2$ and $M = 1$.

Step 2: Next we substitute both ϕ, given in Equation (7), and its derivatives $\phi_\xi, \phi_{\xi\xi}, \ldots$, in Equation (6) to obtain the polynomial equation:

$$P(Q(\xi)) = 0. \quad (9)$$

Step 3: We select all the terms having the same algebraic power in Q from the polynomial Equation (9), setting them equal to zero, and obtain a system of algebraic equations with the following set of unknowns, $\{a_0, a_1, a_2, b_0, b_1, \omega\}$ depending on the value of α. We use algebraic manipulation software such as Mathematica to solve the system with the model constraints, considering that $a_2 \neq 0$ and $b_1 \neq 0$ are also required.

Step 4: Using the previous results and considering Equation (7) together with Equation (8), we obtain the possible exact solutions of Equation (6) and consequently those of Equation (1).

Due to the fact that the generalized Kudryashov method is defined by the rational form of finite series given by Equation (7), it provides a greater number of exact and more general solutions in an identical manner as the classical Kudryashov method, which is a significant advantage [28].

Solutions Obtained by the Generalized Kudryashov Technique

The system of nonlinear algebraic equations resulting from this method is shown in Appendix C in Equation (A27). Next, we present the solutions obtained for different values of the parameters. The first set of solutions is for $\alpha = 0$.

Solution 1. If $\alpha = 0$, we have $a_0 = a_0$, $a_1 = -a_2 - b_0$, $a_2 = a_2$, $b_0 = a_0$, $b_1 = -a_2$, and $\omega = 2$, from which we obtain the solution

$$u_1(x,t) = \cosh(2t - x) - \sinh(2t - x) + 1. \tag{10}$$

Solution 2. If $\alpha = 0$, we have $a_0 = 0$, $a_1 = -b_0$, $a_2 = a_2$, $b_0 = b_0$, $b_1 = -a_2$, and $\omega = -2$, from which we obtain the solution

$$u_2(x,t) = -\sinh(2t + x) + \cosh(2t + x) + 1. \tag{11}$$

Solution 3. If $\alpha = 0$, we have $a_0 = 0$, $a_1 = 0$, $a_2 = 2b_0$, $b_0 = b_0$, $b_1 = -a_2$, and $\omega = -10$, from which we obtain the solution

$$u_3(x,t) = -\sinh(20t + 2x) + \cosh(20t + 2x) - 1. \tag{12}$$

Solution 4. If $\alpha = 0$, we have $a_0 = 2b_0$, $a_1 = -4b_0$, $a_2 = 2b_0$, $b_0 = b_0$, $b_1 = -a_2$, and $\omega = 10$, from which we obtain the solution

$$u_4(x,t) = \sinh(20t - 2x) - \cosh(20t - 2x) + 1. \tag{13}$$

In all cases, non-stationary waves propagating in different directions were obtained. To illustrate, let us consider Solution 4. In Figure 1, we show the plot of traveling wave solution $u_4(x,t)$.

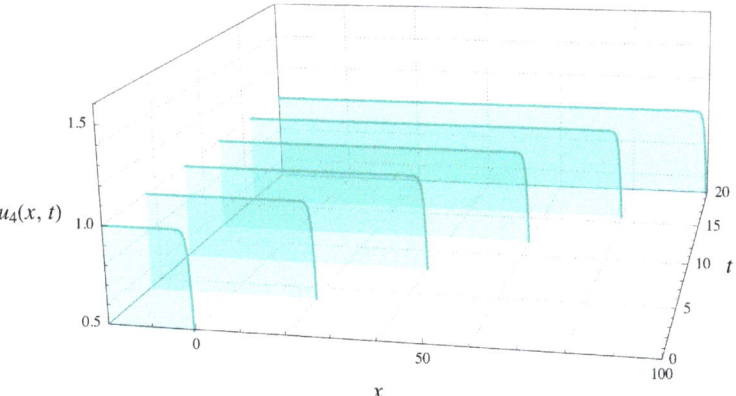

Figure 1. Solution 4 for $\alpha = 1$. Although no aggregate is produced, the wavefront propagates to the right with velocity $\omega = 10$.

Next we present the solutions for $\alpha \neq 0$.

Solution 5. If $\alpha = 1$, we have $a_0 = \frac{b_0(a_1 b_1 - a_2 b_0)}{b_1^2}$, $a_1 = a_1$, $a_2 = a_2$, $b_0 = b_0$, $b_1 = b_1$, and $\omega = 0$, from which we obtain the solution

$$u_5(x) = \cosh\left(\frac{1}{4}x(\beta + x)\right) - \sinh\left(\frac{1}{4}x(\beta + x)\right), \quad \beta = \frac{4a_2 b_0 - 4b_1(2a_2 + a_1)}{b_1^2}. \tag{14}$$

Solution 6. If $\alpha > 1$, we have $a_0 = \frac{1}{4}(-2a_1 - a_2)$, $a_1 = a_1$, $a_2 = a_2$, $b_0 = -a_1 - \frac{1}{2}a_2$, $b_1 = -a_2$, and $\omega = 0$, from which we obtain the solutions

$$u_6(x) = C\cosh(\gamma x), \quad C \neq 0 \text{ and } \gamma = \pm\frac{1}{\sqrt{\alpha - 1}}. \tag{15}$$

Solution 7. *If $\alpha > 1$, we have $a_0 = \frac{1}{2}a_2$, $a_1 = -a_2$, $a_2 = a_2$, $b_0 = -a_1 - \frac{1}{2}a_2$, $b_1 = -a_2$, and $\omega = 0$, from which we obtain the solutions*

$$u_7(x) = C \sinh(\gamma x), \quad C \neq 0 \text{ and } \gamma = \pm \frac{1}{\sqrt{\alpha - 1}}. \tag{16}$$

Solution 8. *If $\alpha > 1$, we have $a_0 = \frac{1}{4}(-2a_1 - a_2)$, $a_1 = a_1$, $a_2 = a_2$, $b_0 = \frac{1}{4}(\alpha - 1)(2a_1 + a_2)$, $b_1 = \frac{1}{2}(\alpha - 1)a_2$, and $\omega = 0$, from which we obtain the solutions*

$$u_8(x) = C \operatorname{sech}^m(\gamma x), \quad C \neq 0, \; m = \frac{2}{\alpha - 1} \text{ and } \gamma = \frac{\sqrt{\alpha - 1}}{2}. \tag{17}$$

Here only stationary solutions with $\omega = 0$ were obtained, recovering especially the finger-like distribution from [14] in Solution 8. Figure 2 shows that the bell-shaped curve's distribution becomes progressively wider as the value of alpha increases. This suggests that the bacteria exhibit a preference for being farther away. In other words, as alpha increases, the bacteria tend to distribute themselves over a larger area, indicating a lower degree of clustering.

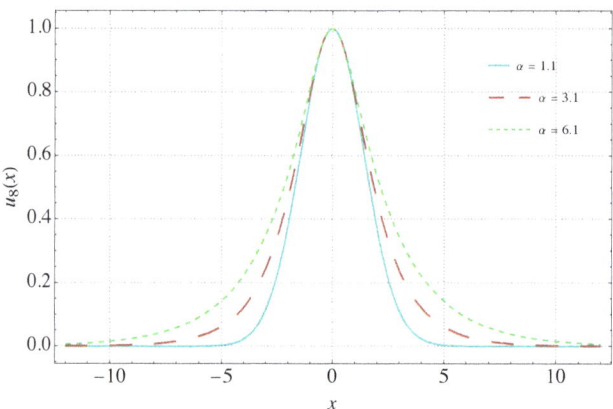

Figure 2. Solution 8 reproduces the stationary finger-like distribution obtained in [14]. Values of $\alpha = 1.1, 3.1, 6.1$ are presented. As α grows, the distribution becomes increasingly wider.

Earlier, we mentioned that when $\alpha = 3$, Equation (4) for v_x can be directly integrated. For this special case, the following solutions were found.

Solution 9. *If $\alpha = 3$, we have $a_0 = \frac{a_2}{12 - 6\sqrt{3}}$, $a_1 = -\frac{1}{3}(\sqrt{3} + 3)a_2$, $a_2 = a_2$, $b_0 = -a_1 - \frac{1}{2}a_2$, $b_1 = -a_2$, and $\omega = \frac{1}{3\sqrt{3}}$, from which we obtain the solution*

$$u_9(x,t) = -\frac{e^{\frac{x}{\sqrt{3}} - \frac{t}{9}}\left(e^{\frac{t}{3\sqrt{3}}} + e^x\right)}{\left(2\sqrt{3} - 3\right)e^{\frac{t}{3\sqrt{3}}} + \left(2\sqrt{3} + 3\right)e^x} \tag{18}$$

Solution 10. *If $\alpha = 3$, we have $a_0 = \frac{a_2}{6(\sqrt{3} + 2)}$, $a_1 = \frac{1}{3}(\sqrt{3} - 3)a_2$, $a_2 = a_2$, $b_0 = -a_1 - \frac{1}{2}a_2$, $b_1 = -a_2$, $\beta \in \mathbb{R}$, $h = \pm 1$, and $\omega = -\frac{1}{3\sqrt{3}}$, from which we obtain the solution*

$$u_{10}(x,t) = \beta\left[\sinh\left(\frac{t}{3\sqrt{3}} + hx\right) + \cosh\left(\frac{t}{3\sqrt{3}} + hx\right) + 1\right]\left[\sqrt{3}\sinh\left(\frac{t}{3\sqrt{3}} + hx\right)\right.$$
$$+ \sqrt{3}\cosh\left(\frac{t}{3\sqrt{3}} + hx\right) + 7\sqrt{3} + 12\right]^{\frac{1}{2\sqrt{3}}-\frac{1}{2}}\left[(2\sqrt{3}+3)\left(\sinh\left(\frac{t}{3\sqrt{3}} + hx\right)\right.\right.$$
$$\left.\left.+ \cosh\left(\frac{t}{3\sqrt{3}} + hx\right)\right) + 26\sqrt{3} + 45\right]^{-\frac{1}{2}-\frac{1}{2\sqrt{3}}}\left[\cosh\left(\frac{t}{9} + \frac{hx}{\sqrt{3}}\right) - \sinh\left(\frac{t}{9} + \frac{hx}{\sqrt{3}}\right)\right] \quad (19)$$

Solution 11. If $\alpha = 3$, we have $a_0 = \pm\frac{1}{6}(\sqrt{3}\pm 2)a_2$, $a_1 = \mp\frac{1}{3}(\sqrt{3}\pm 3)a_2$, $a_2 = a_2$, $b_0 = \frac{1}{4}(\alpha-1)(2a_1 + a_2)$, $b_1 = \frac{1}{2}(\alpha-1)a_2$, and $\omega = \mp\frac{1}{3\sqrt{3}}$, from which we obtain the solution

$$u_{11\mp}(x,t) = \mp\left(3\tanh\left(\frac{1}{18}\left(\sqrt{3}t \pm 9x\right)\right) + 2\sqrt{3}\right)e^{\mp\frac{x}{\sqrt{3}} - \frac{t}{9}}. \quad (20)$$

The above solutions exhibit similar behaviors at different scales. Although they have exponential growth, near zero, there is a small propagating pulse. To illustrate this, we consider the solution $u_{11-}(x,t)$. In Figure 3, we present the graph of the traveling pulse of Solution 11; notice how it moves to the right.

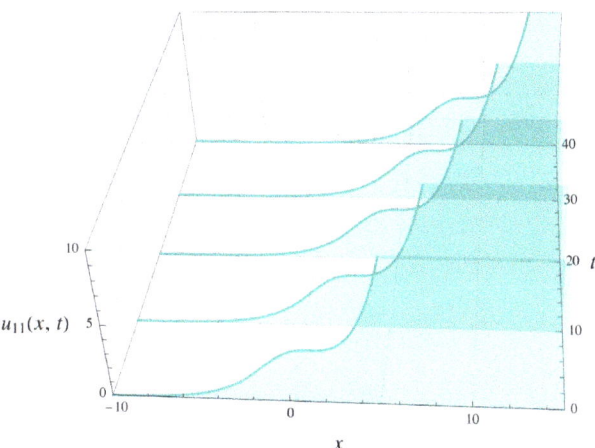

Figure 3. Solution 11 where a small pulse propagates to the right with velocity $\omega = \frac{1}{3\sqrt{3}}$.

Since the method allows specific solutions for particular values of the parameters, here we present the stationary solution for $\alpha = 5$, being a particular case for $\alpha > 1$.

Solution 12. If $\alpha = 5$, we have $a_0 = \frac{1}{2}a_2$, $a_1 = -a_2$, $a_2 = a_2$, $b_0 = \frac{1}{4}(\alpha-1)(2a_1 + a_2)$, $b_1 = \frac{1}{2}(\alpha-1)a_2$, and $\omega = 0$, from which we obtain the solution

$$u_{12}(x) = \frac{\sinh\left(\frac{x}{2}\right) + \cosh\left(\frac{x}{2}\right)}{\sqrt{-2\sinh^2(x) - 2\sinh(x)\cosh(x)}}. \quad (21)$$

3.2. Brief Description of the $e^{-R(\xi)}$-Expansion Method

Among the methods for finding analytical solutions to nonlinear equations is the so-called $e^{-R(\xi)}$-expansion, which has been used to find solitary wave-like solutions in some fluid problems [29,30].

Step 1: The $e^{-R(\xi)}$-expansion method assumes that the solution of Equation (6) is expressed as

$$\phi(\xi) = \sum_{i=0}^{N} a_i (e^{-R(\xi)})^i \qquad (22)$$

where a_i is an arbitrary constant with $a_N \neq 0$, and the function R satisfies the following differential equation [31]:

$$R_\xi = \lambda + \mu e^{R(\xi)} + e^{-R(\xi)}. \qquad (23)$$

Consequently, the function R can be given by

$$R(\xi) = \begin{cases} \ln\left(-\frac{\sqrt{\lambda^2-4\mu}\tanh\left(\frac{1}{2}(\xi+A)\sqrt{\lambda^2-4\mu}\right)}{2\mu} - \frac{\lambda}{2\mu}\right) & \text{if } \lambda^2 - 4\mu > 0,\ \mu \neq 0 \\[4pt] \ln\left(-\frac{\sqrt{\lambda^2-4\mu}\coth\left(\frac{1}{2}(\xi+A)\sqrt{\lambda^2-4\mu}\right)}{2\mu} - \frac{\lambda}{2\mu}\right) & \text{if } \lambda^2 - 4\mu > 0,\ \mu \neq 0 \\[4pt] \ln\left(\frac{\sqrt{4\mu-\lambda^2}\tan\left(\frac{1}{2}(\xi+A)\sqrt{4\mu-\lambda^2}\right)}{2\mu} - \frac{\lambda}{2\mu}\right) & \text{if } \lambda^2 - 4\mu < 0,\ \mu \neq 0 \\[4pt] \ln\left(\frac{\sqrt{4\mu-\lambda^2}\cot\left(\frac{1}{2}(\xi+A)\sqrt{4\mu-\lambda^2}\right)}{2\mu} - \frac{\lambda}{2\mu}\right) & \text{if } \lambda^2 - 4\mu < 0,\ \mu \neq 0 \\[4pt] -\ln\left(\frac{\lambda}{e^{\lambda(\xi+A)}-1}\right) & \text{if } \mu = 0,\ \lambda > 0 \\[4pt] \ln\left(-\frac{2(\lambda(\xi+A)+2)}{\lambda^2(\xi+A)}\right) & \text{if } \lambda \neq 0,\ \lambda^2 - 4\mu = 0 \\[4pt] \ln(\xi+A) & \text{if } \mu = 0,\ \lambda = 0. \end{cases} \qquad (24)$$

As previously said, to compute the positive integer N, consider the homogeneous balance between the higher-order derivatives and the nonlinear parts in Equation (6). In this case, $N = 1$.

Step 2: In this method we consider ϕ given in Equation (22) and the necessary derivatives $\phi_\xi, \phi_{\xi\xi}, \ldots$, then we substitute them into Equation (6) to obtain the following polynomial equation:

$$P\left(e^{-R(\xi)}\right) = 0. \qquad (25)$$

Step 3: We select from the polynomial Equation (25) all terms having the same algebraic power of $e^{-R(\xi)}$, set them equal to zero, and obtain a system of algebraic equations with the set of unknowns $\{a_0, a_1, \omega\}$ depending on α. In the same way as the previous method, we use Mathematica to solve the system with its natural constraints, assuming $a_1 \neq 0$.

Step 4: With the results obtained in the previous step and taking Equation (22) along with Equation (23), we obtain the possible exact solutions of Equation (6), and hence those of Equation (1).

Solutions Found by the $e^{-R(\xi)}$-Expansion Method

The resulting nonlinear algebraic system of equations resulting from this method is presented in Equation (A28) of Appendix D; here we present the solutions obtained by this method. First for the case $\alpha = 0$:

Solution 13. *If $\alpha = 0$, we have $a_0 = 0$, $a_1 = 1$, $\lambda > 0$, $\mu = 0$, and $\omega = -\lambda^3 - \lambda$, from which we obtain the solution*

$$u_{13}(x,t) = e^{-\lambda\left((\lambda^3+\lambda)t+x\right)} - e^{A\lambda}, \quad A \in \mathbb{R}. \qquad (26)$$

Solution 14. *If $\alpha = 0$, we have $a_0 > 0$, $a_1 = 1$, $\lambda = a_0$, $\mu = a_0(\lambda - a_0)$, and $\omega = 6a_0\lambda^2 - 12a_0^2\lambda + 8a_0^3 + 2a_0 - \lambda^3 - \lambda$, from which we obtain the solution*

$$u_{14}(x,t) = -\sinh\left(a_0(x+A) - a_0^2 t(a_0^2+1)\right) - \cosh\left(a_0(x+A) - a_0^2 t(a_0^2+1)\right) + 1, \quad A \in \mathbb{R}. \tag{27}$$

The first two solutions are similar to $u_4(x,t)$, with wavefronts propagating to one side. Figure 4 shows, with fixed values of the parameters, a constant unit density over time.

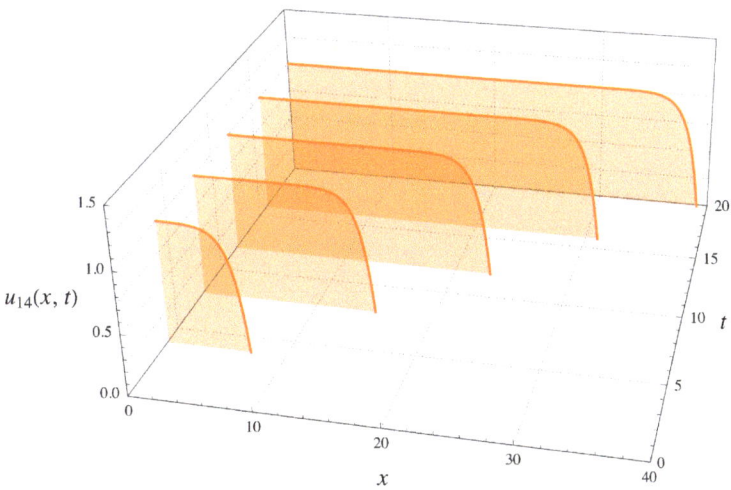

Figure 4. Solution 14 for $A = 1$ and $a_0 = 1$. Propagating wave front behavior is observed.

Solution 15. *If $\alpha = 0$, we have $a_0 = a_0$, $a_1 = 2$, $\lambda = a_0$, $\mu = \frac{1}{4}(a_0^2+1)$, and $\omega = 0$, from which we obtain the solution*

$$u_{15}(x) = \left(\sin\left(\frac{x+A}{2}\right) - a_0 \cos\left(\frac{x+A}{2}\right)\right)^2, \quad A \in \mathbb{R}. \tag{28}$$

The solution $u_{15}(x)$ is an oscillatory function; evidently, the constants A and a_0 are the phase and amplitude of a standing wave. Notably, this solution arises only from the reverse diffusion and the fourth-order term. Thus, although each maximum represents the bacterial concentration, this distribution is preserved from the beginning of the process.

This method made it possible to find two stationary solutions for $\alpha < 1$. While this clearly does not correspond to the region of instability, and therefore we cannot expect the formation of aggregates, we can think of α as a perturbation parameter in an intermediate region between reverse diffusion alone and pattern formation.

Solution 16. *If $\alpha = 1 - \frac{2}{a_1}$, we have $a_0 = a_0$, $a_1 > 0$, $\lambda = \frac{2a_0}{a_1}$, $\mu = \frac{2a_0^2+a_1}{2a_1^2}$, and $\omega = 0$, from which we obtain the solution*

$$u_{16}(x) = \left(\sqrt{2}\sin\left(\frac{x+A}{\sqrt{2a_1}}\right) - 2a_0\sqrt{\frac{1}{a_1}}\cos\left(\frac{x+A}{\sqrt{2a_1}}\right)\right)^{a_1}, \quad A \in \mathbb{R}. \tag{29}$$

Particularly, it makes sense for $a_1 \geq 2$, which implies $\alpha < 1$.

Solution 17. *If* $\alpha = \frac{1}{3}$, *we have* $a_0 = a_0$, $a_1 = 3$, $\lambda = \frac{2a_0}{3}$, $\mu = \frac{1}{18}\left(2a_0^2 + 3\right)$, *and* $\omega = 0$, *from which we obtain the solution*

$$u_{17}(x) = \left(\sqrt{6}\sin\left(\frac{x+A}{\sqrt{6}}\right) - 2a_0\cos\left(\frac{x+A}{\sqrt{6}}\right)\right)^3, \quad A \in \mathbb{R}. \tag{30}$$

Interestingly, the solutions in this regime are also oscillatory, with Solution 16 having the same structure as u_{17} for even values of a_1. However, for odd a_1, negative values occur, and the parity of a_1 must be considered to interpret u_{16} as a distribution.

Figure 5 illustrates the solution with different values of a_1, which represents stationary distributions of bacteria aggregates. As the value of a_1 increases, the number of bacterial aggregates decreases while the amplitude of each curve increases. This leads to a higher density of bacteria within each curve.

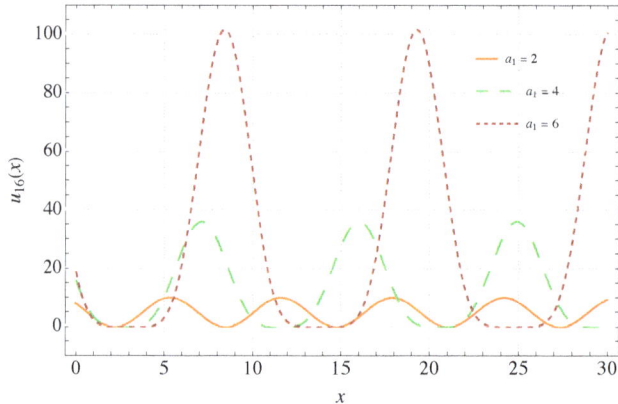

Figure 5. Solution 16 for fixed $A = 0$, $a_0 = 2$, and $a_1 = 2, 4, 6$, where increasing the value of a_1 increases the amplitude of each curve.

Finally, in the region of structure formation, when $\alpha > 1$, we obtain five stationary solutions, which also depend on method parameters.

Solution 18. *If* $\alpha > 1$, *we have* $a_0 = a_0$, $a_1 = -\frac{2}{\alpha-1}$, $\lambda = \frac{2a_0}{a_1}$, $\mu = \frac{2a_0^2 + a_1}{2a_1^2}$, *and* $\omega = 0$, *from which we obtain the solution*

$$u_{18}(x) = \left[\frac{e^{-\sqrt{\alpha-1}} - e^{\sqrt{\alpha-1}}}{\sqrt{\alpha-1}} + a_0 e^{-\frac{1}{2}\sqrt{\alpha-1}(A+x)}\left(1 + e^{\sqrt{\alpha-1}(A+x)}\right)\right]^{-\frac{2}{\alpha-1}}, \quad A \in \mathbb{R}. \tag{31}$$

Solution 19. *If* $\alpha > 1$, *we have* $a_0 = a_0$, $a_1 = 1$, $\lambda = 2a_0$, $\mu = a_0^2 - \frac{1}{1-\alpha}$, *and* $\omega = 0$, *from which we obtain the solution*

$$u_{19}(x) = \frac{1}{\sqrt{\alpha-1}}\sinh\left(\frac{x+A}{\sqrt{\alpha-1}}\right) \mp a_0\cosh\left(\frac{x+A}{\sqrt{\alpha-1}}\right), \quad A \in \mathbb{R}. \tag{32}$$

Solution 20. *If* $\alpha = 1 + \frac{1}{a_0^2} > 1$, *we have* $a_0 > 0$, $a_1 = 1$, $\lambda = 2a_0$, $\mu = a_0^2 - \frac{1}{1-\alpha}$, *and* $\omega = 0$, *from which we obtain the solution*

$$u_{20}(x) = e^{-a_0 x}\left(1 - e^{2a_0(A+x)}\right), \quad A \in \mathbb{R}. \tag{33}$$

Solution 21. If $\alpha = 1 - \frac{2}{a_1^2}$, we have $a_0 < 0$, $a_1 = -2a_0^2$, $\lambda = \frac{2a_0}{a_1}$, $\mu = \frac{2a_0^2 + a_1}{2a_1^2}$, and $\omega = 0$, from which we obtain the solution

$$u_{21}(x) = e^{-a_0 x}\left(1 - e^{-\frac{x+A}{a_0}}\right)^{2a_0}, \quad A \in \mathbb{R}. \tag{34}$$

Note that given the restriction for a_1, $\alpha = 1 + \frac{1}{a_1^2} > 1$.

Solution 22. If $\alpha = 1 - \frac{2}{a_1}$, we have $a_0 = a_0$, $a_1 < 0$, $\lambda = \frac{2a_0}{a_1}$, $\mu = \frac{2a_0^2 + a_1}{2a_1^2}$, and $\omega = 0$, from which we obtain the solution

$$u_{22}(x) = \left(\sqrt{-\frac{2}{a_1}}\, a_1 \cosh\left(\frac{x+A}{\sqrt{-2a_1}}\right) + 2a_0 \sinh\left(\frac{x+A}{\sqrt{-2a_1}}\right)\right)^{a_1}, \quad A \in \mathbb{R}. \tag{35}$$

Note that $\alpha > 1$, given that $a_1 < 0$.

Some of the solutions are exponential, but there are also spike solutions, as in Solution 18.

Figure 6 illustrates, for $\alpha = 5$, that the distribution of the bacterial population takes a bell-shaped curve in the steady state. In this scenario, the bacteria form an aggregate, and the density of the aggregate is determined by the value of a_0. When this value increases, the distance required for the bacteria to join and form an aggregate also increases. As a result, the bacteria are farther apart from each other, leading to a lower overall density of aggregates.

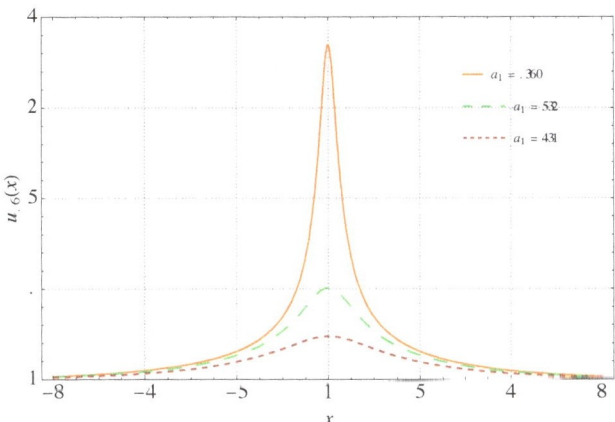

Figure 6. Solution 18 for fixed $A = 0$ and $\alpha = 5$. We show tree cases for $a_0 = 1.85, 2.3, 4$, as a_0 increases the amplitude of the spike decreases.

3.3. Brief Description of the Modified Exponential Function Method

The Exp-method was introduced to find solitary, compact, and periodic solutions of nonlinear wave-like equations [32]. It has been applied, for instance, to obtain soliton-type solutions for the Allen–Cahn equation, a reaction–diffusion equation describing phase separation in multi-alloy systems, and plasma dynamics [33]. The algorithm of the method is given below.

Step 1: We assume the exact solutions to Equation (6) can also be formulated as follows:

$$\phi(\xi) = \frac{\sum_{i=0}^{N} a_i (e^{-Q(\xi)})^i}{\sum_{j=0}^{M} b_i (e^{-Q(\xi)})^j}, \tag{36}$$

where the a_i and b_j are arbitrary constants with $a_N \neq 0$, $b_M \neq 0$, and the function Q satisfies the differential equation [32,33]:

$$Q_\xi = \lambda + \mu e^{Q(\xi)} + e^{-Q(\xi)}. \tag{37}$$

Consequently, the function Q satisfies the same differential equation given in Equation (24). The integers N and M that appear in this method can be determined in the same way as before by considering the homogeneous balance between the higher-order derivatives and the nonlinear factors in Equation (6). In this case, $N = 2$ and $M = 1$.

The second, third, and fourth steps of the current procedure are identical to those outlined in Section 3.2.

Solutions Found by the Modified Exponential Function Method

The nonlinear algebraic system of equations necessary to obtain solutions according to the exponential function method can be seen in Equation (A29) of Appendix E. Next we show the solutions we obtain by this method. For $\alpha = 0$, we find three stationary and three traveling solutions below.

Solution 23. *If* $\alpha = 0$, $a_0 = 0$, $a_1 = a_1$, $a_2 = 2b_1$, $b_0 = 0$, $b_1 \neq 0$, $\lambda = \frac{a_1}{b_1}$, $\mu = \frac{a_1^2 + b_1^2}{4b_1^2}$ *and* $\omega = 0$, *from which we obtain the solution*

$$u_{23}(x) = \left(a_1 \cos\left(\frac{x+A}{2}\right) - b_1 \sin\left(\frac{x+A}{2}\right) \right)^2, \quad A \in \mathbb{R}. \tag{38}$$

Solution 24. *If* $\alpha = 0$, $a_0 \neq 0$, $a_1 = 0$, $a_2 = -\frac{a_0}{\mu}$, $b_0 = 0$, $b_1 = -\frac{a_0}{\mu}$, $\lambda = \mp\sqrt{4\mu - 1}$, $\mu \neq 0$ *and* $\omega = 0$, *from which we obtain the solution*

$$u_{24}(x) = \frac{1}{2}\left(\sqrt{4\mu - 1}\cos(x+A) \pm \sin(x+A) + \sqrt{4\mu - 1} \right), \quad A \in \mathbb{R}. \tag{39}$$

Solution 25. *If* $\alpha = 0$, $a_0 \neq 0$, $a_1 = 0$, $a_2 = -\frac{a_0}{\mu}$, $b_0 = 0$, $b_1 = -\frac{a_0}{\mu}$, $\lambda = \sqrt{4\mu - 1}$, $\mu \neq 0$ *and* $\omega = 0$, *from which we obtain the solution*

$$u_{25}(x) = \frac{1}{2}\left(\sqrt{4\mu - 1}\cos(x+A) - \sin(x+A) + \sqrt{4\mu - 1} \right), \quad A \in \mathbb{R}. \tag{40}$$

Solution 26. *If* $\alpha = 0$, $a_0 = 0$, $a_1 = a_1$, $a_2 = b_1$, $b_0 = a_1$, $b_1 \neq 0$, $\lambda \neq 0$, $\mu = 0$ *and* $\omega = -\lambda^3 - \lambda$, *from which we obtain the solution*

$$u_{26}(x,t) = \sinh(A\lambda) + \cosh(A\lambda) + \sinh\left(\lambda^4 t + \lambda^2 t + \lambda x\right) - \cosh\left(\lambda^4 t + \lambda^2 t + \lambda x\right), \quad A \in \mathbb{R}. \tag{41}$$

Solution 27. *If* $\alpha = 0$, $a_0 = 0$, $a_1 = 0$, $a_2 = b_1$, $b_0 = \frac{b_1 \lambda}{2}$, $b_1 \neq 0$, $\lambda \neq 0$, $\mu = 0$ *and* $\omega = -2(4\lambda^3 + \lambda)$, *from which we obtain the solution*

$$u_{27}(x,t) = \sinh(2A\lambda) + \cosh(2A\lambda) + \sinh\left(16\lambda^4 t + 4\lambda^2 t + 2\lambda x\right) - \cosh\left(16\lambda^4 t + 4\lambda^2 t + 2\lambda x\right), \quad A \in \mathbb{R}. \tag{42}$$

Solution 28. *If* $\alpha = 0$, $a_0 = 0$, $a_1 \neq 0$, $a_2 = b_1$, $b_0 = 0$, $b_1 \neq 0$, $\lambda = \frac{a_1}{b_1}$, $\mu = 0$ *and* $\omega = \frac{a_1(a_1^2 + b_1^2)}{b_1^3}$, *from which we obtain the solution*

$$u_{28}(x,t) = \sinh\left(-\lambda A + \lambda^2(\lambda^2 + 1)t - \lambda x\right) - \cosh\left(-\lambda A + \lambda^2(\lambda^2 + 1)t - \lambda x\right) + 1, \quad A \in \mathbb{R}. \tag{43}$$

In this case, we have three standing wave-like solutions and three traveling wavefront-like solutions, close to those obtained with previous methods. Additionally, these solutions also depend on the parameters of the method.

Seven stationary solutions were found for the pre-pattern formation region, $\alpha < 1$, all oscillatory functions, which are presented next.

Solution 29. *If $\alpha < 1$, $a_0 = -\frac{b_1}{8}$, $a_1 = 0$, $a_2 = b_1$, $b_0 = 0$, $b_1 \neq 0$, $\lambda = 0$, $\mu = \frac{1}{8}$ and $\omega = 0$, from which we obtain the solution*

$$u_{29}(x) = C \sin\left(\frac{x+B}{\sqrt{1-\alpha}}\right), \quad C \neq 0, \quad B \in \mathbb{R}. \tag{44}$$

Solution 30. *If $\alpha < 1$, $a_0 = 0$, $a_1 = a_1$, $a_2 = b_1$, $b_0 = 0$, $b_1 \neq 0$, $\lambda = \frac{2a_1}{b_1}$, $\mu = \frac{\alpha a_1^2 - a_1^2 - b_1^2}{(\alpha-1)b_1^2}$ and $\omega = 0$, from which we obtain the solution*

$$u_{30}(x) = a_1 \cos\left(\sqrt{\frac{1}{1-\alpha}}(x+A)\right) - \sqrt{\frac{1}{1-\alpha}} b_1 \sin\left(\sqrt{\frac{1}{1-\alpha}}(x+A)\right), \quad A \in \mathbb{R}. \tag{45}$$

Solution 31. *If $\alpha < 1$, $a_0 = 0$, $a_1 = a_1$, $a_2 = -\frac{2b_1}{\alpha-1}$, $b_0 = 0$, $b_1 \neq 0$, $\lambda = \frac{a_1 - \alpha a_1}{b_1}$, $\mu = -\frac{(\alpha-1)\left(-\alpha a_1^2 + a_1^2 + b_1^2\right)}{4b_1^2}$ and $\omega = 0$, from which we obtain the solution*

$$u_{31}(x) = \left(-(1-\alpha)a_1 \cos\left(\frac{1}{2}\sqrt{1-\alpha}(A+x)\right) + b_1\sqrt{1-\alpha}\sin\left(\frac{1}{2}\sqrt{1-\alpha}(A+x)\right)\right)^{\frac{2}{1-\alpha}}, \quad A \in \mathbb{R}. \tag{46}$$

Solution 32. *If $\alpha < 1$, $a_0 \neq 0$, $a_1 = 0$, $a_2 = -\frac{a_0}{\mu}$, $b_0 = 0$, $b_1 = -\frac{a_0}{\mu}$, $\lambda = 0$, $\mu = -\frac{1}{4(\alpha-1)}$ and $\omega = 0$, from which we obtain the solution*

$$u_{32}(x) = \frac{1}{2}\sin\left(\sqrt{\frac{1}{1-\alpha}}(x+A)\right), \quad A \in \mathbb{R}. \tag{47}$$

Solution 33. *If $\alpha = \frac{1}{3}$, $a_0 = 0$, $a_1 = a_1$, $a_2 = 3b_1$, $b_0 = 0$, $b_1 \neq 0$, $\lambda = \frac{2a_1}{3b_1}$, $\mu = \frac{2a_1^2 + 3b_1^2}{18b_1^2}$ and $\omega = 0$, from which we obtain the solution*

$$u_{33}(x) = \left(2a_1 \cos\left(\frac{x+A}{\sqrt{6}}\right) - \sqrt{6}b_1 \sin\left(\frac{x+A}{\sqrt{6}}\right)\right)^3, \quad A \in \mathbb{R}. \tag{48}$$

Solution 34. *If $\alpha = \frac{1}{2}$, $a_0 \neq 0$, $a_1 = 0$, $a_2 = -\frac{3a_0}{\mu}$, $b_0 = 0$, $b_1 - \frac{a_0}{\mu}$, $\lambda = 0$, $\mu = \frac{1}{8}$ and $\omega = 0$, from which we obtain the solution*

$$u_{34}(x) = \sin^3\left(\frac{x+A}{2\sqrt{2}}\right)\cos\left(\frac{x+A}{2\sqrt{2}}\right), \quad A \in \mathbb{R}. \tag{49}$$

Solution 35. *If $\alpha = \frac{1}{2}$, $a_0 \neq 0$, $a_1 = 0$, $a_2 = -\frac{a_0}{3\mu}$, $b_0 = 0$, $b_1 = -\frac{a_0}{3\mu}$, $\lambda = 0$, $\mu = \frac{1}{8}$ and $\omega = 0$, from which we obtain the solution*

$$u_{35}(x) = \frac{1}{8}\left(\sin\left(\sqrt{2}(A+x)\right) + 2\sin\left(\frac{x+A}{\sqrt{2}}\right)\right), \quad A \in \mathbb{R}. \tag{50}$$

Three of the five solutions in the instability region are time-independent, and two are time-dependent. With these solutions, one of the difficulties is that they involve increasingly more parameters external to the model.

Solution 36. If $\alpha > 1$, $a_0 = 0$, $a_1 = -\frac{b_1}{\sqrt{\alpha-1}}$, $a_2 = -\frac{2b_1}{\alpha-1}$, $b_0 = 0$, $b_1 \neq 0$, $\lambda = \sqrt{\alpha-1}$, $\mu = 0$ and $\omega = 0$, from which we obtain the solution

$$u_{36}(x) = e^{\frac{x}{\sqrt{\alpha-1}}} \left(1 - e^{\sqrt{\alpha-1}(A+x)}\right)^{\frac{2}{1-\alpha}}, \quad A \in \mathbb{R}. \tag{51}$$

Solution 37. If $\alpha = \frac{a_1^2 + b_1^2}{a_1^2}$, $a_0 = 0$, $a_1 \neq 0$, $a_2 = b_1$, $b_0 = 0$, $b_1 \neq 0$, $\lambda = \frac{2a_1}{b_1}$, $\mu = 0$ and $\omega = 0$, from which we obtain the solution

$$u_{37}(x) = e^{-\frac{\lambda x}{2}} \left(1 - e^{\lambda(x+A)}\right), \quad A \in \mathbb{R}. \tag{52}$$

Solution 38. If $\alpha = \frac{a_1^2 + b_1^2}{a_1^2}$, $a_0 = 0$, $a_1 \neq 0$, $a_2 = \frac{2b_1}{1-\alpha}$, $b_0 = 0$, $b_1 \neq 0$, $\lambda = \frac{a_1 - \alpha a_1}{b_1}$, $\mu = -\frac{(\alpha-1)\left(-\alpha a_1^2 + a_1^2 + b_1^2\right)}{4b_1^2}$ and $\omega = 0$, from which we obtain the solution

$$u_{38}(x) = \frac{e^{\frac{a_1}{b_1} x}}{\left(1 - e^{\frac{a_1}{b_1}(x+A)}\right)^{\frac{2a_1^2}{b_1^2}}}, \quad A \in \mathbb{R}. \tag{53}$$

Solution 39. If $\alpha = 3$, we have $a_0 = \frac{b_1}{6}$, $a_1 = \mp \frac{b_1}{\sqrt{6}}$, $a_2 = b_1$, $b_0 = 0$, $b_1 \neq 0$, $\lambda = \mp\sqrt{\frac{2}{3}}$, $\mu = \frac{1}{6}$, and $\omega = \pm\frac{1}{3}\sqrt{\frac{2b_1}{3}}$, from which we obtain the solution

$$u_{39}(x,t) = \frac{3e^{\pm\left(\frac{A}{\sqrt{6}} - \frac{t}{9} + \frac{x}{\sqrt{6}}\right)} \left(3\sqrt{6}A \mp 2t + 3\sqrt{6}x \mp 18\right)}{9A \mp \sqrt{6}t + 9x}, \quad A \in \mathbb{R}. \tag{54}$$

Solution 40. If $\alpha \neq 1$, $a_0 = a_0$, $a_1 \neq 0$, $b_0 = 0$, $b_1 = 0$, $a_2 = b_2$, $\lambda = \frac{a_1}{\alpha-1}$, $\mu = \frac{(\alpha-1)}{2}$ and $\omega = a_0^3(\alpha-1) + a_0$, from which we obtain the solution

$$u_{40}(x,t) = Ae^{\left(a_0 x + a_0^2 t(a_0^2(\alpha-1)-1)\right)}, \quad A \in \mathbb{R}. \tag{55}$$

These solutions are combinations of exponentials; however, for several parameter values, no spike or wavelet patterns occur, and as a result, these combinations cannot be considered as a distribution.

4. Summary and Conclusions

In this work, we find several families of analytical solutions to the CWK equation for different values of the parameters, not only in the instability region. For this purpose, we use the generalized Kudryashov method, the $e^{-R(\xi)}$-expansion, and exponential function methods, which allows us to find exact solutions of nonlinear differential equations, including those with variable coefficients, non-integer powers, singular perturbation problems, and non-polynomial nonlinearities. These methods allow us to find analytical solutions to the CWK equation that have not been previously reported in the literature. Specifically, when $\alpha \neq 0$, the nonlinearity in the CWK equation cannot be analyzed with conventional methods. Our solutions are important because they provide insights into the behavior of the system and can be used in numerical simulations or experiments. Moreover, they can be used to develop new mathematical tools and techniques for analyzing and solving other nonlinear differential equations in fluid mechanics and related fields.

We found twenty-seven analytical solutions in the case $\alpha \neq 0$ by using the three methods. In the $\alpha < 1$ case, the nonlinear term can be considered a perturbation of the linear behavior where inverse diffusion and fourth-order terms drive the dynamics. Although structure formation is not expected here, we find several wave-like stationary solutions.

Thus, this region can be considered a pre-pattern formation region, and the solutions are budding patterns. The instability region $\alpha > 1$ is where this model's aggregate formation is expected. We first recover the stationary solution found in [14] and a pulse propagating without deformation by the generalized Kudryashov method. Some similar spike-like solutions were found by the e^{-R}-expansion method. The exponential function method did not yield any new physical solutions beyond those obtained by previous methods. This is not surprising, given that N.A. Kudryashov observed this in [27].

It is worth emphasizing that these methods allow us to obtain a wide range of behaviors, some previously obtained and that qualitatively resemble what was seen in the experiments. Furthermore, reverse diffusion and fourth-order terms still need to be explored since the traveling solutions were mainly found in this regime. The pattern formation and pulse motion mechanism could be better understood by studying each case in depth. On the other hand, the shortcoming of these methods is the large number of free parameters that appear in the solutions. One only way to fix them is to consider initial and boundary value problems, making the solutions more realistic and closer to the experimental phototaxis conditions, even in simple models like the one-dimensional CWK equation. We strongly believe the collection of physically meaningful solutions can guide the study of bacterial aggregate formation in phototaxis.

Author Contributions: Methodology, Software, Formal analysis, Writing—Original Draft, Visualization, A.L.-R.; Conceptualization, Methodology, Investigation, Supervision, O.G.-G.; Conceptualization, Methodology, Investigation, Supervision, G.C.-A. All authors have read and agreed to the published version of the manuscript.

Funding: This research received no external funding.

Data Availability Statement: Not applicable.

Acknowledgments: ALR declares that he received support from the Mexican Council of Science and Technology (CONACyT), through scholarship No. 798462.

Conflicts of Interest: The authors declare no conflict of interest.

Appendix A. Stability Analysis

In [14], the authors derive Equation (1) from the continuum limit of the system of differential equations over a lattice formed by n bins, which is given by

$$\begin{cases} \dfrac{dR_j}{dt} = aR_{j-1} - (a+c)R_j + cU_{j-1}\eta_{j-1}^+ \\ \dfrac{dL_j}{dt} = aL_{j+1} - (a+c)L_j + cU_{j+1}\eta_{j+1}^- \end{cases} \quad (A1)$$

where

$$\eta_j^\pm = \frac{\sum_{k=1}^d U_{j\pm k}}{\sum_{k=1}^d (U_{j+k} + U_{j-k})} \quad \text{and} \quad U_j = L_j + R_j. \quad (A2)$$

Here, $R_j(t)$ and $L_j(t)$ represent the density of right- and left-moving bacteria in the bin $j = 1, ..., n$ at time t; a represents the rate at which the bacterium moves one bin according to its orientation; and c represents the rate at which the bacterium moves after transitioning to a new orientation. The parameter d is the sensing radius of the bacterium.

Considering that $U_j = L_j + R_j$ and adding the two equalities of the system (A1), we obtain

$$\frac{dU_j}{dt} = a(R_{j-1} + L_{j+1}) - (a+c)U_j + c(U_{j-1}\eta_{j-1}^+ + U_{j+1}\eta_{j+1}^-). \quad (A3)$$

A closed system can be constructed by defining

$$V_j = R_{j+1} + L_{j-1}. \quad (A4)$$

Observe that immediately from system (A1) and (A2) we have

$$\begin{cases} \dfrac{dR_{j+1}}{dt} = aR_j - (a+c)R_{j+1} + cU_j\eta_j^+ \\ \dfrac{dL_{j-1}}{dt} = aL_j - (a+c)L_{j-1} + cU_j\eta_j^-. \end{cases} \quad (A5)$$

Now, adding the two equations in (A5), we obtain

$$\dfrac{dV_j}{dt} = (a+c)(U_j - V_j). \quad (A6)$$

Now, rewriting

$$R_{j-1} + L_{j+1} = U_{j-1} + U_{j+1} - V_j, \quad (A7)$$

we conclude that the system (A1) is equivalent to

$$\begin{cases} \dfrac{dU_j}{dt} = a(U_{j-1} + U_{j+1} - V_j) - (a+c)U_j + c(U_{j-1}\eta_{j-1}^+ + U_{j+1}\eta_{j+1}^-) \\ \dfrac{dV_j}{dt} = (a+c)(U_j - V_j). \end{cases} \quad (A8)$$

Model (A1) clearly allows for a homogeneous equilibrium $L_j = R_j = C$ for any constant C. Now, we will analyze the stability of this equilibrium. It is easier and more practical to conduct the analysis for the system (A8) whose steady state is given by $U_j = V_j = V$. Consider the following perturbations:

$$U_j = V + \xi_j(t); \quad V_j = V + \rho_j(t), \quad j = 1, 2, \ldots, n \quad (A9)$$

where $|\xi_j|, |\rho_j| \ll 1$. We now obtain the linearized system from the system (A8):

$$\dfrac{d\xi_k}{dt} = (a+c/2)(\xi_{k-1} + \xi_{j+1}) - a\rho_j - (a+c)\xi_j$$
$$+ \dfrac{c}{2d}(2\xi_j + \xi_{j-1} + \xi_{j+1} - \xi_{j+d} - \xi_{j-d} - \xi_{j+d+1} - \xi_{j-d-1}) \quad (A10)$$

$$\dfrac{d\rho_j}{dt} = (a+c)(\xi_j - \rho_j). \quad (A11)$$

This $(2n) \times (2n)$ linear problem can be divided down into n subproblems of 2×2. Make an ansatz

$$\xi_j = \xi e^{\lambda t} e^{\frac{2\pi m j i}{n}}; \quad \rho_j = \rho e^{\lambda t} e^{\frac{2\pi m j i}{n}}, \quad m = 0, 1, \ldots, n-1 \quad (A12)$$

to obtain

$$\lambda \xi = (2a+c)\xi \cos(\theta) - a\rho - (a+c)\xi$$
$$+ \dfrac{c}{2d}\xi(1 + \cos(\theta) - \cos(d\theta) - \cos((d+1)\theta)) \quad (A13)$$

$$\lambda \rho = (a+c)(\xi - \rho) \quad (A14)$$

Here, $\theta = \dfrac{2\pi m}{n}$ with $m = 0, 1, \ldots, n-1$.

There are two eigenvalues for each possible value of m, for a total of $2n$ eigenvalues. The quadratic equation

$$\lambda^2 - (g(\theta) - c)\lambda - (a+c)g(\theta) = 0 \quad (A15)$$

gives the solution to the 2×2 eigenvalue Problems (A13) and (A14), where function g is defined as

$$g(\theta) = (2a+c)\big(\cos(\theta)-1\big) + \frac{c}{2d}\big(1+\cos(\theta)-\cos(d\theta)-\cos((d+1)\theta)\big). \tag{A16}$$

Note that $g(\theta) - c \leq 0$ for all θ so that a sufficient and necessary condition for stability is that $g(\theta) < 0$ for all θ.

Computations reveal that the instability occurs for the first time at $\theta = 0$. Because $g(0) = g'(0) = 0$, the value of the threshold can be determined by setting $g''(0) = dc - 2a = 0$. Consequently, we conclude that the critical value of the threshold is $c_0 = \frac{2a}{d}$. The homogeneous steady state is therefore stable when $c < c_0$ and unstable when $c > c_0$, i.e., it is unstable if $c > \frac{2a}{d}$. The conclusion is obtained by spectral equivalence.

Appendix B. Separation of Variables Method for the Linear Case $\alpha = 0$

Here, we discuss the case $\alpha = 0$ occurring when, after changing orientation, the bacterium stops $c = 0$, or when the rate of motion without changing orientation is very large $a \to \infty$, both for all finite d. In this case, Equation (1) reduces to the linear differential equation $u_t = -u_{xx} - u_{xxxx}$, i.e., only the reverse diffusion and long-range terms. The aggregate size is controlled by α, so we cannot refer here to finger-like solutions. This equation can be solved by the well-known method of separation of variables where $u(x,t) = f(x)g(t)$ leads to the following:

$$\frac{g'}{g} = -\frac{(f''+f'''')}{f} = \gamma^2, \tag{A17}$$

where the solutions can be directly obtained by considering the three possible cases for the separation parameter γ^2:

Case A1. $\gamma^2 = 0$

$$g' = 0 \quad \text{and} \quad f'''' + f'' = 0. \tag{A18}$$

solving two linear differential equations gives

$$g(t) = c_1 \quad \text{and} \quad f(x) = k_1 + k_2 x + k_3 \cos(x) + k_4 \sin(x) \tag{A19}$$

from which we obtain the family of solutions

$$u_A(x,t) = C_1 + C_2 x + C_3 \cos(x) + C_4 \sin(x), \quad C_1, C_2, C_3, C_4 \subset \mathbb{R}. \tag{A20}$$

Case A2. $\gamma^2 > 0$

$$g' - \gamma^2 g = 0 \quad \text{and} \quad f'''' + f'' + \gamma^2 f = 0. \tag{A21}$$

solving two linear differential equations gives

$$g(t) = c_1 e^{\gamma^2 t} \quad \text{and} \quad f(x) = k_1 e^{\left(\frac{-1-\beta}{2}\right)x} + k_2 e^{\left(\frac{-1+\beta}{2}\right)x} + k_3 x e^{\left(\frac{-1-\beta}{2}\right)x} + k_4 x e^{\left(\frac{-1+\beta}{2}\right)x} \tag{A22}$$

from which, considering $\beta = \sqrt{1-4\gamma^2}$, we obtain the family of solutions

$$u_B(x,t) = e^{\gamma^2 t}\bigg(C_1 e^{\left(\frac{-1-\beta}{2}\right)x} + C_2 e^{\left(\frac{-1+\beta}{2}\right)x} + C_3 x e^{\left(\frac{-1-\beta}{2}\right)x} + C_4 x e^{\left(\frac{-1+\beta}{2}\right)x}\bigg), \quad C_1, C_2, C_3, C_4 \in \mathbb{R}. \tag{A23}$$

Case A3. $\gamma^2 < 0$

$$g' + \gamma^2 g = 0 \quad \text{and} \quad f'''' + f'' - \gamma^2 f = 0. \tag{A24}$$

solving two linear differential equations gives

$$g(t) = c_1 e^{-\gamma^2 t} \quad \text{and} \quad f(x) = k_1 e^{\left(\frac{-1-\delta}{2}\right)x} + k_2 e^{\left(\frac{-1+\delta}{2}\right)x} + k_3 x e^{\left(\frac{-1-\delta}{2}\right)x} + k_4 x e^{\left(\frac{-1+\delta}{2}\right)x} \quad \text{(A25)}$$

from which, considering $\delta = \sqrt{1 + 4\gamma^2}$, we obtain the family of solutions

$$u_C(x,t) = e^{-\gamma^2 t} \left(C_1 e^{\left(\frac{-1-\delta}{2}\right)x} + C_2 e^{\left(\frac{-1+\delta}{2}\right)x} + C_3 x e^{\left(\frac{-1-\delta}{2}\right)x} + C_4 x e^{\left(\frac{-1+\delta}{2}\right)x} \right), \quad C_1, C_2, C_3, C_4 \in \mathbb{R}. \quad \text{(A26)}$$

All five constants in each case can be fixed through the corresponding initial and boundary conditions. We generally observe that, according to the sign of γ^2, we can have oscillatory solutions or increasing and decreasing exponential solutions. Consider also that the principle of superposition of solutions is valid for the present linear case. We have one family of standing wave-like solutions and two families of traveling wavefront-like solutions, similar to those obtained with the previous methods. Moreover, these solutions coincide with those obtained with the proposed methods. We show some examples of this below.

Example A1. *If we consider the family of solutions u_1:*

$$u_1(x,t) = \cosh(2t - x) - \sinh(2t - x) = e^{-(2t-x)} + 1,$$

this is derived from the present method using u_C and considering $C_1 = 0$, $C_2 = 1$, $\delta - 1 = 2$, $\gamma^2 = 4$, $C_3 = C_4 = 0$.

Example A2. *If we consider the family of solutions u_3:*

$$u_3(x,t) = \cosh(20t + 2x) - \sinh(20t + 2x) = e^{-(2x+20t)} - 1,$$

this is derived from the present method using u_C and considering $C_1 = 0$, $C_2 = 1$, $\delta - 1 = -4$, $\gamma^2 = 20$, $C_3 = C_4 = 0$.

Example A3. *If we consider the family of solutions u_{13}:*

$$u_{13}(x) = e^{-\lambda\left((\lambda^3 + \lambda)t + x\right)} - e^{\lambda A},$$

this is derived from the present method using u_C and considering $C_1 = 1$, $C_2 = 0$, $\delta + 1 = 2\lambda$, $\gamma^2 = \lambda^4 + \lambda^2$, $C_3 = C_4 = 0$; moreover, $e^{\lambda A}$ is a constant.

Example A4. *If we consider the family of solutions u_{28}:*

$$u_{28}(x,t) = \sinh\left(-\lambda A + \lambda^2(\lambda^2 + 1)t - \lambda x\right) - \cosh\left(-\lambda A + \lambda^2(\lambda^2 + 1)t - \lambda x\right) + 1,$$

this is derived from the present method using u_C and considering $C_1 = 0$, $C_2 = -e^{\lambda A}$, $\delta - 1 = 2\lambda$, $\gamma^2 = \lambda^2(\lambda^2 + 1)$, $C_3 = C_4 = 0$.

The other families for $\alpha = 0$ are obtained similarly and consider the superposition principle. In the present case of $\alpha = 0$, aggregate formation is not expected when the nonlinear term does not appear in the CWK equation. However, among the solutions found are time-propagating wavefront solutions and some standing wave solutions that could be interpreted as finger-shaped distributions. Such solutions are interesting but cannot be considered a final steady state; they must start with that form.

Unfortunately, for $\alpha \neq 0$, Equation (1) is nonlinear. Note that when the derivative is expanded, the nonlinearity becomes more involved:

$$u_t = -u_{xx} - u_{xxxx} + \alpha \left[\frac{u u_x u_{xxx} + u u_{xx}^2 - u_x^2 u_{xx}}{u^2} \right].$$

This equation cannot always be solved by the method of separation of variables, nor can all the families of solutions found in this work be obtained.

Appendix C. Algebraic System for Kudryashov Method

The Kudryashov method algorithm requires solving the following system of equations for the unknowns $\{a_0, a_1, a_2, b_0, b_1, \omega\}$.

$$Q^0: \quad \alpha a_0^4 + a_0 b_0^3 \omega - a_0^2 b_0^2 - a_0^4 = 0,$$

$$\begin{aligned}Q^1: \quad & 4\alpha a_1 a_0^3 + 4\alpha a_0^3 b_1 - 4\alpha a_1 a_0^2 b_0 - \alpha a_0^2 b_0 b_1 + \alpha a_1 a_0 b_0^2 + 3 a_0 b_0^2 b_1 \omega + a_1 b_0^3 \omega - 6 a_0^3 b_1 \\ & + 6 a_1 a_0^2 b_0 + 2 a_0^2 b_0 b_1 - 6 a_1 a_0 b_0^2 - 2 a_0 b_0^2 b_1 + 2 a_1 b_0^3 - 4 a_1 a_0^3 = 0,\end{aligned}$$

$$\begin{aligned}Q^2: \quad & 4\alpha a_2 a_0^3 + 6\alpha a_1^2 a_0^2 - 4\alpha a_0^3 b_1 + 2\alpha a_0^2 b_1^2 + 4\alpha a_1 a_0^2 b_0 - 8\alpha a_2 a_0^2 b_0 + 8\alpha a_1 a_0^2 b_1 + 3\alpha a_0^2 b_0 b_1 \\ & - 3\alpha a_1 a_0 b_0^2 + 4\alpha a_2 a_0 b_0^2 - 8\alpha a_1^2 a_0 b_0 - 4\alpha a_1 a_0 b_0 b_1 + 2\alpha a_1^2 b_0^2 + 3 a_0 b_0 b_1^2 \omega \\ & + a_2 b_0^3 \omega + 3 a_1 b_0^2 b_1 \omega + 6 a_0^3 b_1 - 8 a_0^2 b_1^2 - 6 a_1 a_0^2 b_0 + 12 a_2 a_0^2 b_0 - 12 a_1 a_0^2 b_1 \\ & - 12 a_0^2 b_0 b_1 + 12 a_1 a_0 b_0^2 - 18 a_2 a_0 b_0^2 + 2 a_0 b_0 b_1^2 + 12 a_1^2 a_0 b_0 + 8 a_0 b_0^2 b_1 \\ & + 10 a_1 a_0 b_0 b_1 - 8 a_1 b_0^3 + 10 a_2 b_0^3 - 8 a_1^2 b_0^2 - 2 a_1 b_0^2 b_1 - 4 a_2 a_0^3 - 6 a_1^2 a_0^2 = 0,\end{aligned} \quad \text{(A27)}$$

$$\begin{aligned}Q^3: \quad & 4\alpha a_0 a_1^3 + 12\alpha a_0^2 a_2 a_1 - 4\alpha a_1^3 b_0 - 5\alpha a_1^2 b_0^2 + 8\alpha a_0 a_1^2 b_0 + 4\alpha a_0 a_1^2 b_1 - \alpha a_1^2 b_0 b_1 \\ & + 2\alpha a_0 a_1 b_0^2 + 9\alpha a_2 a_1 b_0^2 + \alpha a_0 a_1 b_1^2 - 24\alpha a_0 a_2 a_1 b_0 - 8\alpha a_0^2 a_1 b_1 + 8\alpha a_0 a_1 b_0 b_1 \\ & - 10\alpha a_0 a_2 b_0^2 - 3\alpha a_0^2 b_1^2 + 8\alpha a_0^2 a_2 b_0 + 4\alpha a_0^2 a_2 b_1 - 2\alpha a_0^2 b_0 b_1 - 2\alpha a_0 a_2 b_0 b_1 \\ & + 3 a_1 b_0 b_1^2 \omega + a_0 b_1^3 \omega + 3 a_2 b_0^2 b_1 \omega + 6 a_1^3 b_0 + 18 a_1^2 b_0^2 - 12 a_0 a_1^2 b_0 - 6 a_0 a_1^2 b_1 \\ & + 2 a_1^2 b_0 b_1 + 12 a_1 b_0^3 - 8 a_0 a_1 b_0^2 - 34 a_2 a_1 b_0^2 - 6 a_0 a_1 b_1^2 + 2 a_1 b_0 b_1^2 + 36 a_0 a_2 a_1 b_0 \\ & + 12 a_0^2 a_1 b_1 + 8 a_1 b_0^2 b_1 - 28 a_0 a_1 b_0 b_1 - 40 a_2 b_0^3 - 2 a_0 b_1^3 + 40 a_0 a_2 b_0^2 + 10 a_0^2 b_1^2 - 8 a_0 b_0 b_1^2 \\ & - 12 a_0^2 a_2 b_0 - 12 a_0 b_0^2 b_1 + 10 a_2 b_0^2 b_1 - 6 a_0^2 a_2 b_1 + 8 a_0^2 b_0 b_1 - 4 a_0 a_1^3 - 12 a_0^2 a_2 a_1 = 0,\end{aligned}$$

$$\begin{aligned}Q^4: \quad & \alpha a_1^4 + 12\alpha a_0 a_2 a_1^2 + 6\alpha a_0^2 a_2^2 + 4\alpha a_1^3 b_0 + 3\alpha a_1^2 b_0^2 - 16\alpha a_2 a_1^2 b_0 - 4\alpha a_0 a_1^2 b_1 \\ & + \alpha a_1^2 b_0 b_1 - 21\alpha a_2 a_1 b_0^2 - \alpha a_0 a_1 b_1^2 + 24\alpha a_0 a_2 a_1 b_0 - 4\alpha a_0 a_1 b_0 b_1 - 18 a_2 a_1 b_0 b_1 \\ & - 4 a_1^2 b_0 b_1 + 4\alpha a_2 a_1 b_0 b_1 + 8\alpha a_2^2 b_0^2 + 6\alpha a_0 a_2 b_0^2 + \alpha a_0^2 b_1^2 - 16\alpha a_0 a_2^2 b_0 - 4\alpha a_0^2 a_2 b_1 \\ & + 2\alpha a_0 a_2 b_0 b_1 + a_1 b_1^3 \omega + 3 a_2 b_0 b_1^2 \omega - 6 a_1^3 b_0 - 11 a_1^2 b_0^2 - a_1^2 b_1^2 + 24 a_2 a_1^2 b_0 + 6 a_0 a_1^2 b_1 \\ & - 6 a_1 b_0^3 + 76 a_2 a_1 b_0^2 + 4 a_0 a_1 b_1^2 - 2 a_1 b_0 b_1^2 - 36 a_0 a_2 a_1 b_0 - 6 a_1 b_0^2 b_1 + 14 a_0 a_1 b_0 b_1 \\ & + 54 a_2 b_0^3 + 2 a_0 b_1^3 - 29 a_2^2 b_0^2 - 24 a_0 a_2 b_0^2 - 3 a_0^2 b_1^2 - 4 a_0 a_2 b_1^2 + 6 a_0 b_0 b_1^2 + 8 a_2 b_0 b_1^2 \\ & + 24 a_0 a_2^2 b_0 + 6 a_0 b_0^2 b_1 - 46 a_2 b_0^2 b_1 + 6 a_0^2 a_2 b_1 - a_1^4 - 12 a_0 a_2 a_1^2 - 6 a_0^2 a_2^2 = 0,\end{aligned}$$

$$\begin{aligned}Q^5: \quad & 4\alpha a_2 a_1^3 + 12\alpha a_0 a_2^2 a_1 + 16\alpha a_2 a_1^2 b_0 - 4\alpha a_2 a_1^2 b_1 + 12\alpha a_2 a_1 b_0^2 + \alpha a_2 a_1 b_1^2 \\ & + 44 a_2 a_1 b_0 b_1 - 20\alpha a_2^2 a_1 b_0 - 12\alpha a_2 a_1 b_0 b_1 - 18 a_2 b_0^2 + 16\alpha a_0 a_2^2 b_0 - 4\alpha a_0 a_2^2 b_1 \\ & + 7\alpha a_2^2 b_0 b_1 + a_2 b_1^3 \omega - 24 a_2 a_1^2 b_0 + 6 a_2 a_1^2 b_1 - 44 a_2 a_1 b_0^2 - 6 a_2 a_1 b_1^2 + 30 a_2^2 a_1 b_0 \\ & - 24 a_2 b_0^3 + 2 a_2 b_1^3 + 64 a_2^2 b_0^2 + 4 a_0 a_2 b_1^2 - 32 a_2 b_0 b_1^2 - 24 a_0 a_2^2 b_0 + 6 a_0 a_2^2 b_1 \\ & + 72 a_2 b_0^2 b_1 - 26 a_2^2 b_0 b_1 - 4 a_0 a_2 b_0 b_1 - 4 a_2 a_1^3 - 12 a_0 a_2^2 a_1 = 0,\end{aligned}$$

$$Q^6: \quad 4\alpha a_0 a_2^3 + 6\alpha a_1^2 a_2^2 - 8\alpha a_2^3 b_0 + 10\alpha a_2^2 b_0^2 + 2\alpha a_2^2 b_1^2 + 20\alpha a_1 a_2^2 b_0 + 12 a_2^3 b_0$$
$$+ 4\alpha a_0 a_2^2 b_1 - 8\alpha a_1 a_2^2 b_1 - 17\alpha a_2^2 b_0 b_1 - 3\alpha a_1 a_2 b_1^2 + 4\alpha a_1^2 a_2 b_1 + 8\alpha a_1 a_2 b_0 b_1$$
$$- 36 a_2^2 b_0^2 - 8 a_2^2 b_1^2 - 30 a_1 a_2^2 b_0 - 6 a_0 a_2^2 b_1 + 12 a_1 a_2^2 b_1 + 60 a_2^2 b_0 b_1 - 8 a_2 b_1^3 - 2 a_0 a_2 b_1^2$$
$$+ 12 a_1 a_2 b_1^2 + 48 a_2 b_0 b_1^2 - 6 a_1^2 a_2 b_1 - 36 a_2 b_0^2 b_1 - 30 a_1 a_2 b_0 b_1 - 4 a_0 a_2^3 - 6 a_1^2 a_2^2 = 0,$$

$$Q^7: \quad 4\alpha a_1 a_2^3 + 8\alpha a_2^3 b_0 - 4\alpha a_2^3 b_1 - 5\alpha a_2^2 b_1^2 + 8\alpha a_1 a_2^2 b_1 + 10\alpha a_2^2 b_0 b_1 + 2\alpha a_1 a_2 b_1^2 - 12 a_2^3 b_0$$
$$+ 6 a_2^3 b_1 + 18 a_2^2 b_1^2 - 12 a_1 a_2^2 b_1 - 36 a_2^2 b_0 b_1 + 12 a_2 b_1^3 - 8 a_1 a_2 b_1^2 - 24 a_2 b_0 b_1^2 - 4 a_1 a_2^3 = 0,$$

$$Q^8: \quad \alpha a_2^4 + 4\alpha a_2^3 b_1 + 3\alpha a_2^2 b_1^2 - 6 a_2^3 b_1 - 11 a_2^2 b_1^2 - 6 a_2 b_1^3 - a_2^4 = 0.$$

Appendix D. Algebraic System for the $e^{-R(\xi)}$-Expansion Method

In the algorithm of the $e^{-R(\xi)}$-expansion method, the algorithm needs to solve the following system of equations for the a_0, a_1, and ω; here we present the system for each power of $e^{-R(\xi)}$ from 0 to 4.

$$e^0: \quad a_1\mu\Big((\alpha-3)a_1\mu + \lambda^2 + 2\mu + 1\Big) + a_0((\alpha-4)a_1\lambda\mu + \omega)$$
$$+ a_0^2((6-4\alpha)a_1\mu - 1) + (\alpha-1)a_0^4 = 0,$$

$$e^{-R(z)}: \quad \alpha a_0 a_1 \lambda^2 + 3\alpha a_1^2 \lambda\mu - 4\alpha a_0^2 a_1 \lambda - 8\alpha a_0 a_1^2 \mu + 2\alpha a_0 a_1 \mu$$
$$+ 4\alpha a_0^3 a_1 + a_1 \lambda^3 - 4 a_0 a_1 \lambda^2 - 10 a_1^2 \lambda\mu + 8 a_1 \lambda\mu + 6 a_0^2 a_1 \lambda$$
$$+ a_1 \lambda + 12 a_0 a_1^2 \mu - 8 a_0 a_1 \mu + a_1 \omega - 4 a_0^3 a_1 - 2 a_0 a_1 = 0,$$

$$e^{-2R(z)}: \quad 2\alpha a_1^2 \lambda^2 - 8\alpha a_0 a_1^2 \lambda + 3\alpha a_0 a_1 \lambda - 4\alpha a_1^3 \mu + 4\alpha a_1^2 \mu$$
$$+ 6\alpha a_0^2 a_1^2 - 4\alpha a_0^2 a_1 - 7 a_1^2 \lambda^2 + 7 a_1 \lambda^2 + 12 a_0 a_1^2 \lambda - 12 a_0 a_1 \lambda \quad \text{(A28)}$$
$$+ 6 a_1^3 \mu - 14 a_1^2 \mu + 8 a_1 \mu - 6 a_0^2 a_1^2 - a_1^2 + 6 a_0^2 a_1 + a_1 = 0,$$

$$e^{-3R(z)}: \quad -4\alpha a_1^3 \lambda + 5\alpha a_1^2 \lambda + 4\alpha a_0 a_1^3 - 8\alpha a_0 a_1^2 + 2\alpha a_0 a_1$$
$$+ 6 a_1^3 \lambda - 18 a_1^2 \lambda + 12 a_1 \lambda - 4 a_0 a_1^3 + 12 a_0 a_1^2 - 8 a_0 a_1 = 0,$$

$$e^{-4R(z)}: \quad \alpha a_1^4 - 4\alpha a_1^3 + 3\alpha a_1^2 - a_1^4 + 6 a_1^3 - 11 a_1^2 + 6 a_1 = 0.$$

Appendix E. System of Equations for Exponential Function Method

To obtain solution through the exponential function method, the following nonlinear algebraic system needs to be solved:

$$e^0: \quad a_2\Big(-4a_2 b_1 + a_2^2 + 3 b_1^2\Big)((\alpha-1)a_2 + 2 b_1) = 0,$$

$$e^{Q(z)}: \quad 4\alpha a_1 a_2^3 - 4\alpha a_2^3 b_1 \lambda + 5\alpha a_2^2 b_1^2 \lambda - 8\alpha a_2^3 b_0 - 8\alpha a_1 a_2^2 b_1 + 10\alpha a_2^2 b_0 b_1 + 2\alpha a_1 a_2 b_1^2 + 6 a_2^3 b_1 \lambda$$
$$- 18 a_2^2 b_1^2 \lambda + 12 a_2 b_1^3 \lambda + 12 a_2^3 b_0 + 12 a_1 a_2^2 b_1 - 36 a_2^2 b_0 b_1 - 8 a_1 a_2 b_1^2 + 24 a_2 b_0 b_1^2 - 4 a_1 a_2^3 = 0,$$

$e^{2Q(z)}:$ $\quad 4\alpha a_0 a_2^3 + 6\alpha a_1^2 a_2^2 + 2\alpha a_2^2 b_1^2 \lambda^2 - 8\alpha a_2^3 b_0 \lambda - 8\alpha a_1 a_2^2 b_1 \lambda + 17\alpha a_2^2 b_0 b_1 \lambda + 3\alpha a_1 a_2 b_1^2 \lambda$
$\quad - 4\alpha a_2^3 b_1 \mu + 4\alpha a_2^2 b_1^2 \mu + 10\alpha a_2^2 b_0^2 - 20\alpha a_1 a_2^2 b_0 - 4\alpha a_0 a_2^2 b_1 - 4\alpha a_1^2 a_2 b_1 + 8\alpha a_1 a_2 b_0 b_1$
$\quad - 7 a_2^2 b_1^2 \lambda^2 + 7 a_2 b_1^3 \lambda^2 + 12 a_2^3 b_0 \lambda + 12 a_1 a_2^2 b_1 \lambda - 60 a_2^2 b_0 b_1 \lambda - 12 a_1 a_2 b_1^2 \lambda + 48 a_2 b_0 b_1^2 \lambda$
$\quad + 6 a_2^3 b_1 \mu - 14 a_2^2 b_1^2 \mu + 8 a_2 b_1^3 \mu - 36 a_2^2 b_0^2 - a_2^2 b_1^2 + 30 a_1 a_2^2 b_0 + 6 a_0 a_2^2 b_1 + a_2 b_1^3 - 2 a_0 a_2 b_1^2$
$\quad + 6 a_1^2 a_2 b_1 + 36 a_2 b_0^2 b_1 - 30 a_1 a_2 b_0 b_1 - 4 a_0 a_2^3 - 6 a_1^2 a_2^2 = 0,$

$e^{3Q(z)}:$ $\quad 4\alpha a_2 a_1^3 + 12\alpha a_0 a_2^2 a_1 + \alpha a_2 a_1 b_1^2 \lambda^2 + 7\alpha a_2^2 b_0 b_1 \lambda^2 + 3\alpha a_2^2 b_1^2 \lambda \mu - 4\alpha a_2 a_1^2 b_1 \lambda$
$\quad - 20\alpha a_2^2 a_1 b_0 \lambda + 12\alpha a_2 a_1 b_0 b_1 \lambda + 18\alpha a_2^2 b_0^2 \lambda - 4\alpha a_0 a_2^2 b_1 \lambda + 2\alpha a_2 a_1 b_1^2 \mu$
$\quad - 8\alpha a_2^2 a_1 b_1 \mu - 8\alpha a_2^2 b_0 \mu + 14\alpha a_2^2 b_0 b_1 \mu - 16\alpha a_2 a_1^2 b_0 + 12\alpha a_2 a_1 b_0^2 - 16\alpha a_0 a_2^2 b_0$
$\quad + a_2 b_1^3 \lambda^3 - 4 a_2 a_1 b_1^2 \lambda^2 + 28 a_2 b_0 b_1^2 \lambda^2 - 24 a_2^2 b_0 b_1 \lambda^2 + 8 a_2 b_1^3 \lambda \mu - 10 a_2^2 b_1^2 \lambda \mu$
$\quad + 6 a_2 a_1^2 b_1 \lambda + 30 a_2^2 a_1 b_0 \lambda - 44 a_2 a_1 b_0 b_1 \lambda + a_2 b_1^3 \lambda - 64 a_2^2 b_0^2 \lambda - 4 a_0 a_2 b_1^2 \lambda + 6 a_0 a_2^2 b_1 \lambda$
$\quad + 72 a_2 b_0^2 b_1 \lambda - 8 a_2 a_1 b_1^2 \mu + 12 a_2^2 a_1 b_1 \mu + 32 a_2 b_0 b_1^2 \mu + 12 a_2^3 b_0 \mu - 48 a_2^2 b_0 b_1 \mu$
$\quad + a_2 b_1^3 \omega + 24 a_2 a_1^2 b_0 - 44 a_2 a_1 b_0^2 - 2 a_2 a_1 b_1^2 + 24 a_2 b_0^3 + 4 a_2 b_0 b_1^2$
$\quad + 24 a_0 a_2^2 b_0 - 2 a_2^2 b_0 b_1 - 4 a_0 a_2 b_0 b_1 - 4 a_2 a_1^3 - 12 a_0 a_2^2 a_1 = 0,$

$e^{4Q(z)}:$ $\quad \alpha a_1^4 - a_1^4 - 4\alpha b_0 a_1^3 + 6 b_0 a_1^3 + 3\alpha b_1^2 a_1^2 - 11 b_1^2 a_1^2 - b_1^2 a_1^2 + 12\alpha a_0 a_2 a_1^2 - 12 a_0 a_2 a_1^2$
$\quad - 16\alpha \lambda a_2 b_0 a_1^2 + 24 \lambda a_2 b_0 a_1^2 + 4\alpha a_0 b_1 a_1^2 - 6 a_0 b_1 a_1^2 - 4\alpha \mu a_2 b_1 a_1^2 + 6\mu a_2 b_1 a_1^2$
$\quad - \alpha \lambda b_0 b_1 a_1^2 + 4 \lambda b_0 b_1 a_1^2 + 6 b_0^3 a_1 + \omega b_1^3 a_1 + 21\alpha \lambda a_2 b_0^2 a_1 - 76 \lambda a_2 b_0^2 a_1$
$\quad + \alpha \lambda a_0 b_1^2 a_1 - 4 \lambda a_0 b_1^2 a_1 + \alpha \lambda \mu a_2 b_1^2 a_1 - 4 \lambda \mu a_2 b_1^2 a_1 + \lambda^2 b_0 b_1^2 a_1 + 2\mu b_0 b_1^2 a_1$
$\quad + b_0 b_1^2 a_1 - 20\alpha \mu a_2^2 b_0 a_1 + 30\mu a_2^2 b_0 a_1 - 24\alpha a_0 a_2 b_0 a_1 + 36 a_0 a_2 b_0 a_1 - 6 \lambda b_0^2 b_1 a_1$
$\quad - 4\alpha a_0 b_0 b_1 a_1 + 14 a_0 b_0 b_1 a_1 + 4\alpha \lambda^2 a_2 b_0 b_1 a_1 - 14 \lambda^2 a_2 b_0 b_1 a_1 + 8\alpha \mu a_2 b_0 b_1 a_1$
$\quad - 28\mu a_2 b_0 b_1 a_1 - 4 a_2 b_0 b_1 a_1 + 54 \lambda a_2 b_0^3 - \lambda^2 a_0 b_1^3 - 2\mu a_0 b_1^3 - a_0 b_1^3 + 2\mu^2 a_2 b_1^3$
$\quad + \lambda^2 \mu a_2 b_1^3 + \mu a_2 b_1^3 + 6\alpha a_0^2 a_2^2 - 6 a_0^2 a_2^2 + 8\alpha \lambda^2 a_2^2 b_0^2 - 28 \lambda^2 a_2^2 b_0^2 + 16\alpha a_2^2 b_0^2$
$\quad - 56\mu a_2^2 b_0^2 - a_2^2 b_0^2 + 6\alpha a_0 a_2 b_0^2 - 24 a_0 a_2 b_0^2 + \alpha a_0^2 b_1^2 - 3 a_0^2 b_1^2 + \alpha \mu^2 a_2^2 b_1^2$
$\quad - 3\mu^2 a_2^2 b_1^2 - 2 \lambda^2 a_0 a_2 b_1^2 - 4\mu a_0 a_2 b_1^2 - 2 a_0 a_2 b_1^2 + 6 \lambda a_0 b_0 b_1^2 + 4 \lambda^3 a_2 b_0 b_1^2$
$\quad + 4 \lambda a_2 b_0 b_1^2 + 32 \lambda \mu a_2 b_0 b_1^2 + 3\omega a_2 b_0 b_1^2 - 16\alpha \lambda a_0 a_2^2 b_0 + 24 \lambda a_0 a_2^2 b_0$
$\quad - 4\alpha \mu a_0 a_2^2 b_1 + 6\mu a_0 a_2^2 b_1 - 6 a_0 b_0^2 b_1 + 41 \lambda^2 a_2 b_0^2 b_1 + 46\mu a_2 b_0^2 b_1 + 5 a_2 b_0^2 b_1$
$\quad + 4\alpha a_0^2 a_2 b_1 - 6 a_0^2 a_2 b_1 + 11\alpha \lambda \mu a_2^2 b_0 h_1 - 36 \lambda \mu a_2^2 h_0 h_1 - 2\alpha \lambda a_0 a_2 h_0 h_1 = 0,$

$e^{5Q(z)}:$ $\quad -a_0b_1^3\lambda^3 + a_1b_0b_1^2\lambda^3 + 5a_2b_0^2b_1\lambda^3 + 38a_2b_0^3\lambda^2 + 9\alpha a_1a_2b_0^2\lambda^2 - 32a_1a_2b_0^2\lambda^2$
$\quad + \alpha a_0a_1b_1^2\lambda^2 - 4a_0a_1b_1^2\lambda^2 + 10a_0b_0b_1^2\lambda^2 + 4\mu a_2b_0b_1^2\lambda^2 - 10a_1b_0^2b_1\lambda^2$
$\quad - \alpha a_1^2b_0b_1\lambda^2 + 4a_1^2b_0b_1\lambda^2 - 2\alpha a_0a_2b_0b_1\lambda^2 + 4a_0a_2b_0b_1\lambda^2 + 12a_1b_0^3\lambda$
$\quad - 8\mu a_0b_1^3\lambda - a_0b_1^3\lambda + 5\alpha a_1^2b_0^2\lambda - 18a_1^2b_0^2\lambda + 14\alpha\mu a_2^2b_0^2\lambda - 48\mu a_2^2b_0^2\lambda$
$\quad + 10\alpha a_0a_2b_0^2\lambda - 40a_0a_2b_0^2\lambda + 3\alpha a_0^2b_1^2\lambda - 10a_0^2b_1^2\lambda - 4\mu a_0a_2b_1^2\lambda + 8\mu a_1b_0b_1^2\lambda$
$\quad + a_1b_0b_1^2\lambda - 4\alpha a_1^3b_0\lambda + 6a_1^3b_0\lambda - 24\alpha a_0a_1a_2b_0\lambda + 36a_0a_1a_2b_0\lambda + 4\alpha a_0a_1^2b_1\lambda$
$\quad - 6a_0a_1^2b_1\lambda - 12a_0b_0^2b_1\lambda + 40\mu a_2b_0^2b_1\lambda + 5a_2b_0^2b_1\lambda + 4\alpha a_0^2a_2b_1\lambda - 6a_0^2a_2b_1\lambda$
$\quad - 8\alpha a_0a_1b_0b_1\lambda + 28a_0a_1b_0b_1\lambda + 4\alpha\mu a_1a_2b_0b_1\lambda - 12\mu a_1a_2b_0b_1\lambda + 4\alpha a_0a_1^3$
$\quad - 4a_0a_1^3 + 40\mu a_2b_0^3 + 2a_2b_0^3 + \omega a_0b_1^3 + 2\alpha a_0a_1b_0^2 - 8a_0a_1b_0^2 + 18\alpha\mu a_1a_2b_0^2$
$\quad - 64\mu a_1a_2b_0^2 - 2a_1a_2b_0^2 + 2\alpha\mu a_0a_1b_1^2 - 8\mu a_0a_1b_1^2 - 2a_0a_1b_1^2 + 8\mu a_0b_0b_1^2 - 2a_0b_0b_1^2$
$\quad + 3\omega a_1b_0b_1^2 + 8\mu^2 a_2b_0b_1^2 + 4\mu a_2b_0b_1^2 + 12\alpha a_0^2a_1a_2 - 12a_0^2a_1a_2 - 8\alpha a_0a_1^2b_0$
$\quad + 12a_0a_1^2b_0 - 16\alpha\mu a_0a_2b_0^2 + 24\mu a_0a_2b_0^2 - 8\alpha a_0^2a_2b_0 + 12a_0^2a_2b_0 - 16\mu a_1^2a_2b_0$
$\quad + 24\mu a_1^2a_2b_0 - 8\mu a_1b_0^2b_1 + 2a_1b_0^2b_1 + 3\omega a_2b_0^2b_1 + 8\alpha a_0^2a_1b_1 - 12a_0^2a_1b_1$
$\quad - 2\alpha a_0^2b_0b_1 + 8a_0^2b_0b_1 - 2\alpha\mu a_1^2b_0b_1 + 8\mu a_1^2b_0b_1 - 2a_1^2b_0b_1 + 4\alpha\mu^2 a_2^2b_0b_1$
$\quad - 12\mu^2 a_2^2b_0b_1 - 4\alpha\mu a_0a_2b_0b_1 + 8\mu a_0a_2b_0b_1 - 4a_0a_2b_0b_1 = 0,$ \hfill (A29)

$e^{6Q(z)}:$ $\quad 8a_2b_0^3\lambda^3 + 4a_0b_0b_1^2\lambda^3 - 4a_1b_0^2b_1\lambda^3 + 7a_1b_0^3\lambda^2 - 7\mu a_0b_1^3\lambda^2 + 2\alpha a_1^2b_0^2\lambda^2 - 7a_1^2b_0^2\lambda^2$
$\quad + 4\alpha a_0a_2b_0^2\lambda^2 - 16a_0a_2b_0^2\lambda^2 + 2\alpha a_0^2b_1^2\lambda^2 - 7a_0^2b_1^2\lambda^2 + 7\mu a_1b_0b_1^2\lambda^2 - 7a_0b_0b_1\lambda^2$
$\quad - \mu a_2b_0^2b_1\lambda^2 - 4\alpha a_0a_1b_0b_1\lambda^2 + 14a_0a_1b_0b_1\lambda^2 + 52\mu a_2b_0^3\lambda + 2a_2b_0^3\lambda + 3\alpha a_0a_1b_0^2\lambda$
$\quad - 12a_0a_1b_0^2\lambda + 15\alpha\mu a_1a_2b_0^2\lambda - 52\mu a_1a_2b_0^2\lambda + 3\alpha\mu a_0a_1b_1^2\lambda - 12\mu a_0a_1b_1^2\lambda$
$\quad + 20\mu a_0b_0b_1^2\lambda - 2a_0b_0b_1^2\lambda - 8\alpha a_0a_1^2b_0\lambda + 12a_0a_1^2b_0\lambda - 8\alpha a_0^2a_2b_0\lambda + 12a_0^2a_2b_0\lambda$
$\quad - 20\mu a_1b_0^2b_1\lambda + 2a_1b_0^2b_1\lambda + 8\alpha a_0^2a_1b_1\lambda - 12a_0^2a_1b_1\lambda - 3\alpha a_0^2b_0b_1\lambda + 12a_0^2b_0b_1\lambda$
$\quad - 3\alpha\mu a_1^2b_0b_1\lambda + 12\mu a_1^2b_0b_1\lambda - 6\alpha\mu a_0a_2b_0b_1\lambda + 16\mu a_0a_2b_0b_1\lambda + 8\mu a_1b_0^3 + a_1b_0^3$
$\quad + \omega a_2b_0^3 - 8\mu^2 a_0b_1^3 - \mu a_0b_1^3 + 6\alpha a_0^2a_1^2 - 6a_0^2a_1^2 + 4\alpha\mu a_1^2b_0^2 - 14\mu a_1^2b_0^2 - a_1^2b_0^2$
$\quad + 6\alpha\mu^2 a_2^2b_0^2 - 20\mu^2 a_2^2b_0^2 + 8\mu a_0a_2b_0^2 - 32\mu a_0a_2b_0^2 - 2a_0a_2b_0^2 + 4\alpha\mu a_0^2b_1^2 - 14\mu a_0^2b_1^2$
$\quad - a_0^2b_1^2 - 2\mu^2 a_0a_2b_1^2 + 3\omega a_0b_0b_1^2 + 8\mu^2 a_1b_0b_1^2 + \mu a_1b_0b_1^2 + 4\alpha a_0^3a_2 - 4a_0^3a_2 - 4\alpha\mu a_1^3b_0$
$\quad + 6\mu a_1^3b_0 - 4\alpha a_0^2a_1b_0 + 6a_0^2a_1b_0 - 24\alpha\mu a_0a_1a_2b_0 + 36\mu a_0a_1a_2b_0 + 4\alpha a_0^3b_1 - 6a_0^3b_1$
$\quad + 4\alpha\mu a_0a_1^2b_1 - 6\mu a_0a_1^2b_1 - 8\mu a_0b_0^2b_1 - a_0b_0^2b_1 + 3\omega a_1b_0^2b_1 + 4\mu^2 a_2b_0^2b_1$
$\quad + 5\mu a_2b_0^2b_1 + 4\alpha\mu a_0^2a_2b_1 - 6\mu a_0^2a_2b_1 - 8\alpha\mu a_0a_1b_0b_1$
$\quad + 28\mu a_0a_1b_0b_1 - 4a_0a_1b_0b_1 + 2\mu^2 a_1a_2b_0b_1 = 0,$

$e^{7Q(z)}$: $a_1 b_0^3 \lambda^3 - a_0 b_0^2 b_1 \lambda^3 + 14\mu a_2 b_0^3 \lambda^2 + \alpha a_0 a_1 b_0^2 \lambda^2 - 4 a_0 a_1 b_0^2 \lambda^2 + 10\mu a_0 b_0 b_1^2 \lambda^2$
$- 10\mu a_1 b_0^2 b_1 \lambda^2 - \alpha a_0^2 b_0 b_1 \lambda^2 + 4 a_0^2 b_0 b_1 \lambda^2 + 8\mu a_1 b_0^3 \lambda + a_1 b_0^3 \lambda - 12\mu^2 a_0 b_1^3 \lambda$
$+ 3\alpha\mu a_1^2 b_0^2 \lambda - 10\mu a_1^2 b_0^2 \lambda + 6\alpha\mu a_0 a_2 b_0^2 \lambda - 24\mu a_0 a_2 b_0^2 \lambda + 5\alpha\mu a_0^2 b_1^2 \lambda$
$- 18\mu a_0^2 b_1^2 \lambda + 12\mu^2 a_1 b_0 b_1^2 \lambda - 4\alpha a_0^2 a_1 b_0 \lambda + 6 a_0^2 a_1 b_0 \lambda + 4\alpha a_0^3 b_1 \lambda - 6 a_0^3 b_1 \lambda$
$- 8\mu a_0 b_0^2 b_1 \lambda - a_0 b_0^2 b_1 \lambda - 12\mu^2 a_2 b_0^2 b_1 \lambda - 8\alpha\mu a_0 a_1 b_0 b_1 \lambda + 28\mu a_0 a_1 b_0 b_1 \lambda$
$+ \omega a_1 b_0^3 + 16\mu^2 a_2 b_0^3 + 2\mu a_2 b_0^3 + 2\alpha\mu a_0 a_1 b_0^2 - 8\mu a_0 a_1 b_0^2 - 2 a_0 a_1 b_0^2 + 6\alpha\mu^2 a_1 a_2 b_0^2$
$- 20\mu^2 a_1 a_2 b_0^2 + 2\alpha\mu^2 a_0 a_1 b_1^2 - 8\mu^2 a_0 a_1 b_1^2 + 8\mu^2 a_0 b_0 b_1^2 - 2\mu a_0 b_0 b_1^2 + 4\alpha a_0^3 a_1$
$- 4 a_0^3 a_1 - 8\alpha\mu a_0 a_1^2 b_0 + 12\mu a_0 a_1^2 b_0 - 8\mu a_0^2 a_2 b_0 + 12\mu a_0^2 a_2 b_0 + 3\omega a_0 b_0^2 b_1$
$- 8\mu^2 a_1 b_0^2 b_1 + 2\mu a_1 b_0^2 b_1 + 8\alpha\mu a_0^2 a_1 b_1 - 12\mu a_0^2 a_1 b_1 - 2\alpha\mu a_0^2 b_0 b_1 + 8\mu a_0^2 b_0 b_1$
$- 2 a_0^2 b_0 b_1 - 2\alpha\mu^2 a_1^2 b_0 b_1 + 8\mu^2 a_1^2 b_0 b_1 - 4\alpha\mu^2 a_0 a_2 b_0 b_1 + 12\mu^2 a_0 a_2 b_0 b_1 = 0,$

$e^{8Q(z)}$: $\alpha a_0^4 - \alpha a_0^2 b_0 b_1 \lambda \mu + \alpha a_1 a_0 b_0^2 \lambda \mu + 3\alpha a_0^2 b_1^2 \mu^2 + 2\alpha a_2 a_0 b_0^2 \mu^2 - 4\alpha a_1 a_0 b_0 b_1 \mu^2$
$+ \alpha a_1^2 b_0^2 \mu^2 + 4\alpha a_0^3 b_1 \mu - 4\alpha a_1 a_0^2 b_0 \mu - a_0 b_0^2 b_1 \lambda^2 \mu + a_1 b_0^3 \lambda^2 \mu + 6 a_0 b_0 b_1^2 \lambda \mu^2$
$+ 6 a_2 b_0^3 \lambda \mu^2 - 6 a_1 b_0^2 b_1 \lambda \mu^2 + 4 a_0^2 b_0 b_1 \lambda \mu - 4 a_1 a_0 b_0^2 \lambda \mu - 6 a_0 b_1^3 \mu^3 + 6 a_1 b_0 b_1^2 \mu^3$
$- 6 a_2 b_0^2 b_1 \mu^3 - 11 a_0^2 b_1^2 \mu^2 - 8 a_2 a_0 b_0^2 \mu^2 - 2 a_0 b_0^2 b_1 \mu^2 + 14 a_1 a_0 b_0 b_1 \mu^2 + 2 a_1 b_0^3 \mu^2$
$- 3 a_1^2 b_0^2 \mu^2 - 6 a_0^3 b_1 \mu + 6 a_1 a_0^2 b_0 \mu - a_0 b_0^2 b_1 \mu + a_1 b_0^3 \mu + a_0 b_0^3 \omega - a_0^2 b_0^2 - a_0^4 = 0.$

References

1. Keller, E.F.; Segel, L.A. Traveling bands of chemotactic bacteria: A theoretical analysis. *J. Theor. Biol.* **1971**, *30*, 235–248. [CrossRef] [PubMed]
2. Arumugam, G.; Tyagi, J. Keller-Segel Chemotaxis Models: A Review. *Acta Appl. Math.* **2020**, *171*, 6. [CrossRef]
3. Bhaya, D.; Takahashi, A.; Grossman, A.R. Light regulation of type IV pilus-dependent motility by chemosensor-like elements in Synechocystis PCC6803. *Proc. Natl. Acad. Sci. USA* **2001**, *98*, 7540–7545. [CrossRef] [PubMed]
4. Varuni, P.; Menon, S.N.; Menon, G.I. Phototaxis as a collective phenomenon in Cyanobacterial colonies. *Sci. Rep.* **2017**, *7*, 17799. [CrossRef] [PubMed]
5. Levy, D.; Requeijo, T. Modeling group dynamics of phototaxis: From particle systems to PDEs. *Discret. Contin. Dyn. Syst.-B* **2008**, *9*, 103–128. [CrossRef]
6. Levy, D.; Requeijo, T. Stochastic models for phototaxis. *Bull. Math. Biol.* **2008**, *70*, 1684–1706. [CrossRef]
7. Ha, S.; Levy, D. Particle, kinetic and fluid models for phototaxis. *Discret. Contin. Dyn. Syst.-B* **2009**, *12*, 77–108. [CrossRef]
8. Galante, A.; Wisen, S.; Bhaya, D.; Levy, D. Modeling local interactions during the motion of cyanobacteria. *J. Theor. Biol.* **2012**, *309*, 147–158. [CrossRef]
9. Galante, A.; Levy, D. Modeling selective local interactions with memory. *Phys. D Nonlinear Phenom.* **2013**, *260*, 176–190. [CrossRef] [PubMed]
10. Weinberg, D.; Levy, D. Modeling selective local interactions with memory: Motion on a 2d lattice. *Phys. D Nonlinear Phenom.* **2014**, *278–279*, 13–30. [CrossRef]
11. Drescher, K.; Goldstein, R.; Tuval, I. Fidelity of adaptive phototaxis. *Proc. Natl. Acad. Sci. USA* **2010**, *107*, 11171–11176. [CrossRef] [PubMed]
12. Giometto, A.; Altermatt, F.; Maritan, A.; Stocker, R.; Rinaldo, A. Generalized receptor law governs phototaxis in the phytoplankton Euglena gracilis. *Proc. Natl. Acad. Sci. USA* **2015**, *112*, 7045–7050. [CrossRef]
13. Dervaux, J.; Resta, M.C.; Brunet, P. Light-controlled flows in active fluids. *Nat. Phys.* **2017**, *13*, 306–312. [CrossRef]
14. Chavy-Waddy, P.; Kolokolnikov, T. A local PDE model of aggregation formation in bacterial colonies. *Nonlinearity* **2016**, *29*, 3174. [CrossRef]
15. Bernoff, A.J.; Topaz, C.M. Biological aggregation driven by social and environmental factors: A nonlocal model and its degenerate Cahn–Hilliard approximation. *SIAM J. Appl. Dyn. Syst.* **2016**, *15*, 1528–1562. [CrossRef]
16. Taranets, R.; Chugunova, M. Longtime dynamics of the PDE model for the motion toward light of bacterial colonies. *Nonlinearity* **2018**, *31*, 887. [CrossRef]
17. Leptos, K.C.; Chioccioli, M.; Furlan, S.; Pesci, A.I.; Goldstein, R.E. Phototaxis of chlamydomonas arises from a tuned adaptive photoresponse shared with multicellular volvocine green algae. *Phys. Rev. E* **2023**, *107*, 014404. [CrossRef]
18. Ali, K.K.; Osman, M.; Baskonus, H.M.; Elazab, N.; Ilhan, E. Analytical and numerical study of the HIV-1 infection of CD4+ T-cells conformable fractional mathematical model that causes acquired immunodeficiency syndrome (AIDS) with the effect of antiviral drug therapy. *Math. Methods Appl. Sci.* **2020**, *46*, 7654–67670. [CrossRef]

19. Kumar, D.; Seadawy, A.R.; Joardar, A.K. Modified Kudryashov method via new exact solutions for some conformable fractional differential equations arising in mathematical biology. *Chin. J. Phys.* **2018**, *56*, 75–85. [CrossRef]
20. Lee, D.; Huh, J.; Jeong, D.; Shin, J.; Yun, A.; Kim, J. Physical, mathematical, and numerical derivations of the Cahn–Hilliard equation. *Comput. Mater. Sci.* **2014**, *81*, 216–225. [CrossRef]
21. Murray, J.D. *Mathematical Biology I. An Introduction, Volume 17 of Interdisciplinary Applied Mathematics*; Springer: Berlin/Heidelberg, Germany, 2002.
22. Murray, J.D. *Mathematical Biology II: Spatial Models and Biomedical Applications, Volume 18 of Interdisciplinary Applied Mathematics*; Springer: Berlin/Heidelberg, Germany, 2003.
23. Couzin, I.D.; Krause, J.; James, R.; Ruxton, G.D.; Franks, N.R. Collective memory and spatial sorting in animal groups. *J. Theor. Biol.* **2002**, *218*, 1–11. [CrossRef] [PubMed]
24. Mogilner, A.; Edelstein-Keshet, L.; Bent, L.; Spiros, A. Mutual interactions, potentials, and individual distance in a social aggregation. *J. Math. Biol.* **2003**, *47*, 353–389. [CrossRef] [PubMed]
25. Volpert, V.A.; Volpert, A.I. Application of the Leray-Schauder method to the proof of the existence of wave solutions of parabolic systems. *Sov. Math.* **1988**, *37*, 138–141.
26. Volpert, A.I.; Volpert, V.A.; Volpert, V.A. Traveling Wave Solutions of Parabolic Systems. In *Translations of Mathematical Monographs*; American Mathematical Society: Providence, RI, USA, 1994.
27. Kudryashov, N.A. One method for finding exact solutions of nonlinear differential equations. *Commun. Nonlinear Sci. Numer. Simul.* **2012**, *17*, 2248–2253. [CrossRef]
28. Kaplan, M.; Bekir, A.; Akbulut, A. A generalized kudryashov method to some nonlinear evolution equations in mathematical physics. *Nonlinear Dyn.* **2016**, *85*, 2843–2850. [CrossRef]
29. Akbar, M.A.; Ali, N.H.M. Solitary wave solutions of the fourth order Boussinesq equation through the $\exp(-\phi(\eta))$-expansion method. *SpringerPlus* **2014**, *3*, 344. [CrossRef]
30. Uddin, S.; Alam, N.; Hossain, S.M.S.; Hasan, S. Some New Exact Traveling Wave Solutions to the (3+1)-Dimensional Zakharov-Kuznetsov Equation and the Burgers Equations via $\text{Exp}(-\phi(\eta))$-Expansion Method. *Front. Math. Its Appl.* **2014**, *1*, 1–8.
31. Hafez, M.; Alam, M.N.; Akbar, M.A. Traveling wave solutions for some important coupled nonlinear physical models via the coupled Higgs equation and the Maccari system. *J. King Saud Univ. Sci.* **2015**, *27*, 105–112. [CrossRef]
32. He, J.; Wu, X. Exp-function method for nonlinear wave equations. *Chaos Solitons Fractals* **2006**, *30*, 700–708. [CrossRef]
33. Bulut, H. Application of the modified exponential function method to the Cahn-Allen equation. *AIP Conf. Proc.* **2017**, *1798*, 020033.

Disclaimer/Publisher's Note: The statements, opinions and data contained in all publications are solely those of the individual author(s) and contributor(s) and not of MDPI and/or the editor(s). MDPI and/or the editor(s) disclaim responsibility for any injury to people or property resulting from any ideas, methods, instructions or products referred to in the content.

Article
Global Boundedness in a Logarithmic Keller–Segel System

Jinyang Liu [1,2], Boping Tian [1], Deqi Wang [2,*], Jiaxin Tang [2] and Yujin Wu [3]

1. School of Mathematics, Harbin Institute of Technology, Harbin 150001, China; lista@cuit.edu.cn (J.L.); bopingt361147@hit.edu.cn (B.T.)
2. School of Statistics, Chengdu University of Information Technology, Chengdu 610103, China; m17358660205@163.com
3. School of Economics and Management, Zhejiang Sci-Tech University, Hangzhou 310018, China; wyj215837583@163.com
* Correspondence: wangdeqi9@126.com

Abstract: In this paper, we propose a user-friendly integral inequality to study the coupled parabolic chemotaxis system with singular sensitivity under the Neumann boundary condition. Under a low diffusion rate, the classical solution of this system is uniformly bounded. Our proof replies on the construction of the energy functional containing $\int_\Omega \frac{|v|^4}{v^2}$ with $v > 0$. It is noteworthy that the inequality used in the paper may be applied to study other chemotaxis systems.

Keywords: chemotaxis model; energy functional; integral inequality; global uniform boundedness

MSC: 35A01; 35A02

1. Introduction

Our work considers the coupled parabolic chemotaxis system with singular sensitivity

$$\begin{cases} u_t = \nabla \cdot (\nabla u - \chi \frac{u}{v} \nabla v), & x \in \Omega, t > 0, \\ v_t = k\Delta v - v + u, & x \in \Omega, t > 0, \\ \partial_\nu u = \partial_\nu v = 0, & x \in \partial\Omega, t > 0, \\ u(x,0) = u_0, \quad v(x,0) = v_0, & x \in \Omega, \end{cases} \quad (1)$$

for parameters $\chi, k > 0$ with the Neumann boundary condition, where $\Omega \subset \mathbb{R}^2$ is a bounded domain with a smooth boundary. u and v are the cell density and concentration of chemical stimulus with respect to time t and x, respectively. k represents the diffusion rate of the chemical signal. The initial functions $u_0 \in C^0(\bar{\Omega})$ and $v_0 \in W^{1,\infty}(\Omega)$ satisfy $u_0 \geq 0$ and $v_0 > 0$.

In 1970, Keller and Segel [1] originally introduced the system

$$\begin{cases} u_t = \nabla \cdot (\nabla u - u\chi(v)\nabla v), & x \in \Omega, t > 0, \\ \tau v_t = k\Delta v - \alpha v + \beta u, & x \in \Omega, t > 0, \end{cases} \quad (2)$$

to describe chemotaxis, the oriented movement of cells in response to the concentration of chemical signal produced by themselves and self-diffusion, where $\tau, k, \alpha, \beta > 0$ are parameters. The chemical signal experiences random diffusion and decay. Particular cases and derivatives of chemotaixs models have been developed extensively, such as the parabolic–elliptic case [2–5], the fully parabolic case [6–10] and other extensive versions [11–13]. Some studies have focused on the problem of whether the solution to the respective model undergoes a chemotactic collapse in the sense that the cell density becomes unbounded in finite or infinite time [3,6,7,12]. Given the initial conditions $u_0 \geq 0, v_0 > 0$ and the Neumann boundary conditions, others have concentrated on the aggregation effect of the chemotactic sensitivity $\chi(v)$.

If $\chi(v) = \chi$ with $\tau = k = \alpha = \beta = 1$, Osaki and Yagi [14] showed the global boundedness of solutions to (2) for $n = 1$ and Nagai et al. [15] proved the results if $\int_\Omega u_0 < 4\pi$ for $n = 2$. For $n \geq 3$, if $\|u_0\|_{L^{\frac{n}{2}}(\Omega)}$ is small enough, there exist global weak solutions [16]. Another form of sensitivity function is

$$\chi(v) = \frac{\chi_0}{(c + \alpha v)^k}$$

for $c, \chi_0 > 0, k > 1$ and $\alpha > 0$, which is non-singular. In this case, the global existence is established for $k = 2, c = 1$ by [17] and for $k = 1, \alpha = 1$ by [12]. Furthermore, if $\chi(v) = \frac{\chi_0}{v^k}$ for $k > 1, \chi_0 > 0$, there exist global classical solutions to (2) [18].

The logarithmic sensitivity function $\chi(v) = \frac{\chi}{v}$ with $\chi > 0$ is commonly considered because it is in compliance with the Weber–Fechner law [19]. Taking this form with $\tau = k = \alpha = \beta = 1$, the chemotaxis model becomes the classical version:

$$\begin{cases} u_t = \nabla \cdot (\nabla u - \chi u \frac{\nabla v}{v}), & x \in \Omega, t > 0, \\ v_t = \Delta v - v + u, & x \in \Omega, t > 0, \\ \partial_\nu u = \partial_\nu v = 0, & x \in \partial\Omega, t > 0, \\ u(x,0) = u_0, \quad v(x,0) = v_0, & x \in \Omega. \end{cases} \quad (3)$$

Global bounded solutions to (3) are provided by Osaki and Yagi [14] in a one-dimensional case. As for $n = 2$, Lankeit [7] introduced an energy functional and proved that the solutions are uniform bounded in a convex domain with the range of χ extending to slightly more than one. Moreover, Winkler [20] proved that there exist global classical solutions if $0 < \chi < \sqrt{\frac{2}{n}}$, and Fujie [6] showed the solutions are uniformly time bounded. In [21], global bounded solutions are constructed under the the condition of $\chi \leq \frac{4}{n}$ with $\Omega \subset \mathbb{R}^n$ being the convex domain. Furthermore, (3) employs global weak solutions when $\chi < \sqrt{\frac{n+2}{3n-4}}$ [20]. In the radially symmetric setting, weak solutions are constructed by [22] under the condition $\chi < \sqrt{\frac{n}{n-2}}$. These results imply that there is a balance between χ and dimension n for the establishment of global solutions to classic models (3). The work to extend both χ and n is laborious without giving any condition of (3). Lankeit and Winkler [23] extended the range of χ to

$$\chi < \begin{cases} \infty & \text{if } n = 2 \\ \sqrt{8} & \text{if } n = 3, \\ \frac{n}{n-2} & \text{if } n \geq 4 \end{cases}$$

under the definition of the generalized solution, which is constructed on the basis of the global weak solution.

There are also other results established on the changing of parameters, referring to [9,24]. Indeed, the parameters in (2) have an impact on the aggregation of cell density. Xiangdong [25] constructed global solutions to (1) with $n \leq 8$ under some conditions, where the relationship between k and χ is established. However, if $n = 2$, the diffusion rate of the concentration of chemicals k does not work, since χ is still less than one, as in [25].

In [26], the estimates containing $\int_\Omega |\nabla v|^2$ are established to study the system where the chemotactic sensitivity is a constant and the source of the signal is modeled by v. In the work of Winkler [27], the only evident global quasi-dissipative structure involving $\int_\Omega \frac{|\nabla v|^2}{v^2}, (v > 0)$ is established to address the difficulty brought about by the nonlinear source of signal. However, the system with logarithmic sensitivity presents more challenges, and the structure of $\int_\Omega f(v)|\nabla v|^n$ (n is even) is essential to the estimates. Hence, motivated by Lankeit [7] and Nagai [15], we establish an energy-type functional containing

$$\int_\Omega \frac{|\nabla v|^4}{v^2}.$$

The fractional term of v in the energy-type functional may alleviate the difficulty of preventing the aggregation caused by nonlinear kinetics in some derivate systems such as [27,28], where the source of the signal is modeled by uv.

In this paper, the global existence and uniform boundedness of the classical solutions of (1) are established as follows:

Theorem 1. *Let Ω be a bounded domain with a smooth boundary $\partial\Omega$ on $\mathbb{R}^2$, initial data $v_0 > 0$ and $u_0 \geq, \not\equiv 0$ in Ω with $u_0 \in C^0(\bar{\Omega})$ and $v_0 \in W^{1,\infty}(\Omega)$. For all $\chi > 0$, there exists a constant C_k that depends on u_0, v_0, Ω and χ, such that whenever*

$$k \geq C_k,$$

then (1) admits a unique classical solution $(u,v) \in C^0(\bar{\Omega} \times [0,\infty)) \cap C^{2,1}(\bar{\Omega} \times (0,\infty))$. Moreover, there exist constants $\delta, C > 0$ such that $\delta \leq v < C$ and $0 \leq u < C$ for all $t \in (0,\infty)$.

Intuitively, this shows that the large diffusion rate of chemical signals can prevent the aggregation of cell density resulting from a large χ.

In the paper, we first demonstrate the local existence of and recall some inequalities in the preliminaries. Then, we prove our key integral inequality in the Section 3 and give some useful a priori estimates in the Section 4. Finally, we prove the uniform boundedness of the solutions.

2. Preliminaries

2.1. Local Existence

The local existence of classical solutions to chemotaxis systems has been well-established using the methods of standard parabolic regularity theory and an appropriate fixed-point framework, which is shown in the following. Details of proof can be seen in Theorem 2.1 of [7] or [20].

Proposition 1. *Let $\Omega \subset \mathbb{R}^n$ be a bounded domain with a smooth boundary, and $u_0 \in C^0(\bar{\Omega})$ and $v_0 \in W^{1,q}(\Omega), q > n \geq 1$ are non-negative; then, for any $k, \chi > 0$, there exists $T_{\max} \in (0,\infty]$ and a pair of unique non-negative solutions satisfying*

$$\begin{cases} u \in C^0(\bar{\Omega} \times [0, T_{\max})) \cap C^{2,1}(\bar{\Omega} \times (0, T_{\max})), \\ v \in C^0(\bar{\Omega} \times [0, T_{\max})) \cap C^{2,1}(\bar{\Omega} \times (0, T_{\max})) \cap L^\infty_{loc}([0, T_{\max}); W^{1,q}(\Omega)), \end{cases}$$

such that (u,v) solves (1) classically in $\Omega \times [0, T_{\max})$ and, moreover, if $T_{\max} < \infty$, then
$$\lim_{t \to T_{\max}} \|u(\cdot,t)\|_{L^\infty(\Omega)} + \|v(\cdot,t)\|_{W^{1,q}(\Omega)} = \infty.$$

2.2. The Positive Lower Boundedness of v

In order to prove the lower boundedness of v in (1), we first prove the boundedness of $\|u\|_{L^1}$ and $\|v\|_{L^1}$. Integrating the first and the second PDE in (1), we have the mass identities

$$\int_\Omega u = \int_\Omega u_0 =: m, \ t > 0$$

and

$$\int_\Omega v = \int_\Omega u_0 + \left(\int_\Omega v_0 - \int_\Omega u_0\right) \cdot e^{-t}, \ t > 0.$$

Based on these facts, one can deduce the non-negative lower boundedness of v from the abstract representation formula of the v equation. Copying Lemma 2.2 of [7], we write it as follows:

Lemma 1. *Let (u,v) satisfy Proposition 1; then, there exists $T_{\max} > 0$ and a positive constant δ depending on v_0 such that*

$$v(x,t) \geq \delta > 0, \ \forall (x,t) \in \bar{\Omega} \times [0, T_{\max}). \tag{4}$$

Proof. Firstly, by the comparison principle and the fact of $v_0 > 0$ on $\bar{\Omega}$, we have for a small t

$$v(x,t) \geq \min_{x \in \Omega} v_0 \cdot e^{-t} > 0.$$

Let us fix $\tau = \tau(u_0, v_0)$. Then, it follows that

$$v(x,t) \geq \min_{x \in \Omega} v_0 \cdot e^{-\tau} := \delta_1 > 0, \ \forall t \in [0, \tau).$$

Now, from the well-known Neumann heat semigroup estimate for $e^{t\Delta}$ (see Lemma 1.3 in [29] and Lemma 2.2 in [20]), we denote by d the diameter of the Ω and have for $\Omega \subset \mathbb{R}^2$ that

$$(e^{t\Delta}\omega) \geq \frac{1}{4\pi t}e^{-\frac{d^2}{4t}} \cdot \int_\Omega \omega > 0, \ \omega \in C^0(\Omega).$$

Then, the abstract representation formula of v shows

$$\begin{aligned} v(\cdot, t) &= e^{t(\Delta-1)}v_0 + \int_\Omega e^{(t-s)(\Delta-1)}u(\cdot,t)ds \\ &\geq \int_0^t \frac{1}{4\pi(t-s)}e^{-((t-s)+\frac{d^2}{4(t-s)})}(\int_\Omega u(\cdot,t))ds \\ &\geq m \int_0^t \frac{1}{4\pi r}e^{-(r+\frac{d^2}{4r})}dr := \delta_2 > 0, \ \forall t \in [\tau, \infty), \end{aligned} \tag{5}$$

where $r := t - s$. Choosing $\delta = \min\{\delta_1, \delta_2\}$, we deduce (4). □

2.3. Recall of Useful Theorems

The well-known general Young's inequality [30] is recalled.

Lemma 2. *Let $f, g \geq 0$ be the continuous function with $p, q > 0$ satisfying $\frac{1}{p} + \frac{1}{q} = 1$, then*

$$fg \leq \epsilon f^p + \frac{1}{q}(\epsilon p)^{-\frac{q}{p}}g^q \tag{6}$$

holds for all $\epsilon > 0$. Moreover, for continuous $h > 0$ and any $\epsilon_1, \epsilon_2 > 0$, taking $p = 2, q = 3, r = 6$ such that $\frac{1}{p} + \frac{1}{q} + \frac{1}{r} = 1$, we have

$$fgh \leq \epsilon_1 f^2 + \frac{\epsilon_2}{4\epsilon_1}g^3 + \frac{\sqrt{6}}{36\epsilon_1\sqrt{\epsilon_2}}h^6. \tag{7}$$

Proof. In (7) is given the result of the straightforward calculation of the well-known inequality (6). □

Lemma 3. *Let $\Omega \subset \mathbb{R}^n$, $n \geq 1$ be a smooth bounded domain. Any function $f \in C^2(\Omega)$ satisfies*

$$i.\ \nabla |\nabla f|^2 = 2\nabla f \cdot D^2 f, \tag{8}$$

$$ii.\ (\Delta f)^2 \leq n |D^2 f|^2, \tag{9}$$

$$iii.\ \nabla f \cdot \nabla \Delta f = \frac{1}{2}\Delta |\nabla f|^2 - |D^2 f|^2. \tag{10}$$

All the identities and inequalities in the above lemma can be obtained from straightforward calculation. One can see [7,31] and Lemma 3.1 in [8] for their application. We could not find a precise reference in the literature that covers all that is necessary for our purpose; therefore, we conclude with a short lemma here.

3. A User-Friendly Integral Inequality

The proof of Theorem 1 is based on the extension and application of an integral inequality, which is generated within one dimension by Q. Wang [28]. The following theorem has a multidimensional form. It is worth noting that the integral inequality connects the fraction of the gradient and the second derivative. A similar inequality can be found in [7]. Furthermore, the explicit coefficient in the integral inequality is easy to use for readers.

Theorem 2. *Let $\Omega \subset \mathbb{R}^n$ be a smooth bounded domain with $w > 0$ satisfying $w \in C^2(\bar{\Omega})$ and $\frac{\partial w}{\partial \nu} = 0$ on $\partial \Omega$. Then,*

$$\int_\Omega \frac{|\nabla w|^{2p+2}}{w^{q+2}} \leq \frac{n + 4p\epsilon}{2q + 1 - \frac{p}{\epsilon}} \int_\Omega \frac{|D^2 w|^2 |\nabla w|^{2p-2}}{w^q} \tag{11}$$

for all $p \geq 1$, $q > -\frac{1}{2}$ and $\epsilon > \frac{p}{2q+1} > 0$.

Proof. Let $J := \int_\Omega |\Delta \log w|^2 \frac{|\nabla w|^{2p-2}}{w^{q-2}} > 0$ for $p \geq 1$. Directly calculating $|\Delta \log w|^2$ leads to

$$J = \int_\Omega \frac{|\Delta w|^2 |\nabla w|^{2p-2}}{w^q} \overbrace{-2 \int_\Omega \frac{|\nabla w|^{2p} \Delta w}{w^{q+1}}}^{J_0} + \int_\Omega \frac{|\nabla w|^{2p+2}}{w^{q+2}}. \tag{12}$$

Since $\frac{\partial w}{\partial \nu} = 0$ on $\partial \Omega$, integration by parts gives

$$J_0 = 2 \int_\Omega \frac{\nabla |\nabla w|^{2p} \cdot \nabla w}{w^{q+1}} - 2(q+1) \int_\Omega \frac{|\nabla w|^{2p+2}}{w^{q+2}}$$

$$= 2p \int_\Omega \frac{|\nabla w|^{2p-2} \nabla |\nabla w|^2 \cdot \nabla w}{w^{q+1}} - 2(q+1) \int_\Omega \frac{|\nabla w|^{2p+2}}{w^{q+2}}.$$

By (8) of Lemma 3 and (6), we have for $\epsilon > 0$ that

$$\begin{aligned} J_0 =& 4p \int_\Omega \frac{|\nabla w|^{2p} \cdot D^2 w}{w^{q+1}} - 2(q+1) \int_\Omega \frac{|\nabla w|^{2p+2}}{w^{q+2}} \\ \leq& 4p\epsilon \int_\Omega \frac{|\nabla w|^{2p-2} |D^2 w|^2}{w^q} - \left(2(q+1) - \frac{p}{\epsilon}\right) \int_\Omega \frac{|\nabla w|^{2p+2}}{w^{q+2}}. \end{aligned} \tag{13}$$

By (9), substituting (13) into (12) gives

$$J \leq (n + 4p\epsilon) \int_\Omega \frac{|\nabla w|^{2p-2} |D^2 w|^2}{w^q} - \left((2q+1) - \frac{p}{\epsilon}\right) \int_\Omega \frac{|\nabla w|^{2p+2}}{w^{q+2}}.$$

Due to $q > -\frac{1}{2}$, $\epsilon > \frac{p}{2q+1} > 0$; thus, $(2q+1) - \frac{p}{\epsilon} > 0$, and we conclude with (11). □

Remark 1. Letting $\Omega \subset \mathbb{R}^2$ and taking $q = p = 2, \epsilon > \frac{2}{5}$, then $\frac{n+4p\epsilon}{2q+1-\frac{p}{\epsilon}} = \frac{2+8\epsilon}{5-\frac{2}{\epsilon}}$. Note that $\frac{2+8\epsilon}{5-\frac{2}{\epsilon}}$ achieves its global minimum over $(\frac{2}{5}, \infty)$ at $\epsilon = \frac{4+\sqrt{26}}{10} (\approx 0.9099)$ with the value $\frac{2}{21-4\sqrt{26}} (\approx 3.3117)$. Therefore,

$$\int_\Omega \frac{|\nabla w|^6}{w^4} \leq \frac{2}{21 - 4\sqrt{26}} \int_\Omega \frac{|D^2 w|^2 |\nabla w|^2}{w^2}. \tag{14}$$

4. Some Useful A Priori Estimates

Let us first give an inequality to estimate the boundary integration.

Lemma 4. Let $\Omega \subset \mathbb{R}^2$ be a bounded smooth domain. If $v \in C^2(\bar{\Omega})$ satisfies $\frac{\partial v}{\partial \nu} = 0$, the for any $\hat{\epsilon} > 0$, there exists $C(\hat{\epsilon})$ depending on Ω such that

$$\int_{\partial \Omega} \frac{|\nabla v|^2}{v^2} \frac{\partial(|\nabla v|^2)}{\partial \nu} \leq \hat{\epsilon} \int_\Omega \frac{|\nabla v|^2 |D^2 v|^2}{v^2} + C(\hat{\epsilon}) \tag{15}$$

for all $t \in (0, T_{\max})$ and $n \geq 1$.

Proof. Firstly, we show that

$$\int_{\partial \Omega} \frac{|\nabla v|^2}{v^2} \frac{\partial(|\nabla v|^2)}{\partial \nu} = 16 \int_{\partial \Omega} |\nabla \sqrt{v}|^2 \frac{\partial(|\nabla \sqrt{v}|^2)}{\partial \nu}. \tag{16}$$

From the Neumann boundary condition, we calculate the right-hand side, obtaining

$$16 \int_{\partial \Omega} |\nabla \sqrt{v}|^2 \frac{\partial(|\nabla \sqrt{v}|^2)}{\partial \nu} = \int_{\partial \Omega} \frac{|\nabla v|^2}{v} \frac{\partial \frac{|\nabla v|^2}{v}}{\partial \nu}$$

$$= \int_{\partial \Omega} \frac{|\nabla v|^2}{v} \frac{\frac{\partial |\nabla v|^2}{\partial \nu} v - \frac{\partial v}{\partial \nu} |\nabla v|^2}{v^2} = \int_{\partial \Omega} \frac{|\nabla v|^2}{v^2} \frac{\partial(|\nabla v|^2)}{\partial \nu}$$

for all $t \in (0, T_{\max})$.

Now, according to (3.17) in [11], we have for any $\varepsilon > 0$ and constant $C_\varepsilon > 0$ depending on Ω that

$$\int_{\partial \Omega} |\nabla \sqrt{v}|^2 \frac{\partial(|\nabla \sqrt{v}|^2)}{\partial \nu} \leq \varepsilon \int_\Omega \left| \nabla |\nabla \sqrt{v}|^2 \right|^2 + C_\varepsilon \quad \text{for all } t \in (0, T_{\max}). \tag{17}$$

By straightforward calculation, we have

$$\int_\Omega \left| \nabla |\nabla \sqrt{v}|^2 \right|^2 = \frac{1}{16} \int_\Omega \left| \nabla \left(\frac{|\nabla v|^2}{v} \right) \right|^2 = \frac{1}{16} \int_\Omega \left| \frac{\nabla(|\nabla v|^2)}{v} - \frac{\nabla v |\nabla v|^2}{v^2} \right|^2$$

$$= \frac{1}{16} \int_\Omega \left(\frac{|\nabla |\nabla v|^2|^2}{v^2} - 2 \frac{\nabla |\nabla v|^2 \cdot \nabla v |\nabla v|^2}{v^3} + \frac{|\nabla v|^6}{v^4} \right)$$

$$\leq \frac{1}{16} \int_\Omega \left((2\varepsilon_1 + 1) \frac{|\nabla |\nabla v|^2|^2}{v^2} + (\frac{1}{2\varepsilon_1} + 1) \frac{|\nabla v|^6}{v^4} \right)$$

for $\varepsilon_1 > 0$. Then, we have from (14) that

$$\int_\Omega \left| \nabla |\nabla \sqrt{v}|^2 \right|^2 \leq \frac{1}{16} \left(2\varepsilon_1 + 1 + \frac{\tilde{\epsilon}}{8\varepsilon_1} + \frac{\tilde{\epsilon}}{4} \right) \int_\Omega \frac{|\nabla |\nabla v|^2|^2}{v^2} \tag{18}$$

for all $t \in (0, T_{\max})$, where $\tilde{\epsilon} = \frac{2}{21-4\sqrt{26}}$ for simplicity. Combining (18) and (17) with (16), we can obtain that

$$\int_{\partial \Omega} \frac{|\nabla v|^2}{v^2} \frac{\partial(|\nabla v|^2)}{\partial \nu} \leq \varepsilon \left(2\varepsilon_1 + 1 + \frac{\tilde{\epsilon}}{8\varepsilon_1} + \frac{\tilde{\epsilon}}{4}\right) \int_{\Omega} \frac{|\nabla |\nabla v|^2|^2}{v^2} + 16C_{\varepsilon}.$$

Denoting $\hat{\epsilon} = \varepsilon(2\varepsilon_1 + 1 + \frac{\tilde{\epsilon}}{8\varepsilon_1} + \frac{\tilde{\epsilon}}{4})$ and $C(\hat{\epsilon}) = 16C_{\varepsilon}$, we prove (15) for any $\hat{\epsilon} > 0$. □

In preparation for the construction and estimation of energy-type functionals, some important *a priori* estimates are provided and collected into two lemmas in the following.

Lemma 5. *Let $k > 0$ and (u, v) be the solutions of (1) satisfying Proposition 1. Then, we have for any $\hat{\epsilon} > 0$ that*

$$\frac{d}{dt} \int_{\Omega} \frac{|\nabla v|^4}{v^2} + \int_{\Omega} \frac{|\nabla v|^4}{v^2} \leq -\left(\frac{4k}{3} - 2k\hat{\epsilon}\right) \int_{\Omega} \frac{|\nabla v|^2 |D^2 v|^2}{v^2} - 2 \int_{\Omega} \frac{|\nabla v|^4 u}{v^3} \\ + 4 \int_{\Omega} \frac{|\nabla v|^2 \nabla v \cdot \nabla u}{v^2} + C(\hat{\epsilon}). \tag{19}$$

Proof. Through straightforward calculation, we can show

$$\frac{d}{dt} \int_{\Omega} \frac{|\nabla v|^4}{v^2} = 4 \int_{\Omega} \underbrace{\frac{|\nabla v|^2 \nabla v \cdot \nabla v_t}{v^2}}_{I_1} - 2 \int_{\Omega} \frac{|\nabla v|^4 v_t}{v^3}$$

$$= 4k \int_{\Omega} \underbrace{\frac{|\nabla v|^2 \nabla v \cdot \nabla \Delta v}{v^2}}_{I_2} - 2 \int_{\Omega} \frac{|\nabla v|^4}{v^2} + 4 \int_{\Omega} \frac{|\nabla v|^2 \nabla v \nabla u}{v^2} \tag{20}$$

$$- 2k \int_{\Omega} \frac{|\nabla v|^4 \Delta v}{v^3} - 2 \int_{\Omega} \frac{|\nabla v|^4 u}{v^3}.$$

In light of (10), we have from (15) that

$$I_1 = 2k \int_{\Omega} \frac{|\nabla v|^2 \Delta |\nabla v|^2}{v^2} - 4k \int_{\Omega} \frac{|\nabla v|^2 |D^2 v|^2}{v^2}$$

$$= 2k \int_{\partial \Omega} \frac{|\nabla v|^2}{v^2} \frac{\partial(|\nabla v|^2)}{\partial \nu} - 2k \int_{\Omega} \nabla\left(\frac{|\nabla v|^2}{v^2}\right) \cdot \nabla |\nabla v|^2 - 4k \int_{\Omega} \frac{|\nabla v|^2 |D^2 v|^2}{v^2}$$

$$= 2k \int_{\partial \Omega} \frac{|\nabla v|^2}{v^2} \frac{\partial(|\nabla v|^2)}{\partial \nu} - 2k \int_{\Omega} \underbrace{\frac{(\nabla |\nabla v|^2)^2}{v^2}}_{I_3} \tag{21}$$

$$+ 4k \int_{\Omega} \frac{|\nabla v|^2 \nabla v \cdot \nabla |\nabla v|^2}{v^3} - 4k \int_{\Omega} \frac{|\nabla v|^2 |D^2 v|^2}{v^2}$$

$$\leq -(12k - 2k\hat{\epsilon}) \int_{\Omega} \frac{|\nabla v|^2 |D^2 v|^2}{v^2} + 4k \int_{\Omega} \overbrace{\frac{\nabla v |\nabla v|^2 \cdot \nabla |\nabla v|^2}{v^3}}^{I_3} + C(\hat{\epsilon}).$$

Similarly, we calculate that

$$I_2 = 2k \int_{\Omega} \nabla\left(\frac{|\nabla v|^4}{v^3}\right) \nabla v = 4k \int_{\Omega} \frac{|\nabla v|^2 \nabla v \cdot \nabla |\nabla v|^2}{v^3} - 6k \int_{\Omega} \frac{|\nabla v|^6}{v^4}.$$

Given by the sum of I_2 and I_3 and taking $\epsilon = \frac{1}{3}$, (6) implies that

$$\begin{aligned} I_2 + I_3 =& 8k \int_\Omega \frac{|\nabla v|^2 \nabla v \cdot \nabla |\nabla v|^2}{v^3} - 6k \int_\Omega \frac{|\nabla v|^6}{v^4} \\ \leq & 8k\epsilon \int_\Omega \frac{(\nabla |\nabla v|^2)^2}{v^2} + \left(\frac{2k}{\epsilon} - 6k\right) \int_\Omega \frac{|\nabla v|^6}{v^4} \\ =& \frac{32k}{3} \int_\Omega \frac{|\nabla v|^2 |D^2 v|^2}{v^2}. \end{aligned} \quad (22)$$

Substituting (22) and (21) into (20), we finish the proof by taking the first identity of Lemma 3. □

Lemma 6. *Supposing that (u,v) solves (1) and all conditions of Proposition 1 hold, then there exist small $\epsilon_1, \epsilon_2 > 0$ and $\delta > 0$ such that*

$$\frac{1}{2}\frac{d}{dt}\int_\Omega u^2 \leq -(1 - \chi\epsilon_1\delta^*)\int_\Omega |\nabla u|^2 + \frac{\chi\epsilon_2}{4\epsilon_1}\int_\Omega u^3 + \frac{\chi\sqrt{6}}{36\epsilon_1\sqrt{\epsilon_2}}\int_\Omega \frac{|\nabla v|^6}{v^4}. \quad (23)$$

Proof. In light of the u equation of (1) and integration by parts, we can show that

$$\frac{1}{2}\frac{d}{dt}\int_\Omega u^2 = \int_\Omega u\nabla \cdot \left(\nabla u - \chi\frac{\nabla v}{v}u\right) = -\int_\Omega |\nabla u|^2 + \int_\Omega \chi u \frac{\nabla u \cdot \nabla v}{v}. \quad (24)$$

The employment of (7) implies

$$\int_\Omega \chi u \frac{\nabla u \cdot \nabla v}{v} \leq \chi\epsilon_1 \int_\Omega \frac{|\nabla u|^2}{v^{\frac{2}{3}}} + \frac{\chi\epsilon_2}{4\epsilon_1}\int_\Omega u^3 + \frac{\chi\sqrt{6}}{36\epsilon_1\sqrt{\epsilon_2}}\int_\Omega \frac{|\nabla v|^6}{v^4} \quad (25)$$

for small $\epsilon_1, \epsilon_2 > 0$. Note that v has the lower bound for any $t > 0$. Let $\delta^* := \delta^{-\frac{2}{3}}$ be the upper bound of $v^{-\frac{2}{3}}$ and substitute (25) into (24) to obtain (23). □

5. Uniform Boundedness

In this section, we shall finish the proof of Theorem 1. Firstly, we construct the energy functional and prove that each item of the functional is uniform bounded.

Theorem 3. *For $\alpha > 0$, let $\mathcal{F}_\alpha(u,v)$ take the following form:*

$$\mathcal{F}_\alpha(u,v) = \alpha \int_\Omega u^2 + \int_\Omega \frac{|\nabla v|^4}{v^2}.$$

Then, for $\Omega \subset \mathbb{R}^2$ and any $\chi > 0$, there exists a constant $C_k(u_0, v_0, \Omega, \chi) > 0$ such that if $k > C_k(u_0, v_0, \Omega, \chi)$, then for some $C > 0$

$$\frac{d}{dt}\mathcal{F}_\alpha(u,v) + \mathcal{F}_\alpha(u,v) < C \text{ for all } t \in (0, T_{\max}). \quad (26)$$

Proof. Combining (19) and (23), we achieve

$$\frac{d}{dt}(\alpha \int_\Omega u^2 + \int_\Omega \frac{|\nabla v|^4}{v^2}) + (\alpha \int_\Omega u^2 + \int_\Omega \frac{|\nabla v|^4}{v^2})$$

$$\leq -(2\alpha - 2\alpha\chi\epsilon_1\delta^*)\int_\Omega |\nabla u|^2 + \overbrace{\frac{\alpha\chi\epsilon_2}{2\epsilon_1}\int_\Omega u^3}^{I_1} + \overbrace{\frac{\alpha\chi\sqrt{6}}{18\epsilon_1\sqrt{\epsilon_2}}\int_\Omega \frac{|\nabla v|^6}{v^4}}^{I_2} \qquad (27)$$

$$-(\frac{4k}{3} - 2k\hat{e})\int_\Omega \frac{|\nabla v|^2|D^2v|^2}{v^2} - 2\int_\Omega \frac{|\nabla v|^4 u}{v^3} + 4\overbrace{\int_\Omega \frac{|\nabla v|^2 \nabla v \cdot \nabla u}{v^2}}^{I_3}$$

$$+ \alpha \int_\Omega u^2 + C(\hat{e}).$$

The Gagliardo–Nirenberg inequality and the boundedness of $\|u\|_{L^1(\Omega)}$ imply that there exists $C > 0$ depending on $\|u_0\|_{L^1(\Omega)}, \Omega$ such that

$$\int_\Omega u^2 \leq \eta \int_\Omega |\nabla u|^2 + C$$

for some small $\eta > 0$ and

$$I_1 = \frac{\alpha\chi\epsilon_2}{2\epsilon_1}\|u\|^3_{L^3(\Omega)} \leq \frac{\alpha\chi\epsilon_2}{2\epsilon_1}(C_1\|\nabla u\|^2_{L^2(\Omega)} + C_2), \qquad (28)$$

where $C_1, C_2 > 0$, depending on $\|u_0\|_{L^1(\Omega)}$ and Ω. For I_3, we employ Lemma 2 to obtain

$$I_3 \leq \frac{1}{\epsilon_3}\int_\Omega \frac{|\nabla v|^6}{v^4} + 4\epsilon_3\int_\Omega |\nabla u|^2 \qquad (29)$$

for any $\epsilon_3 > 0$. Combining the first item of (29) with I_2 and employing (14), we have

$$(\frac{\alpha\chi\sqrt{6}}{18\epsilon_1\sqrt{\epsilon_2}} + \frac{1}{\epsilon_3})\int_\Omega \frac{|\nabla v|^6}{v^4} \leq (\frac{\alpha\chi\sqrt{6}}{18\epsilon_1\sqrt{\epsilon_2}} + \frac{1}{\epsilon_3})\tilde{\epsilon}\int_\Omega \frac{|\nabla v|^2|D^2v|^2}{v^2}, \qquad (30)$$

where we denote $\tilde{\epsilon} = \frac{2}{21 - 4\sqrt{26}}$ for simplicity. Thus, substituting (28)–(30) into (27) gives

$$\frac{d}{dt}(\alpha \int_\Omega u^2 + \int_\Omega \frac{|\nabla v|^4}{v^2}) + (\alpha \int_\Omega u^2 + \int_\Omega \frac{|\nabla v|^4}{v^2})$$

$$\leq -\overbrace{(2\alpha(1 - \chi\epsilon_1\delta^* - \frac{\chi\epsilon_2}{4\epsilon_1}C_1 - \eta) - 4\epsilon_3)}^{\kappa_1}\int_\Omega |\nabla u|^2 \qquad (31)$$

$$-\overbrace{(\frac{4k}{3} - 2k\hat{e} - \frac{\alpha\chi\sqrt{6}}{18\epsilon_1\sqrt{\epsilon_2}}\tilde{\epsilon} - \frac{1}{\epsilon_3}\tilde{\epsilon})}^{\kappa_2}\int_\Omega \frac{|\nabla v|^2|D^2v|^2}{v^2} + C.$$

Let ϵ_1, ϵ_2 and ϵ_3 be small, such that $\kappa_1 = 0$. Then, taking a small $\hat{e}$ such that $\frac{2}{3} > \hat{e}$, we denote

$$C_{(\epsilon_1,\epsilon_2,\epsilon_3)} := \frac{\alpha\chi\sqrt{6}}{6\epsilon_1\sqrt{\epsilon_2}(4 - 6\hat{e})}\tilde{\epsilon} + \frac{3}{\epsilon_3(4 - 6\hat{e})}\tilde{\epsilon} > 0,$$

and let C_k depending on u_0, v_0, Ω, χ be the lower bound of $C_{(\epsilon_1,\epsilon_2,\epsilon_3)}$ provided $\kappa_1 = 0$. Therefore, for any $k \geq C_k > 0$, we have $\kappa_2 \geq 0$ and can then deduce (26). □

Theorem 4. *Let (u,v) be the solutions of (1) satisfying all conditions in Proposition 1. Then,*

$$\int_\Omega u^2(\cdot,t) \leq C \quad \text{and} \quad \int_\Omega |\nabla v(\cdot,t)|^2 \leq C, \tag{32}$$

with $t \in (0, T_{\max})$.

Proof. According to (26), there is $C > 0$ such that

$$\int_\Omega u^2(\cdot,t) \leq C \quad \text{and} \quad \int_\Omega \frac{|\nabla v|^4}{v^2}(\cdot,t) \leq C,$$

for all $t \in (0, T_{\max})$. From Young's inequality and the Gagliardo–Nirenberg inequality, there exist $\epsilon_4, \epsilon_{GN} > 0$ and $C > 0$ such that

$$\begin{aligned}\int_\Omega |\nabla v(\cdot,t)|^2 &\leq C_{\epsilon_4} \int_\Omega \frac{|\nabla v|^4}{v^2}(\cdot,t) + \epsilon_4 \int_\Omega v^2(\cdot,t) \\ &\leq C_{\epsilon_4} \int_\Omega \frac{|\nabla v|^4}{v^2}(\cdot,t) + \epsilon_4 \epsilon_{GN} \int_\Omega |\nabla v(\cdot,t)|^2 + C\end{aligned} \tag{33}$$

for all $t \in (0, T_{\max})$. Taking $\epsilon_4 < \frac{1}{2\epsilon_{GN}}$, then we have $\epsilon_4 \epsilon_{GN} < \frac{1}{2}$ and prove (32). □

Proof of Theorem 1. Using the well-known Moser's technique [32], the L^∞ boundedness of u follows from Theorem 4. Indeed, one can follow the estimates of Nagai [15] or directly employ Lemma 2.3 in [7] to prove the theorem. □

6. Conclusions

Our paper proves the uniform boundedness of solutions of the chemotaxis system with singular sensitivity under a small diffusion rate of the chemical signal. We prove a user-friendly inequality that has certain parameters, and construct a new energy functional that is applicable to the double Keller–Segel model with nonlinear sources.

Author Contributions: Conceptualization, J.L., B.T. and D.W.; Methodology, D.W.; Validation, J.L., B.T. and J.T.; Formal analysis, J.L., J.T. and Y.W.; Writing—original draft, B.T. and D.W.; Writing—review & editing, J.L., J.T. and Y.W. All authors have read and agreed to the published version of the manuscript.

Funding: This research received no external funding.

Data Availability Statement: Not applicable.

Conflicts of Interest: The authors declare no conflict of interest.

References

1. Keller, E.F.; Segel, L.A. Initiation of slime mold aggregation viewed as an instability. *J. Theor. Biol.* **1970**, *26*, 399–415. [CrossRef] [PubMed]
2. Biler, P. Global solutions to some parabolic-elliptic systems of chemotaxis. *Adv. Math. Sci. Appl.* **1999**, *9*, 347–359.
3. Fujie, K.; Winkler, M.; Yokota, T. Blow-up prevention by logistic sources in a parabolic–elliptic Keller-Segel system with singular sensitivity. *Nonlinear Anal. Theory Methods Appl.* **2014**, *109*, 56–71. [CrossRef]
4. Fujie, K.; Winkler, M.; Yokota, T. Boundedness of solutions to parabolic–elliptic Keller-Segel systems with signal-dependent sensitivity. *Math. Methods Appl. Sci.* **2015**, *38*, 1212–1224. [CrossRef]
5. Zhigun, A. Generalised supersolutions with mass control for the Keller–Segel system with logarithmic sensitivity. *J. Math. Anal. Appl.* **2018**, *467*, 1270–1286. [CrossRef]
6. Fujie, K. Boundedness in a fully parabolic chemotaxis system with singular sensitivity. *J. Math. Anal. Appl.* **2015**, *424*, 675–684. [CrossRef]
7. Lankeit, J. A new approach toward boundedness in a two-dimensional parabolic chemotaxis system with singular sensitivity. *Math. Methods Appl. Sci.* **2015**, *39*, 394–404. [CrossRef]
8. Marras, M.; Viglialoro, G. Boundedness in a fully parabolic chemotaxis-consumption system with nonlinear diffusion and sensitivity, and logistic source. *Math. Nachrichten* **2018**, *291*, 2318–2333. [CrossRef]

9. Zhang, Q. Global bounded solutions to a Keller-Segel system with singular sensitivity. *Appl. Math. Lett.* **2020**, *107*, 106397. [CrossRef]
10. Liujie, G.; Fei, G.; Hui, Z. Existence, uniqueness and L∞-bound for weak solutions of a time fractional Keller-Segel system. *Chaos Solitons Fractals* **2022**, *160*, 112–185.
11. Liu, D.; Tao, Y. Global boundedness in a fully parabolic attraction–repulsion chemotaxis model. *Math. Methods Appl. Sci.* **2015**, *38*, 2537–2546. [CrossRef]
12. Wang, Q. Global solutions of a Keller-Segel system with saturated logarithmic sensitivity function. *Commun. Pure Appl. Anal.* **2015**, *14*, 383–396. [CrossRef]
13. Xu, J.; Liu, Z.; Shi, S. Large time behavior of solutions for the attraction–repulsion Keller-Segel system with large initial data. *Appl. Math. Lett.* **2019**, *87*, 13–19. [CrossRef]
14. Osaki, K.; Yagi, A. Finite dimensional attractor for one-dimensional Keller-Segel equations. *Funkc. Ekvacioj* **2001**, *44*, 441–469.
15. Nagai, T.; Senba, T.; Yoshida, K. Application of the Trudinger-Moser inequality to a parabolic system of chemotaxis. *Funkc. Ekvacioj* **1997**, *40*, 411–434.
16. Corrias, L.; Perthame, B.; Zaag, H. Global solutions of some chemotaxis and angiogenesis systems in high space dimensions. *Milan J. Math.* **2004**, *72*, 1–28. [CrossRef]
17. Winkler, M. Absence of collapse in a parabolic chemotaxis system with signal-dependent sensitivity. *Math. Nachrichten* **2010**, *283*, 1664–1673. [CrossRef]
18. Fujie, K.; Yokota, T. Boundedness in a fully parabolic chemotaxis system with strongly singular sensitivity. *J. Math. Anal. Appl.* **2014**, *38*, 140–143. [CrossRef]
19. Keller, E.F.; Segel, L.A. Traveling bands of chemotactic bacteria: A theoretical analysis. *J. Theor. Biol.* **1971**, *30*, 235–248. [CrossRef]
20. Winkler, M. Global solutions in a fully parabolic chemotaxis system with singular sensitivity. *Math. Methods Appl. Sci.* **2011**, *34*, 176–190. [CrossRef]
21. Ahn, J.; Kang, K.; Lee, J. Global well-posedness of logarithmic Keller-Segel type systems. *J. Differ. Equ.* **2021**, *287*, 185–211. [CrossRef]
22. Stinner, C.; Winkler, M. Global weak solutions in a chemotaxis system with large singular sensitivity. *Nonlinear Anal. Real World Appl.* **2011**, *12*, 3727–3740. [CrossRef]
23. Lankeit, J.; Winkler, M. A generalized solution concept for the Keller-Segel system with logarithmic sensitivity: Global solvability for large nonradial data. *Nonlinear Differ. Equ. Appl.* **2017**, *24*, 49–73. [CrossRef]
24. Fujie, K.; Senba, T. Global existence and boundedness of radial solutions to a two dimensional fully parabolic chemotaxis system with general sensitivity. *Nonlinearity* **2016**, *29*, 2417–2450. [CrossRef]
25. Zhao, X.; Zheng, S. Global boundedness of solutions in a parabolic-parabolic chemotaxis system with singular sensitivity. *J. Math. Anal. Appl.* **2016**, *443*, 445–452. [CrossRef]
26. Horstmann, D.; Winkler, M. Boundedness vs. blow-up in a chemotaxis system. *J. Differ. Equ.* **2005**, *215*, 52–107. [CrossRef]
27. Winkler, M. The two-dimensional Keller–Segel system with singular sensitivity and signal absorption: Global large-data solutions and their relaxation properties. *Math. Model. Methods Appl. Sci.* **2016**, *26*, 987–1024. [CrossRef]
28. Wang, Q.; Wang, D.; Feng, Y. Global well-posedness and uniform boundedness of urban crime models: One-dimensional case. *J. Differ. Equ.* **2020**, *269*, 6216–6235. [CrossRef]
29. Winkler, M. Aggregation vs. global diffusive behavior in the higher-dimensional Keller-Segel model. *J. Differ. Equ.* **2010**, *248*, 2889–2905. [CrossRef]
30. Young, W.H. On classes of summable functions and their Fourier series. *Proc. R. Soc. Lond. Ser. A Contain. Pap. Math. Phys. Character* **1912**, *87*, 225–229.
31. Winkler, M. Global Large-Data Solutions in a Chemotaxis-(Navier–)Stokes System Modeling Cellular Swimming in Fluid Drops. *Commun. Partial. Differ. Equ.* **2012**, *37*, 319–351. [CrossRef]
32. Alikakos, N.D. L_p bounds of solutions of reaction-diffusion equations. *Commun. Partial. Differ. Equ.* **1979**, *4*, 827–868. [CrossRef]

Disclaimer/Publisher's Note: The statements, opinions and data contained in all publications are solely those of the individual author(s) and contributor(s) and not of MDPI and/or the editor(s). MDPI and/or the editor(s) disclaim responsibility for any injury to people or property resulting from any ideas, methods, instructions or products referred to in the content.

Article

Lump-Type Solutions, Lump Solutions, and Mixed Rogue Waves for Coupled Nonlinear Generalized Zakharov Equations

Aly R. Seadawy [1,*], Syed T. R. Rizvi [2] and Hanadi Zahed [1]

[1] Mathematics Department, Faculty of Science, Taibah University, Al-Madinah Al-Munawarah 41411, Saudi Arabia
[2] Department of Mathematics, COMSATS University Islamabad, Lahore Campus, Islamabad 45550, Pakistan
* Correspondence: aabdelalim@taibahu.edu.sa

Abstract: This article studies diverse forms of lump-type solutions for coupled nonlinear generalized Zakharov equations (CNL-GZEs) in plasma physics through an appropriate transformation approach and bilinear equations. By utilizing the positive quadratic assumption in the bilinear equation, the lump-type solutions are derived. Similarly, by employing a single exponential transformation in the bilinear equation, the lump one-soliton solutions are derived. Furthermore, by choosing the double exponential ansatz in the bilinear equation, the lump two-soliton solutions are found. Interaction behaviors are observed and we also establish a few new solutions in various dimensions (3D and contour). Furthermore, we compute rogue-wave solutions and lump periodic solutions by employing proper hyperbolic and trigonometric functions.

Keywords: CNL-GZE; lump-type solitons; rogue wave; appropriate transformation technique

MSC: 35J05; 35J10; 35K05; 35L05

1. Introduction

The study of partial differential equations (PDEs) occurs in various fields such as theoretical physics, applied mathematics, biological sciences, and engineering sciences. These PDEs play a crucial role in explaining key scientific phenomena. For instance, the Korteweg–de Vries equation governs shallow water wave dynamics near ocean shores and beaches, and the nonlinear Schrödinger's equation governs the propagation of solitons through optical fibers. Some examples of PDEs and their applications can be found in [1–8].

Although the above-mentioned PDEs are scalar, a large number of PDEs are coupled. Some of them are two coupled PDEs such as the Gear–Grimshaw equation, whereas others are three-coupled PDEs. An example of a three-coupled PDE is the Wu–Zhang equation. These coupled PDEs are also calculated in distinct areas of theoretical physics. In this paper, we will study CNL-GZE used in plasmas.

Lump waves (LWs), as superior nonlinear wave phenomena, have been visualized in various fields. LWs are theoretically viewed as a limited type of soliton and move with higher propagating energy compared to general solitons. Consequently, LWs can be destructive and even catastrophic in certain systems, such as in the ocean and finance. It is important to be able to find and anticipate LWs in practical applications. In recent years, studies on lump solutions have increased, leading to more specialized investigations. Therefore, theoretical investigations of LWs are instrumental in enhancing our understanding and predicting possible extremes in nonlinear systems [9–13].

Finding the lump solutions of PDEs has become a primary focus in recent years. As a result, several mathematical experts have developed important schemes in order to solve PDEs [14–16].

In this article, we consider the CNL-GZE for the complex envelope $u(x,t)$ of the high-frequency wave and the real low-frequency field $v(x,t)$, as follows [17]:

$$\begin{cases} ih_1\psi_t + \psi_{xx} - 2h_2|\phi|^2\psi + 2\psi\phi = 0, \\ \phi_{tt} - \psi_{xx} - (|\phi|^2)_{xx} = 0. \end{cases} \quad (1)$$

where h_1 and h_1 are real constants. The cubic term in Equation (1) represents the nonlinear self-interaction in the high-frequency subsystem, which corresponds to a self-focusing effect in plasma physics.

Several researchers have worked on the stated model. For instance, Wang et al. evaluated periodic wave solutions for GZEs using the extended F-expansion method [17]. Zheng et al. performed a numerical simulation of a GZ system [18]. Bao et al. developed numerical schemes for a GZ system [19]. Bhrawy et al. constructed an efficient Jacobi pseudospectral approximation for a nonlinear complex GZ system [20]. Zhang et al. studied solitary wave solutions through a variational approach [21]. Similarly, Yildirim et al. studied some newly discovered soliton solutions of GZEs by applying He's variational approach [22]. Li et al. computed additional exact solutions of GZEs through the Exp-function method [23]. Buhe et al. studied symmetry reductions, conservation laws, and exact solutions for GZEs [24]. Lin et al. constructed some additional exact solutions for GZEs through the Exp-function method [23]. Wu et al. studied exact solutions for GZEs using a variational approach [25]. However, in this paper, we will explore lump, lump-type, lump one-strip, and lump two-strip solutions for CNL-GZEs through appropriate transformation methods and bilinear equations. We compute the lump solutions by choosing the appropriate polynomial function. In addition, we compute lump-periodic and rogue-wave solutions by using logarithmic transformation.

This article is organized as follows. In Section 2, we form bilinear equations and evaluate lump solutions for the coupled nonlinear generalized Zakharov equations in plasma physics through appropriate transformation approaches. The solutions are presented along with with their corresponding graphs. The mixed solutions of soliton and lump waves are provided in Section 3. We evaluate the lump one-strip and lump two-strip solutions using suitable profiles in Section 3. By employing a trigonometric ansatz in the bilinear equation, we compute lump periodic solutions in Section 4. By utilizing a hyperbolic ansatz in the bilinear equation, we explore rogue-wave solutions in Section 5. Section 6 discusses the results of the obtained solutions, and finally, in Section 7, we present some concluding remarks.

2. Lump Solution

For the lump solutions of Equation (1), we apply the following ansatz: [26–30],

$$\psi(x,t) = \frac{h_3 e^{(ict)} p(x,t)}{q(x,t)}, \quad \phi(x,t) = 2[\ln q(x,t)]_x - c, \quad (2)$$

then, we obtain the bilinear equations,

$$2h_2 h_3^2 p^3 + 2ch_3 pqt^2 + ch_1 h_3 pq^2 - ih_1 h_3 q^2 + p_t + ih_1 h_3 pqq_t - 4h_3 pqq_x \\ + 2h_3 q p_x q_x - 2h_3 pq_x^2 - h_3 q^2 p_{xx} + h_3 pqq_{xx} = 0, \quad (3)$$

and

$$h_3^2 q^2 p_x^2 q_t^2 q_x - q^2 q_{tt} q_x - 4h_3^2 pq p_x q_x + 3h_3^3 p^2 q_x^2 - 2qq_x^3 - 2q^2 q_t q_{xt} + q^3 q_{xtt} \\ + h_3^2 pq^2 p_{xx} - h_3^2 p^2 qq_{xx} + 3q^2 q_x q_{xx} - q^3 q_{xxx} = 0, \quad (4)$$

respectively.

Now, to obtain the LP solution, the functions p and q in Equations (3) and (4) are assumed to be [27,28],

$$p = \zeta_1^2 + \zeta_2^2 + a_2, \quad q = \zeta_1^2 + \zeta_2^2 + a_3, \tag{5}$$

where $\zeta_1 = a_0 x + t$, $\zeta_2 = a_1 x + t$.

In addition, $a_i (1 \leq i \leq 3)$ are specific constants. Now, by substituting Equation (5) into Equations (3) and (4) and solving the equations obtained from the coefficients of x and t, we obtain:

Set I. The values of unknowns for Equations (3) and (4), respectively, are as follows:

$$\begin{cases} a_0 = \frac{-1+i\sqrt{3}}{2},\ h_1 = -\frac{2(h_2 h_3^2 + c)}{c},\ a_2 = a_2,\ a_3 = a_3,\ a_0 = a_0. \\ \text{and} \\ a_0 = \frac{1-i}{2},\ a_1 = \frac{1+i}{2},\ h_3 = 0,\ a_2 = a_2,\ a_3 = a_3. \end{cases} \tag{6}$$

Then, the values in Equation (6) generate the required solutions for Equations (3) and (4), which are, respectively,

$$\begin{cases} \psi_{1,1} = -\dfrac{2e^{ict}(c + h_2 h_3^2)\left(a_2 + \left(t + \frac{(-1+i\sqrt{3})}{2} x\right)^2 + (t + a_1 x)^2\right)}{c\left(a_3 + \left(t + \frac{(-1+i\sqrt{3})x}{2}\right)^2 + (t + a_1 x)^2\right)}, \\ \text{and} \\ \phi_{1,1} = \dfrac{2(-1+i\sqrt{3})\left(\left(t + \frac{(-1+i\sqrt{3})}{2} x\right)^2 + 2a_1(t + a_1 x)\right)}{a_3 + \left(t + \frac{(-1+i\sqrt{3})x}{2}\right)^2 + (t + a_1 x)^2} - c. \end{cases} \tag{7}$$

and

$$\begin{cases} \psi_{1,2} = \dfrac{e^{ict} h_1 \left(a_2 + \left(t + \left(\frac{1-i}{2}\right)x\right)^2 + \left(t + \left(\frac{1+i}{2}\right)x\right)^2\right)}{a_3 + \left(t + \left(\frac{1-i}{2}\right)x\right)^2 + \left(t + \left(\frac{1+i}{2}\right)x\right)^2}, \\ \text{and} \\ \phi_{1,2} = \dfrac{2\left((1-i)\left(t + \left(\frac{1-i}{2}\right)x\right) + (1+i)\left(t + \left(\frac{1+i}{2}\right)x\right)\right)}{a_3 + \left(t + \left(\frac{1-i}{2}\right)x\right)^2 + \left(t + \left(\frac{1+i}{2}\right)x\right)^2} - c. \end{cases} \tag{8}$$

Set II. The values of the parameters in Equations (3) and (4) are, respectively,

$$\begin{cases} a_0 = \frac{-3+3i}{4},\ a_1 = \frac{3+3i}{4},\ h_1 = -2,\ a_2 = 0,\ a_3 = a_3. \\ \text{and} \\ a_0 = 1,\ a_1 = 1,\ h_3 = h_3,\ a_2 = a_2,\ a_3 = a_3. \end{cases} \tag{9}$$

Then, the values in Equation (9) generate the required solutions for Equations (3) and (4), which are, respectively,

$$\begin{cases} \psi_{2,1} = -\dfrac{2e^{ict}\left(\left(t - \left(\frac{3-3i}{4}\right)x\right)^2 + \left(t + \left(\frac{3+3i}{4}\right)x\right)^2\right)}{a_3 + \left(t - \left(\frac{3-3i}{4}\right)x\right)^2 + \left(t + \left(\frac{3+3i}{4}\right)x\right)^2}, \\ \text{and} \\ \phi_{2,1} = \dfrac{2\left(\left(\frac{-3+3i}{2}\right)\left(t - \left(\frac{3-3i}{4}\right)x\right) + \left(\frac{3+3i}{2}\right)\left(t + \left(\frac{3+3i}{4}\right)x\right)\right)}{a_3 + \left(t - \left(\frac{3-3i}{4}\right)x\right)^2 + \left(t + \left(\frac{3+3i}{4}\right)x\right)^2} - c. \end{cases} \tag{10}$$

and

$$\begin{cases} \psi_{2,2} = \frac{e^{ict}h_1\left(a_2+2(t+x)^2\right)}{a_3+2(t+x)^2}, \\ \text{and} \\ \phi_{2,2} = -c + \frac{8(t+x)}{a_3+2(t+x)^2}. \end{cases} \tag{11}$$

3. Mixed Solutions of Soliton and Lump Waves

In this section, we study the interaction of a lump soliton with a single kink wave and the interaction of a lump soliton with double kink waves.

3.1. Lump One-Strip Soliton Interaction Solution

To obtain the lump one-strip solution, we use the transformations given in Equations (3) and (4) [22,27–30]:

$$p = \xi_1^2 + \xi_2^2 + a_2 + b_0 e^{k_1 x + k_2 t}, \quad q = \xi_1^2 + \xi_2^2 + a_3 + b_0 e^{k_1 x + k_2 t}, \tag{12}$$

where $\xi_1 = a_0 x + t$, $\xi_2 = a_1 x + t$, and $a_i (1 \leq i \leq 3)$, k_1, k_2, and b_0 are any constants. Now, from Equations (12) and (4), we obtain the coefficients of x and t and solve the equations as follows:

Set I. The values of the parameters in Equations (3) and (4) are, respectively,

$$\begin{cases} c = \frac{-18h_2h_3^2+8+4\sqrt{-9ih_1k_2-72h_2h_3^2+4}}{9h_1+18}, \; k_1 = \frac{2+\sqrt{-9ih_1k_2-72h_2h_3^2+4}}{3}, \; a_0 = ia_1, \; h_3 = h_3, \; a_2 = a_2, \\ \text{and} \\ a_0 = \frac{1-2i\sqrt{5}}{3}, a_1 = \frac{1+2i\sqrt{5}}{3}, a_2 = -\frac{69300}{19h_3^4}, a_3 = -\frac{62100}{19h_3^4}, k_1 = -\frac{19}{90}h_3^2, k_2 = -\frac{19}{90}h_3^2. \end{cases} \tag{13}$$

Then, the values in Equation (13) generate the required results for Equations (3) and (4), which are, respectively,

$$\begin{cases} \psi_{3,1} = \dfrac{e^{i\frac{\left(-18h_2h_3^2+8+4\sqrt{-9ih_1k_2-72h_2h_3^2+4}\right)t}{9h_1+18}} h_1 \left(a_2+b_0 e^{k_2 t+\frac{\left(2+\sqrt{-9ih_1k_2-72h_2h_3^2+4}\right)x}{3}}+(t+ia_1 x)^2+(t+a_1 x)^2\right)}{a_3+b_0 e^{k_2 t+\frac{\left(2+\sqrt{-9ih_1k_2-72h_2h_3^2+4}\right)x}{3}}+(t+ia_1 x)^2+(t+a_1 x)^2}, \\ \text{and} \\ \phi_{3,1} = -\dfrac{-18h_2h_3^2+8+4\sqrt{-9ih_1k_2-72h_2h_3^2+4}}{9h_1+18} + \dfrac{2\left(\frac{1}{3}b_0 e^{k_2 t+\frac{\left(2+\sqrt{-9ih_1k_2-72h_2h_3^2+4}\right)x}{3}}\Pi_1\right)}{a_3+b_0 e^{k_2 t+\frac{\left(2+\sqrt{-9ih_1k_2-72h_2h_3^2+4}\right)x}{3}}+(t+ia_1 x)^2+(t+a_1 x)^2}, \\ \Pi_1 = \left(2+\sqrt{-9ih_1k_2-72h_2h_3^2+4}\right)+2ia_1(t+ia_1 x)+2a_1(t+a_1 x). \end{cases} \tag{14}$$

and

$$\begin{cases} \psi_{4,1} = \dfrac{e^{ict}h_1\left(b_0 e^{\frac{19h_3^2 t}{90} - \frac{19h_3^2 x}{90}} - \frac{69300}{19h_3^4} + \left(t + \frac{(1-2i\sqrt{5})x}{3}\right)^2 + \left(t + \frac{(1+2i\sqrt{5})x}{3}\right)^2\right)}{b_0 e^{\frac{19h_3^2 t}{90} - \frac{19h_3^2 x}{90}} - \frac{69300}{19h_3^4} + \left(t + \frac{(1-2i\sqrt{5})x}{3}\right)^2 + \left(t + \frac{(1+2i\sqrt{5})x}{3}\right)^2}, \\ \text{and} \\ \phi_{4,1} = \dfrac{2\left(-\frac{19}{90} b_0 e^{\frac{19h_3^2 t}{90} - \frac{19h_3^2 x}{90}} h_3^2 + \frac{2(1-2i\sqrt{5})}{3}\left(t + \frac{(1-2i\sqrt{5})x}{3}\right) + \Pi_2\right)}{b_0 e^{\frac{19h_3^2 t}{90} - \frac{19h_3^2 x}{90}} - \frac{62100}{19h_3^4} + \left(t + \frac{(1-2i\sqrt{5})x}{3}\right)^2 + \left(t + \frac{(1+2i\sqrt{5})x}{3}\right)^2} - c, \\ \Pi_2 = \dfrac{2(1+2i\sqrt{5})}{3}\left(t + \dfrac{(1-2i\sqrt{5})x}{3}\right). \end{cases} \quad (15)$$

Set II. The values of the parameters in Equations (3) and (4) are, respectively,

$$\begin{cases} a_0 = ia_1,\ k_1 = \dfrac{6h_2 h_3^2 + 3ch_1 + 6c}{4},\ a_3 = a_3,\ h_3 = h_3,\ a_2 = a_2. \\ \text{and} \\ a_0 = \dfrac{-1-2i\sqrt{5}}{3},\ a_1 = \dfrac{-1+2i\sqrt{5}}{3},\ a_2 = -\dfrac{69300}{19h_3^4},\ a_3 = -\dfrac{62100}{19h_3^4},\ k_1 = -\dfrac{19}{90}h_3^2,\ k_2 = -\dfrac{19}{90}h_3^2. \end{cases} \quad (16)$$

Then, the values in Equation (16) generate the required results for Equations (3) and (4), which are, respectively,

$$\begin{cases} \psi_{5,1} = \dfrac{e^{ict}h_1\left(a_2 + b_0 e^{k_2 t + \frac{(6h_2 h_3^2 + 3ch_1 + 6c)x}{4}} + (t + ia_1 x)^2 + (t + a_1 x)^2\right)}{a_3 + b_0 e^{k_2 t + \frac{(6h_2 h_3^2 + 3ch_1 + 6c)x}{4}} + (t + ia_1 x)^2 + (t + a_1 x)^2}, \\ \text{and} \\ \phi_{5,1} = \dfrac{2\left(\frac{1}{4} b_0 e^{k_2 t + \frac{(6h_2 h_3^2 + 3ch_1 + 6c)x}{4}} + (6h_2 h_3^2 + 3ch_1 + 6c) + 2ia_1(t + ia_1 x)^2 + 2a_1(t + a_1 x)^2\right)}{a_3 + b_0 e^{k_2 t + \frac{(6h_2 h_3^2 + 3ch_1 + 6c)x}{4}} + (t + ia_1 x)^2 + (t + a_1 x)^2} - c. \end{cases} \quad (17)$$

and

$$\begin{cases} \psi_{5,2} = \dfrac{e^{ict}h_1\left(b_0 e^{\frac{19h_3^2 t}{90} - \frac{19h_3^2 x}{90}} - \frac{69300}{19h_3^4} + \left(t + \frac{(-1-2i\sqrt{5})x}{3}\right)^2 + \left(t + \frac{(-1+2i\sqrt{5})x}{3}\right)^2\right)}{b_0 e^{\frac{19h_3^2 t}{90} - \frac{19h_3^2 x}{90}} - \frac{69300}{19h_3^4} + \left(t + \frac{(-1-2i\sqrt{5})x}{3}\right)^2 + \left(t + \frac{(-1+2i\sqrt{5})x}{3}\right)^2}, \\ \text{and} \\ \phi_{5,2} = \dfrac{2\left(-\frac{19}{90} b_0 e^{\frac{19h_3^2 t}{90} - \frac{19h_3^2 x}{90}} h_3^2 + \frac{2(-1-2i\sqrt{5})}{3}\left(t + \frac{(-1-2i\sqrt{5})x}{3}\right) + \Pi_3\right)}{b_0 e^{\frac{19h_3^2 t}{90} - \frac{19h_3^2 x}{90}} - \frac{62100}{19h_3^4} + \left(t + \frac{(-1-2i\sqrt{5})x}{3}\right)^2 + \left(t + \frac{(-1+2i\sqrt{5})x}{3}\right)^2} - c, \\ \Pi_3 = \dfrac{2(-1+2i\sqrt{5})}{3}\left(t + \dfrac{(-1-2i\sqrt{5})x}{3}\right). \end{cases} \quad (18)$$

3.2. Lump Double-Strip Soliton Interaction Solution

To obtain the lump two-strip solution, we assume the following transformation [22,27–30]:

$$p = \bigwedge_{1}^{2} + \bigwedge_{2}^{2} + a_3 + m_1 e^{k_1 x + k_2 t + k_3} + m_2 e^{k_4 x + k_5 t + k_6},\quad q = \bigwedge_{1}^{2} + \bigwedge_{2}^{2} + a_4 + m_1 e^{k_1 x + k_2 t + k_3} + m_2 e^{k_4 x + k_5 t + k_6}, \quad (19)$$

where $\Lambda_1 = a_1 x + a_2 t$, $\Lambda_2 = a_1 x + a_2 t$, and $a_i (1 \leq i \leq 4)$, $k_i (1 \leq i \leq 6)$, m_1, and m_2 are specific real parameters. Now, from Equation (19) and Equation (4), we obtain the coefficients of x, t, and exp and solve these equations as follows:

Set I. When $k_5 = k_4 = a_1 = 0$ for Equation (3) and $k_3 = k_6 = a_1 = 0$ for Equation (4), the values of the parameters are, respectively,

$$\begin{cases} a_4 = -\frac{i\left(9ih_2h_3^2k_1^2 - 3a_2a_3h_2h_3^2 + ia_2^2a_3\right)}{\left(3ih_2h_3^2 + a_2\right)a_2}, \ k_2 = \frac{2k_1\left(3ih_2h_3^2 - 2a_2\right)}{3h_2h_3^2}, \ m_1 = -\frac{a_2 m_2 \left(3ih_2h_3^2 m_2 + 2a_2\right)}{-a_2 + 3ih_2h_3^2}. \\ \text{and} \\ a_2 = \frac{\sqrt{6}h_3^2}{60}, \ k_1 = -\frac{\sqrt{6}k_4^2 - \frac{2}{3}\sqrt{6}k_5^2 + 3k_4k_5}{5\sqrt{\frac{2}{5}\sqrt{6}k_4k_5 - \frac{6}{5}k_4^2 - \frac{1}{5}k_5^2}}, \ k_2 = \sqrt{\frac{2}{5}\sqrt{6}k_4k_5 - \frac{6}{5}k_4^2 - \frac{1}{5}k_5^2}, \ a_4 = 0. \end{cases} \quad (20)$$

Then, the values in Equation (20) generate the required results for Equations (3) and (4), which are, respectively,

$$\begin{cases} \psi_{5,1} = \frac{e^{ict}h_1 \left(a_3 + k_6^2 + e^{a_2 t}m_2 - \frac{a_2 m_2 e^{a_2 t}\left(3ih_2h_3^2 m_2 + 2a_2\right)}{-a_2 + 3ih_2h_3^2} + \left(k_3 + \frac{2k_1\left(3ih_2h_3^2 - 2a_2\right)t}{3h_2h_3^2} + k_1 x\right)^2\right)}{2e^{a_2 t} - \frac{i\left(9ih_2h_3^2k_1^2 - 3a_2a_3h_2h_3^2 + ia_2^2a_3\right)}{\left(3ih_2h_3^2 + a_2\right)a_2} + k_6^2 + \left(k_3 + \frac{2k_1\left(3ih_2h_3^2 - 2a_2\right)t}{3h_2h_3^2} + k_1 x\right)^2}, \\ \phi_{5,1} = \frac{4k_1\left(k_3 + \frac{2k_1\left(3ih_2h_3^2 - 2a_2\right)t}{3h_2h_3^2} + k_1 x\right)}{2e^{a_2 t} - \frac{i\left(9ih_2h_3^2k_1^2 - 3a_2a_3h_2h_3^2 + ia_2^2a_3\right)}{\left(3ih_2h_3^2 + a_2\right)a_2} + k_6^2 + \left(k_3 + \frac{2k_1\left(3ih_2h_3^2 - 2a_2\right)t}{3h_2h_3^2} + k_1 x\right)^2} - c. \end{cases} \quad (21)$$

and

$$\begin{cases} \psi_{6,1} = \frac{e^{ict}h_1 \left(\Delta_1 + \left(\sqrt{\frac{2}{5}\sqrt{6}k_4k_5 - \frac{6}{5}k_4^2 - \frac{1}{5}k_5^2} t - \frac{\left(\sqrt{6}k_4^2 - \frac{2}{3}\sqrt{6}k_5^2 + 3k_4k_5\right)x}{5\sqrt{\frac{2}{5}\sqrt{6}k_4k_5 - \frac{6}{5}k_4^2 - \frac{1}{5}k_5^2}}\right)^2\right)}{2e^{\frac{h_3^2 t}{10\sqrt{6}}} + (k_5 t + k_4 x)^2 + \left(\sqrt{\frac{2}{5}\sqrt{6}k_4k_5 - \frac{6}{5}k_4^2 - \frac{1}{5}k_5^2} t - \frac{\left(\sqrt{6}k_4^2 - \frac{2}{3}\sqrt{6}k_5^2 + 3k_4k_5\right)x}{5\sqrt{\frac{2}{5}\sqrt{6}k_4k_5 - \frac{6}{5}k_4^2 - \frac{1}{5}k_5^2}}\right)^2}, \\ \Delta_1 = a_3 + e^{\frac{h_3^2 t}{10\sqrt{6}}} m_1 + e^{\frac{h_3^2 t}{10\sqrt{6}}} m_2 + (k_5 t + k_4 x)^2. \\ \text{and} \\ \phi_{6,1} = \frac{2\left(\Delta_2 - \frac{\left(\sqrt{6}k_4^2 - \frac{2}{3}\sqrt{6}k_5^2 + 3k_4k_5\right)\left(\sqrt{\frac{2}{5}\sqrt{6}k_4k_5 - \frac{6}{5}k_4^2 - \frac{1}{5}k_5^2} t - \frac{\left(\sqrt{6}k_4^2 - \frac{2}{3}\sqrt{6}k_5^2 + 3k_4k_5\right)x}{5\sqrt{\frac{2}{5}\sqrt{6}k_4k_5 - \frac{6}{5}k_4^2 - \frac{1}{5}k_5^2}}\right)}{5\sqrt{\frac{2}{5}\sqrt{6}k_4k_5 - \frac{6}{5}k_4^2 - \frac{1}{5}k_5^2}}\right)}{2e^{\frac{h_3^2 t}{10\sqrt{6}}} + (k_5 t + k_4 x)^2 + \left(\sqrt{\frac{2}{5}\sqrt{6}k_4k_5 - \frac{6}{5}k_4^2 - \frac{1}{5}k_5^2} t - \frac{\left(\sqrt{6}k_4^2 - \frac{2}{3}\sqrt{6}k_5^2 + 3k_4k_5\right)x}{5\sqrt{\frac{2}{5}\sqrt{6}k_4k_5 - \frac{6}{5}k_4^2 - \frac{1}{5}k_5^2}}\right)^2} - c, \\ \Delta_2 = 2k_4(k_5 t + k_4 x). \end{cases} \quad (22)$$

Set II. When $k_5 = k_4 = a_1 = 0$ for Equation (3) and $k_3 = k_6 = a_1 = 0$ for Equation (4), the values of the parameters are, respectively,

$$\begin{cases} a_2 = \frac{4ih_2h_3^2 c(a_3 - a_4)}{-10a_3 h_2 h_3^2 + 10a_4 h_2 h_3^2 + 2a_3 c - 2a_4 c + 9k_1^2}, \ h_1 = -\frac{-10a_3 h_2 h_3^2 + 10a_4 h_2 h_3^2 + 2a_3 c - 2a_4 c + 9k_1^2}{c(a_3 - a_4)}, \\ k_2 = -\frac{\frac{4}{3}ick_1(a_3 - a_4)}{-10a_3 h_2 h_3^2 + 10a_4 h_2 h_3^2 + 2a_3 c - 2a_4 c + 9k_1^2}, \ m_1 = -m_2 - 4. \\ \text{and} \\ m_1 = -\frac{5a_3 m_2 - 4a_4 m_2 - 8a_3 + 6a_4}{5a_3 - 4a_4}, \ k_1 = ik_4, k_2 = ik_5, a_2 = 0. \end{cases} \quad (23)$$

Then, the values in Equation (23) generate the required results for Equations (3) and (4), which are, respectively,

$$\begin{cases}
\psi_{7,1} = \dfrac{-\left(e^{ict}D_1\left(a_3+k_6^2+(-m_2-4)e^{\frac{4ih_2h_3^2c(a_3-a_4)t}{-10a_3h_2h_3^2+10a_4h_2h_3^2+2a_3c-2a_4c+9k_1^2}}+m_2e^{\frac{4ih_2h_3^2c(a_3-a_4)t}{-10a_3h_2h_3^2+10a_4h_2h_3^2+2a_3c-2a_4c+9k_1^2}}D_2\right)\right)}{(a_3-a_4)c\left(a_4+k_6^2+2e^{\frac{4ih_2h_3^2c(a_3-a_4)t}{-10a_3h_2h_3^2+10a_4h_2h_3^2+2a_3c-2a_4c+9k_1^2}}D_2\right)}, \\
D_1 = -10a_3h_2h_3^2+10a_4h_2h_3^2+2a_3c-2a_4c+9k_1^2, \\
D_2 = \left(k_3 - \dfrac{4ik_1c(a_3-a_4)t}{3\left(-10a_3h_2h_3^2+10a_4h_2h_3^2+2a_3c-2a_4c+9k_1^2\right)} + k_1x\right)^2, \\
\text{and} \\
\phi_{7,1} = -c + \dfrac{4k_1\left(k_3 - \dfrac{4ik_1c(a_3-a_4)t}{3\left(-10a_3h_2h_3^2+10a_4h_2h_3^2+2a_3c-2a_4c+9k_1^2\right)} + k_1x\right)}{\left(a_4+k_6^2+2e^{\frac{4ih_2h_3^2c(a_3-a_4)t}{-10a_3h_2h_3^2+10a_4h_2h_3^2+2a_3c-2a_4c+9k_1^2}}D_2\right)}.
\end{cases} \quad (24)$$

and

$$\begin{cases}
\psi_{8,1} = \dfrac{e^{ict}h_1\left(a_3+m_2-\frac{5a_3m_2-4a_4m_2-8a_3+6a_4}{5a_3-4a_4}+(ik_5t+ik_4x)^2+(k_5t+k_4x)^2\right)}{2+a_4+(ik_5t+ik_4x)^2+(k_5t+k_4x)^2}, \\
\text{and} \\
\phi_{8,1} = \dfrac{2\left(2ik_4(ik_5t+ik_4x)^2+2k_4(k_5t+k_4x)^2\right)}{2+a_4+(ik_5t+ik_4x)^2+(k_5t+k_4x)^2} - c.
\end{cases} \quad (25)$$

4. Lump Periodic Soliton Solution

To compute the LPS solution, we use the following supposition in Equations (3) and (4) [22,27–30]:

$$p = \bigwedge_1^2 + \bigwedge_2^2 + a_2 + a_3\cos(n_1x+t), \quad q = \bigwedge_1^2 + \bigwedge_2^2 + a_4 + a_5\cos(n_1x+t) \quad (26)$$

where $\wedge_1 = B_0x+t$, $\wedge_2 = B_1x+t$. In addition, $a_i\,(1 \leq i \leq 5)$ and n_1 are various parameters to be determined. Now, by substituting Equation (26) into Equations (3) and (4) and then examining the coefficients of x, cos function, and t, we obtain the following:

Set I. The values of the parameters for Equations (3) and (4) are, respectively,

$$\begin{cases}
n_1 = -\dfrac{\frac{1}{4}ih_1(a_4-a_5)}{a_4+a_5},\ a_0 = -a_1,\ c = c,\ a_4 = a_4. \\
\text{and} \\
n_1 = -\dfrac{4(a_0^2+a_1^2)}{(a_1+a_0)(3a_0^2+3a_1^2-2)},\ a_0 = a_0,\ c = c,\ a_4 = a_4,\ a_3 = a_3.
\end{cases} \quad (27)$$

Then, the values in Equation (27) generate the required results for Equations (3) and (4), which are, respectively,

$$\begin{cases}
\psi_{9,1} = \dfrac{e^{ict}h_1\left(a_2+(t+a_0x)^2+(t+a_1x)^2+a_4\cos\left(t-\frac{i(a_4-a_5)h_1x}{4(a_4+a_5)}\right)\right)}{\left(a_3+(t+a_0x)^2+(t+a_1x)^2+a_5\cos\left(t-\frac{i(a_4-a_5)h_1x}{4(a_4+a_5)}\right)\right)}, \\
\text{and} \\
\phi_{9,1} = -c + \dfrac{2\left(2a_0(t+a_0x)+2a_1(t+a_1x)+\frac{i(a_4-a_5)h_1a_5\sin\left(t-\frac{i(a_4-a_5)h_1x}{4(a_4+a_5)}\right)}{4(a_4+a_5)}\right)}{\left(a_3+(t+a_0x)^2+(t+a_1x)^2+a_5\cos\left(t-\frac{i(a_4-a_5)h_1x}{4(a_4+a_5)}\right)\right)}.
\end{cases} \quad (28)$$

and

$$\begin{cases} \psi_{10,1} = \dfrac{e^{ict}h_1\left(a_2+(t+a_0x)^2+(t+a_1x)^2+a_4\cos\left(t+\dfrac{4\left(a_0^2+a_1^2\right)x}{(a_1+a_0)\left(3a_0^2+3a_1^2-2\right)}\right)\right)}{\left(a_3+(t+a_0x)^2+(t+a_1x)^2+a_5\cos\left(t+\dfrac{4\left(a_0^2+a_1^2\right)x}{(a_1+a_0)\left(3a_0^2+3a_1^2-2\right)}\right)\right)}, \\ \text{and} \\ \phi_{10,1} = -c + \dfrac{2\left(2a_0(t+a_0x)+2a_1(t+a_1x)-\dfrac{4\left(a_0^2+a_1^2\right)a_5\sin\left(t+\dfrac{4\left(a_0^2+a_1^2\right)x}{(a_1+a_0)\left(3a_0^2+3a_1^2-2\right)}\right)}{(a_1+a_0)\left(3a_0^2+3a_1^2-2\right)}\right)}{\left(a_3+(t+a_0x)^2+(t+a_1x)^2+a_5\cos\left(t+\dfrac{4\left(a_0^2+a_1^2\right)x}{(a_1+a_0)\left(3a_0^2+3a_1^2-2\right)}\right)\right)}. \end{cases} \quad (29)$$

5. Rogue-Wave Solutions

To compute the LPS solution, we use the following supposition in Equations (3) and (4) [22,27–30]:

$$p = \bigwedge_1^2 + \bigwedge_2^2 + a_2 + a_3 \cosh(n_1 x + t), \quad q = \bigwedge_1^2 + \bigwedge_2^2 + a_4 + a_5 \cosh(n_1 x + t) \quad (30)$$

where $\bigwedge_1 = a_0 x + t$, $\bigwedge_2 = a_1 x + t$. In addition, $a_i(1 \leq i \leq 5)$ and n_1 are various parameters to be determined. Now, by substituting Equation (26) into Equations (3) and (4) and then examining the coefficients of x, cos function, and t, we obtain the following:

Set I. The values of the parameters for Equations (3) and (4), are, respectively,

$$\begin{cases} a_4 = -\dfrac{a_5(4in_1+h_1)}{(4in_1-h_1)}, \ a_0 = -a_1, \ a_2 = a_2, \ a_4 = a_4, \ a_3 = a_3. \\ \text{and} \\ a_1 = ia_0, \ a_4 = 0, \ n_1 = 1, \ a_3 = a_3, \ a_5 = a_5. \end{cases} \quad (31)$$

Then, the values in Equation (31) generate the solutions for Equations (3) and (4), which are, respectively,

$$\begin{cases} \psi_{11,1} = \dfrac{e^{ict}h_1\left(a_2+(t-a_1x)^2+(t+a_1x)^2-\dfrac{a_5(4in_1+h_1)\cosh(t+n_1x)}{(4in_1-h_1)}\right)}{\left(a_3+(t-a_1x)^2+(t+a_1x)^2+a_5\cosh(t+n_2x)\right)}, \\ \text{and} \\ \phi_{11,1} = \dfrac{2(-2a_1(t-a_1x)+2a_1(t+a_1x)+a_5n_2\sinh(t+n_2x))}{\left(a_3+(t-a_1x)^2+(t+a_1x)^2+a_5\cosh(t+n_2x)\right)} - c. \end{cases} \quad (32)$$

and

$$\begin{cases} \psi_{12,1} = \dfrac{e^{ict}h_1\left(a_2+(t+ia_0x)^2+(t+a_1x)^2\right)}{\left(a_3+(t+ia_0x)^2+(t+a_1x)^2+a_5\cosh(t+n_2x)\right)}, \\ \text{and} \\ \phi_{12,1} = -c + \dfrac{2(2ia_0(t+ia_0x)+2a_0(t+a_0x)+a_5n_2\sinh(t+n_2x))}{\left(a_3+(t+ia_0x)^2+(t+a_1x)^2+a_5\cosh(t+n_2x)\right)}. \end{cases} \quad (33)$$

6. Results and Discussion

We observed that the solution $\psi_{1,1}(x,t)$ in Equation (7) with $a_1 = 10, h_2 = -2, h_3 = 2$, $a_3 = 2$, and $c = 3$ formed two lump waves (LWs) known as upper-bright and lower-dark LWs, and that the bright and dark LWs were symmetrical about the coordinate plane. As a_2 varied from a minimum to a maximum number, the two LWs rotated counterclockwise. When $a_2 = 0$, the LW disappeared, but at $a_2 = 5$, the LW gradually reappeared (see Figure 1). The contour lump-wave profiles for $\psi_{1,1}(x,t)$ are plotted for $a_1 = 10, h_2 = -2$, $h_3 = 2, a_3 = 2$, and $c = 3$ in Figure 2. The mixed solutions of soliton and lump waves were successfully obtained. Notice that our solution $\phi_{3,1}(x,t)$ in Equation (14) with

$h_1 = 10, b_0 = 10$, and $c = 5$ formed lump one-strip waves (LSWs) known as upper-bright LSWs. The lump one-strip wave profiles for $\phi_{2,1}(x,t)$ are depicted for $h_1 = 10, b_0 = 10$, and $c = 5$ in Figures 3 and 4. The lump double-strip wave profiles for $\phi_{5,1}(x,t)$ are plotted for $k_3 = 4, h_2 = 2, h_1 = 4, h_3 = 3, a_2 = 20, a_3 = 5, k_6 = 2, m_2 = 2$, and $c = 5$ in Figures 3, 5 and 6. By utilizing the assumption of the cosine function in bilinear equations in Equations (3) and (4), we have obtained the lump periodic solutions. We have successfully obtained the lump periodic graphs for $\phi_{9,1}(x,t)$, which are plotted for $a_0 = 10, a_1 = 5, a_2 = 4, a_3 = 2, a_4 = 3, a_5 = 5$, and $h_1 = 20$ in Figure 7. The lump periodic contour graphs for $\phi_{9,1}(x,t)$ are plotted for $a_0 = 10, a_1 = 5, a_2 = 4, a_3 = 2, a_4 = 3, a_5 = 5$, and $h_1 = 20$ in Figure 8. By utilizing the assumption of cosine hyperbolic functions in bilinear equations in Equations (3) and (4), we have obtained the lump periodic solutions. As a_1 varied from -10 to 10, the rogue wave rotated, and its behavior can be seen for $\psi_{11,1}(x,t)$ for $h_1 = 4, a_2 = 3, a_3 = 1.5, a_5 = 5, n_1 = 3, n_2 = 4$, and $c = 5$ in Figure 9.

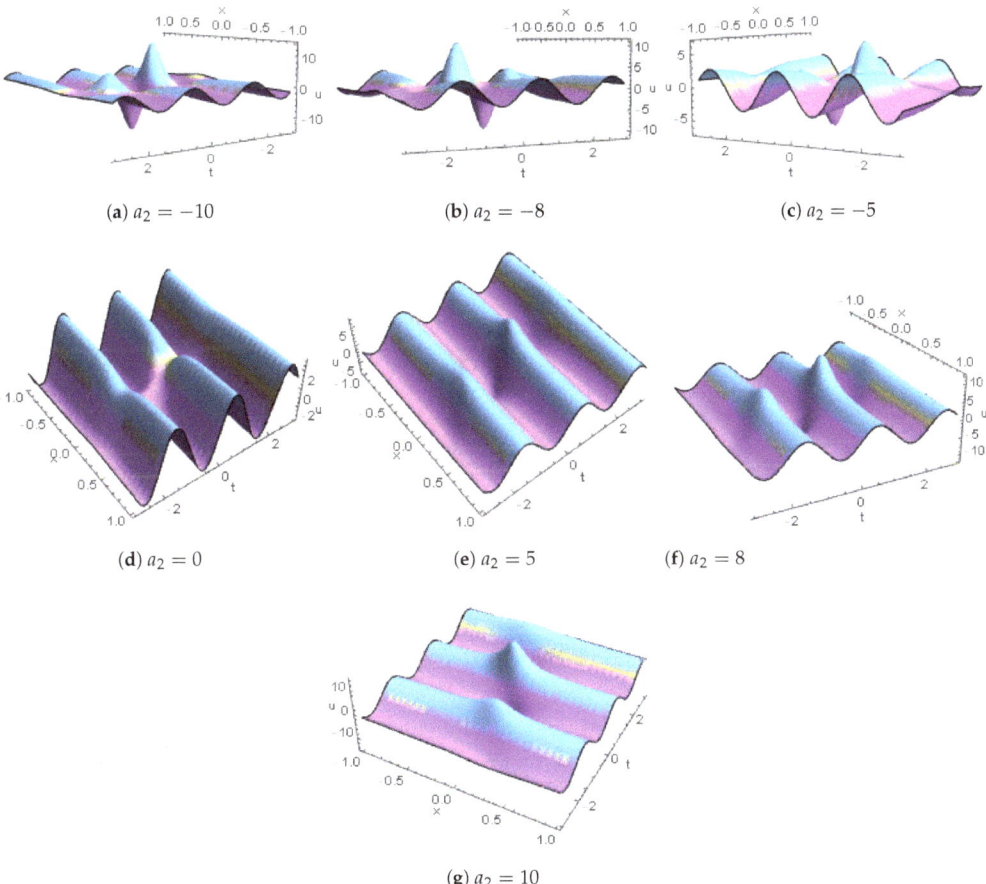

(a) $a_2 = -10$　　(b) $a_2 = -8$　　(c) $a_2 = -5$

(d) $a_2 = 0$　　(e) $a_2 = 5$　　(f) $a_2 = 8$

(g) $a_2 = 10$

Figure 1. Lump-wave profiles for $\psi_{1,1}(x,t)$ are plotted for $a_1 = 10, h_2 = -2, h_3 = 2, a_3 = 2, c = 3$.

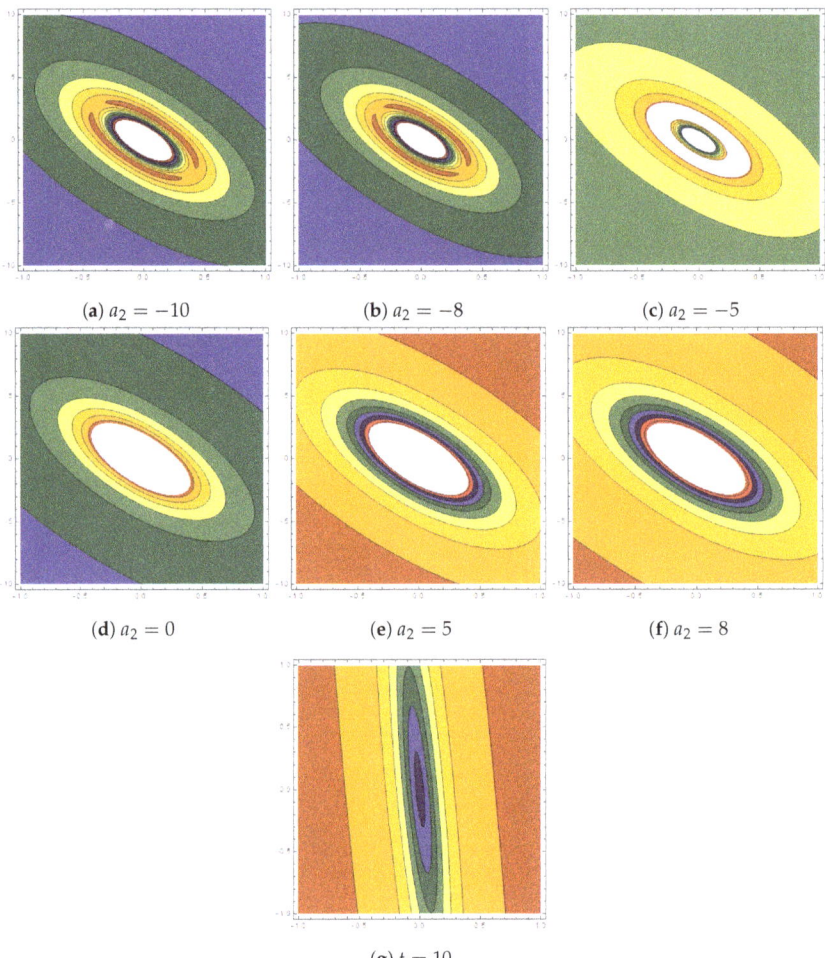

Figure 2. Contour lump-wave profiles for $\psi_{1,1}(x,t)$ are plotted for $a_1 = 10, h_2 = -2, h_3 = 2, a_3 = 2, c = 3$.

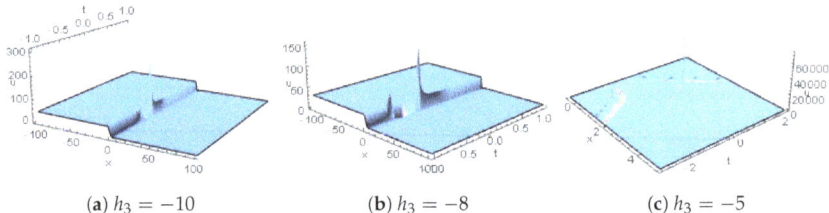

Figure 3. *Cont.*

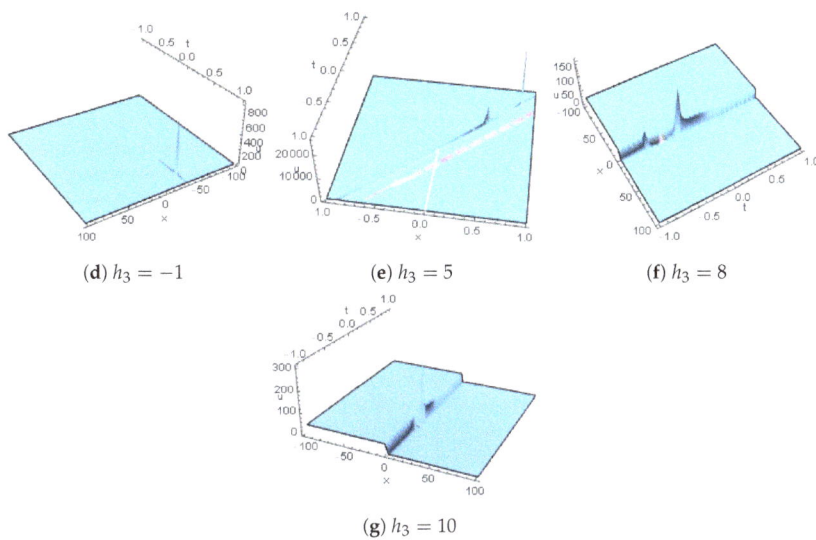

(d) $h_3 = -1$ (e) $h_3 = 5$ (f) $h_3 = 8$

(g) $h_3 = 10$

Figure 3. Lump one-strip wave profiles for $\phi_{3,1}(x,t)$ are plotted for $h_1 = 10, b_0 = 10, c = 5$.

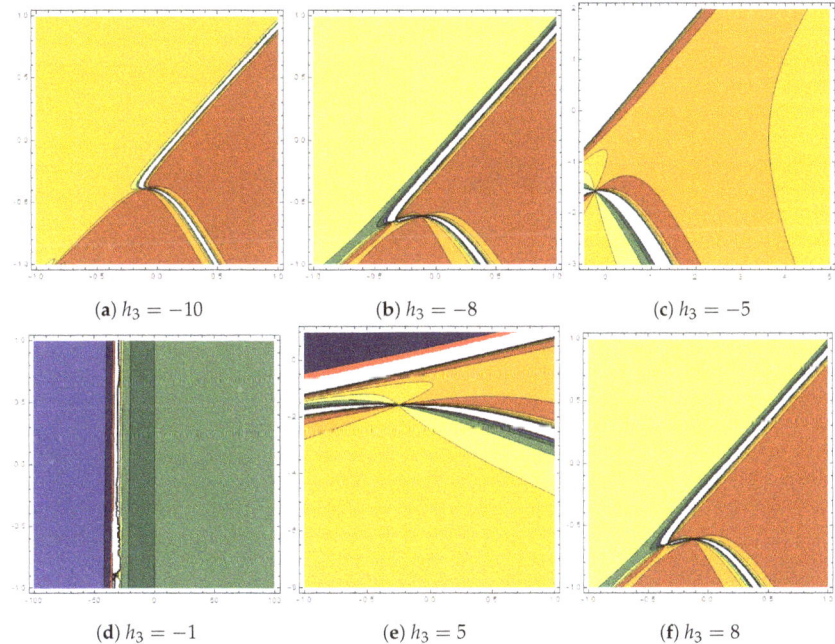

(a) $h_3 = -10$ (b) $h_3 = -8$ (c) $h_3 = -5$

(d) $h_3 = -1$ (e) $h_3 = 5$ (f) $h_3 = 8$

Figure 4. *Cont.*

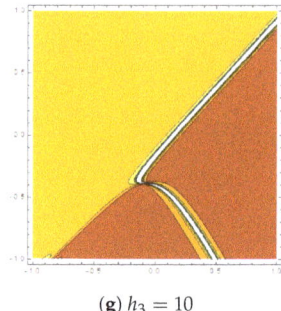

(**g**) $h_3 = 10$

Figure 4. Contour lump one-strip wave profiles for $\phi_{3,1}(x,t)$ are plotted for $h_1 = 10, b_0 = 10, c = 5$.

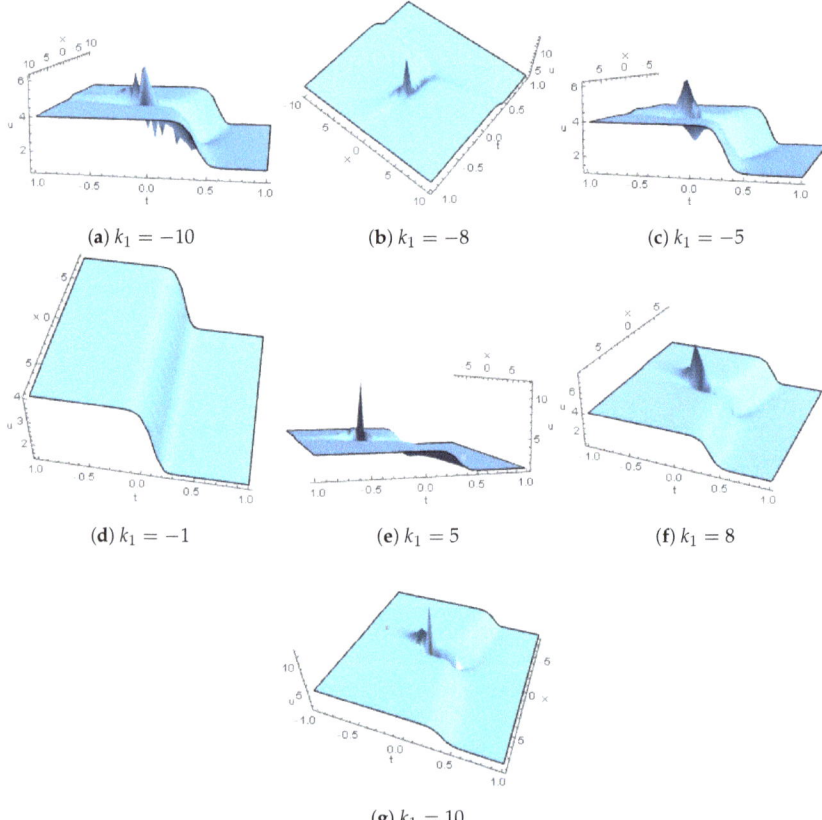

(**a**) $k_1 = -10$ (**b**) $k_1 = -8$ (**c**) $k_1 = -5$

(**d**) $k_1 = -1$ (**e**) $k_1 = 5$ (**f**) $k_1 = 8$

(**g**) $k_1 = 10$

Figure 5. Lump double-strip wave profiles for $\phi_{5,1}(x,t)$ are plotted for $k_3 = 4, h_2 = 2, h_1 = 4, h_3 = 3, a_2 = 20, a_3 = 5, k_6 = 2, m_2 = 2, c = 5$.

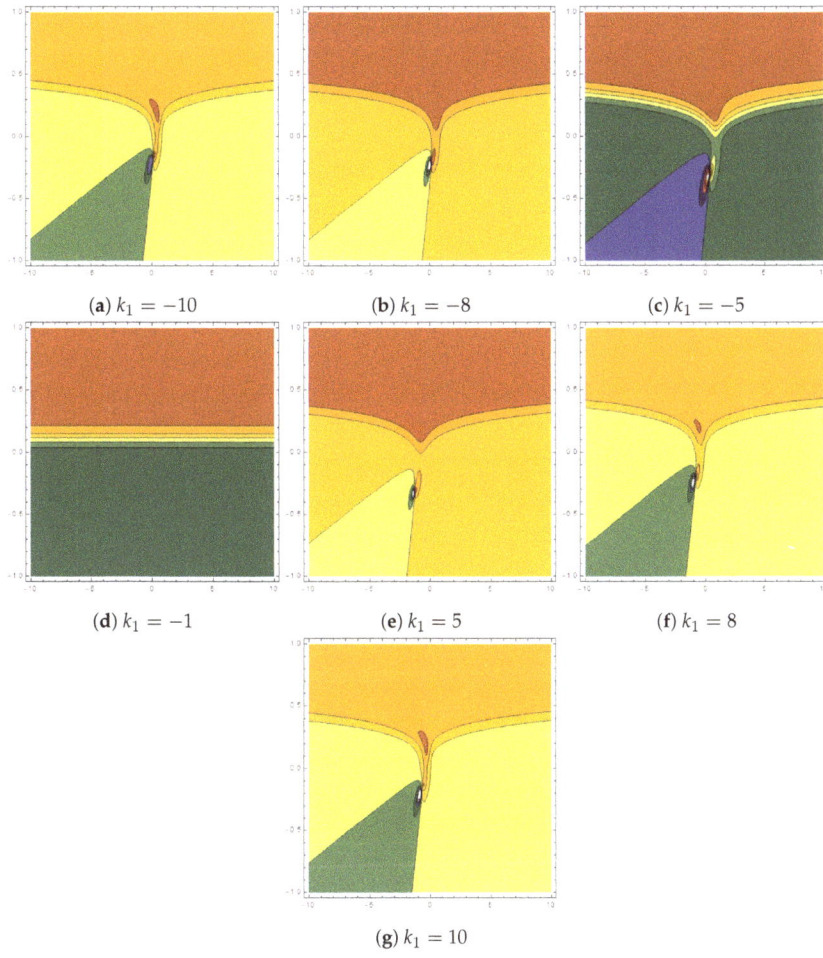

Figure 6. Contour profiles for Figure 5.

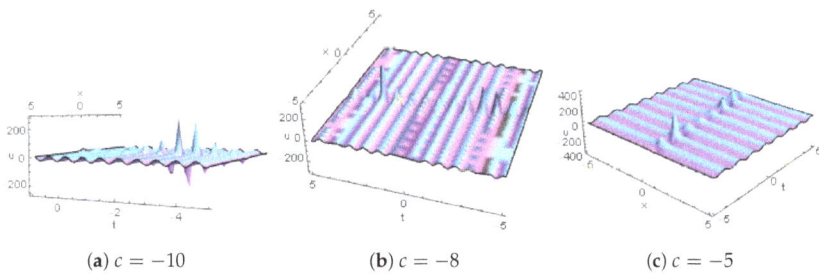

Figure 7. *Cont.*

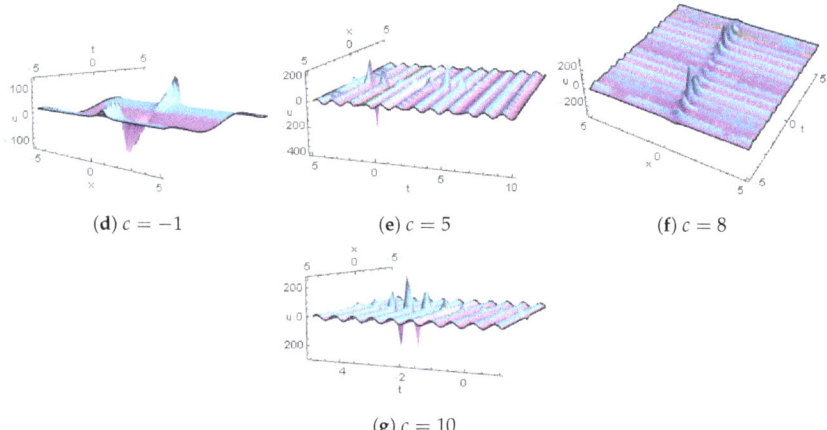

Figure 7. Lump periodic graphs for $\phi_{9,1}(x,t)$ are plotted for $a_0 = 10, a_1 = 5, a_2 = 4, a_3 = 2, a_4 = 3, a_5 = 5, h_1 = 20$.

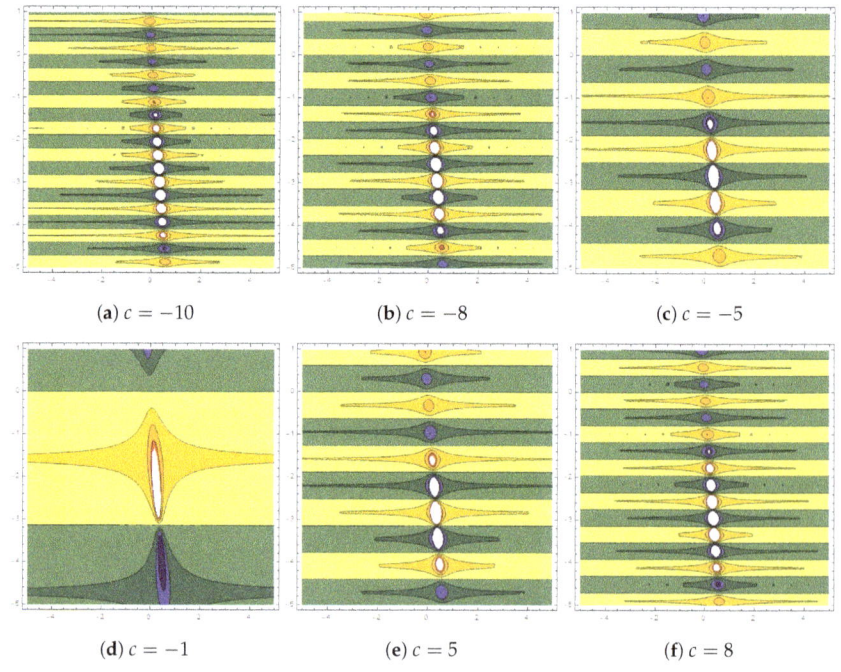

Figure 8. *Cont.*

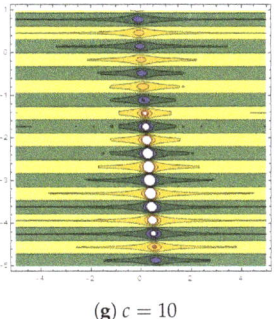

(**g**) $c = 10$

Figure 8. Lump periodic contour graphs for $\phi_{9,1}(x,t)$ are plotted for $a_0 = 10, a_1 = 5, a_2 = 4, a_3 = 2, a_4 = 3, a_5 = 5, h_1 = 20$.

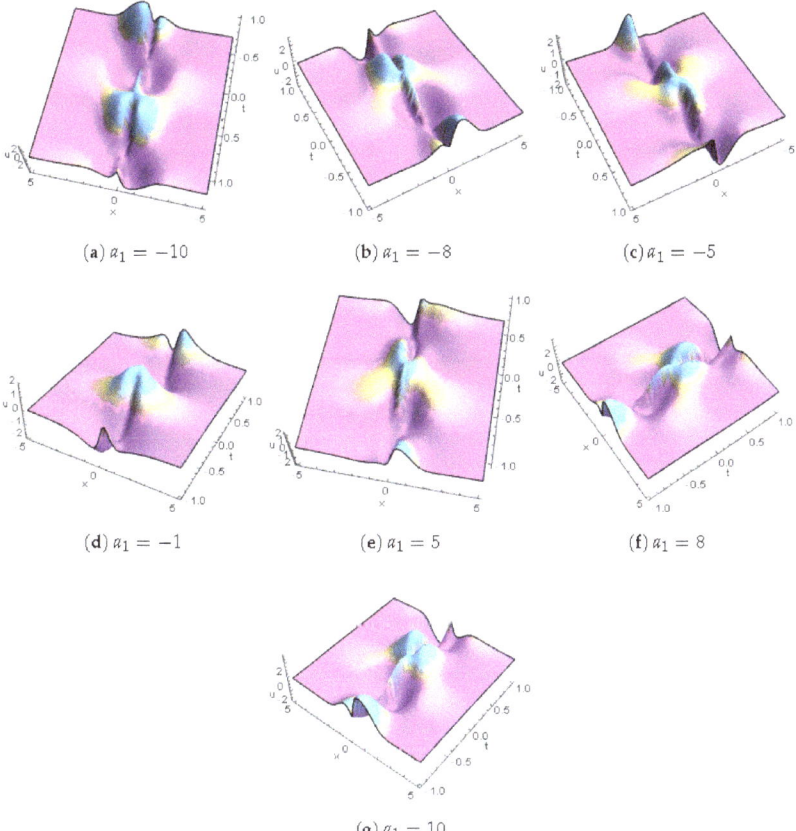

(**a**) $a_1 = -10$ (**b**) $a_1 = -8$ (**c**) $a_1 = -5$

(**d**) $a_1 = -1$ (**e**) $a_1 = 5$ (**f**) $a_1 = 8$

(**g**) $a_1 = 10$

Figure 9. Rogue-wave profiles for $\psi_{11,1}(x,t)$ are plotted for $h_1 = 4, a_2 = 3, a_3 = 1.5, a_5 = 5, n_1 = 3, n_2 = 4, c = 5$.

7. Concluding Remarks

In this paper, we have studied multiple forms of lump solutions for CNL-GZEs in plasma physics using appropriate transformation approaches, bilinear equations, and symbolic computations. By utilizing the positive quadratic assumption in the bilinear equation, we have derived the lump-type solutions. We have evaluated the lump one-soliton solutions through a single exponential function transformation in the bilinear equation. Similarly, we have computed the lump two-soliton solutions using a double exponential function transformation in the bilinear equation. Mixed solutions of lump waves and solitons have been successfully evaluated. Furthermore, we have computed rogue-wave solutions and lump periodic solutions by utilizing appropriate hyperbolic and trigonometric functions. We have identified certain constraint values throughout the derivation of the solutions that must hold for the soliton solution to exist. The presented solutions have valuable uses in plasma physics.

Author Contributions: Methodology, Methodology and Writing—review & editing, S.T.R.R.; Formal analysis, H.Z.; Supervision, A.R.S. All authors have read and agreed to the published version of the manuscript.

Funding: The Deputyship for Research and Innovation in the Ministry of Education in Saudi Arabia for funding this research work under project number 141/442.

Data Availability Statement: Not applicable.

Acknowledgments: The authors extend their appreciation to the Deputyship for Research and Innovation in the Ministry of Education in Saudi Arabia for funding this research work under project number 141/442. Furthermore, the authors would like to extend their appreciation to Taibah University for its supervisory support.

Conflicts of Interest: The authors declare no conflict of interest.

References

1. Ahmed, S.; Seadawy, A.R.; Rizvi, S.T. Study of breathers, rogue waves and lump solutions for the nonlinear chains of atoms. *Opt. Quantum Electron.* **2022**, *54*, 320. [CrossRef]
2. Ding, Q.; Wong, P.J. A higher order numerical scheme for solving fractional Bagley-Torvik equation. *Math. Methods Appl. Sci.* **2022**, *45*, 1241–1258. [CrossRef]
3. Seadawy, A.R.; Rizvi, S.T.; Ahmed, S. Weierstrass and Jacobi elliptic, bell and kink type, lumps, Ma and Kuznetsov breathers with rogue wave solutions to the dissipative nonlinear Schrödinger equation. *Chaos Solitons Fractals* **2022**, *160*, 112258. [CrossRef]
4. Seadawy, A.R.; Ahmed, S.; Rizvi, S.T.; Ali, K. Various forms of lumps and interaction solutions to generalized Vakhnenko Parkes equation arising from high-frequency wave propagation in electromagnetic physics. *J. Geom. Phys.* **2022**, *176*, 104507. [CrossRef]
5. Seadawy, A.R.; Ahmed, S.; Rizvi, S.T.; Ali, K. Lumps, breathers, interactions and rogue wave solutions for a stochastic gene evolution in double chain deoxyribonucleic acid system. *Chaos Solitons Fractals* **2022**, *161*, 112307. [CrossRef]
6. Seadawy, A.R.; Rizvi, S.T.; Ahmed, S. Multiple lump, generalized breathers, Akhmediev breather, manifold periodic and rogue wave solutions for generalized Fitzhugh-Nagumo equation: Applications in nuclear reactor theory. *Chaos Solitons Fractals* **2022**, *161*, 112326. [CrossRef]
7. Seadawy, A.R.; Rizvi, S.T.; Ahmed, S.; Younas, M. Applications of lump and interaction soliton solutions to the Model of liquid crystals and nerve fibers. *Encycl. Complex. Syst. Sci.* **2022**, 1–20.
8. Bashir, A.; Seadawy, A.R.; Ahmed, S.; Rizvi, S.T. The Weierstrass and Jacobi elliptic solutions along with multiwave, homoclinic breather, kink-periodic-cross rational and other solitary wave solutions to Fornberg Whitham equation. *Chaos Solitons Fractals* **2022**, *163*, 112538. [CrossRef]
9. Seadawy, A.R.; Rizvi, S.T.R.; Ahmad, S.; Younis, M.; Baleanu, D. Lump, lump-one stripe, multiwave and breather solutions for the Hunter–Saxton equation. *Open Phys.* **2021**, *19*, 1–10. [CrossRef]
10. Li, X.; Wong, P.J. Generalized Alikhanov's approximation and numerical treatment of generalized fractional sub-diffusion equations. *Commun. Nonlinear Sci. Numer. Simul.* **2021**, *97*, 105719. [CrossRef]
11. Ahmad, H.; Seadawy, A.R.; Khan, T.A. Numerical Solution of Korteweg-de Vries-Burgers Equation by the Modified Variational Iteration Algorithm-II arising in shallow water waves. *Phys. Scr.* **2020**, *95*, 45210. [CrossRef]
12. Li, X.; Wong, P.J. gL1 Scheme for Solving a Class of Generalized Time-Fractional Diffusion Equations. *Mathematics* **2022**, *10*, 1219. [CrossRef]
13. Soundararajan, R.; Subburayan, V.; Wong, P.J. Streamline Diffusion Finite Element Method for Singularly Perturbed 1D-Parabolic Convection Diffusion Differential Equations with Line Discontinuous Source. *Mathematics* **2023**, *11*, 2034. [CrossRef]
14. Liu, Y.; Li, B.; Wazwaz, A.M. Novel high-order breathers and rogue waves in the Boussinesq equation via determinants. *Int. J. Mod. Phys.* **2020**, *43*, 3701–3715. [CrossRef]
15. Younas, U.; Seadawy, A.R.; Younis, M.; Rizvi, S.T.R. Optical solitons and closed form solutions to (3+1)-dimensional resonant Schrodinger equation. *Int. J. Mod. Phys.* **2020**, *34*, 2050291. [CrossRef]
16. Ghaffar, A.; Ali, A.; Ahmed, S.; Akram, S.; Baleanu, D.; Nisar, K.S. A novel analytical technique to obtain the solitary solutions for nonlinear evolution equation of fractional order. *Adv. Differ. Equ.* **2020**, *1*, 308. [CrossRef]

17. Wang, M.; Li, X. Extended F-expansion method and periodic wave solutions for the generalized Zakharov equations. *Phys. Lett. A* **2005**, *343*, 48–54. [CrossRef]
18. Jin, S.; Markowich, P.A.; Zheng, C. Numerical simulation of a generalized Zakharov system. *J. Comput. Phys.* **2004**, *201*, 376–395. [CrossRef]
19. Bao, W.; Sun, F.; Wei, G.W. Numerical methods for the generalized Zakharov system. *J. Comput. Phys.* **2003**, *190*, 201–228. [CrossRef]
20. Bhrawy, A.H. An efficient Jacobi pseudospectral approximation for nonlinear complex generalized Zakharov system. *Appl. Math. Comput.* **2014**, *247*, 30–46. [CrossRef]
21. Zhang, J. Variational approach to solitary wave solution of the generalized Zakharov equation. *Comput. Math. Appl.* **2007**, *54*, 1043–1046. [CrossRef]
22. Khan, Y.; Faraz, N.; Yildirim, A. New soliton solutions of the generalized Zakharov equations using He's variational approach. *Appl. Math. Lett.* **2011**, *24*, 965–968. [CrossRef]
23. Li, Y.Z.; Li, K.M.; Lin, C. Exp-function method for solving the generalized-Zakharov equations. *Appl. Math. Comput.* **2008**, *205*, 197–201. [CrossRef]
24. Buhe, E.; Bluman, G.W. Symmetry reductions, exact solutions, and conservation laws of the generalized Zakharov equations. *J. Math. Phys.* **2015**, *56*, 101501. [CrossRef]
25. Wu, Y. Variational approach to the generalized Zakharov equations. *Int. J. Nonlinear Sci. Numer. Simul.* **2009**, *10*, 1245–1248. [CrossRef]
26. Seadawy, A.R.; Rizvi, S.T.; Ashraf, M.A.; Younis, M.; Hanif, M. Rational solutions and their interactions with kink and periodic waves for a nonlinear dynamical phenomenon. *Int. J. Mod. Phys. B* **2021**, *35*, 2150236. [CrossRef]
27. Wang, H. Lump and interaction solutions to the $(2+1)$-dimensional Burgers equation. *Appl. Math. Lett.* **2018**, *85*, 27–34. [CrossRef]
28. Zhou, Y.; Manukure, S.; Ma, W.X. Lump and lump-soliton solutions to the Hirota Satsuma equation. *Commun. Nonlinear Sci. Numer. Simul.* **2019**, *68*, 56–62. [CrossRef]
29. Wu, P.; Zhang, Y.; Muhammad, I.; Yin, Q. Lump, periodic lump and interaction lump stripe solutions to the $(2+1)$-dimensional B-type Kadomtsev–Petviashvili equation. *Mod. Phys. Lett. B* **2018**, *32*, 1850106. [CrossRef]
30. Li, B.Q.; Ma, Y.L. multiple-lump waves for a $(3+1)$-dimensional Boiti–Leon–Manna–Pempinelli equation arising from incompressible fluid. *Comput. Math. Appl.* **2018**, *76*, 204–214. [CrossRef]

Disclaimer/Publisher's Note: The statements, opinions and data contained in all publications are solely those of the individual author(s) and contributor(s) and not of MDPI and/or the editor(s). MDPI and/or the editor(s) disclaim responsibility for any injury to people or property resulting from any ideas, methods, instructions or products referred to in the content.

Article

General Stability for the Viscoelastic Wave Equation with Nonlinear Time-Varying Delay, Nonlinear Damping and Acoustic Boundary Conditions

Mi Jin Lee [1] and Jum-Ran Kang [2,*]

[1] Department of Mathematics, Pusan National University, Busan 46241, Republic of Korea; jin0624@pusan.ac.kr
[2] Department of Applied Mathematics, Pukyong National University, Busan 48513, Republic of Korea
* Correspondence: jrkang@pknu.ac.kr

Abstract: This paper is focused on energy decay rates for the viscoelastic wave equation that includes nonlinear time-varying delay, nonlinear damping at the boundary, and acoustic boundary conditions. We derive general decay rate results without requiring the condition $a_2 > 0$ and without imposing any restrictive growth assumption on the damping term f_1, using the multiplier method and some properties of the convex functions. Here we investigate the relaxation function ψ, namely $\psi'(t) \leq -\mu(t)G(\psi(t))$, where G is a convex and increasing function near the origin, and μ is a positive nonincreasing function. Moreover, the energy decay rates depend on the functions μ and G, as well as the function F defined by f_0, which characterizes the growth behavior of f_1 at the origin.

Keywords: optimal decay; viscoelastic wave equation; nonlinear time-varying delay; nonlinear damping; acoustic boundary conditions

MSC: 35B40; 35L05; 37L45; 74D99

1. Introduction

In this paper, we study the energy decay rates for the viscoelastic wave equation with nonlinear time-varying delay, nonlinear damping at the boundary, and acoustic boundary conditions

$$u_{tt}(x,t) - \Delta u(x,t) + \int_0^t \psi(t-s)\Delta u(x,s)ds = 0, \quad \text{in } \Omega \times (0,\infty), \tag{1}$$

$$u(x,t) = 0, \quad \text{on } \Gamma_0 \times (0,\infty), \tag{2}$$

$$\frac{\partial u}{\partial \nu}(x,t) - \int_0^t \psi(t-s)\frac{\partial u}{\partial \nu}(x,s)ds + a_1 f_1(u_t(x,t)) + a_2 f_2(u_t(x,t-\varrho(t)))$$
$$= w_t(x,t), \quad \text{on } \Gamma_1 \times (0,\infty), \tag{3}$$

$$u_t(x,t) + h(x)w_t(x,t) + m(x)w(x,t) = 0, \quad \text{on } \Gamma_1 \times (0,\infty), \tag{4}$$

$$u(x,0) = u_0(x), \quad u_t(x,0) = u_1(x), \quad \text{in } \Omega, \tag{5}$$

$$u_t(x,t) = j_0(x,t), \quad \text{in } \Gamma_1 \times (-\varrho(0), 0), \tag{6}$$

where Ω is a bounded domain in $\mathbb{R}^n (n \geq 1)$ with smooth boundary Γ of class C^2; $\Gamma = \Gamma_0 \cup \Gamma_1$, where Γ_0 and Γ_1 are closed and disjoint; $w(x,t)$ is the normal displacement into the domain of a point $x \in \Gamma_1$ at time t; and $h, m : \Gamma_1 \to \mathbb{R}$ are essential bounded functions that represent resistivity and spring constant per unit area, respectively. $f_1, f_2 : \mathbb{R} \to \mathbb{R}$ are given functions, and f_1 represents the nonlinear frictional damping. a_1, a_2 are real numbers with $a_1 > 0, a_2 \neq 0$. The integral term is the memory responsible for the viscoelastic damping. The functions ψ and $\varrho(t)$ represent the kernel of the memory term and the time-varying delay, respectively. ν is the outward unit normal vector to Γ. The initial data

(u_0, u_1, j_0) belong to a suitable space. Boundary conditions (3) and (4) are called acoustic boundary conditions.

In the past decades, the non-delayed wave equation with a viscoelastic term has garnered significant attention in the field of partial differential equations. Research on the energy decay rate of the solution to the viscoelastic wave equation is vital in various fields, contributing to technological advancements, safety assurance, environmental protection, energy efficiency, and academic exploration. The stability of solutions for such equations has recently been studied by many authors (see [1–3] and references therein). When $a_1 = a_2 = 0$, models (1)–(5) are pertinent to noise control and suppression in practical applications. The noise propagates through some acoustic medium, like air, in a room that is defined by a bounded domain Ω and whose floor, walls, and ceiling are determined by the boundary conditions [4,5]. Under the conditions that $\int_0^\infty \psi(s)ds < \frac{1}{2}$ and $\psi'(t) \leq -\mu(t)\psi(t)$, for $t \geq 0$, Park and Park [6] considered the general decay for problems (1)–(5). Liu [7] improved the research of [6] by achieving arbitrary rates of decay, which may not necessarily be an exponential or a polynomial one. Recently, Yoon et al. [8] generalized the work of [6,7] without the assumption condition $\int_0^\infty \psi(s)ds < \frac{1}{2}$. The assumption on relaxation function ψ has been weakened compared to the conditions assumed in previous literature [6,7].

Numerous phenomena are influenced by both the current state and the previous occurrences of the system. There has been a notable increase in the research on the equation with delay effects, which frequently arise in various physical, biological, chemical, medical, and economic problems [9–11]. However, the delay effects can generally be considered a cause of instability. In order to stabilize a system containing delay terms, additional control terms will be necessary. Kirane and Said-Houari [12] showed the global existence and asymptotic stability for the following wave equation with memory and constant delay,

$$u_{tt}(x,t) - \Delta u(x,t) + \int_0^t \psi(t-s)\Delta u(x,s)ds + a_1 u_t(x,t) + a_2 u_t(x,t-\varrho) = 0,$$

where a_1, a_2, and ϱ are positive constants. They used the damping term $a_1 u_t(x,t)$ to control the delay term in obtaining the decay estimate of the energy. They proved that its energy was exponentially decaying when $a_2 \leq a_1$. Dai and Yang [13] investigated the exponential decay of an unsolved problem proposed by Kirane and Said-Houari [12], namely, the problem with $a_1 = 0$. In the case of constant weight and constant delay, the delay term typically considers the past history of strain, only up to some finite time $\varrho(t) \equiv \varrho$. Nicaise and Pignotti [14] investigated the following wave equation with internal time-varying delay instead of constant delay,

$$u_{tt}(x,t) - \Delta u(x,t) + a_1 u_t(x,t) + a_2 u_t(x,t-\varrho(t)) = 0,$$

where $\varrho(t) > 0$, a_1, and a_2 are real numbers with $a_1 > 0$. They proved the exponential stability result for the wave equation under the condition $|a_2| < \sqrt{1-\zeta_0}\, a_1$, where the constant ζ_0 satisfies $\varrho'(t) \leq \zeta_0 < 1, \forall t > 0$. Liu [15] studied the following wave equation involving memory and time-varying delay:

$$u_{tt}(x,t) - \Delta u(x,t) + \alpha(t)\int_0^t \psi(t-s)\Delta u(x,s)ds + a_1 u_t(x,t) + a_2 u_t(x,t-\varrho(t)) = 0.$$

Systems with time-varying delays have been extensively considered by many authors (see [16–22] and references therein). Recently, Zennir [23] considered the stability for solutions of plate equations with a time-varying delay and weak viscoelasticity in $\mathbb{R}^n$. Moreover, Benaissa et al. [24] proved the global existence and stability for solutions of the following wave equation with a time-varying delay in the weakly nonlinear feedback,

$$u_{tt}(x,t) - \Delta u(x,t) + a_1 \sigma(t) f_1(u_t(x,t)) + a_2 \sigma(t) f_2(u_t(x,t-\varrho(t))) = 0,$$

where $\varrho(t) > 0$, a_1, and a_2 are positive real numbers, and f_1, f_2 satisfy some conditions. This result extended the previous work [10,14]. Park [25] investigated the decay result of the energy for a von Karman equation with time-varying delay by dropping the restriction $a_2 > 0$ under the same conditions as ϱ, f_1, and f_2 in [24]. For the viscoelastic problem with time-varying delay in the nonlinear internal or boundary feedback, we also refer to [26,27]. As far as we know, there are few results for the viscoelastic wave equation with a nonlinear time-varying delay. Recently, Djeradi et al. [28] and Mukiawa et al. [29] showed the stability of the thermoelastic laminated beam and thermoelastic Timoshenko beam with nonlinear time-varying delay, respectively. The papers introduced so far have studied the energy decay rate of the solution for the equation with nonlinear time-varying delay in the Dirichlet boundary condition.

Motivated by these results, we study the general decay rates of the solution for problems (1)–(6) with a nonlinear time-varying delay term, nonlinear damping at the boundary, and acoustic boundary conditions. Research on the energy decay rate of solutions for the viscoelastic wave equation with nonlinear time-delay terms plays a critical role in various application areas, including stability assessment, understanding complex behaviors, advancing neuroscience, disaster preparedness, and improving energy efficiency. We consider the general assumption on the relaxation function ψ,

$$\psi'(t) \leq -\mu(t) G(\psi(t)), \tag{7}$$

where $\mu : \mathbb{R}^+ \to \mathbb{R}^+$ is a positive nonincreasing function, and G is linear or is a strictly increasing and strictly convex function. We derive the general decay rate results without requiring the condition $a_2 > 0$ and without imposing any restrictive growth assumption on the damping term f_1. The energy decay rates depend on the functions μ and G, as well as the function F defined by f_0, which represents the growth f_1 at the origin. Our result improves upon previous work [6–8].

This paper is composed of the following. In Section 2, we prepare some notations and materials needed for our work. In Section 3, we introduce some technical lemmas to prove our stability result. In Section 4, we state and prove the general energy decay.

2. Preliminaries

In this section, we present some materials required for our results. Throughout this paper, we use the notation

$$V = \{u \in H^1(\Omega) : u = 0 \text{ on } \Gamma_0\}.$$

For simplicity, we denote $\|\cdot\|_{L^2(\Omega)}$ and $\|\cdot\|_{L^2(\Gamma_1)}$ by $\|\cdot\|$ and $\|\cdot\|_{\Gamma_1}$, respectively.

The Poincaré inequality holds in V; that is, there exist the positive constants λ_0 and λ_1 such that

$$\|u\|^2 \leq \lambda_0 \|\nabla u\|^2 \quad \text{and} \quad \|u\|_{\Gamma_1}^2 \leq \lambda_1 \|\nabla u\|^2 \quad \text{for all } u \in V. \tag{8}$$

As in [1,3,8,26,30], we consider the following assumptions for $\psi, f_1, f_2, \varrho, h$, and m.
(H1) $\psi : [0, \infty) \to \mathbb{R}^+$ is a differentiable function satisfying

$$1 - \int_0^\infty \psi(s) ds = l > 0, \tag{9}$$

and there exists a C^1 function $G : \mathbb{R}^+ \to \mathbb{R}^+$ that is linear or is a strictly convex and strictly increasing C^2 function on $(0, r_0]$, $r_0 \leq \psi(0)$ such that

$$\psi'(t) \leq -\mu(t) G(\psi(t)), \quad \forall t \geq 0, \tag{10}$$

where $G(0) = G'(0) = 0$, and μ is a positive nonincreasing differentiable function. The function G was first introduced in [31]. These are weaker conditions on G than those introduced in [31].

(H2) $f_1 : \mathbb{R} \to \mathbb{R}$ is a nondecreasing C^0 function such that there exists a strictly increasing function $f_0 \in C^1(\mathbb{R}^+)$, with $f_0(0) = 0$, and positive constants c_0, c_1, and ε such that

$$f_0(|s|) \leq |f_1(s)| \leq f_0^{-1}(|s|) \quad \text{for all } |s| \leq \varepsilon, \tag{11}$$

$$c_0|s| \leq |f_1(s)| \leq c_1|s| \quad \text{for all } |s| \geq \varepsilon. \tag{12}$$

Moreover, we assume that the function F, defined by $F(s) = \sqrt{s}f_0(\sqrt{s})$, is a strictly convex C^2 function on $(0, r_1]$, for some $r_1 > 0$, when f_0 is nonlinear.

(H3) $f_2 : \mathbb{R} \to \mathbb{R}$ is an odd nondecreasing C^1 function such that there exist positive constants c_2, c_3, and c_4 that satisfy

$$|f_2'(s)| \leq c_2, \quad c_3 s f_2(s) \leq F_2(s) \leq c_4 s f_1(s), \quad \text{for } s \in \mathbb{R}, \tag{13}$$

where $F_2(s) = \int_0^s f_2(t)dt$.

(H4) $\varrho \in W^{2,\infty}([0,T])$ is a function such that

$$0 < \varrho_1 \leq \varrho(t) \leq \varrho_2 \text{ and } \varrho'(t) \leq \varrho_3 < 1 \text{ for all } t > 0, \tag{14}$$

where T, ϱ_1, and ϱ_2 are positive constants. Moreover, the weight of dissipation and the delay satisfy

$$0 < |a_2| < \frac{c_3(1 - \varrho_3)}{c_4(1 - c_3\varrho_3)} a_1. \tag{15}$$

(H5) We assume that $h, m \in C(\Gamma_1)$, $h(x) > 0$, and $m(x) > 0$ for all $x \in \Gamma_1$. Then, there exist positive constants h_i and $m_i (i = 1, 2)$ such that

$$h_1 \leq h(x) \leq h_2, \quad m_1 \leq m(x) \leq m_2 \text{ for all } x \in \Gamma_1. \tag{16}$$

Remark 1. *1. The assumption (H2) implies that $sf_1(s) > 0$, for all $s \neq 0$.*
2. The assumption (11) of function f_1 has been weakened compared to the condition assumed in [24,25].
3. Since f_2 is an odd nondecreasing function, F_2 is an even and convex function. Furthermore, it is satisfied that $F_2(s) = \int_0^s f_2(t)dt \leq sf_2(s)$. From (13), we find that $c_3 \leq 1$.

Remark 2 ([3])**.** *1. By (H1), we obtain $\lim_{t \to +\infty} \psi(t) = 0$. Then, there exists $t_0 \geq 0$ large enough that*

$$\psi(t_0) = r_0 \Rightarrow \psi(t) \leq r_0, \quad \forall t \geq t_0. \tag{17}$$

Given ψ and μ are positive nonincreasing continuous functions, G is a positive continuous function, and for (10), we have, for some positive constant c_5,

$$\psi'(t) \leq -\mu(t)G(\psi(t)) \leq -c_5\psi(t), \quad \forall t \in [0, t_0]. \tag{18}$$

2. If G is a strictly convex and strictly increasing C^2 function on $(0, r_0]$, with $G(0) = G'(0) = 0$, then it has an extension $\overline{G}$, which is a strictly convex and strictly increasing C^2 function on $(0, \infty)$. The same remark can be established for $\overline{F}$.

We recall the well-known Jensen inequality, which plays a pivotal role in proving our main result. If ϕ is a convex function on $[a, b]$, $p : \Omega \to [a, b]$ and k represents integrable functions on Ω such that $k(x) \geq 0$ and $\int_\Omega k(x)dx = k_0 > 0$, then Jensen's inequality holds:

$$\phi\left[\frac{1}{k_0}\int_\Omega p(x)k(x)dx\right] \leq \frac{1}{k_0}\int_\Omega \phi[p(x)]k(x)dx. \tag{19}$$

Let H^* be the conjugate of the convex function H defined by $H^*(s) = \sup_{r \geq 0}(sr - H(r))$, then

$$sr \leq H^*(s) + H(r), \quad \forall s, r \geq 0. \tag{20}$$

Moreover, due to the argument provided in [32], it holds that

$$H^*(s) = s(H')^{-1}(s) - H((H')^{-1}(s)), \quad \forall s \geq 0. \tag{21}$$

As in [10,14], we introduce the following new function:

$$v(x, \kappa, t) = u_t(x, t - \kappa \varrho(t)), \text{ for } (x, \kappa, t) \in \Gamma_1 \times (0,1) \times (0, \infty).$$

Then, problems (1)–(6) can be expressed as follows:

$$u_{tt}(x,t) - \Delta u(x,t) + \int_0^t \psi(t-s) \Delta u(x,s) ds = 0, \text{ in } \Omega \times (0, \infty), \tag{22}$$

$$\varrho(t) v_t(x, \kappa, t) + (1 - \kappa \varrho'(t)) v_\kappa(x, \kappa, t) = 0, \text{ in } \Gamma_1 \times (0,1) \times (0, \infty), \tag{23}$$

$$u(x,t) = 0, \text{ in } \Gamma_0 \times (0, \infty), \tag{24}$$

$$\frac{\partial u}{\partial \nu}(x,t) - \int_0^t \psi(t-s) \frac{\partial u}{\partial \nu}(x,s) ds + a_1 f_1(u_t(x,t)) + a_2 f_2(v(x,1,t)) = w_t(x,t), \text{ on } \Gamma_1 \times (0, \infty), \tag{25}$$

$$u_t(x,t) + h(x) w_t(x,t) + m(x) w(x,t) = 0, \text{ on } \Gamma_1 \times (0, \infty), \tag{26}$$

$$u(x,0) = u_0(x), \quad u_t(x,0) = u_1(x), \text{ in } \Omega, \tag{27}$$

$$v(x, \kappa, 0) = j_0(x, -\kappa \varrho(0)), \text{ in } \Gamma_1 \times (0,1). \tag{28}$$

We state the global existence result that can be established by the arguments of [24,33].

Theorem 1. Let initial data $(u_0, u_1) \in (V \cap H^2(\Omega)) \times V$ and $j_0 \in L^2(\Gamma_1 \times (0,1))$. Suppose that (H1)–(H5) hold. Then, for any $T > 0$, there exists a unique pair of functions (u, w, v) that are the solution to problems (22)–(28) in the class

$$u \in L^\infty(0,T; V \cap H^2(\Omega)), \quad u_t \in L^\infty(0,T; V), \quad u_{tt} \in L^\infty(0,T; L^2(\Omega)),$$

$$v \in L^\infty(0,T; L^2(\Gamma_1 \times (0,1))), \quad w, w_t \in L^2(0, \infty; L^2(\Gamma_1)).$$

As in [6,25], we introduce the energy for problems (22)–(28),

$$E(t) = \frac{1}{2} \|u_t(t)\|^2 + \frac{1}{2}\left(1 - \int_0^t \psi(s) ds\right) \|\nabla u(t)\|^2 + \frac{1}{2}(\psi \circ \nabla u)(t)$$

$$+ \frac{1}{2} \int_{\Gamma_1} m(x) w^2(t) d\Gamma + \frac{\zeta \varrho(t)}{2} \int_{\Gamma_1} \int_0^1 F_2(v(x, \kappa, t)) d\kappa d\Gamma, \tag{29}$$

where

$$(\psi \circ \nabla u)(t) = \int_0^t \psi(t-s) \|\nabla u(t) - \nabla u(s)\|^2 ds$$

and

$$\frac{2|a_2|(1-c_3)}{c_3(1-\varrho_3)} < \zeta < \frac{2(a_1 - |a_2|c_4)}{c_4}. \tag{30}$$

Thanks to (15), this makes sense.

To show the main results of this paper, we need the following lemma.

Lemma 1. *Assume that (H3)–(H5) hold. Then, there exist positive constants γ_0 and γ_1 satisfying*

$$E'(t) \leq \frac{1}{2}(\psi' \circ \nabla u)(t) - \frac{1}{2}\psi(t)\|\nabla u(t)\|^2 - h_1\|w_t(t)\|^2_{\Gamma_1}$$
$$-\gamma_0 \int_{\Gamma_1} f_1(u_t(t))u_t(t)d\Gamma - \gamma_1 \int_{\Gamma_1} f_2(v(x,1,t))v(x,1,t)d\Gamma. \quad (31)$$

Proof. Multiplying by $u_t(t)$ in (22), using Green's formula, (25), and (26), we have

$$\frac{1}{2}\frac{d}{dt}\left[\|u_t(t)\|^2 + \left(1 - \int_0^t \psi(s)ds\right)\|\nabla u(t)\|^2 + (\psi \circ \nabla u)(t) + \int_{\Gamma_1} m(x)w^2(t)d\Gamma\right]$$
$$= \frac{1}{2}(\psi' \circ \nabla u)(t) - \frac{1}{2}\psi(t)\|\nabla u(t)\|^2 - \int_{\Gamma_1} h(x)w_t^2(t)d\Gamma$$
$$-a_1 \int_{\Gamma_1} f_1(u_t(t))u_t(t)d\Gamma - a_2 \int_{\Gamma_1} f_2(v(x,1,t))u_t(t)d\Gamma, \quad (32)$$

where we used the relation

$$-\int_\Omega \nabla u_t(t) \int_0^t \psi(t-s)\nabla u(s)ds dx$$
$$= \frac{d}{dt}\left[\frac{1}{2}(\psi \circ \nabla u)(t) - \frac{1}{2}\int_0^t \psi(s)ds\|\nabla u(t)\|^2\right] - \frac{1}{2}(\psi' \circ \nabla u)(t) + \frac{1}{2}\psi(t)\|\nabla u(t)\|^2.$$

From (29) and (32), we have

$$E'(t) = \frac{1}{2}(\psi' \circ \nabla u)(t) - \frac{1}{2}\psi(t)\|\nabla u(t)\|^2 - \int_{\Gamma_1} h(x)w_t^2(t)d\Gamma$$
$$-a_1 \int_{\Gamma_1} f_1(u_t(t))u_t(t)d\Gamma - a_2 \int_{\Gamma_1} f_2(v(x,1,t))u_t(t)d\Gamma$$
$$+\frac{\zeta \varrho'(t)}{2}\int_{\Gamma_1}\int_0^1 F_2(v(x,\kappa,t))d\kappa d\Gamma + \frac{\zeta \varrho(t)}{2}\int_{\Gamma_1}\int_0^1 f_2(v(x,\kappa,t))v_t(x,\kappa,t)d\kappa d\Gamma, \quad (33)$$

where $F_2(t) = \int_0^t f_2(s)ds$. In (23), we multiply by $f_2(v(x,\kappa,t))$ and integrate over $\Gamma_1 \times (0,1)$ to obtain

$$\frac{\zeta \varrho(t)}{2}\int_{\Gamma_1}\int_0^1 f_2(v(x,\kappa,t))v_t(x,\kappa,t)d\kappa d\Gamma$$
$$= -\frac{\zeta}{2}\int_{\Gamma_1}\left[(1-\varrho'(t))F_2(v(x,1,t)) - F_2(v(x,0,t)) + \int_0^1 \varrho'(t)F_2(v(x,\kappa,t))d\kappa\right]d\Gamma.$$

Applying this to (33) and noting that $v(x,0,t) = u_t(x,t)$, it follows that

$$E'(t) = \frac{1}{2}(\psi' \circ \nabla u)(t) - \frac{1}{2}\psi(t)\|\nabla u(t)\|^2 - \int_{\Gamma_1} h(x)w_t^2(t)d\Gamma - a_1\int_{\Gamma_1} f_1(u_t(t))u_t(t)d\Gamma$$
$$-a_2\int_{\Gamma_1} f_2(v(x,1,t))u_t(t)d\Gamma - \frac{\zeta}{2}\int_{\Gamma_1}\left[(1-\varrho'(t))F_2(v(x,1,t)) - F_2(u_t(x,t))\right]d\Gamma. \quad (34)$$

From (13) and (14), we obtain

$$-\frac{\zeta}{2}\int_{\Gamma_1}\left[(1-\varrho'(t))F_2(v(x,1,t)) - F_2(u_t(x,t))\right]d\Gamma$$
$$\leq -\frac{\zeta c_3}{2}(1-\varrho_3)\int_{\Gamma_1} f_2(v(x,1,t))v(x,1,t)d\Gamma + \frac{\zeta c_4}{2}\int_{\Gamma_1} f_1(u_t(t))u_t(t)d\Gamma. \quad (35)$$

Substituting (35) into (34), we obtain

$$E'(t) \leq \frac{1}{2}(\psi' \circ \nabla u)(t) - \frac{1}{2}\psi(t)\|\nabla u(t)\|^2 - \int_{\Gamma_1} h(x)w_t^2(t)d\Gamma$$
$$- \left(a_1 - \frac{\zeta c_4}{2}\right)\int_{\Gamma_1} f_1(u_t(t))u_t(t)d\Gamma - \frac{\zeta c_3}{2}(1 - \varrho_3)\int_{\Gamma_1} f_2(v(x,1,t))v(x,1,t)d\Gamma$$
$$- a_2 \int_{\Gamma_1} f_2(v(x,1,t))u_t(t)d\Gamma. \tag{36}$$

Now, we estimate the last term in the right-hand side of (36). The definition of F_2 and (21) give

$$F_2^*(s) = sf_2^{-1}(s) - F_2(f_2^{-1}(s)), \quad \text{for } s \geq 0. \tag{37}$$

When $f_2(v(x,1,t)) < 0$ and $u_t(t) \geq 0$, using (20) and (37) with $s = -f_2(v(x,1,t))$ and $r = u_t(t)$, we obtain (see details in [25])

$$a_2 \int_{\Gamma_1} (-f_2(v(x,1,t)))u_t(t)d\Gamma$$
$$\leq |a_2| \int_{\Gamma_1} \left(-f_2(v(x,1,t))(-v(x,1,t)) - F_2(-v(x,1,t)) + F_2(u_t(t))\right)d\Gamma$$
$$= |a_2| \int_{\Gamma_1} \left(f_2(v(x,1,t))v(x,1,t) - F_2(v(x,1,t)) + F_2(u_t(t))\right)d\Gamma, \tag{38}$$

where we used the fact that f_2 is odd and F_2 is even. When $f_2(v(x,1,t)) \geq 0$ and $u_t(t) < 0$, with $s = f_2(v(x,1,t))$ and $r = -u_t(t)$, we obtain

$$a_2 \int_{\Gamma_1} f_2(v(x,1,t))(-u_t(t))d\Gamma$$
$$\leq |a_2| \int_{\Gamma_1} \left(f_2(v(x,1,t))(v(x,1,t)) - F_2(v(x,1,t)) + F_2(-u_t(t))\right)d\Gamma$$
$$= |a_2| \int_{\Gamma_1} \left(f_2(v(x,1,t))v(x,1,t) - F_2(v(x,1,t)) + F_2(u_t(t))\right)d\Gamma. \tag{39}$$

From (38) and (39), for the case $f_2(v(x,1,t))u_t(t) \leq 0$, we have

$$-a_2 \int_{\Gamma_1} f_2(v(x,1,t))u_t(t)d\Gamma \leq |a_2| \int_{\Gamma_1} \left(f_2(v(x,1,t))v(x,1,t) - F_2(v(x,1,t)) + F_2(u_t(t))\right)d\Gamma. \tag{40}$$

Similarly, (40) holds when $f_2(v(x,1,t))u_t(t) \geq 0$. Hence, using (13) and (40), we see that

$$-a_2 \int_{\Gamma_1} f_2(v(x,1,t))u_t(t)d\Gamma$$
$$\leq |a_2|\left((1-c_3)\int_{\Gamma_1} f_2(v(x,1,t))v(x,1,t)d\Gamma + c_4 \int_{\Gamma_1} f_1(u_t(t))u_t(t)d\Gamma\right). \tag{41}$$

By using (16), (36), and (41), and by selecting ζ satisfying (30), we obtain the desired inequality (31) where $\gamma_0 = a_1 - \frac{\zeta c_4}{2} - |a_2|c_4 > 0$ and $\gamma_1 = \frac{\zeta c_3}{2}(1-\varrho_3) - |a_2|(1-c_3) > 0$. □

3. Technical Lemmas

In this section, we prove the following lemmas to obtain the general decay rates of the solution to problems (22)–(28).

Lemma 2. *Under the assumption (H1), the functional Φ_1 defined by*

$$\Phi_1(t) = \int_\Omega u(t)u_t(t)dx + \int_{\Gamma_1} u(t)w(t)d\Gamma + \frac{1}{2}\int_{\Gamma_1} h(x)w^2(t)d\Gamma$$

satisfies

$$\Phi'_1(t) \leq \|u_t(t)\|^2 - \frac{l}{2}\|\nabla u(t)\|^2 + \frac{2C(\xi)}{l}(i \circ \nabla u)(t) + \frac{8\lambda_1}{l}\|w_t(t)\|^2_{\Gamma_1}$$
$$+ \frac{a_1 a_3}{l}\int_{\Gamma_1} f_1^2(u_t(t))d\Gamma + \frac{|a_2|a_3}{l}\int_{\Gamma_1} f_2^2(v(x,1,t))d\Gamma - \int_{\Gamma_1} m(x)w^2(t)d\Gamma, \quad (42)$$

for any $0 < \xi < 1$, where

$$i(t) = \xi\psi(t) - \psi'(t) \text{ and } C(\xi) = \int_0^\infty \frac{\psi^2(s)}{i(s)}ds. \quad (43)$$

Proof. Using Equations (22) and (24)–(26), and utilizing (9) and Young's inequality, we obtain

$$\Phi'_1(t) = \|u_t(t)\|^2 - \left(1 - \int_0^t \psi(s)ds\right)\|\nabla u(t)\|^2 + \int_0^t \psi(t-s)(\nabla u(s) - \nabla u(t), \nabla u(t))ds$$
$$- a_1\int_{\Gamma_1} f_1(u_t(t))u(t)d\Gamma - a_2\int_{\Gamma_1} f_2(v(x,1,t))u(t)d\Gamma + 2\int_{\Gamma_1} u(t)w_t(t)d\Gamma - \int_{\Gamma_1} m(x)w^2(t)d\Gamma$$
$$\leq \|u_t(t)\|^2 - \frac{7l}{8}\|\nabla u(t)\|^2 + \frac{2}{l}\int_\Omega \left(\int_0^t \psi(t-s)|\nabla u(s) - \nabla u(t)|ds\right)^2 dx$$
$$- a_1\int_{\Gamma_1} f_1(u_t(t))u(t)d\Gamma - a_2\int_{\Gamma_1} f_2(v(x,1,t))u(t)d\Gamma + 2\int_{\Gamma_1} u(t)w_t(t)d\Gamma - \int_{\Gamma_1} m(x)w^2(t)d\Gamma.$$

Using the Cauchy–Schwarz inequality and (43), we have (see [3,34])

$$\int_\Omega \left(\int_0^t \psi(t-s)|\nabla u(s) - \nabla u(t)|ds\right)^2 dx \leq \left(\int_0^t \frac{\psi^2(s)}{i(s)}ds\right)(i \circ \nabla u)(t) \leq C(\xi)(i \circ \nabla u)(t). \quad (44)$$

Applying Young's inequality and (8), we obtain, for $\eta > 0$,

$$\left|-a_1\int_{\Gamma_1} f_1(u_t(t))u(t)d\Gamma\right| \leq \eta a_1\lambda_1\|\nabla u(t)\|^2 + \frac{a_1}{4\eta}\int_{\Gamma_1} f_1^2(u_t(t))d\Gamma, \quad (45)$$

$$\left|-a_2\int_{\Gamma_1} f_2(v(x,1,t))u(t)d\Gamma\right| \leq \eta|a_2|\lambda_1\|\nabla u(t)\|^2 + \frac{|a_2|}{4\eta}\int_{\Gamma_1} f_2^2(v(x,1,t))d\Gamma, \quad (46)$$

and

$$2\int_{\Gamma_1} u(t)w_t(t)d\Gamma \leq \frac{l}{8}\|\nabla u(t)\|^2 + \frac{8\lambda_1}{l}\|w_t(t)\|^2_{\Gamma_1}. \quad (47)$$

Combining estimates (44)–(47), we see that

$$\Phi'_1(t) \leq \|u_t(t)\|^2 - \left(\frac{3l}{4} - \eta a_1\lambda_1 - \eta|a_2|\lambda_1\right)\|\nabla u(t)\|^2 + \frac{2C(\xi)}{l}(i \circ \nabla u)(t) + \frac{8\lambda_1}{l}\|w_t(t)\|^2_{\Gamma_1}$$
$$+ \frac{a_1}{4\eta}\int_{\Gamma_1} f_1^2(u_t(t))d\Gamma + \frac{|a_2|}{4\eta}\int_{\Gamma_1} f_2^2(v(x,1,t))d\Gamma - \int_{\Gamma_1} m(x)w^2(t)d\Gamma.$$

Setting $a_3 = (a_1 + |a_2|)\lambda_1$ and choosing $\eta = \frac{l}{4a_3}$ leads to (42). □

Lemma 3. *Under the assumption (H1), the functional Φ_2 defined by*

$$\Phi_2(t) = -\int_\Omega u_t(t)\int_0^t \psi(t-s)(u(t) - u(s))dsdx$$

satisfies

$$\Phi_2'(t) \leq -\left(\int_0^t \psi(s)ds - \delta\right)\|u_t(t)\|^2 + \delta\|\nabla u(t)\|^2 + \frac{C_1(1+C(\xi))}{\delta}(i \circ \nabla u)(t)$$
$$+ \delta\lambda_1\|w_t(t)\|_{\Gamma_1}^2 + \delta a_1\lambda_1 \int_{\Gamma_1} f_1^2(u_t(t))d\Gamma + \delta|a_2|\lambda_1 \int_{\Gamma_1} f_2^2(v(x,1,t))d\Gamma, \tag{48}$$

for any $0 < \delta < 1$.

Proof. Using Equations (22), (24), and (25), we obtain

$$\Phi_2'(t) = \left(1 - \int_0^t \psi(s)ds\right) \int_\Omega \nabla u \cdot \int_0^t \psi(t-s)(\nabla u(t) - \nabla u(s))dsdx$$
$$+ \int_\Omega \left(\int_0^t \psi(t-s)(\nabla u(t) - \nabla u(s))ds\right)^2 dx - \int_{\Gamma_1} w_t(t) \int_0^t \psi(t-s)(u(t) - u(s))dsd\Gamma$$
$$+ a_1 \int_{\Gamma_1} f_1(u_t(t)) \int_0^t \psi(t-s)(u(t) - u(s))dsd\Gamma + a_2 \int_{\Gamma_1} f_2(v(x,1,t)) \int_0^t \psi(t-s)(u(t) - u(s))dsd\Gamma$$
$$- \int_\Omega u_t(t) \int_0^t \psi'(t-s)(u(t) - u(s))dsdx - \left(\int_0^t \psi(s)ds\right)\|u_t(t)\|^2$$
$$= \vartheta_1 + \vartheta_2 + \cdots + \vartheta_6 - \left(\int_0^t \psi(s)ds\right)\|u_t(t)\|^2.$$

By Young's inequality, (8), and (44), we obtain, for $\delta > 0$,

$$\vartheta_1 \leq \delta\|\nabla u(t)\|^2 + \frac{C(\xi)}{4\delta}(i \circ \nabla u)(t),$$
$$\vartheta_2 \leq C(\xi)(i \circ \nabla u)(t),$$
$$|\vartheta_3| \leq \delta\lambda_1\|w_t(t)\|_{\Gamma_1}^2 + \frac{C(\xi)}{4\delta}(i \circ \nabla u)(t),$$
$$|\vartheta_4| \leq \delta a_1\lambda_1 \int_{\Gamma_1} f_1^2(u_t(t))d\Gamma + \frac{a_1 C(\xi)}{4\delta}(i \circ \nabla u)(t),$$
$$|\vartheta_5| \leq \delta|a_2|\lambda_1 \int_{\Gamma_1} f_2^2(v(x,1,t))d\Gamma + \frac{|a_2|C(\xi)}{4\delta}(i \circ \nabla u)(t).$$

Using Young's inequality, (8), (9), (43), and (44), we see that

$$\vartheta_6 = \int_\Omega u_t(t) \int_0^t i(t-s)(u(t) - u(s))dsdx - \xi \int_\Omega u_t(t) \int_0^t \psi(t-s)(u(t) - u(s))dsdx$$
$$\leq \delta\|u_t(t)\|^2 + \frac{1}{2\delta}\int_\Omega \left(\int_0^t i(t-s)|u(s) - u(t)|ds\right)^2 dx + \frac{\xi^2}{2\delta}\int_\Omega \left(\int_0^t \psi(t-s)|u(t) - u(s)|ds\right)^2 dx$$
$$\leq \delta\|u_t(t)\|^2 + \frac{\lambda_0(\psi(0)+\xi)}{2\delta}(i \circ \nabla u)(t) + \frac{\lambda_0\xi^2 C(\xi)}{2\delta}(i \circ \nabla u)(t).$$

Combining all above estimates and taking $C_1 = \max\{\frac{\lambda_0(\psi(0)+\xi)}{2}, \delta + \frac{1+\lambda_0\xi^2}{2} + \frac{a_1+|a_2|}{4}\}$, the desired inequality (48) is established. □

Lemma 4. *Under the assumptions (H3) and (H4), the functional Φ_3 defined by*

$$\Phi_3(t) = \varrho(t)\int_{\Gamma_1}\int_0^1 e^{-\kappa\varrho(t)}F_2(v(x,\kappa,t))d\kappa d\Gamma$$

satisfies

$$\Phi_3'(t) \leq -e^{-\varrho_2}\varrho(t)\int_{\Gamma_1}\int_0^1 F_2(v(x,\kappa,t))d\kappa d\Gamma - c_3(1-\varrho_3)e^{-\varrho_2}\int_{\Gamma_1} f_2(v(x,1,t))v(x,1,t)d\Gamma$$
$$+c_4\int_{\Gamma_1} f_1(u_t(t))u_t(t)d\Gamma. \tag{49}$$

Proof. Using Equation (23), integration by parts, (13), and (14), we obtain (see [26])

$$\Phi_3'(t) = \varrho'(t)\int_{\Gamma_1}\int_0^1 e^{-\kappa\varrho(t)}F_2(v(x,\kappa,t))d\kappa d\Gamma - \varrho(t)\int_{\Gamma_1}\int_0^1 \kappa\varrho'(t)e^{-\kappa\varrho(t)}F_2(v(x,\kappa,t))d\kappa d\Gamma$$
$$-\int_{\Gamma_1}\int_0^1 e^{-\kappa\varrho(t)}(1-\kappa\varrho'(t))\frac{d}{d\kappa}F_2(v(x,\kappa,t))d\kappa d\Gamma$$
$$= -\Phi_3(t) - e^{-\varrho(t)}\int_{\Gamma_1}(1-\varrho'(t))F_2(v(x,1,t))d\Gamma + \int_{\Gamma_1} F_2(u_t(x,t))d\Gamma$$
$$\leq -e^{-\varrho_2}\varrho(t)\int_{\Gamma_1}\int_0^1 F_2(v(x,\kappa,t))d\kappa d\Gamma - c_3(1-\varrho_3)e^{-\varrho_2}\int_{\Gamma_1} f_2(v(x,1,t))v(x,1,t)d\Gamma$$
$$+c_4\int_{\Gamma_1} f_1(u_t(t))u_t(t)d\Gamma.$$
$\square$

Lemma 5 ([3])**.** *Under the assumption (H1), the functional Φ_4 defined by*

$$\Phi_4(t) = \int_\Omega \int_0^t G_2(t-s)|\nabla u(s)|^2 ds dx$$

satisfies

$$\Phi_4'(t) \leq 3(1-l)\|\nabla u(t)\|^2 - \frac{1}{2}(\psi \circ \nabla u)(t), \tag{50}$$

where $G_2(t) = \int_t^\infty \psi(s)ds$.

Next, let us define the perturbed modified energy by

$$L(t) = NE(t) + N_1\Phi_1(t) + N_2\Phi_2(t) + \Phi_3(t) + b_1 E(t), \tag{51}$$

where N, N_1, N_2, and b_1 are some positive constants.

As in [6,26], for a large enough $N > 0$, there exist positive constants β_1 and β_2 such that

$$\beta_1 E(t) \leq L(t) \leq \beta_2 E(t).$$

Lemma 6. *Assume that (H1) and (H3)–(H5) hold. Then, there exist positive constants β_3, β_4, and β_5 such that*

$$L'(t) \leq -\beta_3 E(t) + \beta_4 \int_{t_0}^t \psi(s)\int_\Omega |\nabla u(t) - \nabla u(t-s)|^2 dx ds + \beta_5 \int_{\Gamma_1} f_1^2(u_t(t))d\Gamma, \quad \forall t \geq t_0, \tag{52}$$

where t_0 was introduced in (17).

Proof. Let $\psi_0 = \int_0^{t_0} \psi(s)ds$. Using the fact that $i(t) = \xi\psi(t) - \psi'(t)$ and combining (31), (42), (48), (49), and (51), we obtain, for all $t \geq t_0$,

$$L'(t) \leq \frac{\xi N}{2}(\psi \circ \nabla u)(t) - \left(\frac{lN_1}{2} - \delta N_2\right)\|\nabla u(t)\|^2 - \left(\psi_0 N_2 - \delta N_2 - N_1\right)\|u_t(t)\|^2$$
$$- \left(\frac{N}{2} - \frac{2C(\xi)N_1}{l} - \frac{C_1(1+C(\xi))N_2}{\delta}\right)(i \circ \nabla u)(t) - N_1 \int_{\Gamma_1} m(x)w^2(t)d\Gamma + b_1 E'(t)$$
$$- \left(h_1 N - \frac{8\lambda_1 N_1}{l} - \delta \lambda_1 N_2\right)\|w_t(t)\|^2_{\Gamma_1} - e^{-\varrho_2}\varrho(t)\int_{\Gamma_1}\int_0^1 F_2(v(x,\kappa,t))d\kappa d\Gamma \qquad (53)$$
$$- (\gamma_0 N - c_4)\int_{\Gamma_1} f_1(u_t(t))u_t(t)d\Gamma - \left(\gamma_1 N + c_3(1-\varrho_3)e^{-\varrho_2}\right)\int_{\Gamma_1} f_2(v(x,1,t))v(x,1,t)d\Gamma$$
$$+ \left(\frac{a_1 a_3 N_1}{l} + \delta a_1 \lambda_1 N_2\right)\int_{\Gamma_1} f_1^2(u_t(t))d\Gamma + \left(\frac{|a_2|a_3 N_1}{l} + \delta|a_2|\lambda_1 N_2\right)\int_{\Gamma_1} f_2^2(v(x,1,t))d\Gamma.$$

From (13), we find that
$$\int_{\Gamma_1} f_2^2(v(x,1,t))d\Gamma \leq c_2 \int_{\Gamma_1} f_2(v(x,1,t))v(x,1,t)d\Gamma. \qquad (54)$$

Applying (54) to (53) and taking $\delta = \frac{l}{4N_2}$, we obtain, for all $t \geq t_0$,
$$L'(t) \leq \frac{\xi N}{2}(\psi \circ \nabla u)(t) - \left(\frac{lN_1}{2} - \frac{l}{4}\right)\|\nabla u(t)\|^2 - \left(\psi_0 N_2 - N_1 - \frac{l}{4}\right)\|u_t(t)\|^2$$
$$- \left(\frac{N}{2} - \frac{4C_1 N_2^2}{l} - C(\xi)\left[\frac{2N_1}{l} + \frac{4C_1 N_2^2}{l}\right]\right)(i \circ \nabla u)(t) - N_1 \int_{\Gamma_1} m(x)w^2(t)d\Gamma$$
$$- \left(h_1 N - \frac{8\lambda_1 N_1}{l} - \frac{l\lambda_1}{4}\right)\|w_t(t)\|^2_{\Gamma_1} - e^{-\varrho_2}\varrho(t)\int_{\Gamma_1}\int_0^1 F_2(v(x,\kappa,t))d\kappa d\Gamma$$
$$- (\gamma_0 N - c_4)\int_{\Gamma_1} f_1(u_t(t))u_t(t)d\Gamma + \left(\frac{a_1 a_3 N_1}{l} + \frac{a_1 l \lambda_1}{4}\right)\int_{\Gamma_1} f_1^2(u_t(t))d\Gamma + b_1 E'(t)$$
$$- \left(\gamma_1 N + c_3(1-\varrho_3)e^{-\varrho_2} - \frac{|a_2|a_3 c_2 N_1}{l} - \frac{|a_2|c_2 l \lambda_1}{4}\right)\int_{\Gamma_1} f_2(v(x,1,t))v(x,1,t)d\Gamma.$$

We choose N_1 large enough so that
$$\frac{lN_1}{2} - \frac{l}{4} > 4(1-l),$$
then N_2 large enough so that
$$\psi_0 N_2 - N_1 - \frac{l}{4} > 1.$$

Using the fact that $\frac{\xi \psi^2(s)}{i(s)} < \psi(s)$ and the Lebesgue dominated convergence theorem, we deduce that
$$\xi C(\xi) = \int_0^\infty \frac{\xi \psi^2(s)}{i(s)} ds \to 0 \text{ as } \xi \to 0.$$
Hence, there is $0 < \xi_0 < 1$ such that if $\xi < \xi_0$, then
$$\xi C(\xi)\left[\frac{2N_1}{l} + \frac{4C_1 N_2^2}{l}\right] < \frac{1}{8}.$$

Finally, selecting $\xi = \frac{1}{2N}$ and choosing N large enough so that
$$N > \max\left\{\frac{16 C_1 N_2^2}{l}, \frac{1}{h_1}\left(\frac{8\lambda_1 N_1}{l} + \frac{l\lambda_1}{4}\right), \frac{c_4}{\gamma_0}, \frac{1}{\gamma_1}\left(\frac{|a_2|a_3 c_2 N_1}{l} + \frac{|a_2|c_2 l \lambda_1}{4} - c_3(1-\varrho_3)e^{-\varrho_2}\right)\right\},$$
we obtain

$$L'(t) \leq -\|u_t(t)\|^2 - 4(1-l)\|\nabla u(t)\|^2 + \frac{1}{4}(\psi \circ \nabla u)(t) - N_1 \int_{\Gamma_1} m(x)w^2(t)d\Gamma$$
$$-e^{-\varrho_2}\varrho(t) \int_{\Gamma_1} \int_0^1 F_2(v(x,\kappa,t))d\kappa d\Gamma + \beta_5 \int_{\Gamma_1} f_1^2(u_t(t))d\Gamma + b_1 E'(t), \quad \forall t \geq t_0, \tag{55}$$

where $\beta_5 = \frac{a_1 a_3 N_1}{l} + \frac{a_1 l \lambda_1}{4}$. Using (18) and (31), we find that, for any $t \geq t_0$,

$$\int_0^{t_0} \psi(s) \int_\Omega |\nabla u(t) - \nabla u(t-s)|^2 dx ds \leq -\frac{1}{c_5} \int_0^{t_0} \psi'(s) \int_\Omega |\nabla u(t) - \nabla u(t-s)|^2 dx ds \leq -\frac{2}{c_5} E'(t). \tag{56}$$

Combining (29), (55), and (56) and making a suitable choice for b_1, we obtain the estimate (52). □

To evaluate the two terms on the right side of (52), we establish the following lemmas.

Lemma 7 ([1]). *Assume that (H2) holds and $\max\{r_1, f_0(r_1)\} < \varepsilon$, where ε was introduced in (11). Then, there exist positive constants $C_2, C_3,$ and C_4 such that*

$$\int_{\Gamma_1} f_1^2(u_t(t))d\Gamma \leq C_2 \int_{\Gamma_1} f_1(u_t(t))u_t(t)d\Gamma, \quad \text{if } f_0 \text{ is linear}, \tag{57}$$

$$\int_{\Gamma_1} f_1^2(u_t(t))d\Gamma \leq C_3 F^{-1}(\chi(t)) - C_3 E'(t), \quad \text{if } f_0 \text{ is nonlinear}, \tag{58}$$

where

$$\chi(t) = \frac{1}{|\Gamma_{11}|} \int_{\Gamma_{11}} f_1(u_t(t))u_t(t)d\Gamma \leq -C_4 E'(t), \tag{59}$$

$\Gamma_{11} = \{x \in \Gamma_1 : |u_t(t)| \leq \varepsilon_1\}$ *and* $0 < \varepsilon_1 = \min\{r_1, f_0(r_1)\}$.

Lemma 8. *Assume that (H1) and (H3)–(H5) hold and that f_0 is linear. Then, the energy functional satisfies*

$$\int_0^\infty E(s)ds < \infty. \tag{60}$$

Proof. We introduce the functional

$$\mathcal{L}(t) = L(t) + \Phi_4(t),$$

which is nonnegative. From (50) and (55), we see that, for all $t \geq t_0$,

$$\mathcal{L}'(t) \leq -\|u_t(t)\|^2 - (1-l)\|\nabla u(t)\|^2 - \frac{1}{4}(\psi \circ \nabla u)(t) - N_1 \int_{\Gamma_1} m(x)w^2(t)d\Gamma$$
$$-e^{-\varrho_2}\varrho(t) \int_{\Gamma_1} \int_0^1 F_2(v(x,\kappa,t))d\kappa d\Gamma + \beta_5 \int_{\Gamma_1} f_1^2(u_t(t))d\Gamma + b_1 E'(t).$$

Applying (29), (31), and (57), we have

$$\mathcal{L}'(t) \leq -d_1 E(t) + \left(b_1 - \frac{\beta_5 C_2}{\gamma_0}\right) E'(t),$$

where d_1 is some positive constant. Selecting a suitable choice for b_1, we obtain

$$\mathcal{L}'(t) \leq -d_1 E(t).$$

This implies that

$$d_1 \int_{t_0}^{t} E(s)ds \leq \mathcal{L}(t_0) - \mathcal{L}(t) \leq \mathcal{L}(t_0) < \infty.$$

□

Next, we define $Y(t)$ by

$$Y(t) := -\int_{t_0}^{t} \psi'(s) \int_{\Omega} |\nabla u(t) - \nabla u(t-s)|^2 dx ds \leq -2E'(t). \tag{61}$$

Lemma 9. *Assume that (H1) and (H2) hold and that G is nonlinear. Then, the solution to (22)–(28) satisfies the estimates*

$$\int_{t_0}^{t} \psi(s) \int_{\Omega} |\nabla u(t) - \nabla u(t-s)|^2 dx ds \leq \frac{1}{\theta} \overline{G}^{-1}\left(\frac{\theta Y(t)}{\mu(t)}\right), \forall t \geq t_0, \text{ if } f_0 \text{ is linear}, \tag{62}$$

$$\int_{t_0}^{t} \psi(s) \int_{\Omega} |\nabla u(t) - \nabla u(t-s)|^2 dx ds \leq \frac{t-t_0}{\theta} \overline{G}^{-1}\left(\frac{\theta Y(t)}{(t-t_0)\mu(t)}\right), \forall t > t_0, \text{ if } f_0 \text{ is nonlinear}, \tag{63}$$

where $\theta \in (0,1)$, and $\overline{G}$ is an extension of G such that $\overline{G}$ is a strictly convex and strictly increasing C^2 function on $(0,\infty)$.

Proof. First, we prove the estimate (62) when f_0 is linear. For $0 < \theta < 1$, we define $I(t)$ by

$$I(t) := \theta \int_{t_0}^{t} \int_{\Omega} |\nabla u(t) - \nabla u(t-s)|^2 dx ds.$$

By (60), θ is taken so small that, for all $t \geq t_0$,

$$I(t) < 1. \tag{64}$$

Since G is strictly convex on $(0, r_0]$, then

$$G(q\zeta) \leq qG(\zeta), \tag{65}$$

where $0 \leq q \leq 1$ and $\zeta \in (0, r_0]$. Using the fact that μ is a positive nonincreasing function and applying (10), (64), (65), and Jensen's inequality (19), we find that (see details in [1,3])

$$\begin{aligned} Y(t) &\geq \frac{\mu(t)}{\theta I(t)} \int_{t_0}^{t} I(t)G(\psi(s)) \int_{\Omega} \theta |\nabla u(t) - \nabla u(t-s)|^2 dx ds \\ &\geq \frac{\mu(t)}{\theta I(t)} \int_{t_0}^{t} G(I(t)\psi(s)) \int_{\Omega} \theta |\nabla u(t) - \nabla u(t-s)|^2 dx ds \\ &\geq \frac{\mu(t)}{\theta} \overline{G}\left(\theta \int_{t_0}^{t} \psi(s) \int_{\Omega} |\nabla u(t) - \nabla u(t-s)|^2 dx ds\right). \end{aligned} \tag{66}$$

Since $\overline{G}$ is strictly increasing, we obtain

$$\int_{t_0}^{t} \psi(s) \int_{\Omega} |\nabla u(t) - \nabla u(t-s)|^2 dx ds \leq \frac{1}{\theta} \overline{G}^{-1}\left(\frac{\theta Y(t)}{\mu(t)}\right).$$

Now, we show the estimate (63) when f_0 is nonlinear. Since we cannot guarantee (60), we define the following function:

$$I_1(t) := \frac{\theta}{t - t_0} \int_{t_0}^{t} \int_{\Omega} |\nabla u(t) - \nabla u(t-s)|^2 dx ds, \forall t > t_0.$$

Using the fact that $E'(t) \leq 0$ and (29), we have

$$I_1(t) \leq \frac{2\theta}{t-t_0} \int_{t_0}^t (||\nabla u(t)||^2 + ||\nabla u(t-s)||^2) ds \leq \frac{8\theta E(0)}{l}.$$

Choose θ small enough so that, for all $t > t_0$,

$$I_1(t) < 1. \tag{67}$$

Similar to (67), using (10), (65), (67), and Jensen's inequality (19), we obtain

$$\begin{aligned}
Y(t) &= \frac{t-t_0}{\theta I_1(t)} \int_{t_0}^t I_1(t)(-\psi'(s)) \int_\Omega \frac{\theta}{t-t_0} |\nabla u(t) - \nabla u(t-s)|^2 dx ds \\
&\geq \frac{(t-t_0)\mu(t)}{\theta I_1(t)} \int_{t_0}^t G(I_1(t)\psi(s)) \int_\Omega \frac{\theta}{t-t_0} |\nabla u(t) - \nabla u(t-s)|^2 dx ds \\
&\geq \frac{(t-t_0)\mu(t)}{\theta} \overline{G}\left(\frac{\theta}{t-t_0} \int_{t_0}^t \psi(s) \int_\Omega |\nabla u(t) - \nabla u(t-s)|^2 dx ds \right).
\end{aligned}$$

This implies that

$$\int_{t_0}^t \psi(s) \int_\Omega |\nabla u(t) - \nabla u(t-s)|^2 dx ds \leq \frac{t-t_0}{\theta} \overline{G}^{-1}\left(\frac{\theta Y(t)}{(t-t_0)\mu(t)} \right).$$

□

4. General Decay of the Energy

In this section, we state and prove the main result of our work.

Theorem 2. *Assume that (H1)–(H5) hold and that f_0 is linear. Then, there exist positive constants $k_1, k_2, k_3,$ and k_4 such that the energy functional satisfies, for all $t \geq t_0$,*

$$E(t) \leq k_2 e^{-k_1 \int_{t_0}^t \mu(s) ds}, \quad \text{if } G \text{ is linear}, \tag{68}$$

$$E(t) \leq k_4 G_1^{-1}\left(k_3 \int_{t_0}^t \mu(s) ds \right), \quad \text{if } G \text{ is nonlinear}, \tag{69}$$

where $G_1(t) = \int_t^{r_0} \frac{1}{sG'(s)} ds$ is strictly decreasing and convex on $(0, r_0]$.

Proof. Now, we consider the following two cases.
Case 1: $G(t)$ is linear. Multiplying (52) by the positive nonincreasing function $\mu(t)$ and using (10), (31), and (57), we obtain

$$\mu(t)L'(t) \leq -\beta_3 \mu(t)E(t) + \beta_4 \int_{t_0}^t \mu(s)\psi(s) \int_\Omega |\nabla u(t) - \nabla u(t-s)|^2 dx ds + \beta_5 \mu(t) \int_{\Gamma_1} f_1^2(u_t(t)) d\Gamma$$

$$\leq -\beta_3 \mu(t)E(t) - \beta_4 \int_{t_0}^t \psi'(s) \int_\Omega |\nabla u(t) - \nabla u(t-s)|^2 dx ds + \beta_5 C_2 \mu(0) \int_{\Gamma_1} f_1(u_t(t)) u_t(t) d\Gamma$$

$$\leq -\beta_3 \mu(t)E(t) - C_5 E'(t),$$

where $C_5 = 2\beta_4 + \frac{\beta_5 C_2 \mu(0)}{\gamma_0}$ is a positive constant. Since $\mu(t)$ is nonincreasing, we have

$$(\mu L + C_5 E)'(t) \leq -\beta_3 \mu(t) E(t), \quad \forall t \geq t_0.$$

Since $\mu(t)L(t) + C_5 E(t) \sim E(t)$, for some positive constants k_1 and k_2, we obtain

$$E(t) \leq k_2 e^{-k_1 \int_{t_0}^t \mu(s) ds}.$$

Case 2: $G(t)$ is nonlinear. This case is obtained through the ideas presented in [3] as follows. Using (31), (52), (57), and (62), we obtain

$$L'(t) \leq -\beta_3 E(t) + \frac{\beta_4}{\theta}\overline{G}^{-1}\left(\frac{\theta Y(t)}{\mu(t)}\right) - \frac{\beta_5 C_2}{\gamma_0}E'(t), \quad \forall t \geq t_0. \tag{70}$$

Let $L_1(t) = L(t) + \frac{\beta_5 C_2}{\gamma_0}E(t) \sim E(t)$, and then (70) becomes

$$L'_1(t) \leq -\beta_3 E(t) + \frac{\beta_4}{\theta}\overline{G}^{-1}\left(\frac{\theta Y(t)}{\mu(t)}\right), \quad \forall t \geq t_0. \tag{71}$$

For $0 < \varepsilon_0 < r_0$, using (71) and the fact that $E' \leq 0, \overline{G}' > 0$ and $\overline{G}'' > 0$, we find that the functional L_2, defined by

$$L_2(t) := \overline{G}'\left(\varepsilon_0 \frac{E(t)}{E(0)}\right)L_1(t) \sim E(t),$$

satisfies

$$L'_2(t) \leq -\beta_3 E(t)\overline{G}'\left(\varepsilon_0 \frac{E(t)}{E(0)}\right) + \frac{\beta_4}{\theta}\overline{G}'\left(\varepsilon_0 \frac{E(t)}{E(0)}\right)\overline{G}^{-1}\left(\frac{\theta Y(t)}{\mu(t)}\right), \quad \forall t \geq t_0. \tag{72}$$

With $s = \overline{G}'\left(\varepsilon_0 \frac{E(t)}{E(0)}\right)$ and $r = \overline{G}^{-1}\left(\frac{\theta Y(t)}{\mu(t)}\right)$, using (20), (21), and (72), we obtain

$$L'_2(t) \leq -\beta_3 E(t)G'\left(\varepsilon_0 \frac{E(t)}{E(0)}\right) + \frac{\varepsilon_0 \beta_4}{\theta}\frac{E(t)}{E(0)}G'\left(\varepsilon_0 \frac{E(t)}{E(0)}\right) + \frac{\beta_4 Y(t)}{\mu(t)},$$

where we have used that $\varepsilon_0 \frac{E(t)}{E(0)} < r_0$ and $\overline{G}' = G'$ on $(0, r_0]$. Multiplying this by $\mu(t)$ and using (61), we obtain

$$\mu(t)L'_2(t) \leq -\left(\beta_3 E(0) - \frac{\varepsilon_0 \beta_4}{\theta}\right)\frac{\mu(t)E(t)}{E(0)}G'\left(\varepsilon_0 \frac{E(t)}{E(0)}\right) - 2\beta_4 E'(t).$$

By defining $L_3(t) = \mu(t)L_2(t) + 2\beta_4 E(t)$, we see that, for some positive constants γ_2 and γ_3,

$$\gamma_2 L_3(t) \leq E(t) \leq \gamma_3 L_3(t). \tag{73}$$

With a suitable choice of ε_0, we obtain, for some positive constant d_2,

$$L'_3(t) \leq -d_2\mu(t)\frac{E(t)}{E(0)}G'\left(\varepsilon_0 \frac{E(t)}{E(0)}\right) = -d_2\mu(t)G_2\left(\frac{E(t)}{E(0)}\right), \quad \forall t \geq t_0, \tag{74}$$

where $G_2(t) = tG'(\varepsilon_0 t)$. Applying the strict convexity of G on $(0, r_0]$ and $G'_2(t) = G'(\varepsilon_0 t) + \varepsilon_0 tG''(\varepsilon_0 t)$, we see that $G_2(t), G'_2(t) > 0$ on $(0, 1]$. Finally, defining

$$Q(t) = \frac{\gamma_2 L_3(t)}{E(0)}$$

and using (73), we have

$$Q(t) \leq \frac{E(t)}{E(0)} \leq 1 \text{ and } Q(t) \sim E(t). \tag{75}$$

From (74), (75), and the fact that $G'_2(t) > 0$ on $(0, 1]$, we arrive at

$$Q'(t) \leq -k_3\mu(t)G_2(Q(t)), \quad \forall t \geq t_0,$$

where $k_3 = \frac{d_2 \gamma_2}{E(0)}$ is a positive constant. Integrating this over (t_0, t) and using variable transformation, we find that (see details in [3])

$$\int_t^{t_0} \frac{\varepsilon_0 Q'(s)}{\varepsilon_0 Q(s) G'(\varepsilon_0 Q(s))} ds \geq k_3 \int_{t_0}^t \mu(s) ds \implies \int_{\varepsilon_0 Q(t)}^{\varepsilon_0 Q(t_0)} \frac{1}{sG'(s)} ds \geq k_3 \int_{t_0}^t \mu(s) ds.$$

Since $\varepsilon_0 < r_0$ and $Q(t) \leq 1$, for all $t \geq t_0$, we have

$$G_1(\varepsilon_0 Q(t)) = \int_{\varepsilon_0 Q(t)}^{r_0} \frac{1}{sG'(s)} ds \geq k_3 \int_{t_0}^t \mu(s) ds \implies Q(t) \leq \frac{1}{\varepsilon_0} G_1^{-1}\left(k_3 \int_{t_0}^t \mu(s) ds\right), \quad (76)$$

where $G_1(t) = \int_t^{r_0} \frac{1}{sG'(s)} ds$. Here, we have used the fact that G_1 is a strictly decreasing function on $(0, r_0]$. Therefore, using (75) and (76), the estimate (69) is established. □

Theorem 3. Assume that (H1)–(H5) hold and that f_0 is nonlinear. Then, there exist positive constants $\alpha_1, \alpha_2, \alpha_3$, and α_4 such that the energy functional satisfies

$$E(t) \leq \alpha_2 F_1^{-1}\left(\alpha_1 \int_{t_0}^t \mu(s) ds\right), \quad \forall t \geq t_0, \text{ if } G \text{ is linear,} \quad (77)$$

where $F_1(t) = \int_t^{r_1} \frac{1}{sF'(s)} ds$ and

$$E(t) \leq \alpha_4 (t - t_0) K_1^{-1}\left(\frac{\alpha_3}{(t - t_0) \int_{t_1}^t \mu(s) ds}\right), \quad \forall t \geq t_1, \text{ if } G \text{ is nonlinear,} \quad (78)$$

where $K_1(t) = tK'(\varepsilon_2 t)$, $0 < \varepsilon_2 < r_2 = \min\{r_0, r_1\}$ and $K = \left(\overline{G}^{-1} + \overline{F}^{-1}\right)^{-1}$.

Proof. **Case 1**: $G(t)$ is linear. Multiplying (52) by the positive nonincreasing function $\mu(t)$ and using (10), (31), and (58), we obtain

$$\mu(t) L'(t) \leq -\beta_3 \mu(t) E(t) + \beta_5 C_3 \mu(t) F^{-1}(\chi(t)) - C_6 E'(t), \quad (79)$$

where $C_6 = 2\beta_4 + \beta_5 C_3 \mu(0)$ is a positive constant. Since $\mu(t)$ is nonincreasing, (79) becomes

$$F_3'(t) \leq -\beta_3 \mu(t) E(t) + \beta_5 C_3 \mu(t) F^{-1}(\chi(t)), \quad \forall t \geq t_0, \quad (80)$$

where $F_3(t) = \mu(t) L(t) + C_6 E(t) \sim E(t)$. For $0 < \varepsilon_1 < r_1$, using (80) and the fact that $E' \leq 0, F' > 0$ and $F'' > 0$ on $(0, r_1]$, the functional F_4, defined by

$$F_4(t) := F'\left(\varepsilon_1 \frac{E(t)}{E(0)}\right) F_3(t) \sim E(t),$$

satisfies

$$F_4'(t) \leq -\beta_3 \mu(t) E(t) F'\left(\varepsilon_1 \frac{E(t)}{E(0)}\right) + \beta_5 C_3 \mu(t) F'\left(\varepsilon_1 \frac{E(t)}{E(0)}\right) F^{-1}(\chi(t)).$$

Given (20) and (21) with $s = F'\left(\varepsilon_1 \frac{E(t)}{E(0)}\right)$ and $r = F^{-1}(\chi(t))$, using (59), we obtain that

$$F_4'(t) \leq -\beta_3 \mu(t) E(t) F'\left(\varepsilon_1 \frac{E(t)}{E(0)}\right) + \varepsilon_1 \beta_5 C_3 \frac{\mu(t) E(t)}{E(0)} F'\left(\varepsilon_1 \frac{E(t)}{E(0)}\right) + \beta_5 C_3 \mu(0) \chi(t)$$

$$\leq -\left(\beta_3 E(0) - \varepsilon_1 \beta_5 C_3\right) \frac{\mu(t) E(t)}{E(0)} F'\left(\varepsilon_1 \frac{E(t)}{E(0)}\right) - \beta_5 C_3 C_4 \mu(0) E'(t), \quad \forall t \geq t_0.$$

Let $F_5(t) = F_4(t) + \beta_5 C_3 C_4 \mu(0) E(t)$; then it satisfies, for positive constants γ_4 and γ_5,

$$\gamma_4 F_5(t) \leq E(t) \leq \gamma_5 F_5(t). \tag{81}$$

Consequently, with a suitable choice of ε_1, we have, for some positive constant d_3,

$$F_5'(t) \leq -d_3 \mu(t) \frac{E(t)}{E(0)} F'\left(\varepsilon_1 \frac{E(t)}{E(0)}\right) = -d_3 \mu(t) F_0\left(\frac{E(t)}{E(0)}\right), \quad \forall t \geq t_0, \tag{82}$$

where $F_0(t) = tF'(\varepsilon_1 t)$. From the strict convexity of F on $(0, r_1]$, we obtain $F_0(t), F_0'(t) > 0$ on $(0, 1]$. Let

$$J(t) = \frac{\gamma_4 F_5(t)}{E(0)},$$

and from (81) and (82), we obtain

$$J(t) \leq \frac{E(t)}{E(0)} \leq 1 \text{ and } J'(t) \leq -\alpha_1 \mu(t) F_0(J(t)), \quad \forall t \geq t_0,$$

where $\alpha_1 = \frac{d_3 \gamma_4}{E(0)}$ is a positive constant. Then, similar to (76), the integration over (t_0, t) and variable transformation yield

$$J(t) \leq \frac{1}{\varepsilon_1} F_1^{-1}\left(\alpha_1 \int_{t_0}^{t} \mu(s) ds\right), \tag{83}$$

where $F_1(t) = \int_t^{r_1} \frac{1}{sF'(s)} ds$, which is a strictly decreasing function on $(0, r_1]$. Combining (81) and (83), the estimate (77) is proved.

Case 2: $G(t)$ is nonlinear. This case is obtained by the arguments presented in [1] as follows. Using (52), (58), and (63), we obtain

$$L'(t) \leq -\beta_3 E(t) + \frac{\beta_4(t-t_0)}{\theta} \overline{G}^{-1}\left(\frac{\theta Y(t)}{(t-t_0)\mu(t)}\right) + \beta_5 C_3 F^{-1}(\chi(t)) - \beta_5 C_3 E'(t), \quad \forall t > t_0. \tag{84}$$

Since $\lim_{t \to \infty} \frac{1}{t-t_0} = 0$, there exists $t_1 > t_0$ such that

$$\frac{1}{t-t_0} < 1, \quad \forall t \geq t_1. \tag{85}$$

Using the strictly convex and strictly increasing function of $\overline{F}$ and (65) with $q = \frac{1}{t-t_0}$, we see that

$$\overline{F}^{-1}(\chi(t)) \leq (t-t_0) \overline{F}^{-1}\left(\frac{\chi(t)}{t-t_0}\right), \quad \forall t \geq t_1. \tag{86}$$

Combining (84) and (86), we arrive at

$$R_1'(t) \leq -\beta_3 E(t) + \frac{\beta_4(t-t_0)}{\theta} \overline{G}^{-1}\left(\frac{\theta Y(t)}{(t-t_0)\mu(t)}\right) + \beta_5 C_3 (t-t_0) \overline{F}^{-1}\left(\frac{\chi(t)}{t-t_0}\right), \quad \forall t \geq t_1, \tag{87}$$

where $R_1(t) = L(t) + \beta_5 C_3 E(t) \sim E(t)$. Let

$$r_2 = \min\{r_0, r_1\}, \quad \varphi(t) = \max\left\{\frac{\theta Y(t)}{(t-t_0)\mu(t)}, \frac{\chi(t)}{t-t_0}\right\} \text{ and } K = \left(\overline{G}^{-1} + \overline{F}^{-1}\right)^{-1}, \quad \forall t \geq t_1. \tag{88}$$

Therefore, (87) reduces to

$$R_1'(t) \leq -\beta_3 E(t) + C_7(t-t_0) K^{-1}(\varphi(t)), \quad \forall t \geq t_1, \tag{89}$$

where $C_7 = \max\{\frac{\beta_4}{\theta}, \beta_5 C_3\}$. The strictly increasing and strictly convex properties of $\overline{G}$ and $\overline{F}$ imply that
$$K' = \frac{\overline{G}'\overline{F}'}{\overline{G}' + \overline{F}'} > 0 \text{ and } K'' = \frac{\overline{G}''(\overline{F}')^2 + (\overline{G}')^2\overline{F}''}{(\overline{G}' + \overline{F}')^2} > 0, \quad (90)$$

on $(0, r_2]$.

Now, for $0 < \varepsilon_2 < r_2$, using (85), we see that $\frac{\varepsilon_2}{t-t_0}\frac{E(t)}{E(0)} < r_2$. Defining
$$R_2(t) = K'\left(\frac{\varepsilon_2}{t-t_0}\frac{E(t)}{E(0)}\right) R_1(t), \quad \forall t \geq t_1,$$

and using (89) and (90), we find that
$$R_2'(t) = \left(-\frac{\varepsilon_2}{(t-t_0)^2}\frac{E(t)}{E(0)} + \frac{\varepsilon_2}{t-t_0}\frac{E'(t)}{E(0)}\right) K''\left(\frac{\varepsilon_2}{t-t_0}\frac{E(t)}{E(0)}\right) R_1(t) + K'\left(\frac{\varepsilon_2}{t-t_0}\frac{E(t)}{E(0)}\right) R_1'(t)$$
$$\leq -\beta_3 E(t) K'\left(\frac{\varepsilon_2}{t-t_0}\frac{E(t)}{E(0)}\right) + C_7(t-t_0) K'\left(\frac{\varepsilon_2}{t-t_0}\frac{E(t)}{E(0)}\right) K^{-1}(\varphi(t)), \quad \forall t \geq t_1. \quad (91)$$

Using (20) and (21) with $s = K'(\frac{\varepsilon_2}{t-t_0}\frac{E(t)}{E(0)})$ and $r = K^{-1}(\varphi(t))$ and applying (91), we obtain
$$R_2'(t) \leq -\beta_3 E(t) K'\left(\frac{\varepsilon_2}{t-t_0}\frac{E(t)}{E(0)}\right) + \varepsilon_2 C_7 \frac{E(t)}{E(0)} K'\left(\frac{\varepsilon_2}{t-t_0}\frac{E(t)}{E(0)}\right) + C_7(t-t_0)\varphi(t). \quad (92)$$

From (59), (61), and (88), we obtain
$$(t-t_0)\mu(t)\varphi(t) \leq -C_8 E'(t), \quad (93)$$

where $C_8 = \min\{2\theta, C_4\mu(0)\}$. Multiplying (92) by the positive nonincreasing function $\mu(t)$ and using (93), we have
$$R_3'(t) \leq -\left(\beta_3 E(0) - \varepsilon_2 C_7\right)\frac{\mu(t)E(t)}{E(0)} K'\left(\frac{\varepsilon_2}{t-t_0}\frac{E(t)}{E(0)}\right), \quad \forall t \geq t_1,$$

where $R_3(t) = \mu(t)R_2(t) + C_7 C_8 E(t) \sim E(t)$. For a suitable choice of ε_2, we find that
$$R_3'(t) \leq -d_4 \frac{\mu(t)E(t)}{E(0)} K'\left(\frac{\varepsilon_2}{t-t_0}\frac{E(t)}{E(0)}\right), \quad \forall t \geq t_1, \quad (94)$$

where d_4 is a positive constant. An integration of (94) yields
$$\frac{d_4}{E(0)} \int_{t_1}^{t} E(s) K'\left(\frac{\varepsilon_2}{s-t_0}\frac{E(s)}{E(0)}\right) \mu(s) ds \leq \int_{t}^{t_1} R_3'(s) ds \leq R_3(t_1).$$

Using (90) and the non-increasing property of E, we see that the map $t \to E(t) K'(\frac{\varepsilon_2}{t-t_0}\frac{E(t)}{E(0)})$ is non-increasing and, consequently, we obtain
$$d_4 \frac{E(t)}{E(0)} K'\left(\frac{\varepsilon_2}{t-t_0}\frac{E(t)}{E(0)}\right) \int_{t_1}^{t} \mu(s) ds \leq R_3(t_1), \quad \forall t \geq t_1. \quad (95)$$

Multiplying (95) by $\frac{1}{t-t_0}$, we obtain
$$d_4 K_1\left(\frac{1}{t-t_0}\frac{E(t)}{E(0)}\right) \int_{t_1}^{t} \mu(s) ds \leq \frac{R_3(t_1)}{t-t_0}, \quad \forall t \geq t_1,$$

where $K_1(s) = sK'(\varepsilon_2 s)$, which is strictly increasing. Therefore, we deduce that

$$E(t) \leq \alpha_4(t-t_0)K_1^{-1}\left(\frac{\alpha_3}{(t-t_0)\int_{t_1}^t \mu(s)ds}\right), \quad \forall t \geq t_1,$$

where α_3 and α_4 are positive constants. This completes the proof. □

Examples. We provide examples to explain the decay of energy (see [1]).
1. Case: f_0 and G are linear.
Let $\psi(t) = ae^{-b(1+t)}, \mu(t) = b$, and $G(t) = t$, where $b > 0$, and $a > 0$ is small enough. Assume that $f_0(t) = ct$ and $F(t) = \sqrt{t}f_0(\sqrt{t}) = ct$. Then, we can obtain

$$E(t) \leq k_2 e^{-k_1 t}, \text{ for all } t \geq t_0.$$

2. Case: f_0 is linear and G is nonlinear.
Let $\psi(t) = ae^{-t^p}, \mu(t) = 1$, and $G(t) = \frac{p^t}{(\ln(\frac{a}{t}))^{\frac{1}{p}-1}}$, where $0 < p < 1$, and $a > 0$ is small enough. Assume that $f_0(t) = ct$ and $F(t) = \sqrt{t}f_0(\sqrt{t}) = ct$. Then, G satisfies the condition (H1) on $(0, r_0]$ for any $0 < r_0 < a$.

$$G_1(t) = \int_t^{r_0} \frac{1}{sG'(s)}ds = \int_t^{r_0} \frac{[\ln\frac{a}{s}]^{\frac{1}{p}}}{s[1-p+p\ln\frac{a}{s}]}ds = \int_{\ln\frac{a}{r_0}}^{\ln\frac{a}{t}} \frac{u^{\frac{1}{p}}}{1-p+pu}du \leq \left(\ln\frac{a}{t}\right)^{\frac{1}{p}}.$$

Then, we can have

$$E(t) \leq k_4 e^{-k_3 t^p}, \text{ for all } t \geq t_0.$$

3. Case: f_0 is nonlinear and G is linear.
Let $\psi(t) = ae^{-b(1+t)}, \mu(t) = b$, and $G(t) = t$, where $b > 0$, and $a > 0$ is small enough. Assume that $f_0(t) = ct^p$, where $p > 1$ and $F(t) = \sqrt{t}f_0(\sqrt{t}) = ct^{\frac{p+1}{2}}$. Then,

$$F_1(t) = \int_t^{r_1} \frac{1}{sF'(s)}ds = \int_t^{r_1} \frac{2}{c(p+1)}s^{-\frac{p+1}{2}}ds = -\alpha_0\left(r_1^{-\frac{p-1}{2}} - t^{-\frac{p-1}{2}}\right)$$

and

$$F_1^{-1}(t) = (r_1^{-\frac{p-1}{2}} + \frac{1}{\alpha_0}t)^{-\frac{2}{p-1}},$$

where $\alpha_0 = \frac{4}{c(p+1)(p-1)}$. Therefore, we find that

$$E(t) \leq (\alpha_1 t + \alpha_2)^{-\frac{2}{p-1}}, \text{ for all } t \geq t_0.$$

4. Case: f_0 is nonlinear and G is nonlinear.
Let $\psi(t) = \frac{a}{(1+t)^2}, \mu(t) = b$, and $G(t) = t^{\frac{3}{2}}$, where $b > 0$, and $a > 0$ is taken so that (9) remains valid. Assume that $f_0(t) = t^5$ and $F(t) = t^3$. Then,

$$K(s) = (G^{-1} + F^{-1})^{-1}(s) = \left(\frac{-1+\sqrt{1+4s}}{2}\right)^3.$$

Therefore, we see that

$$E(t) \leq \frac{\alpha_3}{(t-t_0)^{\frac{1}{3}}}, \text{ for all } t \geq t_1,$$

where $t_1 > t_0$.

5. Conclusions

Numerous phenomena are influenced by both the current state and the previous occurrences of the system. There has been a notable increase in the research on the equation with delay effects, which frequently arise in various physical, biological, chemical, medical, and economic problems. In this paper, we study the energy decay rates for the viscoelastic wave equation with nonlinear time-varying delay, nonlinear damping at the boundary, and acoustic boundary conditions. We consider the relaxation function ψ, namely $\psi'(t) \leq -\mu(t)G(\psi(t))$, where G is an increasing and convex function near the origin, and μ is a positive nonincreasing function. We establish general decay rate results without the need for the condition $a_2 > 0$ and without imposing any limiting growth assumption on the damping term f_1, using the multiplier method and some properties of the convex functions. Moreover, the energy decay rates depend on the functions μ and G, as well as the function F defined by f_0, which characterizes the growth behavior of f_1 at the origin.

Author Contributions: M.J.L. and J.-R.K. contributed equally to the writing of this paper and reviewed the manuscript. All authors have read and agreed to the published version of the manuscript.

Funding: This work was supported by the Pukyong National University Industry–University Cooperation Research Fund in 2023 (202311540001).

Institutional Review Board Statement: Not applicable.

Informed Consent Statement: Not applicable.

Data Availability Statement: Data are contained within the article.

Acknowledgments: The authors would like to thank the handling editor and the referees for their relevant remarks and corrections in order to improve the final version.

Conflicts of Interest: The authors declare no conflict of interest.

References

1. Al-Gharabli, M.M.; Al-Mahdi, A.M.; Messaoudi, S.A. General and optimal decay result for a viscoelastic problem with nonlinear boundary feedback. *J. Dyn. Control Syst.* **2019**, *25*, 551–572. [CrossRef]
2. Messaoudi, S.A. General decay of solutions of a viscoelastic equation. *J. Math. Anal. Appl.* **2008**, *341*, 1457–1467. [CrossRef]
3. Mustafa, M.I. Optimal decay rates for the viscoelastic wave equation. *Math. Meth. Appl. Sci.* **2018**, *41*, 192–204. [CrossRef]
4. Beale, J.T.; Rosencrans, S.I. Acoustic boundary conditions. *Bull. Am. Math. Soc.* **1974**, *80*, 1276–1278. [CrossRef]
5. Munoz Rivera, J.E.; Qin, Y.M. Polynomial decay for the energy with an acoustic boundary condition. *Appl. Math. Lett.* **2003**, *16*, 249–256. [CrossRef]
6. Park, J.Y.; Park, S.H. Decay rate estimates for wave equation of memory type with acoustic boundary conditions. *Nonlinear Anal. Theory Methods Appl.* **2011**, *74*, 993–998. [CrossRef]
7. Liu, W.J. Arbitrary rate of decay for a viscoelastic equation with acoustic boundary coditions. *Appl. Math. Lett.* **2014**, *38*, 155–161. [CrossRef]
8. Yoon, M.; Lee, M.J.; Kang, J.R. General decay result for the wave equation with memory and acoustic boundary conditions. *Appl. Math. Lett.* **2023**, *135*, 108385. [CrossRef]
9. Feng, B.W. Long-time dynamics of a plate equation with memory and time delay. *Bull. Braz. Math. Soc.* **2018**, *49*, 395–418. [CrossRef]
10. Nicaise, S.; Pignotti, D. Stability and instability results of the wave equation with a delay term in the boundary or internal feedbacks. *SIAM J. Control Optim.* **2006**, *45*, 1561–1585. [CrossRef]
11. Nicaise, S.; Pignotti, C. Stability of the wave equation with boundary or internal distributed delay. *Differ. Integral Equ.* **2008**, *21*, 935–958.
12. Kirane, M.; Said-Houari, B. Existence and asymptotic stability of a viscoelastic wave equation with a delay. *Z. Angew. Math. Phys.* **2011**, *62*, 1065–1082. [CrossRef]
13. Dai, Q.; Yang, Z.F. Global existence and exponential decay of the solution for a viscoelastic wave equation with a delay. *Z. Angew. Math. Phys.* **2014**, *65*, 885–903. [CrossRef]
14. Nicaise, S.; Pignotti, C. Interior feedback stabilization of wave equations with time dependent delay. *Electron. J. Differ. Equ.* **2011**, *2011*, 1–20.
15. Liu, W.J. General decay rate estimate for the energy of a weak viscoelastic equation with an internal time-varying delay term. *Taiwanese J. Math.* **2013**, *17*, 2101–2115. [CrossRef]

16. Feng, B.W. Well-posedness and exponential stability for a plate equation with time-varying delay and past history. *Z. Angew. Math. Phys.* **2017**, *68*, 1–24. [CrossRef]
17. Lee, M.J.; Kim, D.W.; Park, J.Y. General decay of solutions for Kirchhoff type containing Balakrishnan-Taylor damping with a delay and acoustic boundary conditions. *Bound. Value Probl.* **2016**, *2016*, 173. [CrossRef]
18. Liu, G.W.; Diao, L. Energy decay of the solution for a weak viscoelastic equation with a time-varying delay. *Acta Appl. Math.* **2018**, *155*, 9–19. [CrossRef]
19. Mustafa, M.I. Asymptotic behavior of second sound thermoelasticity with internal time-varying delay. *Z. Angew. Math. Phys.* **2013**, *64*, 1353–1362. [CrossRef]
20. Park, S.H. Decay rate estimates for a weak viscoelastic beam equation with time-varying delay. *Appl. Math. Lett.* **2014**, *31*, 46–51. [CrossRef]
21. Park, S.H.; Kang, J.R. General decay for weak viscoelastic Kirchhoff plate equations with delay boundary conditions. *Bound. Value Probl.* **2017**, *2017*, 96. [CrossRef]
22. Zitouni, S.; Zennir, K.; Bouzettouta, L. Uniform decay for a viscoelastic wave equation with density and time-varying delay in $\mathbb{R}^n$. *Filomat.* **2019**, *33*, 961–970. [CrossRef]
23. Zennir, K. Stabilization for Solutions of Plate Equation with Time-Varying Delay and Weak-Viscoelasticity in $\mathbb{R}^n$. *Russ. Math.* **2020**, *64*, 21–33. [CrossRef]
24. Benaissa, A.; Benaissa, A.; Messaoudi, S.A. Global existence and energy decay of solutions for the wave equation with a time varying delay term in the weakly nonlinear internal feedbacks. *J. Math. Phys.* **2012**, *53*, 123514. [CrossRef]
25. Park, S.H. Energy decay for a von Karman equation with time-varying delay. *Appl. Math. Lett.* **2016**, *55*, 10–17. [CrossRef]
26. Kang, J.R.; Lee, M.J.; Park, S.H. Asymptotic stability of a viscoelastic problem with Balakrishnan-Taylor damping and time-varying delay. *Comput. Math. Appl.* **2017**, *74*, 1506–1515. [CrossRef]
27. Lee, M.J.; Park, J.Y.; Park, S.H. General decay of solutions of quasilinear wave equation with time-varying delay in the boundary feedback and acoustic boundary conditions. *Math. Meth. Appl. Sci.* **2017**, *40*, 4560–4576. [CrossRef]
28. Djeradi, F.S.; Yazid, F.; Georgiev, S.G.; Hajjej, Z.; Zennir, K. On the time decay for a thermoelastic laminated beam with microtemperature effects, nonlinear weight, and nonlinear time-varying delay. *AIMS Math.* **2023**, *8*, 26096–26114. [CrossRef]
29. Mukiawa, S.E.; Enyi, C.D.; Messaoudi, S.A. Stability of thermoelastic Timoshenko beam with suspenders and time-varying feedback. *Adv. Contin. Disc. Models.* **2023**, *2023*, 7. [CrossRef]
30. Al-Gharabli, M.M.; Balegh, M.; Feng, B.W.; Hajjej, Z.; Messaoudi, S.A. Existence and general decay of Balakrishnan-Taylor viscoelastic equation with nonlinear frictional damping and logarithmic source term. *Evol. Equ. Control Theory.* **2022**, *11*, 1149–1173. [CrossRef]
31. Alabau-Boussouira, F.; Cannarsa, P. A general method for proving sharp energy decay rates for memory dissipative evolution equations. *Comptes Rendus Math.* **2009**, *347*, 867–872. [CrossRef]
32. Arnold, V.I. *Mathematical Methods of Classical Mechanics*; Springer: New York, NY, USA, 1989.
33. Park, J.Y.; Ha, T.G. Well-posedness and uniform decay rates for the Klein–Gordon equation with damping term and acoustic boundary conditions. *J. Math. Phys.* **2009**, *50*, 013506. [CrossRef]
34. Jin, K.P.; Liang, J.; Xiao, T.J. Coupled second order evolution equations with fading memory: Optimal energy decay rate. *J. Differ. Equ.* **2014**, *257*, 1501–1528. [CrossRef]

Disclaimer/Publisher's Note: The statements, opinions and data contained in all publications are solely those of the individual author(s) and contributor(s) and not of MDPI and/or the editor(s). MDPI and/or the editor(s) disclaim responsibility for any injury to people or property resulting from any ideas, methods, instructions or products referred to in the content.

MDPI
St. Alban-Anlage 66
4052 Basel
Switzerland
www.mdpi.com

Mathematics Editorial Office
E-mail: mathematics@mdpi.com
www.mdpi.com/journal/mathematics

Disclaimer/Publisher's Note: The statements, opinions and data contained in all publications are solely those of the individual author(s) and contributor(s) and not of MDPI and/or the editor(s). MDPI and/or the editor(s) disclaim responsibility for any injury to people or property resulting from any ideas, methods, instructions or products referred to in the content.

www.ingramcontent.com/pod-product-compliance
Lightning Source LLC
LaVergne TN
LVHW070506100526
838202LV00014B/1801